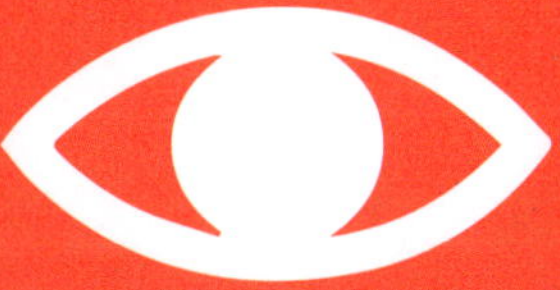

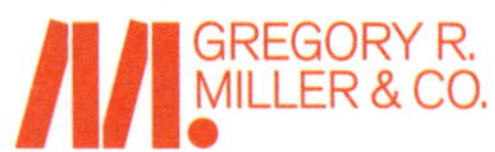
GREGORY R.
MILLER & CO.

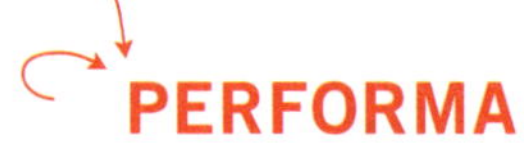
PERFORMA

PERFORMA 13

Surrealism • The Voice • Citizenship

Performa 13:

Surrealism • The Voice • Citizenship

RoseLee Goldberg

Edited by Kathleen Madden
Photographs by Paula Court

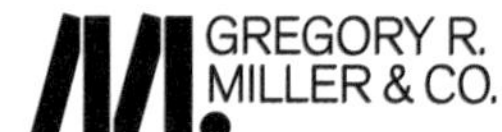

62 Cooper Square
New York, NY 10003
grmandco.com

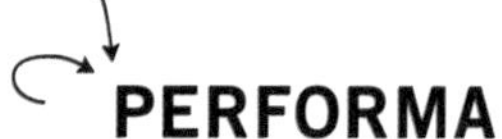

100 West 23rd Street, 5th Floor
New York, NY 10011
performa-arts.org

Performa is a non-profit arts organization dedicated to exploring the critical role of live performance in the history of twentieth-century art and to encouraging new directions in performance for the twenty-first century. Performa launched New York's first performance biennial, Performa 05, in 2005.

Founding Director and Curator RoseLee Goldberg

Editor: Kathleen Madden
Design: Robin Cameron
Photography: Paula Court
Photo Editor: Marc Arthur
Indexer: Onni Nickle
Metroproof
Print by Worzalla, Stevens Point, Wisconsin

PERFORMA 13

SURREALISM / THE VOICE / CITIZENSHIP

CONTENTS

Key to Symbols
▲ Performa Commission
☉ Performa Premiere
△ Performa Project
◑ Biennial Consortium

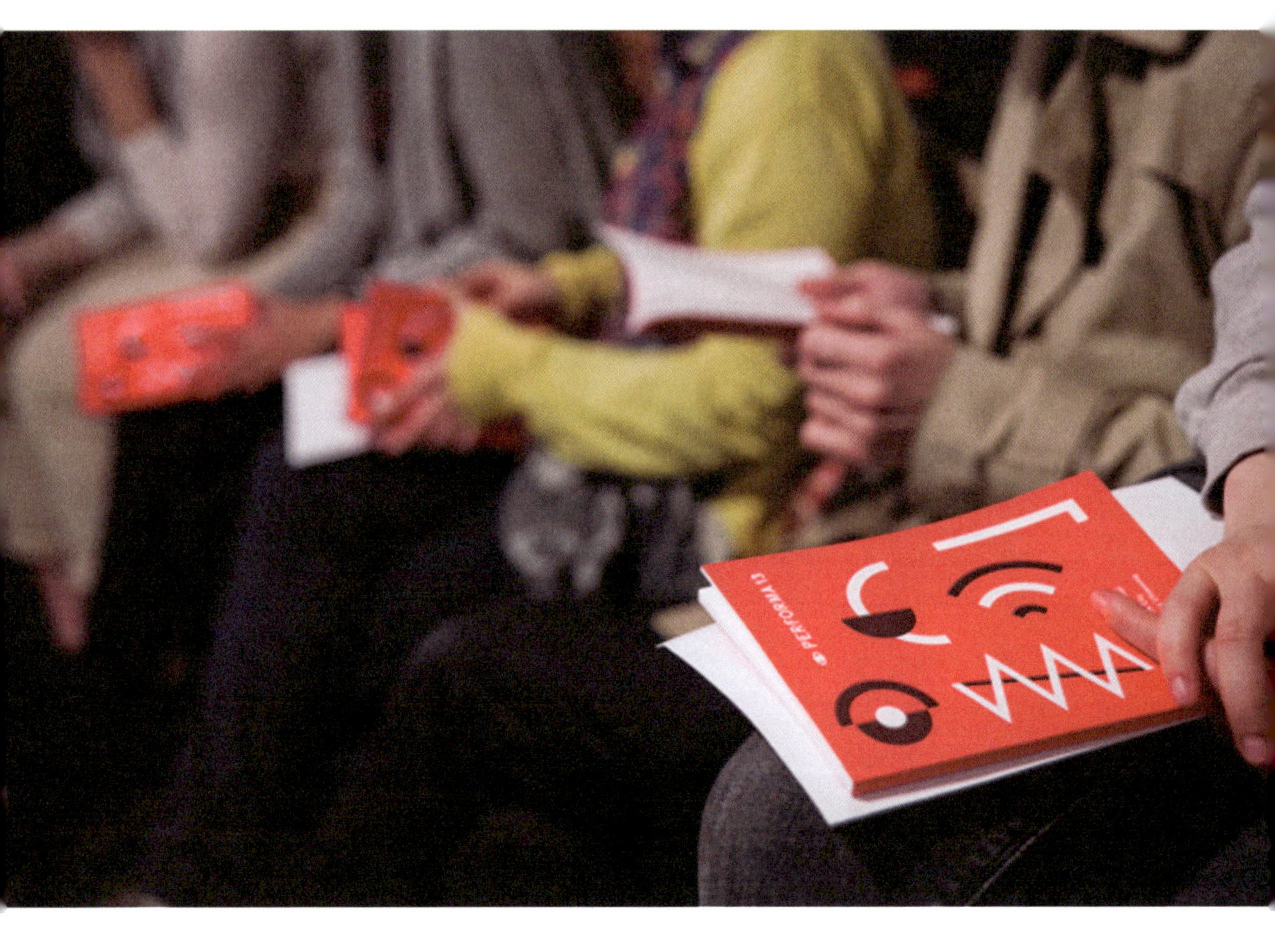

FOREWORD BY JENS HOFFMANN

PERFORMA IN AN EXPANDED FIELD

Performa is in many ways the logical continuation of RoseLee Goldberg's entire life's work. No one else in the last forty years has so strongly insisted on a truly interdisciplinary understanding of art. The fusion of diverse creative disciplines, RoseLee believes, has been key to many of the major milestones in the history of twentieth-century art, from the Bauhaus to Black Mountain College, from Judson Dance Theater to European theater and avant garde dance of the 1990s. The fusion of fields leads to the brightest artistic illuminations. RoseLee is a pioneer in the study of performance work, not only with her thoughtful publications, exhibitions, and programs, but also as a committed teacher and mentor to her many students at New York University.

The hard-and-fast lines that once existed between the proscenium and the museum, the black box and the white cube, have dissolved, and Performa, with its radical appetite to continuously push artistic borders, has spurred this development. From the early avantgardists of the last century, who looked around and saw the world radically changed and began to advocate for an altered artistic practice to mirror their new surroundings, incorporating movement, sound, and self into their expressions, to the pioneers of the postwar era who forcefully placed the artist's body at the center of a dialogue that questioned the very limits of art and life—performative artworks have been at the forefront of artistic practice over the last one hundred years and are finding homes in the world's most prestigious museums. Performa paved the way.

Performa's first biennial spanned several weeks in the fall of 2005. Since then, the five editions of the biennial have presented a wide array of live events throughout New York. Full-scale theatrical productions, presentations of dance, music, and intermedia projects, as well as more subtle interventions cohabitate comfortably under the Performa umbrella. Utilizing a variety of venues and locales, networking and connecting hundreds of artists and performers, and captivating thousands of viewers, Performa has certainly made its mark not only on New York but also on the international contemporary art scene.

Having worked in the field of performing arts for the first years of my career, and having always been interested in visual art, I know from firsthand experience the resistance within museums and theaters to works that blur boundaries. It is thus even more remarkable to witness how forceful and influential Performa has been in presenting and contextualizing performance, from dance to theater, to social practice, to multimedia works and everything in between. By commissioning new, significant works with each iteration, and presenting current and historical works together under the rubric of a single three-week event, Performa allows for a concentrated reflection on performance art's past and present. RoseLee always insists on a wide view that resists established timelines, generational divisions, and ethnic separations.

To me, the new commissions are the highlight of each Performa biennial. Allowing artists to explore often entirely new modalities— not only as a presenter of performing arts but as an advocate for their vitality as well—the organization has worked with many artists for whom performance was, at that point in their careers, an entirely new artistic language. Under the guise of its commissioning program, Performa has facilitated new works by some of contemporary art's most visionary minds, from Francis Alÿs to Mike Kelley, Yvonne Rainer, Paweł Althamer, Simon Fujiwara, and Tacita Dean. Alongside these new commissions, Performa has found itself in a valuable position to revitalize past discourses, presenting for instance a concert of Italian Futurist "noise intoners," the intonarumori, in 2009; reimagining Allan Kaprow's first Happening, *18 Happenings in 6 Parts* (1959), in 2007; or inviting Fluxus pioneer Benjamin Patterson to revisit his own oeuvre through a series of concerts and events in 2013.

While the centrality of the performative within contemporary art can hardly be denied, its radicality still presents difficult questions for artists, curators, critics, viewers, and historians. Breaking out of the medium-specific molds that have defined museum collections and cultural codes for centuries, the expansive practices of artists using performance raise questions about art's value, its collection and preservation, its mediation, and its relationship to audiences. Thanks to the efforts of RoseLee and the staggering advances that Performa has both reflected and created, museums are finally engaging in serious conversations about what it means to collect, exhibit, preserve, and interpret performative actions. Necessitating cooperation across departments, manifesting in sometimes unfamiliar places and engaging the public in vastly different ways than do static works of art, the expansion of performance in contemporary art has changed the conversation within both the studio and the museum.

Great art asks us to consider our limitations, the things we share with others and the things that we withhold. And while we may tire, from time to time, of the endless conversations that dominate art circles—about the role of the museum, the curator, the critic, the artist—in those moments when we are utterly compelled by the irrepressible power of a work, we are reminded that art is still a radical form of expression. It is continually in contention. As we face overwhelming circumstances as a collective, international community—staring down international conflict, global health crises, militarized police forces, infringements on our privacies and personal rights—the great potential of art to produce meaningful moments of exchange, understanding, and confrontation is reinforced, reinscribed. Now setting the course for its next decade of innovative programming, Performa will remain at the forefront of this dialogue: one that extends, ardently, from the art world into the world proper.

LOOK WHO'S TALKING

Even as one Performa biennial comes to an end, we begin to consider a series of research themes that will drive the next one. So it was with the final days of Performa 11, when ideas for Performa 13 began to form. With several commissions that had taken place during Performa 11 on proscenium stages, underlining differences between performance by visual artists in the art world versus performance by actors in the theater world, it was clear how minor a role the voice played in the context of these theater-based art works; hence the decision to investigate "the voice" in the 2013 biennial as a way to examine an element that seemed to be largely missing from artists' performance. Another strong theme of Performa 11, that of translating ideas from one medium to another, from visual concept to three-dimensional live performance, evolved into a discussion about communication across cultures and countries and the meaning of "citizenship" in a world increasingly acknowledged as a collection of immigrant nations.

Our historical anchor, always the critical foundation of our inquiry into performances past, moved along a chronological and geographical timeline from Russian Constructivism for the 2011 biennial to Surrealism, both in its Parisian mode and in its diasporic form, in the Caribbean and in West Africa.

We also launched an entirely new international initiative, the Pavilions Without Walls, a curatorial research program that focuses on artists and cultural practices in particular countries, allowing for the most expansive understanding of nationality in the process. We developed and built upon each of these themes, incorporating curator and producer fellowships to train emerging international professionals from Pavilion countries.

What, we wondered, is "the voice" in the art context? What does it sound like and what can it possibly say? Well, it all depends on who's talking. Such was the starting point for a series of evening-length concerts in venues across town, curated by Mark Beasley, whose accumulated research into "the voice" was given unique exposure. Indeed, these concerts provided countless opportunities to experience a little-known history firsthand: the voice in avant garde art over the past four decades. Considered by some as a solid substance analogous to the materials of painting or sculpture, from delicate trill to guttural cry, soft whisper to cackling laughter, Beasley's curatorial selection revealed the human voice to be an expressive instrument with enormous range and a record of outlandish experimentation. Combining elements of breath and physical fitness, emotion and pitch, song and rhythm, its reach expanding with ever-escalating technologies, the concerts provided an introduction to a range of vocal methods and were also a reminder of the fragility and power of the human voice at a time when texting dominates digital communication on the Internet and on smartphones. A trilogy of concerts presented different strands of vocal performance: one was exclusively for female vocalists, another explored a spectrum of male and female voices from avant garde to pop and death metal, while a third focused on readings lifted off the page.

The question "whose voice?" has also been central to our research into citizenship, and what it means in today's world of shifting cultures and customs across national borders and around the globe. With each crossing, the lines separating countries becomes fainter, nationalism loses its rousing common refrains, and a new citizenry emerges among those who raise and drop roots from one place to another. Mixing cultural mores and histories, several Performa 13 projects reflected on citizenship as a shifting, individualized brew of references that only partially reflect a given location, leaning instead toward citizenship as a worldview. The Norwegian Pavilion included an artist from Lebanon contemplating Norse mythology and "being Norwegian" while the Polish Pavilion showcased a cross-generational spread of ways to be Polish, in a country where political stripes have changed often, especially over the past half-century. The work of Akademia Ruchu, a performance group whose 1970s political happenings questioned "whose Poland?" at a time when the country was under the umbrella of Soviet Communism, contrasted with a younger generation who seemed to ask not only "in which European voice do we speak?" but also "how do we incorporate the colloquialisms of American rock and pop as well?" Citizenship, clearly, is an active status, continually defined and redefined by the citizen himself or herself and perfectly suited as subject matter to the layered tiers of live performance.

Whether experiencing the vitality of a Polish after-hours beer garden along the Williamsburg waterfront (with Paweł Althamer), or a communal Indian feast inside a light-filled sculpture that recalled street festivals in India (with Subodh Gupta), many of the Performa commissions provided moments in which anecdotes were shared, complicated, and exchanged through direct engagement with New York audiences. Raqs Media Collective from New Delhi used a chronicle of labor organizations in New York as the underlying manifesto for *The Last International*, their first major performance in the city, combining storytelling, a sculptural installation, and projections accompanied by recitations of revolutionary politics. In an entirely different vein, choreographer Jérôme Bel's *Disabled Theater* asked how it is that the physically disabled seem so often to be invisible, no matter their citizenship or country of origin. In each instance, personal tales, character, and style provided ingredients for an illuminating range of aesthetic possibilities.

Such individualized citizenry and its attendant forms of aesthetic expression worked its way through other channels, providing a startlingly visceral take on the past—as with Rashid Johnson's restaging of *Dutchman* (1963), an emblematic play on American race relations by Amira Baraka that Johnson presented in the overwhelming heat of the Russian & Turkish Baths on East 10th Street, providing an entirely new reading of a despairing political climate. Black performance and its relationship to sculpture, painting, and the museum was the underlying curatorial concept for a series of paired performances titled *Three Duets: Seven Variations*, organized by Adrienne Edwards and Thomas J. Lax in response to the exhibition *Radical Presence: Black Performance and Contemporary Art* at the Studio Museum in Harlem and Grey Art Gallery at New York University. Linking cross-generational artists, whose work over a thirty-year period shared genealogies and an approach to public space, *Three Duets* foregrounded long overdue acknowledgment of a generation of black artists in the historical art world, placing them firmly in the museum and gallery. In addition, the co-curators asserted that "blackness" was as much an approach to performance as a method to disrupt audience complacency, it was necessary to define they believed a network of black performers, aware that together they would have a broader reach.

Online, citizenship in the twenty-first century falls away almost entirely. Beyond borders, out of range, anywhere, everywhere, time and place are splintered, multiplied, cross-referenced, linked. Translating so much divided attention into a live performance and taking up an entire theater to do so—hallways, backstage, stairwells, balconies— Ryan McNamara's *ME∃M: A Story Ballet About the Internet* surprised everyone who saw it with its ingenious way of transporting each person, one seat at a time, from watching one routine of live dancers— Martha Graham to hip hop to jazzercise—to the next. Yet at the same time, everyone knew exactly what McNamara was getting at with his production that mimicked the multiple screens that we simultaneously keep open on our devices (the greater the number, apparently, the younger the user). For this work, which approached contemporary social media with originality, both intellectual and visceral, McNamara earned our second Malcolm McLaren Award, presented on the final night of the biennial.

As the Internet transforms old visions of the world, collapsing images and texts into a constant stream of data, so the Performa Hub provided an alternate gathering place for live encounters from places far and wide. Like the walkways at an airport, with everyone in constant motion and not always facing the same direction, this SoHo meeting place, with its classroom, kitchen, gallery walls, and large open amphitheater at its center, was the daily check-in point—a place to touch base with fellow viewers in the race around the city, intent on seeing more than one hundred events at over sixty venues. At the Hub, and with a little red book (the program guide) in hand, attendees could find one another, discover new ideas in lectures by artists, and talk from morning until night about the many ways of presenting them.

For three weeks, Performa transformed New York City into the performance capital of the world, building on the extensive foundation of live performance by visual artists in New York's historical avant garde. From uptown to downtown, from the Studio Museum to the New Museum, from the Kitchen on the West Side to artist Marianne Vitale's vast industrial studio across the East River in Long Island City, and to many places in between, including the diminutive theater at 80 St. Marks, the vast now-empty corridors of the James A. Farley Post

Office on Eighth Avenue, or the original home of the United Nations (the great hall in the Queens Museum where a United Nations-styled performance by Pedro Reyes took place), the city map was crisscrossed by visitors going to the essential Biennial Consortium, a network of some of New York City's most adventurous cultural institutions. Visitors from many countries—Australia, Korea, Israel, Norway, Poland, Britain, China, France, Turkey, and Brazil among them—came to witness the visionary programming of more than thirty-five curators and the powerful imagination of more than one hundred artists from New York and around the globe.

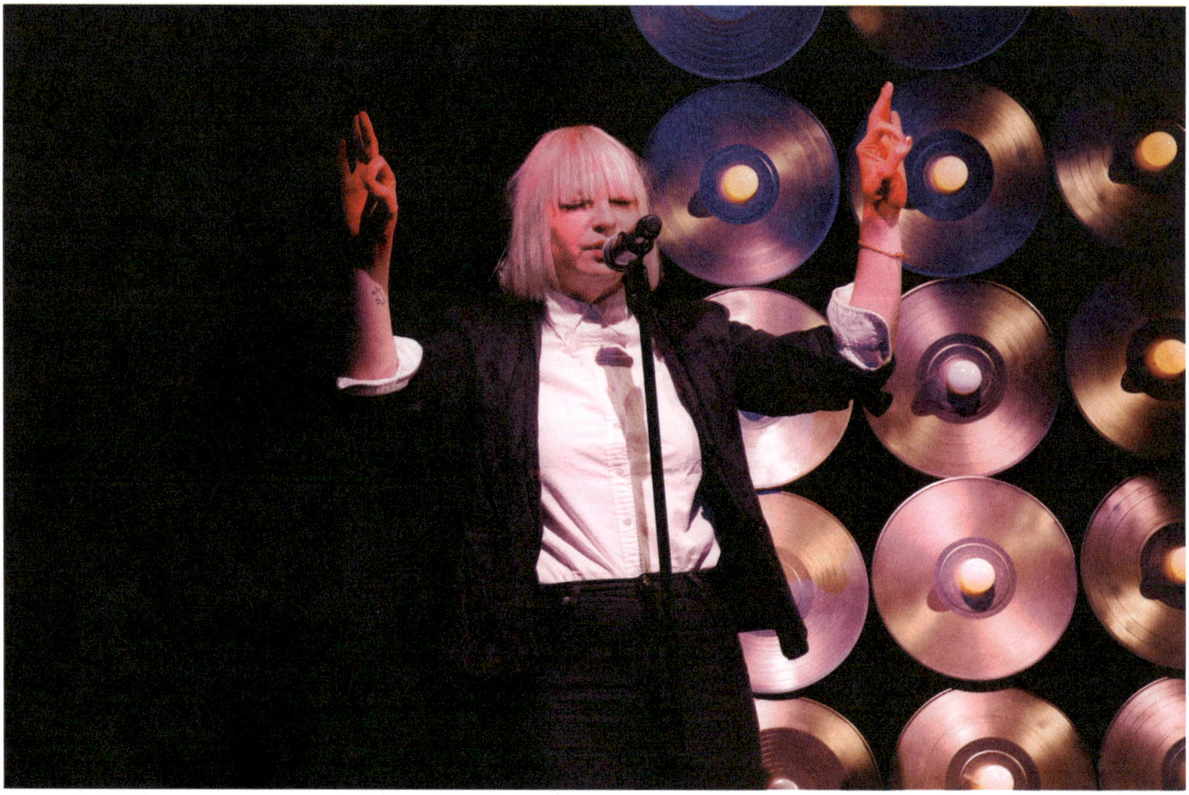

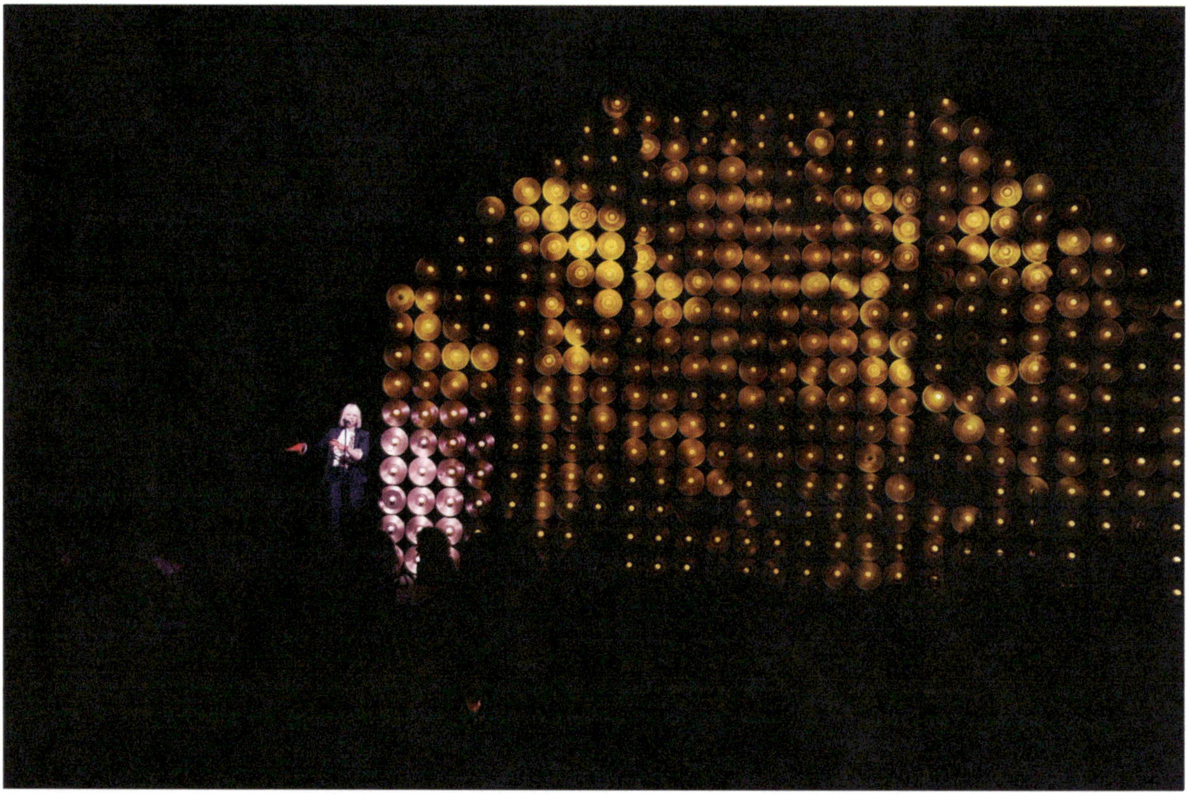

On the evening of November 27, 1924, a large audience, including artists Marcel Duchamp, André Breton, and Fernand Léger, arrived at the Théâtre des Champs Élysées in Paris for the opening of Francis Picabia and Erik Satie's much anticipated *Relâche*. They were surprised to find the theater closed with a large sign bearing "*Relâche*" plastered across the door. There was much confusion; *relâche* is a theater term used to describe a dark night, and audiences assumed the double entendre was another Dada prank. No amount of banging on the doors got the theater to open—rather, the audience was informed that the first performance of *Relâche* was cancelled because the choreographer and lead dancer, Jean Börlin, was ill.

It could not be more ironic that eighty-eight years later, Performa had been forced to postpone its own *Relâche* due to the disastrous aftermath of Hurricane Sandy, which hit New York a few days before the scheduled gala dinner. *Relâche—La Boum* was to be a vibrant, re-imagined reconstruction of that famous evening, which Fernand Léger described as "a lot of kicks in a lot of backsides whether hallowed or not!" in his rave review of the performance when it ran a week later. He also pointed out that this provocative event "burst the watertight division between ballet and music hall. Actor, dancer, acrobat, screen, stage, all these different means for creating a spectacle came together and rearranged themselves," he wrote.

As with *Relâche* in 1924, Performa rescheduled its gala, and for more than three hundred guests, it was an extraordinary introduction to an historic performance, as interpreted and reimagined by artist Ryan McNamara; the set of blazing electric lights was ingeniously recast with gold-painted LPs; fragments from René Clair's film, *Entr'Acte*, from the original, were conjured with acrobats hanging from the ceiling, and the Surrealist-inspired menu, with references to Salvador Dali's cooked birds in gilded cages, and René Magritte's perfectly painted green apples, kept the evening focused on the sheer imagination that drove the artists of Paris in 1920, as it did in New York in 2012. In Picabia's words, the evening offered "perpetual movement, life, the quest for happiness; it is light, riches, luxury, love, removed from prudery and convention; without a moral for the fools, without studied artistic effects for the snobs." For Performa, it was another thrilling occasion to realize one of our key missions: to show the history of performance past, and to bring it into the present in the most immediate and visceral way.

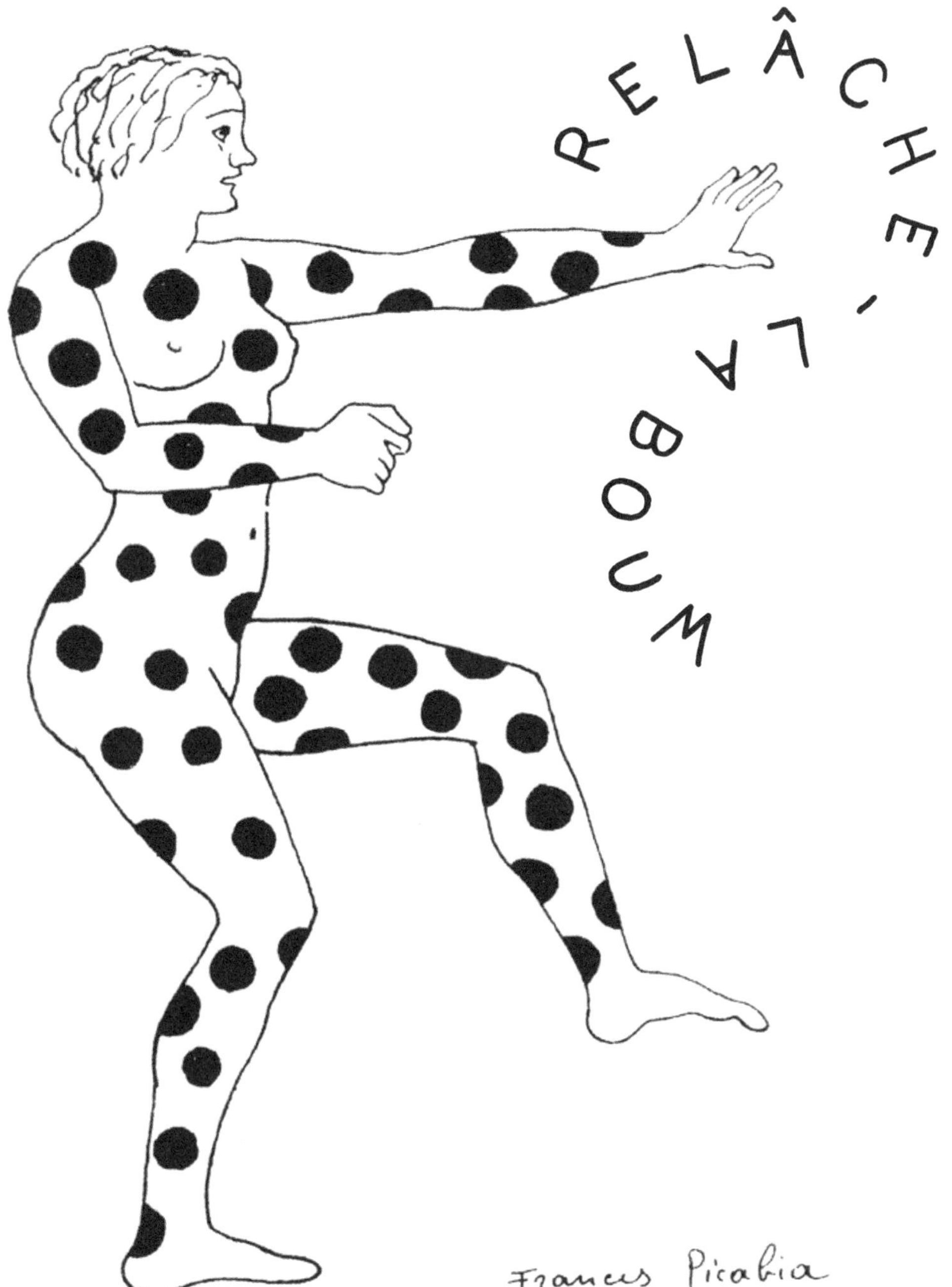

RELÂCHE-
LA
BOUM
Francis Picabia

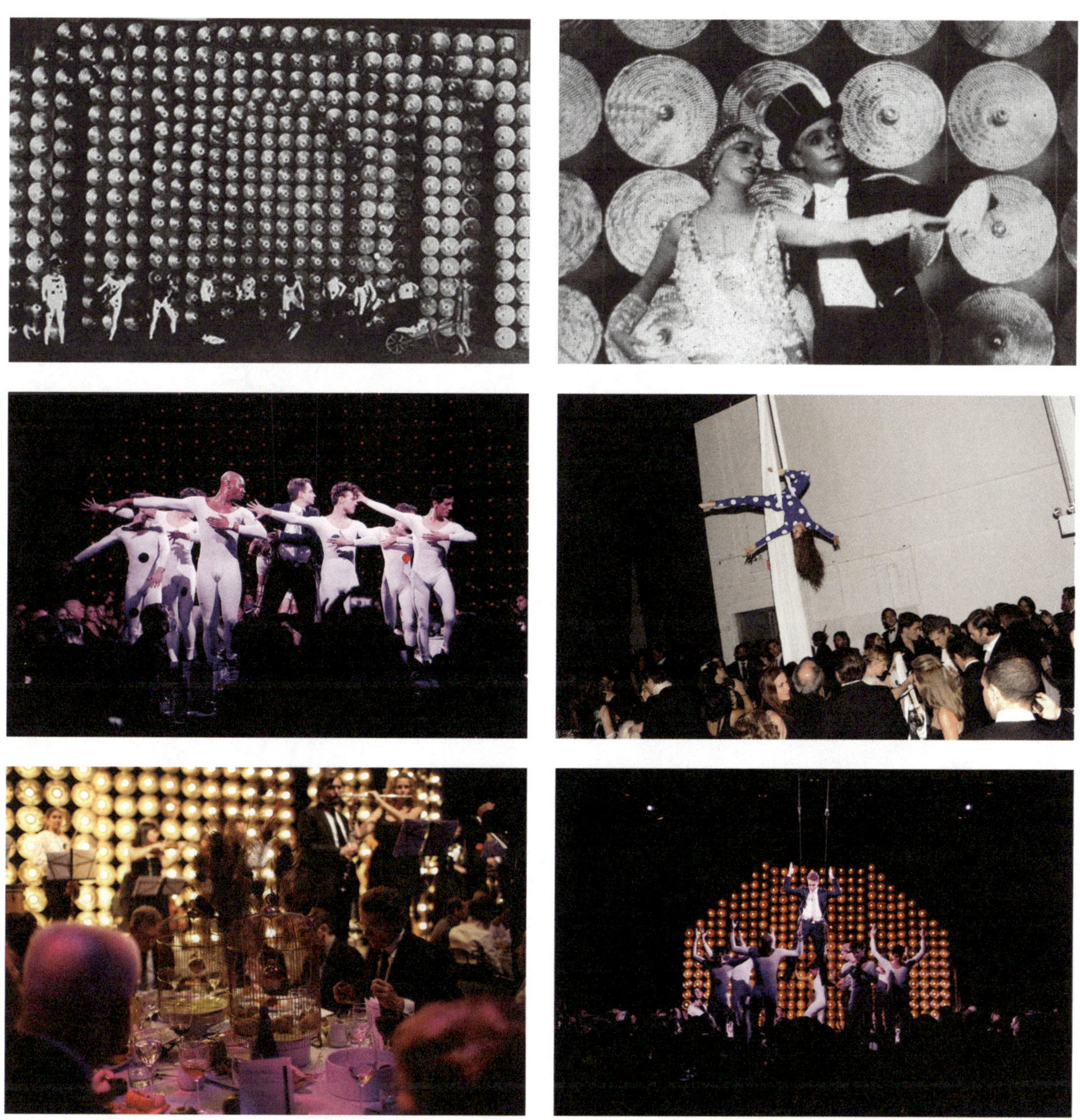

(Above, clockwise) *Relâche* set; Jean Börlin and Edith von Barnsdorff in *Relâche* performance (1924), archival photos, Ryan McNamara and dancers, (2012), aerialist above crowd at *Relâche La Boum* (2012); photo by Patrick McMullan, dinner table (2012); Ryan McNamara and dancers (2012), photos by Paula Court.

(Opposite) Performa Gala Invitation (2012) with Francis Picabia drawing figure for *Relâche*, Paris (1924). India ink, 18 x 14.5cm.

CHAPTER

1

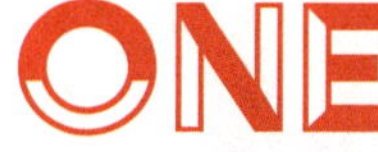

ONE

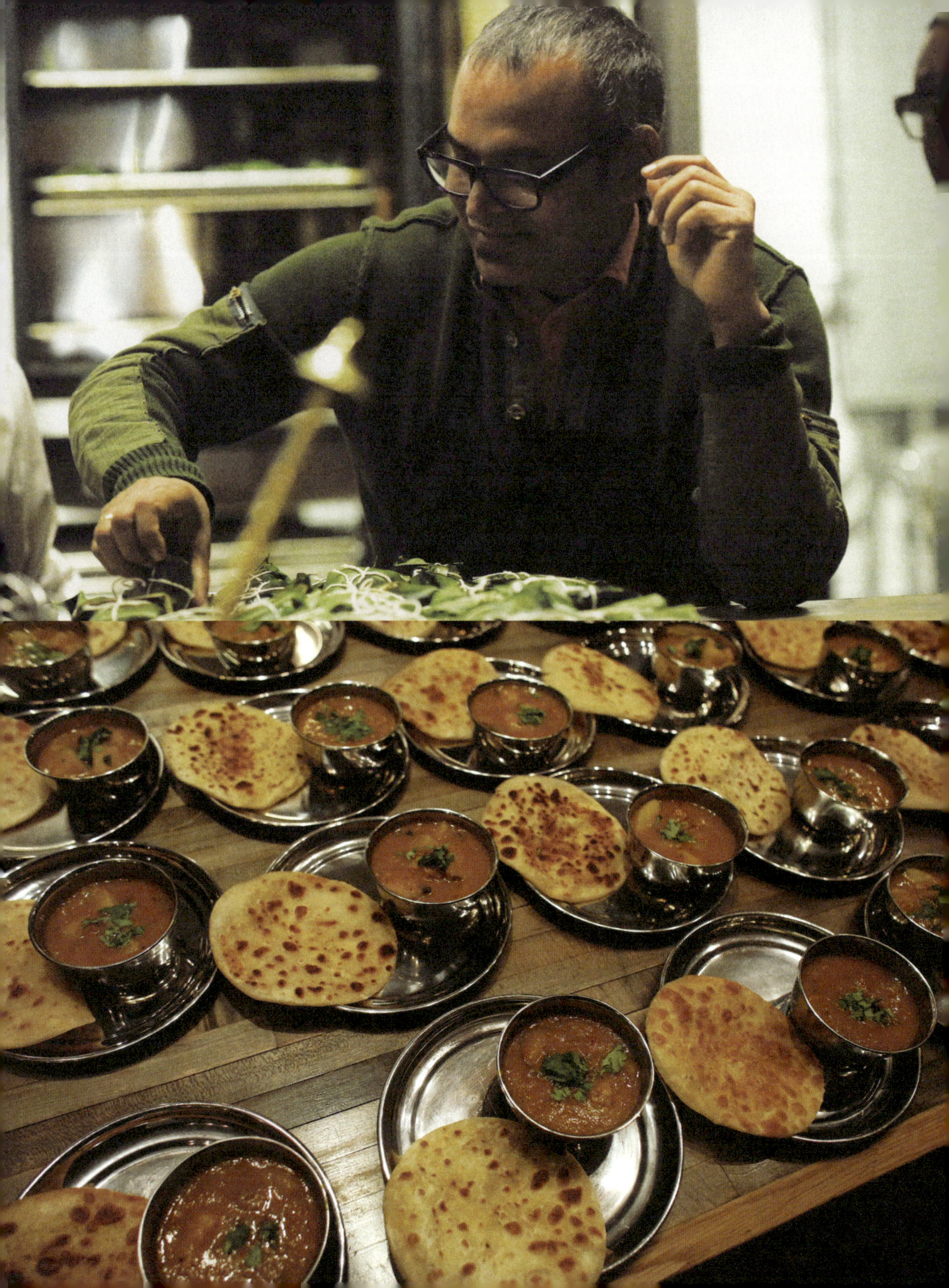

Photo by Paula Court

Subodh Gupta, *Celebration* (2013).

ROSELEE GOLDBERG INTERVIEWS SUBODH GUPTA ▲ THE OLD BOWERY STATION

RoseLee Goldberg: People who attended *Celebration* were surprised to discover that you spent six days prepping a five-course meal—shopping, chopping, cooking, and plating—to be served each evening to sixty people. What inspired you to present such a personally intense event?

Subodh Gupta: Touch is an important element in cooking. Cooking is not just about the food, but also about love, affection, and respect. For food to come together really well, you need the right moment when all these things unite as one—otherwise, you ruin the food. Performa was my first cooking performance and I wasn't going to miss the atmosphere of cooking and interacting with people.

RLG: How does this public dinner relate to traditions of communal eating and celebrations in India?

SG: For me, the Hindi word *utsav* is an apt word that captures this atmosphere of eating, drinking and merry-making with friends, an occasion that is joyous. *Celebration* was precisely this. There are many faces of *utsav* but there is only one mood, and this dinner managed to capture that mood.

RLG: You're clearly a very experienced and sophisticated cook! Where did the recipes come from? Where did you learn to cook?

SG: My mother is my first teacher when it comes to cooking. Most of the recipes are my mother's or from friends. Acquiring a taste for all kinds of food makes you more tuned to one's own traditional cuisine. And one can always improve and experiment with traditional cuisine and give it a different touch. I love doing that.

RLG: Your work often involves utensils—sculptures that include tiffin boxes, bowls, pots, and pans. Do you consider cooking as an extension of your art?

SG: I do consider my cooking as a part of my art. Either consciously or subconsciously, when I started using utensils, I was actually dealing with food, which is consistently part of my work. The utensils and food form a two-way street and narratives live between them, in different layers.

RLG: For this work, we sat inside an immense sculpture surrounded by neon tubes, bright shining utensils, looping light bulbs. Everything seemed to intensify the mood of celebration, or *utsav* as you call it.

SG: At the Performa Institute I heard the excellent talk by Queen Mother aka Dr. Delois Blakely, who said that celebration is a great form of art. It can be a state when everyone is happy, talking and whispering to each other, looking at each other—all these create a great celebration. At that point I thought to myself, yes, she is talking about me. I felt that she was actually giving me answers about my work.

RLG: Your sculpture provided an exquisitely beautiful setting for your food, as though one could not be had without the other. How do these two things come together?

SG: Like in any celebration, we decorate with lights, flowers, and such. For this dinner, I tried gathering all these elements together to make a sculpture out of all the parts. For me as an artist, while cooking and feeding formed a part of my performance, I also wanted to make the atmosphere more lively, so bringing in that element of a sculpture was important for me.

RLG: The dinner was a kind of visceral translation of your ideas about community and creativity—not just as an immersive experience, but as sustenance that actually passed through our bodies. Do you consider food-events a way to get inside your audience?

SG: You know I never thought of it in this way. This performance was an integral part of my journey in art, something that is very important to me. But when I look back, maybe this was not that important to everyone in the room. For some people, maybe this was just a night of food and celebration, leaving a void behind after it was over. But for me, this is the void that stayed with me. This was the strongest result.

RLG: *Celebration* couldn't have been more different from your work

Subodh Gupta, *Celebration* (2013), installation view. Diners were seated amidst the sculpture.

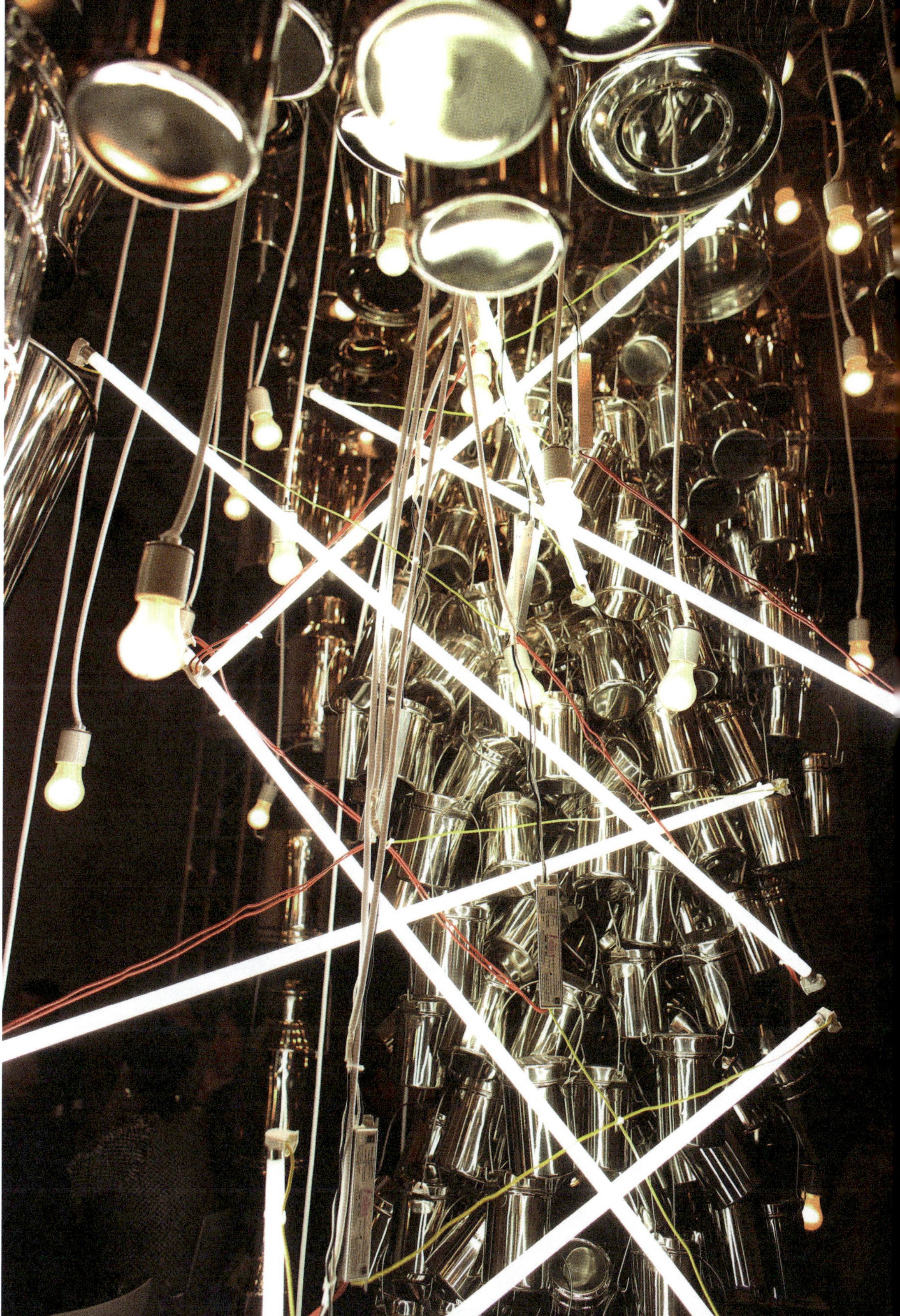

Spirit Eaters that I saw in Delhi in 2012, which involved "spirit eaters" from Northern India being paid to eat in order for a recently deceased person's soul to transition smoothly to the afterlife. It was a riveting exchange that was a bit uncomfortable to watch, as though we were too close to a private ritual, as though this ancient custom could not be staged outside of the context of a funeral. Yet, it was also very beautiful, ritualized and aesthetically arranged, with your aluminum bowls and goblets placed just so, and video cameras focused on the hands and faces of the three "performers" and projected on nearby screens. Can you talk about the different approaches to food in these two pieces?

SG: *Spirit Eaters* was a unique performance for me, as it was not just about bringing an ancient custom into a performance space but also involved my mother and the tension of the proceedings among the spectators. All this formed the performance. My mother cooked the meals for the three spirit eaters, my brother negotiated with them, and on the day of the performance I was completely immersed in it.

Doing this involved a lot of research over a few months. Locating the people who do this and putting the whole performance together was quite intense. Moreover, the fact that this was brought outside the context of a funeral, this was quite a spiritually anxious moment for me, even though I am not that spiritual.

Celebration for me is a script that can be replicated, but *Spirit Eaters* can never be.

RLG: Food becomes a form of communicating—there are very different rituals from country to country. How is sharing food a translation for an international public that doesn't know the details and the intricacies of Indian culture and daily life?

SG: In an increasingly globalized world, food travels more than humans. One doesn't have to travel to different capitals of the world to have cuisines of other countries. I believe this creates a dialogue and maps our awareness. But for an artist, since he belongs to another part of the world, food then is not just about food.

RLG: Your sculptures revolve around the domestic, the everyday, society, and community. What are your thoughts regarding food and its place in society, as an aesthetic as well as political order?

SG: What I try to do is locate the kitchen as a performative space within a larger cultural and artistic order. My own experience as an artist informs my food practice and its performance. I am interested in the entire culture that operates behind food—an everyday performance in the kitchen with people cooking, lighting fires, simmering, touching and smelling food, and of course tasting what is being served.

RLG: What does live performance mean for you in the overall practice of your work?

SG: It shows me that I am still alive doing what I like.

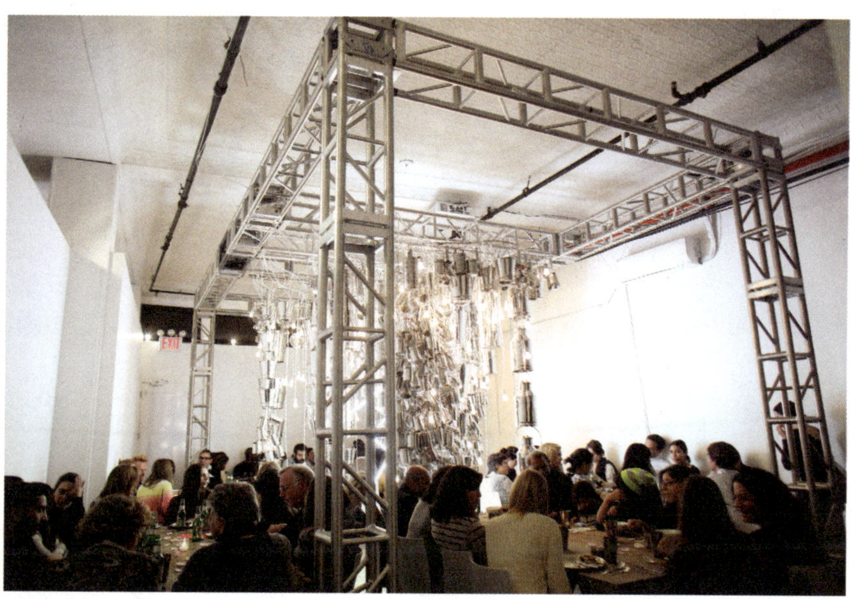

Subodh Gupta, *Celebration* (2013), installation view. With a structure supporting the central sculpture.   Photo by Paula Court

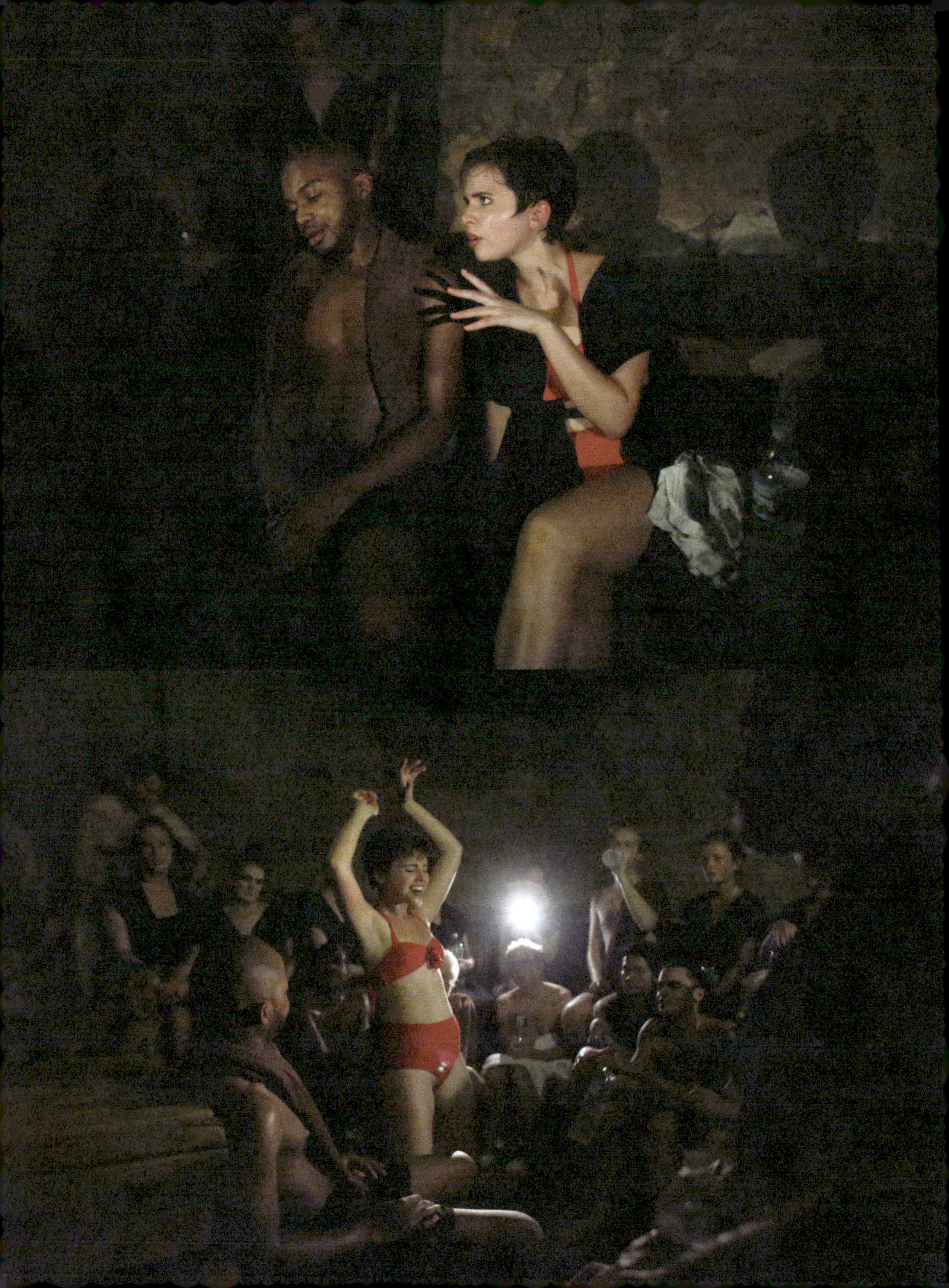

RASHID JOHNSON

DUTCHMAN

Adrienne Edwards: I was immediately intrigued by your idea of doing *Dutchman*, a play first performed almost fifty years ago. How did you encounter Jones/Baraka's writings and who was he—Jones or Baraka?

Rashid Johnson: It was LeRoi Jones. I have had a deep involvement with Baraka's work since I was very young. My mother would read him to me.

AE: Your mother is a professor. What did she teach?

RJ: She taught African Studies with an emphasis on postcolonial and feminist theory. I grew up with real hardcore feminism. I say that kind of jokingly but also lovingly. It was an interesting time. There was malleability. My mother is capable of seeing the grays. It is important for an educated person to be able to see the grays as opposed to seeing things as strictly black and white. Black feminists have a very interesting perspective because their feminism is different from European or Western feminism, which has been formed by a group of women with the input of black female thinkers whose contributions were not necessarily acknowledged nor were their agendas clearly discussed. At the time, feminist black thinkers like my mother were thinking about the complexities, differences, and obstacles that different women have, and insisting on language, strategies, and ultimately an understanding of how to create flexibility in an ideology so that they were equally covered in its discourse. This is an important factor in how one can embrace new ideas.

AE: What you are describing is the notion of intersectionality or simultaneity, which black feminists like the Combahee River Collective theorized. Intersectionality is a productive way to describe your aesthetic.

RJ: In a lot of ways it is. We have the ability to embrace so many different things simultaneously and to put those things together through objects and gestures, as well as systems that seem to flow together and begin to make sense when they can—sometimes intentionally, sometimes not. It's neo-poetry. This is the case for Jones's poems, too. Well into high school I thought of him as a children's poet. One way to understand and experience things is through how we were originally exposed to them. It was Dr. Seuss and LeRoi Jones for me. It wasn't until later that I understood how radical the language was and how complex his concerns were. The things he addressed are relevant today. Despite having a much greater understanding of the struggle of his project and its seriousness, I have that childhood memory of him. Gives me a really fresh perspective on his work, not being introduced to him as a radical, which is the way many people are presented with his work. Thinking about a project for Performa, I wanted to touch on something that was very close to my history and that would be informed by the many different aspects of my experience.

AE: You were always focused and clear about exactly what you wanted this project to be, which made you a true joy to work with. From the start you wanted to direct the play as opposed to acting a character role.

RJ: I wanted to direct a play and work on something I've known for many years. I intimately know Baraka's words and have a comfort level with his language, which gave me the confidence to take it on. I envisioned *Dutchman* before it was finished, which was very rare for me. It's one of the few things I've seen so clearly at an early stage, knowing how it would evolve. I knew I wanted to make an intervention that would color it in some way. I didn't know exactly how. I made the decision to work with the language of the play and to interfere as little as possible.

AE: We had conversations about how the language is shockingly contemporary.

RJ: It really is but also it's kind of dated, which made it complicated. This is the most interesting thing about the writing for me. I was interested in learning as much as possible from the two great performers and the play. I would tell them to repeat the words to bring them to life. Half the time I wasn't rehearsing; I was trying to hear it again, trying to understand it more, and I'd say, "Well, let's just stop there. And, let's, let's do that part again." Doing this play was an opportunity for me to be able to control my ability to witness it. The

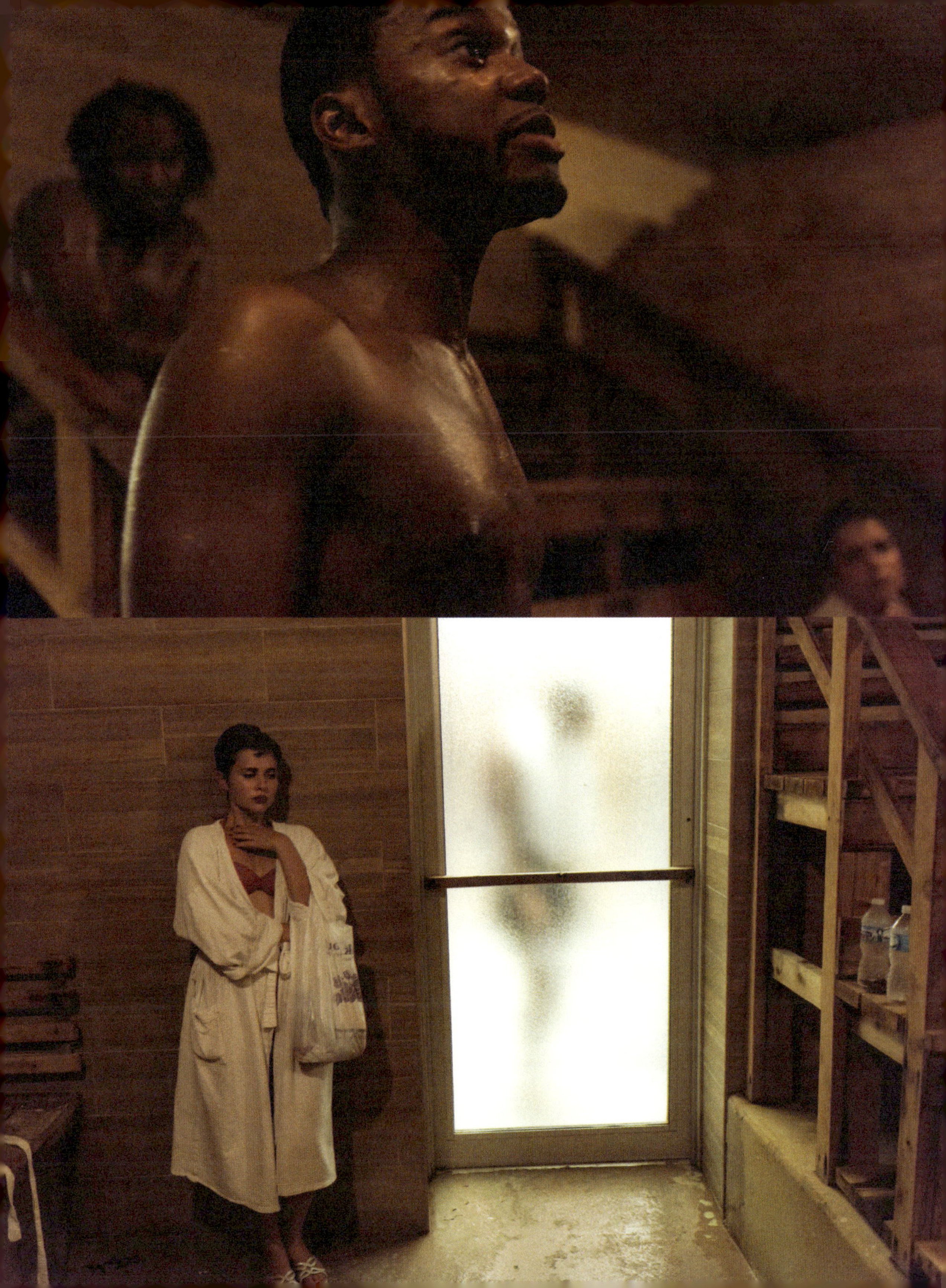

play wasn't being performed anywhere at the time. I needed to make it in order to witness it.

AE: Clearly this was a deeply introspective, personal experience. When did the performance actually begin and end for you?

RJ: It started when I said I wanted to do it. I'm interested in how performance doesn't necessarily have a predictable beginning or ending, especially in the context of performance art. It doesn't revolve around a curtain or have simple definable beginnings and endings. For me, the play began with the idea. Once conversations with you and RoseLee began, it was already performing itself. It was considerably less about the event for me. I didn't even attend all of the performances. In some way I was already done.

AE: Is this because you were most invested in the process?

RJ: Yes. It was about the rehearsals, being able to witness this thing over and over again, coming into being.

AE: The rehearsal process was especially interesting because the bathhouse was fully operational. People would be in the saunas or steam room while the actors went through their lines.

RJ: Other people were there and they would imagine they were witnessing an interaction between two people and I'd sit there watching their reactions as an informed viewer. I was embarrassed for the actors.

AE: Those reactions registered as shock, like, "Why are they talking to each other like that?"

RJ: I was embarrassed to be the catalyst for all of this but I was also thrilled, excited, and energized by the bathhouse customers stumbling upon such an interesting and bizarre scene or what felt like an incident—that was incredibly complex.

AE: Why was it important to stage it in the bathhouse?

RJ: The decision was really personal. I started going to the baths when I began graduate school in Chicago at the age of twenty-four. I had gone one time prior, but in grad school I started to use it as a vehicle. It was a difficult time for me. I was dealing with a lot of anxiety and stress. How was I going to make art? How would I go to school? How was I going to pay rent? How was I going to rebound emotionally from a divorce? All giant questions, which are not unique experiences. A friend of mine said you should go to this Russian bathhouse because it will calm you down. It was in a building three or four blocks away from where I grew up. It's on Division and Damien, and I grew up on Damien and Potomac. I always thought it was a really creepy, old, strange building. I also didn't know the rules. It's just like someone hands you a trumpet and you don't know how to hold your lips. The first time I went with my friend it was the middle of winter. I was under a tremendous amount of pressure and stress. I went in and sat there in heat and it's like everything just went away.

I didn't grow up a religious person. My father is an atheist. He's absolutely an atheist fundamentalist. Eventually, the baths became this ritual place like a temple of some sort. It changed my life. I started going there religiously. I would Xerox my reading for grad school and I would sit on the top row of the Russian room.

AE: The hardcore row—only for the initiated!

RJ: Yeah, the hottest row. I was this young guy and it was all men at that time. It was like walking into a history book, because everyone there knew each other—amazing groups of people. On Mondays, the Communists would come and they would overlap with the Mexican businessmen and then later in the day the judges would come and then Jesse Jackson and the reverends. These guys, they've known each other for thirty years from participating in this ritual. You'd see them rubbing each other down with towels and giving each other *platzas*. One of the Jewish Communists would get a rub down from a South Side reverend. They are taking care of one another and having fascinating conversations, not really debates. There wasn't a lot of high discourse. It was more personal, like, "How are your kids?"

AE: A genuine camaraderie. How did they respond to you? What were your interactions like?

RJ: They called me "The Reader." I would sit up on the top row reading theory like Derrida or Deleuze and Guattari. They always asked, "What are you reading?" No one else was in there reading.

They were all having conversations, they were friends, and had long-standing relationships. I had none of those relationships. But over time they made me feel very welcome.

AE: You moved to New York in 2004, which is when we met.

RJ: Yeah, that's right, and I immediately found the bathhouse where we did the performance—within the first month of being here. I can live in any city as long as there's a bathhouse because it's like a safe house. It's where I've gotten most of my ideas, where I can develop and investigate them. I can be by myself and sit and let the heat soak in. Essentially what we are talking about are two things that are important to me: Baraka and the bathhouse.

When I began thinking about what to do for a performance, I took two of the warmest, most comfortable things that I could wrap myself around and I put them together. It made sense.

AE: What made *Dutchman* remarkable is how these disparate things were reimagined together, alongside one another, how the space of the bathhouse and the language of the play converged, were recontextualized through their relationship to you. How did you convince a bathhouse to host a play? How did you convince two actors to rehearse for weeks and to perform over the course of several days in a sauna?

RJ: Both were very complicated. As far as convincing the bathhouse, I had to make them think it was their idea. They have known me for about nine years. I went in and chatted up the owners and I said, "I'm doing this play and I need something like what they had. But, of course, not this place." And it led to, "Why not this place?" as if something were wrong with it. I replied, "No, you guys are a business and this is an important art project." I think that kind of challenged and intrigued them. So they said yes. They even visited when I did the project in Chicago in 2014. As for the actors, I tried to make them believe this was a normal thing to do. I was lucky to deal with two young actors who did have some experience, but not a ton of expectations for how things should be.

AE: You were clear about working with emerging performers and not celebrities or known actors.

Rashid Johnson, *Dutchman* (2014), Chicago rehearsal views.

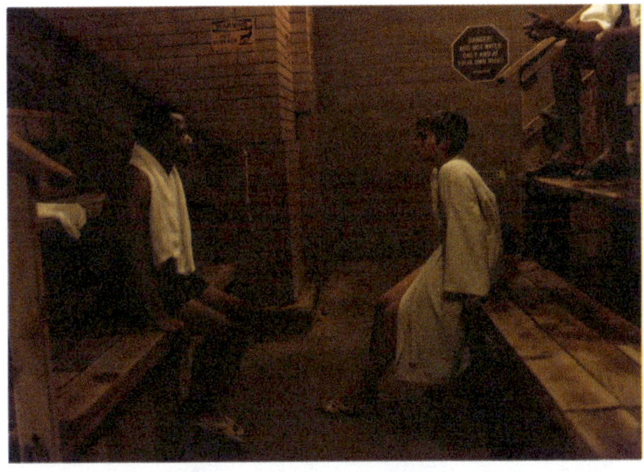
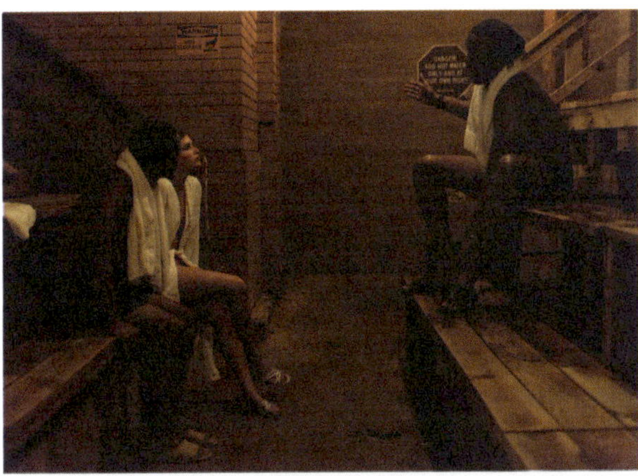
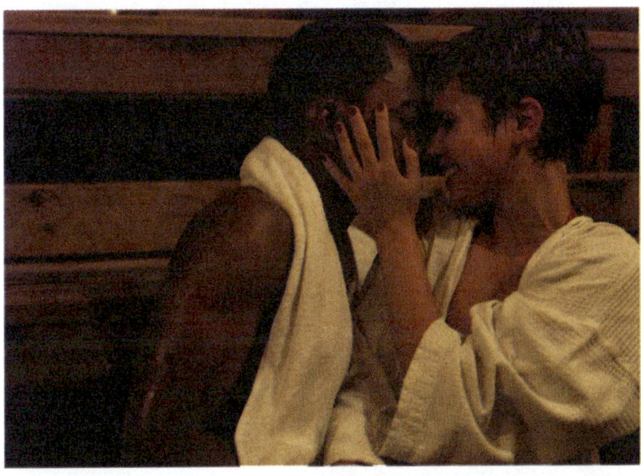
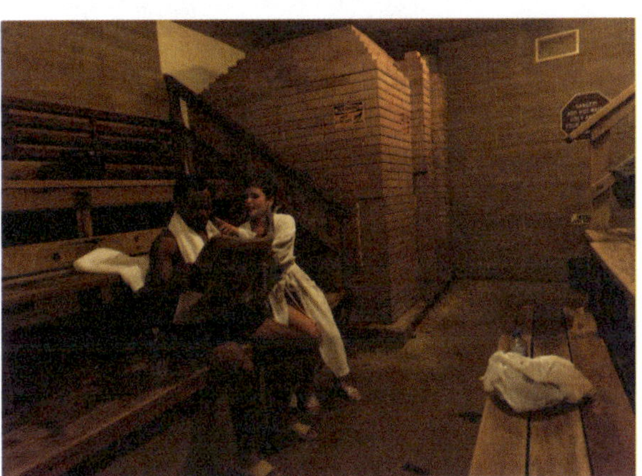
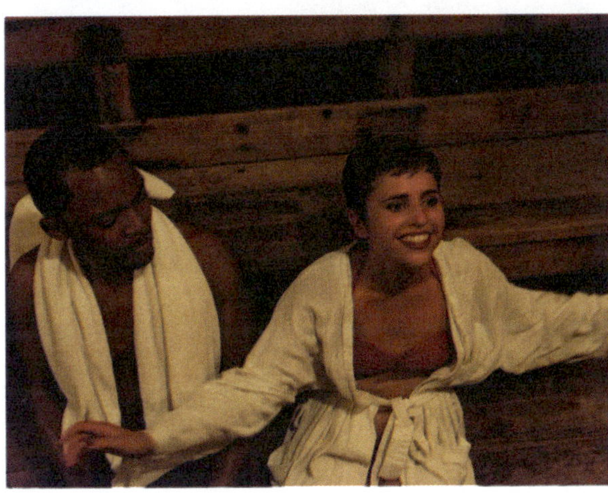
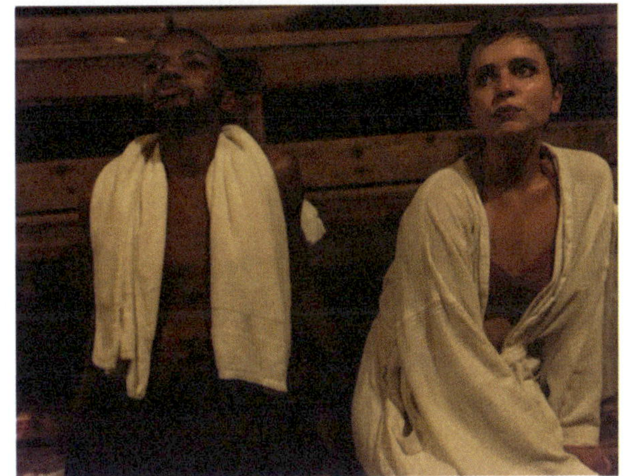

RJ: Absolutely. I wanted two people who were not familiar with the material. I didn't want them to have performed the material or to have witnessed the material performed in a way that wouldn't jive with my expectations for how the performance should function. I wanted them to have some freedom interpreting it, along with me, putting it into their own vision, allowing their interpretations of those characters to develop. I took them to the bathhouse and said, "Do you want to be in here?" You either love or hate a bathhouse. I made clear to them my love of the place. It's really strangely romantic in a way, as is the case with everything I have done. The performance was an opportunity to directly explore the more poetic, romantic side of my work.

AE: Did working in performance feel more experimental to you than the way you think about or approach paintings or sculpture?

RJ: Well, yes. With objects, I have total control. I have never considered myself a control freak until everyone told me I was a control freak. The performance was something that I couldn't control completely, because the characters were out of my hands. I didn't have the skill set to control it in the same way as my other work.

AE: You made deliberate structural choices you would rehearse a lot but your role was very observational, process-driven.

RJ: Absolutely. I was just a witness.

AE: You relish this freedom, which you constructed for yourself.

RJ: It was a totally different experience for me and I loved it. It was cathartic. I had to share the responsibility. As a visual artist, for the most part I am the only one on the hook for everything. It's me, it's my voice, it's my hand. It's a struggle. The artist in the traditional sense as someone by themselves in a room taking something that doesn't exist and making it so.

AE: What was it like to take this piece to Chicago?

RJ: It was amazing. My parents were there and my sister. It really hit me the first night. I was thanking everyone for coming to this place that helped inspire me to do the performance and that has changed my life. As I have gotten older and also have become a father, I'm awfully sentimental. I have these moments when I'm like, wow, this happened here, and this place changed the direction of my work and how my ideas are formed and evolved. It was really beautiful and interesting because the bathhouse in Chicago was very different from the one in New York. The actors did an incredible job adapting to the new environment, where it was no longer a three-part play, occurring in three different zones. In Chicago, it became a play in halves and with an intermission. I played a cameo role in the Chicago version in which I loudly closed a door to start the play. I attended more of the performances because I needed to see the play again, so it became a different experience. The grasp of the characters and the way they evolved for the actors, from the first time and to the second time, was dramatic. It was a different play. A change in venue seems so simple but it's not simple at all. It's a radically different experience. And the fact that it was live continued to be thrilling for me and I'm trying to find a way to do work live again. I still haven't decided which of the two versions I like better. I don't think I'll ever decide. It's not my job.

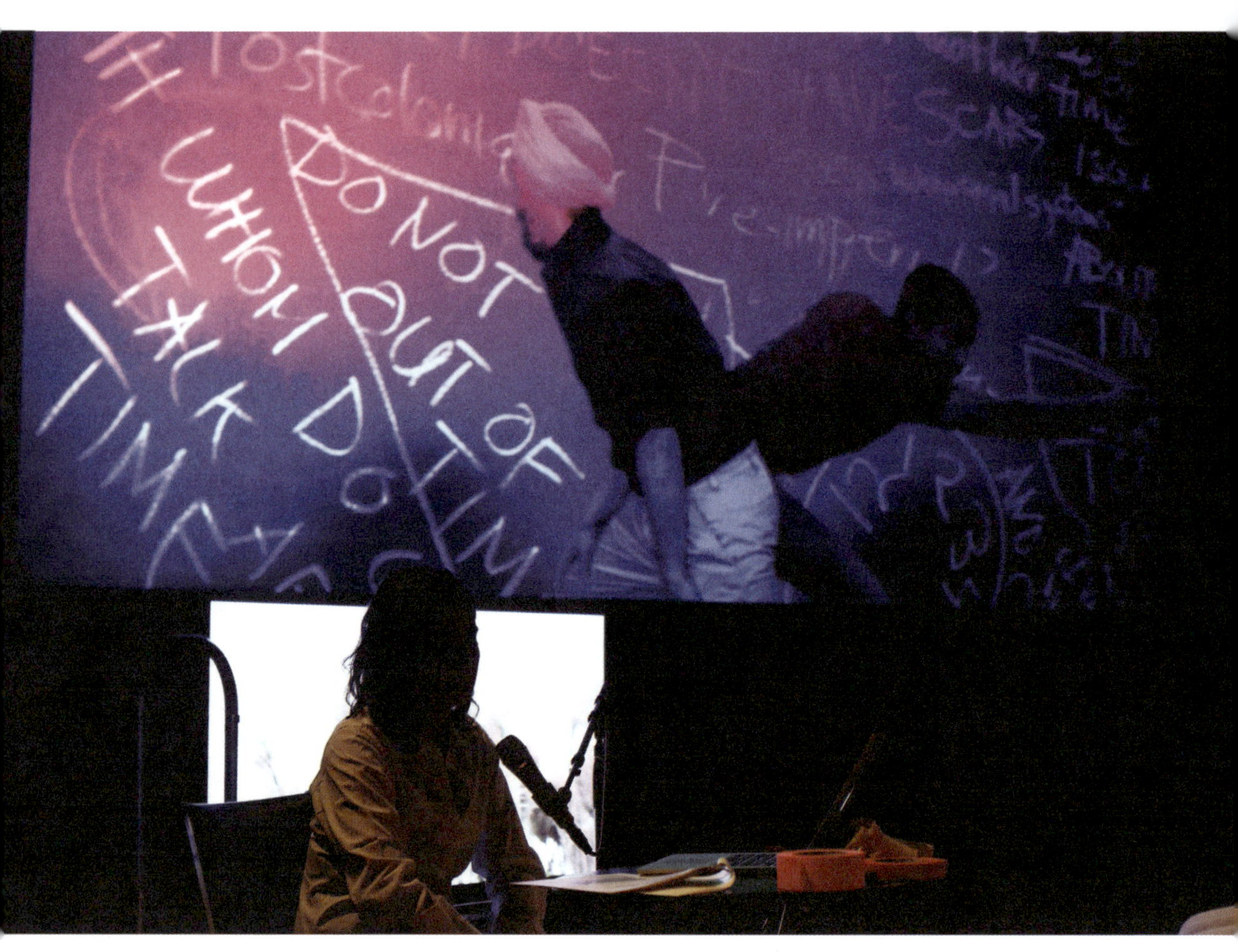

DO NOT
TALK
OUT OF
TIME
WHOM I
DO I
DO I
lost claim
Fire-imprint
scars
TIME

RAQS MEDIA COLLECTIVE

THE LAST INTERNATIONAL

I remember the moment that I got it. I was in the Zurich airport, heading to Dubai, four months after the performance of *The Last International* in Manhattan's once-revolutionary East Village. In this largely generic anyplace, shuttling between two metropolises, I became aware of a meaning, if that's the right word for what I had seen in the East 4th Street theater.

As critics, we're often forced to quickly pass judgment—sometimes weeks later, more often days, increasingly within hours, and nowadays there's the draw to instantly react through tweets and other social media tools. "I was just thinking this performance was abstract then a guy in a vintage diving suit showed up on a bike. #thingscanalwaysgoonestepfurther," I typed into my smartphone during the performance and broadcast to the world with an image through Instagram and Twitter. That curt transmission to over 15,000 people garnered twenty-nine likes on Instagram and two on Twitter. It was one of a small cluster of messages I shot out that evening as I searched for meaning. I use the word "shot" consciously, as such messages feel like bullets into an open field. It's hard to see where these messages go, but where they land feels vast, yet it's space nonetheless, which means it is finite, even if it's impossible to see the horizon. Revolutions, like art and criticism, have an unsuspecting public.

Overhead on the balcony a conversation took place around a table as the audience filed into the old theater. Intellectual types talked in the jargon of symposiums, with their unemotional tones, subtle body language, and congenial insularity. A central performance started a little while later. People in chairs read scripts, a ladder was brought out, colorful tape was stuck on the floor, and a person in a vintage diving suit on a bicycle wheeled in while projections and screens added to the melee. *The Last International* was decentered, even as we, the audience, formed a ring around a cluster of actions.

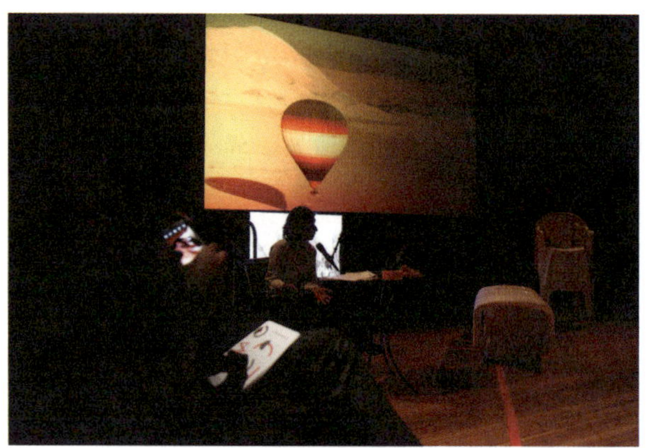
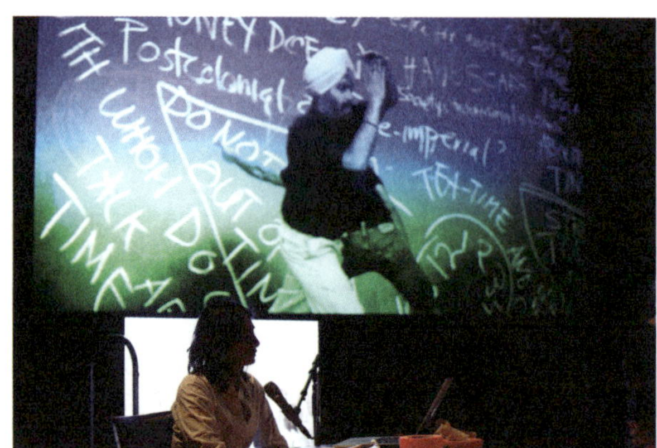
ONEY DO
Postcolonial
e-imperial?
DO NOT
whom
TALK DO
TIME

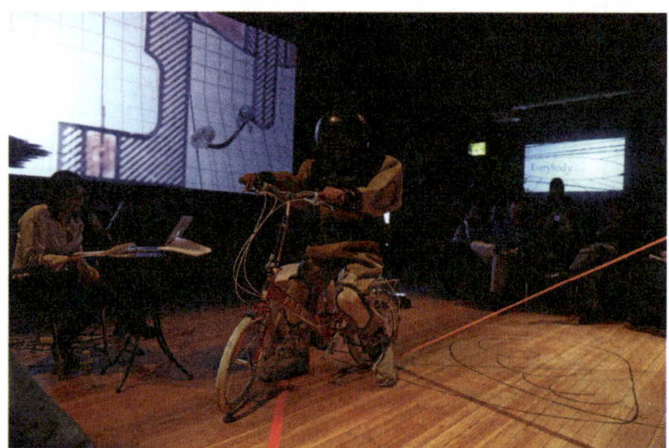
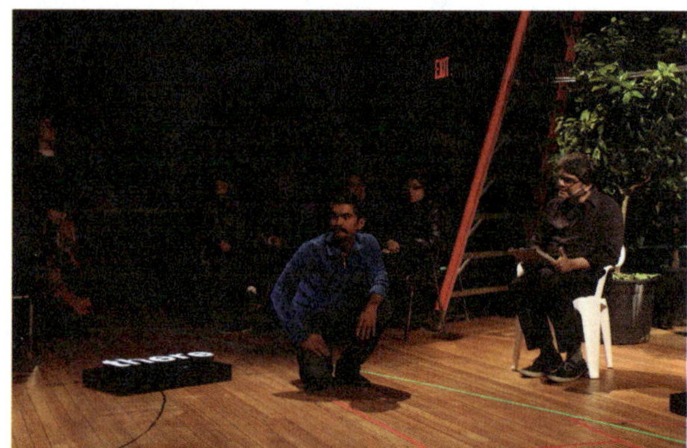
Everybody

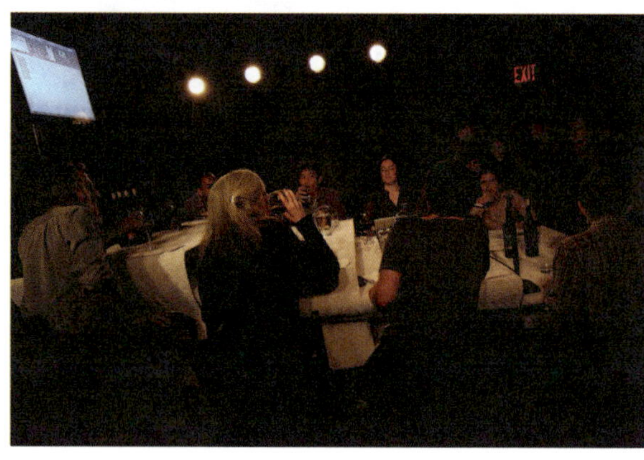
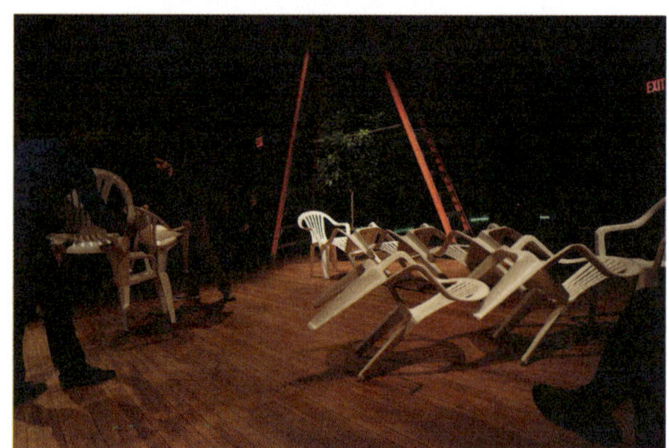

"'I am the recipe for my own marmalade.'—Raqs Media Collective," I tweeted in the haze of the stimuli. The performers promised nineteenth-century utopian politics that evening, while I swam in their lake of words. It was a "performed installation with sculpture, archival documents, actions, newly filmed footage, and music to articulate a possible new aesthetic for political solidarity, debates, and projections." A proposal, it said, "for a new, joyful way of working and thinking with disagreements, solidarities, and projections transformed into poetry, with orchards growing in factories and dancing ideas that connect distant laboring bodies." What I perceived was a series of disjoined elements that mirror the instant revolutions of today unaided by the privilege of hindsight.

That recipe for new aesthetics felt like an educational project, sharing an ambition with many endeavors seeking to change the world. I felt abandoned, floating in a vat of seemingly unrelated ideas. "We saw each other, again, for the first time in Zucotti Park." The work evoked the site of promise for a revolution of the near past, like Shahbag, Sidi Bouzid, and Tahrir.

The lie of performance is that it seems to aspire to universality, like revolution, even though its impact is predominantly personal. The performance of *The Last International* pushed outward into a universe of ideas but triggered visceral reactions. An action is a dispute about rules. Who decides its meaning, and can we see the real impact of its ripples if they continue for hours, days, weeks, months, or years?

I left *The Last International* detesting the didacticism and self-indulgence of the night. The narrative was destabilized to the point of disintegration. Meaning was seemingly shattered on the rocks and all we were left with was the poetics—left in the margins, sharing in the spectacle without a script. As a critic, I'm often mediating the grounds of dispute and debate. Yet here I was in the middle of a hybrid space, where the debate never settled into place. The critical job is often to place art on a scale or spectrum, comparing and contrasting. But in the revolutionary fervor of the moment that scale is perpetually in flux, hard to situate and with shifting boundaries in every dimension. "How does a moment become a movement?"

Modern criticism, according to Terry Eagleton, emerged from the struggle against the absolutist state. It is a distinctive discursive space, borne out of rational judgment and enlightened critique. Today, corporate neocolonialism is ruled by apparatuses of control, so that the rational critic is inadvertently subsumed into its logic. The revolutionary moment seeks to disrupt that structure, which may explain why Surrealism, with its dreams of anti-imperialism, was often a refuge of the postcolonial artist. The allure of escaping into impossible dream-worlds is real, even if its safety is ephemeral.

Revolutions ask us to suspend disbelief as we break the ground beneath us to plant new seeds. We wait for a moment that may never arrive, or project our present into the future. In 1953, Cuba's Fidel Castro ended one of his famous revolutionary speeches with the words, "Condemn me. It does not matter. History will absolve me." The promise of the future substitutes for today—time is the arbiter of that space.

But where does that leave me, the critic? Our role is not anchored to artistic intent—the historical importance of the work is not in the foreground even if it is always on my mind. We react in the present, we witness new worlds before us, often with the language of yesterday. Because *the last international* is nothing when it cannot be everything."

In transit, everything feels possible. Flux is the rule. Walking through the Zurich airport, I remembered the words, "Where does the authority of power, its self-possessed confidence, come from?" It is here, in this space where the systems are simultaneously invisible and clear, where we are traveling through without settling. In that moment confronted with art, we are not historians, or fortunetellers, but witnesses, recording our sliver of the world before us. Yet *The Last International* is not about today, but yesterday and tomorrow. The history it excavates is mercurial, the dreams never realized. During the performance, we learned about Gainda, the runaway rhinoceros, who lives on in the art of Albrecht Dürer. An Indian present for the king of Portugal, the very un-European animal was forced to battle an elephant for royal sport and won. The majestic creature eventually drowned in transit from Lisbon to Rome as he was being shuttled to the

Catholic Pope as a gift. While Gainda died at sea, he did reach Dürer in the landlocked city of Nuremberg through stories and perhaps sketches, an unexpected consequence that made him immortal.

As a critic, I'm asked to find order in chaos, but *The Last International* asked us to sit with the idea of not knowing. As uncomfortable as that may be, I let the memory of the piece wash over me, understanding that the destination is always an imagined oasis.

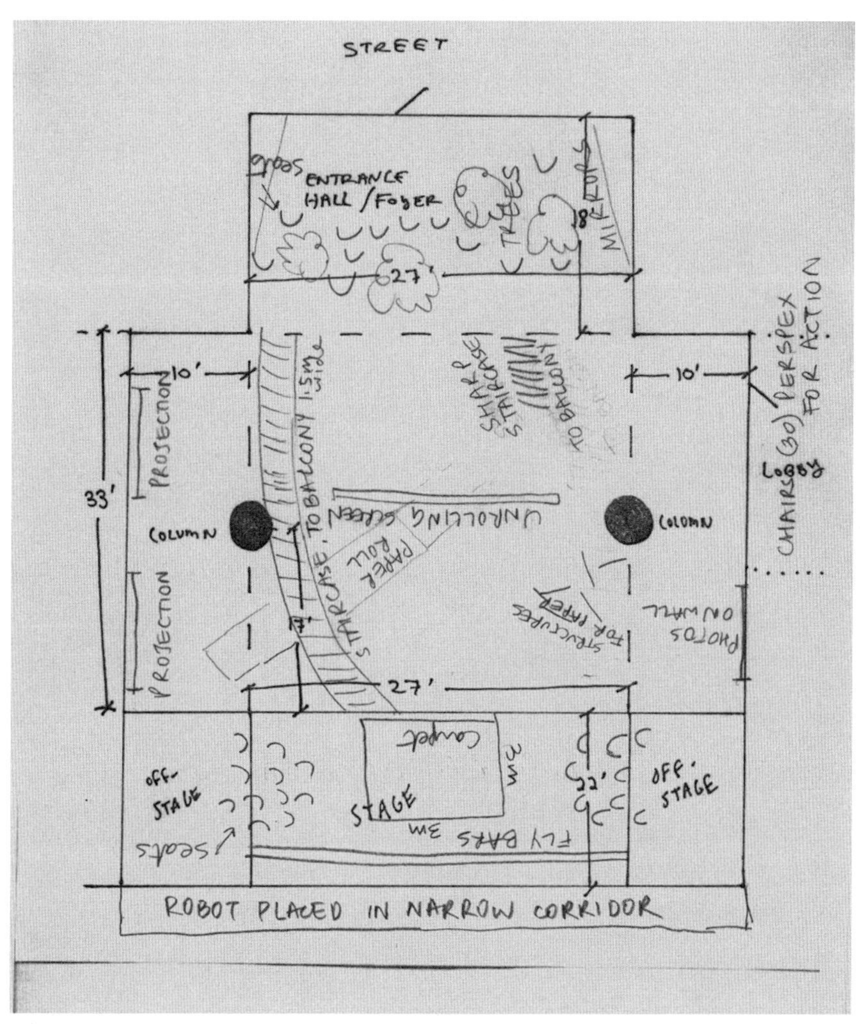

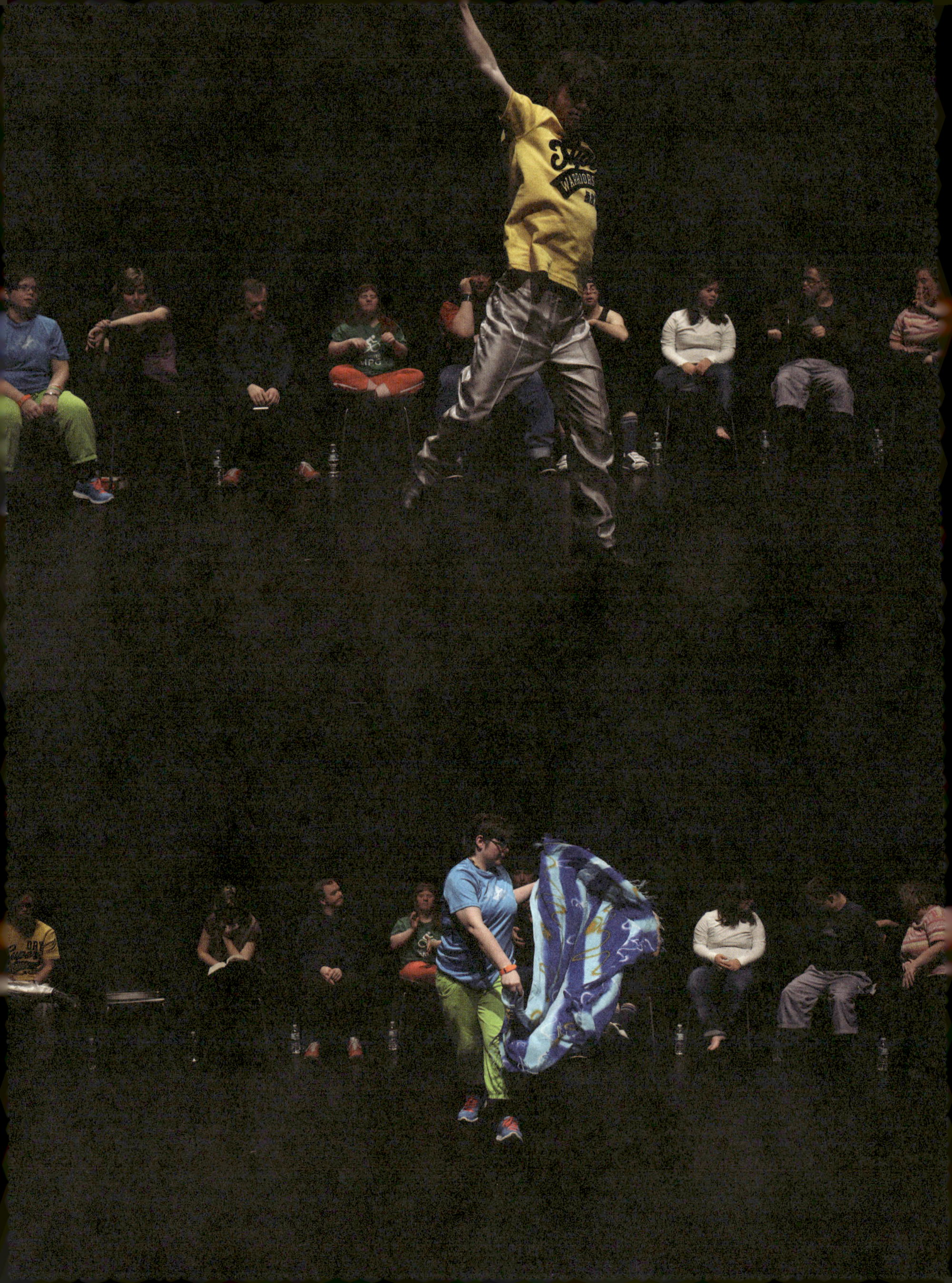

JÉRÔME BEL AND THEATER HORA

DISABLED THEATER

Jens Hoffmann: It is fair to say that a large number of people who saw *Disabled Theater* (2012), which you created together with Theater HORA, a group of actors with developmental disabilities, were highly irritated by the piece. Did you expect this form of reaction and critique? Everyone I spoke to about the piece either loved or hated it.

Jérôme Bel: To tell you the truth I was expecting more aversion from the audience. I noticed irritation, and some people started to insult me in person as well as in the papers or on the Internet, but it was always the same kind of audience: people who are doing theater with disabled actors who could not deal with the idea of me working in a different way. I have seen their work too but I didn't insult them. The tremendous visibility of our piece could have been one of the reasons for their anger. *Disabled Theater* is still on tour and it still produces controversy everywhere.

JH: Was creating controversy part of your objective when directing the piece?

JB: Not at all but once it was there it was totally fine with me. The piece deals with the issue of disability, which is something not many people think about unless it affects them. This discussion is not part of public discourse and that is why it is very difficult for people to establish a relationship to disability. Relations with disability are very personal and emotional, not political or intellectual. That is what I have experienced with the reactions toward the performance, from violent rejection to total empathy.

JH: How did the collaboration begin? What interested you in working with a group of disabled actors?

JB: Marcel Blugiel, the dramaturge of Theater HORA in Zurich, suggested I make a piece for the company. I first rejected the offer since I realized from the start that it would be contentious to work with mentally disabled actors. I had never done it before and was worried it would be overwhelming. I nevertheless asked the company if they could show me material about their work and the productions they had done. Marcel was kind enough to send me videos and once I saw those I changed my mind and got more curious. I asked Marcel if I could meet the actors for a workshop, then a second workshop, and I finally decided to make the piece once I realized the professional attitude and work of the actors. They are paid—they rehearse, perform, and go on tour. The fact that they are socially considered professional actors liberated me from the fear of working with them. Once we started working I used some of my usual strategies as a director/choreographer and it produced good results. The actors were ready to do anything once we started working together. They were trained by the artistic director of the company, Michael Elber, to think about traditional drama but also about physical theater, dance, slapstick, improvisation, and composition. I tried many different things and was improvising a lot. The actors were always ready to try whatever I suggested. It was easy and productive. I made choices from the material we found during the four-week rehearsal. Of course the material was very different from what I found in my other productions. One quality the actors of HORA have in abundance is presence—the most important characteristic for an actor. The HORA actors are more connected with their emotions than any others with whom I have worked. This gives them an incredible energy, which is the most important thing on stage.

JH: How informed were you about critical disability art and the disability rights movement before you started working with HORA?

JB: I was not informed at all about any of it and that was partly the reason why this was so interesting to me. Marcel was very informative and guided me through the process, being present at most rehearsals and helping me when I got stuck.

JH: How has the piece changed from performance to performance and from venue to venue? When I saw it for the first time in Kassel at dOCUMENTA (13) I was very curious how it would be to see it again and again as there is such a high degree of unpredictability to it.

JB: It is actually not so unpredictable. The piece isn't changing. There is a structure maintained by the translators who are on stage, Simone Truong or Chris Weiheimer, yet the actions of the performers might change. Some performers do exactly the same movements and others change their performances. It is fascinating to see them dealing with this process. It is always an experience to see this production; the more I see it the more I like it because I keep discovering new aspects.

JH: To me the work is in essence about communication and about the complexities of communication. Can you speak about the communication between a disabled person and a "neuro-typical" audience?

JB: Yes, that is an important aspect of the piece because it is essentially about my experience interacting with them. As I said, I did not know anything about their disabilities before I started working with them so the whole piece in the end became about my relationship to the actors. How do I find a way to communicate with them and how do they find a way to communicate with me? Since my piece *Veronique Doisneau* (2004), I always ask dancers to talk to me about their work. Here with the mentally disabled actors, the articulation was not that easy. I tried to talk to them but I quickly discovered that language might not be the best form of dialogue. Dance was much more eloquent. Suddenly, unexpectedly, dance was allowing me to see their relation to the world, how they perceive reality and their place within it. Through their dances (they chose their own dances, I did not choreograph or direct anything) I could see their mental structures.

JH: The piece presents a contradiction that challenges the traditional notion of theater. You work with actors but you ask them to be themselves—their so-called authentic selves—rather than to perform a character.

JB: Yes, that is always a question in theater and in the end it is always a bit of both. In this context it becomes even more complicated to know what is real or acted. One of the main lessons I learned from this experience was to be able to accept not knowing what was acted and what was not.

JH: Where do you place this piece within the overall development of your work, where do you see relationships to other pieces, and how did *Disabled Theater* influence thoughts for future performances?

JB: *Disabled Theater* answered questions about performativity that

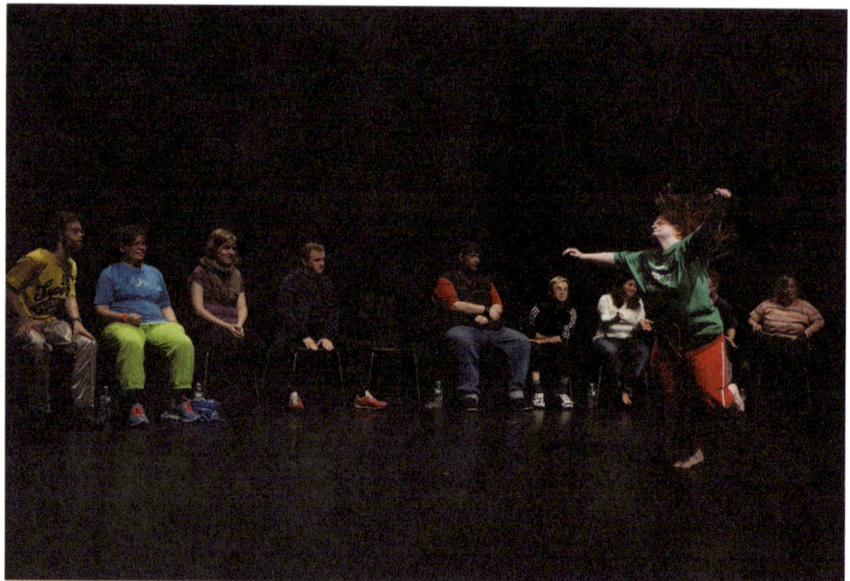

I have been working on for years. The primary question for me is how to find this presence I was mentioning before, this freedom, the emancipation of the performer. The work for me is to find a structure in which the performers could be free, connected with their past, their present, and their feelings. A structure that allowed for an elaborated discourse—decided before and during the rehearsals—but connected with the presence, of the performer. A structure, which could be emancipating—permitting the performers to make decisions, where power and aesthetics would be shared by the performers during the performance.

JH: If you had to name three key elements that characterize your work, what would those be?

JB: I think emancipation, followed by equality and of course interest in the spectators.

JH: Do you still consider yourself a choreographer, and what does that term mean to you?

JB: That is an interesting question. For a long time I did not use that term to describe what I do, but since my work dialogues with the work of other choreographers I decided to use the term. So yes, I am a choreographer, but I have to think more about the meaning of the term.

JH: Who are some of these choreographers that you dialogue with?

JB: There is Xavier Le Roy, with whom I probably have the strongest conversation, but there are many others and some of them are not even alive anymore, for example, Pina Bausch, Merce Cunningham, Raimund Hoghe, Maguy Marin, Steve Paxton, Jonathan Burrows, Anna Halprin, Bruno Beltrao, Lucinda Childs, Isadora Duncan, Trajal Harrell, Yvonne Rainer, Kurt Jooss, Boris Charmatz, and Oskar Schlemmer. I could go on and on.

JH: Please go on!

JB: Fine. Kazuo Ohno, Myriam Gourfink, Eva Meyer-Keller, Michel Fokine, Tatsumi Hijikata, Bob Fosse, Mary Wigman, Léonide Massine, Alain Buffard, Valeska Gert, and Loie Fuller. I think that is it for now.

JH: Is there anyone who is not from the world of dance?

JB: Since you are asking! The influence of artists like Jean-Luc Godard, Marcel Duchamp, Robert Bresson, John Cage, Agnès Varda, Donald Judd, Samuel Beckett, Carl Andre, Daniel Buren, Raymond Roussel, Rainer Werner Fassbinder, Tsai Ming-liang, Felix Gonzalez-Torres, João César Monteiro, Jean Genet, Chantal Akerman, David Hammons, and Alain Guiraudie has been incredibly important.

JH: Don't stop! Give some more names.

JB: Okay! La Monte Young, Bruce Nauman, Michel Houellebecq, Abbas Kiarostami, Jean Echenoz, Herman Melville, Andy Warhol, Pierre Huyghe, Anton Chekhov, Marguerite Duras, Apichatpong Weerasethakul, and Marcel Proust! How is that?

JH: That is excellent. Are you sure you did not forget someone?

JB: If someone else comes to mind I will let you know.

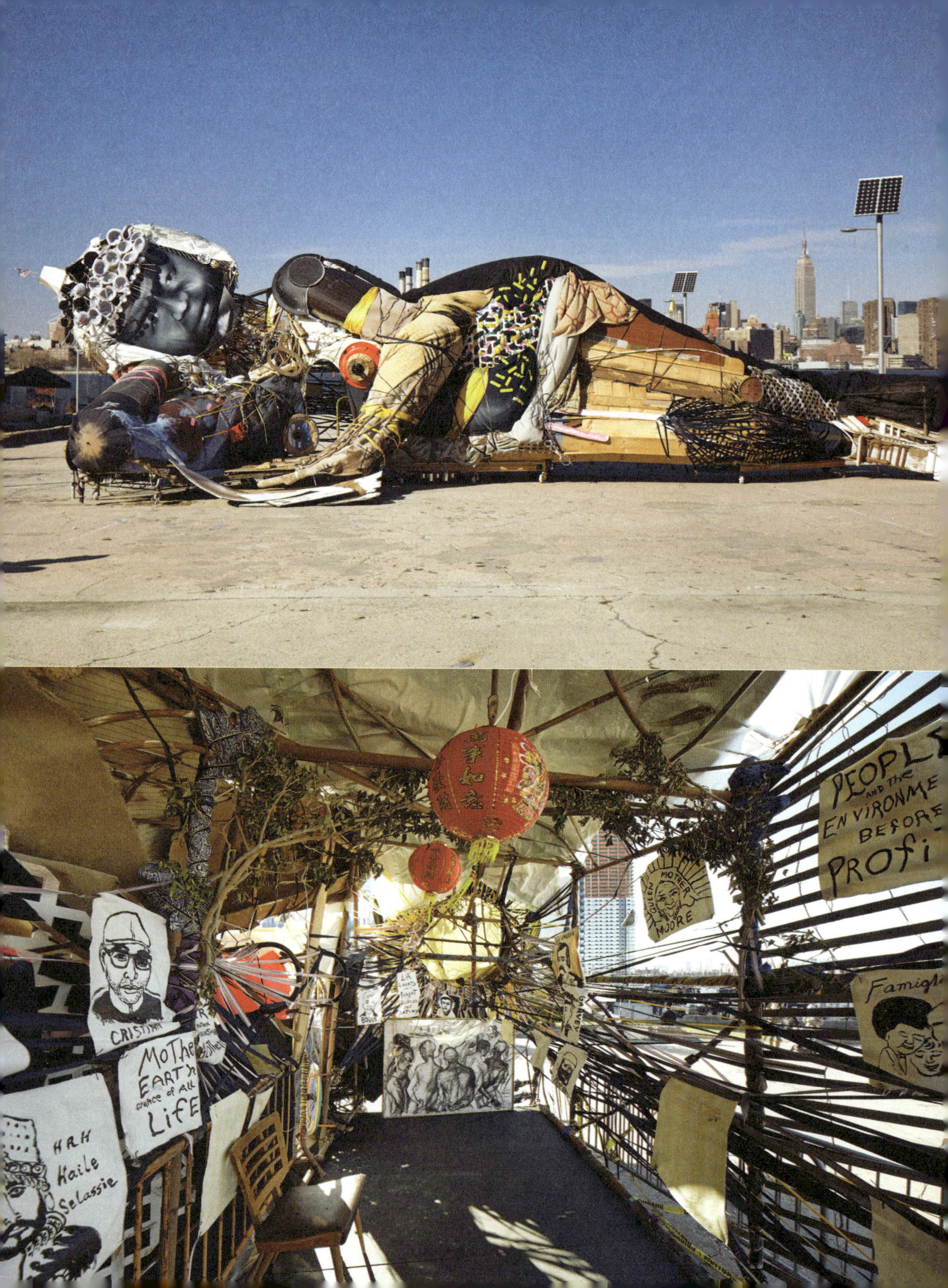

PEOPLE
AND THE
ENVIRONME
BEFORE
PROFI
QUEEN MOTHER MOORE
Famigl
CRISTIAN
MOTHER EARTH
SOURCE OF ALL
LIFE
HRH
Haile
Selassie

PAWEŁ ALTHAMER
WITH BRUNO ALTHAMER, SYMON ALTHAMER, AARON BURR SOCIETY, NOAH FISHER, ROMAN STANÅL CZAK, RAFAL ZWIREK

BIBA PERFORMA

In April 2013, I visited Paweł Althamer's studio in the eastern Warsaw neighborhood Bródno where the artist maintains a studio at his father's plastic-pipe-making factory. That day, Althamer was at work on his "Venetians" series with an audience of eight people from his Nowolipie Group—an organization he founded with individuals with Multiple Sclerosis that convenes weekly. Althamer talked and demonstrated to the group as he worked, a process that involved being handed hot and malleable plastic grey piping that he then quickly shaped to create skeletal and clothing forms on the metal armatures topped with cast masks of the residents of Venice.

With this introduction to the artist, I was struck by the contrasting requirements for community-based artists in English-speaking countries and Scandinavia, compared to artists in Poland, where there is no institutionalized motivation for artists to work with community groups and residents. It was striking that an artist of international renown, who has collaborated with and worked among his neighbors, prioritizes this as an integral part of his process and production. Seeing Althamer's strategies and methods operating in his native habitat was revelatory.

Immersion through the studio visit, combined with a tour of his neighborhood given by the artist the next day, laid the foundations for an unspecified, shapeless adventure in New York for the biennial. We discussed this as we walked through a large preserve where the residents of the surrounding 1970s-era housing blocks maintain small plots of land complete with miniature country houses, fashioned from an array of building materials and found objects twice the size of the average garden shed, each one a marvel of individual style and expression.

In August 2013, Althamer and his wife Julia Matea Petelska visited New York to conceive the idea for his Performa Commission. As evident during my Polish experience, there would be no formal proposal, no written outline or carefully planned budget; rather, we embarked on a tour of the city that we hoped would yield a direction— making observations and many drawings along the way. We ended up on the East River ferry headed to DUMBO, when the tents and activity on the East River Park in Williamsburg caught their attention. It was Smorgasburg—the high-end weekend foodie-fest. Seeking a thirst-quenching drink, Althamer spotted the unmistakable umbrellas of a beer garden. Within ten minutes of being there, we realized we were in a Polish establishment, and within thirty minutes we were talking with the proprietor, Marek Nagawiecki. Althamer was instantly enthralled by the entire scene, where microcosms of divergent communities rub up against each other—the waterfront, the hipsters of Williamsburg, and the old-school Polish operation called Biba, a restored nineteenth-century warehouse with a semi-operational bar and restaurant. Loosely translated from Polish, *biba* means "spree, jag, carousal, souse, razzle dazzle," as well as "do nothing" or "take a break," and had distinctly specific connotations in the Communist era—then an afternoon break in the workday rather than binge partying now.

Biba's atmosphere manages to incorporate all these interpretations—with bare brick, wood beams, salvaged bars, rusty light fixtures, and sartorial furniture with Polish soccer team flags as well as a giant painting of a steam locomotive that once sat next to the building (with Nagawiecki and his son painted in). It is the last vestige of the BEDT (Brooklyn Eastern District Terminal), now the East River State Park, defined by the unparklike concrete slabs that reach from Kent Avenue down to the water's edge. Althamer and his New York collaborator Noah Fischer, the artist/activist and Occupy Museums core member, made a return visit to Biba to meet with Nagawiecki, his wife Barbara, and Joy Glidden, a neighborhood artist and Brooklyn arts scene fixture. A long afternoon of talking, with explanatory drawings, yielded a proposal that Althamer and his band of artist collaborators would rechristen the bar Biba Performa for the duration of the biennial and that it should become home to an unspecified array of activities, from community gatherings, art workshops, and film screenings to dinners and performances, as well as evening bonfires to contemplate the Manhattan skyline. Nagawiecki was simultaneously dubious and charmed by the idea. Althamer left the meeting redoubled in his interest in Nagawiecki as an exceptional figure with many intriguing facets, and in his mission to make Biba Performa a locus of creative activity (the kind of communication through group art-making that he is famous for).

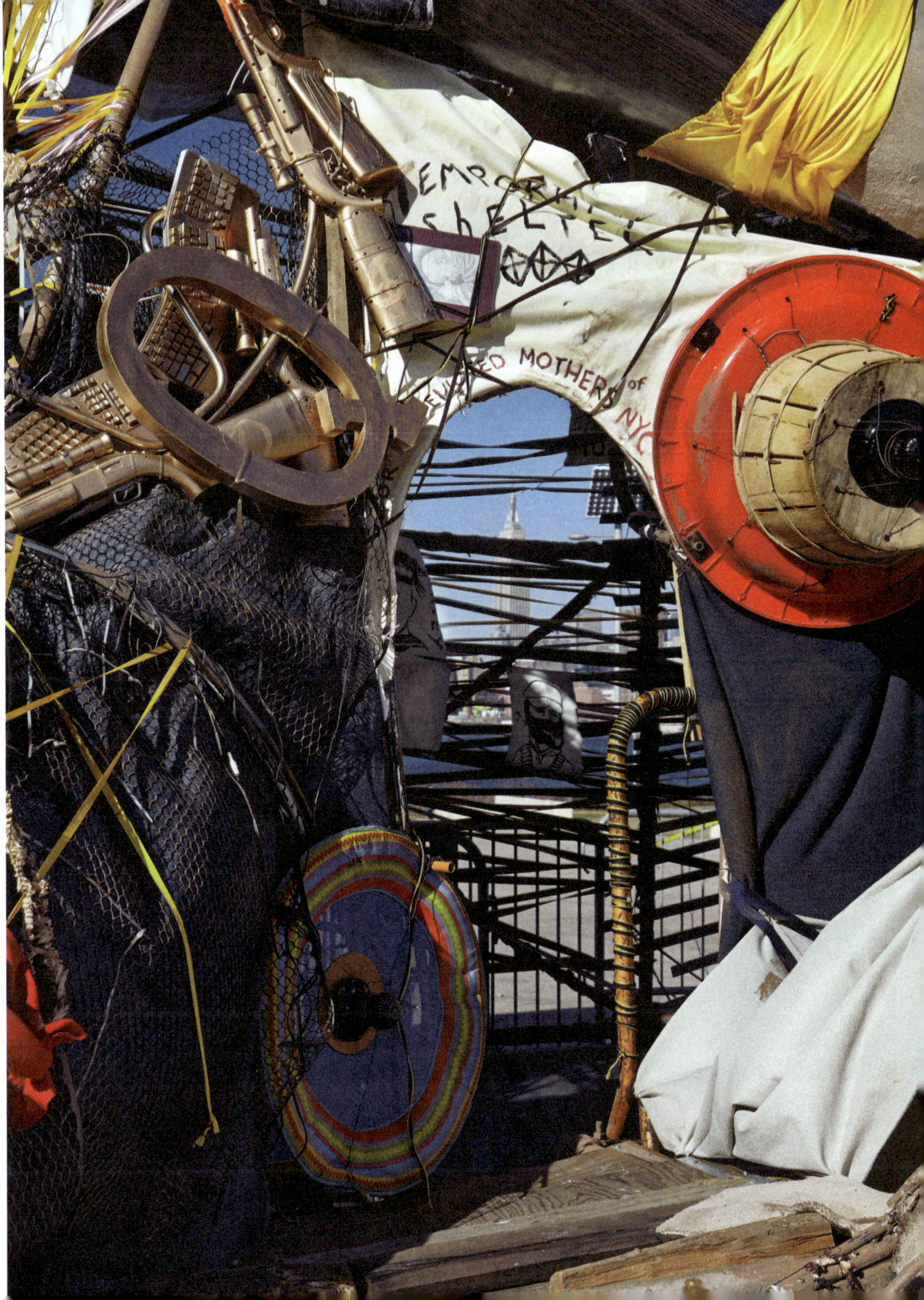
TEMPORARY
SHELTER
MOTHERS of
NYC

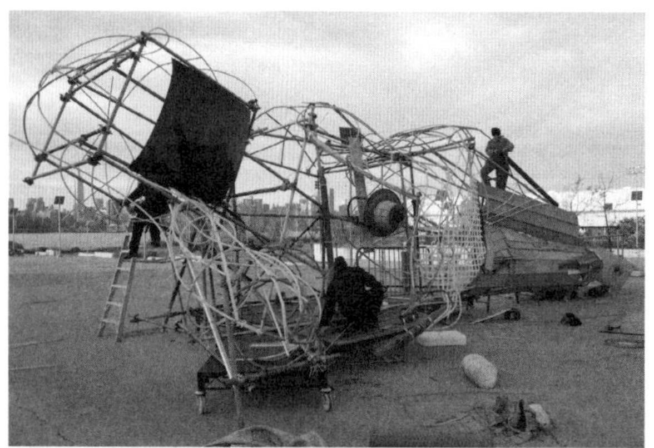
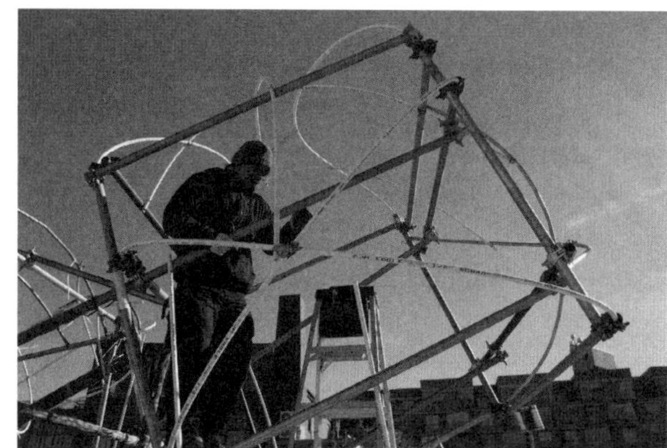
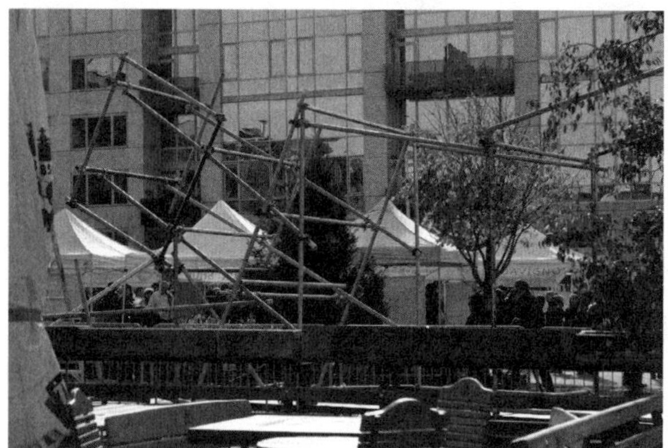
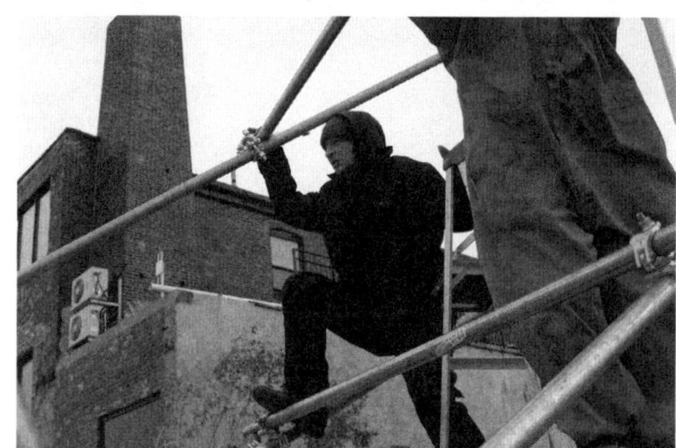
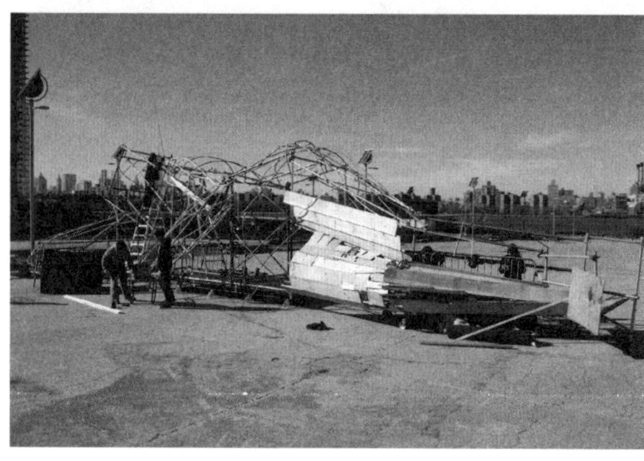
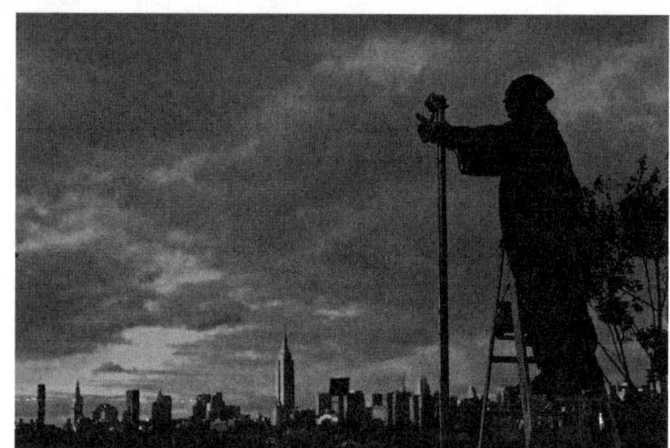

Althamer returned to New York with his two sons, Bruno (an artist) and Symon (a chef), for more planning at Biba. This time he also engaged the small group of New York artists and activists that he had recently begun collaborating with in Warsaw after meeting them at the Berlin Biennial—led by Fischer, who introduced Althamer to Queen Mother aka Dr. Delois Blakely, a former Roman Catholic nun, United Nations delegation representative, and community activist whose inspiring story would give Biba Performa its ultimate trajectory and subject. Queen Mother is a neighborhood hero, a powerful voice for the disenfranchised and homeless members of the Harlem community, and charismatic defender of the rights of women and children of the world. Althamer and Fischer began to organize a loose team around the idea of constructing a larger-than-life portrait of Queen Mother looking out over the East River from the concrete slab in front of Biba. The project was launched with an impromptu parade of the twelve-foot model of the sculpture over the Brooklyn Bridge and through the streets of New York as part of the annual Halloween Parade.

Queen Mother of Reality was constructed over the course of nineteen days out of scaffolding, steel decking, and found materials by a team consisting of Althamer collaborators from Poland (including his two sons and artists Roman Stańczak and Rafal Zwirek) as well as a reluctant but helpful Nagawiecki and Fischer's collaborator Aaron Burr Society (aka Jim Costanzo). Lashed together with fabric, netting, ribbon, and rope that were decorated with plastic hats, umbrellas, planters, wood planks, and a car hood with the image of Dr. Blakely's face, the sculpture was an assemblage of found materials scavenged by the team, and collected from Materials for the Arts. The giant reclining female figure was outfitted with a ramp entrance through her sternum that revealed an intimate inner sanctum decorated with Chinese lanterns and portraits of political heroes, including Marcus Garvey, Haile Selassie, the de Blasio family, Grace Lee Boggs, and Lech Wałesa. High up on a raised platform inside the head of Queen Mother was a small contemplative space with a single chair.

Several events took place at Biba—a launch of the project on November 7 with an informal barbeque, an evening of performances and food on November 14, and a screening of the Tadeuz Kantor documentary *Der Künstler und seine Welt* (1968). The official dedication of *Queen Mother of Reality* took place with a blessing from Dr. Blakely and a Polish feast for one hundred celebrants prepared by Symon Althamer in the basement kitchen of Biba. *Queen Mother of Reality* was given a second life by Socrates Sculpture Park when it was reinstalled just a few miles north of the original location during the summer of 2014.

In the context of Performa, the creation of *Queen Mother of Reality*, a monumental piece of public art, was presented as a performance for the duration of the biennial. Audiences were invited to engage with the process of making a piece rather than to simply visit a finished object. The construction and all attendant conversations, serendipitous meetings, gatherings, bonfires, drawings, dinners, and drinks—in Althamer's distinct way—was the project. What we previously described narrowly as public art, we can now describe as social practice, and what we once described as public participation, we can now call performance.

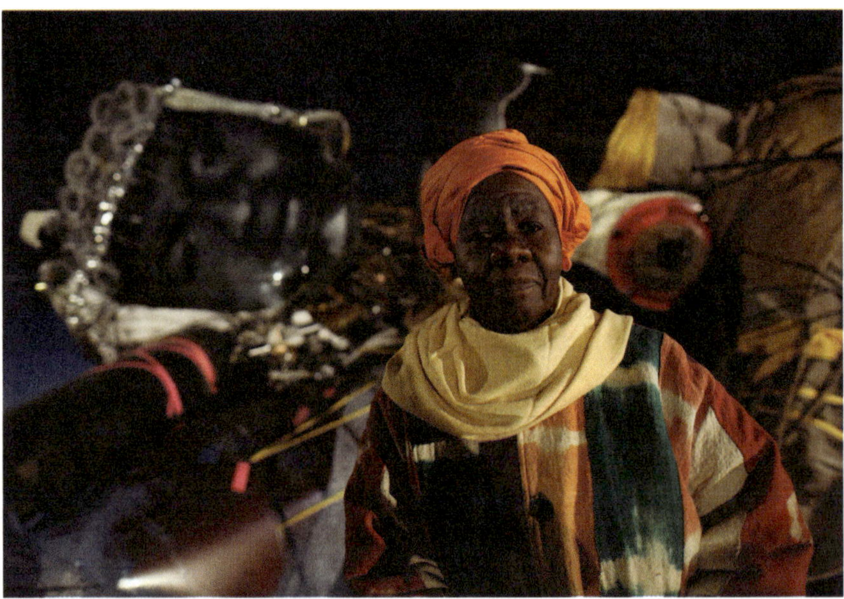

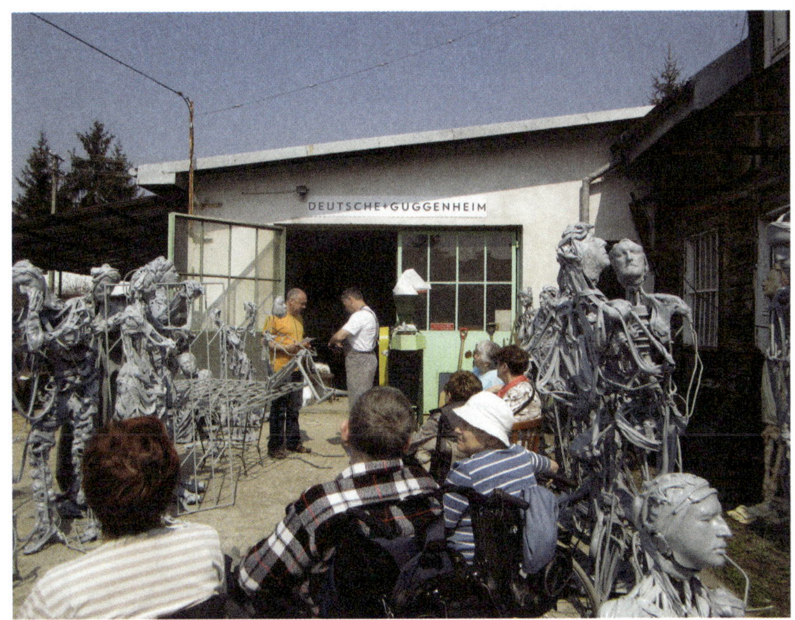

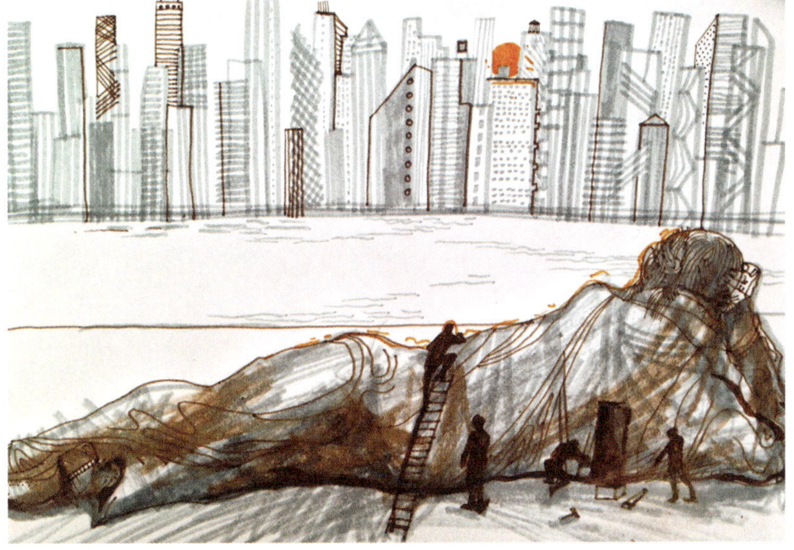

(Above), Althamer Studio, Warsaw, photo by Esa Nickle; (Below) Drawing by Paweł Althamer

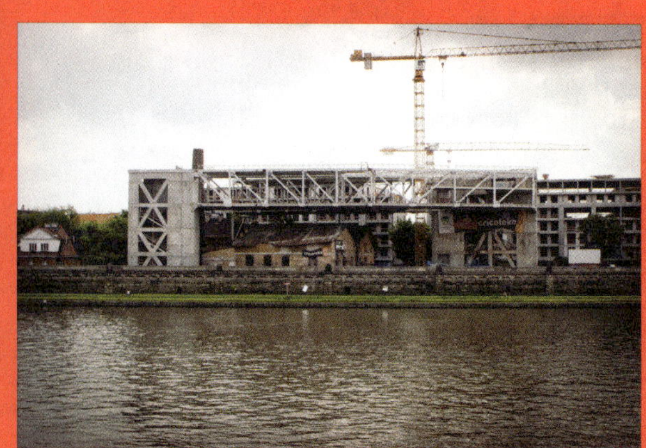

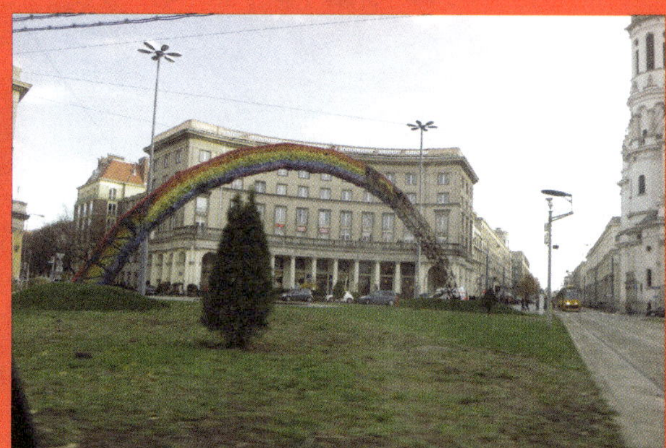

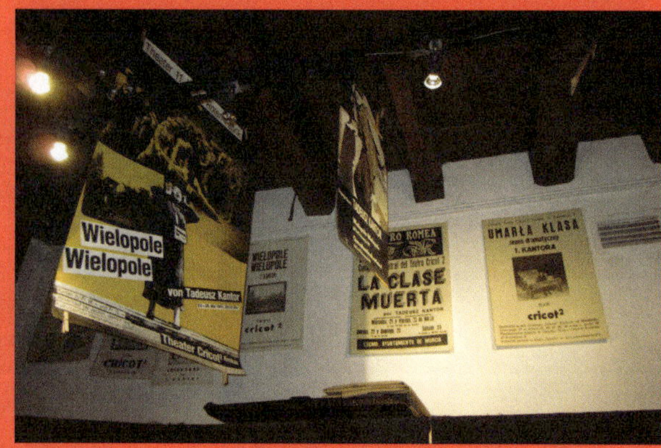
Wielopole
Wielopole
von Tadeusz Kantor
Theater Cricot
cricot
WIELOPOLE
WIELOPOLE
cricot
LA CLASE
MUERTA
por TADEUSZ KANTOR
UMARŁA KLASA
seans dramatyczny
T. KANTORA
cricot2

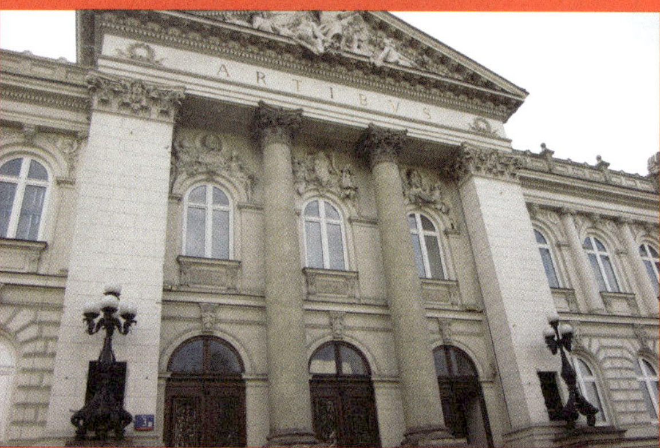
ARTIBVS

PAVILION WITHOUT WALLS

POLAND

Photos by Esa Nickle

Historic sites around Warsaw and Krakow (2012).

ROSELEE GOLDBERG & ESA NICKLE

From the earliest conversation with Jerzy Onuch at the Polish Cultural Institute in New York about the possibilities of a Polish Pavilion, response to our research on the meaning of "citizenship" brought immediate interest. "Citizenship" Onuch agreed, was of vital concern among Poles, especially the younger generation, wondering about national identity amid shifts in Eastern European and Asian politics as well as Poland's place in the debates. From this initial introduction, two research trips were organized to Poland for Performa curators and producers, guided by the Polish Cultural Institute in New York, the Adam Mickielnwicz Institute, the Center for Contemporary Art Ujazdowski Castle in Warsaw, and the new Cricoteka Center for the work of Tadeuz Kantor in Krakow. An overview of current cultural practices was provided by each organization, offering various perspectives and introductions to curators, artists, art historians, and museum directors.

Sifting through the interconnected histories of art, theater, and politics from the past half century provided a rich resource of material from which to curate a Polish Pavilion Without Walls for the biennial in New York. Outstanding historical figures and groups came to the fore, and artists from the following generations reflected on those legacies as well as their own futures: the complexity of Kantor's visual theater of the 1970s; Akademia Ruchu's capacity to interrogate the logics of power under shifting political regimes; Paweł Althamer's post-Communist focus on collaboration and community; and Konrad Smolenski with Radek Szlaga's rowdy response to contemporary Poland that inserted American hip hop into the grey aesthetics of Communist-built suburbs. Performa curators found many artists in Poland who were committed to articulating the relationship between contemporary aesthetics and history, while advancing their ideas in line with progress in new media and technology. The projects selected for the Polish Pavilion represent Performa's longstanding vision acknowledging the role artists play in stimulating social change and championing common justice.

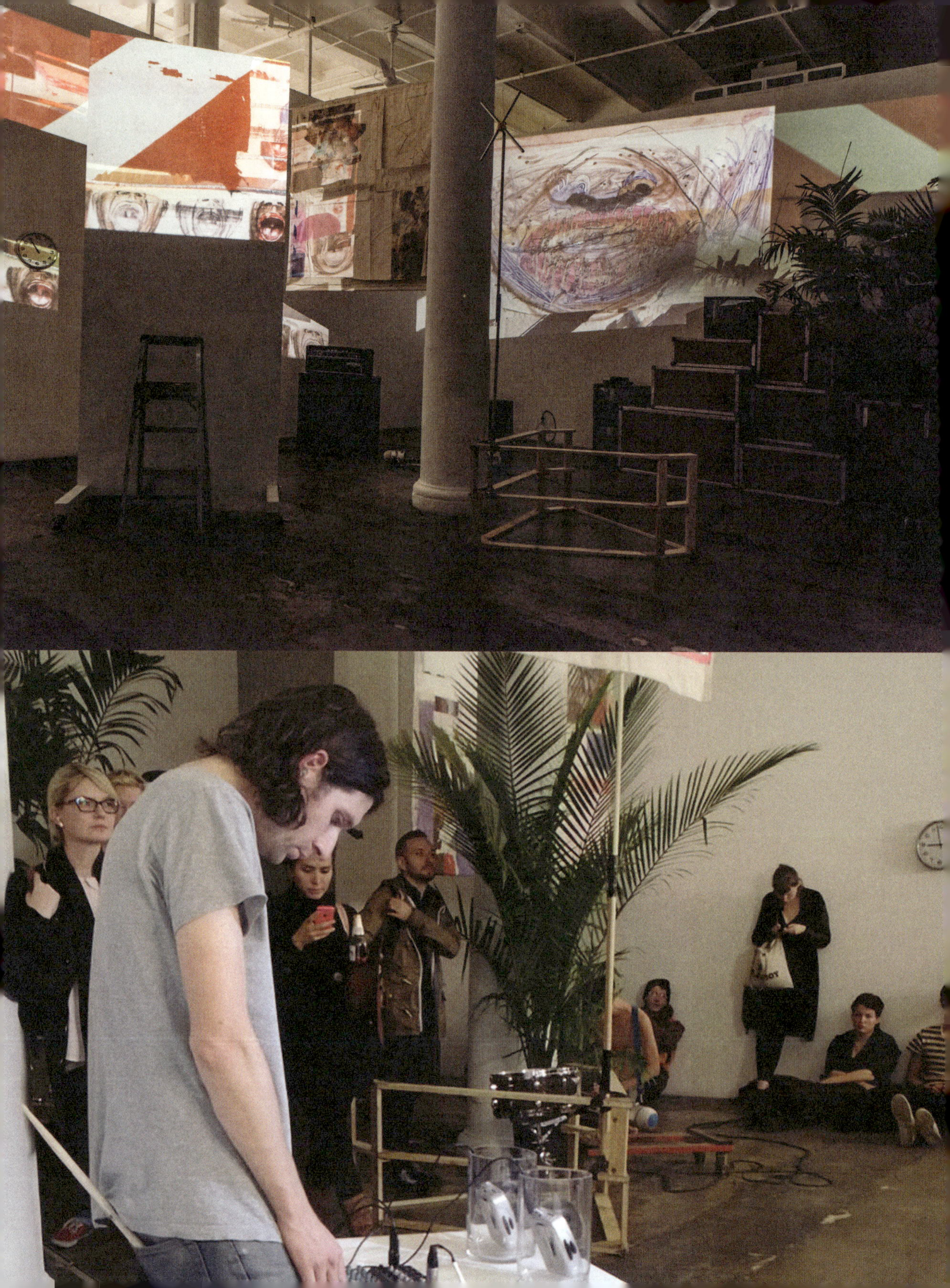

Tribute to Errors and Leftovers was a sound clash experience that bewildered the senses. Set in Fridman Gallery on Spring Street in far West SoHo, the durational performance evolved over the course of a week and concluded with a rowdy concert with guest drummer Dean Spunt of punk band No Age. A menacing pyramid of black speakers stood in front of the gallery entrance. In Radek Szlaga's baroque and immersive installation of scaffoldings, aluminum ladders, wheeled fly cases (often used by musicians on the road), random plants, and 360 degree projections of found images and family photos, this loud sound performance featured Konrad Smoleński's noise band BNNT, which occupied the space every day (through intense amplifications).

Two key members of the Polish artist group Penerstwo (translated as "sensitive boorishness"), Smoleński and Szlaga were the *enfants terribles* of Performa 13's Polish Pavilion Without Walls. Bare-chested and balaclava-clad Smoleński constantly paced the space like a caged animal and shot bursts of noise from his fabricated "missile guitar," while Daniel Swed constructed rapid and intricate poundings on the drums. Both performed with raw energy to a liminal condition where even the architectural structure of the space seemed threatened. Playing with the contrasts between bright and dark, quiet and loud, static and dynamic, Smoleński and Szlaga performed *Tribute to Errors and Leftovers* with an emphasis on the physical experience of music while confusing and challenging the audience.

CURATED BY CHARLES AUBIN △ FRIDMAN GALLERY

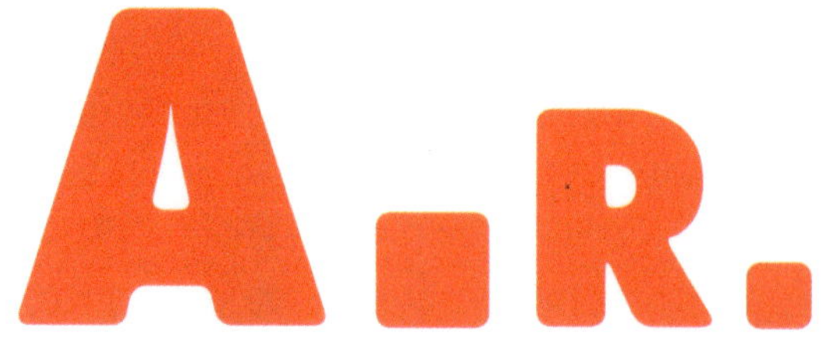

A.R.

40 YEARS OF ARTISTIC PRACTICE.
FROM THE CONTESTATION OF TOTALITARIAN REALITIES TO POSTMODERN DISCOURSES AND AFTER

The Akademia Ruchu artists explore the specificity of the distinction between art and daily life, without, however, striving to equate one with the other (as the avant-garde's radical postulates would have it). Rather, they are interested in the problem of translation, of rendering meaning between the two languages. In their case, testing the language of art and the language of the everyday involves introducing ordinary gestures to the field of theatre, gestures charged with the connotations of their various social applications. According to the AR artists, this virtually anthropological process is related to the necessity of 'noticing the value of the interpenetration of art and life. Not in the repetition of daily life, but in the appreciation of its often unappreciated meaning, in the structures, rhythms and tensions comprising a model of the activity that fills the space of shared experiences, games, communication'.* For Akademia Ruchu, the simplest gestures re-enacted in public space are natural (independent of politics or ideology) mechanisms of the self-regulation of social life — its silent binding agent.
Łukasz Ronduda, Art Critic

* Wojciech Krukowski, lecture 1988

RoseLee Goldberg
Founding Director and Curator, Performa

Operating at the intersection between art, politics, film and theater, Akademia Ruchu, ('Academy of Movement'), was founded in 1973 in Warsaw, Poland, where it brought together a group of performers with a wide range of academic and physical training — from art history and architecture to ballet to martial arts. For Performa 13 the group brings a series of performances to New York, including a set of new works made specifically for the context of Times Square. Active for 40 years, the group, comprising artists Janusz Bałdyga, Jolanta Krukowska, Cezary Marczak, Jan Pieniążek, Zbigniew Olkiewicz, Jarosław and Krzysztof Żwirblis, together with artistic director Wojciech Krukowski, harnesses the appeal of a pared-down, formal visual style, characterized by minimal props and gestures, to engage the general public in critical ways of thinking — a politicization of aesthetics that they have remained committed to from the outset.

1976

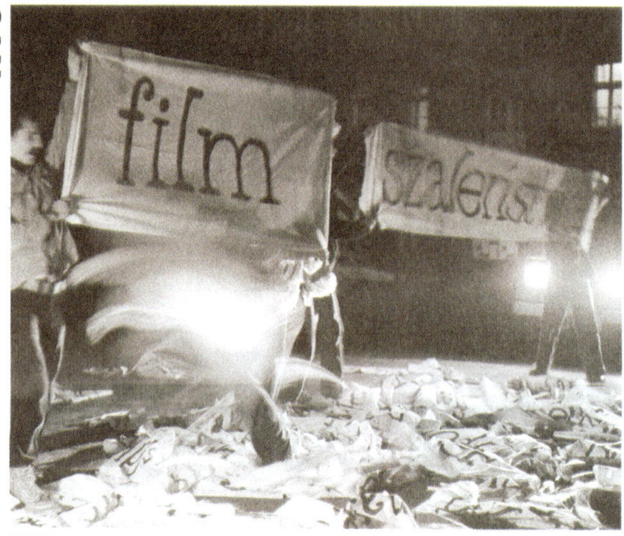

EUROPA

1975

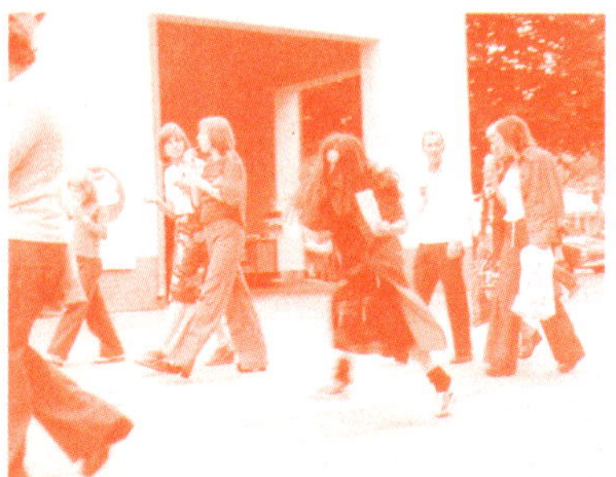

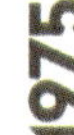

THE STUMBLE
In a place where people usually spend time watching others or arrange to meet each other (a street intersection, a square, a promenade), seemingly accidental passers-by stumbled one after another, at short intervals, at a specific spot, right before the eyes of the 'audience'. The spot was inconspicuous and suggested no danger whatsoever. The inexplicable nature of the repeated accident provoked the hitherto passive viewers to react.

1975

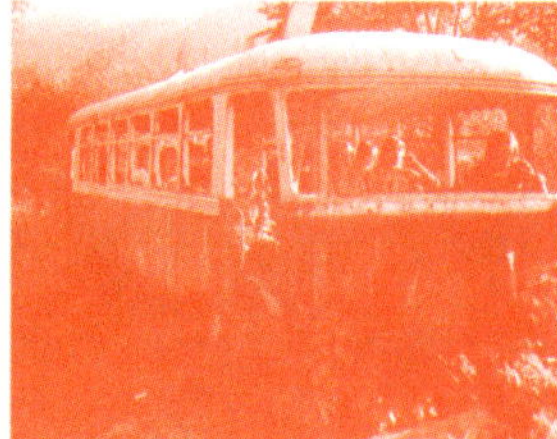

THE BUS II (Wetlina)
An open-space intervention. The wreck of an abandoned bus (situated, at Wetlina, between a train station and a shopping ar and at Hel, near a main road) was filled for the duration of one by 30-40 motionless 'passengers', and, like in *Bus I*, a 'blind' d

1982

ENGLISH LESSON
A 30-minute show modelled upon a typical foreign language lesson (using a tape recorder, improvised linguistic exercises, and dances). Another level implied by the spectacle was a lesson in adapting to an artificial reality — and in creatively interpreting its limited possibilities. In the *English Lesson*'s message, the language, composed of allusions and general stereotypes, becomes mute, and thus but a symbolic means of expression.
The show, designed for a sterile black setting, qualified for the Documenta 8 in Kassel in the 'expanded performance' category, where it was presented in the austere setting of a neglected warehouse. Another non-canonical version was shown in 1984 in Rimini, this time in the middle of a street intersection.

1975

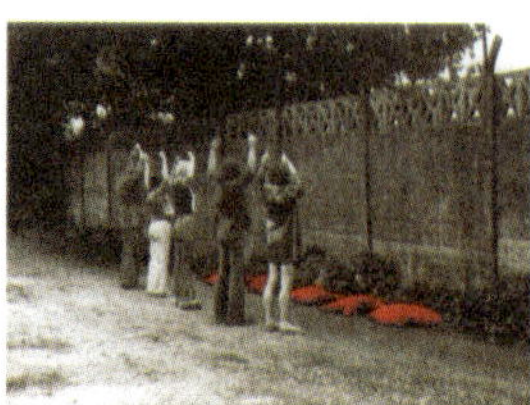

THE VIGIL
A group of peop stood for 30 mi against the wall a house or a wa bordering a pe path, with their raised or claspe behind their ne Between them wall, at a distan to the height of man, large red lay on the grou

A.R.

AKADEMIA RUCHU

THE MARKET OF TOYS

For two days Akademia Ruchu's *The Market of Toys* was performed at ten kiosks located along Broadway in the vicinity of Times Square, a visual retrospective of unique video footage (captured on hidden cameras) of Akademia Ruchu's guerilla actions from the 1970s and '80s presented to passersby. By occupying a zone of constant foot traffic, Akademia Ruchu emphasized the vibrant character of the location and its dense multitude of visitors. Akademia Ruchu was founded in 1973 in Warsaw, Poland, by Wojciech Krukowski, the collective's artistic director. The group consists of seven artists—Janusz Bałdyga, Jolanta Krukowska, Cezary Marczak, Jan Pieniażek, Zbigniew Olkiewicz, Jarosław Żwirblis, and Krzysztof Żwirblis—who have worked together throughout the period of Communism and beyond. Akademia Ruchu turned political repression into a source of inspiration. The collective's initiatives always existed outside any institutional framework that might have been subject to censorship in Communist Poland.

Initiatives such as anonymous performances and installations purposefully interfere with routine city life, transforming any space into a gallery or stage. Since the fall of Communism in 1989, Akademia Ruchu's spirit of critical engagement has not diminished. By transferring art into the streets, the group has made a deep impression on everyday people, engaging with them as co-authors of the work. They use a simple and direct visual language with the goal of establishing clear communication between the collective and members of the public drawn into the performance. *The Market of Toys* was complemented by a newspaper-as-exhibition consisting of original texts, commentaries, and photographs documenting Academia Ruchu's deep history of public performances. The newspaper was distributed in all Performa locations. The purpose of such guerilla action was to activate a sense of civic expression. The collective wants to enrich social connections by promoting creative and independent responses to the reality of everyday life.

The single-element actions of Akademia Ruchu in Times Square were, as Krukowski described, "minimalistic, yet due to the induced

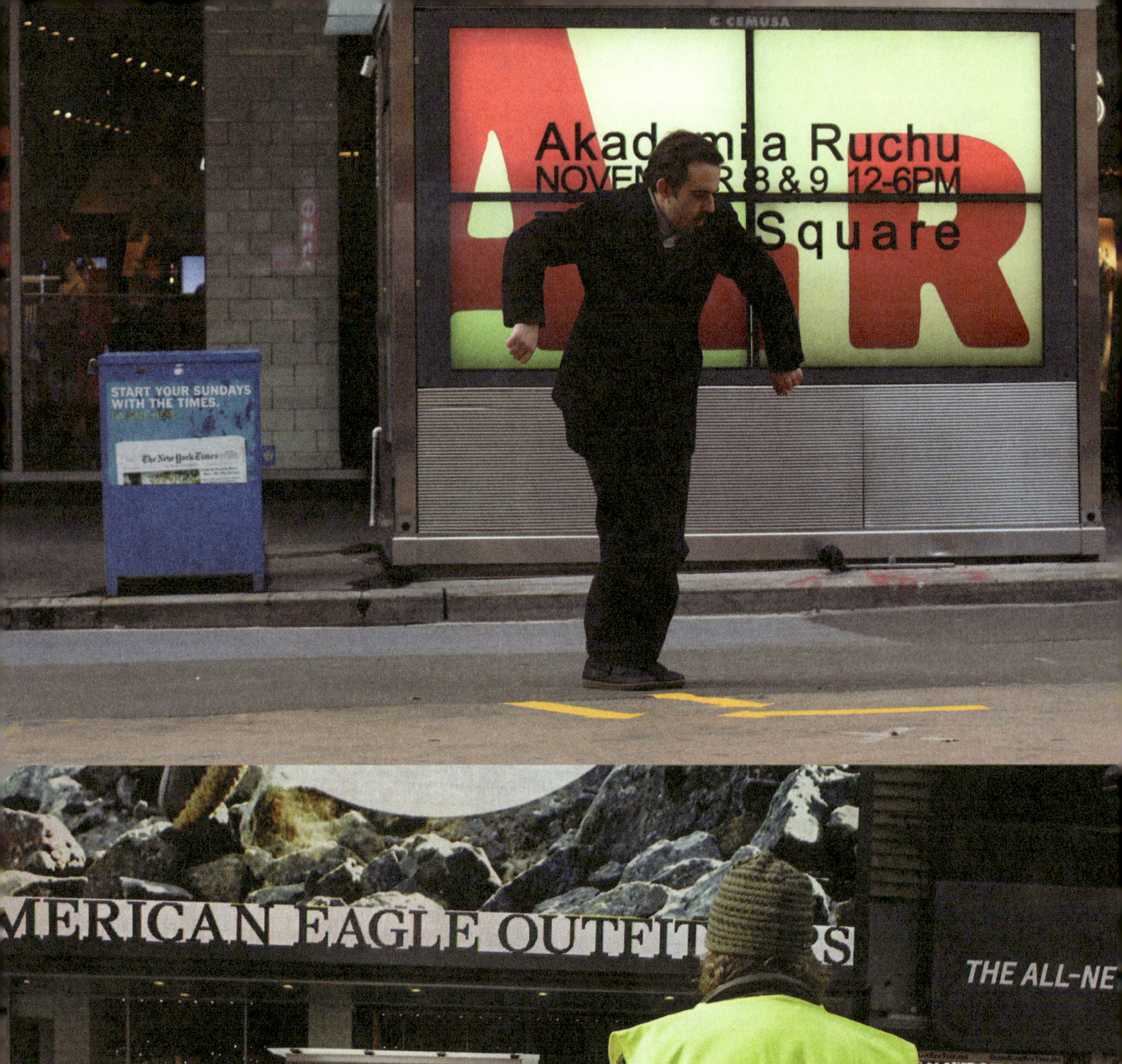
Akademia Ruchu
NOVEMBER 8 & 9 12-6PM
Square
AR
START YOUR SUNDAYS
WITH THE TIMES.
The New York Times
AMERICAN EAGLE OUTFITTERS
THE ALL-NE
EANS
OBSERVER
I ♥ NY

effect of strangeness, the actions were simultaneously legible as a form of visual language." Each action took approximately an hour and was executed by performers scattered throughout Times Square.

1. "Walking people"

The performers stood in pairs, about thirty-five feet apart, connected by a thick, colored ribbon. They lifted the ribbon from the level of the sidewalk to the height of the pedestrians as they were passing by. As the height of the mass of pedestrians differed, this gauging action had an obstinate dynamic. This was performed for about one hour each day.

2. "Standing people"

The performers scattered throughout Times Square, wearing neon-colored safety vests emblazoned with the word "OBSERVER" on the backs. The performers stood motionless, meditative, and observant for fifteen to twenty minutes, after which they calmly moved to a different observation spot. They continued in this fashion for a total of two hours.

3. "Dancing people"

The performers, dressed in regular clothing, dispersed across Times Square and began the action by wiping a three-square-foot area of the sidewalk clean with a white handkerchief. Inside the clean square, the performers taped colorful arrow signs resembling the basic score of a dance lesson. The visual image created by the arrows also resembled military maneuvering plans of action for the great battles of Marathon, Waterloo, Austerlitz, Yorktown, Kanny, and others. Following the arrows, the performers repeatedly execute the choreography over the course of fifteen minutes. The performers then swapped locations and began again.

4. "Smoking people"

The performers, each in a different location, stood motionless with burning incense sticks in their breast pockets. The fragrant smoke covered their faces. From time to time, the performers dispersed the smoke with their hands. The location of each performer shifted every fifteen minutes.

The Market of Toys was the culmination of artistic activities for Krukowski, who passed away at age seventy in January 2014, two months after visiting New York City and taking part in Performa 13.

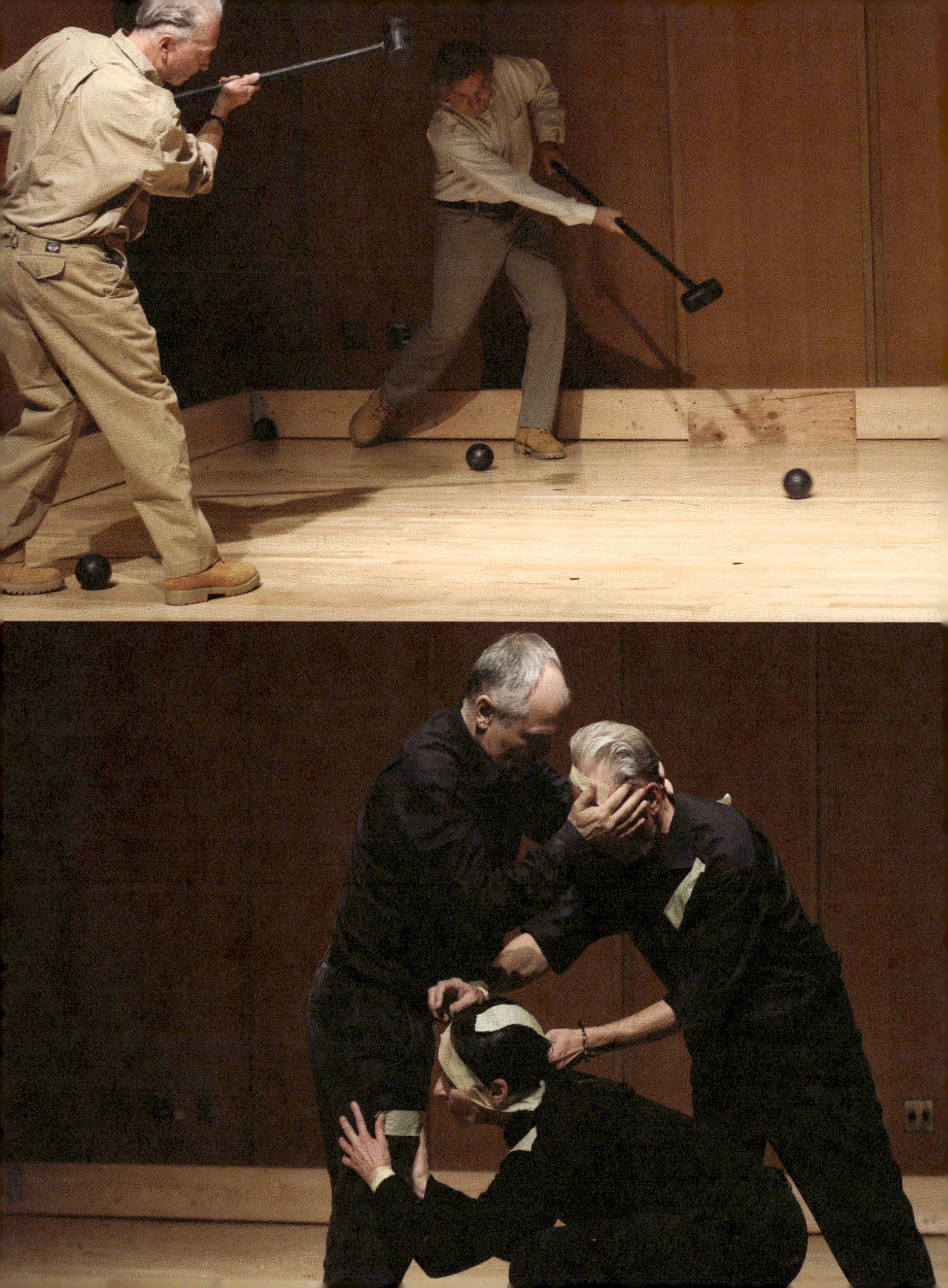

AKADEMIA RUCHU

CHINESE LESSON/ CHIŃSKA LEKCJA

Chinese Lesson/Chińska Lekcja celebrated forty years of one of the most provocative and significant groups to combine theater and politics while simultaneously refusing textual material in favor of visual and movement-based performance languages. Akademia Ruchu was formed in Communist post-war Poland by Wojciech Krowkowski with other artists, actors, activists, historians, and critics to confront the political issues and currents of unrest and rebellion that epitomized Polish society in the late-1960s, '70s and '80s. Rather than producing commentary, their actions and performances generated a reality in the streets and in the theater, blurring practices of everyday life to challenge the status quo. One of Akademia Ruchu's most iconic pieces, *Chinese Lesson/Chińska Lekcja*, elegantly and profoundly brought together art and politics in its exploration of the standardizing and liberating possibilities of gestures, games, and structures of communication, generated through a highly specific language of movement. As curator and historian Łukasz Ronduda said of the piece, "testing the language of art and the language of the everyday involves in their case introducing to the field of theater ordinary gestures, charged with the connotations of their social applications." [*]

The connection to China was vague but provocative. Were the activists of Akademia Ruchu trying to learn something from Chinese dissidents who lived under a similarly oppressive and dangerous Communist regime? Or were they suggesting that translation is a medium for revolutionary politics? Originally created in 1973, *Chinese Lesson/Chińska Lekcja* featured five of the group's oldest members—Wojciech Krukowski, the collective's artistic director, and artists Janusz Bałdyga, Jolanta Krukowska, Cezary Marczak, Jan Pieniażek, Zbigniew Olkiewicz, Jarosław Żwirblis and Krzysztof Żwirblis who all contributed to the work's formation as actors, designers, and directors through collaborative process-based experiments. Performed in the Martin E. Segal Theatre at City University of New York, the piece consisted of a series of scenes of simple and succinct actions, such

[*] "Łukasz Ronduda, "Against the Marginalization of the Art Discourse," European Stages 1, no. 1 (Fall 2013): 69.

TEXT BY MARC ARTHUR △ MARTIN E. SEGAL THEATRE CENTER, AT CITY UNIVERSITY OF NEW YORK

as one in which the stage became a space for black pool balls to be pushed around with croquet mallets—later to be smashed. In another scene, all the performers laid down horizontally on top of tables and chanted the Chinese word for "freedom." These short actions, of which there were twenty or so, have no specific meaning, but they exemplify the group's key tactic of activating the body in the frighteningly conservative and politically dangerous context of post-war Poland through aesthetics and performance. Their visual language, which generally consists of quotidian movements and actions pushed to the limits by political content and violent gestures, has been influential to, and in conversation with, avant garde theater and visual artists across Europe and the United States for over four decades. It has prefigured practices of socially engaged, relational, and participatory art and groups like The Living Theater, The Bread and Puppet Theater, The San Francisco Mime Troupe, Teatro Campesino, the Viennese Actionists, and artists including Bertolt Brecht, Erwin Piscator, John Cage, Allan Kaprow, and Robert Wilson, all of whom have been significantly influenced by Akademia Ruchu's creative and political output.

Akademia Ruchu, *Chinese Lesson/Chińska Lekcja* (2013), performance views.   Photo by Chani Bockwinkel

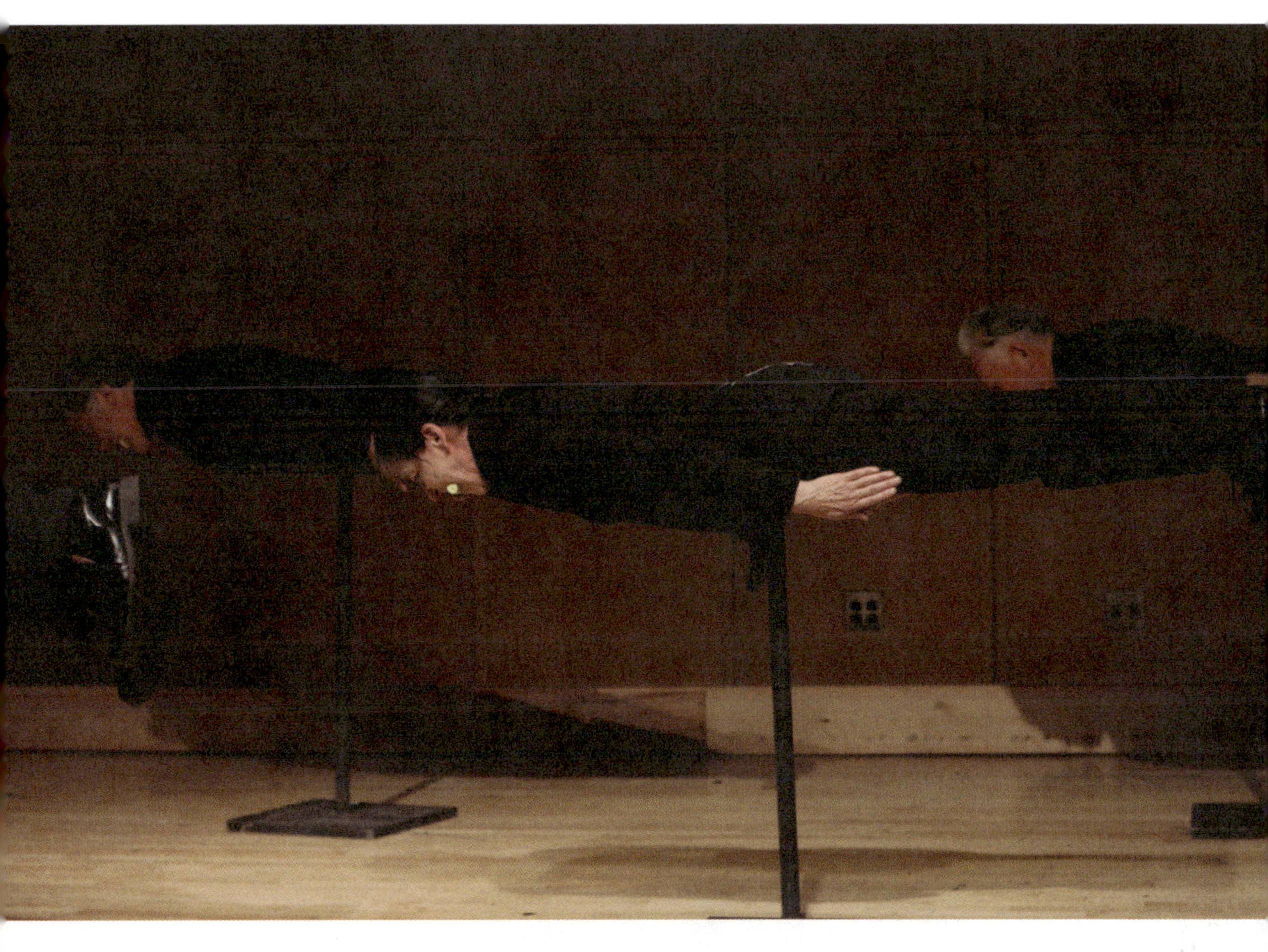

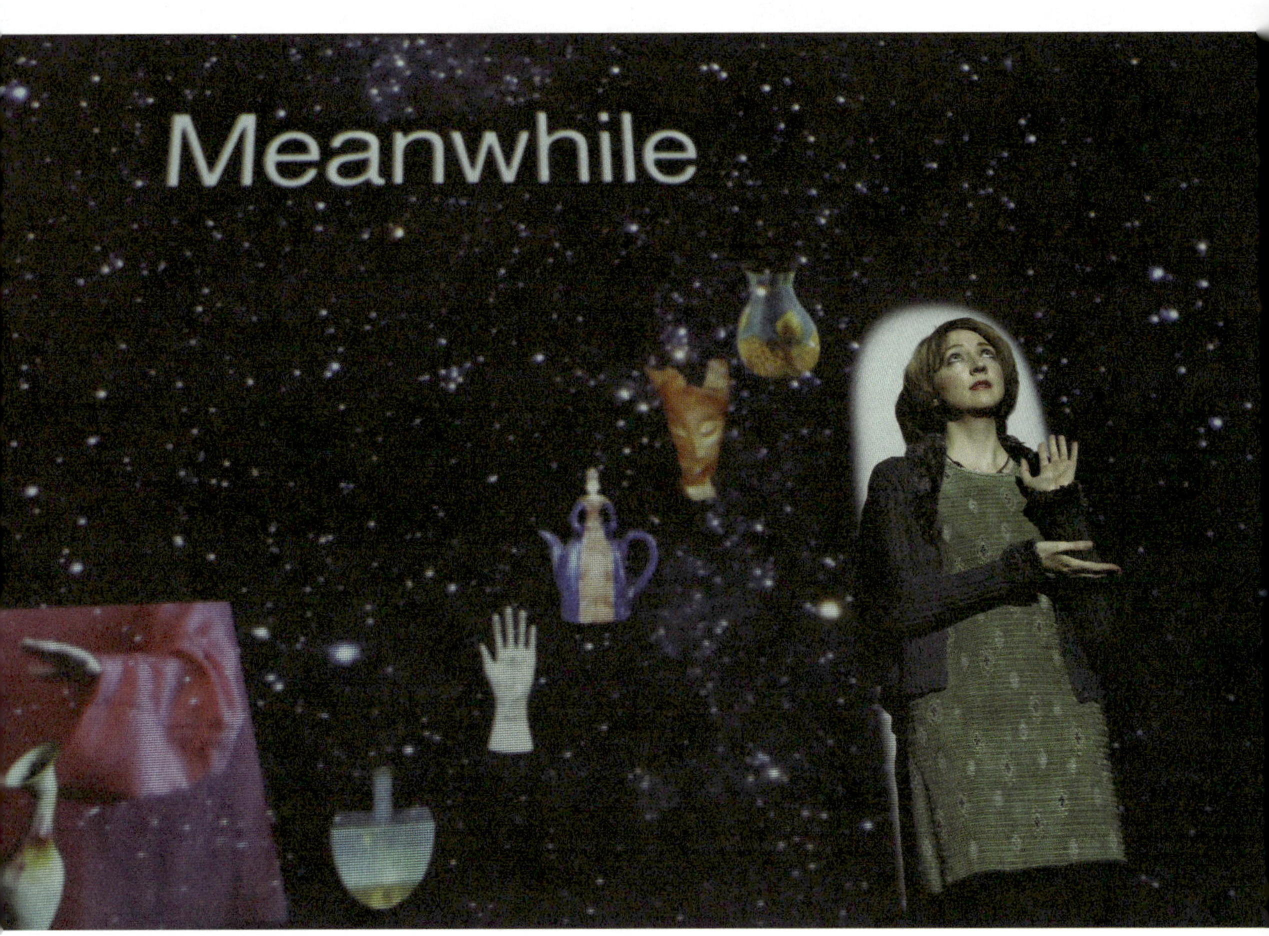
Meanwhile

CAN OBJECTS PERFORM?

To mark the launch of the Cricoteka Museum in Krakow, Poland, that houses the "Living Archive" of theater director Tadeusz Kantor (1915-90), *Can objects perform?*, was an evening-length program of screenings and performances by contemporary artists operating at the intersection of theater, performance and the visual arts, presented at the Performa Hub.

One of the most prominent Polish artists and theater reformers of the twentieth century, Kantor's art and uncompromising stance influenced generations of artists, including Miroslaw Balka, Christian Boltanski, Andrzej Wajda, Robert Wilson, Giselle Vienne, and Catherine Sullivan. In his theater, Kantor introduced numerous revolutionary concepts: "poor object," "bio-object" (person fused with object), "actor-object," or "ready-man." The materials Kantor employed had specific aesthetics—everyday, mundane objects, found or knocked together from sheet metal or bits of wood, that were often assigned to specific protagonists and "united" by their bodies, restricting movement and adding poetic associations. Kantor was interested in Edward Gordon Craig's concept of the "Über-Marionette," which was supposed to replace a living actor on stage. During his groundbreaking performances, these naturalistic dolls confused the viewer, inducing an uncanny feeling.

Can objects perform? began with a keynote lecture by historian Dominika Laster, posing the question about the double nature of the object as both prop and autonomous artwork in Kantor's theater, and went on to feature films, videos and live performances by a series of artists reflecting his legacy.

The film *Future Days* (2013), by Agnieszka Polska, combined elements of animation with images shot on the Swedish island of Gotland. Polska created a fictitious "after-world for artists" where artists from different generations meet after death. Artist discussions there commented on artworks and ironically exposed the limitations of human knowledge.

The application of language is a central theme in Nathaniel Mellors's absurdist scripts, psychedelic theater, film, video, performance,

Shana Moulton, Cricoteka, *Can objects perform?* (2013), performance view, Performa Hub.

Photo by Paula Court

ORGANIZED AND TEXT BY JOANNA ZIELINSKA △ PERFORMA HUB

collage, and sculpture. *The Saprophage* (2012) was shot on an iPhone (in Los Angeles, London, and Greece) and some of the footage was purposely distorted and damaged. Time, place, and action are examined in a maelstrom of words and images. Mellors was frequently on camera as part of this fabulous, absurd saga.

Utilizing handmade costumes and sets, Marvin Gaye Chetwynd's work draws on a wide range of influences from film and television, literature, art history, and philosophy. Chetwynd uses a variety of historical theatrical forms, from Brechtian drama to puppet shows, often within the same performance. A number of Chetwynd's projects have focused on the local environment outside of the gallery space and have embraced the everyday theater, for instance. This strategy is present in her film *Erotics + Bestiality* (2004).

Catherine Sullivan's '*Tis Pity She's a Fluxus Whore* (2003) restaged two confrontational exchanges between performance and audience: a festival of Fluxus events that took place in Aachen, Germany, in 1964 and a performance of a Jacobean drama about incest that was performed in Hartford, Connecticut, in 1943. Sullivan's film brought these two wildly different performance traditions together in the body of one actor who played every role, shifting seamlessly between a purposeful Brechtian directness ("Fluxus style") and a highly mannered theatricality ("Giovanni style").

Many of Shana Moulton's videos and interactive performances feature scenes that play out like old Nintendo video games—the ones where the screen moves in a continuous upward direction and the characters jump and climb between magic carpets and revolving doughnuts. The performance *SPF* (2013) presented at the Performa Hub, tied together videos the artist created for her "Whispering Pines" series and found material from sources including pharmaceutical ads, a TED talk by a neuroscientist who had a stroke and experienced nirvana, an excerpt from Todd Haynes's film *Safe* (1995), a documentary on a DMT research study, HBO, Pink Floyd, and German musical project Enigma.

The program culminated in a walk to Salon de Fleurus, an educational institution dedicated to assembling, preserving, and exhibiting memories of early modern art. Its permanent exhibit, titled *From the Autobiography of Alice B. Toklas*, located at 41 Spring Street, New York, has been open to the public since 1992.

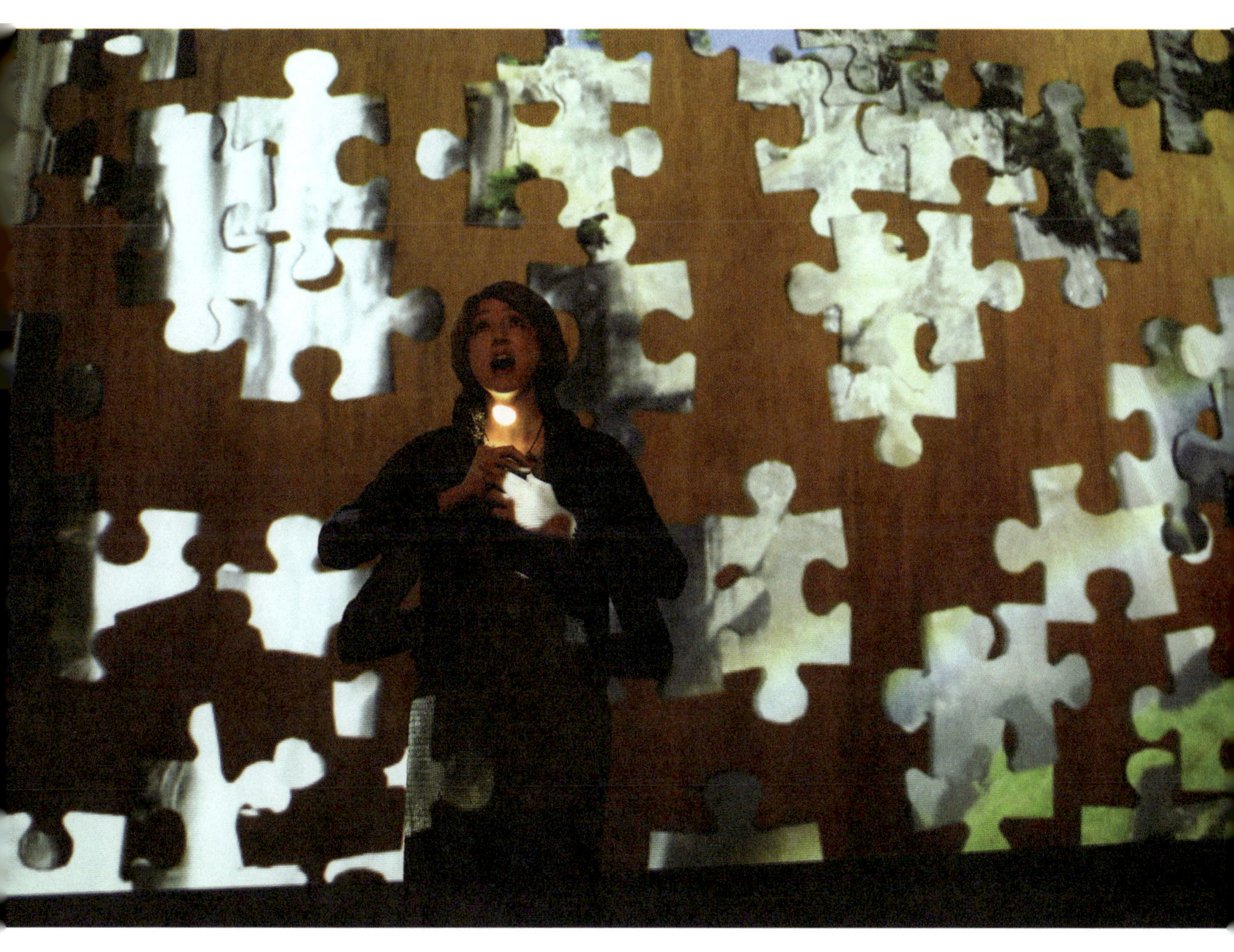

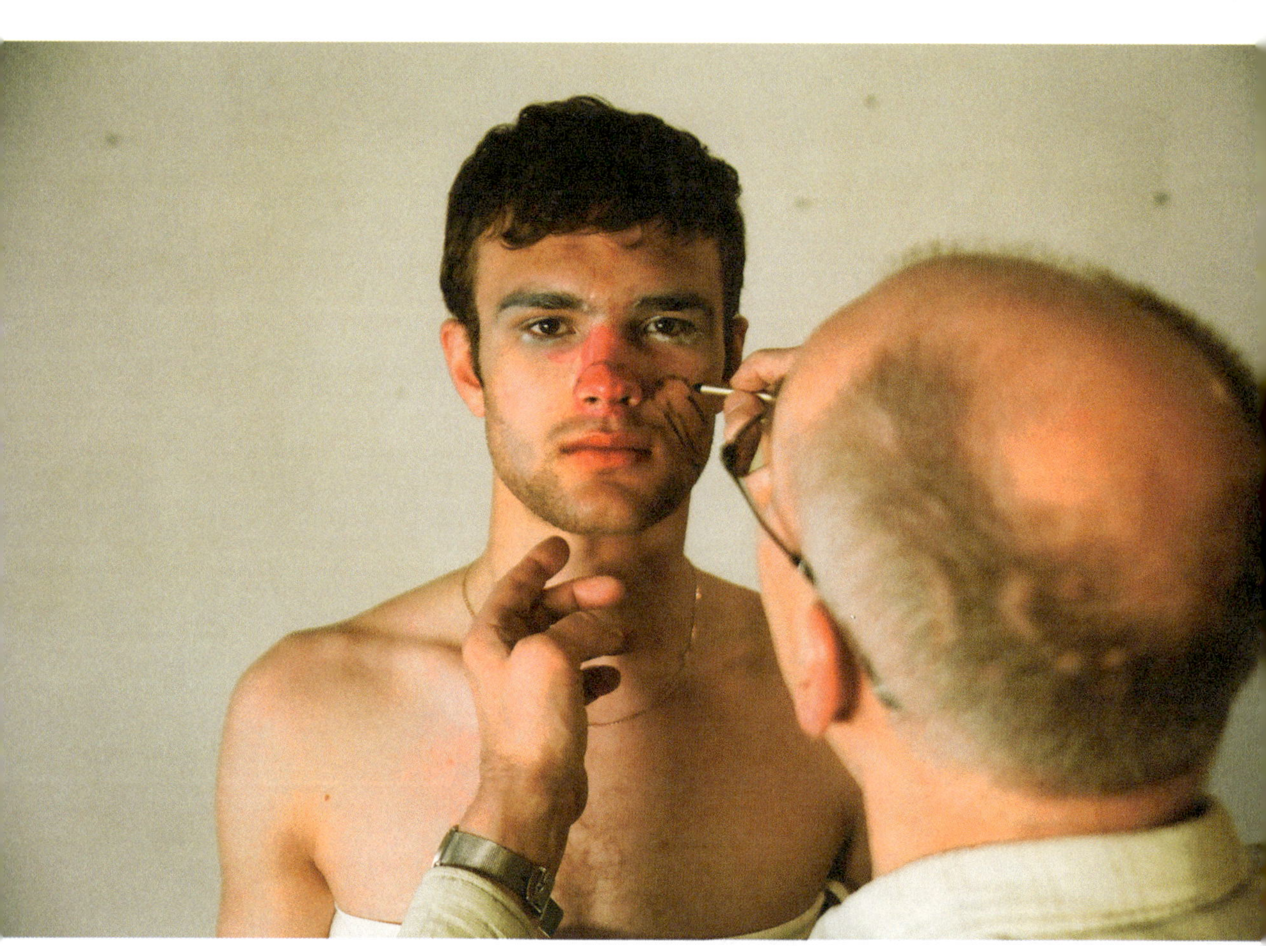

KAROL RADZISZEWSKI

KISIELAND

For Performa 13, the Warsaw-based artist Karol Radziszewski assembled a group of activists and artists, including the American AIDS activist and artist Avram Finkelstein and the Polish documentary filmmaker and gay activist Ryszard Kisiel, who flew especially to New York for the event, to reflect on each country's cultural legacy during the early American AIDS crisis. Radziszewski, whose interdisciplinary practice involves DIY magazines, artist books, fashion, and curatorial projects, conceived this evening of screenings, slideshows, and conversations related to his 2012 documentary film *Kisieland*. The film explores Kisiel's endeavors and artistic output, including his magazines featuring provocatively dressed gay men reproduced during the relentlessly conservative and devastatingly oppressive years of "Operation Hyacinth," during which the ruling Communist Party created a blacklist of homosexuals. Between the years 1985 and 1986, the Polish government's anti-gay crackdown resulted in numerous arrests of homosexuals and the implementation of "pink cards" that gay people were required to carry, stating their sexuality. In 1986, Kisiel founded *Filo*, the first gay magazine published in the Eastern Bloc, with the aim of spreading AIDS awareness, fostering solidarity, and documenting the underground gay community. Subject to arrest and imprisonment for his activities, Kisiel published the zine under a pseudonym until just after the fall of the Soviet Union and the 1990 founding of Lambda, the first official gay rights organization in Poland. Radziszewski's hour-long documentary examines Kisiel's extensive archive of gay propaganda, consisting of dozens of color slides, activist materials, and reenactments of meetings organized by Kisiel and his friends in a private apartment. Such an archive genealogically connects to Radziszewski's own interest in publishing as a platform for art and activism, epitomized by his *DIK Fagzine*, a hugely popular queer zine that scrutinizes queer representation, as well as his campy wallpaper artworks of Donald Duck playing around the word "AIDS," which were installed in the Performa Hub prior to the talk. These cross-generational conversations highlighted the important role of art in activist practices around HIV/AIDS and drew similarities to the work of Finkelstein, whose group Gran Fury used direct action and the production of artistic posters, pamphlets, and other materials to create political change around HIV/AIDS negligence in the 1980s in the United States. During a lively discussion Kisiel, Radziszewski, and Finkelstein commented on the important role of art in communicating the cultural and political history of the AIDS crisis to a younger generation who might not otherwise be aware of this crucial period in GLBTQ history. The event concluded with an interactive group reading by the audience of a story from *Filo*.

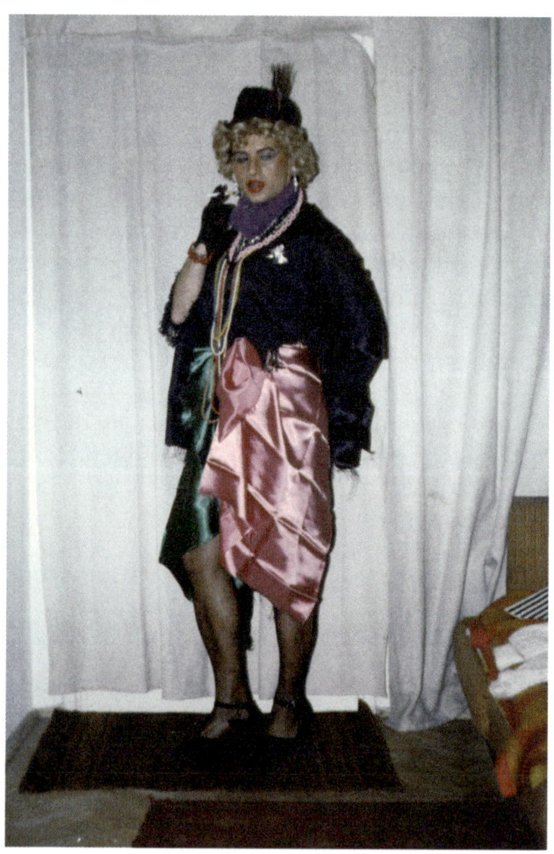

JESZCZE O AIDS

"Prawo i Życie" nr 24 (1171)
z 13 czerwca 1987 przynosi odpowiedź S.Sterkowicza na zarzuty
w artykule "Jeszcze o AIDS.Nieco
futurologii".W tym samym numerze
odpowiedź czytelnika Tadeusza
Olszańskiego na propozycje S.S.
w "AIDS i co dalej?".
Również "Polityka" ustosunkowała
się krytycznie do pomysłów pana
S.S. a także felietonista "Prawa
i Życia".

"Polityka" nie zasypia gruszek w
popiele i co pewien czas drukuje
albo pełne artykuły albo krytyki
albo listy czytelników dotyczące
AIDS. I tak nr 19 przynosi list
czytelniczki z Francji obawiającej
się , że AIDS przysporzy nam u
progu XX wieku nowych trędowatych.

Miesięcznik "Reporter" nr 7 proponuje
ciekawą lekturę dwóch artykułów :
Jacka Walocha "AIDS" i Karola Jackowskiego "Walka o przetrwanie".
Wreszcie publicystyka pozbawiona
pruderii. W artykule Walocha czytamy,
że w Ministerstwie Zdrowia i Opieki
istnieje teczka z listami,jakie napłynęły do MZiOS w sprawie AIDS. Są to
po prostu donosy na homoseksualistów,
zawierające dokładne szczegóły z intymnego życia tych osób.Czyż nie szkoda energii na tak drobiazgowe śledztwa?
W tym samym numerze Witolda Żygulskiego
"Na świecie" o pracach nad leczeniem
AIDS a także wywiad z doc.dr.hab.med.
Jackiem Juszczykiem członkiem rady
d/s AIDS, delegatem Polski na kongres
AIDS w Waszyngtonie.

Dobry poradnik

Pozycją jaką każdy gej powinien sobie
sprawić jest broszura dra hab. med.
Jacka Juszczyka "AIDS - pytania.i
odpowiedzi" 150 zł.Napisana przystępnym językiem,zawiera odpowiedzi na
interesujące nas pytania.

Z PRASY KATOLICKIEJ

Bardzo typowe dla środowisk katolickich
poglądy na AIDS i związane z tą chorobą środowiska homoseksualistów
przedstawił tygodnik katolicki
"Niedziela" nr 36 z 6 IX 1987
w artykule ks. Wacława Gubały
"AIDS - epidemia XX wieku"

KOŚCIÓŁ WOBEC AIDS

Papież w czasie obecnej wizyty w USA,
w San Francisco przyznał,że opieka
nad chorymi na AIDS jest powinnością
moralną chrześcijanina,wypełnia
przykazanie o miłosierdziu i pielęgnowaniu chorych.
Społeczność gejowska San Francisco
zorganizowała demonstrację przeciwko
orędziu Kongregacji Wiary uznające
homoseksualizm za zjawisko niemoralne.

"FORUM" nr 38/87 z 17 września 1987r
przynosi przedruk z włoskiej "Epoki"
"Kościół a AIDS" Z artykułu warto
zacytować stanowisko ojca Davida
Maria Turoldo "...oficjalnego stanowiska Kościoła powinniśmy się
doszukiwać przede wszystkim w dążeniu do postępowania zgodnie z
nauką Ewangelii,która jest księgą
ludzkości.Dlatego starajmy się nie
siać strachu i nie zważajmy na tych,
którzy twierdzą,że AIDS jest produktem moralnego nieładu panującego
w świecie.W przeciwnym razie stalibyśmy się odpowiedzialni za niepotrzebne i nieuzasadnione przypadki
depresji,która była już przyczyną
wielu samobójstw."

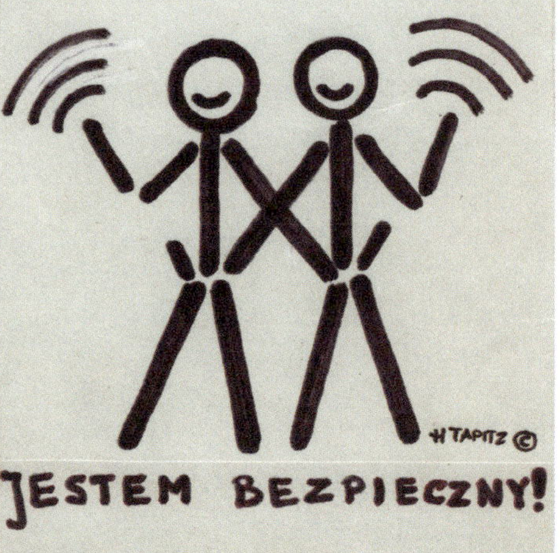

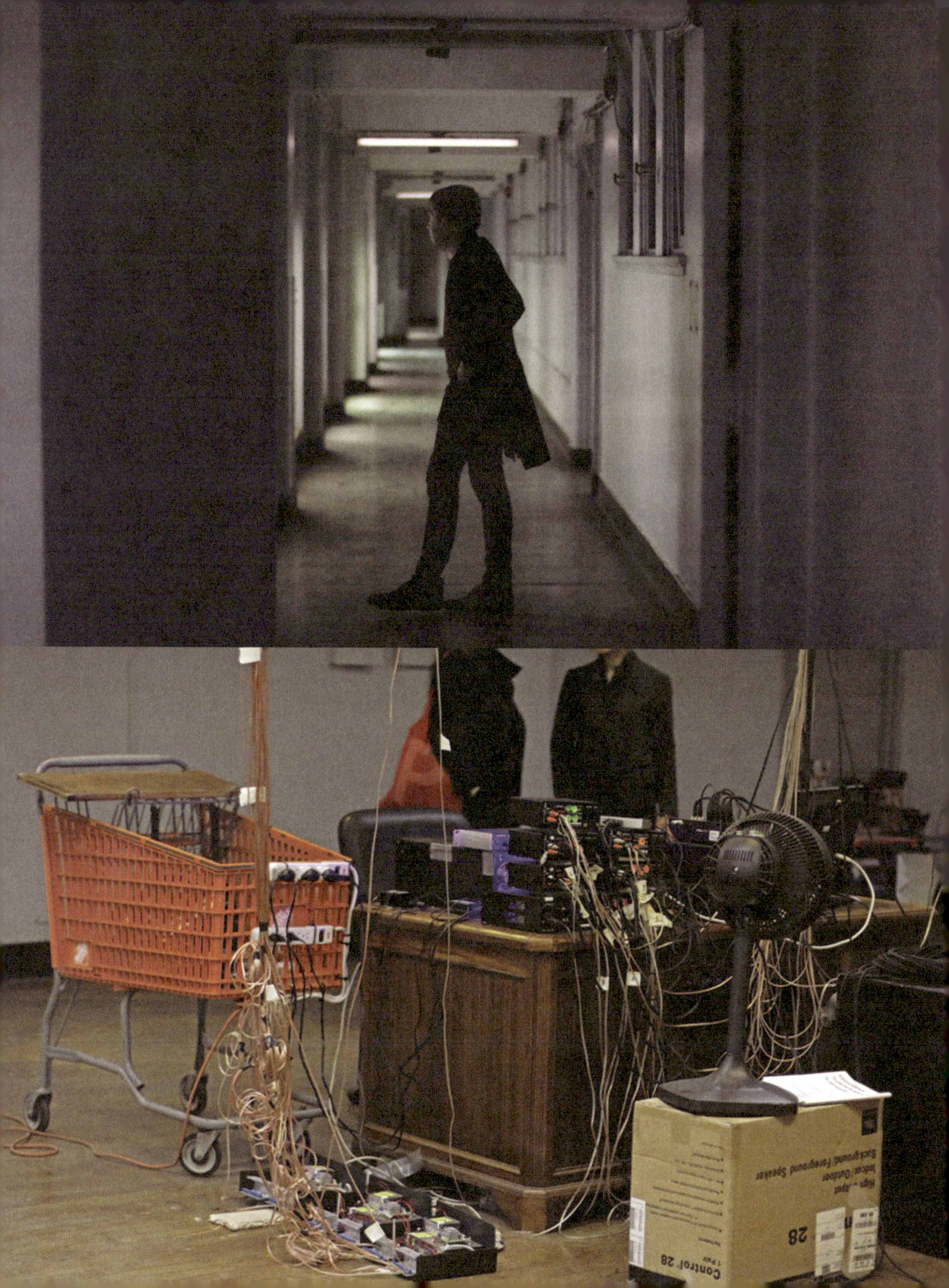
High-output
Indoor/Outdoor
Back ground/Foreground Speaker
Control 28
1 Pair
28

KATARZYNA KRAKOWIAK

THE GREAT AND SECRET SHOW/ THE LOOK OUT GALLERY

The historic James A. Farley Post Office is one of the largest unoccupied buildings in Manhattan. In the mid-twentieth century, more than 16,000 workers inhabited its interiors. Today, fewer than two hundred workers occupy the space, leaving many rooms, corridors, vaults, chambers, and storage spaces vacant.

The Great and Secret Show/The Look Out Gallery took visitors into a closed route of empty rooms and corridors throughout the building. In these spaces, past and present sounds of postal service mechanisms and processes were performed as a fictional sonic reenactment, revealing operational histories of the building and reflecting on the vast scale of its interior spaces. The composition of sounds, as a stenographic archaeology, allowed visitors to reconstruct the territories and routes of the building's past and exposed them to the contemporary silences and sounds of current forms of communication around the globe.

Katarzyna Krakowiak took what workers called "The Look Out Gallery" as the point of departure for her installation. The Look Out Gallery derived its name from a system of secret corridors that connected the thousands of rooms of the old post office building, creating a system of internal surveillance of workers. In the heyday of the post office's operations, small eyeholes enabled assigned postal policemen to control the working environment.

Using a prerecorded collection that included sounds of tasks such as the closing of doors, discarding of cards, stamping of postcards, and other past and present post office activities, the performance transformed the walls of a hallway into a vibrating membrane, producing an intimate experience that synthesized the past and present conditions of the post office. Raising questions of labor, public service, and hierarchy in one of the most visited urban spaces of the past, Krakowiak's installation reminded us that our bodies and memories are also housed in edifices of sound.

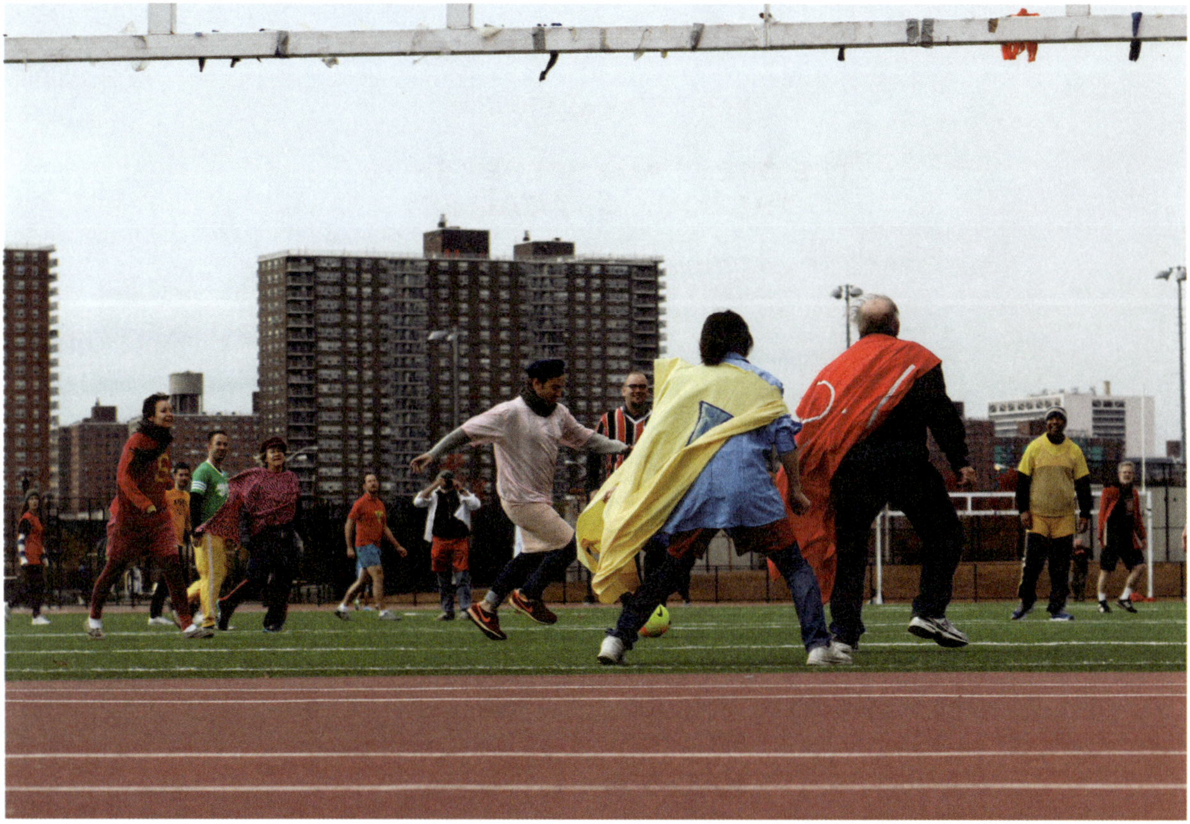

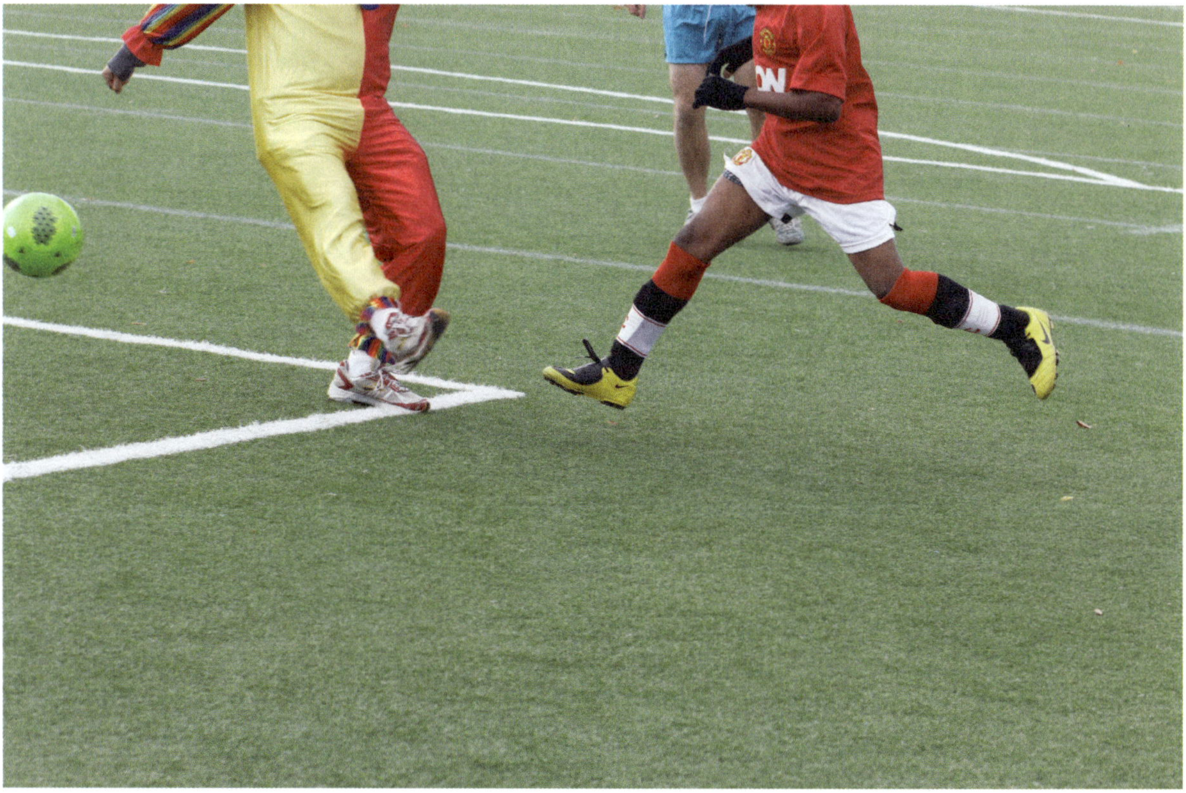

PAULO BRUSCKY

JOGO/PERFORMANCE

For more than four decades, Brazilian artist Paulo Bruscky has created work that engages a keen appreciation for the play within language. The son of a Belarusian father who immigrated to Brazil in the late 1930s, Bruscky has developed a rapport with language that seems to be in a constant state of translation. *Jogo/Performance* (*Game/Performance*, 1971–2013) is a prime example of how Bruscky expands his linguistic investigations into the quirks of everyday rituals. That the game indicated by the title is soccer, which is closely identified with Brazilian culture, is significant. Internationally revered by fans as "the beautiful game," soccer matches are famous for stirring passions among competing teams and their supporters.

In *Jogo/Performance*, however, the situation is confused in that as many as twenty soccer players participate in a match where there are no set teams. Instead, each player is asked to wear a different jersey. Rules and allegiances are thus abolished, and it is every man or woman for himself or herself, running and fighting on the playing field. With this simple, acute twist of the classic soccer rules, Bruscky establishes a situation that resonates with current neo-liberal beliefs in competition as an organizing principle for social structure. Moreover, instead of representing a team, and traditionally, by extension, a country and its value system, each player in *Jogo/Performance* relinquishes his or her citizenship status for the duration of the event. Blurring the thin line between art and life, Paulo Bruscky's performance addresses the politics of friendship, citizenship, and competition. The reenactment of *Jogo/Performance* in the Bronx during Performa 13 was extremely timely as it was prescient in recognizing the social upheaval coming to Brazil in 2014, when urban youths protested the enormous amount invested by the country to host the World Cup, to the detriment of the delivery of adequate public services to city residents.

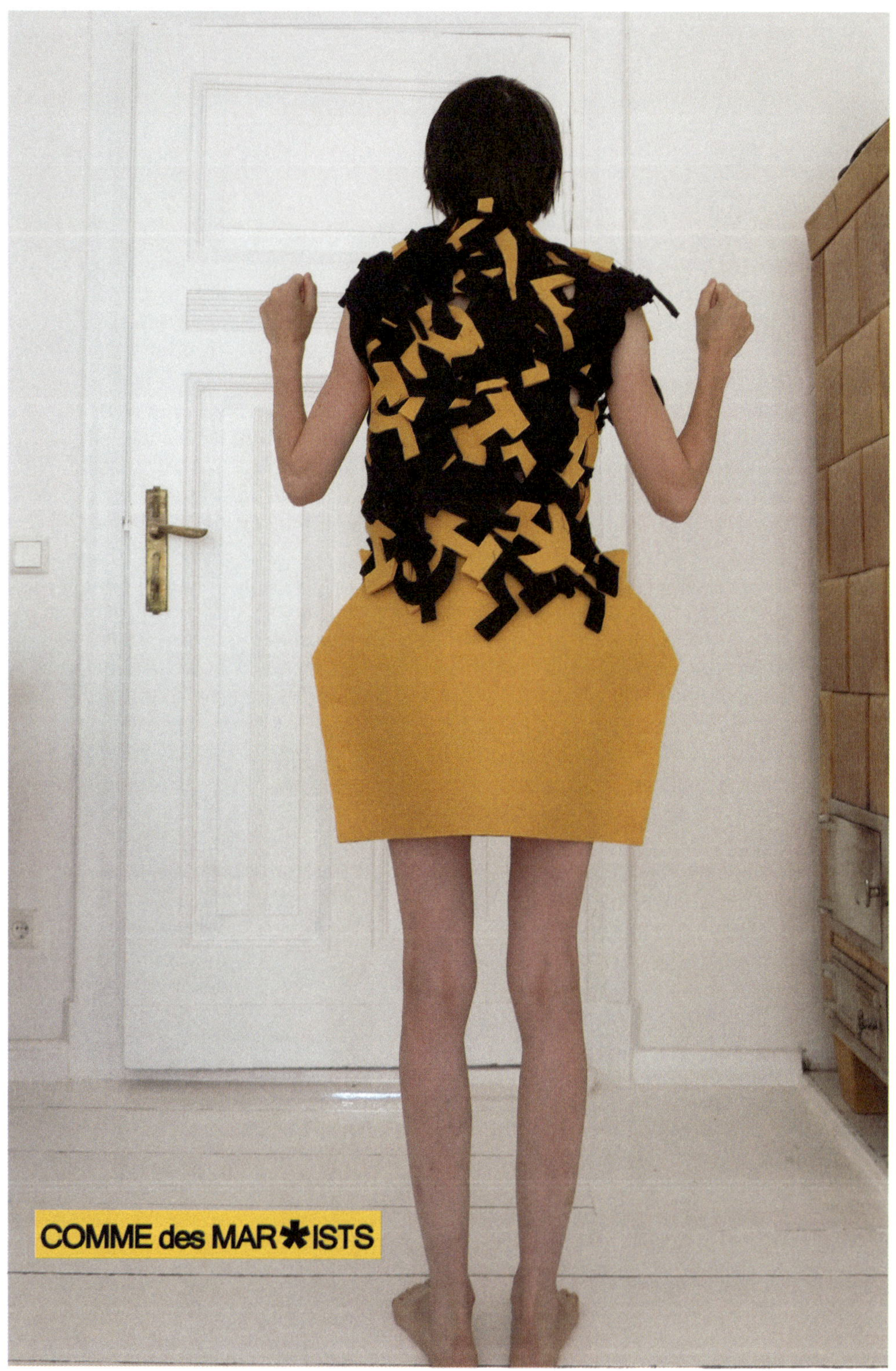
COMME des MAR*ISTS

RAINER GANAHL

COMME DES MARXISTES

The growing swath of common ground shared by the cultural superpowers of fashion and art has yielded some interesting and engaging cultivars in the past decade. Some of these have been performance pieces that manage to engage the audience by exploring the complicated artfulness of identity. The best ones have often drawn revealing and surprising lines between those facets of identity that we neatly sort and label as relating to either our inner or outer selves, making us question value systems like deep-versus-shallow or natural-versus-artificial with new perspectives.

A standout of this exceptional genre was *COMME des MARXISTES*, the chaotically captivating piece that the Austrian-born, New York-based artist Rainer Ganahl produced for two nights at White Columns during Performa 13. Within seconds it was clear that Ganahl would neither be neatly labeling nor sorting anything; instead, he messily mashed together the familiar (but dissimilar) performative acts of the protest march and fashion runway show. The result was a magical melee that managed to be at once hilariously funny, rapturously stylish, and politically inspiring.

Ganahl enlisted dozens of non-model citizens to don his designs, shout leftish Dadaist slogans like "Some boys *like* to play with hammers and sickles," and walk the short runway, outlined in tape on the floor. I was among those who walked, and my cohorts and I were a motley crew of "art-ocratic" men, women, and children, such as Thea Westreich, Linda Yablonsky, Amanda Friedman, Leigh Ledare, Laura Hunt, Peter Fend, Barry Schwabsky, and Karl Holmqvist. I might therefore be biased regarding the success of the endeavor.

Then again, that bias is no accident. I am for the most part seriously underwhelmed by most of the art-fashion hybridizing I see; so often, it's just a thin art idea gussied up to be *au courant*. By contrast, I was sold from the moment that I heard about *COMME des MARXISTES* (and its brilliantly apt title) from Ganahl. He loves to needle our most overinflated beliefs without trying to banish them outright. This is clearly evident in Ganahl's "Seminars/Lectures" series of photographs he made in the 2000s of rock star theoreticians like Noam Chomsky,

Photo by Rainer Ganahl

Rainer Ganahl, *COMME des MARXISTES* (2013).

CURATED BY MATTHEW HIGGS / TEXT BY DAVID COLMAN ● WHITE COLUMNS

Jacques Derrida, and Pierre Bourdieu lecturing to rapt audiences. Invoking two mighty Karls—Marx and Lagerfeld—in the same breath, *COMME des MARXISTES* achieved this same goal, comically pointing out how Marxist ideas are as much a must-have mantle in today's art world as the costly, arty clothes made by COMME des GARÇONS.

But while that observation is hardly newsworthy, Ganahl breathed new life into it with his nonsensical protest rants and—believe it or not—clothes. Employing a patchwork aesthetic and embracing artificial materials like dime-store plastic tote bags and industrial rubber mixed with brightly colored plaid woolens and felts, Ganahl truly delivered an impressive fashion collection. According to the artist, Ganahl spent more than $10,000 on his "samples," and it showed. He had all the requisite categories that a real fashion collection has: day clothes, evening clothes, womenswear, and menswear. There were deconstructed dresses that brought to mind Rodarte's early designs and some snazzy hand-knit sweaters featuring lines like "MARX WALKS WITH A BIG CARBON FOOTPRINT." With a marketer's eye for product extensions, Ganahl even included slogan jewelry and children's clothes with class-tweaking zingers like "I GET A NANNY U GET A TV" and "I GO PRIVATE YOU GO PUBLIC." The black and silver uniforms he created for his "SNOWDEN MARX SECURITY" outfit looked great—smart, stark, snark—and were a vast improvement on the increasingly threadbare cliché of the Joseph Beuys felt suit as an art-fashion statement.

Let's put it this way: I wanted the coat I modeled. Ganahl might actually succeed as a fashion designer; after all, few designers have ever delivered a collection that was this full of ideas and this full of great clothes that you might want to buy. But the problem is that in order to be a success, fashion needs to deliver comfort and fantasy. As anarchic and stylish as COMME des MARXISTES was, part of what Ganahl delivered was something a little uncomfortable—he delivered reality. And that, unfortunately, is a rather hard sell.

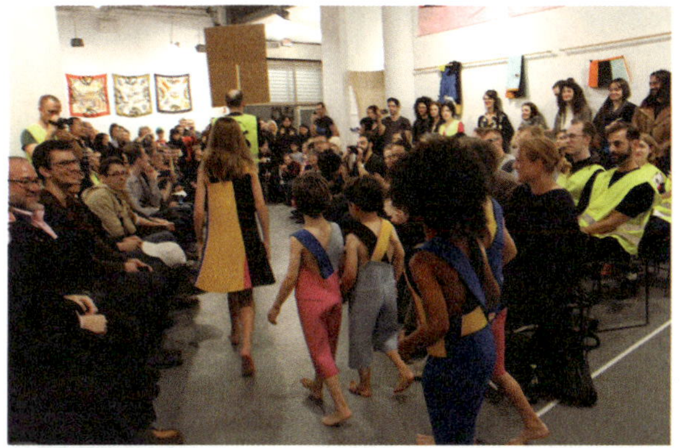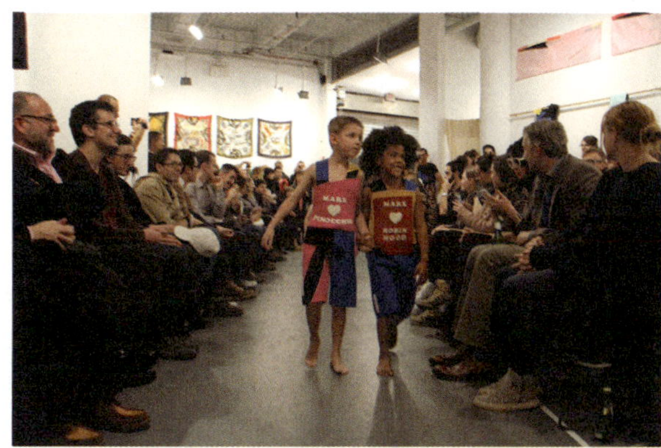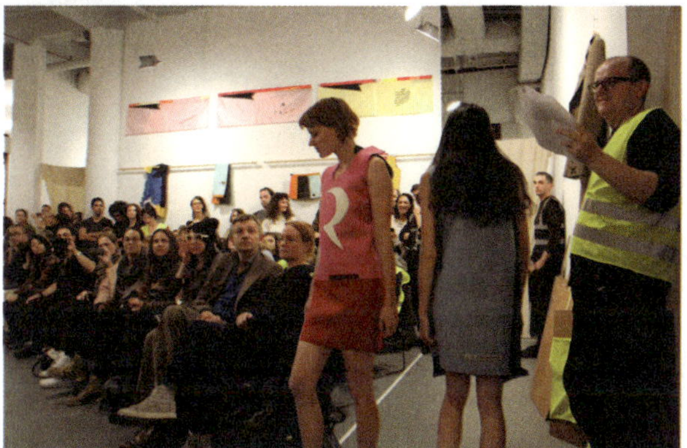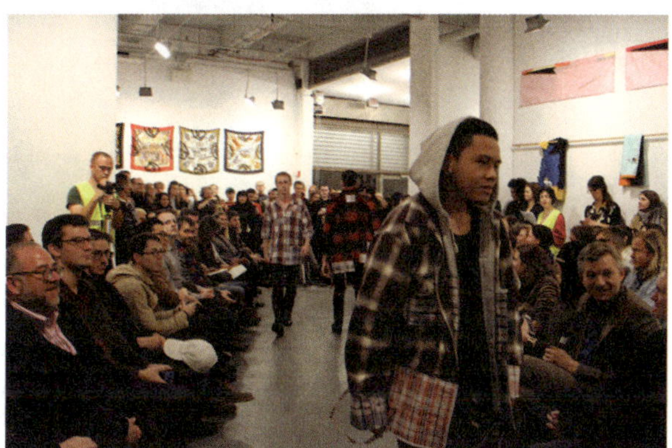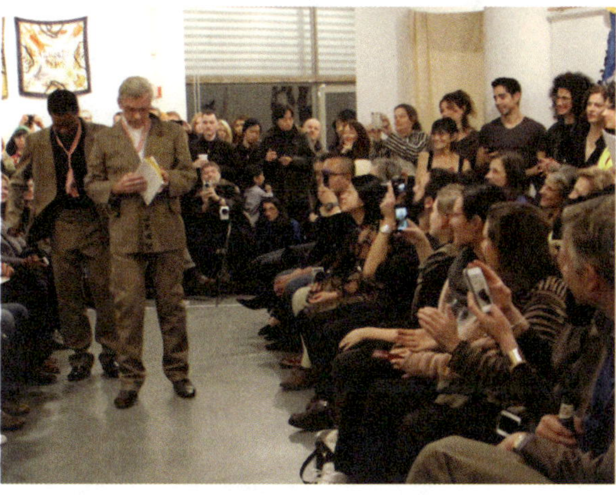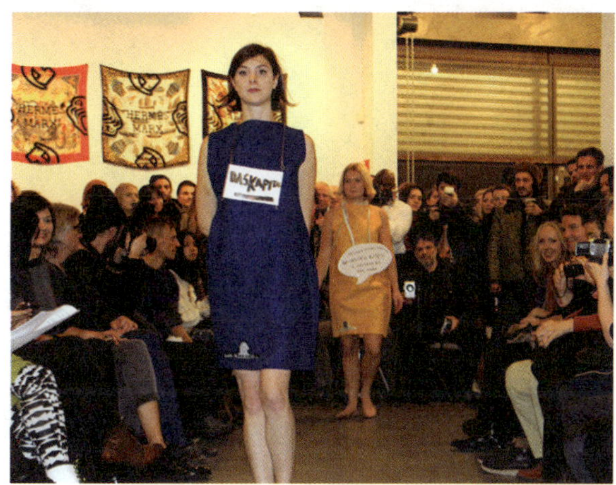

Rainer Ganahl, *COMME des MARXISTES* (2013), performance views.
Photos courtesy of the artist.

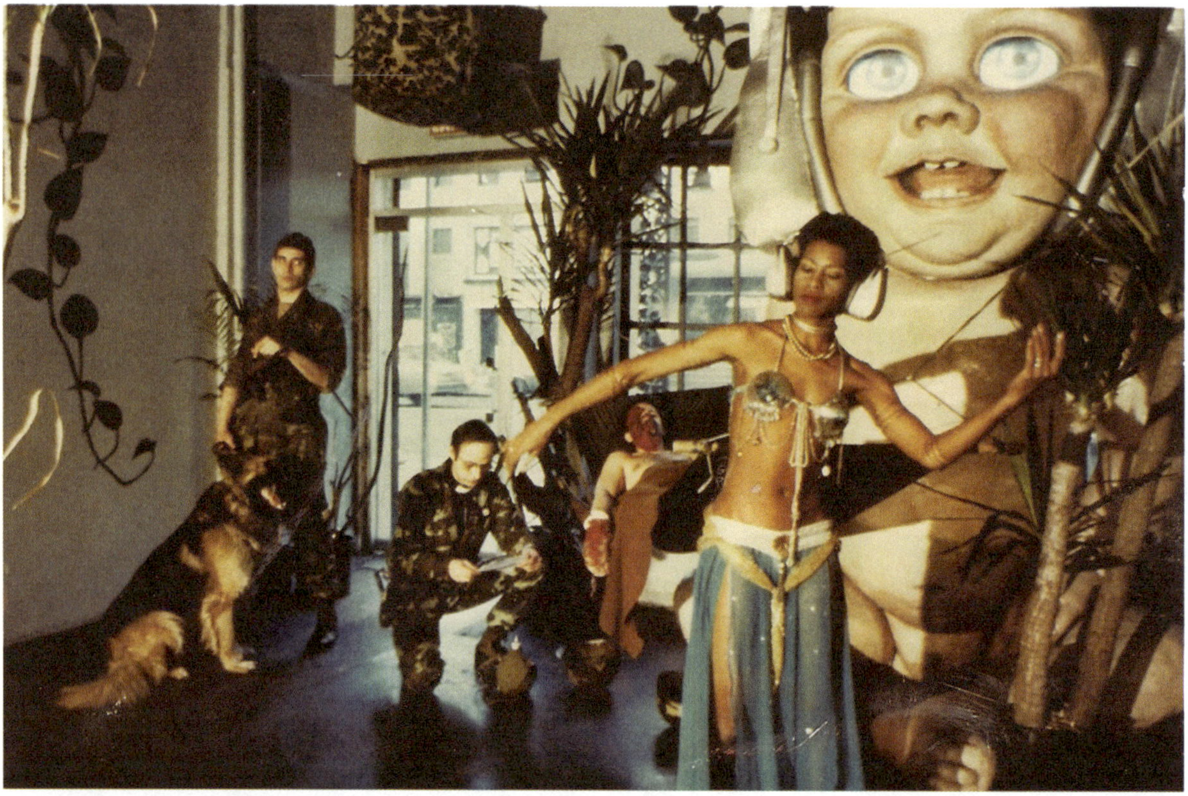

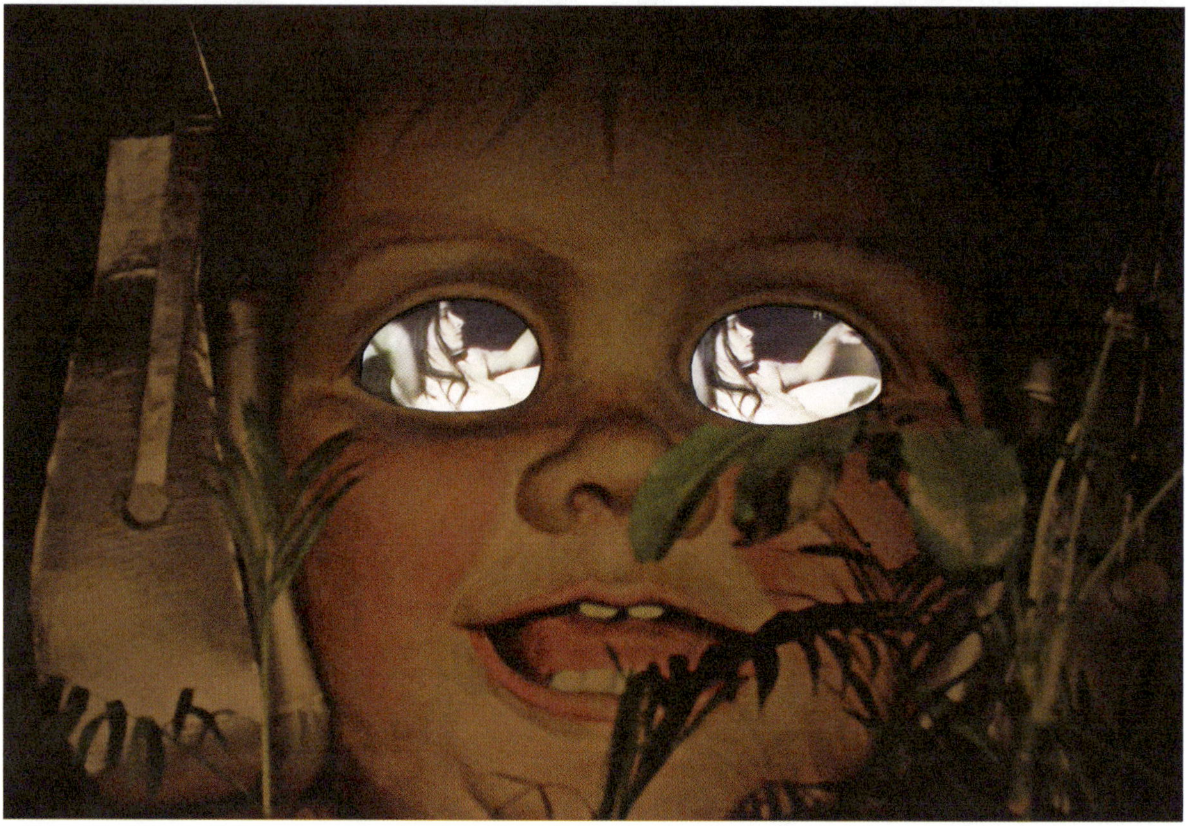

SQUAT THEATRE

Squat Theatre members Anna Koos and Eva Buchmuller screened *Mr. Dead and Mrs. Free,* (1981), followed by a discussion with Jay Sanders and Rebecca Cleman. The two-part video exemplified their multi-part performance approach, featuring a live performance and a film created by the Squat Theatre collective. In 1981, audience members congregated in Squat Theatre's four-story brownstone storefront theater on 23rd Street to experience innovative work by these radical downtown theater artists. The brownstone has been both the primary set and venue for Squat's productions since the late 1970s and early '80s, as well as a residence for the theater group, their children, and visiting artists, including the underground pop icon Nico, who performed *New York, New York* as the finale of *Mr. Dead and Mrs. Free*.

Squat Theatre blurs the lines between life and theater, coming full circle as the group's second generation, now adults, reflected on childhood memories and experiences during this event, many of which were specific scenes and narratives from Squat productions. Notably present for the talk was Sheryl Sutton, along with two members of the second generation of Squat Theatre, Rebecca Major and Judith Halasz. One of the daughters remembered playing in a bedroom, used as a second stage, and brushing her doll's hair, instead of playing outside with other children. Later, this scene was recounted from the parent's perspective as a scene for a particular performance Squat Theare staged that year.

The concluding discussion was peppered with familial arguments, lively talk, and artistic disagreement that seemed like that of any tight-knit family. Despite the fact that they have not lived in the same brownstone for thirty years, their bond remains.

CURATED BY JAY SANDERS / TEXT BY GRETA HARTENSTEIN ◗ ELECTRONIC ARTS INTERMIX AND THE WHITNEY MUSEUM OF AMERICAN ART

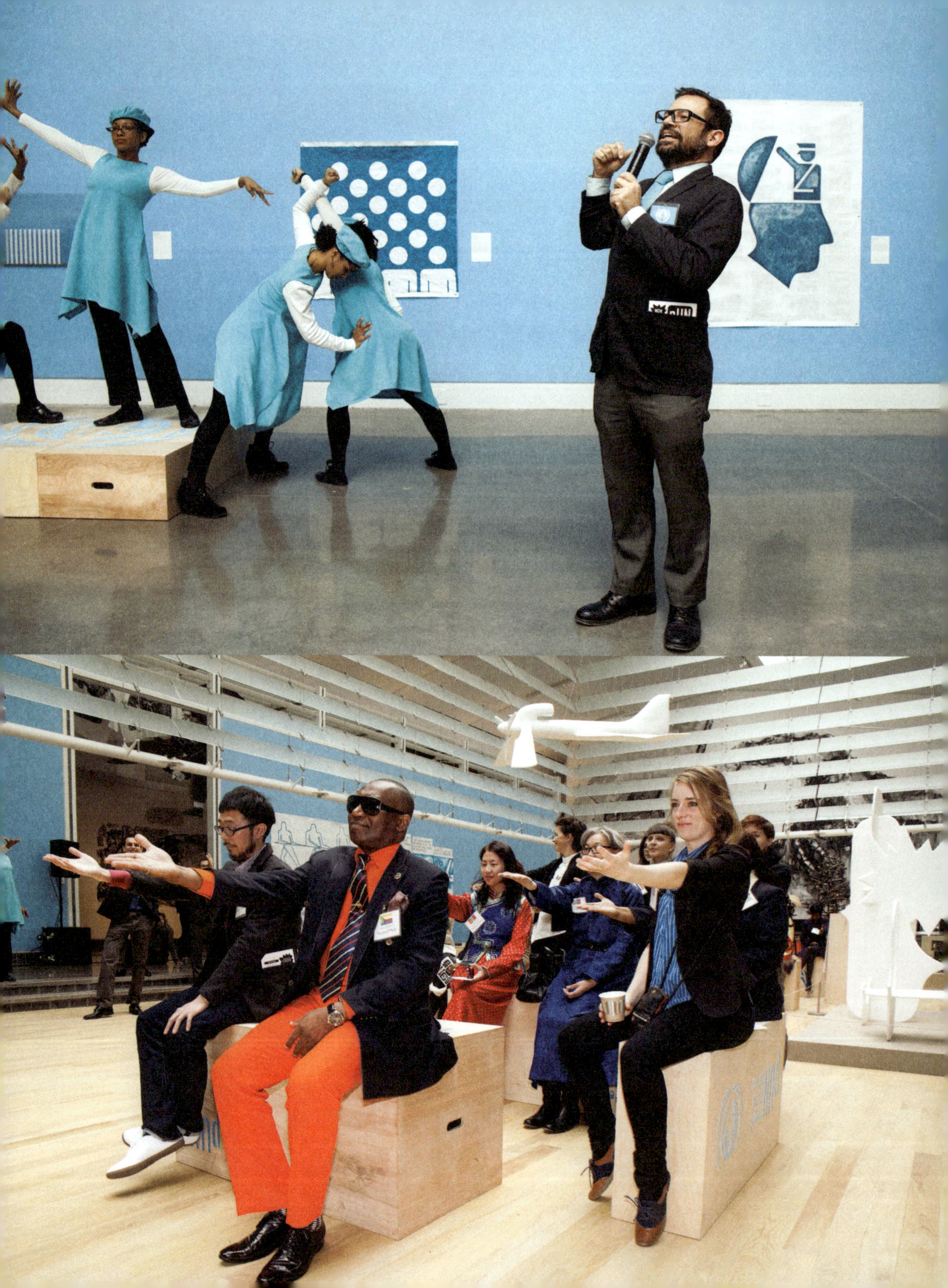

PEDRO REYES

THE PEOPLE'S UNITED NATIONS (pUN)

The People's United Nations (pUN) was an event and exhibition by Mexican artist Pedro Reyes that assembled everyday citizens in a mock UN. A playful homage to the United Nations, inspired by the fact that the global body's General Assembly met from 1946-1950 in the building that later became the Queens Museum, the event brought together 193 New Yorkers who are immigrants from, or have family connections to, the 193 member and observer states that currently make up the UN. This experimental gathering tested Reyes's hypothesis that, since diplomacy has not yet solved the world's problems, conflict resolution techniques proven in other fields should be explored.

Over the course of two days, *pUN* used theater games, group therapy, and techniques from social science to grapple with a set of surprising and provocative proposals as well as the problems the delegates personally brought to the table. A lighthearted spirit of play allowed participants to engage in subjects, the magnitude of which would otherwise overwhelm. Museum visitors were invited to experience the two days of *pUN* activities through special half-hour guided tours. The *pUN* convention took place amid an exhibition specially created by Reyes for the Queens Museum's new atrium, which forms the center of its recently built wing, flooded with light from a massive central skylight. The exhibition included five sculptures that addressed topics like "peace and dialogue" through unexpected combinations of ideas and material. With their frank embrace of symbolism, these sculptures provided a poetic and inspiring backdrop for the *pUN* convention and represented its sincere optimism, serious and playful at once, to the museum visitors even after the event concluded.

CURATED AND TEXT BY LARISSA HARRIS ◗ QUEENS MUSEUM

CHAPTER

2

TWO

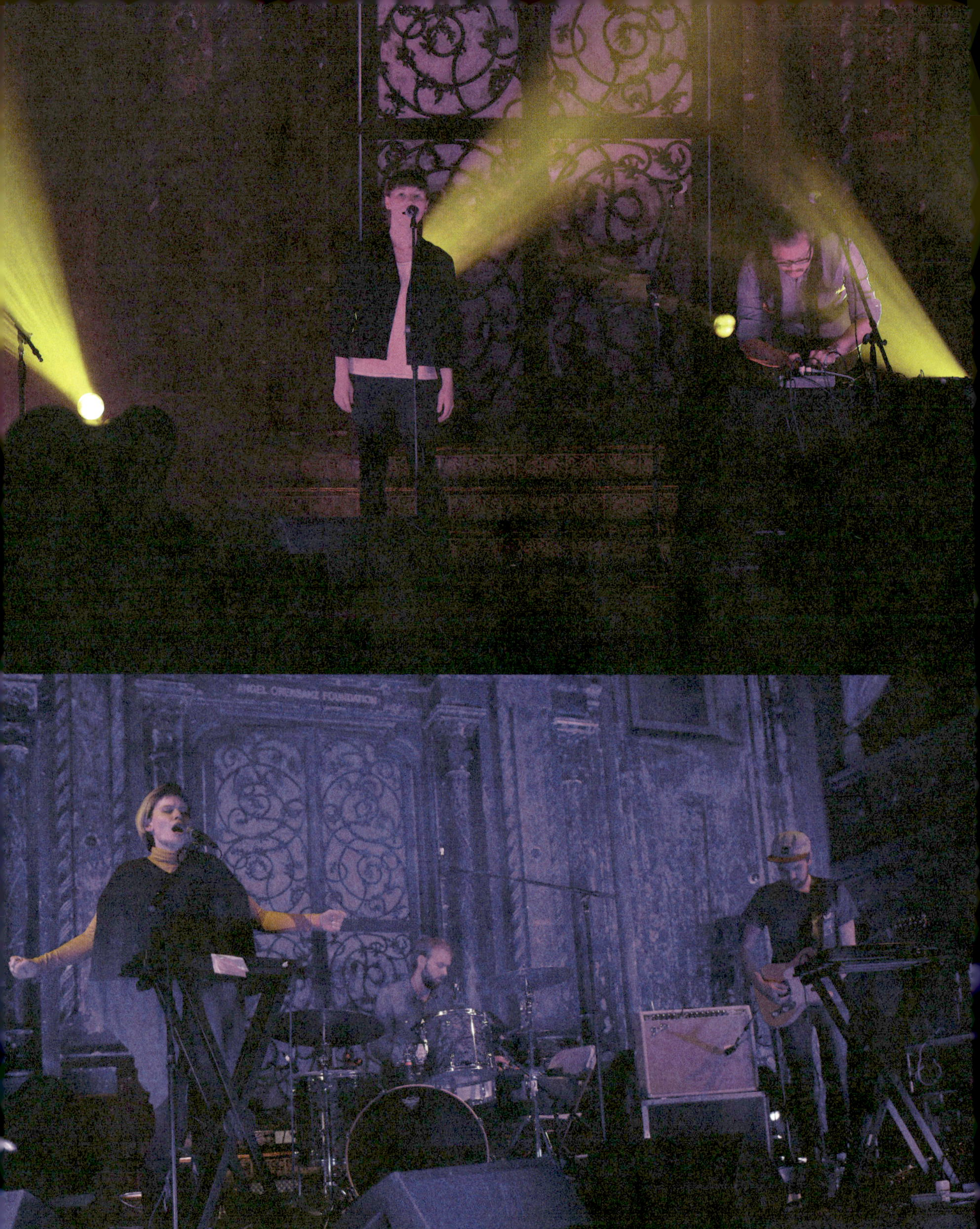

OUT OF BODY

THE VOICE IN PERFORMANCE

Photos by Paula Court

(Above) *In Tones From Light to Dark*, Stine Motland and C. Spencer Yeh (Below) Jenny Hval (2013), performance view.

CURATED BY MARK BEASLEY

"The voice is elusive, always changing, becoming, elapsing, with unclear contours, as opposed to the relative permanence, solidity, and durability of the seen. One could say it is, by its nature, on the side of the event, not of being." So wrote Slovenian philosopher Mladen Dolar in his book, *A Voice and Nothing More* (2006), in which he makes the case for the voice as a form of material—the invisible passing of air particles—that runs like a ribbon up from the lungs, out from the mouth and to the ear of the listener. It is this "materiality" of sound that, when utilized within performance, creates a powerful and often disturbing effect. A central medium of the historic avant garde, the voice as subject in and of itself has been present for many significant moments in performance history: from Alfred Jarry's riotous Parisian spectacle *Ubu Roi* (1896) with the main character Ubu's loud and short opening cry of "Merdre! ;" to Austrian composer Arnold Schoenberg's melodrama *Pierrot Lunaire* (1912), a song cycle of love, sex, religion, and crime for voice and piano set to the words of Belgian poet Albert Giraud; to the first flushes of the American avant garde with John Cage's unique composition *Aria with Fontana Mix* (1958), that let the singer treat the score as a manual for composition, giving them the freedom to expressively roam. The sounds emanating from the human body, whether spoken or sung, have been central to avant garde acts that break faith with old forms and create new and bold styles of expression, and which have had a far-reaching impact on the ways in which the voice is used across a broad spectrum of performance possibilities, from "high art" compositions to popular music.

Vocal performance was the focus—the invisible ribbon—for a series of Performa 13 events and concerts staged throughout Manhattan at the New York Society for Ethical Culture, the Community Church of New York, the Solomon R. Guggenheim Museum, and Angel Orensantz Foundation for the Arts, continuing a history within a city that has long been home to many of the largely female protagonists who have pushed and expanded the vocabulary of vocal performance. From the vocal virtuosity of singer Cathy Berberian, who inspired key compositions from John Cage and Luciano Berio, to the primal screams of Yoko Ono's seminal avant garde pop-inflected *Fly* (1971); from the conceptual art-inflected *études* of Joan La Barbara to the pioneering vocals of Meredith Monk, connecting ancient and modern oral folk culture, the Performa series looked at vocal performances selected from this history, and also from an emerging generation of international artists.

The series began with an opening night concert named after Joan La Barbara's landmark LP, *Voice is The Original Instrument* (1976). Staged at the New York Society for Ethical Culture, the concert opened with *Tablet* (1976), a piece for four voices and a piano presented by The M6: Meredith Monk Music Third Generation. *Tablet* **was a** key work for Monk, as it signaled her move from solo vocalist to choral composer—it was the first work to be performed by Meredith Monk & Vocal Ensemble. Then Maja Ratkje, Norway's leading contemporary vocal improviser, presented a digitally manipulated set that utilized a child's music box. The concert closed with three pieces by La Barbara: *Circular Song* (1974), inspired by the circular breathing techniques of trumpet players; and two later compositions, *Solitary Journeys of the Mind* (2011) and *Windows...* (2013), that demonstrated the move her early, more minimal compositional work made to multi-layered and increasingly complex narratives. *Voice is the Original Instrument* presented the work of three pioneering female vocalists who developed—and continue to push, using digital technologies that fog the voice—the musical genre known as "extended vocal technique" (EVT).

So what is extended vocal technique? Also known as "extra normal vocals" and "extended vocal practices," EVT is the study and categorization of unique singing techniques. Vocal extensions are commonly recognized as techniques arrived at through non-traditional means. An example of extended technique within musical composition might be Cage's works for prepared piano (from *Bacchanale* (1940) to *31'57.9864" For a Pianist* (1954)), in which the piano's timbre has been altered by placing objects "preparations," between or on the strings, hammers or dampers. In EVT the voice is subjected to new articulation and it continually evolves, spurred largely by innovative methods and the advent of new technologies and genre expansion. Recent developments with Auto-Tune have meant that EVT dominates the vocal expression of popular chart music, from the re-tuned vocals of popular R&B to the underground and drastically slowed, "chopped and screwed" musical collages of the late DJ Screw.

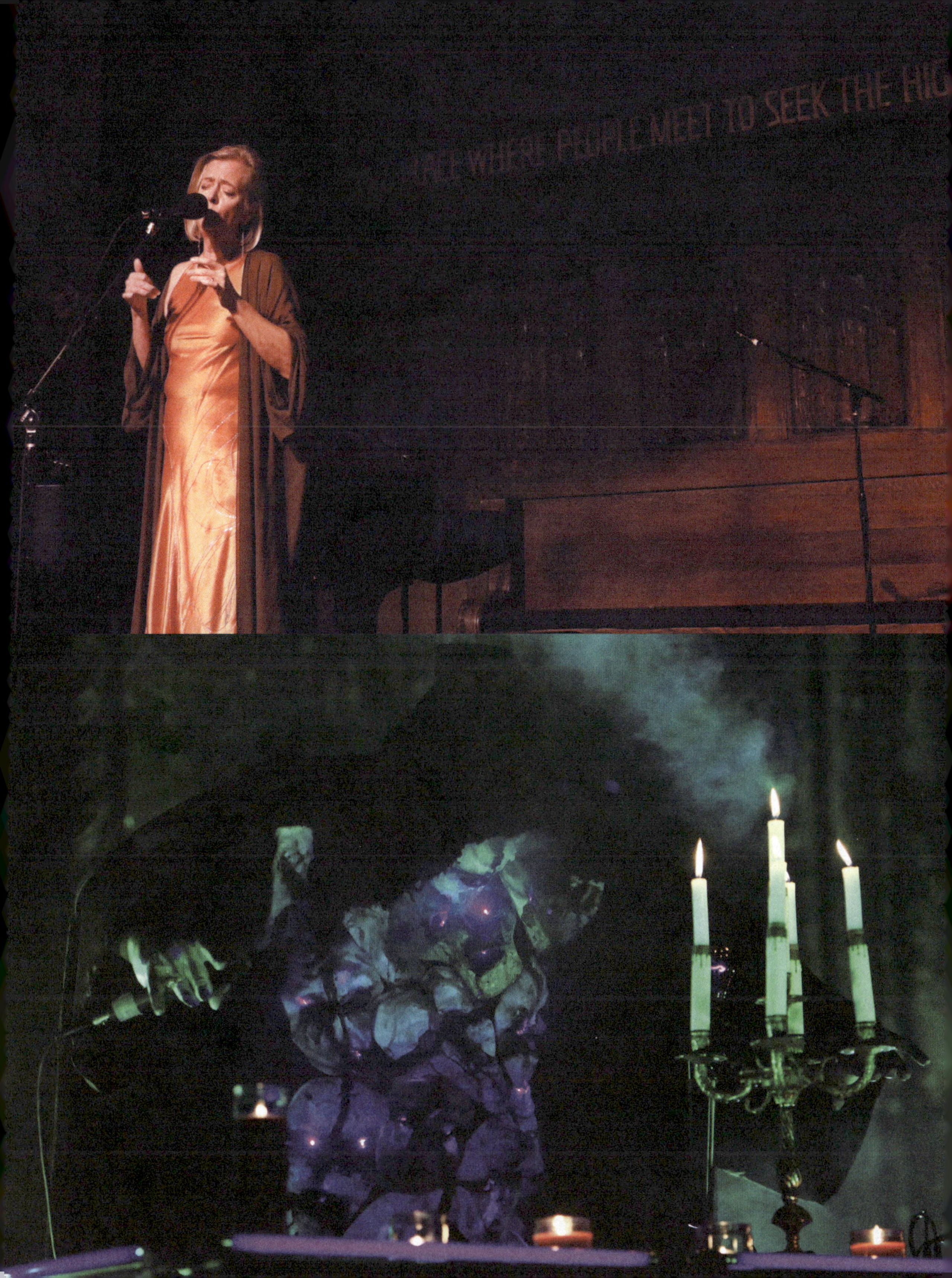
REE WHERE PEOPLE MEET TO SEEK THE HIG

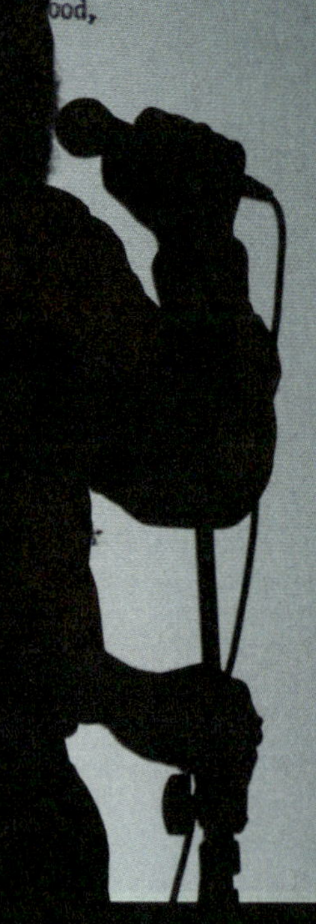

With tranquil restoration :—feelings too
Of unremembered pleasure : such, perhaps,
As may have had no trivial influence
On that best portion of a good man's life ;
His little, nameless, unremembered acts
Of kindness and of love   trust,
To them I may have
Of aspect more subli   ood,
In which the burthen
In which the heavy a
Of all this unin
Is light
In w
U
An
Alm
In b
Wh
Of ha
We

In Tones from Light to Dark, a second concert, was staged at the Lower East Side Angel Orensanz Foundation, and touched upon the interconnected histories of avant garde vocal forms and popular music genres from ART-SCHOOL—inflected experimental vocals to black metal's death growl. Norwegian singer, composer, and lyricist Jenny Hval opened the concert backed by guitar and drums, her *belcanto* (Italian for "beautiful singing") and high-flying octaves further extended with the use of hand-held tape recorders: Oslo-, Stavanger-, and Berlin-based vocalist Stine Motland and New York-based composer and performer C. Spencer Yeh collaboratively employed spontaneous composition, structured improvisation and sound-poetry. The show ended in a cloud of incense smoke, with a vivid light show accompanying the ritualistic dark black metal vocals and growl of Attila Csihar's operatic *Void ov Voices*.

A third and final concert, *To Breathe Is Not Enough*, reflected on the written word, and spoken word practices that propose performance and re-articulation of former texts as a kind of publishing. *To Breathe* featured three artists, writers, and performers who have been key in the contemporary shaping of spoken word performance: Swedish visual artist and poet Karl Holmqvist, British publisher and designer Will Holder (F.R. David) and American writer and editor Angie Keefer (The Serving Library). Keefer ruminated, through an open-letter address—a proposal of collaboration to American singer and songwriter Josephine Foster—upon the work of nineteenth-century American poet Emily Dickinson and its connection to American philosopher Michael Tye's theory of the "explanatory gap": the space between experience and feelings, the space of poetry. (Foster's 2009 LP, *Graphic as a Star* had first introduced Keefer to the work of Dickinson.) Will Holder presented British poet J.H. Prynne's dense and circuitous 2009 lecture *Mental Ears and Poetic Work*. Reading without recourse to the printed word, Holder stumbled over the words of the lecture as he attempted to repeat the words fed to him through an earpiece hidden from the audience. Holder's "mental ears" attempted to hold onto the giddying rhythm of the lecture as piped into his ear while he gripped the microphone stand with both hands. To close the evening Holmqvist read from one of his own publications, turning the pages and reading in exaggerated rhythm: "If you can't be crazy as an artist then what, bankers being bonkers, society out of control, if you can't be crazy as an artist then what, sound poetry, found poetry, bunker madness, the artist is present, sculpting with sound, the artist is present, sculpting with sound, outsider artist, what happens in the head stays in the head." His delivery and text are part poet, part alternative comic, in turn mixing references to contemporary movements and figures in the art world with aphoristic phrases.

Frank Haines and Zeena Schreck's *Live from the Eye of the Storm*, presented at the Community Church of New York, comprised an architectural stage-set of gridded indigo and crimson backdrops, designed by visual artist and performer Haines, and a vocal performance by Schreck. Haines's invitation to collaborate was the first time Schreck had performed in the United States since her 1990 expatriation to Europe. Schreck, who is the daughter of Anton Lavey and Diane Hegarty, co-founders of the Los Angeles-based Church of Satan, is now a practicing Buddhist based in Berlin. She presented a series of musical chants comprised of sacred syllables (unknown to anyone outside of her close circle of friends) accompanied by New York musician Hisham Bharoocha (from the bands Lightning Bolt, Black Dice, and Soft Circle) and Danish musician Anders Hermund.

Two Performa 13 Commissions presented contemporary approaches to vocal extension that were also visual concerts designed to complement and highlight complex voice concerts. Florian Hecker's presentation, *CD: A Script for Synthesis* (2013) was the third and final performance of a trilogy (following *Chimerization* and *Hinge,* both 2012). Staged at the Guggenheim Museum's theater, it featured an experimental and purposefully opaque libretto written by Iranian philosopher Reza Negarestani, pre-recorded as a spoken performance by British actress Charlotte Rampling and piped through monolithic surround-sound airport speakers. Rampling's voice was subjected to digital manipulation as it warped and wended its way around the circular room. A Greek chorus of seven vocalists—clad in textile cloaks designed by Hecker in collaboration with Danish design company Kvadrat—performing vocal arrangements by La Barbara, repeated the central statements of the text, employing La Barbara's signature extended techniques in their delivery. At the center of the Guggenheim stage was a melting pink ice cube, the unknown and abstract center of the performance. What did it mean to consider the slippery essence of a melting form, a phantom of pink water that eluded attempts to be understood? To fully engage synesthetic relations, a scent bound in rubber, devised by Hecker

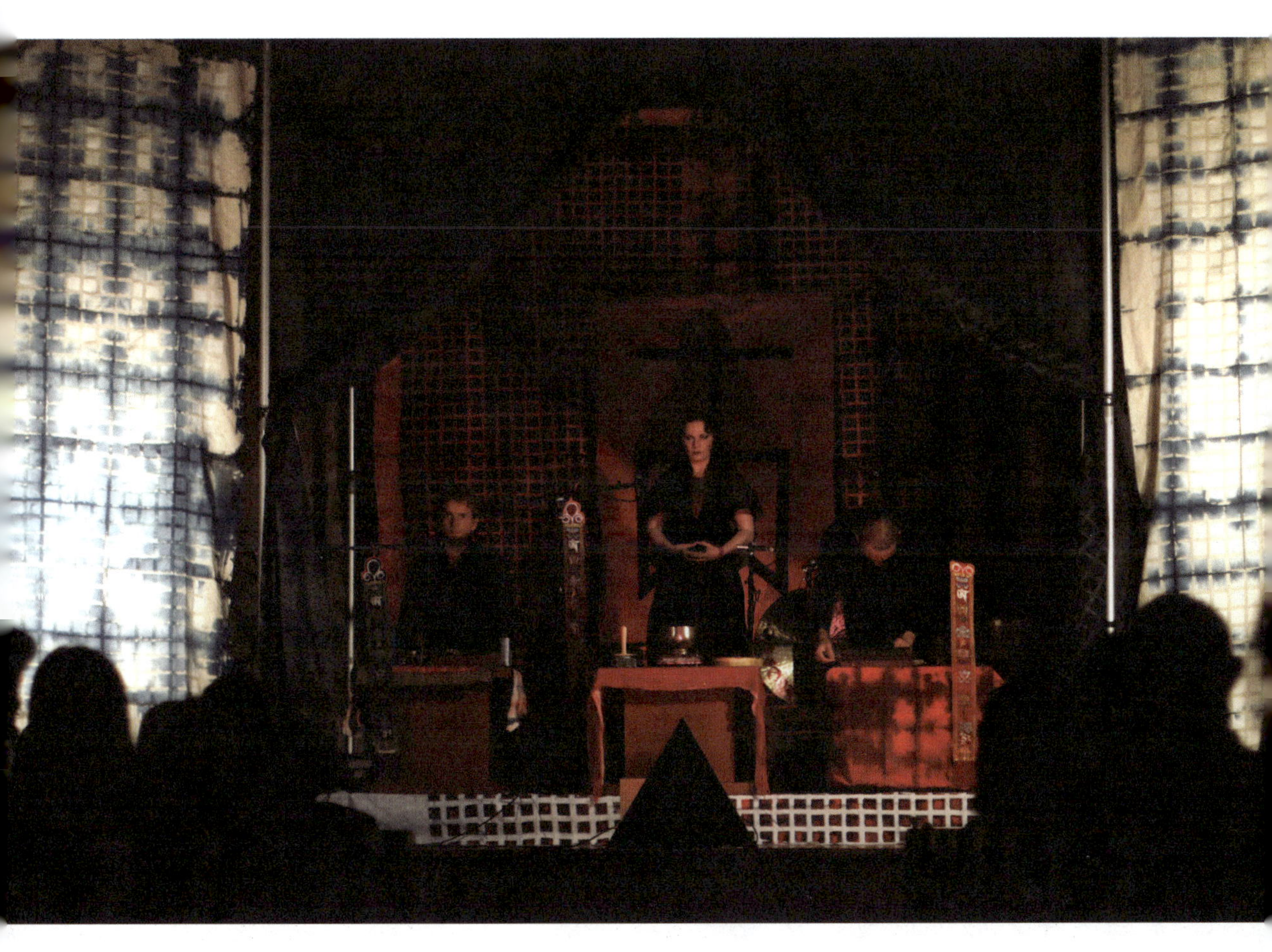

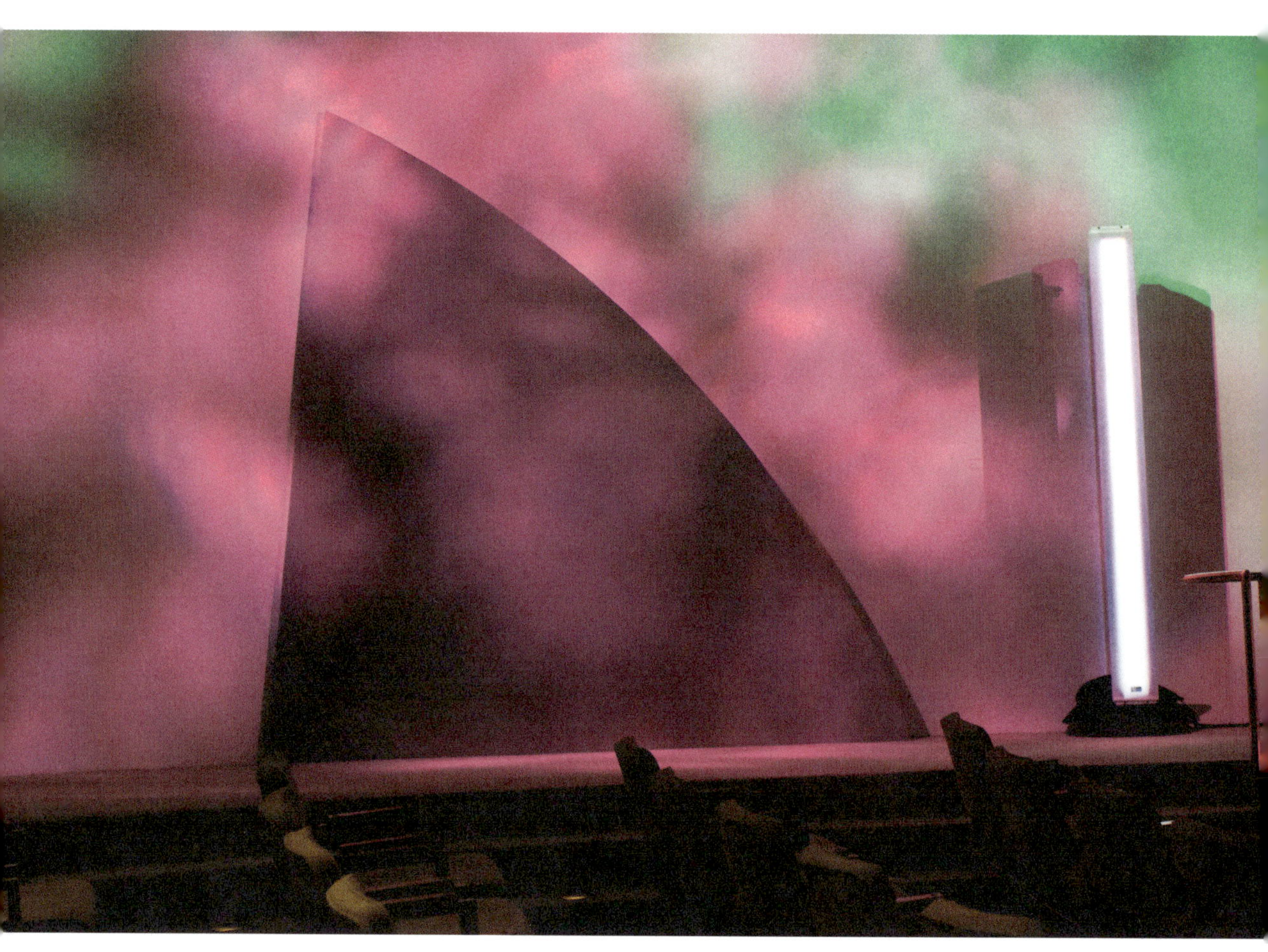

and created by Frédéric Malle (Editions de Parfums) and Carlos Benaïm (International Flavors & Fragrances), accompanied a booklet that included an explicatory text by philosopher Robin Mackay. A sound piece, an experimental drama, and a model of abstraction, *CD* recalled Antonin Artaud's Theater of Cruelty as much as Samuel Beckett's minimalist narratives and Neo-Imagist poetry. The voice became a medium through which there was an attempt to define the unknowable, represented by the pink ice cube, transforming physical space into a site for the dramatization of the hearing process.

The other Performa Commission in this series, Tori Wrånes's epic *Yes Nix*, literally extended the voice in dramatic and utterly unusual ways: she turned it upside down, emitting harmonic tones digitally looped and layered as she was dragged along the floor and swung, by her tied feet, at the end of a rope suspended in the air. Her costume was worn the incorrect way around, her arms in pant legs, her head appearing from the crotch. As she was lowered to the ground a chorus of opera singers astride bicycles circled the room: in low light and guided by bicycle lamps, they mirrored the droning sounds of Wrånes's looped introductory chorus. The bicycles made way for a group of elderly performers, who crossed the path of the cyclists to the center of the room where musical instruments were lowered from the ceiling; flutes were clutched by waiting hands before Wrånes closed out the evening, swinging to and fro from a gantry toward a microphone attached to a flare gun. It was a surreal, looped life journey—from the singing head jutting from the crotch of a pair of pants to the final meeting of head and gun—like a set piece from a David Lynch movie or an imagined lost reel from the Leos Carax fantasy-drama *Holy Motors* (2012). Wrånes's and Hecker's performances indicated the limits of the voice as well as presented new and possible extentions for it, defining its physical contours through spectacular encounter and unlikely circumstance, whether hung from the ceiling or recorded and digitally fractured, a ribbon of material that surrounded the audience.

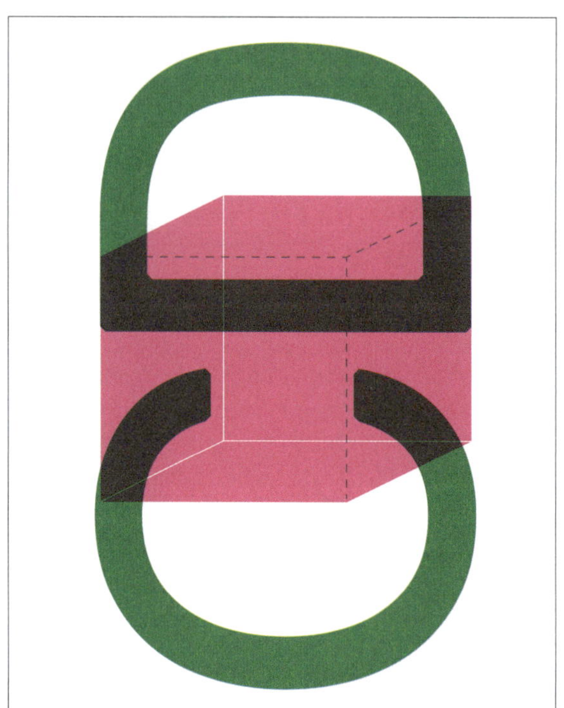

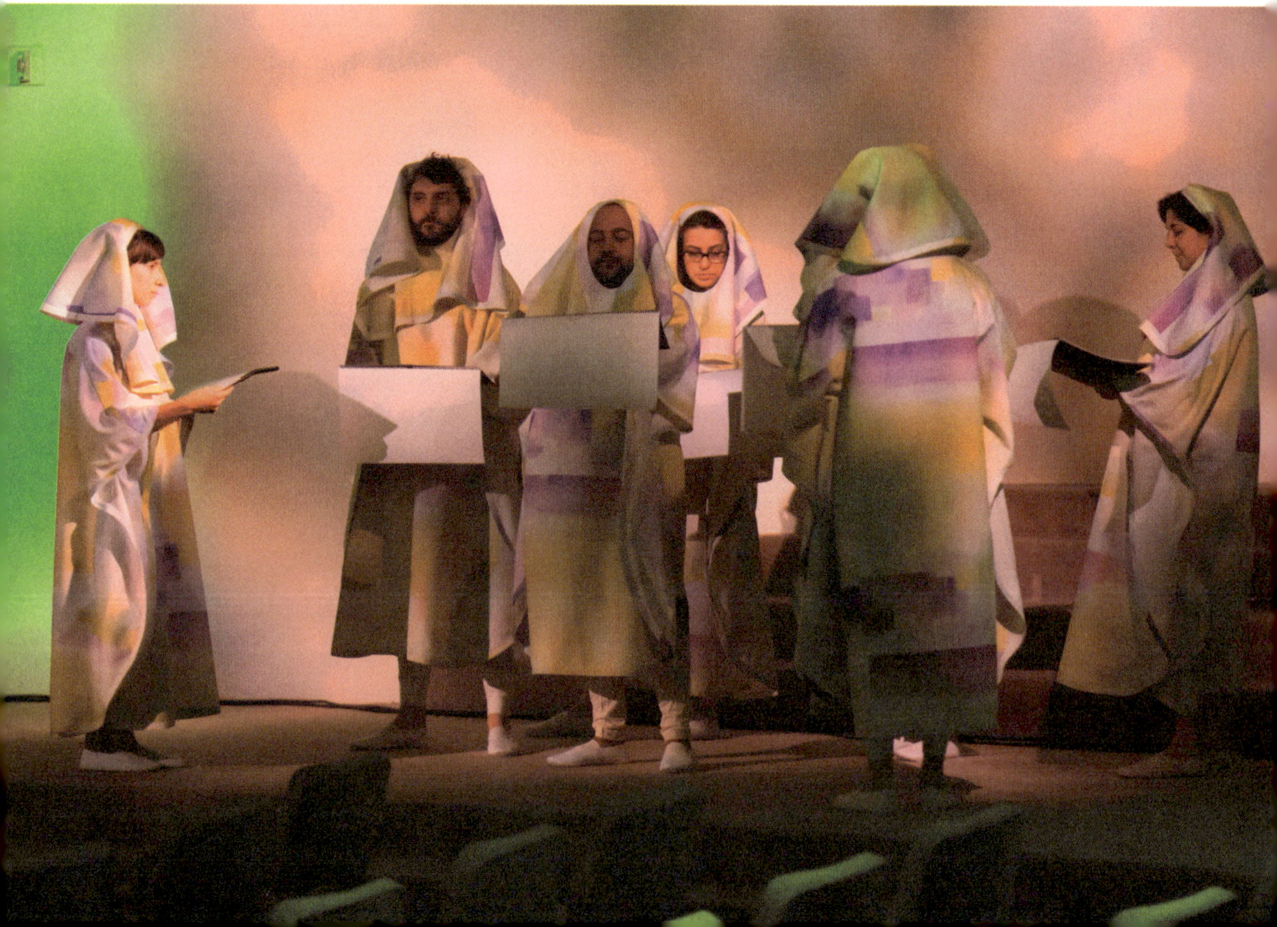

FLORIAN HECKER

CD: A SCRIPT FOR SYNTHESIS

Over the past decade, Florian Hecker has used digital sound technologies to transform physical spaces into sites for the dramatization of the hearing process. In his work, this process itself becomes audible—the human mind's reconstruction (or indeed hallucination) of objects on the basis of auditory cues. Drawing on psychoacoustic research, Hecker carefully designs and controls such cues, using the limit conditions of 'sonic objects' as his material.

In these installations 'it is the auditor who completes the work'; but not because they are interpellated as the artist's helpmeet, tasked with refining the raw matter he presents and fixing its indeterminate meaning—an interpretative role that is said to constitute the 'freedom' of the subject of contemporary art. Rather than offering a spurious perspectival liberation, Hecker amplifies the constraining conditions of the auditor's perceptual apparatus. The subject's occupation of space and reception of material allows it the freedom to explore its own perceptual automatisms.

Perhaps this work can be more profitably compared to the mode of perspective operative in minimalism, where the viewer's perambulations around the 'specific object' awaken them to their own role in constituting it as a perceptual object. The physical sound waves Hecker synthesises are often integrated by the auditor differently, depending upon their position in space and the way they direct their attention, so that sound-matter, auditor, and exhibition space are all components of the work.

Unlike the freeform interpretative play of the readymade, minimalism's theater is one of suspense. Vary her perspective as she may, its viewer never gains access to the specific object, whose 'hollowness,' its reticence to reveal its internal constitution, is precisely what is enthralling: a primed jack-in-the-(black)-box that is never sprung, the object remains opaque and obdurate as the viewer circles it. Minimalism's interrogation of objecthood ends with the simple tension between the gestalt of the object-as-unity and the experiential series of the viewer (a series that is endless, or which, unsatisfactorily, 'just ends').

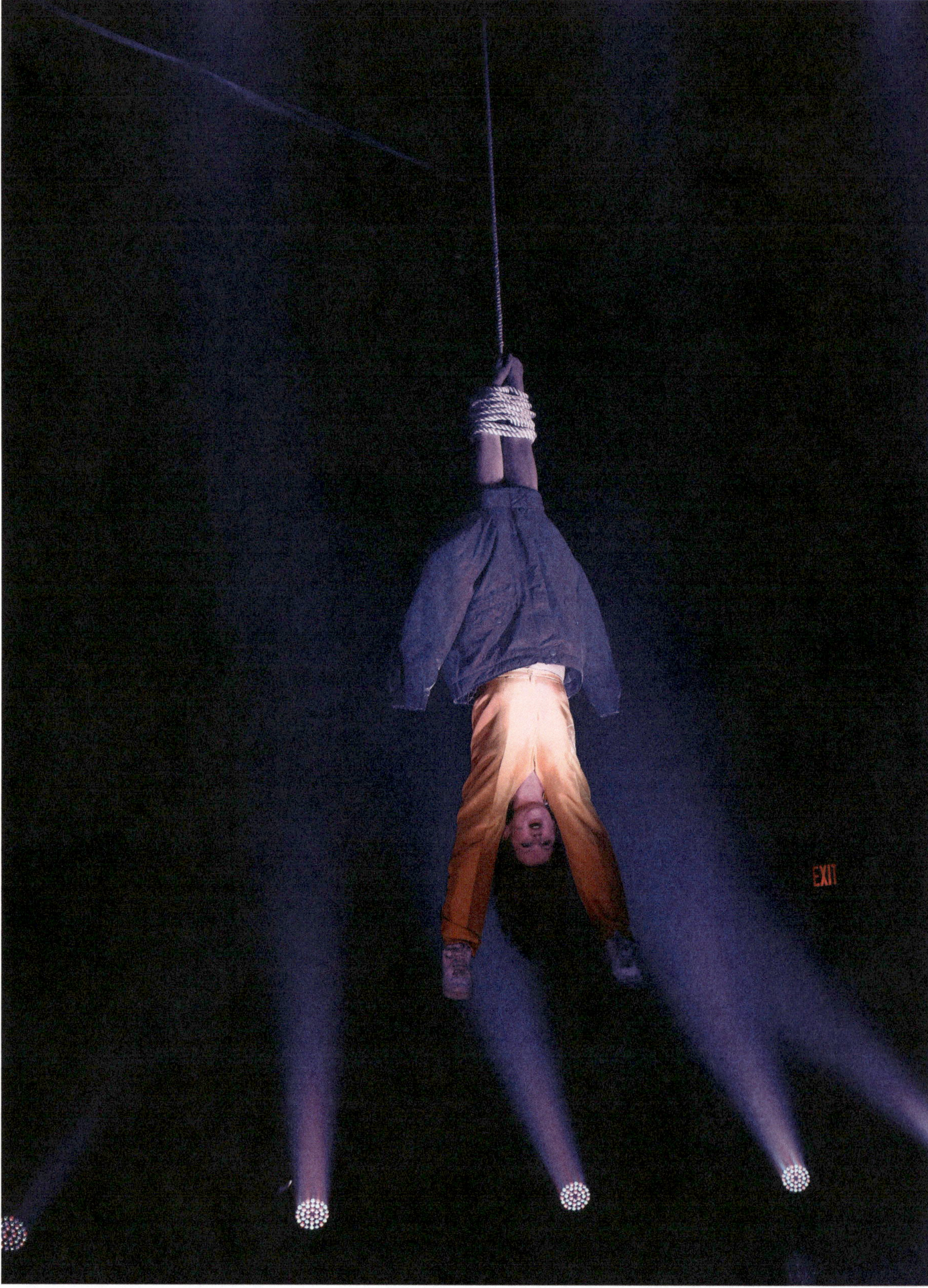
EXIT

Mark Beasley: During the many conversations we've had about vocal performance, we stumbled across what feels like a key fact (perhaps an organizing sensibility) about your early experience of listening. Your father was an ornithologist and, as I understand it, you spent days following him through forests avoiding the snap of branches underfoot while straining—listening for bird song? Can you describe how that experience impacted your decision to become, well … a songbird?

Tori Wrånes: Ha, you're right, and maybe that's why I always wanted to fly too. Yes, my father and I would walk through the forest to map and locate different species—to observe their movements. From their calls and song alone my dad would identify species, their location, gender, and even mood. It meant we had to be extremely quiet. I loved the concentration—it felt like drawing with the ears—to be listening so intently to something in the world. It was like wearing ears for the first time. I mean, the world is the wildest multi-channel sound-system ever!

My dad also worked at sea. He would make records, survey populations, assess the number of different birds, such as eider ducklings. I specifically remember the aggressive calls of the terns. When we went ashore near their nesting sites there would be the wildest concert circling above us. It was a spiral of sounds. The terns would dive, shrieking, toward our heads: we had to wear protective headgear. I didn't think of it as a child, but today and from a distance I can see how it informs the sounds and shapes I'm drawn to. Birdwatching even has a lot to do with choreography.

At the time I absorbed sounds but I also liked to make sound. I remember whistling a lot, and I also sang in three different choirs and played the accordion. Alongside music, I engaged with sport, handball specifically. Handball is very much about rhythm. There is a lot of improvisation in sports, it's very physical and sculptural in relation to sound and movement. Making sound is like building— constructing forms in space.

MB: For many years you performed as a singer in an electro-rock band. When and why did you shift your focus from touring with a band to something more experimental, to the expanded feel of art, performance, and large-scale choreographed works?

TW: I love the rush of a live concert, but it stops being productive or fun if you don't love the music you are playing. I felt this desire to address the needs of the eye, to combine the visual, movement, and sound. As happens with many bands, we were looking for different things and it felt frustrating having to fit into an established format. I wanted to create my own way. I learned a lot about humans from those ten years and the five guys in the band are still my brothers.

When I started at the Art Academy in Oslo in 2004, I worked on pieces that were more jazz- and improvisation-based. I had already experimented a lot with performance in a group called Loop Loop Loop and with an actor named Olav Benestvedt. I presented solo pieces for voice and accordion and always covered my face with hair (wigs) or cloth. It was not my face that defined my identity anymore— when you can't meet the eyes of the audience, you become more sculptural, more of an object.

I was also interested in the body as a sculpture, how to alter the body with clothes or prosthetics to create new characters. I discovered the power of a group in my first big-scale performance called *Beige Birth* in 2003. I invited fifty of my friends to live in my flat and perform with me—ha, I guess you could say I learned too much from this project and experience—but what stayed with me was the power of a group.

Lately I have been thinking of my work as a kind of "human composing," because it involves a lot in terms of psychological engagement. I guess I try to enlarge those qualities that are often overlooked. For example, in *Yes Nix,* the movement of an elderly person has an authentic quality that a young person could only attempt to emulate. At the Art Academy in Oslo, I was lucky to have Sidsel Endresen [the Norwegian composer and singer] visit my studio, and she taught me the importance of creating frames and boundaries for collaboration. Counterintuitively, such limits allow a space for improvisation, for freedom within the work. So when I work with performers, I often create strict structures for movement or specific sounds. That said,

I am trying to get the performers to be as much themselves as possible—I want "full-volume personalities." Endresen also taught me to ignore restrictions or taboos, to essentially work "taboo free." It was a phrase that she used a lot in relation to my work.

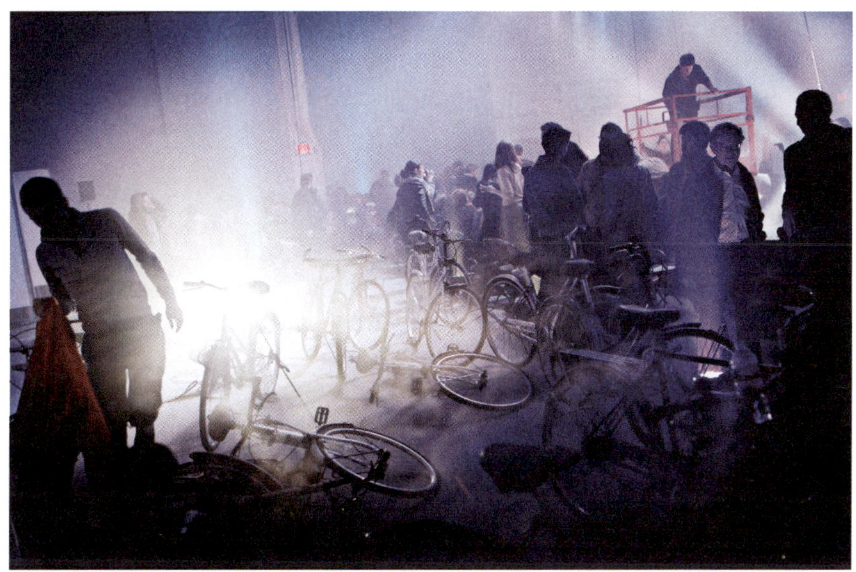

MB: What particularly appeals about your work is the sensitivity to site, both architecturally—your use of a multi-story car park in Los Angeles staged across many levels, as well as hanging off the side of a cliff serenading passengers of a river ferry—but also with regard to the communities you choose to work with, both professional singers and otherwise, in the case of *SPIN ECHO* (2012) at REDCAT in Los Angeles, you worked with professional weightlifters you met socially in Venice Beach, and then with *Yes Nix,* here in New York, you worked with a community of elderly performers. Are social connections and networking with localized communities key for you?

TW: I have a lot of respect and interest in other people's qualities. Often I don't even try to find them—they just bump into me. With *SPIN ECHO*, I needed twenty bikes, and suddenly I was in a Korean sauna with a jobless bike repair specialist. I like to act intuitively. Coincidence can be very rewarding: in Lofoten, in northern Norway, working on *Loose Cannon* (2010), I needed to install a grand piano

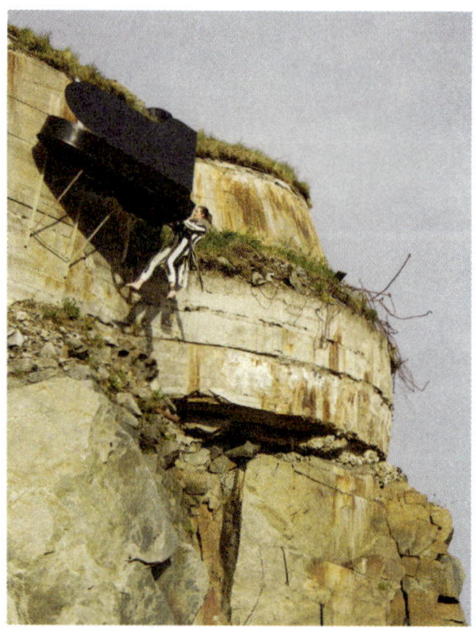

on the edge of a cliff. I drove past the local fire department and it felt natural to knock on the door and speak with them and we ended up collaborating. I also think engaging the local community makes it easier for them to access the piece. I am interested in everyone's opinion, not just the specialists.

MB: What was the reasoning behind your selection of collaborators for *Yes Nix*? You included both elderly saw players and musician cyclists.

TW: To me, the piece is about choreographing sound. It starts with a vertical image and movement—of me hanging upside down, in clothes that suggest I'm hanging the correct way, with my head appearing from the crotch. It shows both a hanging and a birth at the same time, a kind of life loop. The next image and movement is that of a choir on bikes circling the audience, another loop. Then the elderly recorder players enter the stage and they represent a distinct point in the life circle too. They are closer to the end in a way, which means they are also close to the beginning. (Death has the potential to reveal everything we don't know.) Saw players have a wave in their instrument, so it represents the pendulum between a beginning and an end, yes or nix, or tea and coffee if you like. I chose to fly horizontally across the stage at the end, as I wanted to suggest a horizontal movement, of something passing through the circle. It was important to activate the whole space, both physically and, hopefully, psychologically. My use of amplification, of sound, is also a character or participant. I work a lot with combining amplified and acoustic sound to address the physical movement of sound in space. The acoustic bicycle choir provided an analog version of a multi-channel speaker system. The last image, my pendulum back and forth to the microphone situated inside the flare gun, addressed the U.S., where it is legal to carry a gun. Life and death are so very close here, ultimately as they are everywhere, a matter of *Yes Nix*.

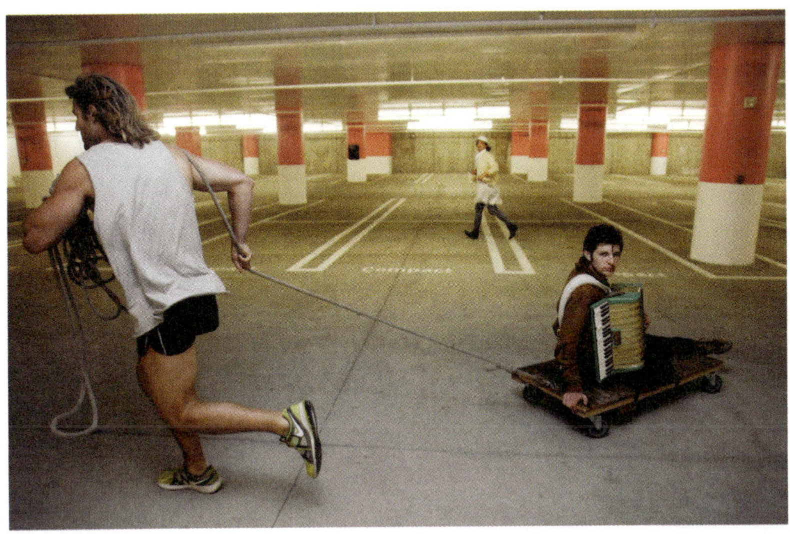

Tori Wrånes, *SPIN ECHO* (2012) Disney Concert Hall parking structure, Los Angeles. Initiated by Warren Neidich, Elena Bajo and Alex Hunt at LAXART; photo by GianPhilippo DeRossi

MB: We talked about your work for Performa as a "visual concert," meaning you are interested in creating both a unique sonic landscape and one that emanates from a visual and physical image: a figure singing while hanging upside down or an orchestra traveling on bicycles. What does the term "visual concert" mean to you?

TW: I am not sure what comes first, sound or image. To me there are no rules—sound and music carry an emotional quality I am interested in. When the two are combined, you can manipulate the meaning or strengthen it. I recently heard Laurie Anderson talk about her work and she said if something wasn't working in a piece it had something to do with the fact that the visual and the sound were in competition with each other, effectively canceling each other out. I understood her meaning to be that one or the other (sound or image) had to be stronger. In my work, I believe in the push and pull in the tension between the two, this is what I look for, not a battle between the senses, but some sort of whole where you can't tell one from the other.

I am not into defining things. I would sooner open up than close down. *Yes Nix* could just as well have been called a work of "sound choreography." I think sometimes performance is a difficult word because it is so indistinct. If you say you work with music, people will ask you: What type of music? It's the same with performance. What type of performance? So maybe "visual concert" is a new subset of performance. It is very difficult to define one's own work, but I love it when others do.

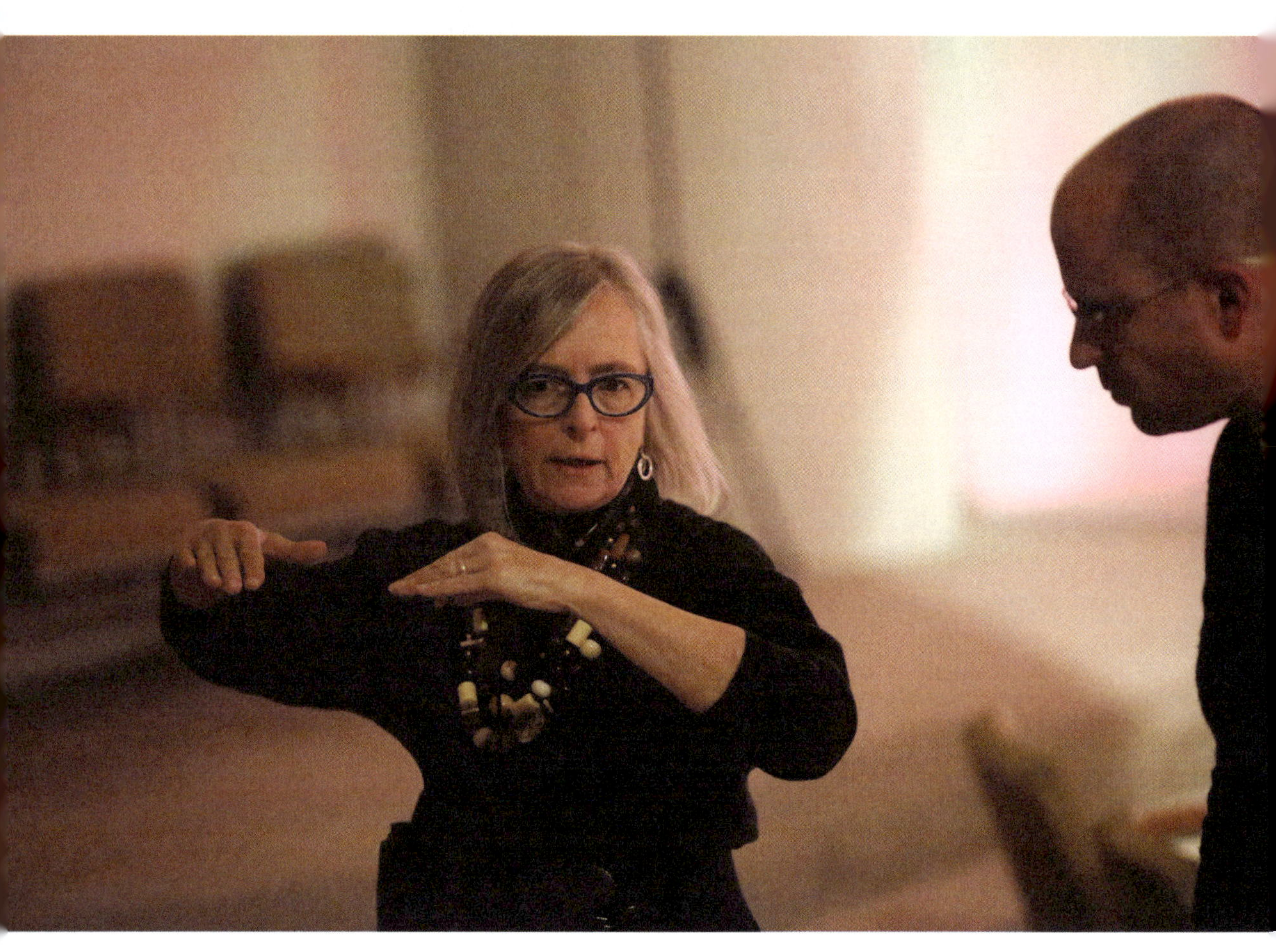

Mark Beasley: At what point did you forego your classical training as too rigid and begin to experiment with your voice?

Joan La Barbara: During college I heard musicians experimenting with instruments—I felt the voice could also be used in that way, as a solo instrument. I started by imitating the sound of instruments. A friend of mine was a composer and trombonist and I imitated his sound and then analyzed how close I came to sounding like that instrument, made adjustments, and continued. This process, surprisingly, allowed me eventually to sing much higher and make sounds I hadn't imagined before.

MB: Post-university you traveled to Europe and performed with emerging American composers Philip Glass and Steve Reich. Interestingly you performed in museum spaces rather than concert halls. How did this impact your approach to performing and composing?

JLB: Working with Steve and Phil in Europe, many of our concerts were in museums or art galleries that were also exhibiting groundbreaking post-war American conceptual art. I became well-acquainted with the work of artists like Bruce Nauman, Vito Acconci, Dennis Oppenheim, John Baldessari, and Douglas Huebler. Their work consisted of more than just what ended up on the walls—the process of getting there was a key component of the work, which felt like a new and fascinating way of approaching art-making. Their approach inspired an early piece of mine titled *Hear What I Feel* (1975). I wanted to surprise sounds out of myself, so I conceived a means of sensory deprivation where I literally taped my eyes shut with cotton balls and masking tape and sat isolated in a room for an hour, also without touching anything, before being led to the stage. I asked someone to choose items to place in six glass dishes, then while touching the substances I emitted new sounds. I wanted to communicate directly and viscerally with the audience on a pre-verbal level. As I touched the material in the dishes, I tried to give an immediate vocal response to what I felt both emotionally and physically, without the benefit of visual information. It was very successful. In inhibiting certain sense responses, I found that my hearing actually expanded and I became attuned to my surroundings in a way I hadn't been before, while discovering new sounds.

MB: As a musician you predominantly performed in art spaces in Europe, especially in the early years. What spaces in New York City did you work with and in?

JLB: The first performance of *Hear What I Feel* was at the Judson Memorial Chuch. At the time it was called "the Peace Church" because during the Vietnam War young men would go there and have counseling sessions on how to avoid the draft. They also staged concerts. I premiered that piece along with other works, such as *One-Note Internal* (1974) *Resonance Investigation* (1975), *Circular Song* (1975), and *Vocal Extensions* (1975), that would eventually be recorded for my first LP, *Voice is The Original Instrument* (1976). I was investigating and exploring the range of vocal possibilities. *One-Note* employed a single pitch, but placing it in different resonance areas—inside my head, nose, various cavities in my face and mouth—resulted in my discovery of reinforced harmonics and multiphonics. *Circular Song* was inspired by watching and listening to horn players and their technique of circular breathing. I started writing short vocal musical compositions, *études* exploring particular techniques, like how *Circular Song* focused upon inhaled singing in a mirror form. The form had a lot to do with process. *Circular Song* was about technique but also about process—as with conceptual art of the time—putting myself in a situation where I wasn't sure if I could get through the piece, so challenging oneself was part of it as well—setting physical tasks.

I also think of my work as literally painting with the voice onto audiotape or into the computer, while recording or performing. I see sound, I see the gestures that I'm singing, it's not quite synesthesia but it has some elements of it, particularly with the graphic scores I produce for each of the compositions.

MB: You are recognized as one of the pioneers of "extended vocal technique" [EVT, non-traditional methods for vocal production]. Can you provide a context for the musical landscape of the time, other vocalists and composers who were also experimenting with vocal extension?

JLB: At the time, the early- to mid-'70s, there were other vocalists who were beginning to experiment with the voice. Cathy Berberian was a touchstone for many, Meredith Monk of course and her early work such as *Our Lady of Late* (1972) for voice and wine glasses. There was a group called the Extended Vocal Techniques Ensemble that was developed at the University of California San Diego, and there was also a vocal quartet, Electric Phoenix, based in London. We were all exploring the voice in different ways.

MB: Extended vocal technique is an ever-expanding field, as each new technology provides more possibilities for expansion and experimentation. There are key techniques, which you helped pioneer, particularly the "vocal fry." Can you talk about some of these techniques?

JLB: Yes, vocal fry: the people who named it thought it sounded like frying an egg; it's a sub-tone so it's below actual pitch. There are other sounds that are similar, like the inhaled glottal click: you don't take in much air but you're actually engaging the vocal cords in this ingressive position (breathing in) as opposed to an egressive position (breathing out). Several years ago I happened to be doing workshops as part of the Institute for Living Voice in Antwerp. A Tuvan singer was there and I took her workshop out of curiosity and was terrified and astonished at the pressure she put on her throat to make certain sounds. My technique for making similar sounds is very relaxed. The Extended Vocal Technique Ensemble in San Diego worked with doctors who photographed the vocal cords in action. They discovered how the false vocal folds were operating, sympathetically vibrating with the primary vocal cords to produce multiphonics. We each produce sounds uniquely, which is what makes the field so vibrant.

MB: Over time you've contributed and been integral to many key works, for example, Philip Glass and Robert Wilson's *Einstein on the Beach* (1975), Steve Reich's *Drumming* (1971) and John Cage's *Solo for Voice 45* (1970). Could you discuss two or three musical collaborations that were key in your development as a solo vocalist?

JLB: We've established that I was trained as a classical vocalist. I was not trained as a composer at school. I took theory, of course, but I didn't take composition lessons. I learned on the job as an apprentice, a very traditional way of learning. So what I brought for instance to Steve Reich was my interest in the imitation of instruments, which also interested him. What Steve did for *Drumming* was to play the tapes on two recording machines and when the patterns would phase into a new interlocking relationship, I sang what I heard. Steve would listen to the recordings and notate the patterns he liked, which became part of the piece.

When I first worked with Philip Glass—who at that point was not working with or composing for vocalists—I sang trumpet parts. He began to write vocal parts around the time of *Music in Twelve Parts* (1971-74), and through collaboration we defined the potential as well as the limitations of EVT. For instance, in discussion with Philip I suggested, "I can sing those two notes for twenty minutes but then in the next section you'll have to take the voice to a different range because essentially the voice is a muscular apparatus. It's prone to fatigue, that's just the way the instrument of the voice works." This is also how I worked with Alvin Lucier—who straddles the territory between science, art, and music. We would discuss certain theories—the first piece we did together was *Still and Moving Lines of Silence in Families of Hyperbolas* (1983), which involved sine tones that were playing from four speakers. We rehearsed at the Merce Cunningham Studios and I explored my vocal response to the sine waves, producing sophisticated beat patterns. It was very much an intellectual exploration of sonic, acoustic, and architectural space, using speaker systems, oscillators, and voice. Alvin introduced my work to Cage, who attended one of my early concerts because of Alvin. I was presenting my *Voice Piece: One-Note Internal Resonance Investigation* (1974) and afterwards he came up to me and said how much he'd enjoyed it and asked if I would like to work with him. So that was when he brought me the *Solo for Voice 45*, from "Song Books (Solos for Voice 3—92)" (1970).

MB: At the time was there a strong and purposeful community of artists, composers, and musicians operating outside of institutions to organize projects and performances?

JLB: Yes, there was an incredible community of like-minded souls who were supporting each other's explorations, experiments, and interests. It was a community; we produced our own concerts. Alvin had a job at Wesleyan but a lot of composers didn't have jobs; they were making a living through performing concerts. Philip had an ensemble, because, as he explained, "I don't want to publish my music so other people can play it; I want to play the music with my group. I want us to get the money not somebody else." That was a political attitude then. If people wanted to hear this particular music the artist had to be present, so it became a different relationship from what had happened before. Because in the academic institutions you had "paper" composers, you know, people who wrote everything on paper and then handed it to someone else to perform—that's part of a tradition. But the tradition of the performer as composer is also a long established one. For instance, artists such as Bach both wrote and performed their music.

MB: What are you working on currently?

JLB: I've been working for a number of years on an opera, actually a collection of operas, with a piece inspired by the life and work of Virginia Woolf. I've performed sections of it already. Some as primary vocalist, with additional vocalists. The piece has now morphed into a new opera inspired by the life/work of Woolf and the life/work of artist Joseph Cornell. I employ what I term "sound paintings," and create "sonic atmospheres," layering not only vocal sounds, but also water and wind, birds and animals, real and electronically-modified instrumental sounds. I'm looking to create a fully realized soundscape that allows the listener space to mentally travel.

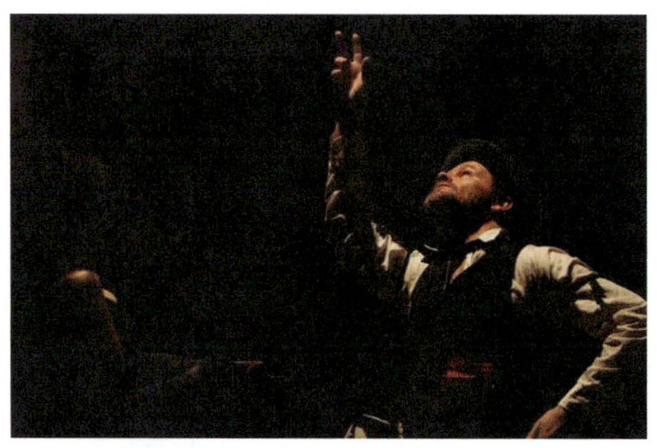 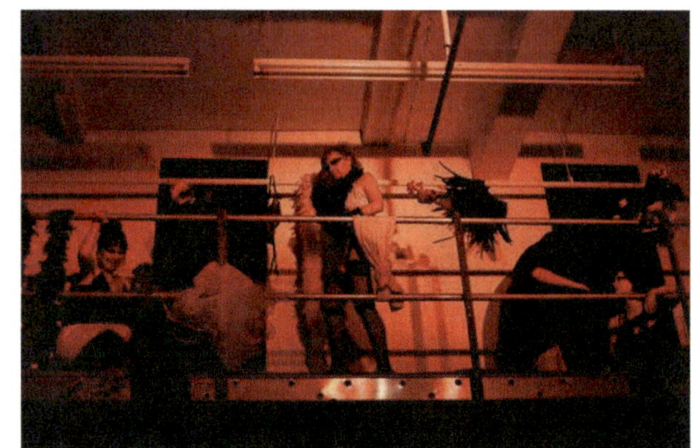

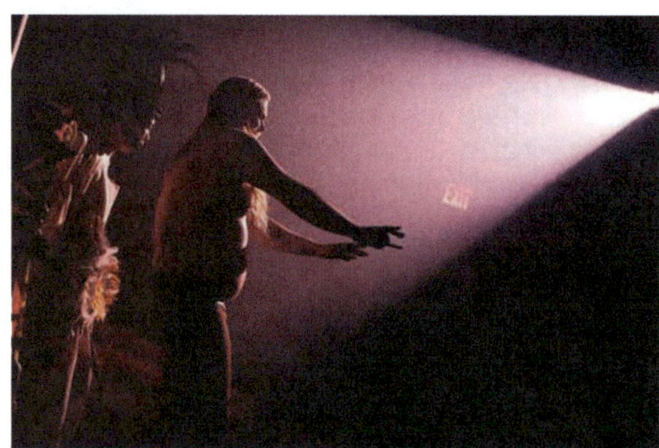 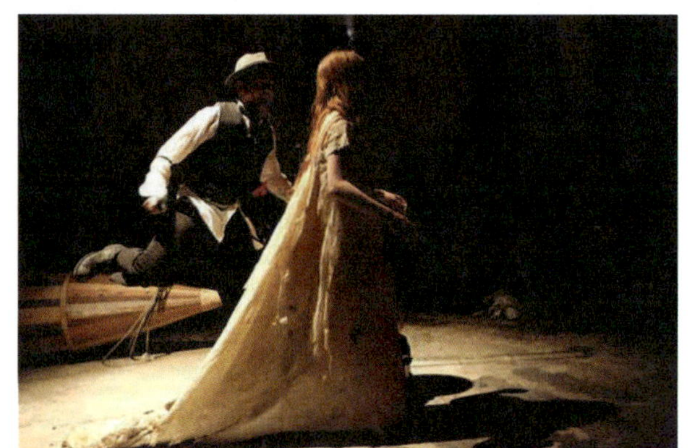

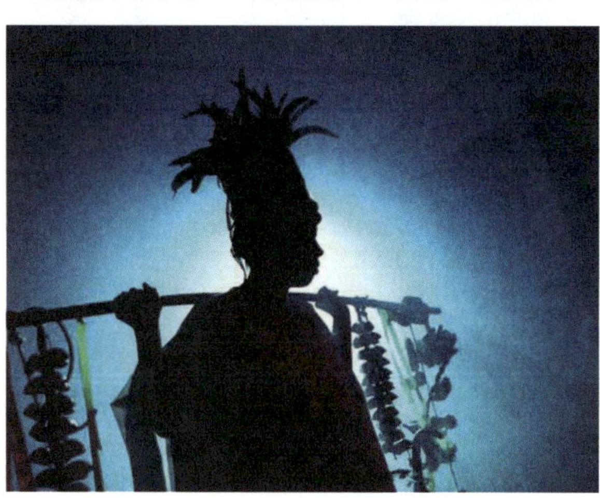 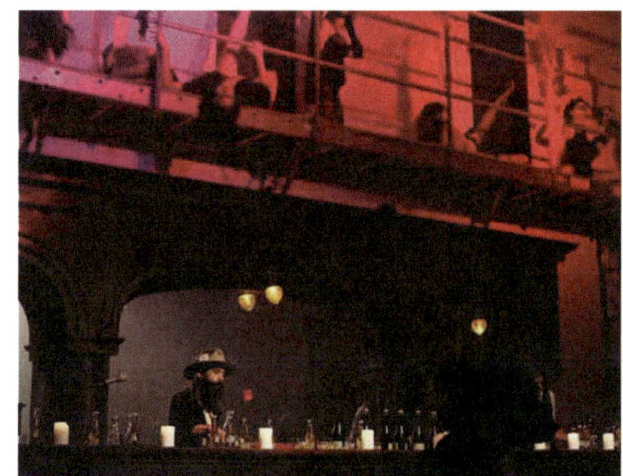

MARIANNE VITALE

THE MISSING BOOK OF SPURS

On a cold night in Long Island City, Marianne Vitale opened her vast industrial studio to an audience of about one hundred for the inauguration of her first live performance—a forty-minute "musical" that took the form of a loose narrative with a specially composed soundtrack, as well as song and dance numbers and spoken word. *The Missing Book of Spurs* took its title from a large picture book about spurs that Vitale once owned and that had literally "gone missing." While a seemingly obscure item, spurs—iconic symbols of the American western frontier—were of interest to Vitale, whose work often engages with historical themes, as manifested in her large-scale sculptures of burnt covered bridges, double outhouses and wooden tombstones.

Visitors were greeted at the entrance to Vitale's studio by a hostess dressed in saloon chic: boots, a belted shirt-dress and apron, with hair piled high. The hostess led the audience into an antechamber, which functioned as a pre-theater bar—however, it was also clearly the artist's working studio, with scraps of metal, wood piles, partial sculptures, and her parked SUV. Guests were given mock playbills, which included advertisements for the artist's favorite eating establishments—Lucien, Corner Bistro, and Junior's—interspersed with fictional ads for an Ad Reinhardt exhibition at David Zwirner, Lorazepam, ("One half pill twice a day and pretty much anything is tolerable") and York Erection Specialists. Typical of Vitale's ironic take on the art establishment, often expressed in the titles of her work, the program reinforced her sardonic nod to theatrical realism—a fictional set conjuring the wild west of an earlier century in the burgeoning art mecca of Queens.

Inside, the "main stage" was a massive, carved, wall-length wooden mirrored bar, built for a mid-Western hotel ballroom that Vitale bought on eBay and had trucked across the country. Scaffolding on either side created a stairway to a temporary catwalk, reaching up to the high-ceilinged studio. The audience sat on bleachers on the other three sides. A cast of misfits, including tired looking whores, spaced-out cowboys, a feather-headdressed Indian, and other apocalyptic, gender-bending characters, some wearing nightdresses and others in chains, even a heavily made-up and "toothless" Vitale, sprawled at one point under the bar, performed the nine "chapters" of *The Missing Book of Spurs*.

These chapters were accompanied by original music composed for the artist by Mike Stroud, one-half of the experimental electronic rock duo Ratatat. These pre-recorded booming electro rock tracks created a loose structure for the ambling performance. One memorable track, "Whoressss," combined the bawdiness of a show tune and the seductiveness of women's voices. The cast of female and male characters catcalled and hissed their way through a raucous number while hanging from the bars of the overhead platform in various states of dishabille. "Slowdance," the final scene, culminated with the cast inviting the audience to join the action—soon regular punters were dancing with the character actors, dissipating the boundary between players and audience. The exaggeratedly formless and anarchic bohemian feel of the performance was indeed a far cry from traditional theater.

Vitale's theater of the absurd was based on the barest of narratives, set in this saloon, which was crossed with a weather station where characters briefly passed through to learn cryptic forecasts and sample the tipple. *The Missing Book of Spurs* was enthralling not for rigor but precisely for the opposite. In a DIY style that harked back to 1970s and '80s loft performances (by Jack Smith or Squat Theatre, for example), Vitale created an atmospheric production where sensuality and outlandishness ruled. The saloon, and the manic actions of its theatrical inhabitants, was also interesting in relation to the artist's large wooden sculptures inspired by architecture and infrastructure from the American frontier. The performance might be considered an outgrowth of her sculptures, a "living sculpture" with the actors reinforcing the three-dimensionality of the artist's aesthetic and its sublimated expressionism. Vitale's performance provided context for understanding her sculptural work. As commentary on the integration of her art and ideas and the place of the artist's studio in bringing these elements into line, Vitale realized, after searching throughout the city for an ideal venue for her performance, her studio was already it.

Marianne Vitale, *The Missing Book of Spurs* (2013), cast view. Photo by Silja Magg

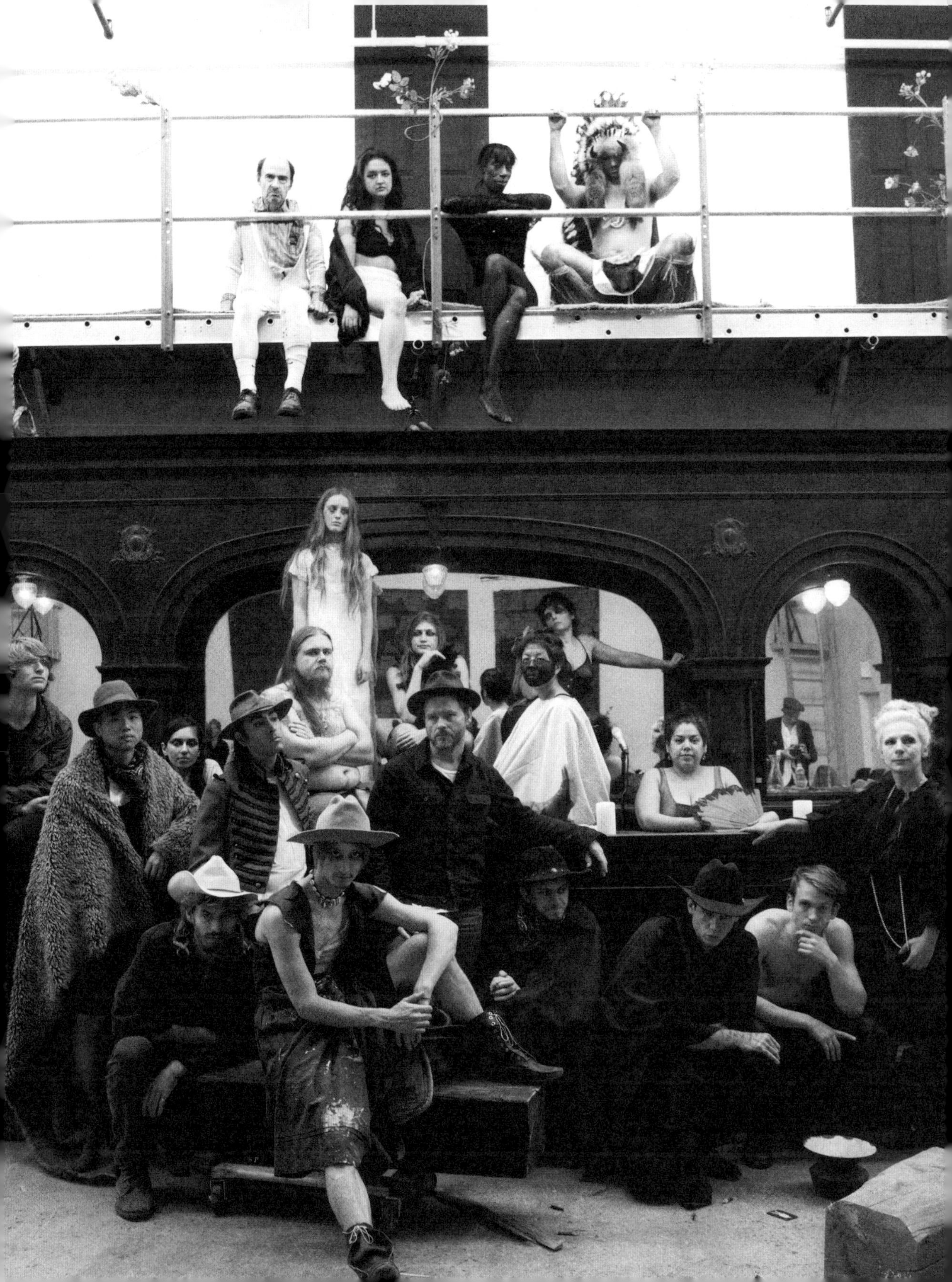

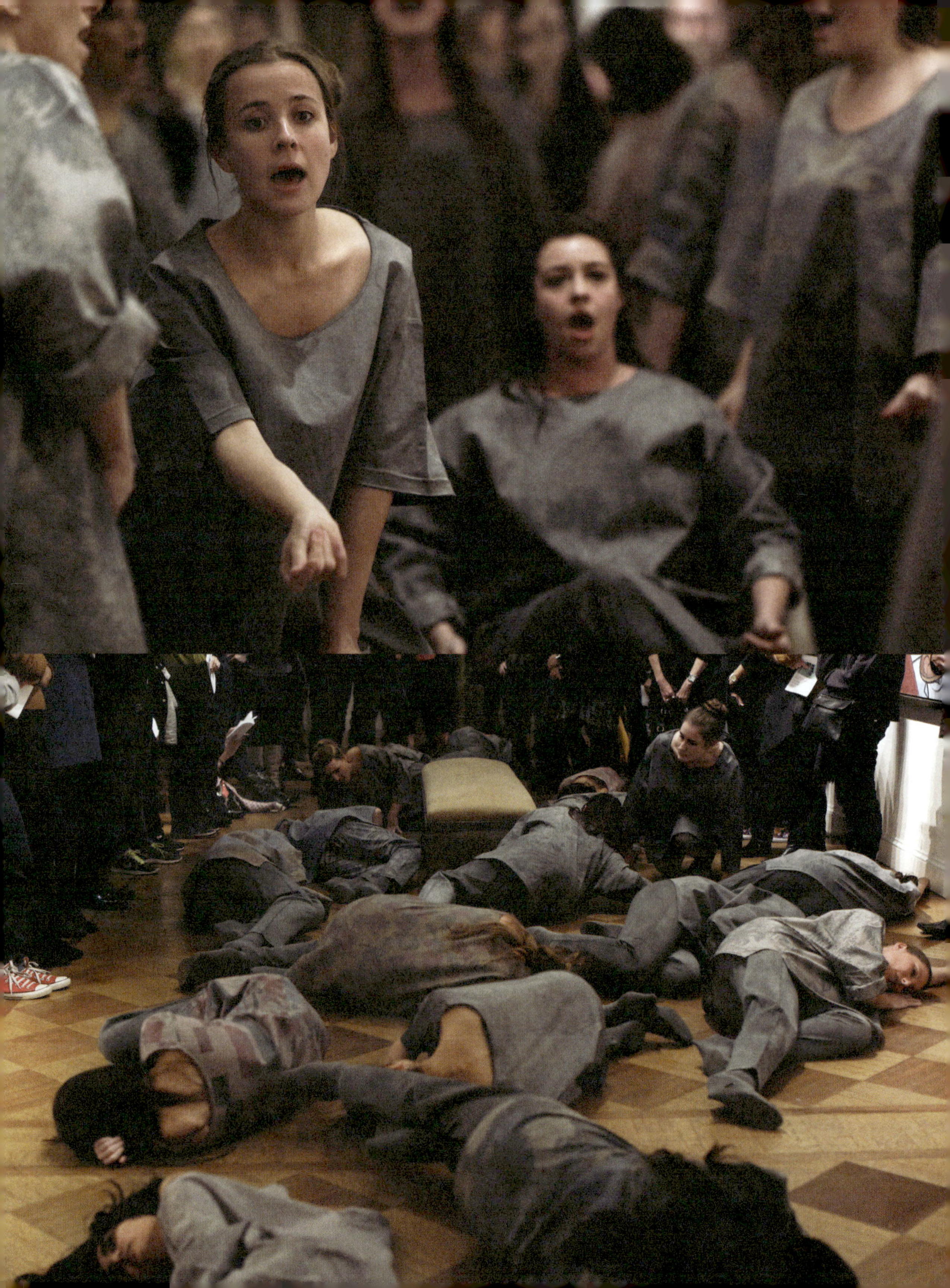

AND YOU WERE WONDERFUL, ON STAGE

A chorus line of eighteen women led Cally Spooner's fifty-minute peripatetic musical, *And You Were Wonderful, On Stage*—but this was no prurient revue, and these were no "Gaiety Girls." Spooner's performers, all classically trained singers, stared vacantly into some opaque beyond, gesturing distractedly and robotically as they delivered an *a cappella* script whose prose drew as much from Kurt Schwitters's sound poetry as it did from political stump speeches and Perez Hilton's headlines. Conflating the Athenian and Broadway valences of the chorus form, Spooner's production (her first musical) moved peripheral gossipers and synchronized filler to the forefront, deploying figures of speech to explore the status of contemporary communication.

The performers—including a core cast of Rhiannon Drake, Helen Hart, Piya Malik, Jenny Minton, Rebecca Thorn, and Chloé Turpin— swarmed the galleries of the National Academy Museum, a pristine Beaux Arts mansion that hosts at its center a dramatic Ogden Codman-designed serpentine staircase, humming an overture that sampled the earworms of Peter Joslyn's original musical score. Suddenly, a voice boomed in the tawdry cadence of a newscaster: "Monday! January 21, 2013. Beyoncé lies to the President!" Thus began a libretto composed of catty YouTube comments dissecting current affairs, punctuated by transcripts "ripped" from an advertising agency on how to usurp true stories for economic gain, all underscored by fragments of French theorist Bernard Stiegler's *For a New Critique of Political Economy*. This textual assemblage—drawing in part from the Russian Constructivist concept of the "living newspaper"—staged something of the precarious condition of expression and exchange under what Bifo Berardi has described as the late-capitalist "financialization and virtualization of communication." It explored the ways in which this social and economic climate has resulted in a growing dependency on "technics," Stiegler's term for those prosthetic aids employed to supplement natural human capacities, such as memory and cognition.

Spooner's efforts have long been invested in locating sites of agency and power within modes of speech, writing, and discourse. Engaging in an atemporal dialogue with Merleau Ponty and Hannah Arendt or Tiger Woods, Spooner's oeuvre aims to parse what occurs when communication is geared toward results rather than exploration. Her previous work has likewise taken the form of scripts or dialogues and staged language that ambiguously occupies ephemeral and inscribed spaces. For her 2011-12 work *Collapsing in Parts*, for example, she wrote a novella over the course of eight months, releasing it to the public (in parts) online as it was produced. She presented at various institutions a series of "footnotes" to the text that materialized as performances, screenings, and conversations. Distributed across many forms of media and across both public and private realms, the resulting novella is the product of a series of Barthesian chess moves and appeals to *jouissance*. In its pages, a copy editor regularly interrupts the narrative so that the material and structural aspects of language—its syntax and its grammar—are constantly insisted upon.

Here, abstracted pop song episodes alluded to various recent social media scandals (Beyoncé's unfortunate lip-synching of *The Star Spangled Banner* at Obama's inauguration, Scooter Braun's damage control of his truant "tool" Justin Bieber, Lance Armstrong's admission to Oprah that he had taken performance-enhancing drugs), and political happenings (the UK Education Secretary Michael Gove's speech on the imperative of rote learning and Obama speechwriter Jon Favreau's decision to leave the White House for Hollywood). Though presented in language that seemed to favor détournement and drift, these sagas began to cohere into a landscape in which public figures traded improvisation (and, in some cases, agency) for the promises of technics—whether a pre-recorded performance, dope, or an educational system that readies young minds to parrot rather than think critically. By pitting real-world examples of political figures legislating the mechanization of knowledge or abandoning the powers of government for those of the spectacle alongside slip-ups of automation in popular culture, Spooner's script suggested the pernicious effects of the making-technical of life.

Converging and dispersing among the audience according to Adam Weinert's minimal choreography, the performers herded visitors as a group from gallery to gallery. Their voices guided the script as protagonists or slipped into the background, effectively fracturing any emergent narrative. Dressed in gray printed hazmat-suit-like latex costumes (designed by Malene List Thomsen), the performers looked factory-ready as they moved before the jewel-toned representational works of Leland Bell and Paul Georges from the concurrent exhibition of Post-War American painters, installed in the museum's galleries.

Intermittently, a voice shouted "Off camera dialogue!" followed by a rapid-fire exchange between two of the gray-clad women, one in the role of an analyst-cum-instructor (Spooner's "brand guardian") and one as a dutiful subject. "Tell me how you've learned," instructed the brand guardian. "Over the past few years, the industry has learned much more," replied the respondent. The guardian corrected her: "Over the last few years, our whole industry, has learned a lot more," and so the respondent re-calibrated her story, "Over the last few years our whole industry has learned a lot—a lot more," the guardian interrupted. This language was extracted directly from notes Spooner took while working years earlier as a copywriter at a London advertising agency. Performa precedents for this staging of appropriated speech might be the French artist collective L'Encyclopédie de la Parole's *Chorale* (2011), a spoken vocal arrangement of collected and indexed speech recordings ranging from movie scenes to political addresses and on to answering machine messages; or perhaps Liz Magic Laser's *I Feel Your Pain* (2011), which restaged dialogues excised from United States political interviews and press conferences as a romantic drama. Spooner's appropriative gesture here evinced the blurring of the parameters of personal expression and the regurgitation of market agendas, demonstrating the ways in which accounts of lived experience are manicured to suit a company's needs, their edges smoothed to function swiftly within capitalist flows. Following suit, the language of the performance began to cohere, and corporate jargon ultimately subsumed the script.

As the audience was ushered out of the galleries and down the National Academy Museum's spiraling staircase, the performers placed themselves in a staggered formation on the stairs and around the stairwell. Their voices reached a crescendo with a cacophonous staccato of the letters "A—S—A—P" and soon were interchangeable as harmonies, struck the contours of the transitional space. The chorus line, finally synchronized, became a production line, mechanically repeating a set of gestural and vocal operations. The women cut to chirp a unified refrain of "Need to finalize" as they marched, single file, down the staircase, past the audience, and out through the front door.

As with all of Spooner's projects, *And You Were Wonderful, On Stage* served as a platform for research, out of which many auxiliary and supplemental works, propositions, and numbers emerged. The musical's preliminary structure was commissioned by and first staged at the Stedelijk Museum in Amsterdam and the work was subsequently performed at Tate Modern in London. Excerpts of the piece were translated to occupy the mediated space of YouTube for the Tate Modern's live broadcast "Performance Room" series, resulting in a six-minute operatic work that served as a trailer, titled *He's in a Great Place!*, for the work's final iteration: an HD feature film, currently in production, based on a live performance before an audience of the musical at EMPAC in Troy, New York. In addition, in 2014 Spooner produced the film *Off-Camera Dialogue*, which isolates and remobilizes the advertising agency transcript from the larger musical, and *It's About You*, a projection of an advertisement featuring latex-clad dancers that was screened on the High Line in New York and was accompanied by several performances. The language in the video was drawn from the confusing accumulation of tweets linked to #PRISM at a moment in 2013 when disclosures were published about the NSA's PRISM program (which extracts personal data from an unwitting public) and Katy Perry was poised to launch her summer album of the same name.

Through these shifting iterations, Spooner reconceived the formal and conceptual stakes of the work as it moved from live performance to live event distributed via a screen, and then on to a cinematic document of a live event, subjected to post-production. When considering Spooner's sprawling and prolific analysis of whatever object she takes up, I'm reminded of Roland Barthes's 1977 description of his own work: "At the crossroads of the entire oeuvre, perhaps the Theater." Barthes meant, of course, not the synthesis and spectacle of dramatic theater, but the semiotic investigations of epic theater. Whether Spooner gives us a musical or a novella, it exposes itself such that we are forced to evaluate our own role as audience- or reader-as-author. Whatever Spooner offers, perhaps it's Theater.

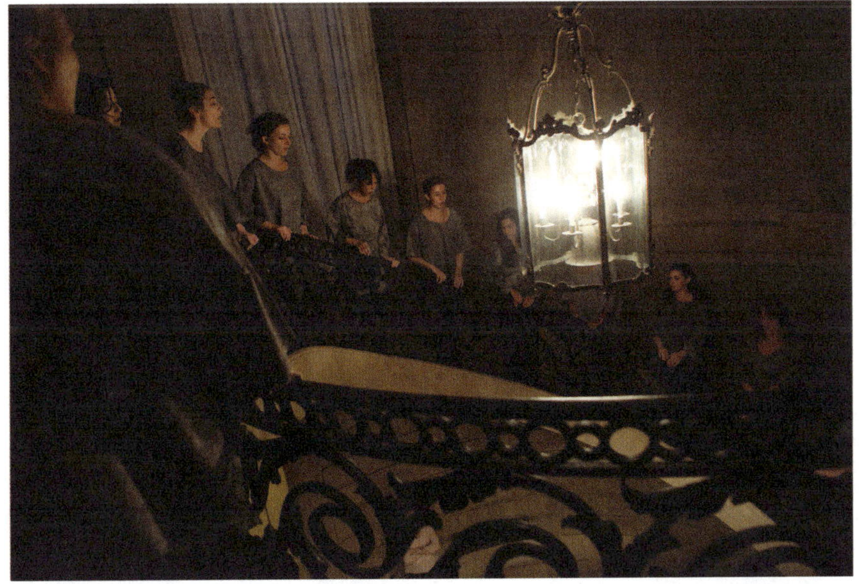

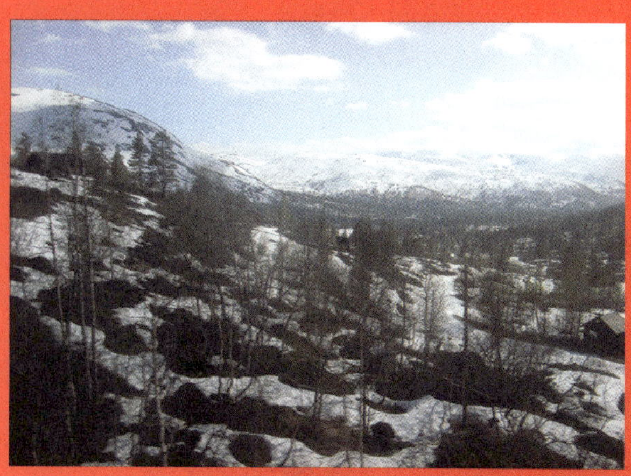
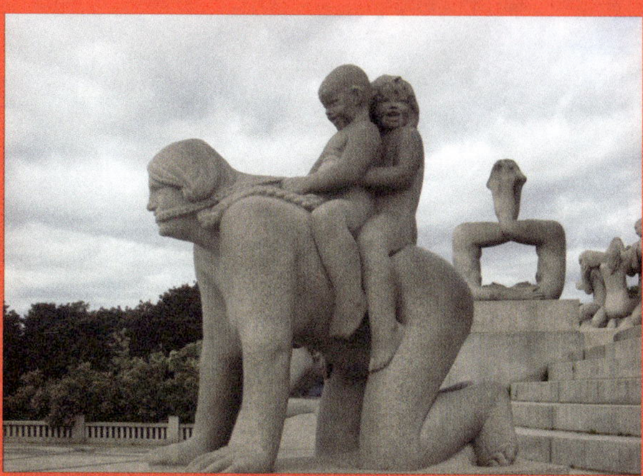
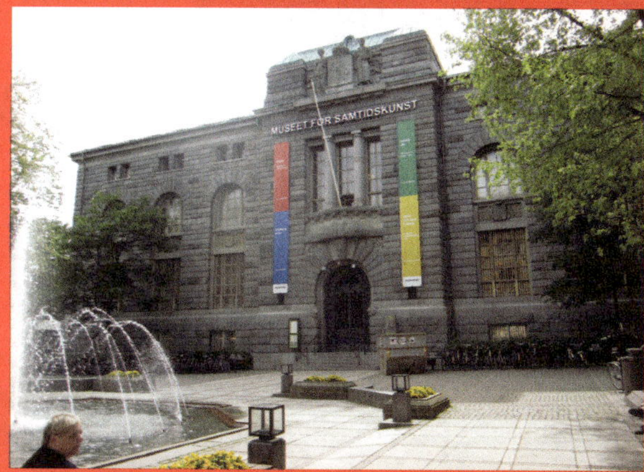
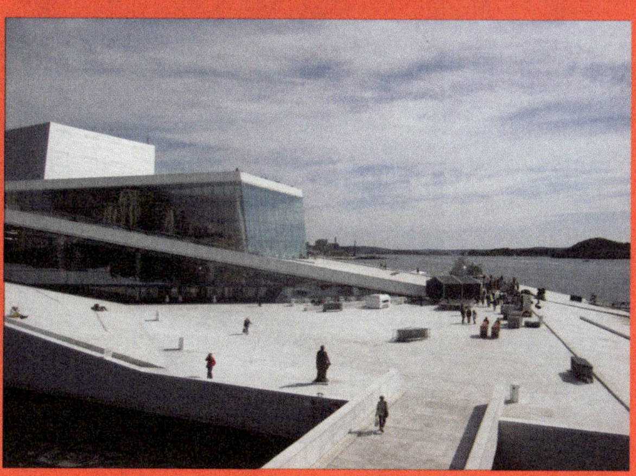

PAVILION WITHOUT WALLS

NORWAY

Photos by Esa Nickle

Historic sites around Oslo and Bergen (2012).

Performa's relationship with the Royal Norwegian Consulate General in New York began with their support of Elmgreen and Dragset's Performa Commission for Performa 11, since one of the artists of the collaborative duo, Ingar Dragset, is Norwegian. This soon developed into a deeper conversation about contemporary art and culture in Norway and what we might learn about it through our Pavilion Without Walls program. Traveling first to Bergen and then to Oslo, in three separate visits to Norway, Performa curators were welcomed by a cross-section of partners (including Queen Sonja of Norway, a photographer and arts patron) to discuss official Norwegian cultural policies and government support of the arts and the considerable interest of a younger generation in contemporary art. Meetings with artists and curators, as well as directors of organizations throughout Norway, such as Ny Musikk, Henie Onstad Kunstsenter (HOK), the Stavanger Kunsthall, Kunsthall Oslo, Hordaland Art Centre, Entrée, and UKS-Unge Kunstneres Samfund, formed the basis for a richly curated program of events that also provided an opportunity for a young Norwegian curator, Randi Grov Berger, to work in New York for several months leading up to the biennial.

The program revealed aesthetic explorations of Norwegian-born artists but also included work by those who might live there only briefly, exhibiting an enlightened international policy on the part of the funders, who supported works such as the visual concert by Tori Wrånes, to a film examining Norway's history by Jumana Manna and Sille Storihle, to the multi-artist Flag NYC project. Performa curators found several sound and vocal artists perfectly suited to one of the main themes of Performa 13, "The Voice," and the resulting program provided an overview of the tonal ecology of a country where popular music, avant garde techniques, and local traditions blend easily in expressive collages. Often without words, it seemed that these collected voices reflected the sparse and severe fjord-filled landscapes of the north.

ROSELEE GOLDBERG AND ESA NICKLE

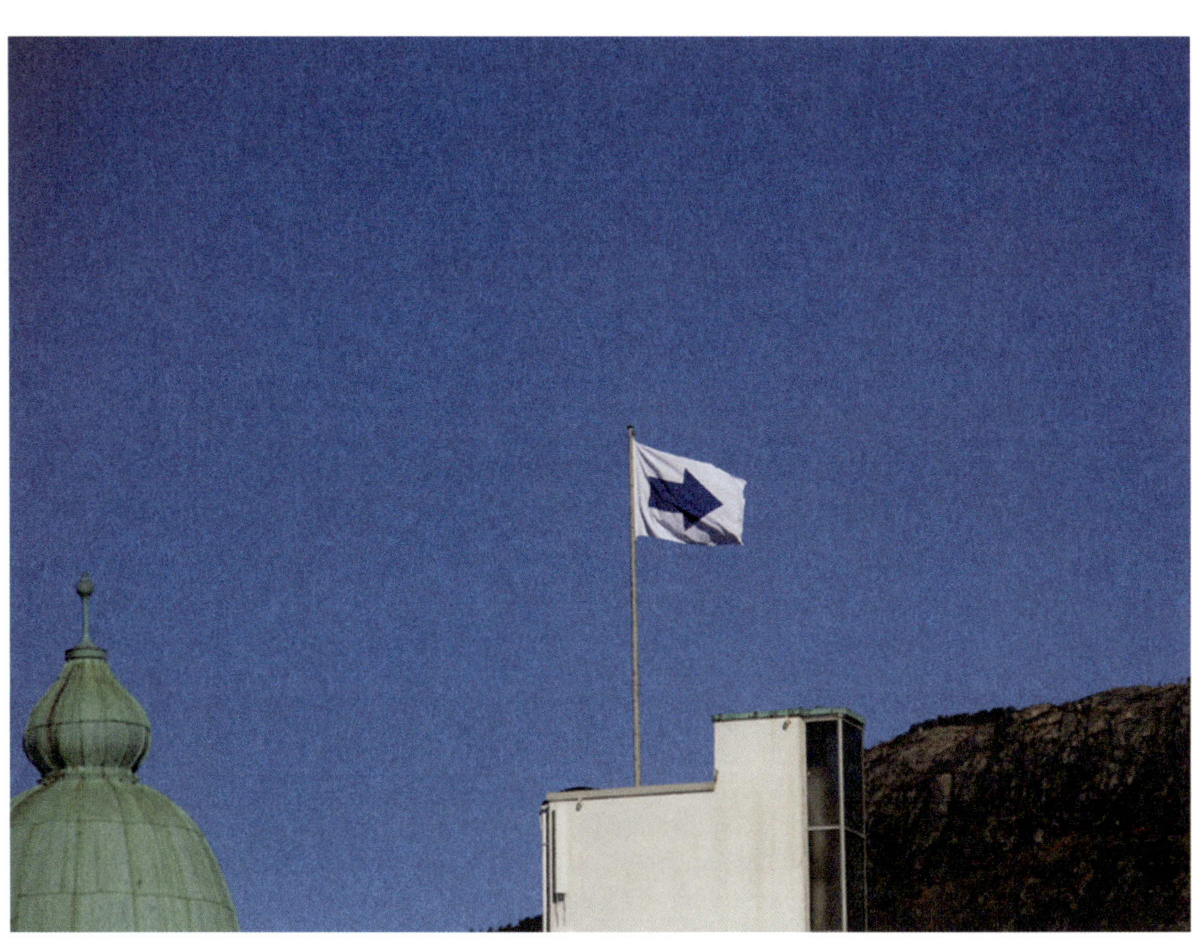

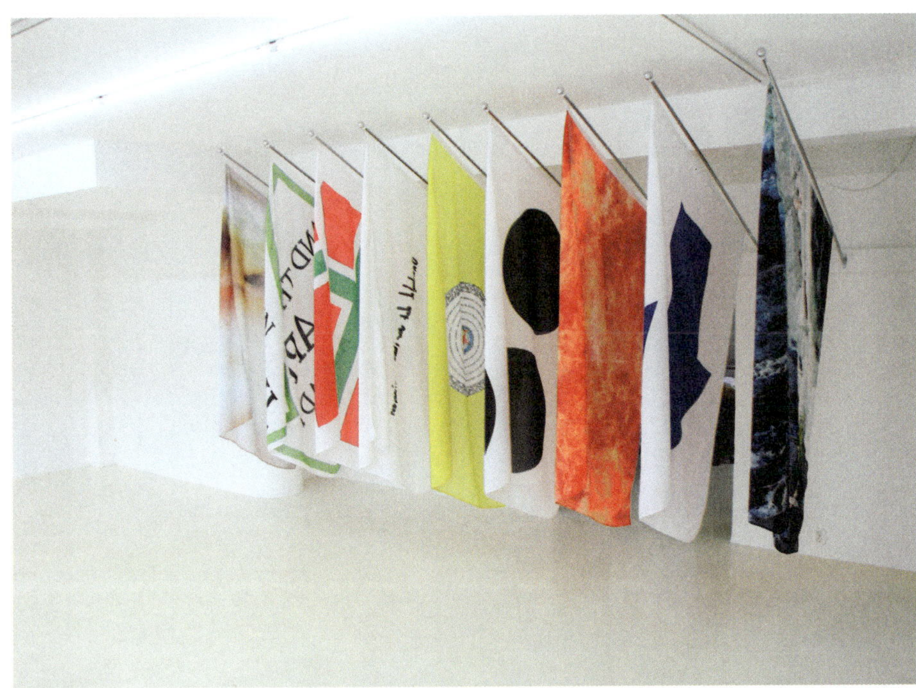

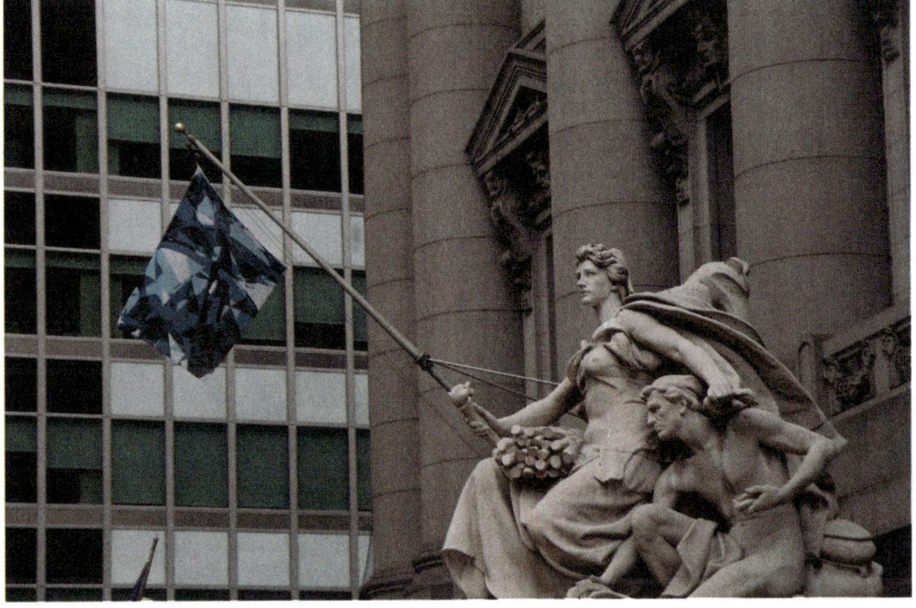

(Left) Flag by Magnhild Øen Nordahl, part of *Flag Bergen*, (2012). Photos by Randi Grov Berger (Right Above) Flag Installation (Right Below) *Espen Dietrichson*, Flag in Situ. New York City (2013).

CURATED BY RANDI GROV BERGER △ LOCATIONS IN AND AROUND NEW YORK CITY

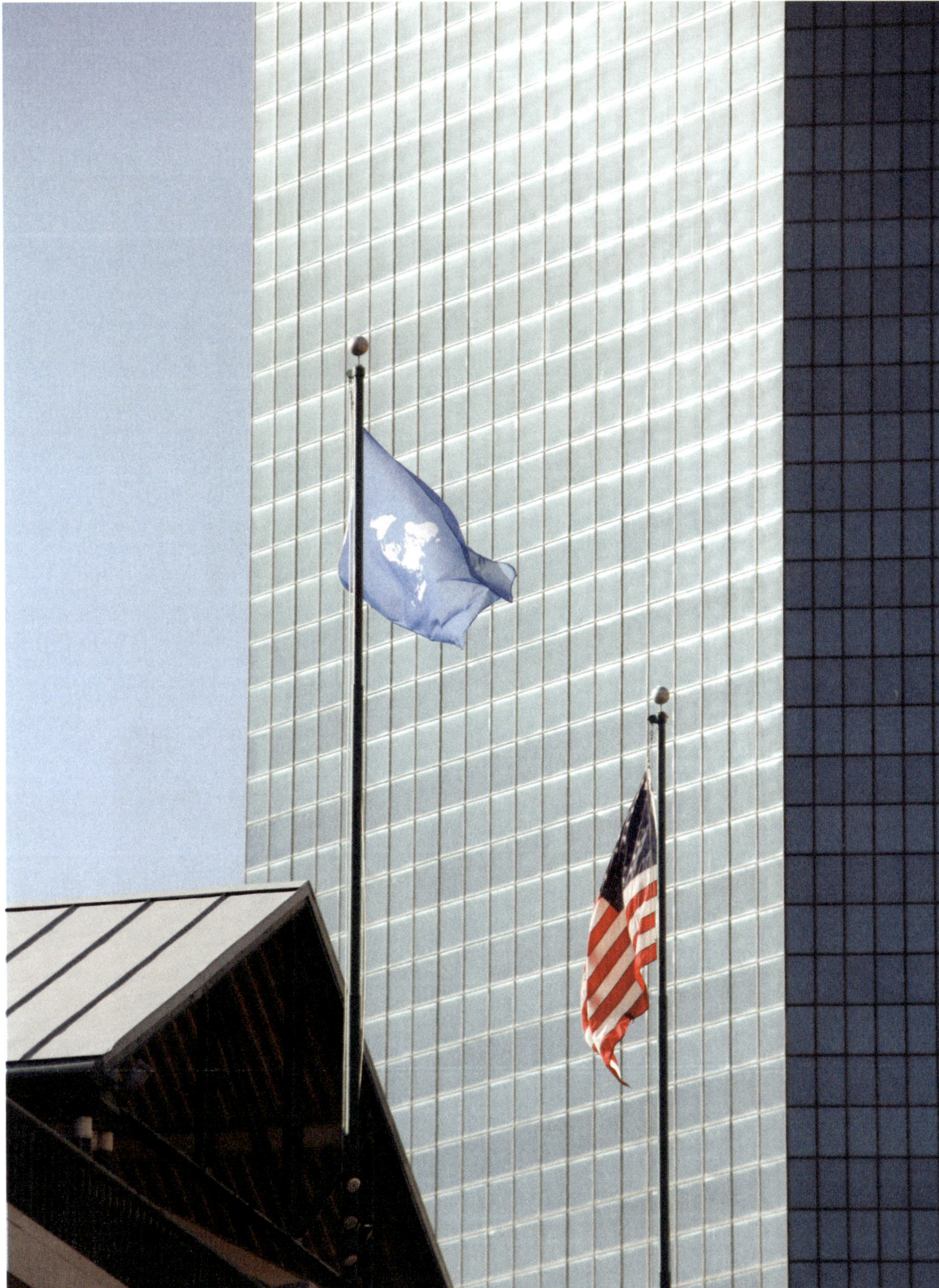

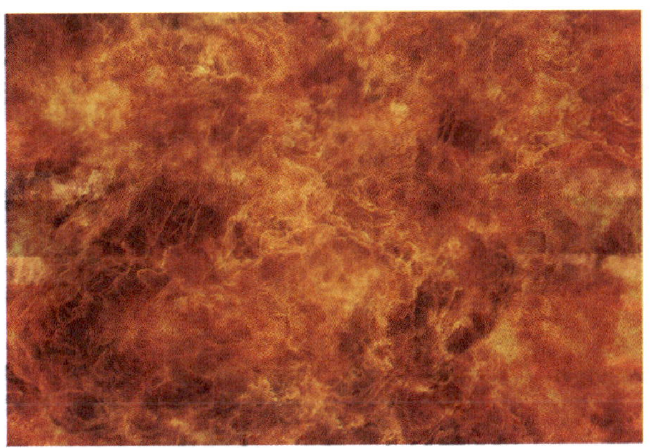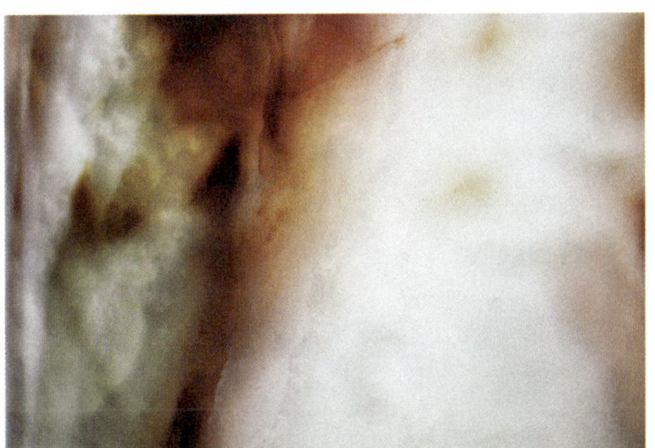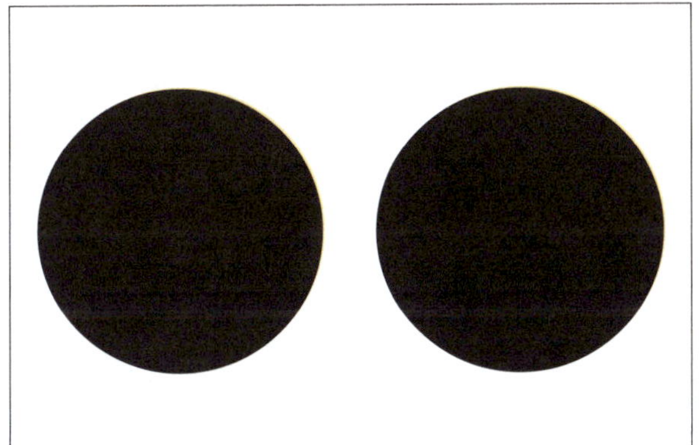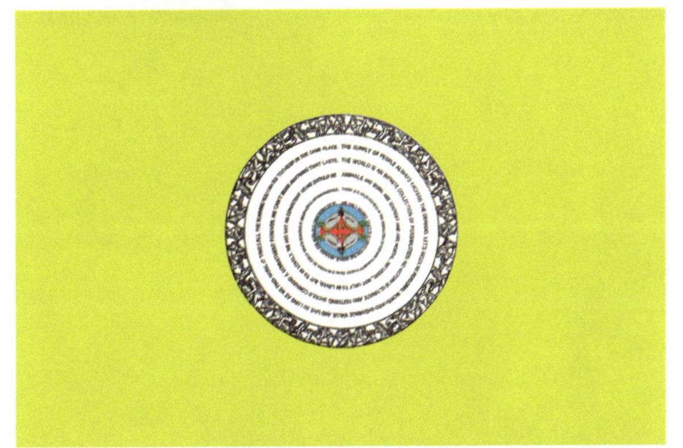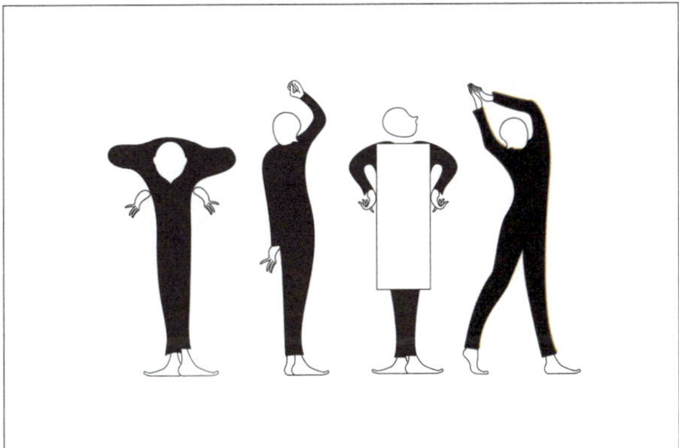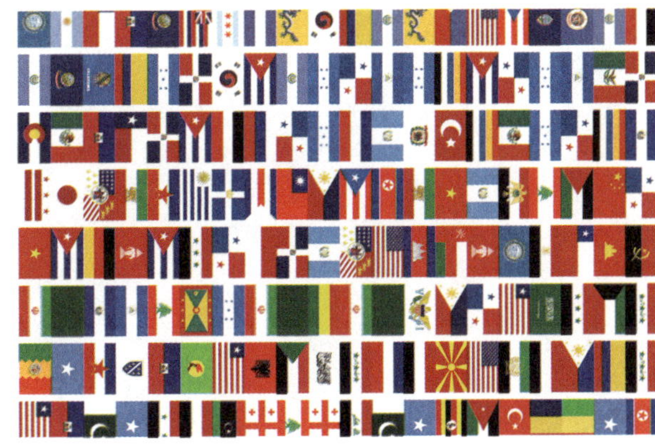

(Above, clockwise) *Flag Designs* by Arne Rygg, Cato Loland, Lewis and Taggart, Lisa Him Jensen, Liz Magic Laser and Sanya Kantarovsky, Andre Tehrani (2013); (Left) *Flag by* Anna Lundh in Situ, New York City (2013), photo by Randi Grov Berger

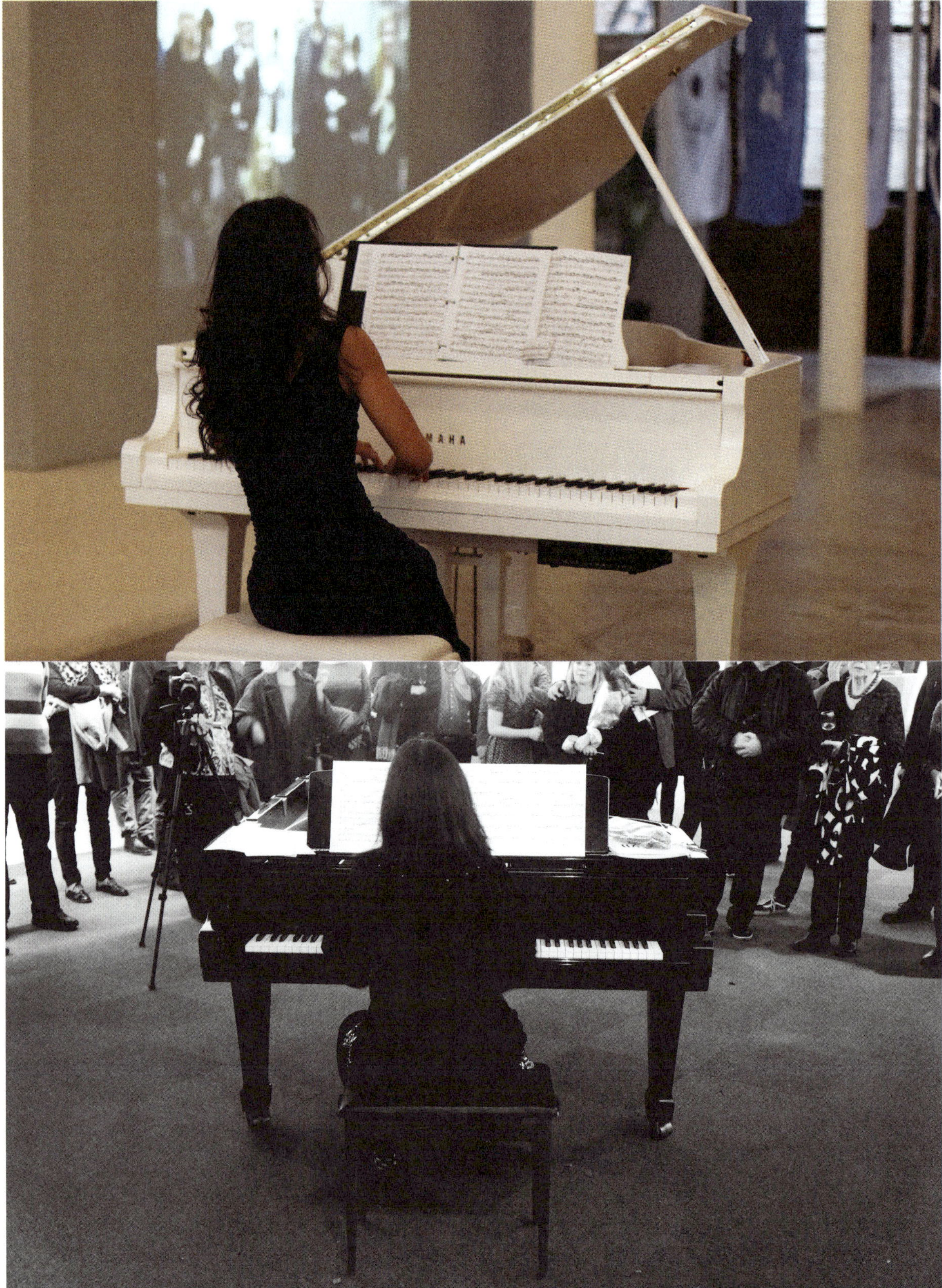

LINA VISTE GRØNLI, PETER CHILD AND ELAINE CHEW

PRACTICING HAYDN
(PIANO SONATA IN EB, HOB XVI:45 FINALE)

Practicing Haydn (Piano Sonata in EB, HOB XVI:45 Finale) was Performa's first intercontinental work, simultaneously performed by two performers, Elaine Kwon in New York at the Performa Hub on Crosby Street, and Elaine Chew at the grand opening of Kunsthall Stavanger in Stavanger, Norway. The performance was part of the Norwegian Pavilion Without Walls.

In Stavanger, at six in the evening, an audience of six hundred watched and listened to *Practicing Haydn* being played at the Kunsthall by Elaine Chew, while a lunch hour audience in New York watched and listened over Skype. Starting at 1pm in New York (7pm Stavanger time), audiences in both cities watched and listened to the same piece being played by prize-winning pianist Elaine Kwon at the Performa Hub—with the Stavanger audience attending via Skype.

Led by artist Lina Viste Grønli and her collaborators Elaine Chew, a concert pianist and digital media professor, and Peter Child, a composer and professor of music at MIT, *Practicing Haydn* was centered on a new piece for solo piano refracting the last movement of a sonata by Joseph Haydn, one of the most prolific and prominent composers of the Classical period. Inspired by the tuning-up of orchestras that happens before a classical concert, the trio set out to capture a similarly chaotic musical chance encounter.

For the piece, a practice session by pianist Elaine Chew was recorded, then transcribed "as is" by composer Peter Child—including all the repetitions, errors, halts, interruptions, etc.—into a new performable score. By making music out of an event that is associated with musical performance but not normally considered "musical," the original eighteenth-century piece transformed and transgressed through time.

The piece exists as a performable score, which was published a week later on Kunsthall Stavanger's website as part of a series of online exhibitions, further making accessible this transformed sonata.

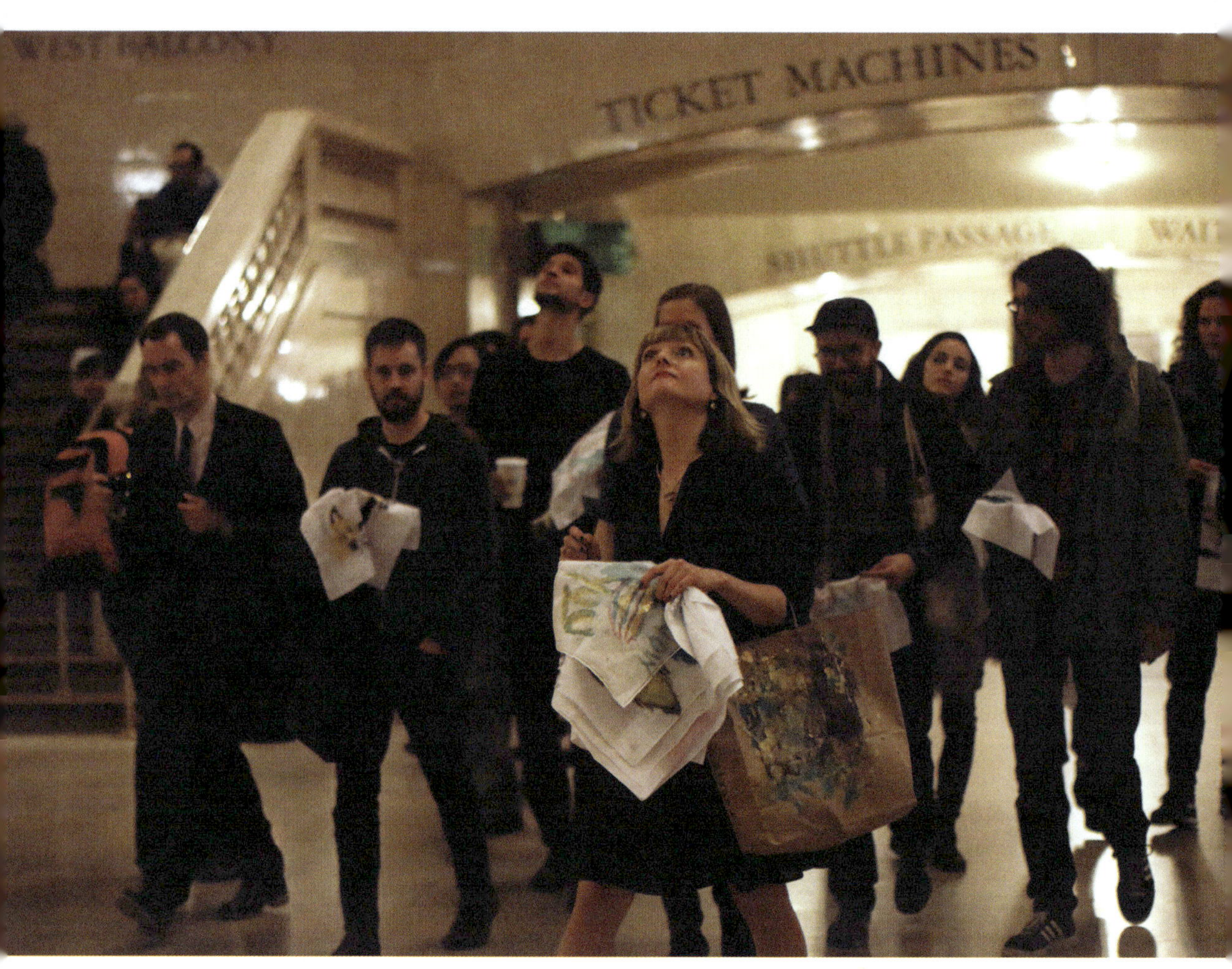

TICKET MACHINES
SHUTTLE PASSAGE
WAIT

MARTHE RAMM FORTUN

INVERTED SKY

It was spring, with our work in New York still months ahead of us, when we met for lunch in Oslo. Marthe presented a proposal for the performance for Performa 13 as part of the Norwegian Pavilion Without Walls—curated by Unge Kunstneres Samfund and co-presented with the biennial. Although short, Marthe's text moved me. She began with a quote from Jackie Kennedy Onassis—"Dear Mayor Beame, is it not cruel to let our city die …?"—and summarized what Marthe wanted to do under the title *Inverted Sky*. Those two words describe the enormous turquoise ceiling hovering above New York's Grand Central Terminal and the celestial drawings there.

Inverted Sky was a performance series hinting at the format of a guided tour for a public place of historical significance, but the history was told with a new set of taxonomies and combinations. With great sophistication, the work knit a tight web from ideas as diverse as the centennials both of Grand Central Terminal and Norwegian women's right to vote; the persona of Jackie Kennedy Onassis and her political role in the dramatic history of the station achieving landmark status; social injustice (current news stories of troubling perspectives on homeless citizens both in New York and Europe); poems and prose by Marthe, Jackie, audience members, Elizabeth Smart (whose cult title *By Grand Central Station I Sat Down and Wept* was published in 1945) and more.

In total, three performances took place in Grand Central Terminal—they were intense, sold out, and inevitably led to the Terminal's famed Oyster Bar—and because of the limited audience size, demanded both for artistic and security purposes, the performances were experienced by far fewer than any curator would ideally prefer. We have published *Inverted Sky—Letters to Jackie* (Unge Kunstneres Samfund/Black Dog, 2014) to expand the audience and magnify the project as a different entity, a new artwork in its own right, created as a book.

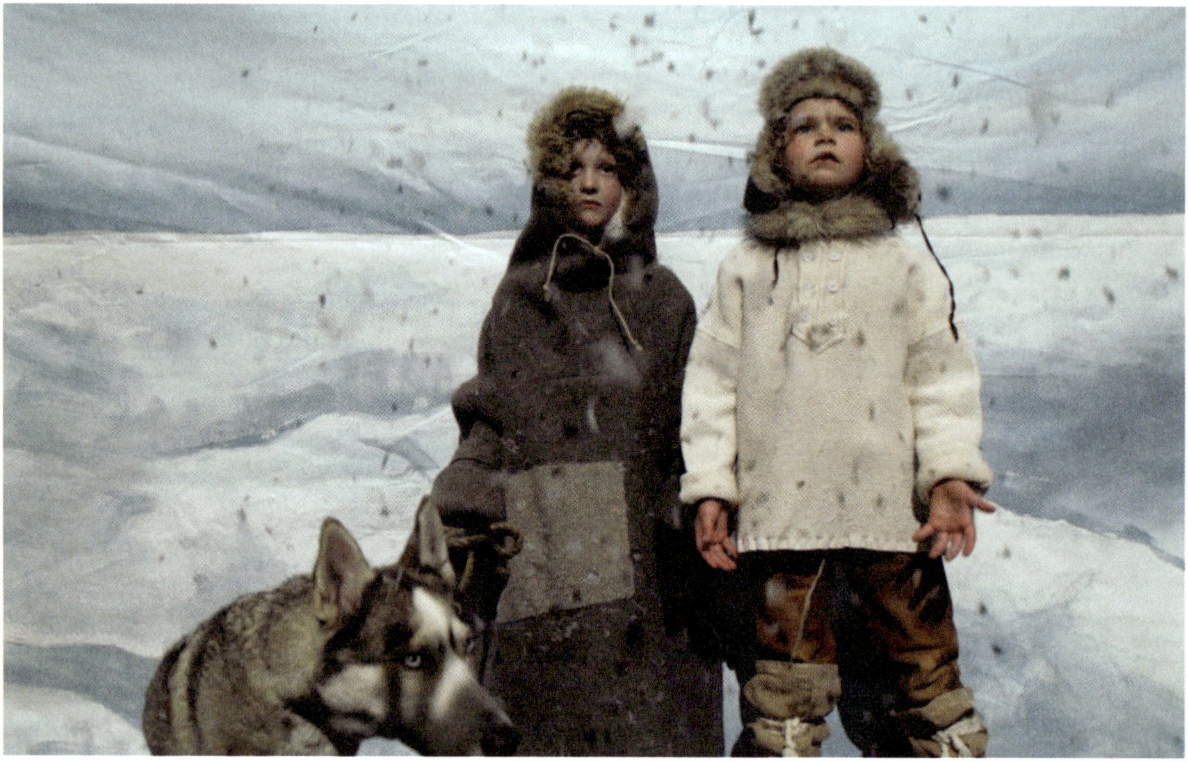

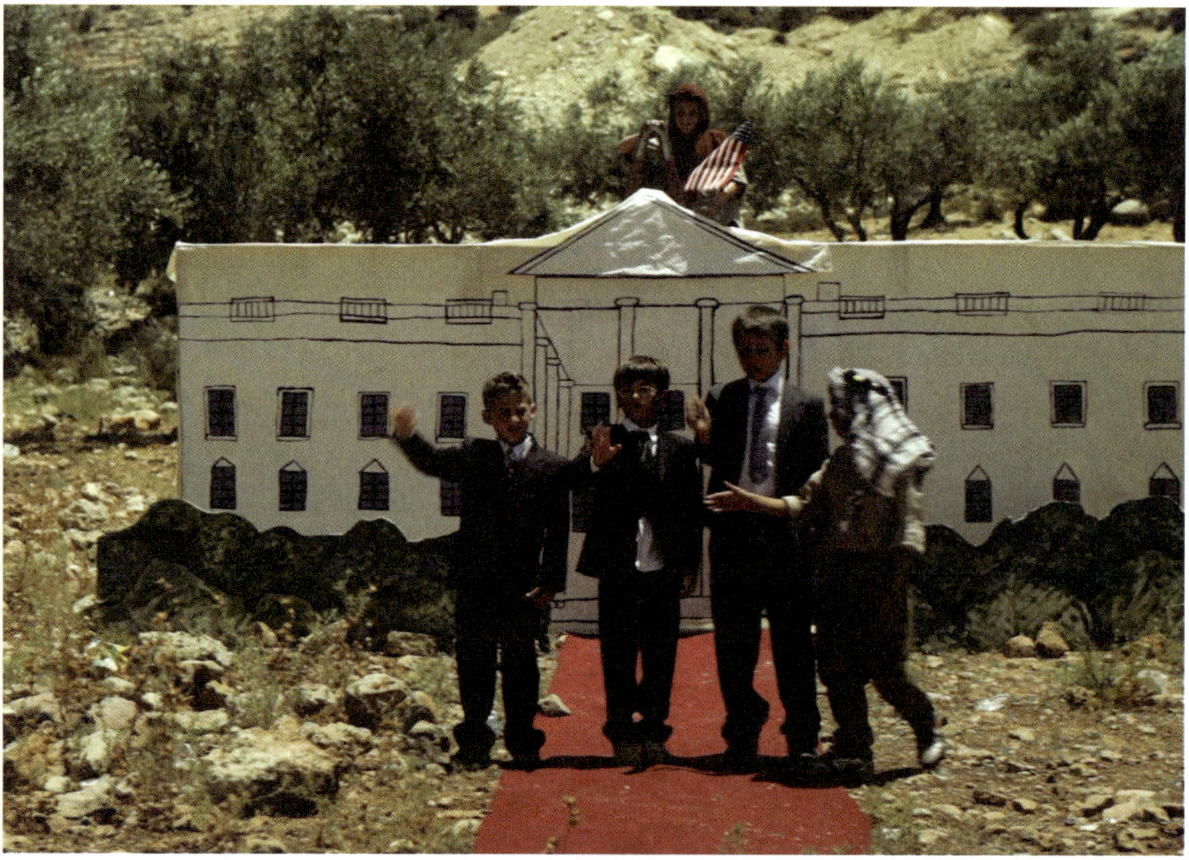

Jumana Mana, an American-born Palestinian grew up in Jerusalem and has lived in Oslo, Los Angeles, and Berlin. "I speak their languages and experience their realities," she has said of the varied geographies and national and political character of each country that has shaped her worldview and aesthetic. But of Norway, where she spent her student years and which she visits regularly, she says, "It is not a place I have ever really left." Finding sympathy with fellow student Norwegian artist Sille Storihle, in Oslo and at Cal Arts where they spent a year together, "studying American society and comparing it to how we felt about Norway, we began to develop a shared critique—and an ambiguity [about Norway]—and this piece is very much about our dialogue and shared experience."

The Goodness Regime, a 21-minute video, is about those reflections as well as the secret Israeli-Palestinian peace talks that took place in Oslo in 1995, in which Norway played a key role. *The Goodness Regime* re-envisions the myths of the country's history and "the goodness" that it represents today as the world's peacekeeper and one of its wealthiest nations. Filmed in both Norway and Palestine, the action unfolds primarily through tableaux of a children's play—with the underage actors undermining the intentions of such grand gestures as the Peace Accords—interwoven with archival footage, including political speeches and voice-overs from Hollywood films describing the quintessential Norway. The video is a satirical examination of ideas about identity that permeate Norwegian society and the way that such national and moral narratives are deeply embedded in the minds of those living in Norway as well as in the minds of those artists from abroad, who are drawn to return precisely for the embracing support of "the good regime."

ORGANIZED BY WILL BRADLEY △ CONNELLY THEATER

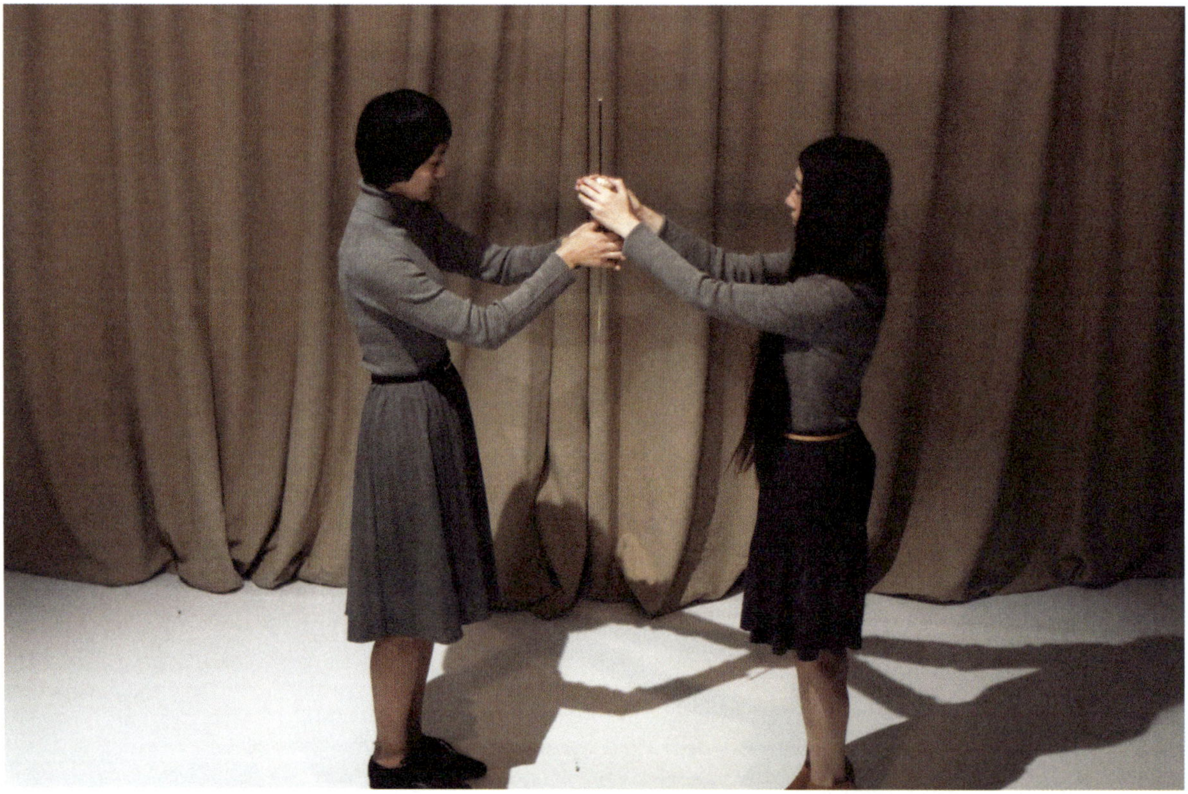

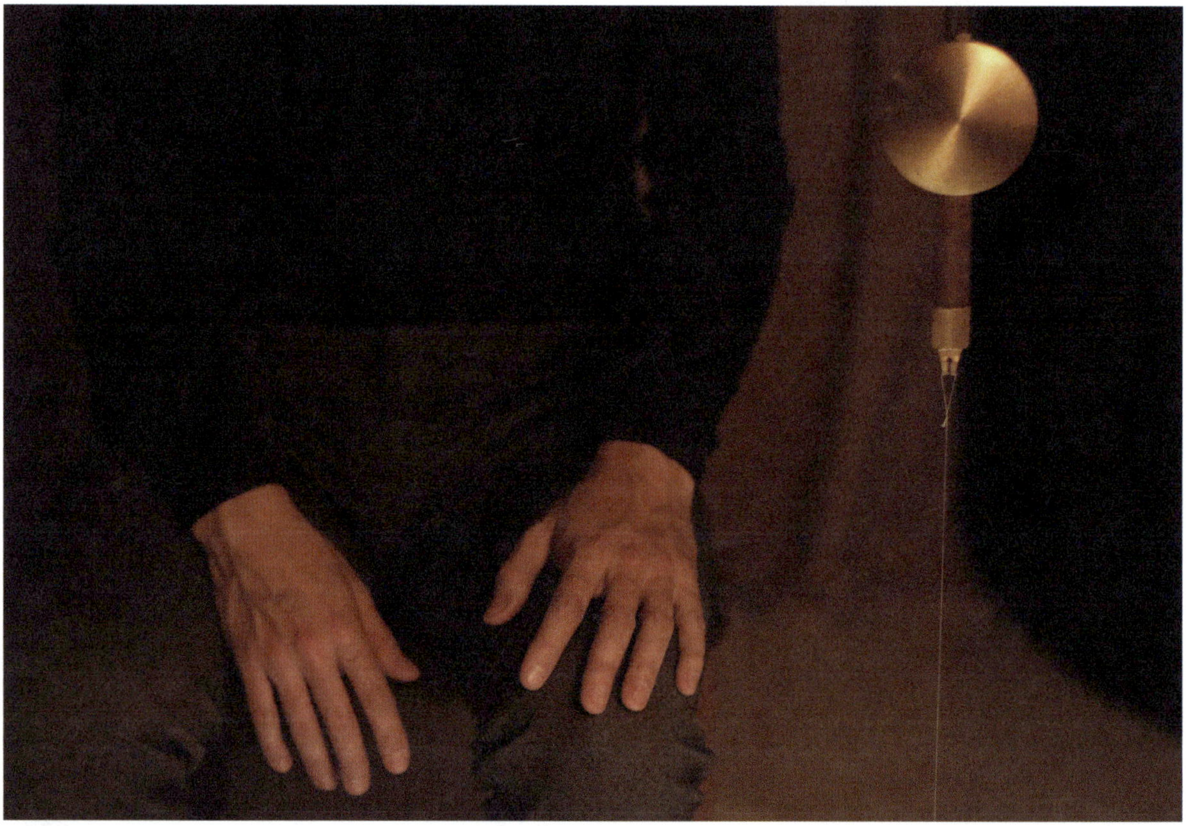

PEDRO GÓMEZ-EGAÑA

OBJECT TO BE DESTROYED

Cut out an eye from a photograph of one who has been loved but is seen no more. Attach the eye to the pendulum of a metronome and regulate the weight to suit the tempo desired. Keep going to the limit of endurance. With a hammer well-aimed, try to destroy the whole at a single blow.

Such were the initial instructions given by the Surrealist artist Man Ray for his much renowned *Object of Destruction*, first presented as a drawing in 1923 representing a metronome with an eye stuck to its pendulum. Today the work is protected behind glass at New York's Museum of Modern Art, but as Pedro Gómez-Egaña suggests,[*] it contains inherent romantic violence expecting to be triggered.

For *Object to Be Destroyed,* Gómez-Egaña instructed a series of ushers to lead small groups of audience members into a dark theater. Standing in a passage for the first part of the piece, they heard but could not see Henri Dutilleux's *Au gré des Ondes* (1946) played tenderly on a piano behind a curtained wall. The wait escalated expectations about what was happening on the other side of the curtain.

Next, the guide gently directed the group beyond the curtain, where chairs were placed in a half-circle facing a performance space about ten feet in front of another wall of beige velvet curtains. The audience was invited to sit down, the lights changed, and two women in gray uniforms moved synchronically as the piano started again repeating the same composition. The women focused on two golden pendulums that each one picked up from the floor. These were ceremoniously and magnetically moved toward each other. As the music ended, the pendulums, which were connected to filaments and fitted with strong neodymium magnets, were suspended in the air with half an inch between them, an arrangement that was arduous to achieve.

[*] Gómez-Egaña referenced Man Ray's *Perpetual Motif (Object of Destruction)* during an introductory lecture about his work *(Artist Class: The Beating Motif)* at the Performa Institute on November 19, 2013 prior to his performance at the Abrons Arts Center.

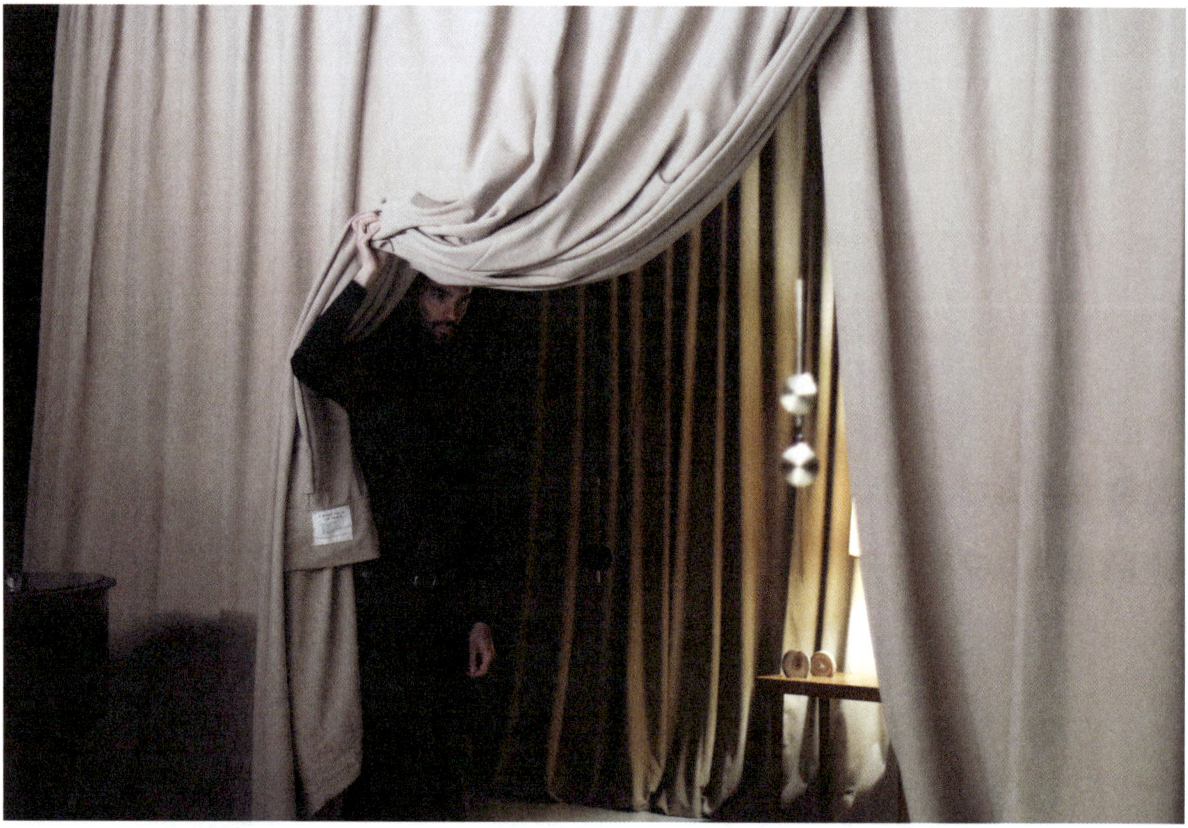

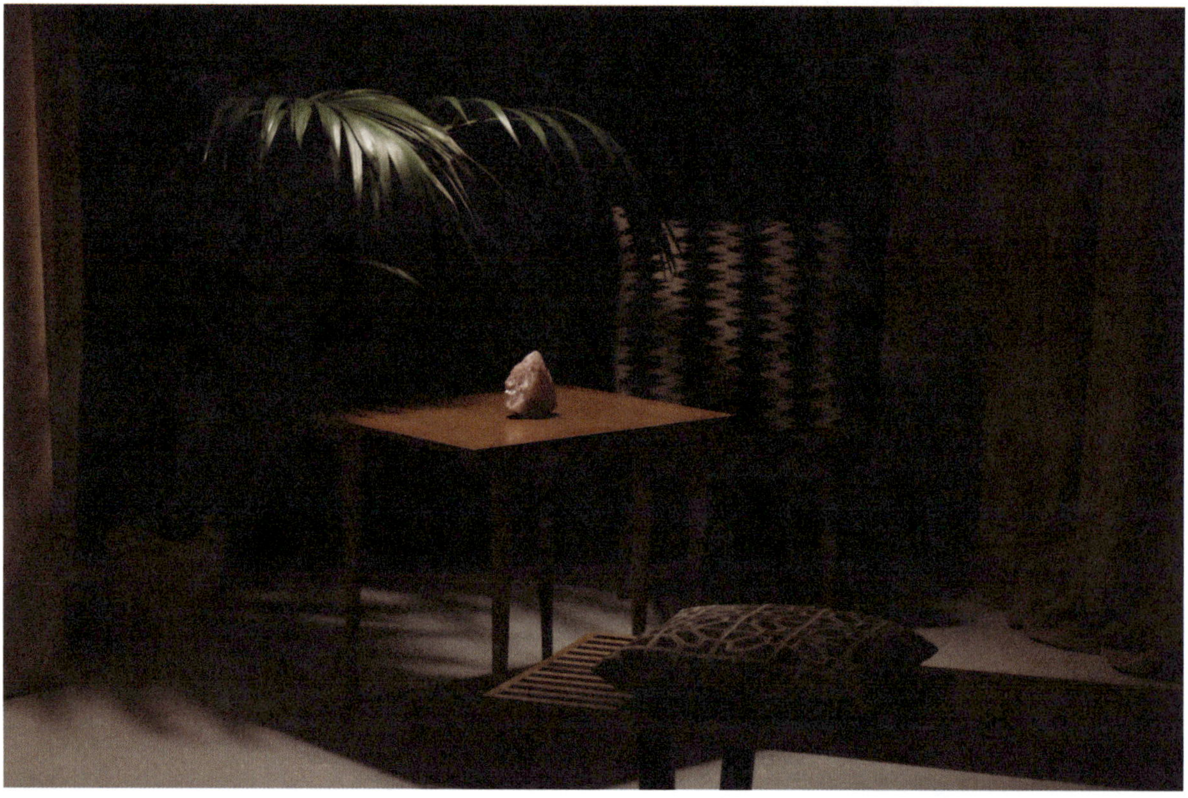

The lights changed and the guide swiftly pulled aside a curtain to access yet another chamber. The "back stage" was arranged as a domestic space with plants, tables, carpets, lamps, and crystals. Again the group was invited to sit, this time on low wooden benches looking back at the curtains through which they had just passed. Once seated, they heard steps behind the curtains. As the piano piece started again, for the third time, now a familiar melody, they sensed another group following behind them. The guide started the same careful process of placing two magnetized pendulums in balance, gently and precisely. The group witnessed the strong magnetism as the pendulums hung in the air. Once Dutilleux's *Au gré des Ondes* concluded for the third time, the group was ushered out by their guide, passing the pendulums in tension when moving out of the room. In the next passageway, a different uniformed man was watching over a table of purple amethyst crystals (each containing their own magnetic field) as the group dispersed from the theater. The audience then walked in a reversed half-circle to where the action of the piece had begun, while simultaneously a new group of audience members were seen entering the performance.

In total, three groups circulated inside this time-machine of Gómez-Egaña's, *Object to be Destroyed*. The performance was like a theater of mirrors, a visual performance arranged as half an hour's journey that brought together symbolic and historical time, mystical fantasies, and the magical experience of science where bearing witness meets spectacle. *Object to be Destroyed* was a reflection on how time has clear signifiers but also, as an experience, how time is the result of flows of actions and perceptions. As Gómez-Egaña has pointed out, "We walk on the street, we go to the train stop, we get in the train, we reach our stop and walk on the sidewalk, we step into an elevator, step out; open the door and we're home. Everyone is doing this, we are like little rivers of people fueling a civic machine administrated by 'stop' and 'go' signs, devices, notifications, and vehicles." In this context, the idea of an interruption of our compulsive everyday habits and routines is what has inspired Gómez-Egaña's recent body of work. He offers the audience a disruption, the possibility for moments to observe and focus, and in these instants of contemplation, the sudden immobility of a gesture might trigger a renewed curiosity toward the familiar magic that we daily experience.

CHAPTER

3

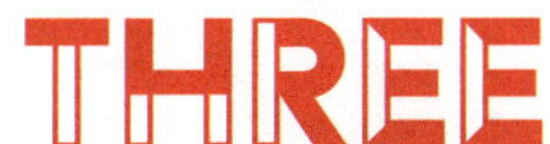

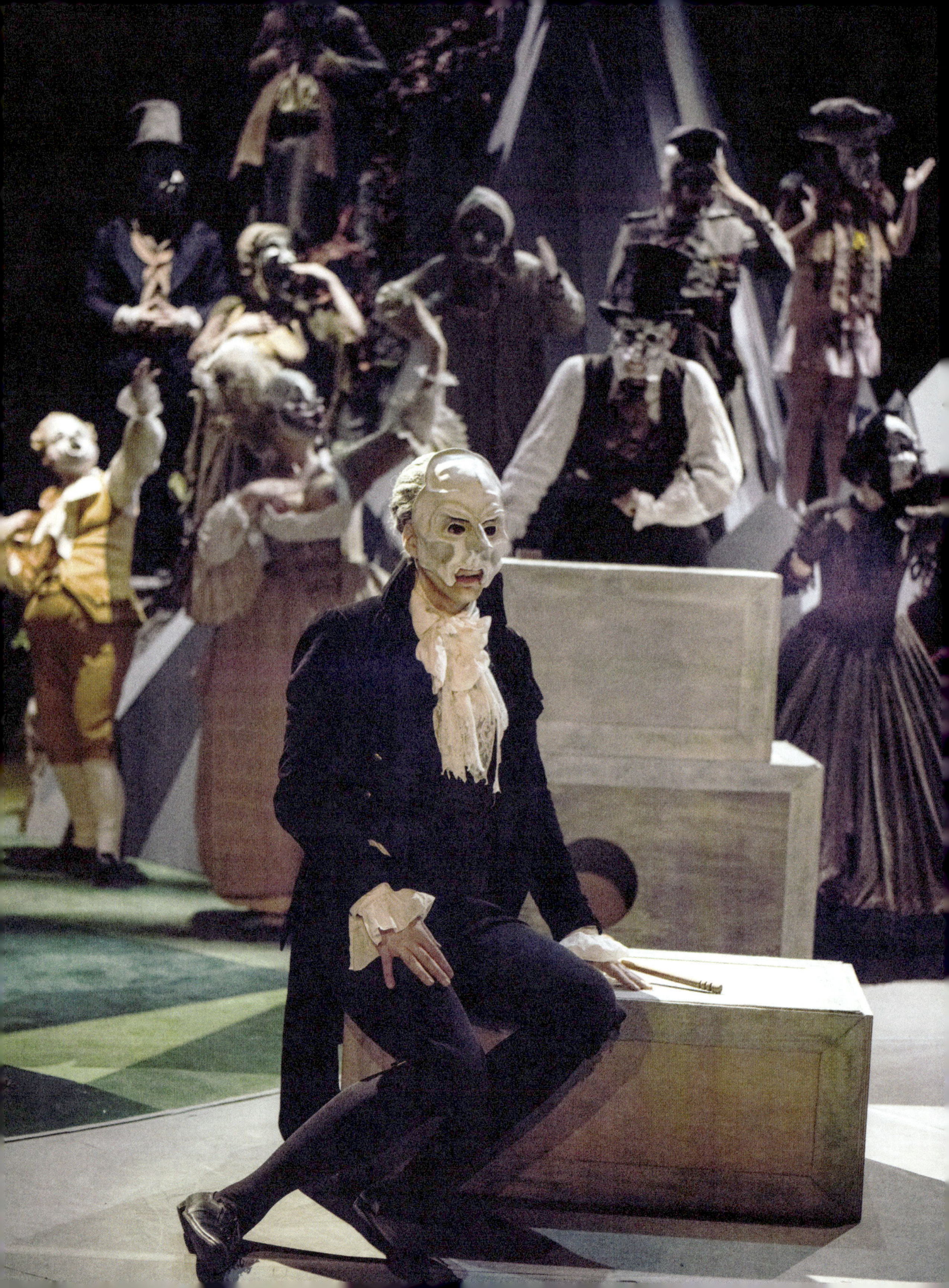

Mined from source material—high and low, ancient and modern—and mixing genres of literature, theater, and visual art, *The Humans*, Alexandre Singh's first play, spun a familiar tale of two doomed lovers in an unfamiliar fashion. Part origin tale, part love story, and set just before the beginning of time, in *The Humans,* the shy young studio assistant Tophole and the bold and beautiful spirit Pantalingua devise a scheme to stop the universe from being created. Trouble enough, but our heroes were born into different worlds: the Dionysian (representing the body, the physical world), and the Apollonian (the intellect and creativity), and it is here that the visual artist Singh took total theatrical license to blend the two.

Divided on stage by a jagged mountain, the imperious Pantalingua and her mother N., a mute rabbit queen, preside over the bucolic Dionysian realm of trees, animals, and nature. Charles Ray (named for the Californian artist) and his diffident assistant Tophole, on the Apollonian side, produce imposing lifelike plaster sculptures in their cool, orderly studio. Amid Gregorian chants extolling the virtue of hard work, Charles Ray recalls his ordination to make sculpture; instructions were received, he explains in verse, from Vox Dei, to create the sun and the moon. Or might those orders have accidentally come from a curious cat by the name of Ms. Chief? Either way this is an impossible task. Instead, the two lovers set their sights on Charles Ray's statues and attempt to teach each other about their separate spheres. She must learn about art and the imagination and he must learn about life, the everyday—and in so doing to defecate, as she does with ease. This exchange inadvertently gives rise to the human race, and the sculptures from Charles Ray's studio become flesh.

As *The Humans* roared into its second act, Charles Ray's studio minions explored their newly-animated human forms and, goaded by an inevitable tyrant in their midst, set off on a path of lust, greed, and murder.

The evolution from statue to human being was paired with a stylistic progression in all aspects of the play: chorus members traded pale

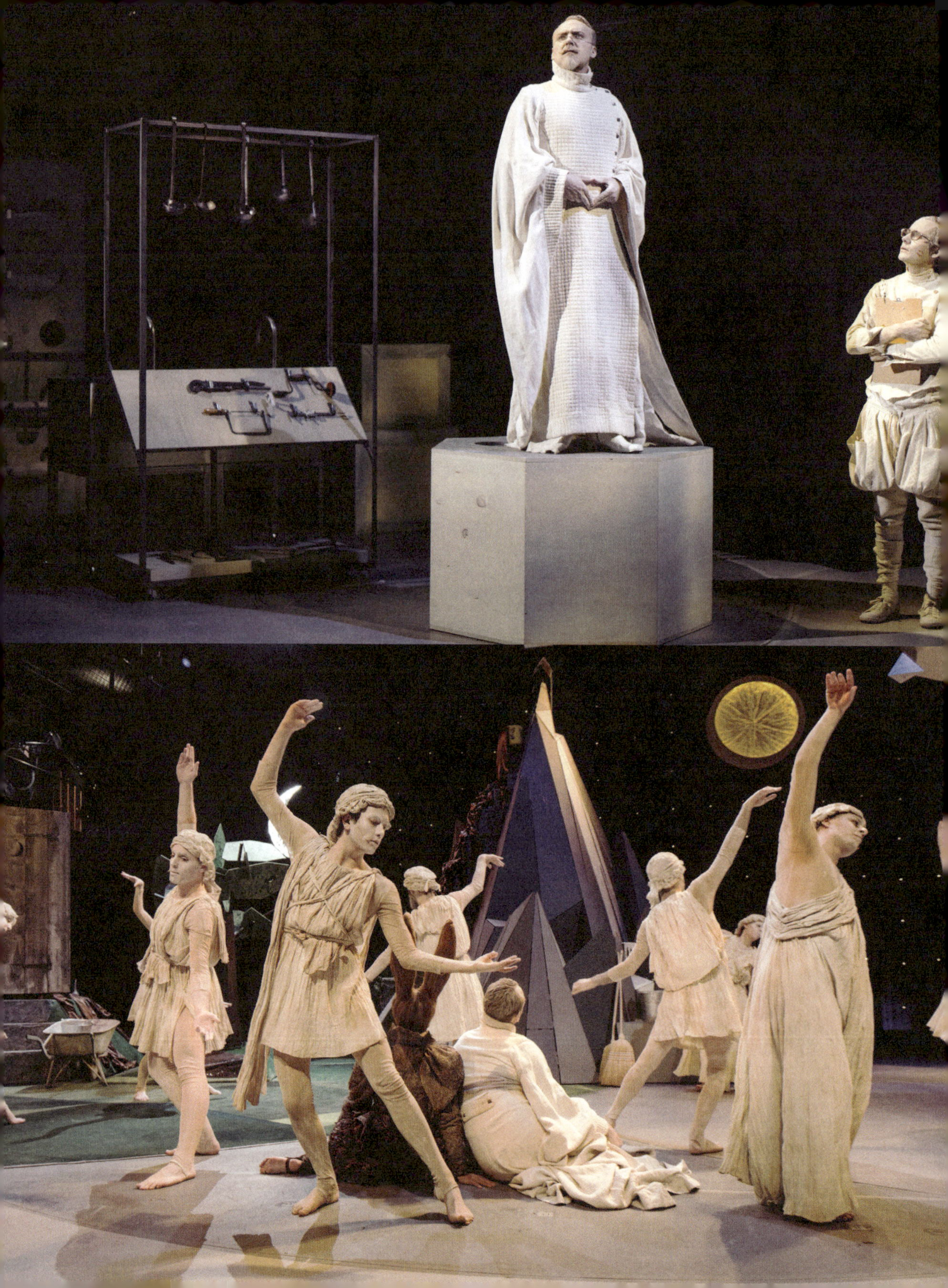

stone visages for garishly colored masks in the manner of Charles Daumier cartoons; Hellenic-inspired robes were swapped for late-nineteenth-century costumes; chants and hymns gave way to big band and swing-influenced musical numbers, swelling into a percussive and aggressively choreographed fight between the humans and N. Upon her mother's death, Pantalingua speculates on what might happen with dozens more humans on earth. With Tophole's master in prison, the two connive to gain control over the humans.

The third act takes on the character of a procedural drama. Pantalingua and Tophole have been captured and put on trial for corrupting the humans and murdering their leader. The twelve-member jury refuses to allow Pantalingua to speak. Instead, Tophole speaks what Pantalingua performs. He says it's better to be than not, despite the trouble borne out of existence. He says she's to blame. He calls his crime a result of his seduction by her, the true curse of existence: "For which is the guiltier? The javelin that kills, or the manicured hand that throws it?" Pantalingua and Tophole part ways, their love unrequited. In a final operatic oratorio, the humans offer themselves as worms to be ruled by the spirits of good and evil and the mountain at the center of the stage splits in two. Pantalingua and Tophole, now spirits, pass through its gaping center, into another realm.

The Humans involved more than one hundred people to realize the three-act play, including volunteers, production and technical assistants, seven principal actors, twelve chorus members, a choreographer, eleven creative team members, two makeup artists, a costume designer with a team of twelve assistants, a producer, and more than twelve people working on the set and props, showing Singh's immense vision of art history and at the same time providing a boisterous live statement, both spectacular and sensual, with attendant metaphysical offerings.

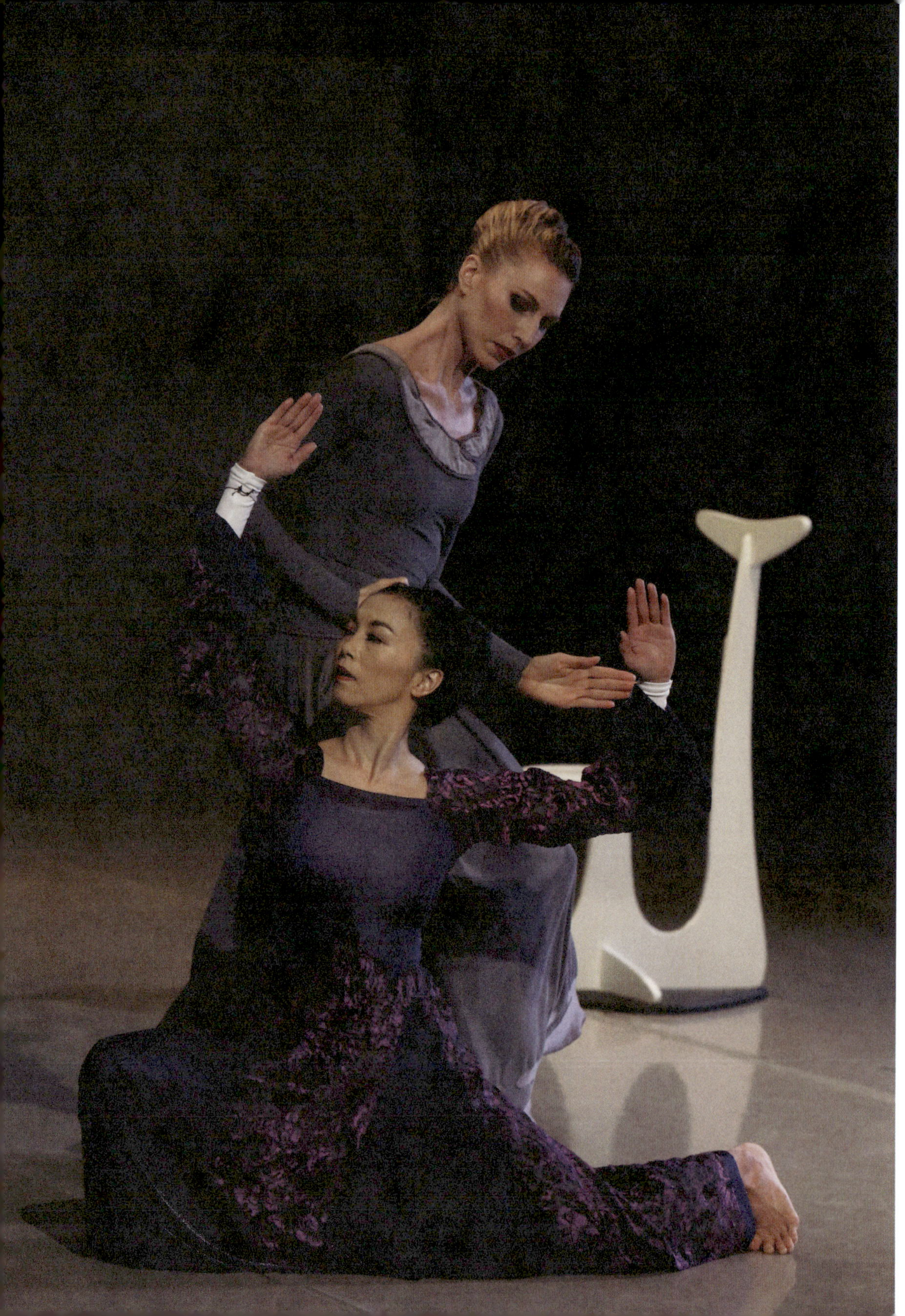

The Martha Graham Dance Company presented *Surreal Graham: Hérodiade* and *Spectre-1914*, two intimate and seminal Graham masterworks choreographed under the influence of Surrealism. *Spectre-1914* (1936) is a premonition of the oncoming Second World War produced the same year as the Museum of Modern Art exhibition *Fantastic Art, Dada and Surrealism*. In the dance, great swirls of red and black skirts, like angel's wings of death, whirled around the solo dancer, Katherine Crockett, the tall blonde principal dancer, who was the Attendant in *Hérodiade* (1944), where she was joined by Miki Orihara, also a principal dancer, far shorter and darker, like Martha Graham, who seemed so much taller when she danced. Orihara played the heroine Hérodiade, a combination of King Herod's daughter and Salomé, with veils metaphorically represented by a great black cloth, first draped over the X-shaped clotheshorse, a sculptural element from the evocative set by Isamu Noguchi.

André Breton's definition of beauty as defined in his beloved prose masterpiece *Nadja* (1928) is relevant here: "Beauty will be convulsive or not be!" This is illustrated in Breton's book by an image of a dancer whirling, and by the idea of motion allied with rest, impossibly, of course. The textual description of a train rushing at full speed into a forest and halted, stopped short, is captured in the dance through the same sensation. The active, violent whirl represents the same motion suspended in its place. Surrealism is made of opposites meeting as if magically, the contraries smashing together, forever joined and in motion. The prediction of war, its hurtling unstoppable movement, impacts the dance, halts and does not halt it. Martha Graham's genius was in being able to combine contraries through this lyricism of terror.

The sets for *Surreal Graham,* the barebones Noguchi pieces, were haunting in their stark simplicity, like so many white bones. Noguchi collaborated with Graham, representing what she saw in the mirror, an immensely narrow standing structure with, at its center, a bird-like form—just a slab of wood with a protrusion against which Hérodiade came to lean as she said, "its beating heart." In the middle of the mirror she saw her "bleached-boned" self. All bare, magnificently dramatic, the "doom-eager" Orihara (Graham)—having sent away her attendant (Crockett) with her smothering and mothering gestures, to enact her self-sacrifice alone—enveloped herself at the end in the black cloak as the lights dimmed. Graham was inspired by the symbolist poet Stéphane Mallarmé's *Hérodiade*, which he began at the age of twenty-two—a long poem about which on his deathbed he requested some unfinished parts be destroyed, saying to his wife and daughter: "Believe me, it would have been very beautiful." The Paul Hindemith music for *Hérodiade* was superbly fitting, stark and ominous. For the hour-long performance of *Surreal Graham,* it was stripped of its sung words, as the set was stripped of any decoration: chair, clotheshorse, mirror, bird. The references of *Surreal Graham* to the Surrealist unconscious and the convulsive dancer of Breton's *Nadja* suggests that this was a legendary period in which "doom" was played out in a way that has preoccupied art and literature since.

One of the enabling actions of Surrealism is the potential of unanticipated violence. It is often performed against the audience: for example, once, when I was on a panel about Surrealism, sharing the stage with Fernando Arrabal, and it was becoming perhaps a bit dull, Arrabal quite gloriously took off his clothes and streaked naked down the aisle. His performance was a direct example of action at once against the spectator and into the fray. The implicit and symbolically enacted violence in Shana Lutker's performance lecture—*The Nose, The Cane, The Broken Left Arm*—at the small and delightful Theatre 80, on the historic St. Mark's Place, based on an incident in which Breton broke his cane over Pierre de Massot's arm—was consistant with the actions of the Surrealists.

The point of the symbolic violence made lots of sense, for Breton wrote and truly believed that if we paid more attention to the feminine side of things, there would not be war. All of Surrealism is double in nature, day and night, death and life—meeting. The violence implicit in the clash of contraries will somehow suffice as a replacement of war. This symbolic violence in the Pierre de Massot episode (like the face-slapping in another Surrealist episode) is meaningful beyond its stage enactment.

Shana Lutker, *The Nose, The Cane, The Broken Left Arm* (2013), performance view.

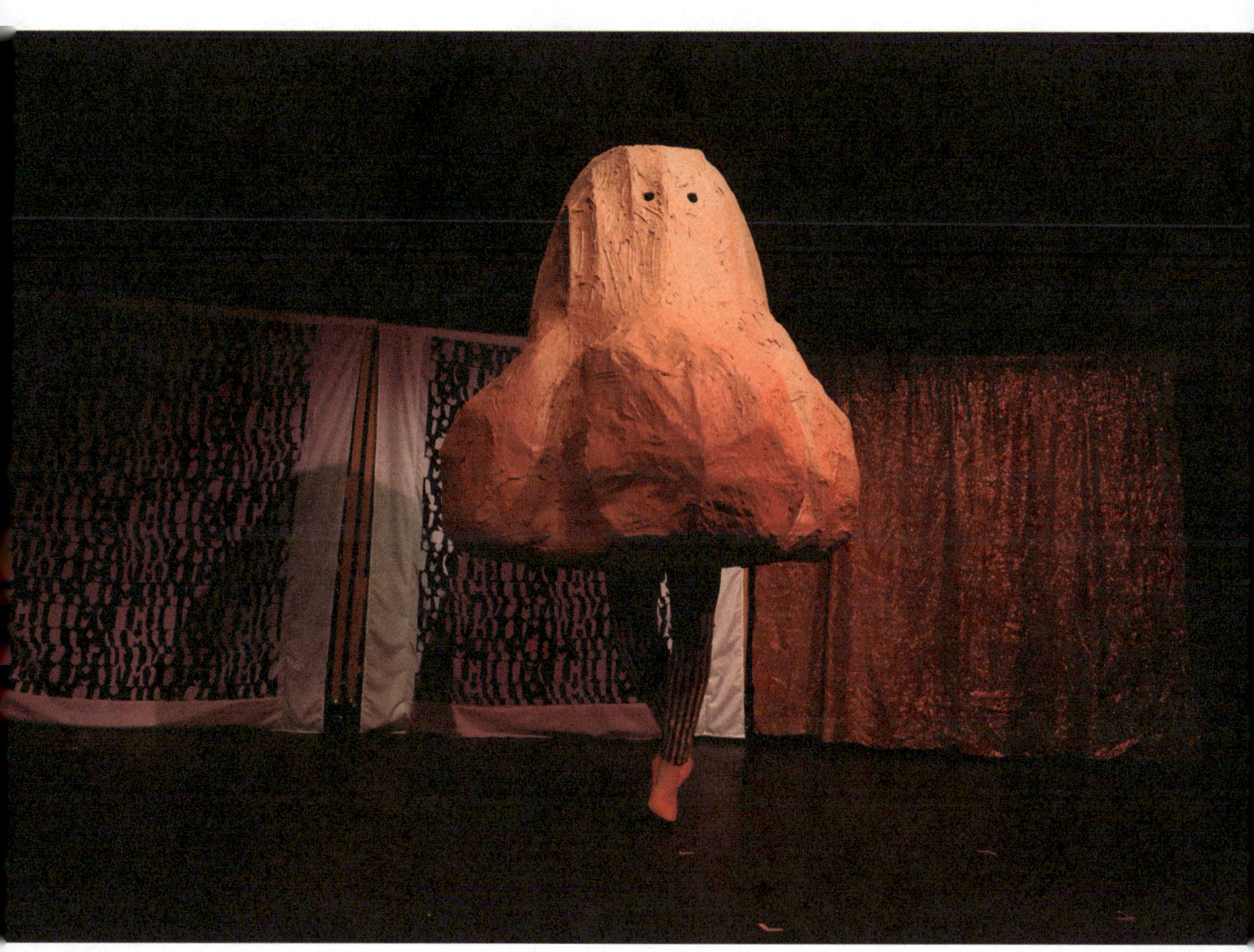

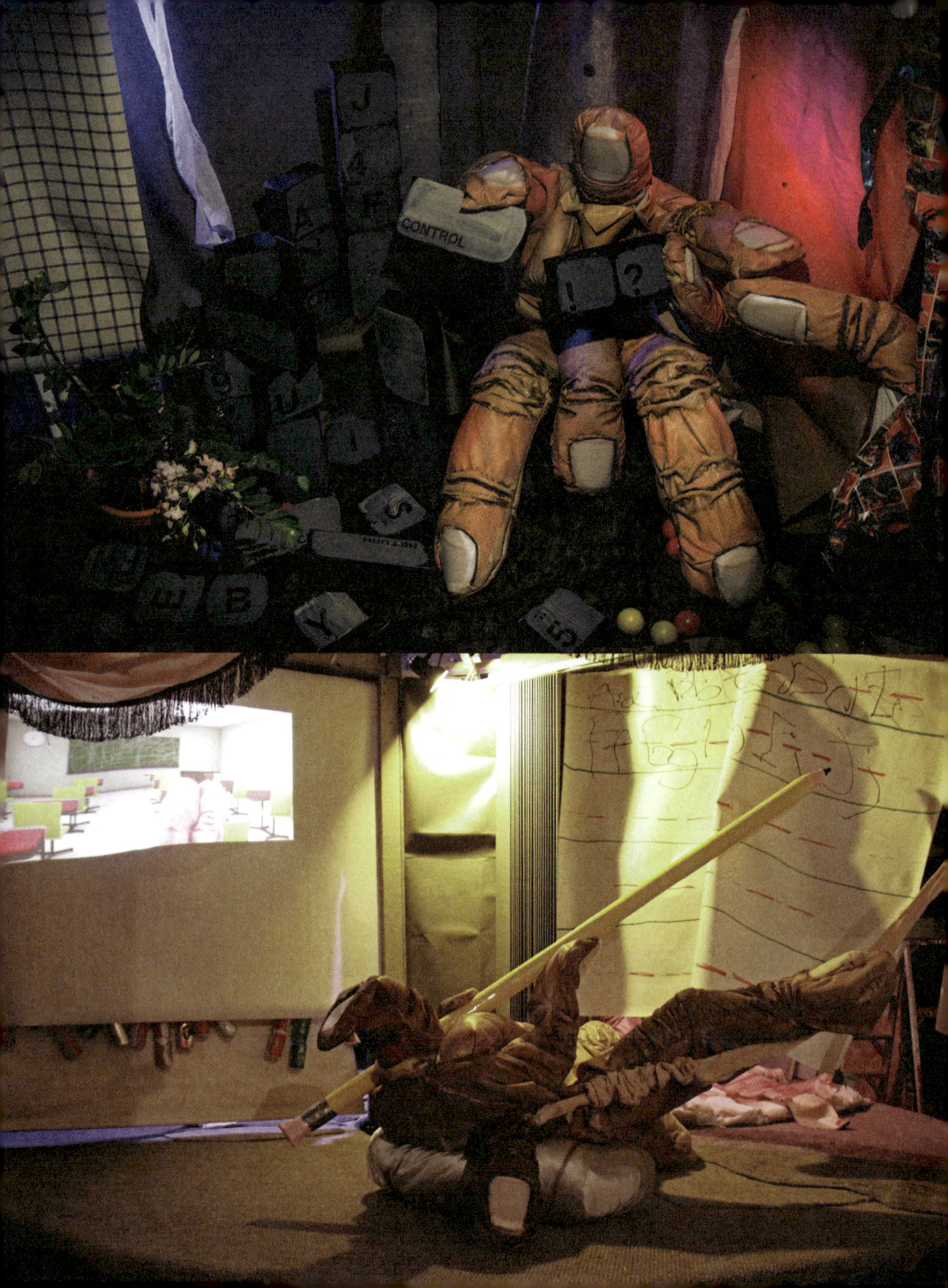
J
4
F
A
CONTROL
!
?
S
B
Y

Jon Kessler: Can you give us a brief description of your *HANDS OFF* performance?

Molly Lowe: *HANDS OFF* involved three performers completely hidden inside giant costumes that I had sewn and painted to resemble human hands, each with five puffy digits. The set was a circular revolving stage, like a carousel, separated into three differently painted and collaged segments, with each hand "inhabiting" one of them. In this unconventional and confined space, each hand was attached with a harness to its section, and each went through various motions, pulling at the painted backdrop behind it, that might be several layers deep, tearing down or peeling back segments as the stage turned. Each hand moved about like a zombie inside its own segment, which also included a video projection on the low walls separating each segment from the other. The scenes were based on repetitive hand motions—such as pressing, tapping, swiping—that we all go through endlessly every day, as we engage directly and addictively with technology. It was a kind of magnification of these unconscious activities.

At the end of the performance, which involved the giant hands going through the same hamster-wheel-like motions, the hands destroyed the walls between them in an attempt to "only connect." Freed from the set, they piled up in a heap, one on top of the other, becoming interconnected at last, but only briefly. In the final scene they retreated to their separate corners, where they curled up in the debris of their own destroyed environments.

JK: So, after this integration, they actually went back into their own separate, technological worlds?

ML: Right, the three giant hands are completely broken and useless after all their interaction with technology.

JK: The audience sat 360 degrees around the stage. Was it important for the viewers to be seated and passive while the actions were playing out in front of them?

ML: Yes, I wanted to create a performance that felt like surfing the Internet … an exquisite corpse carousel, an Internet rabbit hole.

JK: Was the timing of the piece based on the actors dismantling the set so that the audience would eventually see all the segments at once?

ML: Depending on where you sat, you had a different experience. The scenes unfolded for everyone in a different order and way. You could usually hear the sounds from another scene, which were comprised of abstracted vocals and music. But yes, in the end, the whole set was visible.

JK: The destructive element really struck me, and how you created potential for porous events to happen through those walls. How did that work into the bigger ideas of the project?

ML: At every rehearsal and performance the whole set got torn to shreds and built back up again. I had to repaint and remake all the backdrops every time! It was handmade. It seemed that the signature "hand touch" was essential, in contrast to our high tech world. The stage itself was on the verge of completely breaking down and falling over on many occasions, which certainly was destabilizing for the audience, especially for those in the first row. Goodbye fourth wall!

Also, tearing down the walls in between them was the only way for the hands to recognize that they were in on this together.

JK: How do those haptic movements in *HANDS OFF* relate to culture at large?

ML: I see a lot of humor in how transfixed we are by screens and I wanted to shift that hyper focus away from the virtual digital interface, back into the physical, hands-on, handmade world. Performance is really hot in a special way now, because it's unmediated. So in going live I made an over-the-top, wild/messy/magic spectacle of a show about the extraordinary-now-mundane technologies we use to do very ordinary human things.

Our hands are the most agile tools of our bodies. But in comparison to the sleek efficiency of screens, they seem clumsy, fumbly, flawed.

The hand costumes impaired the actors' movements drastically; they served as reminders that being human is being imperfect. Our technology is a constant reflection of that.

JK: Let's talk about your inspirations for *HANDS OFF*. I thought of two important theaters in the round. The first was the pavilion Disney designed for General Electric for the 1964 World's Fair, where the history of electricity was played out by animatronic figures as the audience rotated around it. The second is Christoph Schlingenshief's video theater work, *Animatograph* (2005), where viewers were invited to walk into the immersive theatrical installation. Both of these were brilliant *gesamtkunstwerks*, where the audience is heavily involved. That seems to be an interest of yours as well?

ML: Yes, coming from a video, costume, installation, and sculptural background, a *gesamtkunstwerk* seemed like the only way to do this. I was also interested in obstacle course TV shows like *Double Dare*, multiple-narrative movies like *Magnolia*, artists like you, Jon, also Mike Kelley and Paul McCarthy. I was even inspired by the fantasy world of children's theater and puppetry, specifically Mummenschanz.

JK: The thing with Paul McCarthy or even Mike Kelley is that even when they dressed up like Heidi and her grandfather, they're still figures, images in a video. Not yours. You sent us through a microscope so that we're actually looking at something really close up—the figure becomes very abstract, the scale of the hand disorients us to the point of disconnecting us from the human figure. There were certain points where it became very hard to find the human figure within the hand costumes.

ML: Yes, that's good, because they were meant to look like hands in action, but the soul of the piece, the grounding element, is that there really was a human inside. It's way more terrifying than a puppet or animation, it gives the viewer an empathetic porthole. Some poor human being is actually trapped inside that hand—perhaps that's a condition we can relate to.

JK: It is interesting seeing these bodies become hands, and that in this world the hands are the only thing available to express ourselves online or to access the virtual world. One could imagine a time when our bodies become totally useless—only there to keep our hands alive.

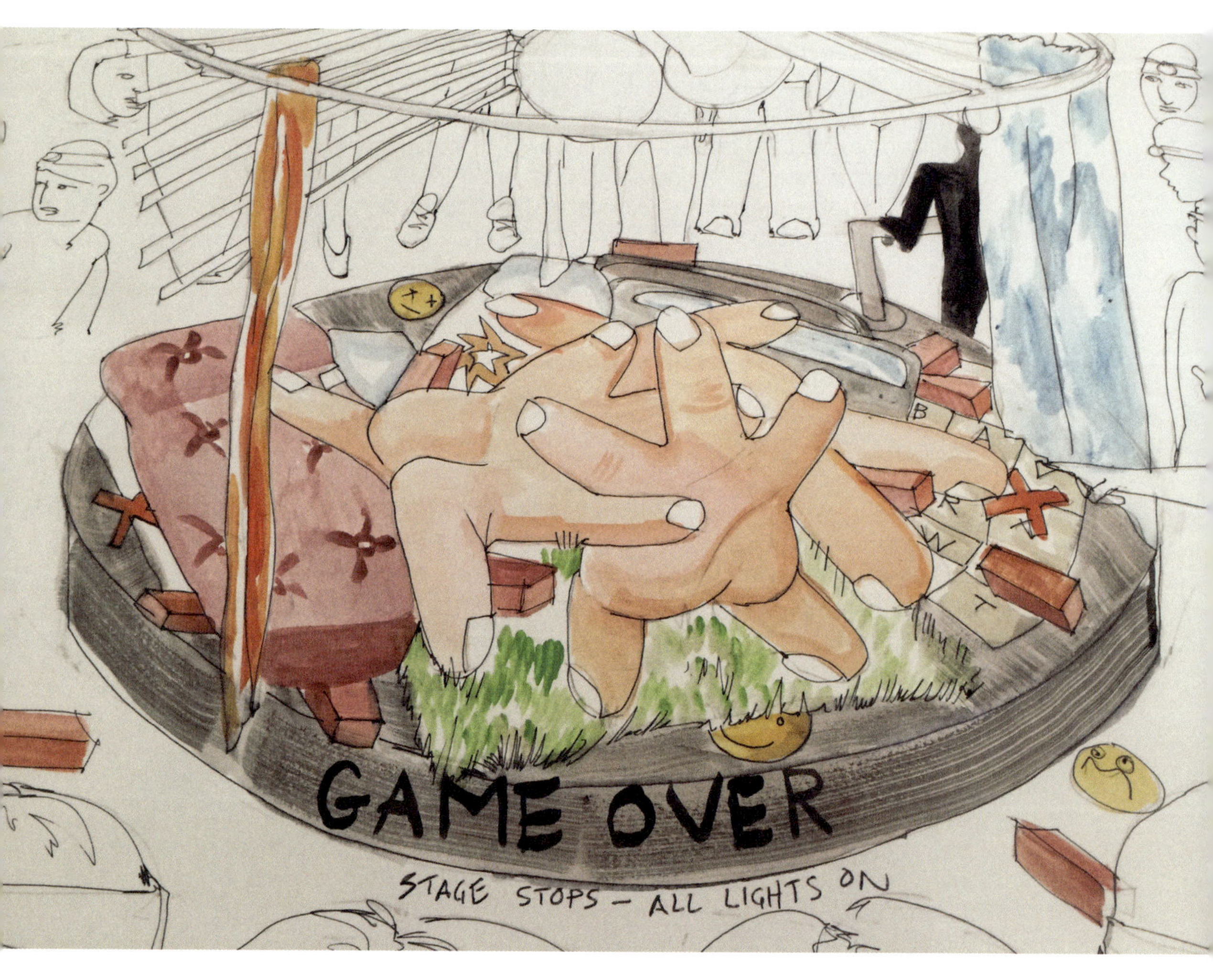

(Left) Molly Lowe, artist rendering of *HANDS OFF*, (2013).

(Right) Molly Lowe, *HANDS OFF* (2013), performance view, courtesy of Molly Lowe.

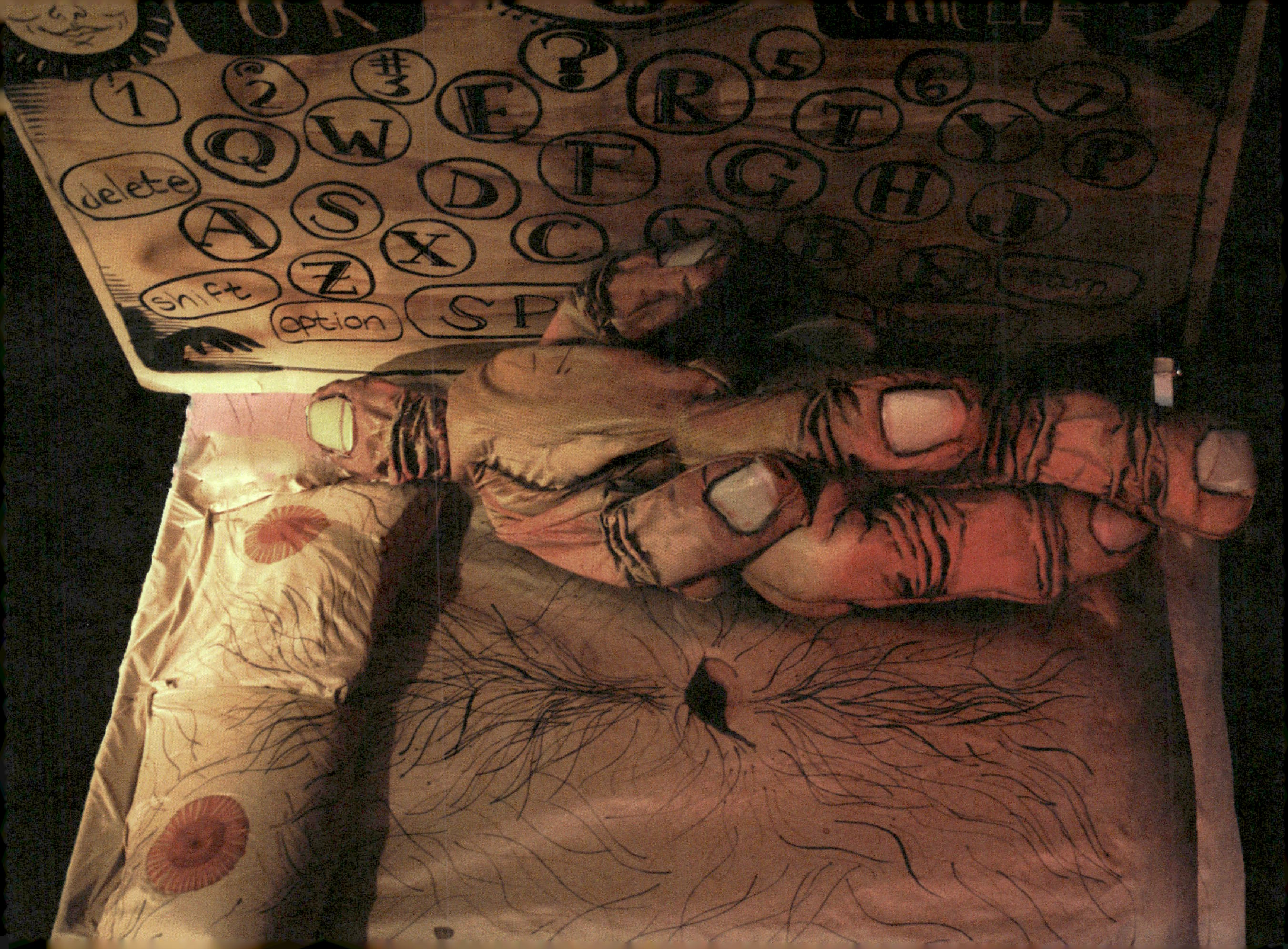

1
2
#3
?
R
5
6
7
Q
W
E
T
Y
P
delete
D
F
G
H
J
A
S
X
C
V
B
Z
shift
option
SP
return

ML: That was the idea, to reduce the whole figure to our fingertips, because that seems like where all the power is now. It's not even about eye contact or body language any more. It's about what buttons you're touching, what screens you're swiping. I wanted to make this entire performance as visceral, absurd, dark, and twisted as possible, to shock people into an awareness of their bodies and the environments they inhabit.

JK: Can you talk about your connection to Surrealism?

ML: I believe in the power of dreams and play, but at the same time I care about real life issues within my work. Stream of consciousness is the most honest, generative, and natural way for me to tap into my own perspective. I let my thoughts run completely wild, and then wrangle them together later based on …

JK: … juxtapositions that are suggestive, or ring true?

ML: Exactly, sometimes I have to mentally hang upside down, or imagine I'm some sort of alien anthropologist and make my observations from that place. When you are disoriented you rely on instincts to connect the dots. It can be very telling. I think a lot of people in this day and age would like to be mindful and perceptive but are often drowning in overstimulation, distracted and scattered. It's a reality now. I wanted the structure of the stage to reflect that.

Photo by Paula Court

Molly Lowe, *HANDS OFF* (2013), performance view.

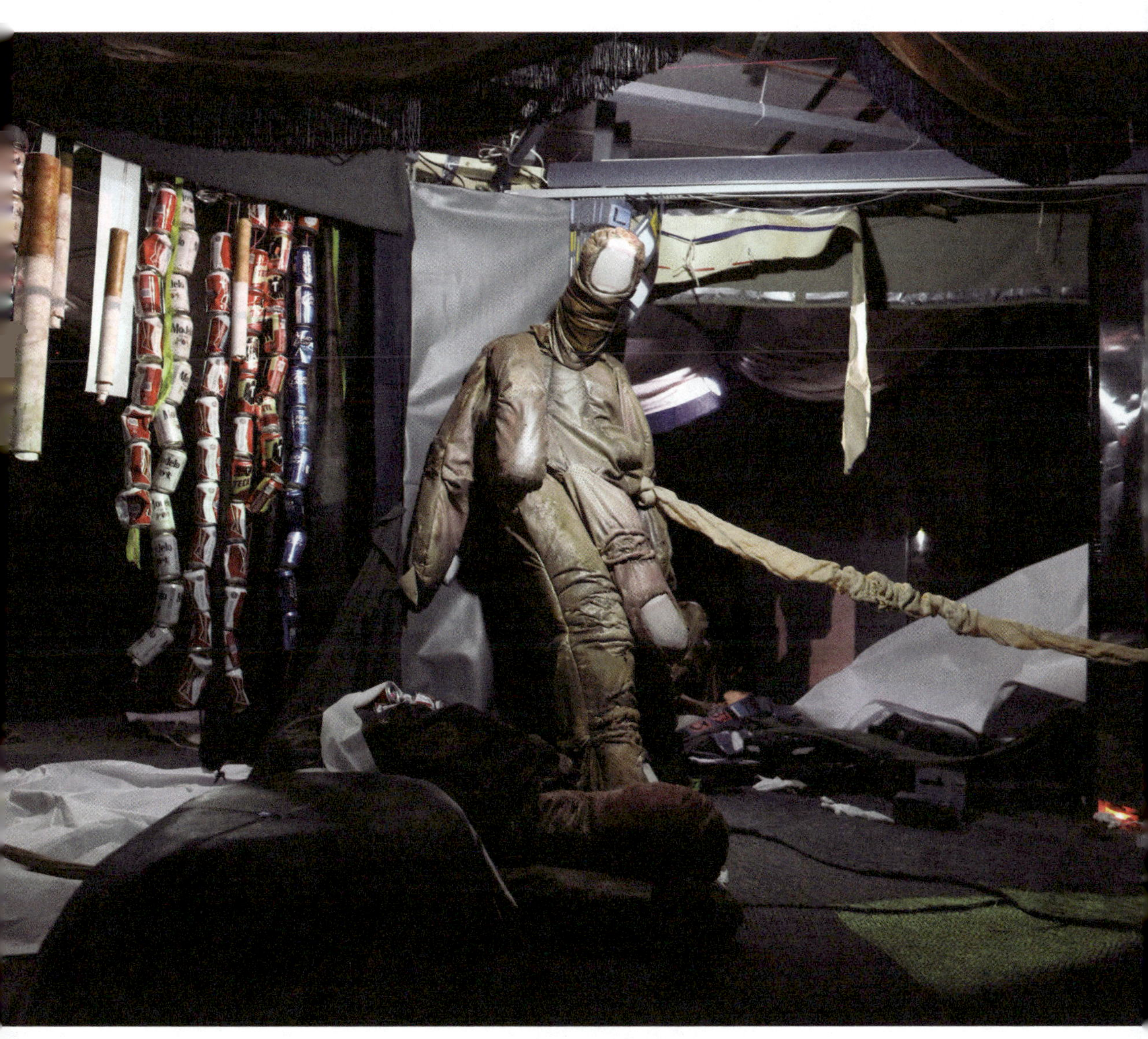

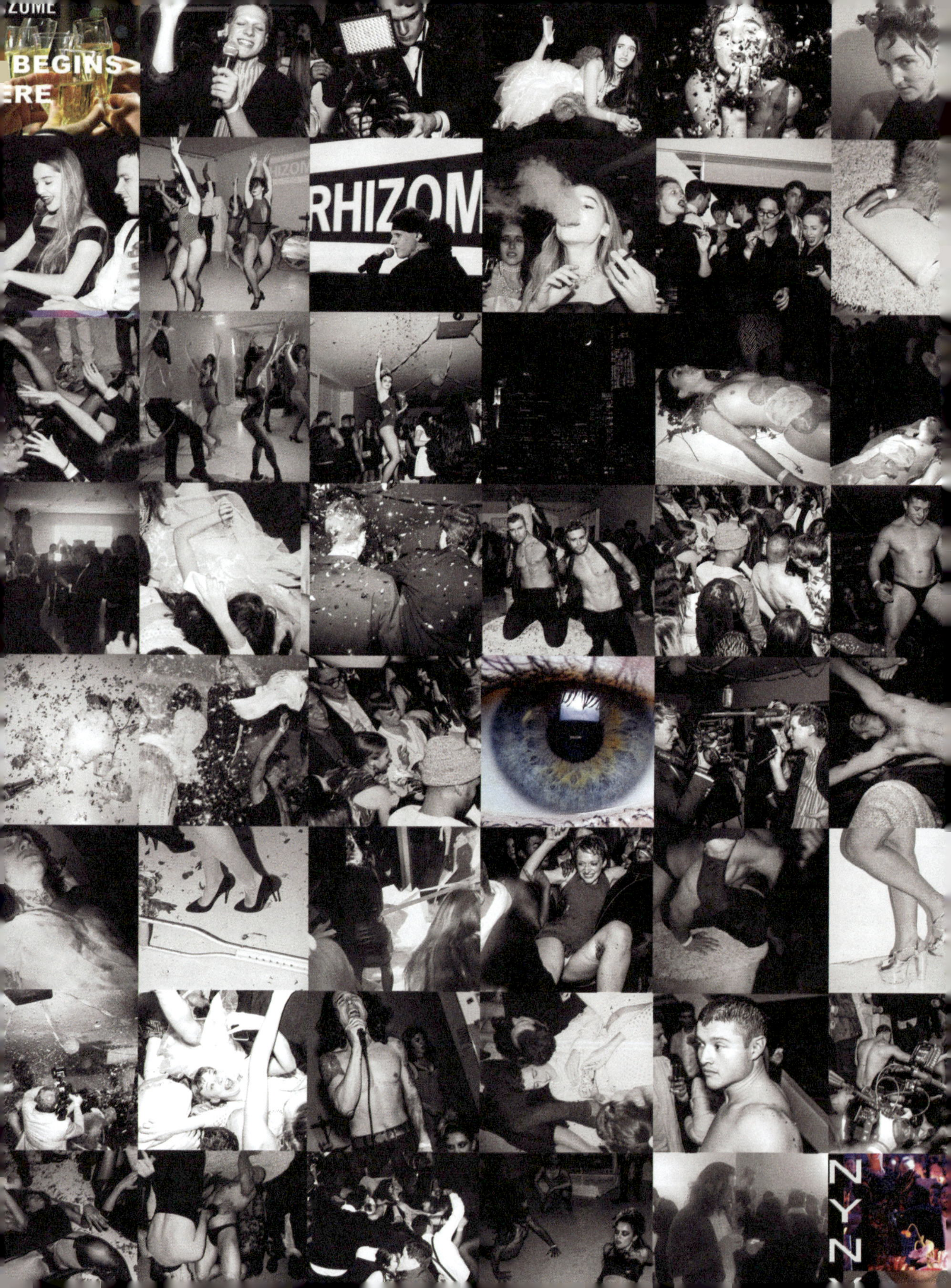
ZUME
BEGINS
ERE
RHIZOM
RHIZOM
NYN

ED FORNIELES

NY NY HP HP

"LARP can change the world." So wrote a Norwegian government official of "Live Action Role-Playing" (LARP), a kind of participatory performance that is partly scripted and partly generated by its participants. As such, it may be used for fantasy role-playing (à la Dungeons & Dragons) to model new outcomes for drawn-from-life situations, or even by business and policy makers (such as the aforementioned official), who recognize the potential of allowing groups to explore different perspectives without real-world consequences.

Ed Fornieles's work has more in common with drawn-from-life LARP than it does with fantasy LARP, but in the context of his work to date, the suggestion that "LARP can change the world" takes on a darker cast. As critic Brian Droitcour noted of an earlier Fornieles LARP, the "familiarity and proximity of the resulting simulations can be discomfiting."

Like his previous work, *Dreamy Awards* (2012), for the Serpentine Gallery, London, Ed Fornieles's *NY NY HP HP* took the form of a live-action role-playing experience. Whereas the former project took on the so-called "creative industries," *NY NY HP HP* was set in a heightened version of an already hyped New York art world event, "the charity gala." With Rhizome and its host organization, the New Museum, Fornieles's performance would be a real charity gala with all its trappings: a host committee, cocktails, entertainment, and dress code, to be held in the museum's Sky Room with its sweeping downtown views.

NY NY HP HP began several weeks before the event when Fornieles took over Rhizome's Instagram account, announcing the time, date, and title of the event. He then posted triumphal image macros that celebrated glamour, the future, and technology in ways intended to attract guests to the gala. Rhizome was central to *NY NY HP HP*, playing an amplified version of itself as an art and technology organization floating uncritically in the ether between the tech bubble and the New York cultural elite. The gala was also a legitimate fundraiser, with all proceeds going to Rhizome.

The evening began at 8 pm with a large crowd arriving at the New Museum, all of whom had been called by telephone beforehand and briefed about the activities that would take place. Many attendees were specially invited performers: dancers, twerkers, models, male strippers, a healer, musicians, and an emcee, who had additionally attended rehearsals, although there was no way to distinguish those "working" from the rest of the approximately 250 guests. Performers and ticket-buyers alike were given prompts by Fornieles such as, "take a right-wing view on issues, be critical of the left," as well as key words to guide their behavior, all of which evoked a hyper-extroverted or sociopathic way of behaving.

Certain scripted moments were mapped out on a spreadsheet, including "21:20: buffet bodies" (a nod to when Samantha in *Sex and the City* covered herself in sushi, or to a Surrealist dinner organized by Meret Oppenheim in 1959), when a man and a woman, lying on tables with their flesh covered in lunch meats, were carried into the space and placed on a larger table.

Despite these instructions, *NY NY HP HP* was not a controlled event. "Loss of control is an important element of the work," Fornieles said. "The performance becomes a structured platform that is inhabited. It's not a group of people to be directed." As the evening progressed, the festivities devolved into an exaggerated and at times grotesque bacchanal as the actions became increasingly physical with undercurrents of sex and violence.

This came to a head at 22:40 when the emcee announced STRIP, at which point participants followed instructions to forcibly undress male and female volunteers in an equal-opportunity sexual violence LARP. This was followed at 22:50 by ORGY, with a song that called everyone to the center of the floor, to make out with whomever was closest. A scrum soon formed, with people pushing and pulling, ripping down the ceiling decorations and knocking over tables as they went.

The ethics of *NY NY HP HP*, like its aesthetics, were ready made. In all his decisions for the project, Fornieles adopted what he believed to be the ethics of the project's milieu, the world where art and tech meet high society in an over-the-top gala. By "accelerating" all aspects of the event, he held to the notion of "accelerationism" as advocated by

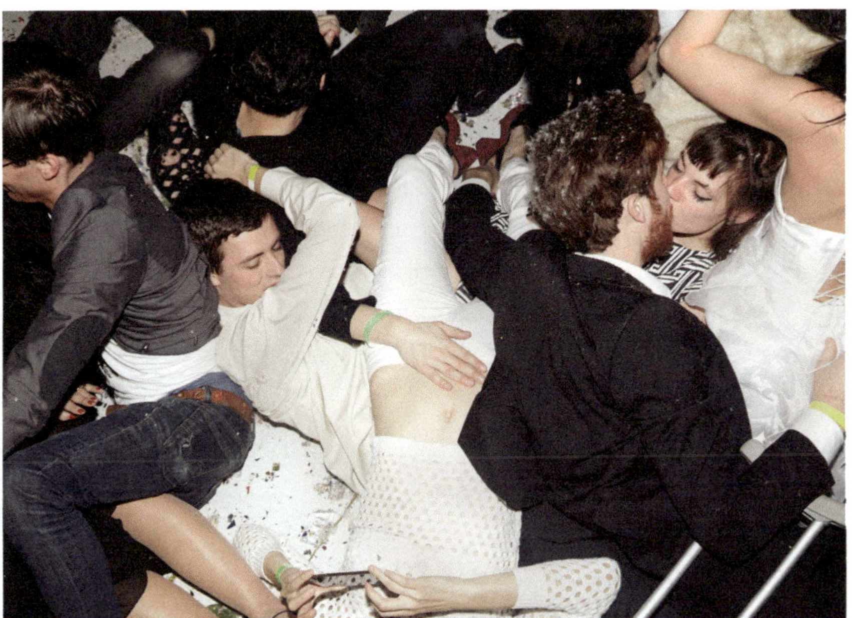

British philosopher Nick Land and others, which proposes that the only possibility for radical social change is through capitalism itself. In other words, the goal is to intensify the internal contradictions of the capitalist system, in order to bring about its collapse and possible rebirth. So *NY NY HP HP* intensified the typical gala's evocation of power and desire, until desire became a goal in itself.

The subject matter of *NY NY HP HP* is easy enough to critique—the gala, the tech industry, and the attention economy all have their problems. The participatory aspect of *NY NY HP HP* gave those in attendance an opportunity not just to make the issues inherent to these contexts visible, but to role-play their acceleration and destruction. For many, this pointed to the hollowness of the radical or redemptive promise of "collapse" that's at the heart of accelerationism, and this was perhaps the point. If *NY NY HP HP* revealed desires, impulses, and forces that are normally unacknowledged yet underpin social interactions, it showed these to be not so much a lurking instability within the capitalist system as the raw material that makes it hum.

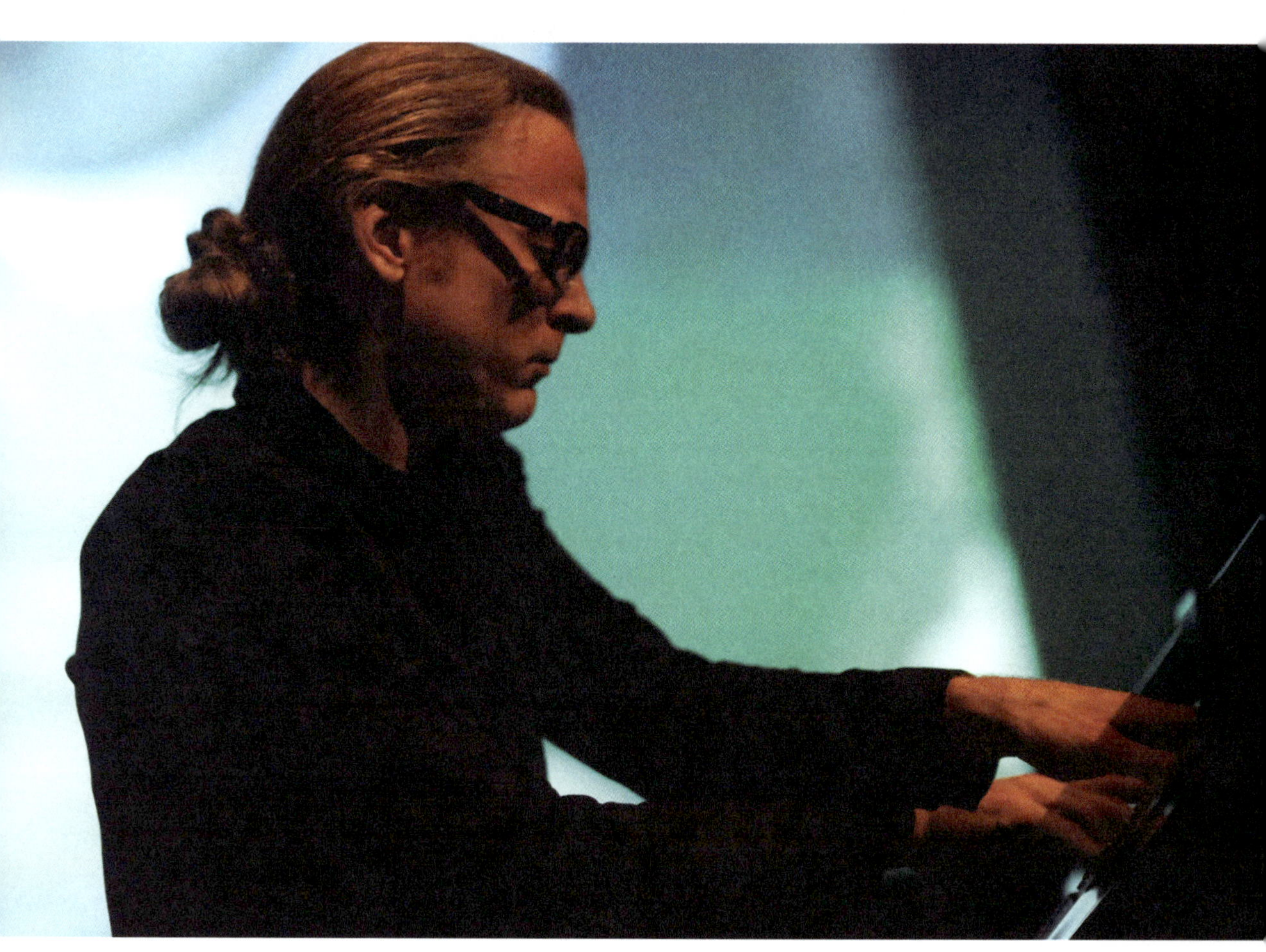

PETE DRUNGLE

DREAM SEQUENCES FOR SOLO PIANO

Luis Buñuel—the Spanish-born filmmaker who died in 1983 in Mexico, but had mostly lived and worked in France—once said, "If someone were to tell me I had twenty years left, and ask me how I'd like to spend them, I'd reply: 'Give me two hours a day of activity, and I'll take the other twenty-two in dreams.'" Composer and pianist Pete Drungle, a longtime admirer of how Buñuel's films dove into the unconscious, was inspired to create a compendium of sequences drawn from them to be used as the point of departure for a "total performance" unlike anything Drungle had done before.

Performa has a long history with Drungle, beginning with Performa 07, when he presented *24-Hour Continuous Solo Piano Improvisation* at SculptureCenter, using the gallery setting to transform a piano concert into a work of durational performance art. He improvised without pause for twenty-four hours, except for three short breaks (totaling twelve minutes) during which he left a vibrator on the strings inside the piano, sustaining a drone so that the continuity of the sound was never broken. By the end of the performance, his fingers were bleeding and he could no longer feel his arms or hands. For Performa 09, Drungle provided live scores for a collection of rare Italian Futurist films and collaborated with video and performance artist Lilibeth Cuenca Rasmussen on her feminist-architecture-inspired one-woman show. And for Performa 11, he composed the music for Alterazioni Video's short film *Blind Barber* and, as part of an installation by visual artist Marianne Vitale, performed in a room full of dead fish.

Why does Drungle gravitate so frequently to the art world? It is because, despite the fact that he is an incredible craftsman—classically trained, he likes to play piano for eight hours a day—he approaches music with the conceptual rigor of a visual artist and a constant awareness of how context shapes what we see and hear. With *Dream Sequences for Solo Piano*, Drungle sought to subvert the traditional mode of music accompanying a movie, and instead create a concert where it felt like the film images were accompanying him. He also, as he explained in his initial proposal to Performa, wanted to blur the line between composition and improvisation, with certain musical themes developed in advance, but the way in which they would come together not predetermined at all. "Improvisation is composition, except that the process is vastly sped up," Drungle once said. "I find that the more I improvise, the better I can compose; and the reverse is equally true."

It might be said that Buñuel, too, loved exploring the boundaries between the purely intuitive and the meticulously staged. As part of the larger Surrealist movement, whose members he met regularly in Parisian cafés in the late-1920s, Buñuel began making films because they were a way to explore the more irrational and intuitive forms of expression that Surrealism was interested in. His work ranged from lavish, name-cast productions skewering the lives of the bourgeoisie to low-budget quasi-documentaries exposing the realities of rural poverty—and throughout all of these were dreams. His first film, *Un Chien Andalou* (1928), resulted from comparing notes on dreams with Salvador Dali—the famous imagery of slicing an eyeball and a hand covered in ants comes directly out of their own visions one night—and many of Buñuel's later films attempt to reconstruct other dreams of his, presenting them for audiences exactly as they were, without efforts to decode them. The dream sequences in Buñuel's films, as a result, don't serve a clear narrative function like they do in classical Hollywood films. Instead they are complex, ambiguous, and unsettling to the core.

For Drungle, Buñuel's dream sequences were not only a tool for deepening his own exploration of the unconscious as a musician, they also presented him with an entirely new challenge, of creating the visual accompaniment for his own concert, and to that end he carefully designed the lighting and stage set-up to support it. Working with Austin-based filmmaker Toby Rymkus, Drungle edited selections from Buñuel's dream sequences with an imaginative, kinetic eye, sometimes cutting back and forth between different dreams from different films, and at one point even creating a Ken Jacobs-like strobe effect during the climax of the forty-five-minute montage. He decided to place the piano in the well-lit foreground of the stage, to visually emphasize that the images were accompanying a concert instead of the other way around. And he used saturated colors in the lighting to draw the mood of each dream sequence out into the larger space—dark greens with spots of gold enhanced a sequence set in a forest, for example, and a deep fuchsia blush rose when Catherine Deneuve woke up in bed, slowly opening her eyes.

On the night of the performance (in the recently renovated Roulette in downtown Brooklyn), Drungle's playing—on a stunning nine-foot Steinway grand—moved through dozens of different recognizable modes, frequently evoking the style of silent film scores. Above him, in the film, were some of the most famous images from Buñuel's work—a bearded man prays on top of a stone column, raising his hands to the sky (*Simón del desierto*, (1965)), a beautiful woman stands tied up in a pristine white gown while men throw mud at her (*Belle de Jour*, (1967)), and a man desperately throws objects out of an apartment window: a pine tree on fire, a stuffed giraffe, and armfuls of downy white feathers (*L'Age d'Or*, (1930)). During one section of abstract geometric shapes, Drungle played only the strings inside the body of the piano, creating an intricate, percussive composition, and during another scene depicting a proper young woman (whose clothes would soon disappear) playing piano, Drungle cleverly riffed on the kind of song an affluent parlor guest might have performed in the 1920s. Drungle's playing not only enhanced the drama and emotion of what we saw on screen, it also had the cohesive effect of weaving all of these images together into a single series of events—a meta-dream sequence that felt even more dizzying than the originals.

By the time of the virtuosic finale, Drungle was pouring with sweat, his hands flying over the keys. As soon as the performance ended, Drungle, backstage, said after his exertions he had absolutely no memory of what had just unfolded. It was almost like a dream.

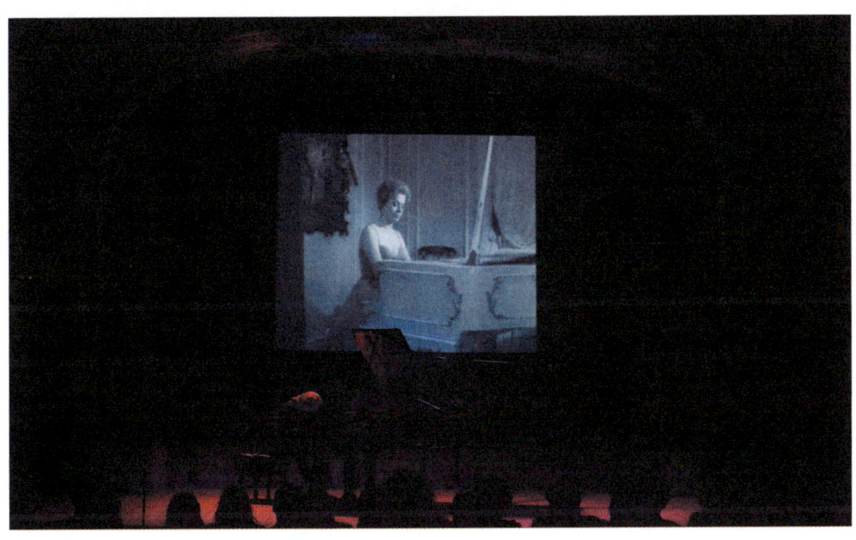

Pete Drunglee, *Dream Sequence for Solo Piano* (2013), performance view.

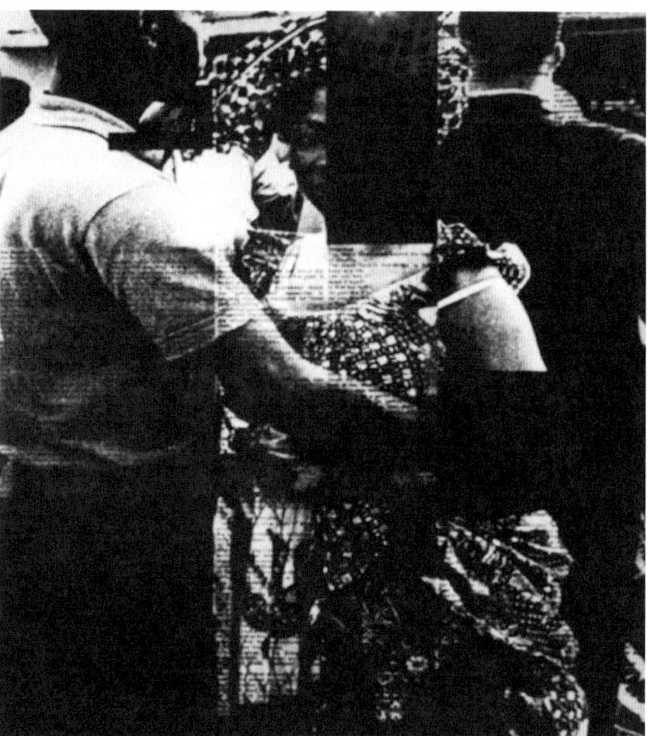
LÉGITIME
DÉFENSE

Textes de :
étienne léro
rené ménil
jules-marcel monnerot
maurice-sabas quitman
simone yoyotte

GET READY FOR THE MARVELOUS

BLACK SURREALISM IN DAKAR, FORT-DE-FRANCE, HAVANA, JOHANNESBURG, NEW YORK CITY, PARIS, PORT-AU-PRINCE, 1932–2013

Get Ready for the Marvelous, a groundbreaking conference exploring historical Surrealism in the African diaspora and its relevance to contemporary art, was presented by the Performa Institute on February 8-9, 2013, at New York University's Steinhardt School of Culture, Education and Human Development in the Einstein Auditorium. Undeterred, over 400 attendees were present to hear elaborations by a group of international black artists who were directly or tangentially involved in Surrealism, engaging with it as an ideology, an artistic movement, and a state of mind—a way of being in the world—and their influence on contemporary art and culture throughout the African diaspora between 1932 and 2013.

As Performa's first entirely self-organized conference, *Get Ready for the Marvelous* was pivotal to the curatorial work and program-planning for Performa 13's historical anchor—Surrealism. Necessarily ambitious, the program explicated and traced black artists' involvement in historical Surrealism and their impact on those creating art today, providing a resonant understanding of the movement in all its complexity. Since its inception in Paris in the mid-1920s, Surrealism expanded through the years to incorporate a range of cultural figures as a truly transdisciplinary movement, including painting, sculpture, poetry, prose, film, theater, dance, and music. Surrealism extended geographically to New York City, Latin America, and the African Diaspora. Despite "the vast critical literature on Surrealism," as historians Robin D.G. Kelley and Franklin Rosemont noted in their introduction to *Black, Brown and Beige: Surrealist Writings from Africa and the Diaspora* (2010), "all but a few black Surrealists have been invisible … Occasional token mentions aside, people of color—and more particularly those from Africa or the Diaspora—have been excluded from most of the so-called standard works on the subject."

The conference title was inspired by Suzanne Césaire's poetic description: "Surrealism is permanent readiness for the Marvelous." It was also informed by Marxist theorist Antonio Gramsci's *The Prison Notebooks* (1929-35), in which he wrote, "The starting-point of critical

NYU STEINHARDT SCHOOL OF CULTURE, EDUCATION AND HUMAN DEVELOPMENT ◉ ORGANIZED BY ADRIENNE EDWARDS

elaboration is the consciousness of what one really is, and is 'knowing thyself' as a product of the historical processes to date, which has deposited in you an infinity of traces, without leaving an inventory." Accordingly, those convening illuminated the complex heterogeneity of historical Surrealism, its circuits of artistic and political exchange in Africa, the Caribbean, Europe, and the United States, and its accumulations as manifested in interdisciplinary art created in relation to ideas of the sublime, the miraculous, the supernatural, the surprising, and the wondrous as expressed in political and socially oriented works by black contemporary artists.

On the first day, Kelley delivered a rousing keynote address titled "Blues People and the Poetic Sprit: Recovering Surrealism's Revolutionary Politics" in which he asked vitally important questions, establishing a context that permeated the entire proceedings, such as: "What is behind the impulse to rediscover, resurrect, and embrace Surrealism as an expression of an Afro-diasporic imagination? How do we reconcile the notion of 'Black Surrealism' as a revolutionary movement with the prevailing criticism that Surrealism is a retreat from real-world political struggle, a kind of dreamscape in which emancipation is limited to the word, line, form, and prison-house of identity?" Kelley redirected Surrealism through writers such as Jayne Cortez, Richard Wright, and Adrienne Kennedy, added blues and jazz music to the aesthetic purview, and cast aside key words such as "marvelous" and "magical" for "freedom" and "revolution," while tracing Surrealism through Negritude and Marxism.

Artist Adam Pendleton was commissioned to write and perform a text in honor of playwright Adrienne Kennedy. Following the prelude of celebrated signer Marian Anderson's recording "Trampin'," Pendleton combined excerpts of Kennedy's prose, drawn from her plays *Funny House of the Negro, A Movie Star Has to Star in Black and White, The Owl Answers,* and *Rat's Mass,* and her autobiography, *The People Who Led to my Plays,* in the non-linear fashion for which Pendleton's and her art are known, enabling the language to beautifully speak to many selves, times, and places.

For the panel "Black Surrealist Beginnings: Dance, Theater and Visual Art," Theater and Africana Studies scholar Awam Ampka probed the multiple and off-center creative activities of black artists and thinkers living in Paris during historical Surrealism who resisted artistic and social conventions in his lecture "Tinkering with Time

Get Ready for the Marvelous (2013), panel discussion. With RoseLee Goldberg, Barbara Browning, Lowery Stokes Sims, and Awam Amkpa. Photo by Ian Douglas

and Place: Pan-Africanism and the Aesthetics of Fragmentation." Curator Lowery Stokes Sims spoke on "Wifredo Lam: Performing the Primitive in Primitivism," exploring the Afro-Chinese-Cuban artist's Surrealist aesthetics and the influence of African art on the work of André Breton and Pablo Picasso. Rounding out this introductory panel, performance studies scholar Barbara Browning delved into the desire and imagination of black American choreographers Katherine Dunham and Ralph Lemon as evinced in their distinct yet related ethnographic research approaches to Haitian dance. Concluding the first day's event was a film screening of Maya Deren's *Divine Horsemen: The Living Gods of Haiti* (1985), a documentary film about dance and possession in Haitian Vodoun compiled from footage Deren shot during her fieldwork on the island between 1947 and 1954.

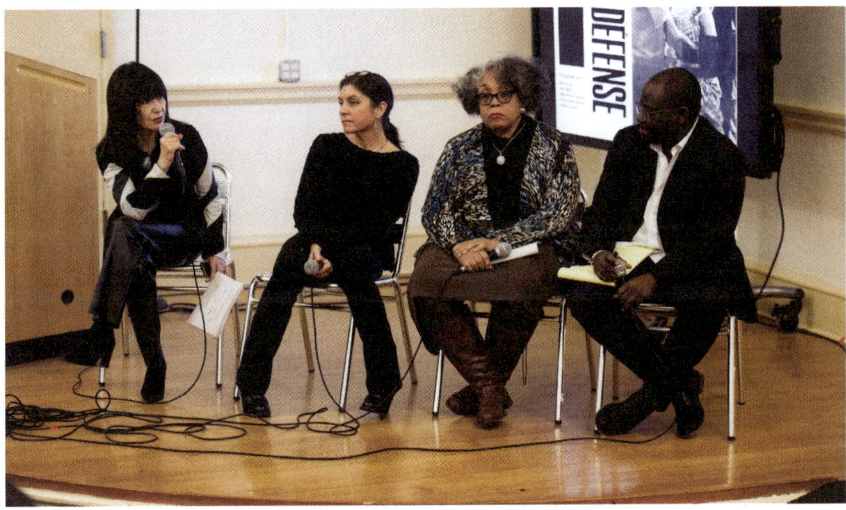

The second day began with a breakfast film program that paired one historical and one contemporary documentary film. William Greave's *The First World Festival of Negro Arts* (1967), the official record of the 1966 festival held in Dakar, Senegal, which included over two thousand writers, artists, and performers from throughout the African diaspora, including Duke Ellington, Langston Hughes, Alvin Ailey, Léopold Sédar Senghor, and Aimé Césaire, as well as other artists, performers, and dignitaries from thirty countries, was shown first. It was followed by Gilles Elie-dit-Cosaque's *Zétwal* (2008), which tells the Afrofuturist tale of local Martinican legend Robert Saint-Rose's attempt to propel himself to outer space through the poetry of Aimé Césaire.

Performance studies scholar Tavia Nyong'o illuminated the affinity between blackness and darkness within the Surrealist dream-image in a three-part talk, "Dream, Collage, Lightning: Dark Future for Black Performance." Nyong'o interwove the interpenetration of dream worlds and capitalist subjectivity through the music of R&B star Frank Ocean and the photo-fictions of Afro-Brazilian Surrealist Washington Silvera, and tracked the figure of the woman within and beyond historical Surrealism in the collages of Wangechi Mutu. I followed with an in-depth "portrait" of Mutu, tracing the "ornamental feminist" qualities of her various bodies of work—drawings, collages, and performances—through the myriad complex references and concepts that inform them such as anthropology, auto-ethnography, post-colonial discourse, fetish, and women's immaterial labor.

Artist Paul D. Miller aka DJ Spooky joined celebrated film director Melvin Van Peebles in a conversation entitled "The Blood of a Poet: Poetry, Cinema, and Sampling." The amusing duo brought levity to the proceedings, inserting a sly sense of humor into the conference as they provided a multimedia stroll through their respective aesthetics and Surrealist dimensions.

The concluding conference program focused on contemporary manifestations of Surrealism by artists from the United States and South Africa in curating, music, and visual arts. Artist Simone Leigh evocatively analyzed how historical Surrealism's proclivity for ethnography and anthropology rendered its appropriated African-cultural references in particular as intriguingly exotic, more corporeal, and excessively sensual, as well as how these have impacted her installations, ceramic objects, and videos. Echoing Nyong'o's remarks, curator Gabi Ngcobo discussed the speculative venture that is the Center for Historical Reenactments, an enigmatic organization she founded based in Johannesburg that makes propositions about history, suggesting future possibilities for living and creating art. Musician and writer Greg Tate delivered the culminating talk with dazzling visuals and beats, linking the sensibilities of historical Surrealism as it came into being in the African diaspora to Afrofuturism, enveloping and bringing full circle the magical imagery of the film *Zétwal (2008)*, screened that morning to the sensational music of Sun Ra, and everything in between.

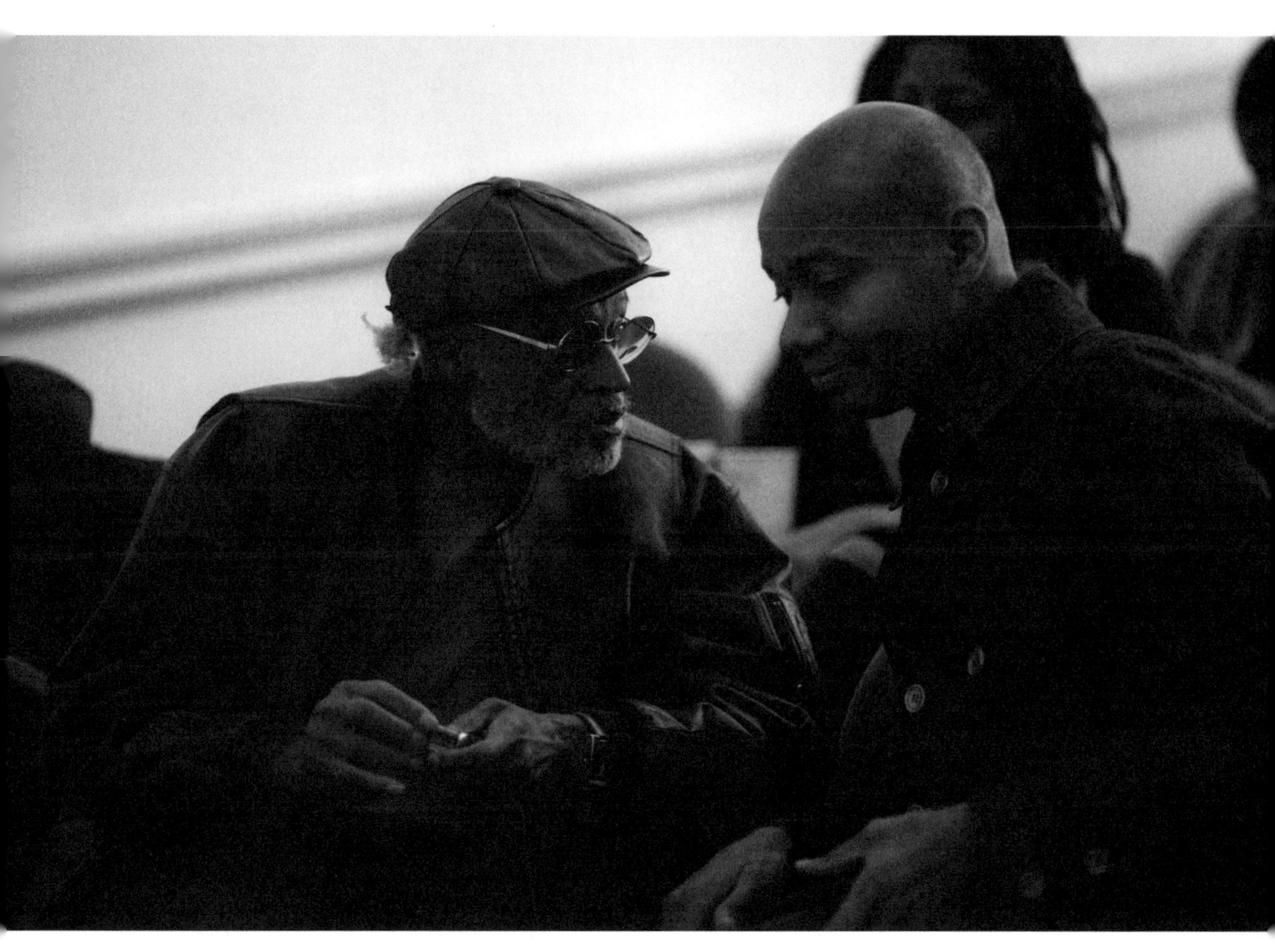

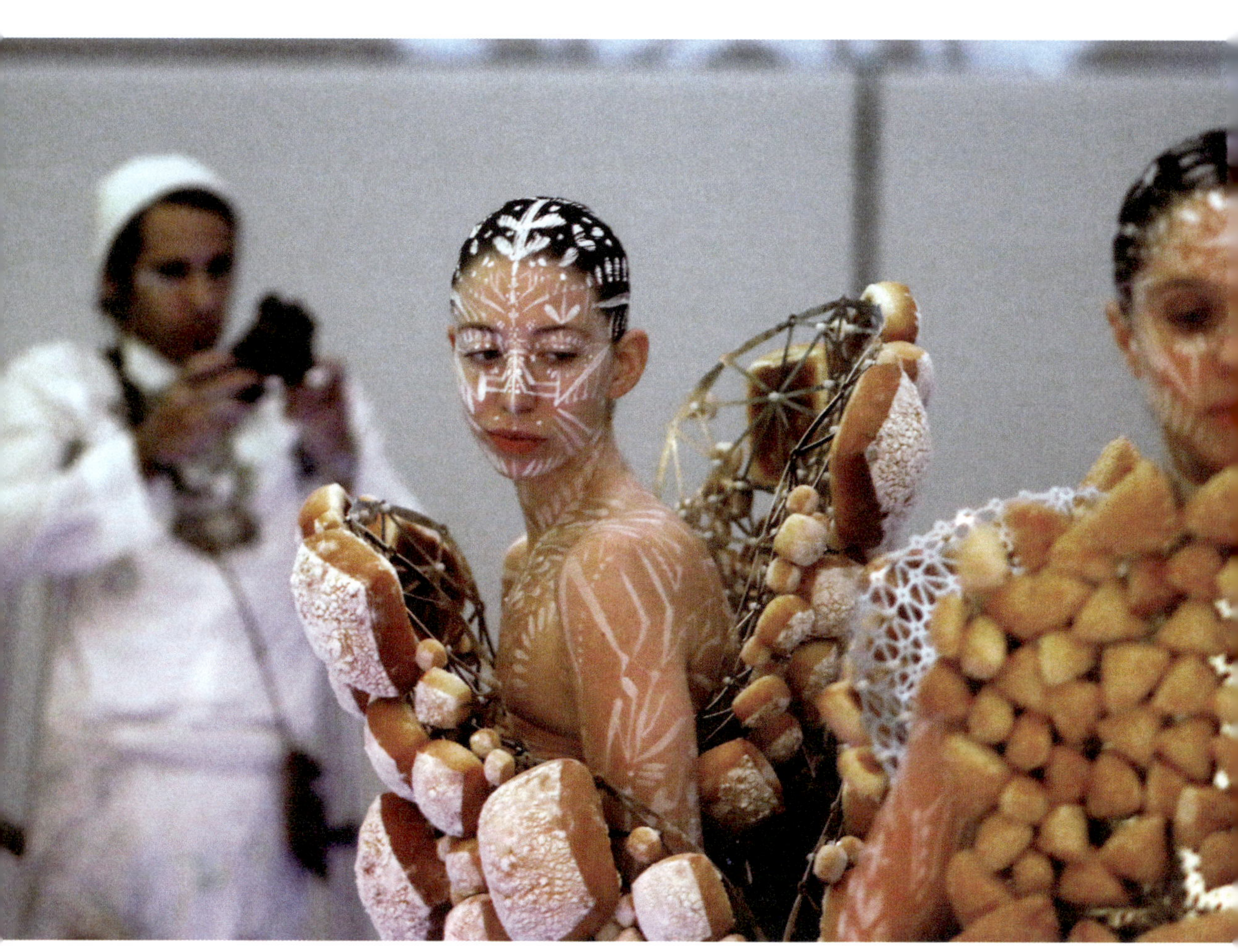

threeASFOUR

FEST

Fashion designers threeASFOUR (Gabi Asfour, Adi Gil, and Angela Donhauser, who joined forces in 1998) are known for challenging expectations in both fashion and design with complex and futuristic creations hand crafted in their downtown New York atelier. Combining ancient motifs with contemporary tailoring, threeASFOUR challenge expectations, for example by constructing accessories from musical instruments such as the "harp belt" worn by Björk on her *biophilia* album cover. Cognoscenti from the spheres of art, music, and media wear each season's small collection, which is based on concepts ranging from crop circles and world religions to cellular growth and architectural ornamentation.

Hailing from Israel, Lebanon, and Tajikistan, respectively, these three trained designers take inspiration from their own ethnic traditions as well as from other world cultures, clashing different ethnic patterns within one print and creating designs that effortlessly combine deconstruction with intricate tailoring. threeASFOUR, unlike many other designers, present their lines in museums and gallery spaces, exhibiting more in the context of art than commercial fashion, having collaborated with Yoko Ono, Matthew Barney, and Jessica Mitrani, among other artists. In one memorable instance, Ono created an abstract drawing that was made into a printed fabric from which the designers later recreated the artist's seminal *Cut Piece* (1964) using a dress that could be dis and reassembled.

Their Performa Project, *Fest*, incorporated traditional breadbreaking rituals constructed as wearable garments. An extension of the threesome's first New York solo museum exhibition, *Mer Ka Ba*, at the Jewish Museum, the exhibition and the performance, set in adjacent spaces, shared a fascination with ancient symbols and cutting edge technology. A handful of 3-D-printed dresses were shown in a sweeping futuristic infrastructure in one dimly lit gallery of the exhibition. At the back of this gallery a mirrored pyramidal structure, where visitors' reflections were refracted into infinity, became a more intimate space devoid of garments, creating an interactive engagement with the audience.

Fest, the performance, touched on the exhibition concept of *mer ka ba,* the union of body, mind, and soul. On the evening when *Fest* was performed, the audience entered the elegant wood-paneled second floor of the former Warburg mansion, where the smell of freshly baked bread permeated the space. Bread—a food common in some form to all cultures and nations—may be a metonym for the diverse backgrounds of threeASFOUR themselves, who spent months collaborating with local baker Uri Scheft near their Lower East Side studio, refining *Fest* into an edible fashion event. The design trio created an immersive environment where all five senses were stimulated. The room was arranged like a five-point star with a central space. This configuration was reminiscent of shapes found in Arabic patterns; if one connects the five points a circle is created.

Inside the circle three models wore dresses of "sacred" shapes—a circle, a square, and a triangle—into which baked creations, in scores of differently-sized rolls, had been intricately woven into the designers' signature elaborate patterns, reminiscent of the geometric shapes found in their designs and anchored on a light metal crinoline infrastructure. Each type of bread was accompanied by a garnish: the circle dress was covered in black Nigella seeds, the triangle dress with sesame seeds, and the square dress was dusted with fine white flour. The communal aspect of breaking bread directly from the dresses threeASFOUR had fashioned related to the concept of *mer ka ba,* literally joining the physical and spiritual realms.

Standing back-to-back, the three models formed the inner triangle of a large circle manned by five "spice boys," representing the five elements: fire, earth, ether, water, and air. They were dressed druid-style, with black hooded *djellabas* holding crystal bowls of condiments. Visitors were invited into the circle in groups of three to break bread from one of the dresses, dip it into one of the spices, and eat it. An electronic soundtrack by Brian Close and Justin Tripp played while abstract-patterned projections that resembled threeASFOUR prints, designed by Alex Czetwertynski, enveloped much of the room and ceiling, completing the notion of an all-senses culinary experience.

Fest began as an ordered, choreographed experience, which over more than two hours slowly devolved into something less so, as an enthusiastic audience closed in on the edible garments at its center.

As the bread dresses were gradually stripped, more of the models' bodies were exposed, giving the bread-eating audience the feeling of participating in an erotic, Dionysian rite. Indeed, the ancient and symbolic ritual of drinking wine that was served at an adjacent bar and breaking bread on this occasion became the simplest way to create a community.

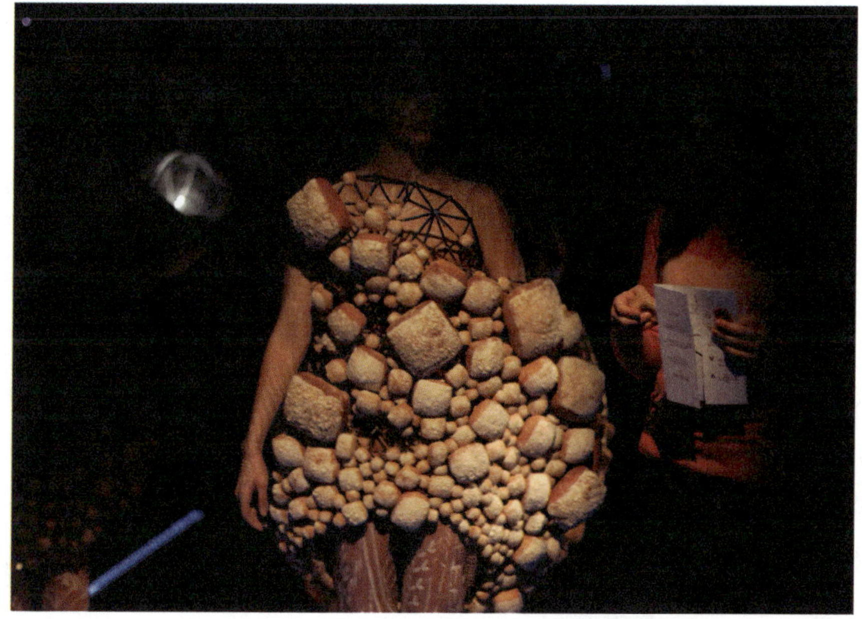

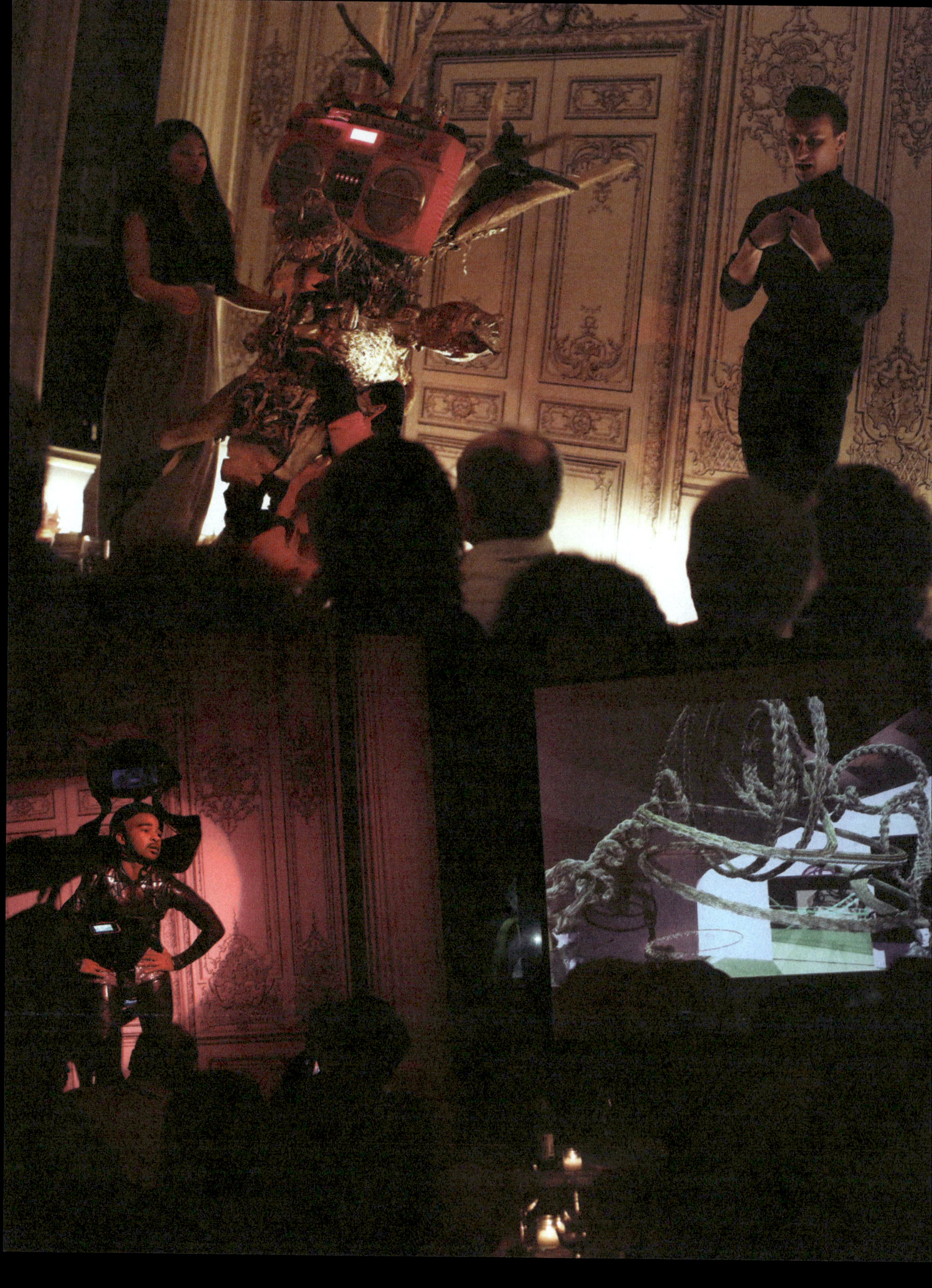

A SURREALIST CAFÉ

Playwright, filmmaker, novelist, poet, and reverent chess player, Paris-based Spanish illuminati Fernando Arrabal has over the past fifty years produced a singular *oeuvre* that defies categorization, utilizing humor, shock, and confrontation while embracing excess, irrationality, and the grotesque. Acquainted with René Magritte, Octavio Paz, Tristan Tzara, Andy Warhol, Allen Ginsberg, Milan Kundera, and Michel Houellebecq, Arrabal spent three years with the Surrealist group in Paris before joining forces in 1962 with Roland Topor and Alejandro Jodorowsky to form a dissident collective called "Panic Movement," in homage to the lascivious Greek God Pan.

Drawing inspiration from Arrabal's 1992 epic film *Farewell Babylon!*, in which a modern-day version of the character Nadja (from André Breton's eponymous 1928 novel set in Paris) traverses the streets of New York, placing her in the chaos of the city—a backdrop for eccentric characters and Surrealist situations—*Two Arrabalesques* featured a live collage of vibrant performers. Hosted in the Bowery Poetry Club, a storied meeting place for the contemporary literary scene in the East Village, the night followed the non-sequitur structure of *Farewell Babylon!*, in which the "main" footage was interspersed with readings of literary texts, philosophical interviews, and excerpts from Arrabal's previous works, resulting in a broken and provocative narrative.

Poet Todd Colby emceed this evening of poetry, cabaret interventions, and impromptu performances. All aspects of the candlelit den for artists were explored during the event, from the ingenious rotating stage to the dramatic stairwell. Artist ITEM IDEM opened the program with a procession for a lobster and soon Amanda Alfieri, who embodied the character of Nadja, stood up from the seated crowd and performed a reading based on the book. Phantasmagorical appearances by visual artist Irvin Moravan and nightlife creature Gage of the Boone mesmerized the audience with aerial performances while Jacolby Satterwhite took everyone by surprise with a multimedia act that encompassed projection, music, and club dance. Opera singer Joseph Keckler and contemporary poet Ariana Reines chimed in with atmospheric numbers. The night also paid tribute to poet Benjamin Péret and Surrealist dissident René Daumal to celebrate Arrabal's constellation of rebellious minds.

Photos by Paula Court

Two Arrabelesques: A Surrealist Café (2013), performance views.

BOWERY POETRY CLUB △ ORGANIZED BY MARC ARTHUR AND CHARLES AUBIN

CHAPTER

4

FOUR

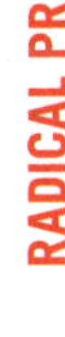

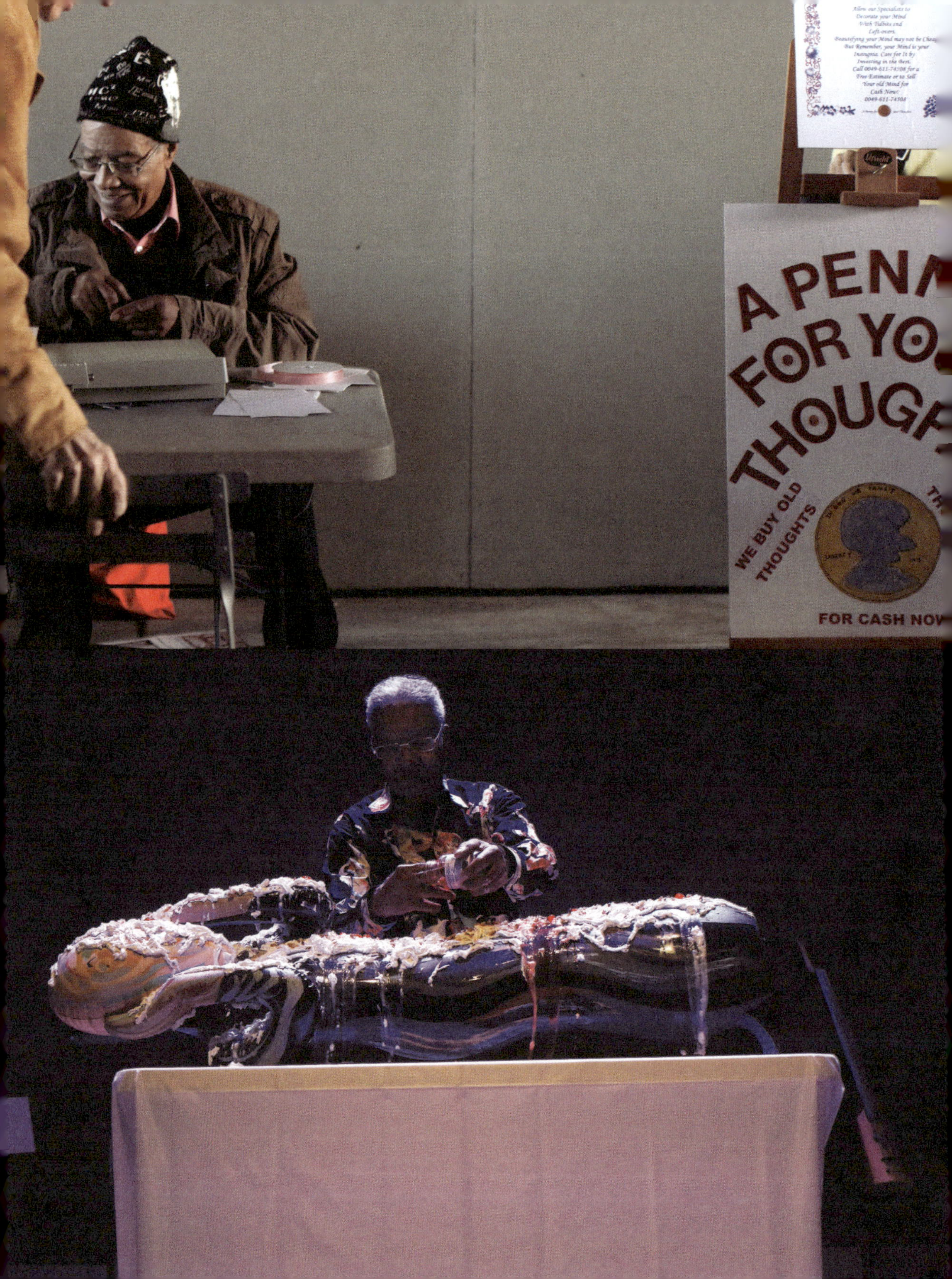
Allow our Specialists to
Decorate your Mind
With Tidbits and
Left-overs.
Beautifying your Mind may not be Cheap
But Remember, your Mind is your
Insignia. Care for It by
Investing in the Best.
Call 0049-611-74508 for a
Free Estimate or to Sell
Your old Mind for
Cash Now!
0049-611-74508
A PENNY
FOR YOUR
THOUGHTS
WE BUY OLD
THOUGHTS
FOR CASH NOW

THREE DUETS

SEVEN VARIATIONS

Three Duets, Seven Variations was a week-long miniseries within the Performa 13 biennial, presented on the occasion of *Radical Presence: Black Performance in Contemporary Art*, an exhibition conceived and organized by Valerie Cassel Oliver, Senior Curator at the Contemporary Art Museum Houston, that originated in Texas and was presented at the Studio Museum in Harlem and New York University's Grey Art Gallery. A visionary endeavor, *Radical Presence* was the first survey of contemporary performance by visual artists of African descent in the United States and the Caribbean, covering work from the 1960s to the present.

Taking the intergenerational focus of the exhibition as a starting point, *Three Duets* was structured in three pairings of artists whose performances were conceptually and formally in dialogue—Benjamin Patterson and Jamal Cyrus, Senga Nengudi and Tameka Norris, and William Pope.L and Zachary Fabri—while *Seven Variations* referred to the number of individual performances on the program. In this series and the exhibition as a whole, "blackness" was not merely a way of naming an artist's identity, but rather an orientation toward performance as a medium. It also related to a network of relationships that was the model for the curatorial process in selecting these artists. Furthermore, it stressed the fact that Nengudi, Patterson, and Pope.L had not received the kind of reception to their performances among New York museums that their long-established careers clearly deserved.

Founding Fluxus member Benjamin Patterson opened the program at Roulette with *Action as Composition*, his first retrospective concert in the U.S., including works from the 1960s such as *Paper Piece* (1961) and *Duo for Voice and a String Instrument* (1961) and new Fluxus-style reimaginings of moments from classic grand operas such as Bizet's *Carmen* or Puccini's *Madame Butterfly*. Patterson later performed *Pond* (1962) at the Grey Art Gallery, with a black grid painted on the floor. Written for nine performers (any spectator who wished to participate), who followed instructions to move from one square to the other, the action included toy wind-up frogs hopping indeterminately among the players.

The indomitable Patterson (now eighty years old) also presented *A Penny for Your Thoughts* at the 14th Street Passage on the High Line alongside Jamal Cyrus's *Texas Fried Tenor* (2012). Interacting with visitors, Patterson constructed hats from newspapers "in exchange for an idea," with typical Fluxus humor, while Cyrus, wearing a jumpsuit and standing on a platform, proceeded to immerse a flour-battered tenor saxophone into a vat of boiling oil; the result was a cacophonous symphony of crackling, hissing, and fizzling noises amplified by the microphones encircling it, that recalled not only southern cuisine but also the improvisatory aesthetics of blues and jazz.

Tameka Norris (trained as a painter) and Senga Nengudi (trained in dance and Japanese theater), despite divergent specialties, nonetheless revealed similar sensibilities in their performances. For Norris, the wall of the Studio Museum's mezzanine gallery became her canvas: dressed in an orange jumpsuit, she cut her tongue with the single stroke of a knife blade and on bent knees, dragged her tongue deliberately along the gallery wall, an act of replacing brush and paint with her mouth and bodily fluids that was reminiscent of performances by artists of the 1970s such as Gina Pane, Marina Abramović, and Ana Mendieta, reflecting on the social position of women with similarly sensual gore.

Nengudi's reconstruction of *RSVP*, originally made in Los Angeles in the 1970s, was its first appearance in New York. Comprising sculptural objects made from pantyhose filled with sand, then twisted, stretched, and attached to the wall, it referred to the inevitable changes to flesh over time and the restraint women experience when wearing nylons. Artist Maren Hassinger, who has long collaborated with Nengudi, performed various body arrangements, exploring this flexible yet restrictive material, along with dancers and choreographers Regina Rocke and Marya Wethers, who had been introduced to the piece by Nengudi in a series of movement workshops in advance of the event.

Pope.L and Fabri share a complex, ephemeral, and nearly illegible choreographic sensibility in the ways in which each artist intervenes in public spaces. While Pope.L is often associated with the abject force of the body and Fabri is known for his effervescent presence,

Jamal Cyrus, *Texas Fried Tenor* (2013), performance views, the Highline.

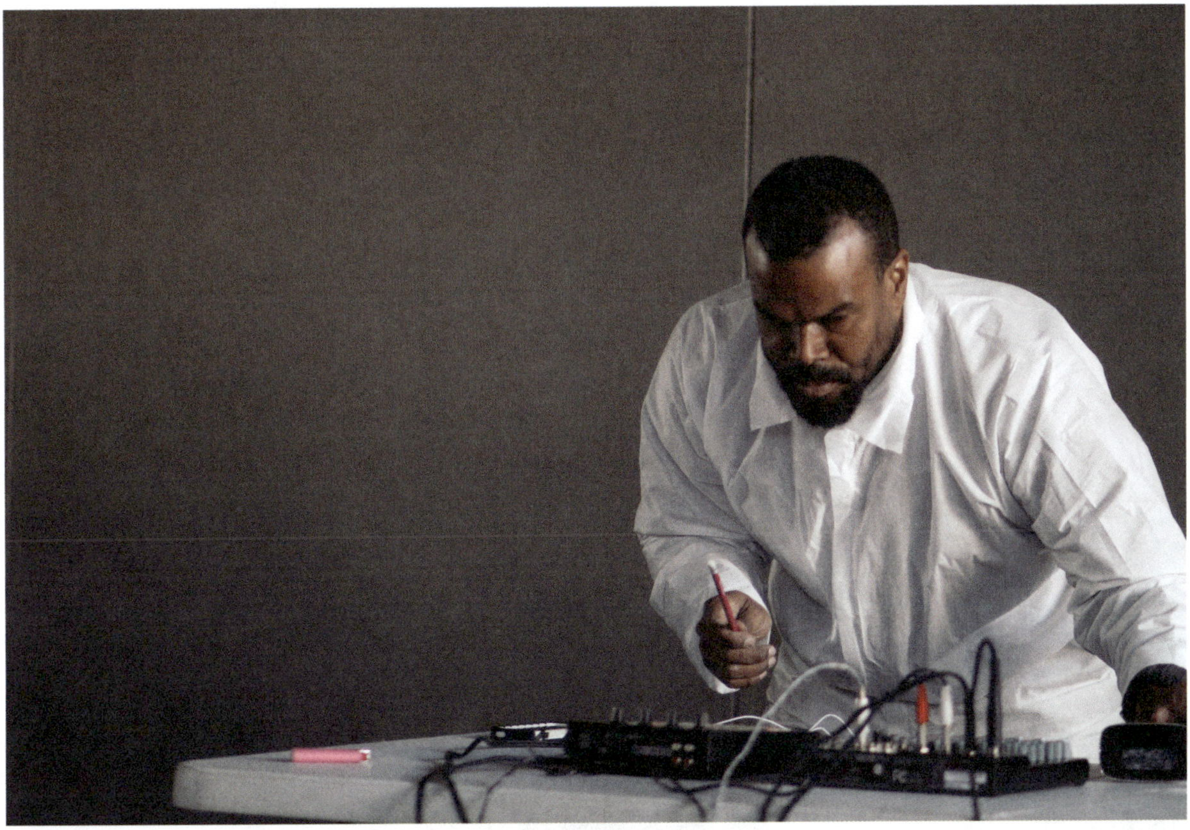

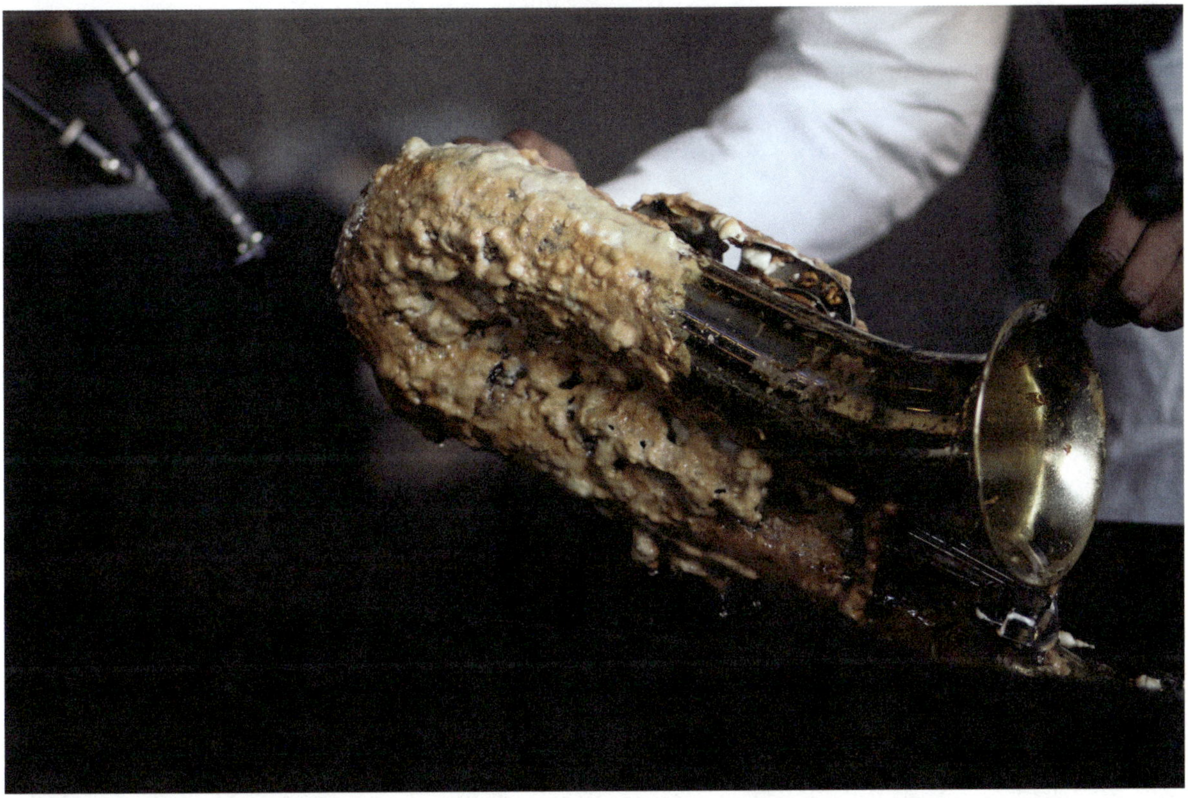

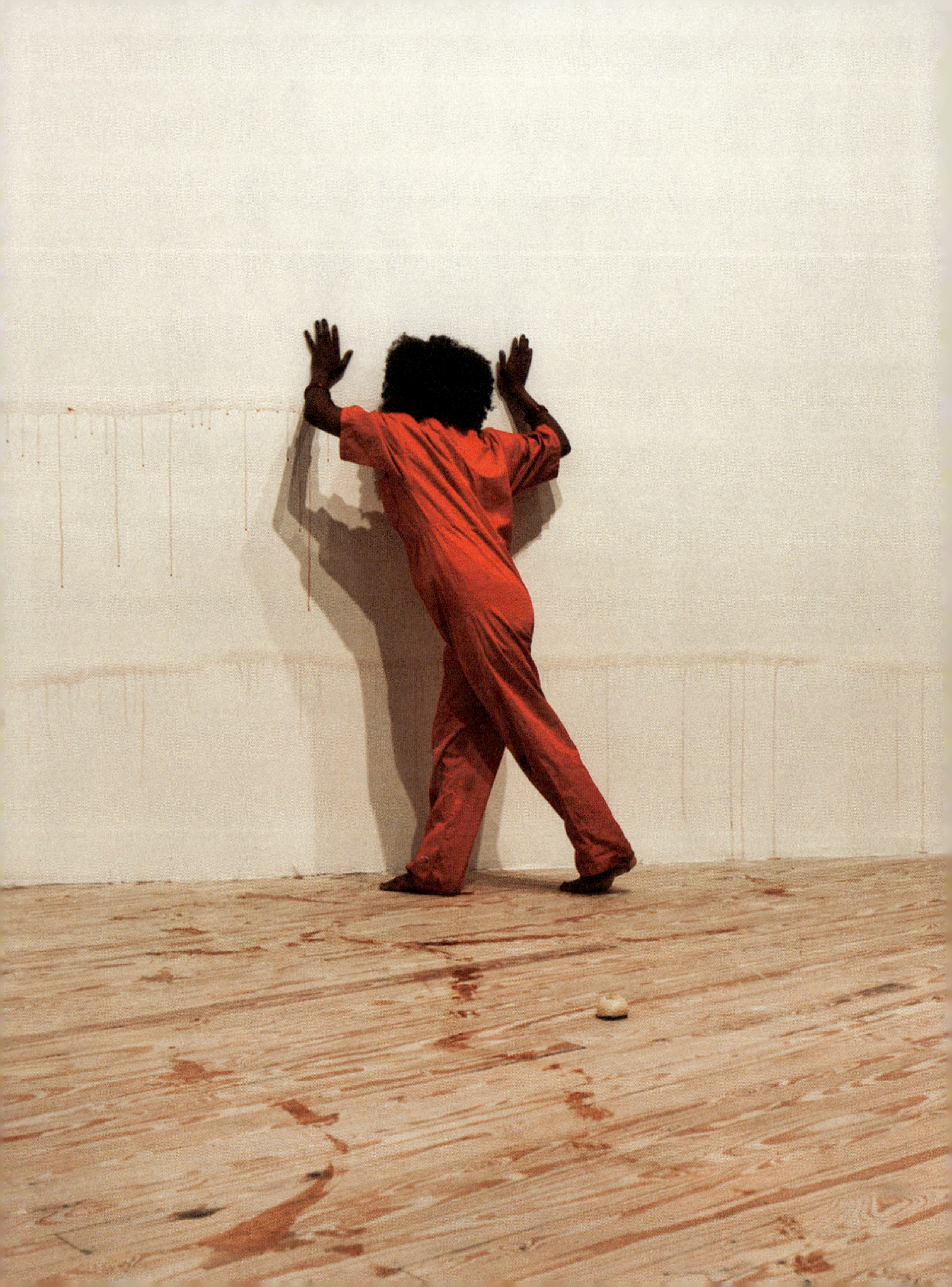

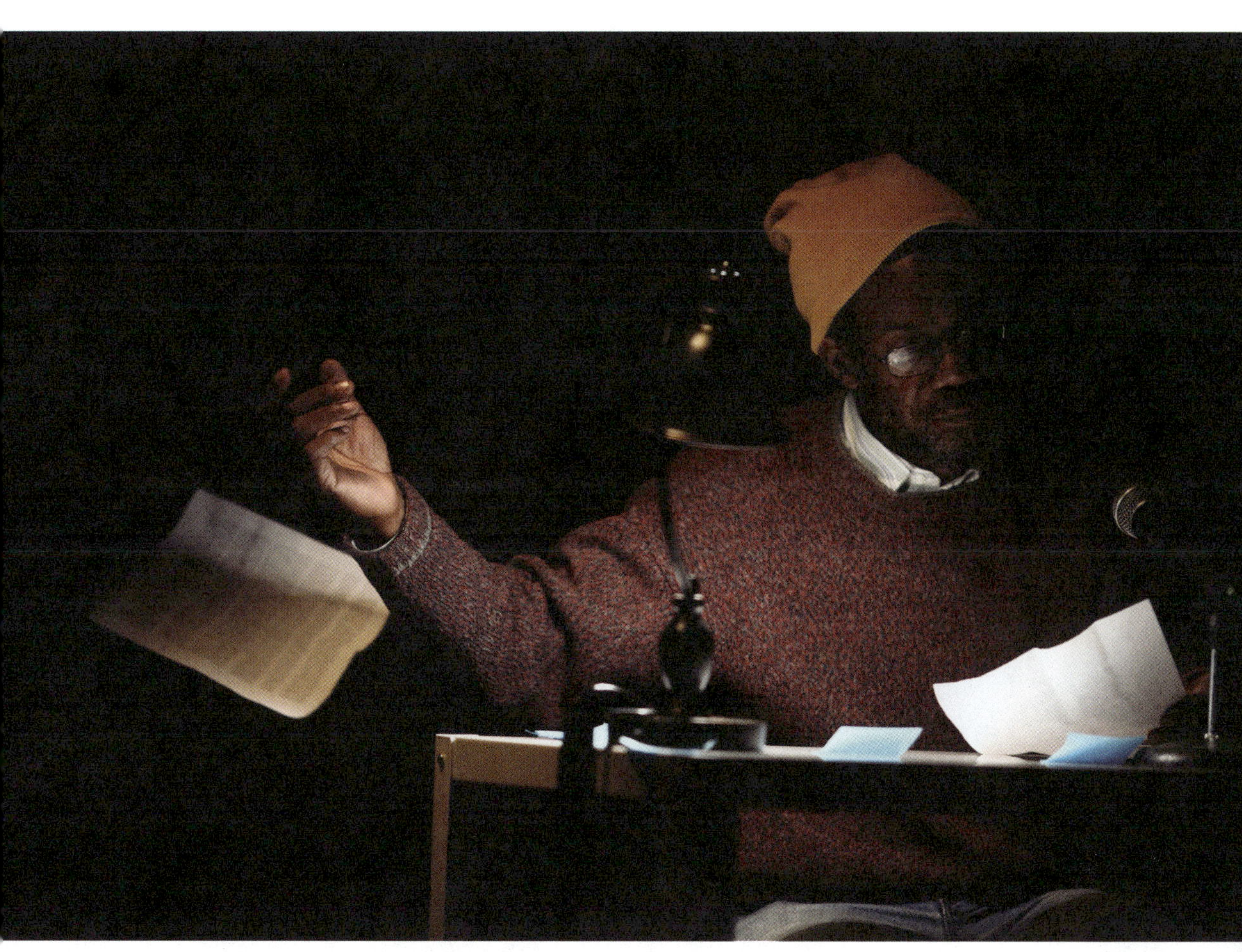

(Left) Tameka Norris, *Untitled* (2013), performance view, Studio Museum in Harlem. Photo by Chani Bockwinkle
(Above) William Pope.L, *Cage Unrequited* (2013), performance view at Clemente Soto Vélez Cultural and Educational Center.
Photo by Paula Court, courtesy of William Pope.L.

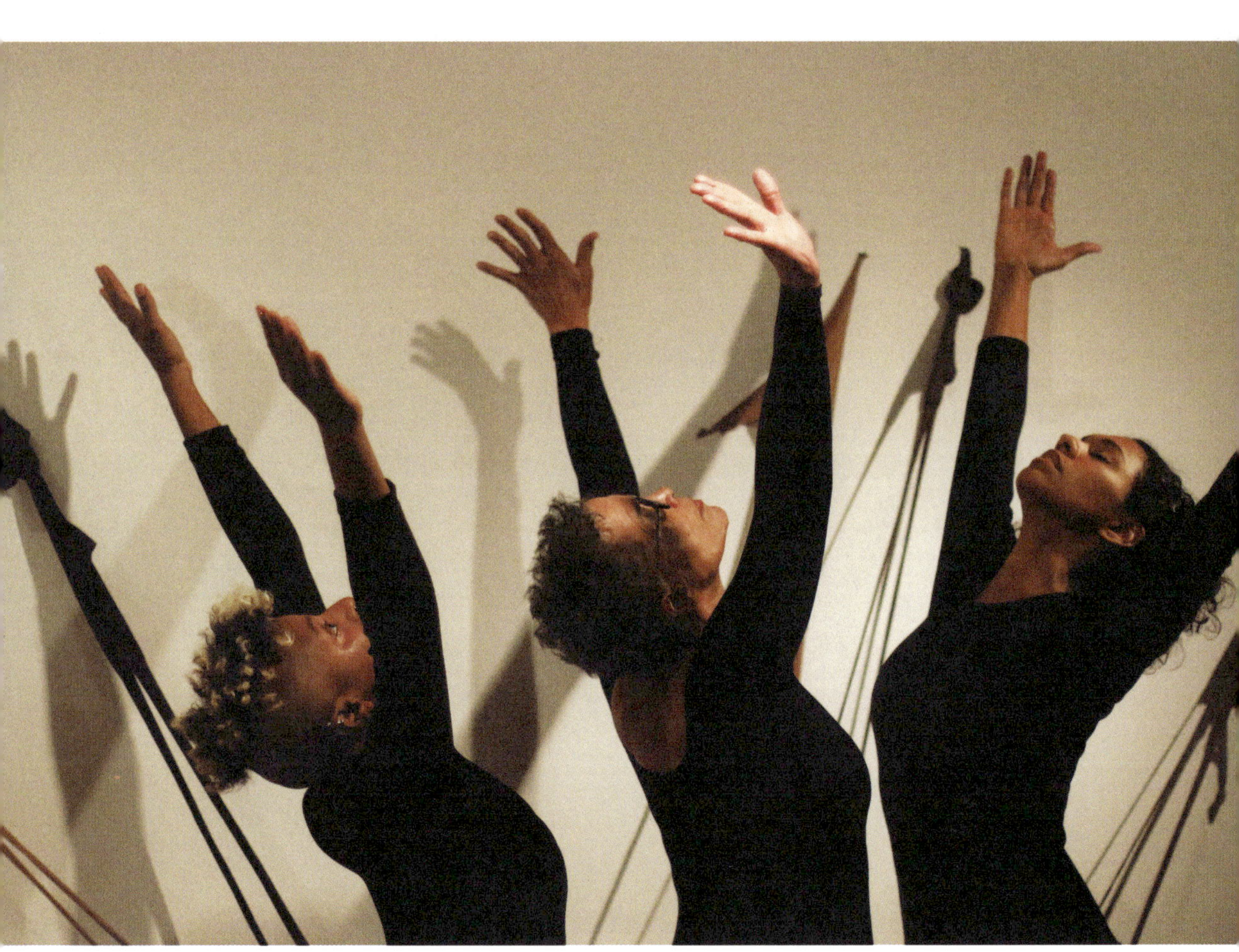

Senga Nengudi, *Untitled (RSVP)* (2013), performance view, Studio Museum in Harlem. Photo by Chani Bockwinkel.

William Pope.L, page from *Another Kind of Love: Cage's "Silence," By Hand* (2013). Photo Courtesy of the artist and Mitchell-Innes & Nash.

they both point to a range of contradictions associated with their particular presences in the world.

Pope.L's *Cage Unrequited* was a twenty-five-hour marathon reading of John Cage's anthology *Silence: Lectures and Writings* (1961) by seventy-four invited guests—curators, scholars, artists, former students, and friends. Presented in the intimate black-box theater in the Clemente Soto Vélez Cultural and Educational Center on the LES, the performance was staged in near darkness, with only a dim glow cast from strands of fairy lights that crossed the middle of the space and hung from the ceiling over the seat risers encircling an open center stage. A reading lamp on a centrally placed desk also punctuated the space. Each participant read for twenty minutes and, if they finished before their allotted time, sat in silence. At times, Pope.L occupied a second desk, transcribing the book by hand onto yellow legal pads, tearing off a page as each one filled and casting it over his shoulder into the darkness.

Halfway through this performance, the artist proceeded to give a lecture on the black, gay, and experimental musician and composer Julius Eastman, whose notorious 1975 performance of Cage's *Song Books* (1970) apparently displeased Cage. In response, Pope.L raised questions of devotion, belonging, a general tendency toward easy cartographies of artistic influence, and the necessary effort to question, or even defile them.

Fabri's performance at the Studio Museum concluded the series. Dressed in a white cotton T-shirt, ash-blue pants, and white sport socks, Fabri presented *Shiny Shoes*, which began in drizzling rain with several pairs of old shoes in varying sizes lined up along the Museum's façade on 125th Street. Trying on and wearing some of them, he fell, tripped, jumped, and slipped with each attempt, his repeated failures, along with a deadpan monologue, inciting laughter from those gathered along the popular Harlem artery. The playful mood was tempered by contorted actions (such as hopping violently to shake off a wet sock) as well as manic sprints through the museum's courtyard. The performance concluded inside the building in the downstairs theater, where chairs lined the perimeter, leaving a narrow corridor for Fabri's final maneuverings in the dark space.

Zachary Fabri, *Shiny Shoes* (2013), performance view, Studio Museum in Harlem.

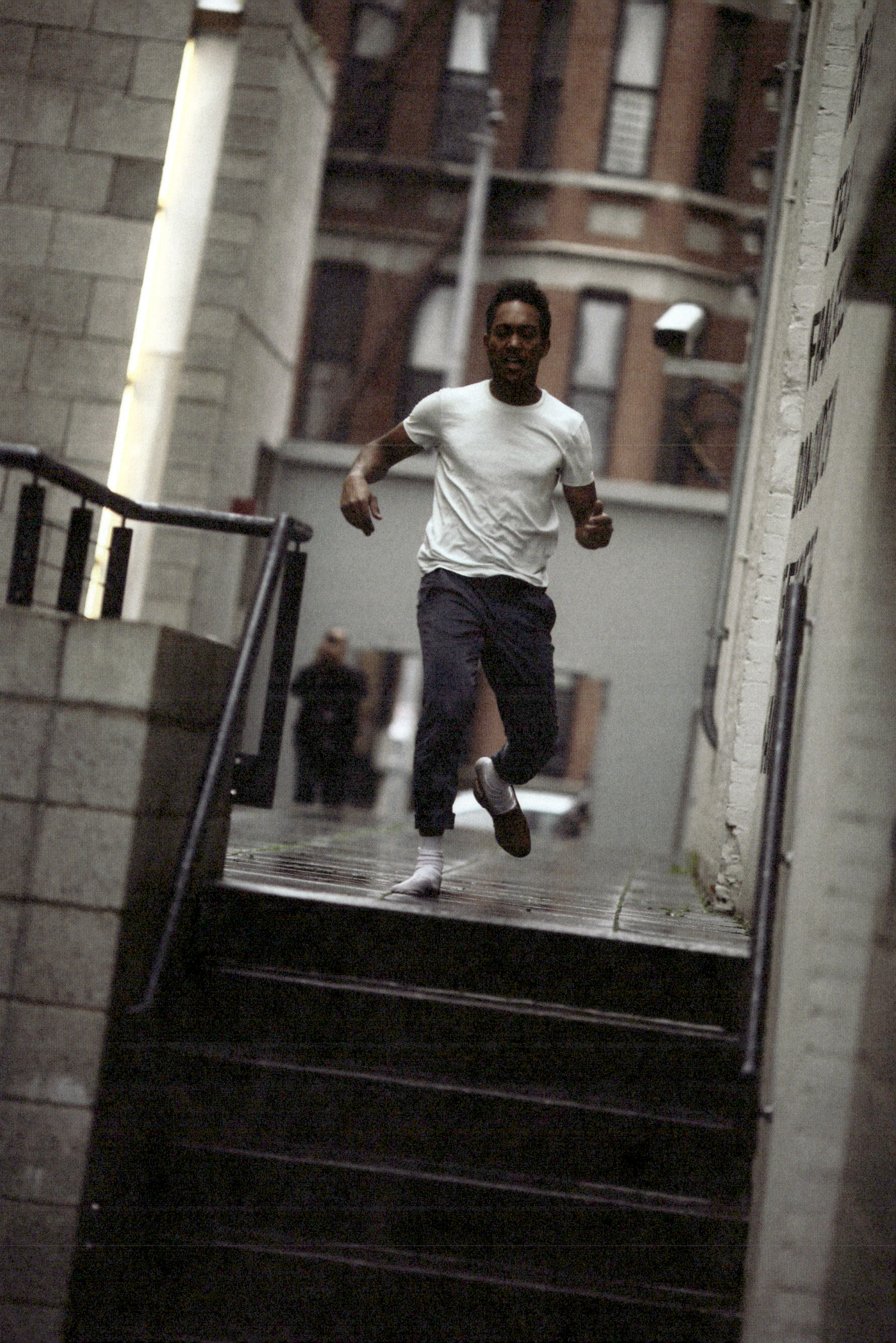

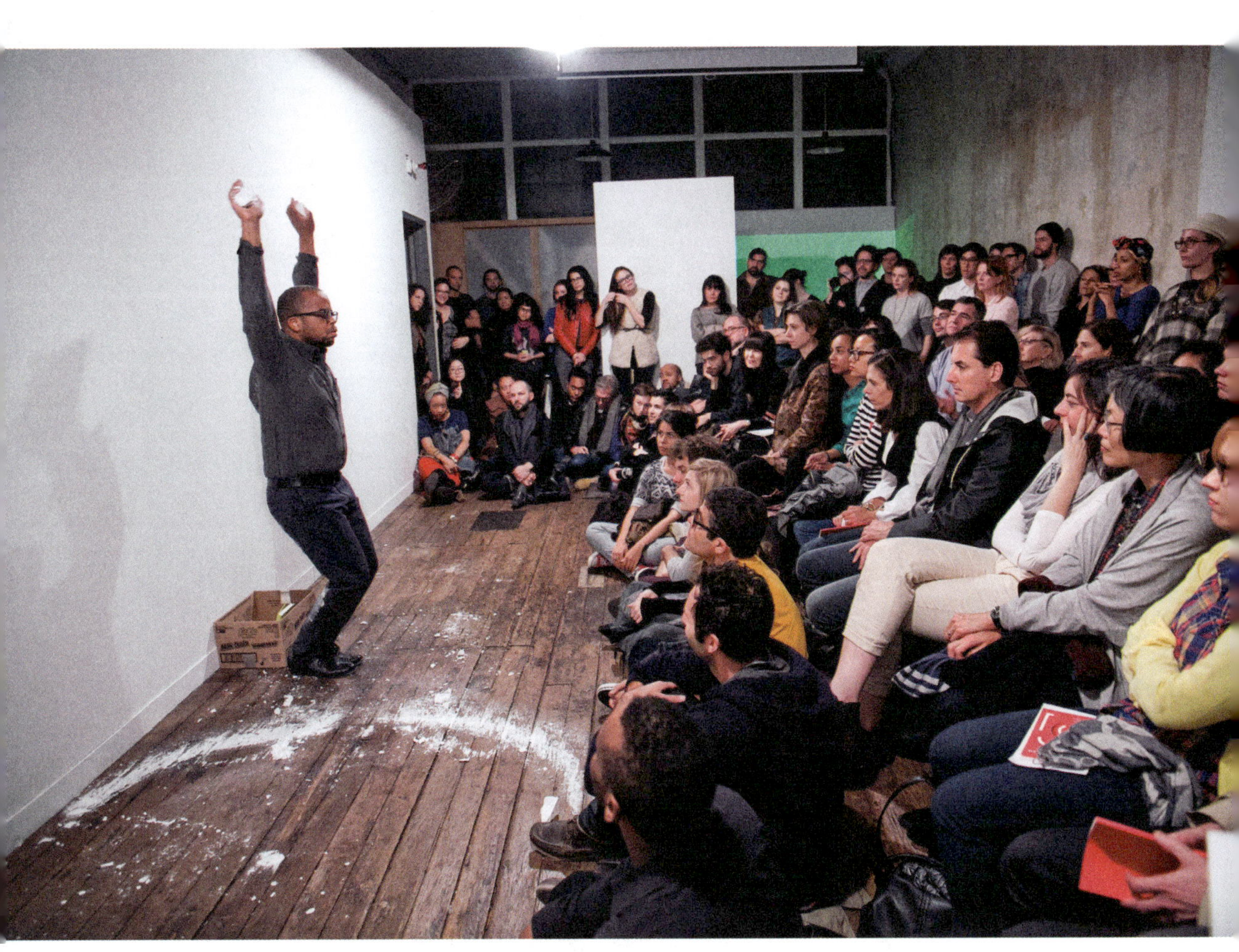

There is a striking and surprising correlation between Jamaican-American artist Dave McKenzie's performances and his training as a printmaker. In McKenzie's live artworks, there is the impression that the repetition of language and movement is meant to have an effect similar to the printing process. McKenzie's repeatedly performed gestures retain a semblance of originality, while also being utterly reduced—through their incessant reiterations—to merely referencing movement or text. His use of repetition is distinctive because the objective is not toward some escalating, accumulating, or dramatic conclusion. Rather, repetition is an elusive circulating link of a mere citational reference to that which occurred prior to its present manifestation, only to conclude when it has reached the point of exhaustion.

Such play with repetition was especially evident in McKenzie's Performa 13 work, *All the King's horses … none of his men*, which was commissioned and presented by Biennial Consortium member Third Streaming as part of a suite of related programming for *Radical Presence: Black Performance in Contemporary Art*. With more than 100 people seated in a crescent shape, occupying over half of the gallery space, McKenzie walked around, navigating various objects—including a cardboard candy box, slabs of chalk, and a book—while delivering a text he wrote especially for the piece.

The performance commenced with McKenzie, who had only episodically attended tap dancing classes as part of his research, replete in black tap shoes, a button down gray oxford shirt, and indigo pants, entering the compressed gallery with the classic heel-toe-shuffle-ball-change maneuver, striking the well-worn wood floors, but bothered by the patched areas of tin squares, where he tended to linger and his foot stuttered. His movements were flat, deadpan, apathetic even. There was no syncopation, no flying swingouts to awe us, rather just the bare essentials meted out bit by bit, over and over again. This antipodal treatment of tap dance was compounded by the pleasantly warm recorded voice of a woman, accompanied by guitar, singing The

Notorious B.I.G.'s anthem "Suicidal Thoughts" from his 1994 debut album *Ready to Die*. Other audible interventions over the course of the performance included a recording of Heathcliff Huxtable, Bill Cosby's character from *The Cosby Show*, in particular his declaration to his on-camera son Theo, "I brought you in this world and I'll take you out," a hit phrase from the show's first episode in 1984.

With the bricks of chalk, McKenzie swept the floor, marking arches of white across its timbers, rubbed them on his head, made snow angels, and clapped them overhead, causing them to crumble, ultimately returning to his interpretation of classic tap dance moves, although with a far more exaggerated execution. Instead of lackadaisical steps, there were large, giant ones, while he repeated "Heel. Brush. Step. Heel." For McKenzie, "Tap is something I am vaguely familiar with but also something that I can't do. Still, I find tap to be beautiful while I am trying to do it. There is this desire to connect the mental part of tapping (following steps) to the physical part (staying in rhythm and balance). I wanted to use this dancing failure as a language—as something that I could struggle with and make my own. Saying the few steps and positions out loud became a kind of script."

Next McKenzie engaged with a wry meditation on the frequent New York City subway performances in which mostly boys, but sometimes girls, sell candy. He said, to the cadence of his heel, brush, step movement, "Ladies and gentlemen. If you be ladies and gentlemen. Money in my pocket. Heel. Brush. Step. Twix," exaggerating certain phrases as he saw fit.

The conceptual paradigm of the performance pivoted on the capacity of the body as material or, more precisely, on subjects transformed into a type of material, either image or symbol, highlighting American culture's obsession with objectifying people. The objectification of black Americans, notably the fetishization of media personalities within commercial and social media spaces, was particularly captivating for McKenzie. However, none of these concerns were overtly presented. Instead the work was imbued with McKenzie's unique sense of ambiguity and contradiction, which he remixed and transformed into a powerful critique of the complexities and contradictions inherent in such ubiquitous images and clichés.

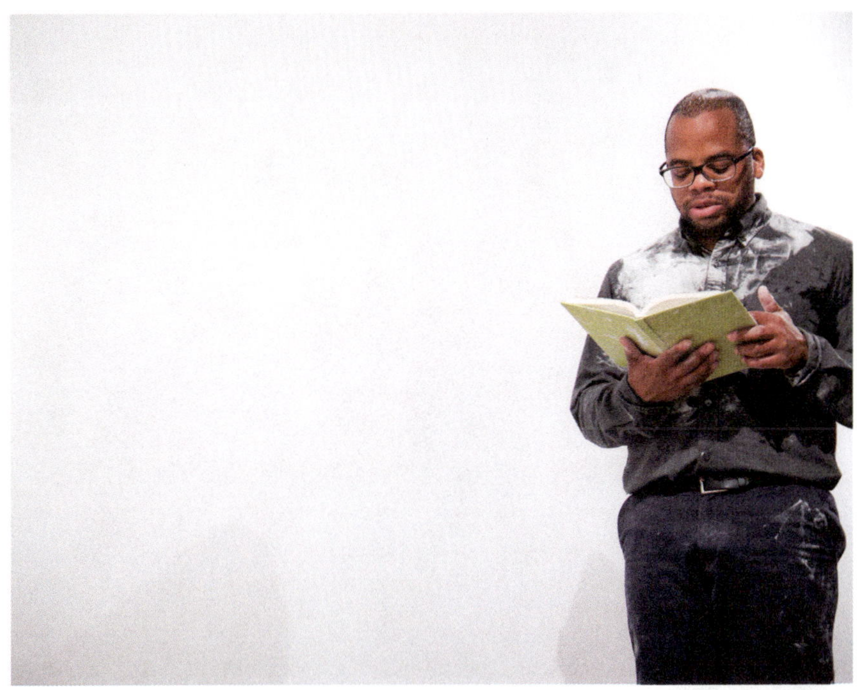

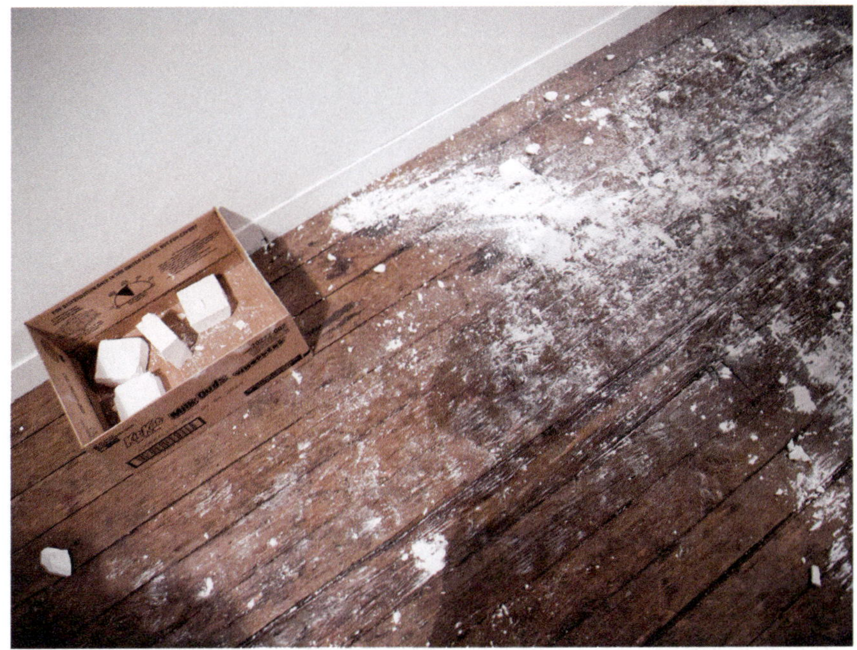

Dave McKenzie, *All the King's horses ... none of his men* (2013), performance views.

CHAPTER

5

FIVE

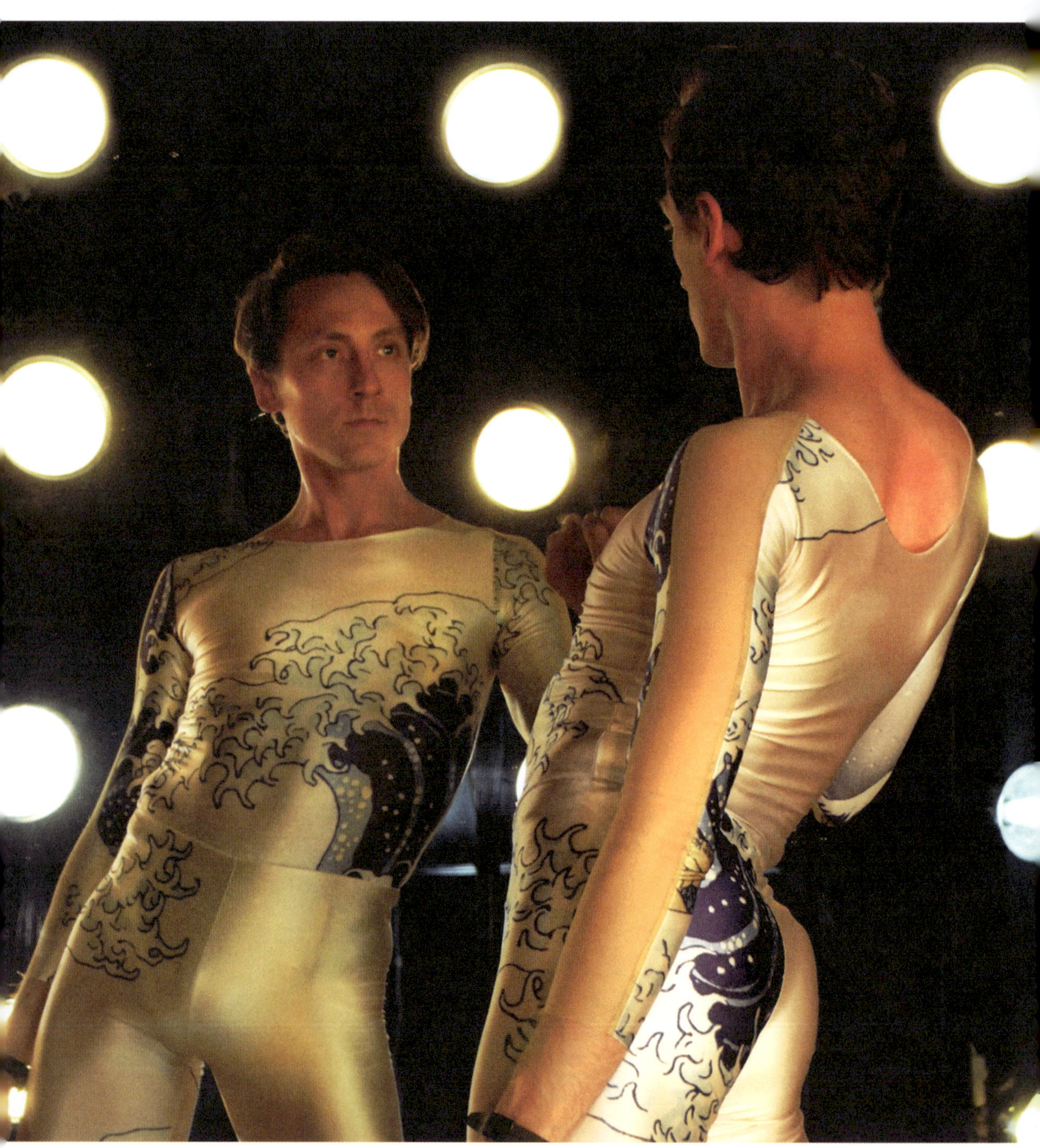

ME∃M: A STORY BALLET
ABOUT THE INTERNET

Ryan McNamara was one of the first artists to be awarded a Performa Commission for the 2013 biennial. Early in 2012, we talked about his developing a major new work, following an earlier project he had created for Performa 09, *Ecks, Ecks, Ecks—AKA Sacred Band of Thebes,* as well as a guest appearance in *Three Performances in Search of Tennessee*, a work by Laurel Nakadate and James Franco for Performa 11. These and other activities showed McNamara always reinventing himself. With every new endeavor, he seems to start from scratch—making things that look like nothing that has come before. A fascination with dance history and dancers, popular music, and MTV as well as a love of art history were recognizable touchstones. Always evident was his prodigious imagination and the speed with which he worked. McNamara seemed to pull ideas out of nowhere, catching an image or an object and making a sculpture, a photograph, a collage from a hybrid combination, as he did nonstop for several weeks in a Chelsea gallery in 2012, arranging a tableaux every twenty minutes or so with whomever walked into the gallery, all the while engaging with social media to assert the presence of what he was undertaking. An easy rapport developed over several years of watching each other in action, but when we got together to discuss the Commission, McNamara went very quiet. The problem, he explained, was that he had never before been given so much advance notice to make a work. That, he said, was unnerving.

The approximately twenty months of development to germinate and grow was clearly apparent in *ME∃M: A Story Ballet About the Internet* when it opened at the Connelly Theater in November 2013. It was hailed as a startlingly original work, a game changer, some said, presented seamlessly and without a hitch on opening night. It showed McNamara to have mastery over an extraordinarily complex range of materials and concepts in unexpected ways. McNamara carved a small theater into eleven separate stages, each with its own dedicated performers dancing to their own tunes: anteroom, proscenium apron, wings, balcony, staircase, seating areas, and aisles. With all these parts fully known only to McNamara, he essentially pulled off a magic trick when he brought them together for the first time. Nothing was

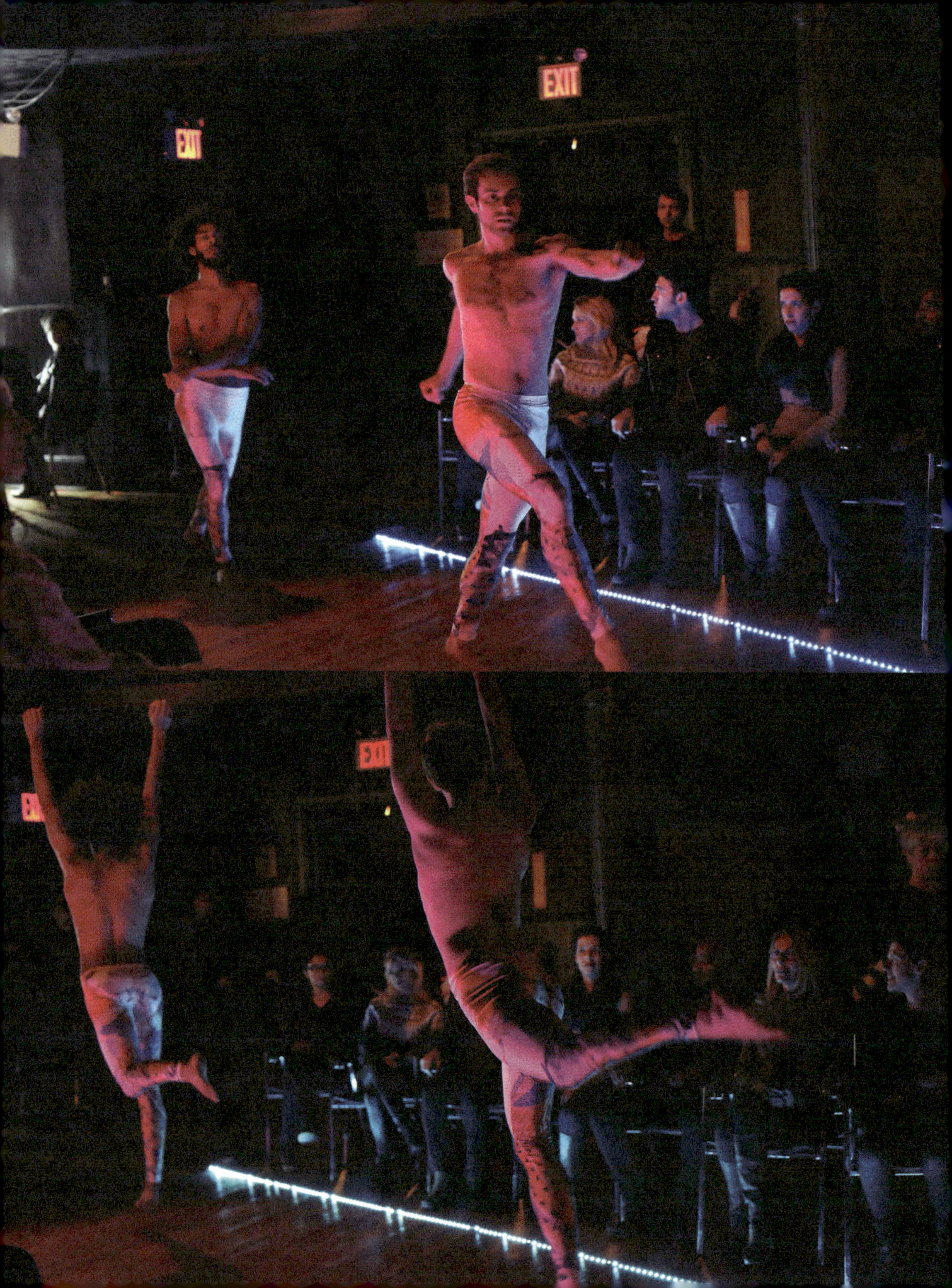

Photos by Paula Court

Ryan McNamara, MEƎM: *A Story Ballet About the Internet* (2013), performance views, showing "People Movers".

as it seemed. Perhaps there were five, ten, twenty ballets, an entire repertoire of unexpected choreographies within a single evening. What McNamara planned was a history not just of dance but of dancing, a way of viewing the world with the same immersive layering of images, information, samplings, styles, and content, appropriated and repeated, as those to be found inside the digital architecture of our online world. Making them his own, in this "utopic commons of unfettered communication," and as he described the space of the Internet, he piled everything into a single theater all at once, like some swirling Piranesi folly.

The audience was asked to wait in the anteroom to the theater until every person who had reserved a ticket was accounted for before being ushered to their seats, where surprises lay ahead. A single dancer in a bright leotard and patterned tights was poised on stage atop a high platform, while others, also in multicolored dancewear, surrounded by bright stage lights, prepared in different parts of the theater, each with its own seating arrangement. Some audience members faced the stage, others the back wall, another group sat in parallel rows on a diagonal, facing each other, while others were back in the anteroom. People turned their heads this way and that, leaning over the backs of their chairs to watch friends being led to one or another staging area. When the music began, eleven separate dance spectacles erupted simultaneously.

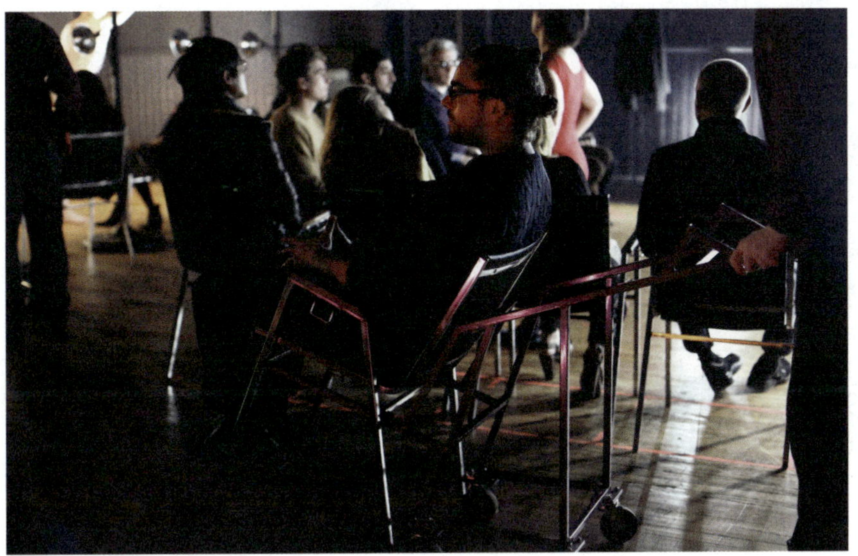

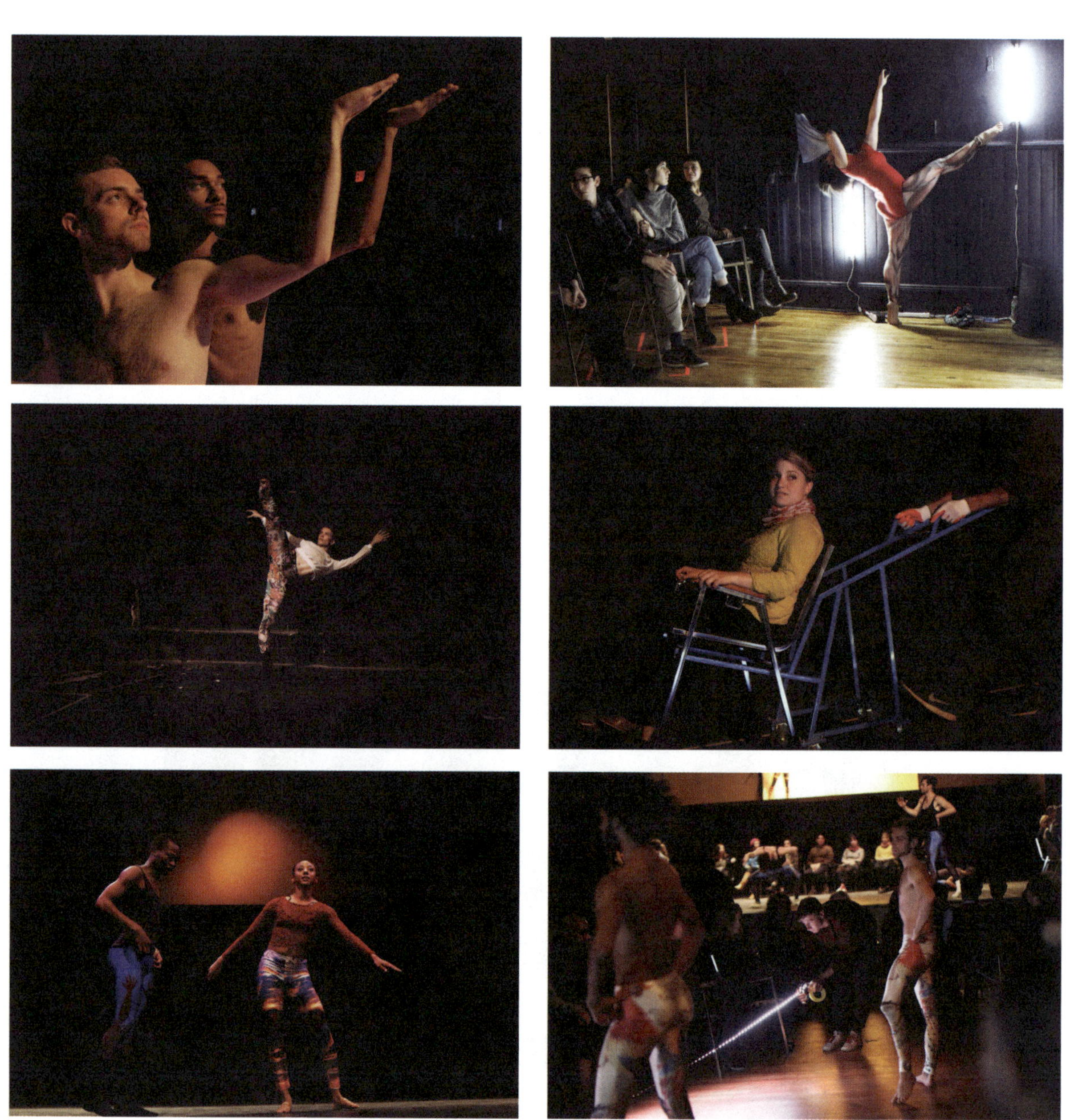

Ryan McNamara, *MEƎM: A Story Ballet About the Internet* (2013), performance views.
Photo credits clockwise from top to bottom: Ryan McNamara, Paula Court, Ryan McNamara, Paula Court, Paula Court, Paula Court.

A modern dance soloist, a pop duet, a trio of disco dancers, and a Martha Graham troupe were all dancing according to their different methods throughout the house. Stealthily, and without warning, the entire place began to change shape, and it seemed as though the floor itself was moving: people in their chairs were lifted a few inches off the ground by "People Movers," a team of strong men and women with custom-designed chair hoists on wheels with which they took individual audience members to other parts of the space to view other performances. Some were pushed up a ramp and deposited on stage before returning to their previous position in the audience soon after, while others were moved just a few rows or were turned around, but over the hour-long performance, all of the approximately 100 viewers had been transported and rearranged, some several times, in front of one dance set or another. By the end, the spectators left the theater laughing, talking loudly—wondering about what exactly had happened in that small theater on the LES. Out into the night they went, the pieces of the puzzle still changing places in their minds, as memories to consider all the way home—exactly as McNamara had imagined it. He said he wanted the viewer to be so immersed in every aspect of *MEƎM: A Story Ballet About the Internet*, that it would not leave them for days. Indeed, it did not, and would remain in the imagination of many for months to come.

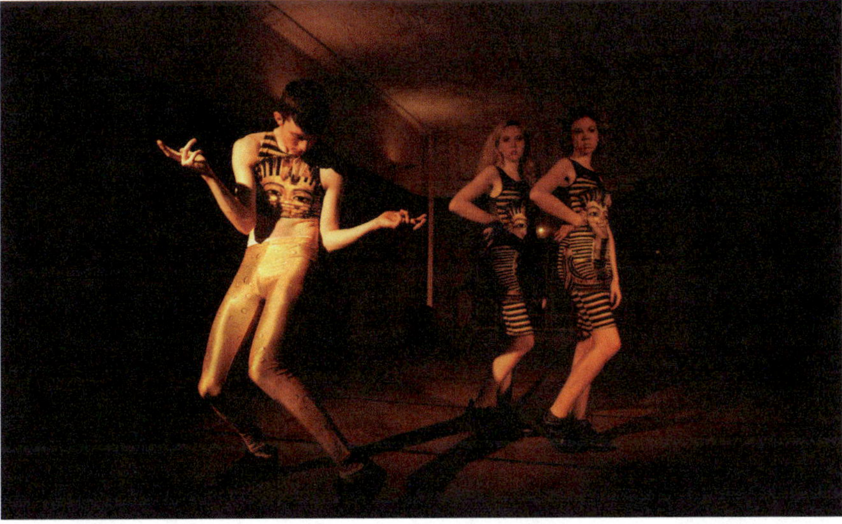

Ryan McNamara, *MEƎM: A Story Ballet About the Internet* (2013), performance view.
Photo by Ryan McNamara.

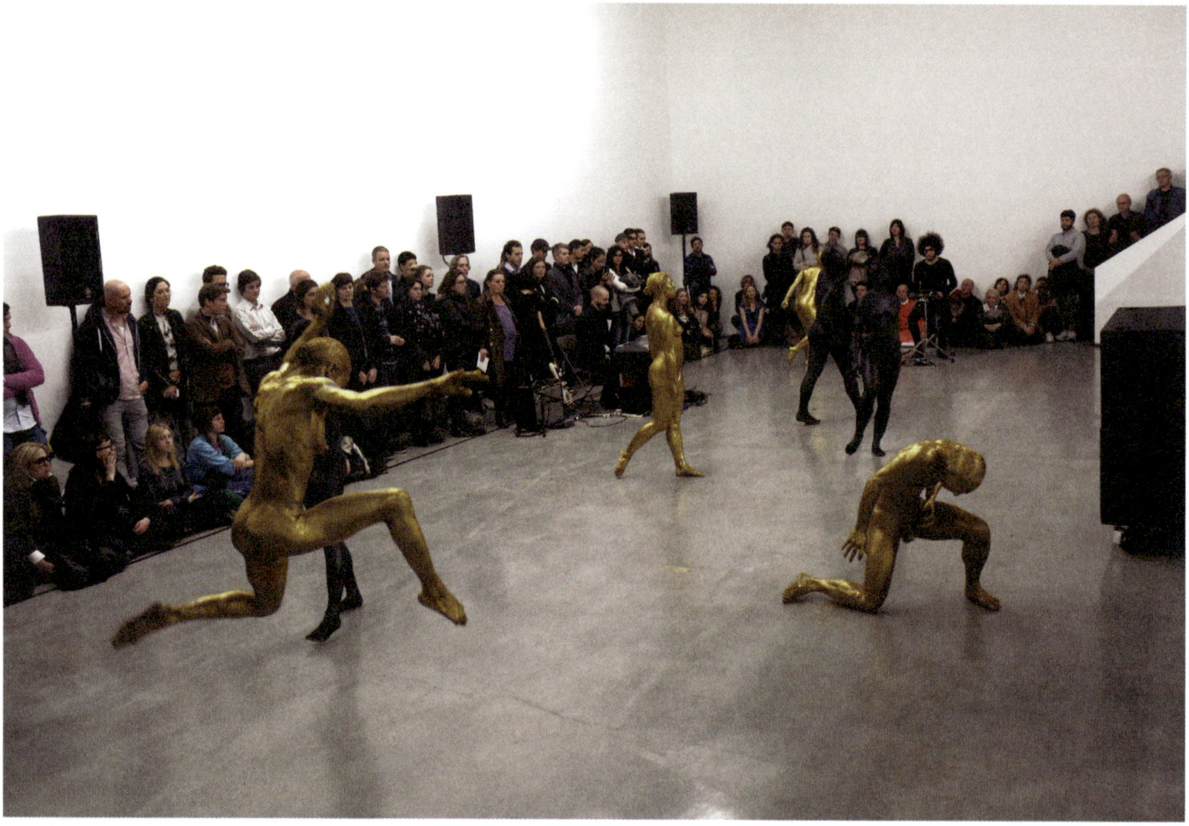

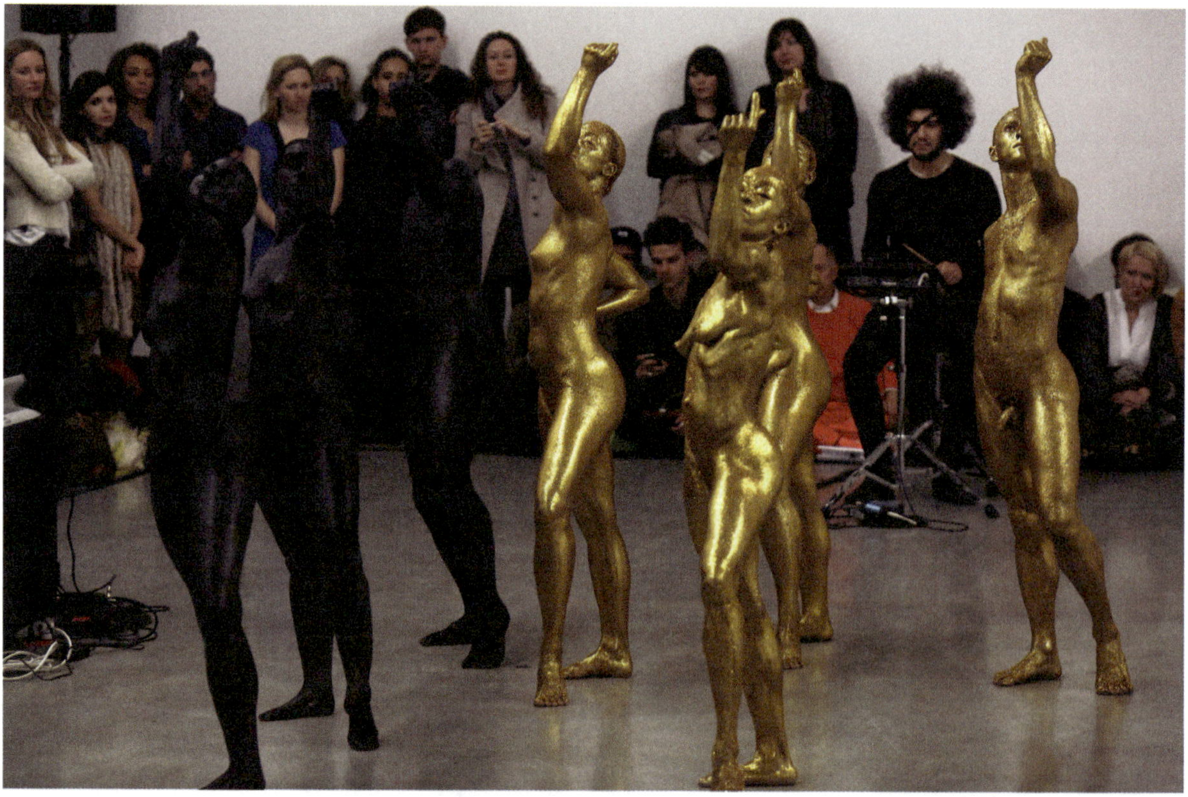

EDDIE PEAKE

ENDYMION

Seven dancers, each naked save for a full coat of body paint—three in black, four in gold—stalked in quiet procession, close to the edges of the bright, white architecture of the Swiss Institute on Wooster Street as the audience entered, finding standing room for themselves in single rows up against the walls. The dancers would occasionally pause, posing, with chins and right arms raised, fingers snapping in the air, before moving on. Paint coverage was total—toes, genitals, hair, eyelids—and thick, like a second skin, so that the bodies seemed alien with not a sliver of bare skin visible. Light sparked off the gold paint, rendering those bodies a metallic sculptural physicality, while the deep, matte black painted figures sucked in the light, creating an impression of dark impenetrable shadows. Even as they warmed up, walking and stopping to hold a hand in the air, or to clap in unison, three musicians took their place at the far end of the space. Long, drawn out, bass-heavy electronic tones, and slow rhythmic beats, accompanied by occasional firings of blips and taut smatterings of drums, built a dense atmosphere of sound that filled the spaces between performers and audience.

Eddie Peake's performers moved through the space in set combinations, all gold, all black, sometimes mixed, three by four, or two by two by three, well aware of the pictures they were making; they might form a row in full *contrapposto*, reminiscent of the lines of dancing figures in a Roman frieze or of Michelangelo's *David*; they might leap into the air, crossing diagonally in the center of the space. Sometimes they let out a gleeful yelp of pleasure or made shushing or oohing and aahing sounds, followed, as frequently occurs in Peake's work, by violent street language, as in a brawl: "Motherfucker, I'll explode!" shouted one male dancer, which was answered by the others in chorus: "Explode Motherfucker!"—ending with a final "You'll never see me again, Motherfucker!" For Peake, the surprisingly aggressive outbursts intentionally contrast with the exquisite elegance of each element of the performance. "I like to elicit strong visceral responses from the audience, to have a broad spectrum of feelings," Peake explained. "It's the one moment of dialogue in the whole piece and if you sonically blink, you've missed it."

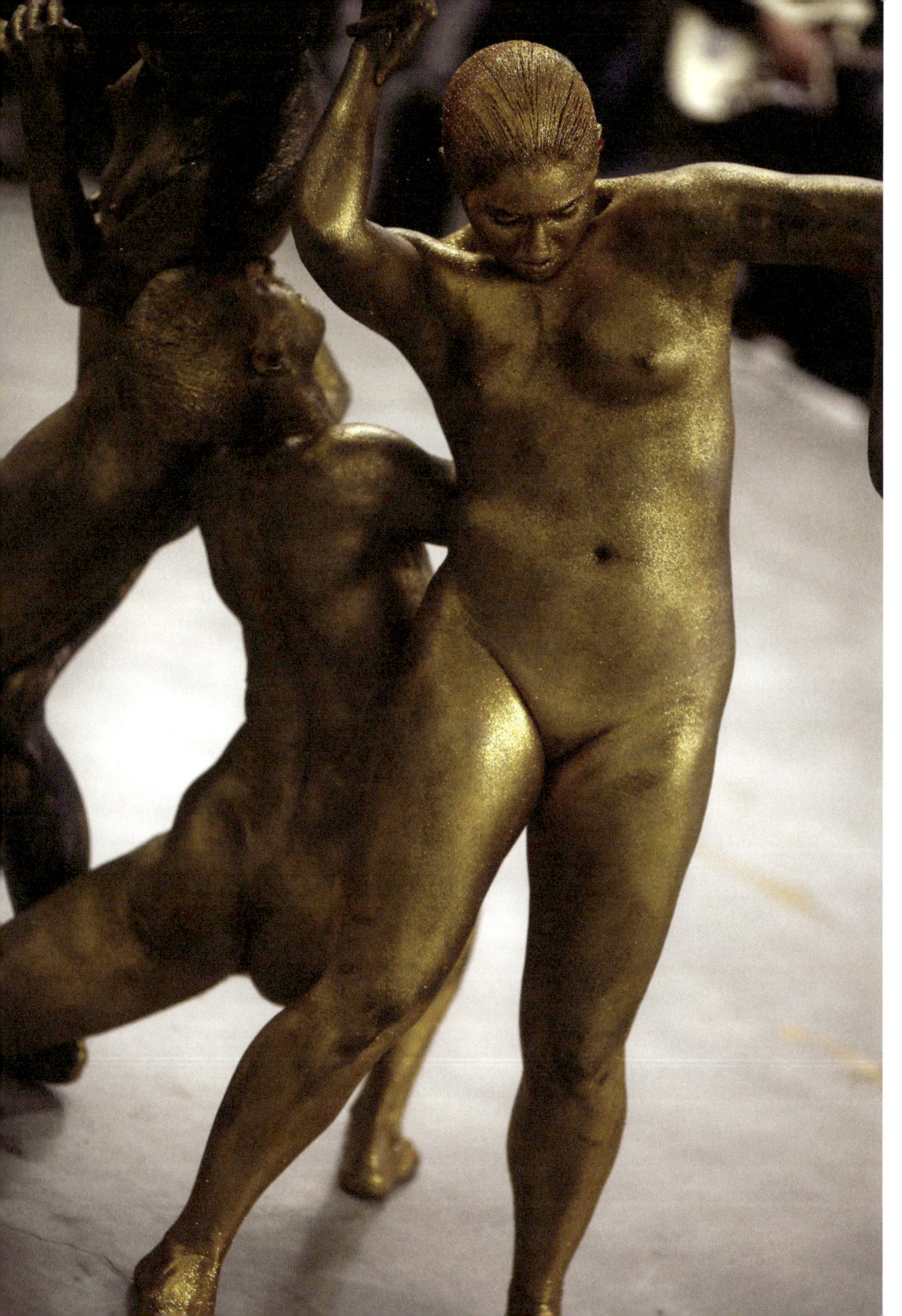

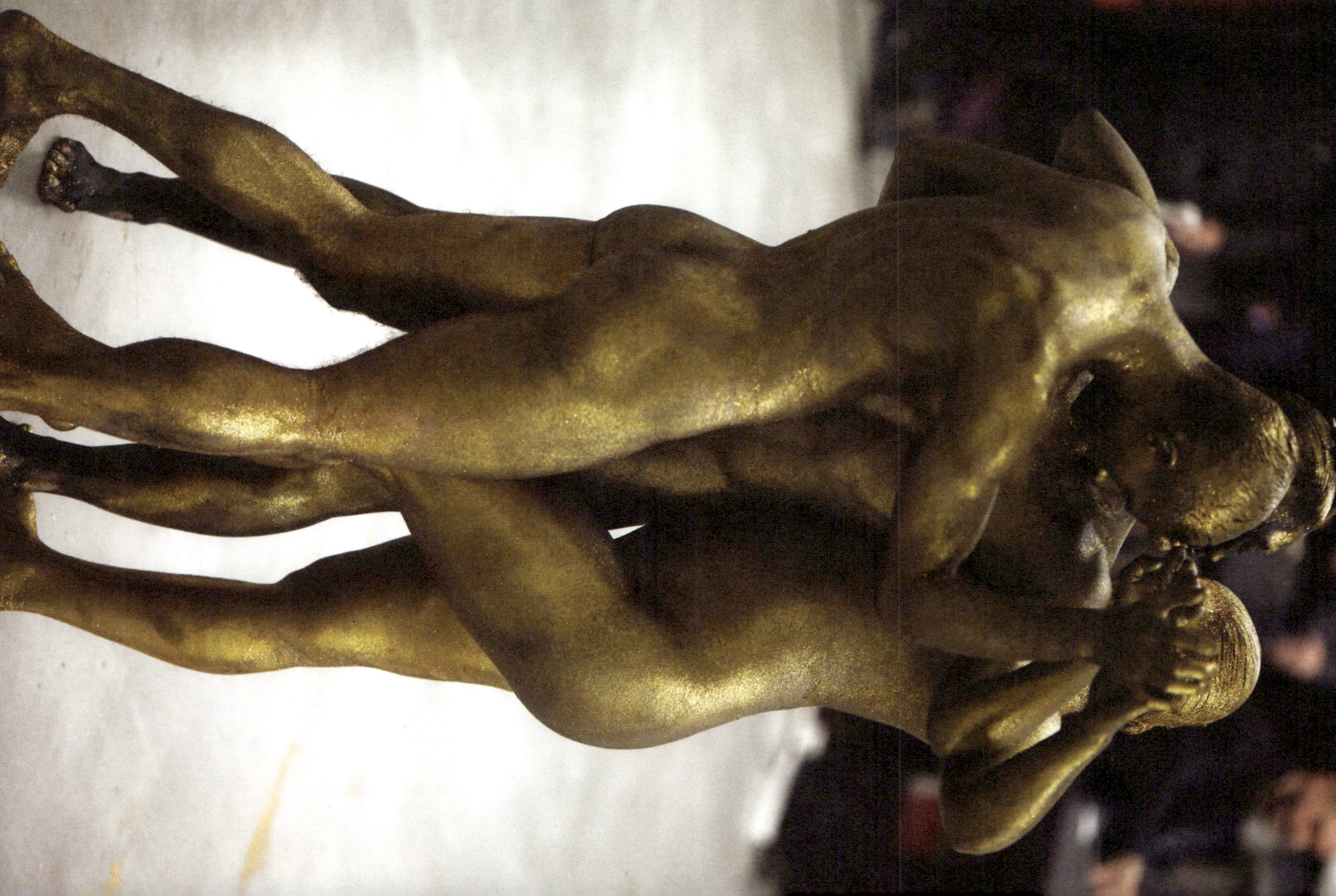

Eddie Peake, *Endymion* (2013), performance views.

Photos by Paula Court.

The clash of art history and poetry with the quotidian is another signature of the artist's work. The title, *Endymion*, an eponymous poem by John Keats about an eternally youthful boy, is also a street name in Finsbury Park, London, where Peake grew up and which he describes as "once a slum, very cosmopolitan, diverse in terms of cultures, classes, races," so it is a recurrent narrative about relationships. Indeed, desire was the throbbing heart of the hour-long performance of *Endymion*, a fact that was made literal as dancers, in pairs or trios, closed in on one another, rubbing edges of thigh and underarm, neck and fingers, with black and gold merging, burnishing all the figures equally so that they looked like they transformed into a collection of Nineteenth-century academic sculptures. Striking tableaux in the familiar style of *The Three Graces* or *The Laocoön*, these otherworldly, perfected object-humans began to watch and scrutinize the audience and each other. As one dancer caressed another, mixing body paint, the action immediately indicated the formation of alliances, jealousies, and the dissolution of edges between individuals. Writhing and grinding orgiastically, the complex group patterning of libidinous action pushed the work to a climax. True, too, there was salaciousness in watching—the audience's eagerness to see black and gold paint mixed in a warm bodily mess was palpable—a deep-seated attraction of human subjects to alchemy, lust, or both.

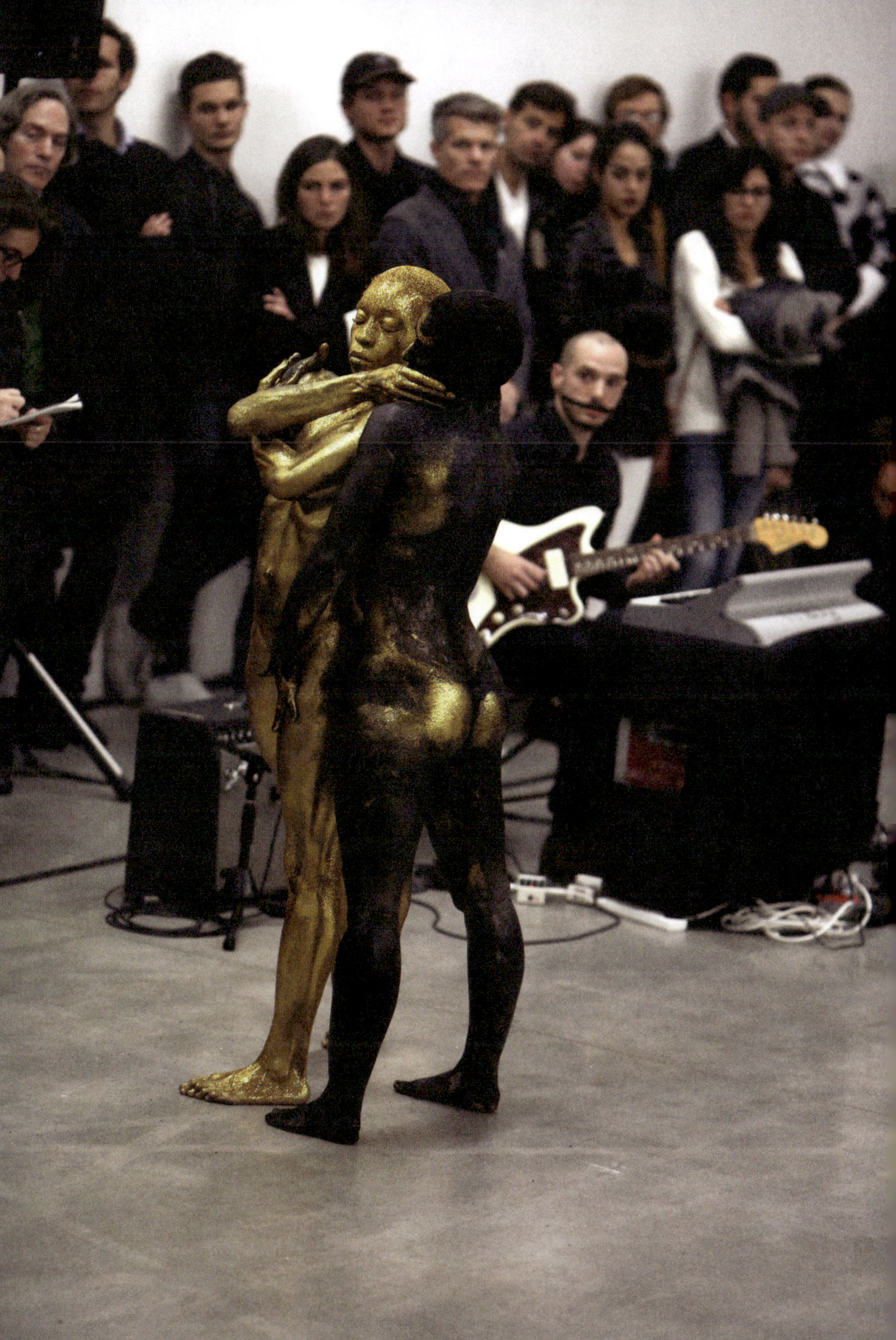

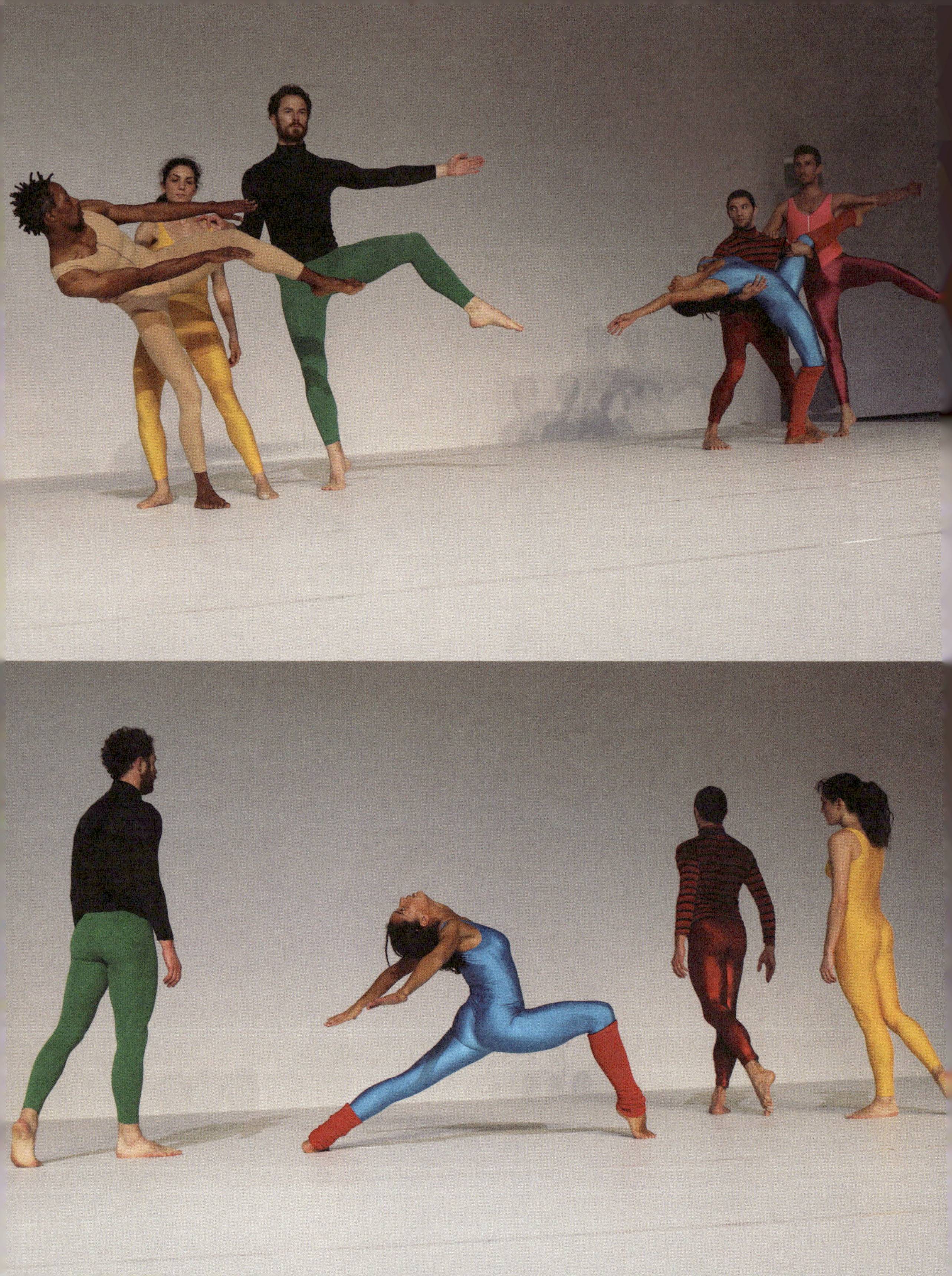

BORIS CHARMATZ

FLIP BOOK, PART OF MUSÉE DE LA DANSE, THREE COLLECTIVE GESTURES

During three long weekends, the *Musée de la Danse* was in residence at MoMA with *Three Collective Gestures*. This temporary occupation challenged ideas about the museum: first, that museums are about a "permanent collection;" second, that we know where the art begins and ends (a boundary strictly policed by guards and barriers); and last, that what is seen is certified by connoisseurs.

Where we expect to see art objects, we found the first of three "gestures"—*20 Dancers for the Twentieth Century*. Dancers were positioned on, within, or next to artworks, performing as moving, "living archives" (or "temporary storage facilities" according to Yvonne Rainer's more prosaic contestation at one of the public discussions) of dances learned as part of their training. *20 Dancers for the Twentieth Century* did not follow a chronological progression, Rainer's own *Trio A* (1966) and Trisha Brown's *Group Primary Accumulation* (1973) appeared, danced by Shelley Senter next to a Richard Serra floor piece; Lynn Hershman Leeson's *Roberta Breitmore* (1974–78) was performed by Lenio Kaklea, and Jim Flecher sat slumped, naked, against the wall biting his arms in a reenactment of Vito Acconci's *Trademarks* (1970), while on the concourse Mani M. Mungai alternated between performing traditional Kenyan dances and the moves of Michael Jackson. This "pop/up" collection of danced gestures and forms did not respond to the material artworks in its proximity, but rather inserted itself at a meta-level that alternately complemented and challenged the static objects on display. These living artworks not only licensed new kinds of movement in the museum, but also introduced mutation, as iterations of one style of dance morphed into another, channeled through the same bodies. Such portability of historical form took attention away from the museum's architecture as a defining frame within which periods and styles might be gathered and posed—the body as a self-possessed museum in its own right, in which art and life are truly blurred.

Boris Charmatz's large-scale 2009 choreographic work, *Levée des Conflits*, was performed the following week as the second gesture in

ORGANIZED BY ANA JANEVSKI / TEXT BY CATHERINE WOOD ◐ DONALD B. & CATHERINE C. MARRON ATRIUM, MOMA

the atrium—a space associated with the display of sculpture after opening in 2004 with Barnett Newman's *Broken Obelisk* (1963–69). The dance expanded and contracted as a live monument, Smithson-like in its entropic swell and drain of centrifugal movement. Twenty-four dancers bled into a fragile proximity, at times merging with viewers fringed around the edges.

One might have expected MoMA to offer the assurance that works shown are "originals," but Charmatz inserted a flagrant "fake" with his third "gesture." *Flip Book* was an irreverent (some said sacrilegious) take on the fifty-year career of Merce Cunningham. Charmatz and his dancers performed a bastardized version of Cunningham's vocabulary and method by copying poses from photographs in a 2005 "coffee table" book and interpolating the gaps; their movements invented shifts between elegantly poised abstractions—*Torque and Variations V* (1965)—producing impressions from incidental snapshots, with a sense of fun and permissive pleasure—all set to a mixed pop soundtrack. Some complained that its compositional method was not "Cunninghamesque." But this was to confuse the material Charmatz was using as a score (the Cunningham book) with his intention. Rather, he took an approach more akin to Mike Kelley's work with found high school yearbooks in *Day is Done* (2005): taking permission to imaginatively "re-enact," from stills, the lost, performative "in-betweens." Charmatz's method proposed an eloquent if melancholic take on the impossibility of capturing performance history through photography, showing the disjunction between its documents and any experience of "liveness." Instead of treating this question of the misleading nature of stilled moments culled from time-based form as a problem, Charmatz cast it as an opportunity. And watching his "amateur" version with an assortment of volunteer audience members (who on Saturday included Rainer) was pure joy.

Flip Book was, at times, disorienting—messy in its blurring of dancers with the crowd and in apparently being worked out live in public. In the context of a modern art collection, "revelation of process" is not new (Hans Namuth photographed Jackson Pollock at work, an image now arguably more famous than the painted originals), but here it was boldly evident, because "performance" is so often about performing certainty. By skewing attention away from things (art objects) and toward people (both the dancers and the audience), and by planting dancers who could do extraordinary things among the crowd standing on the same floor plane, or having them roll and crawl across the grand sweep of the atrium's concrete floor—

familiar as a pedestrian navigational axis—*Flip Book*'s itinerant nature effected awareness of the thinnest boundary between art and not-art, creating nuanced disturbances and elaborations of the given mass of bodies that is always there, unacknowledged, within the museum. In this reconfiguration of form, the constellations of visitors forming around the dancers became the walls, the new "gallery spaces," the alternative frames.

The *Musée* within the Museum became a conceptual *mise-en-abyme*. Superficially, it operated within the boundaries of MoMA, but it fostered an internal insurgency, chafing against the institution's conventions. To encounter *Flip Book* was thus not a straightforward experience. Brian O'Doherty pointed out that the body is neatly banished in the ideal art installation shot "inside the white cube," in favor of the "disembodied eye." The dance museum conversely is founded on a culture of bodies in spatial movement. By introducing transitory and ephemeral movements we focus on the museum as a living entity, with ritualistic behavioral patterns. Such a gesture opens the museum up with new breathing space for social encounters that the twenty-four dancers suggested might deepen rather than negate our relationship with the material things in the permanent collection.

The depth of Charmatz's project is rooted in the line he draws between his own singular capacity and desire as a dancer—evident in his extraordinary solo in *Levée des Conflits*—and a broader investigation of dance's social and cultural frames. Inside this given institutional setting, the *Musée de la Danse* introduced its own terms of time, space, viewing, interaction, and presence through a combination of aesthetic intensity and analytic propositions regarding where dance might sit in a historical narrative and how it might force such an institution to change. The continuously moving mass of *Levée des Conflits* turned around an elliptical but ever-shifting cycle of bodily rotations on different axes and variable speeds that return to a core stasis. In this work alone, one could—as a visual pun on its entangled mass of figures—see performance entering the canonical arena as the new Laocoön while it definitely refuted Greenberg's medium-specific terms. Being made of dances, Charmatz's museum vanished from MoMA while the artworks on display around it remain. The very impermanence of *Musée de la Danse*, its confidence in indistinctness and its sense of permission, create the unalterable perception of an alternative set of aesthetic values that permanently remain.

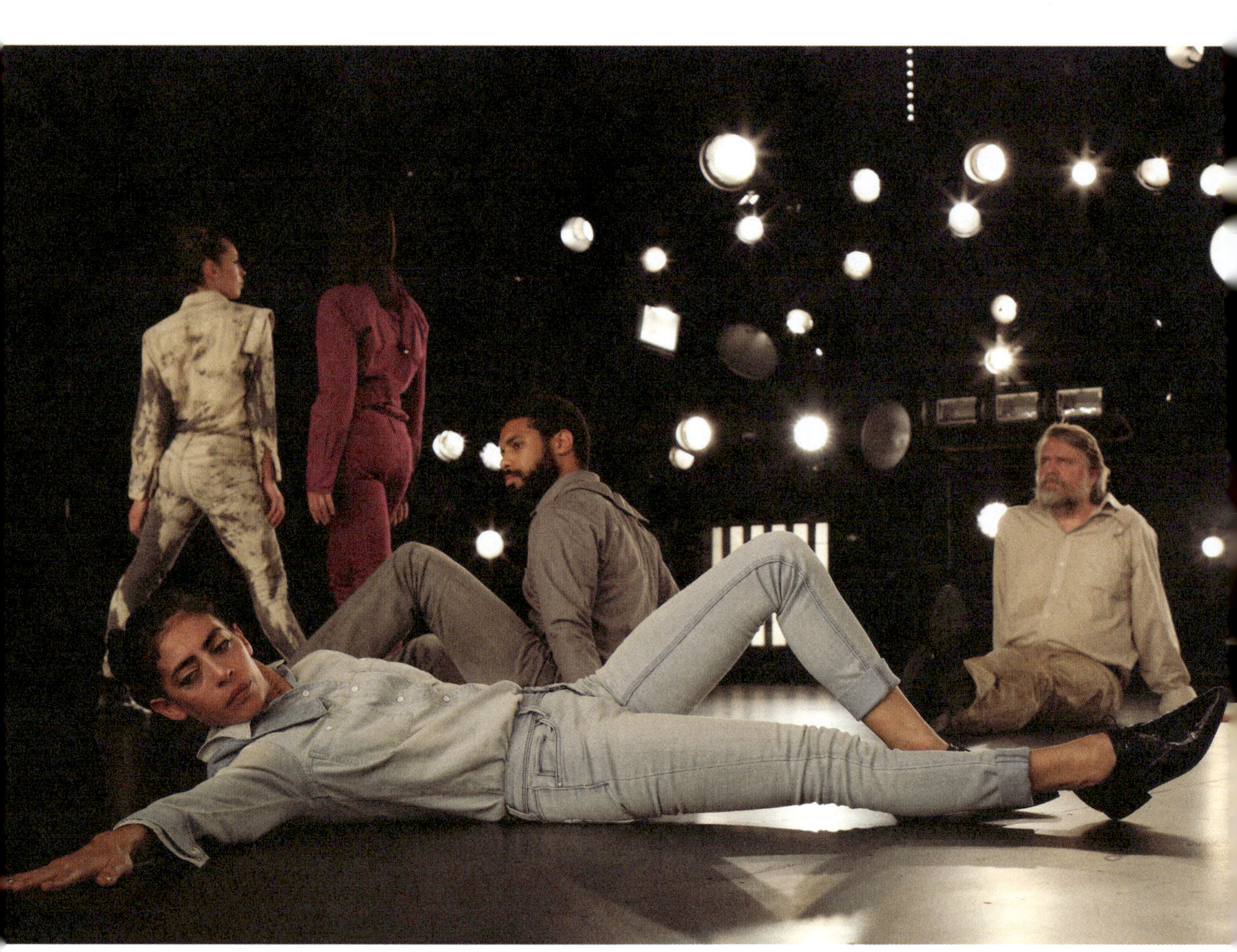

MARIA HASSABI

PREMIERE

It was after curtain time. The lobby of The Kitchen was packed, but the house remained shut. At last, the double doors opened to choreographer Maria Hassabi's *Premiere* (2013), and the crowd was faced with a striking tableau: a line of five dancers, staring back at the audience. Arranged in the center of the black-box space and illuminated by walls of bright lights to the left and the right, the performers—Hassabi, Biba Bell, Hristoula Harakas, Robert Steijn, and Andros Zins-Browne—stood, sat, or reclined, remaining motionless as theatergoers walked around them, through the brilliant heat, to the bleachers along the opposite side.

When the viewers were seated, the sole element of stage design became apparent: the footprints of audience members, tracking their routes from the entrance, stood out starkly on the bare, dark floor and framed the dancers in a circle. After a long, still silence, the group of performers started to shift and turn; their movements were minute, precise, and excruciatingly protracted, occasionally punctuated by the squeak of a rubber sole. Nearly ninety minutes later, the dancers had rotated only 180 degrees; in this literal about-face, they confronted the audience from the same positions in which they had begun—in a sense, ending the performance with an *encore*.

Premiere belongs to a series of works by Hassabi that emphasizes arresting images and sculptural poses. If these words seem to come more from the realm of the plastic arts than from dance, that's no accident. Born in Cyprus, Hassabi studied at CalArts in the early-1990s, and she frequently collaborates with visual artists, such as Scott Lyall, her longtime dramaturge. Today, she is among a handful of choreographers who performs as often in galleries as in theaters. Yet Hassabi remains dedicated to the theatrical *dispositif*. She expresses this commitment, however, by challenging the limits of what is needed to create theater: what is the minimum required to fill a space, make a show, hold an audience?

Hassabi's brand of minimalism is very different from that famously practiced by Judson Dance Theater in the 1960s, in particular, choreographer Steve Paxton. In his *Satisfyin' Lover* (1967), forty people simply walk across the performance space; in *State* (1968), they just stand still. Critic Jill Johnston famously described these works as celebrating "the any old bodies of our any old lives."[1] But while Hassabi's *Premiere* foregrounds the performers' bodies, showing how stillness is disrupted by every breath and quiver, there is nothing "ordinary everyday" about it.[2] The piece is highly theatrical in appearance, from the dramatic lighting to the dancers' denim clothes (styled by threeASFOUR); each movement is carefully choreographed and technically demanding.

Explicitly avoiding the adjective "slow," Hassabi has said that her choreography is "about paring things down" and bringing "precision and clarity to each action."[3] It is a technique that she has been developing over the past five years—initially on her own, then steadily expanding to duets and, subsequently, to ensemble pieces. In *Solo* (2009), a Persian carpet serves as Hassabi's only prop and partner; a companion piece, *SoloShow* (2009)—first presented at Performa 09— was danced by Harakas in a few early performances. Two years later, Hassabi and Harakas performed together in *SHOW*, an augmentation in cast that is echoed in the enlargement of the performance area: the choreographer removed the seating, eliminating the distance between the audience and the performers, who move among them. This device is inverted in *Intermission* (2013), created for the joint Cyprus-Lithuania pavilion at that year's Venice Biennale; in the original "live installation," three dancers gradually rolled down the risers in a gymnasium, again sharing the same space as spectators—exhibition visitors who came in and out over the course of the day.

[1] Jill Johnston, "Paxton's People," *Village Voice*, April 4, 1968; reprinted in Jill Johnston, *Marmalade Me* (New York: Dutton, 1971), 135–37.

[2] Ibid.

[3] Maria Hassabi, quoted in Lauren Grace Bakst, "Scott Lyall and Maria Hassabi," *BOMB Daily*, February 11, 2014: http://bombmagazine.org/article/1000022/scott-lyall-and-maria-hassabi.

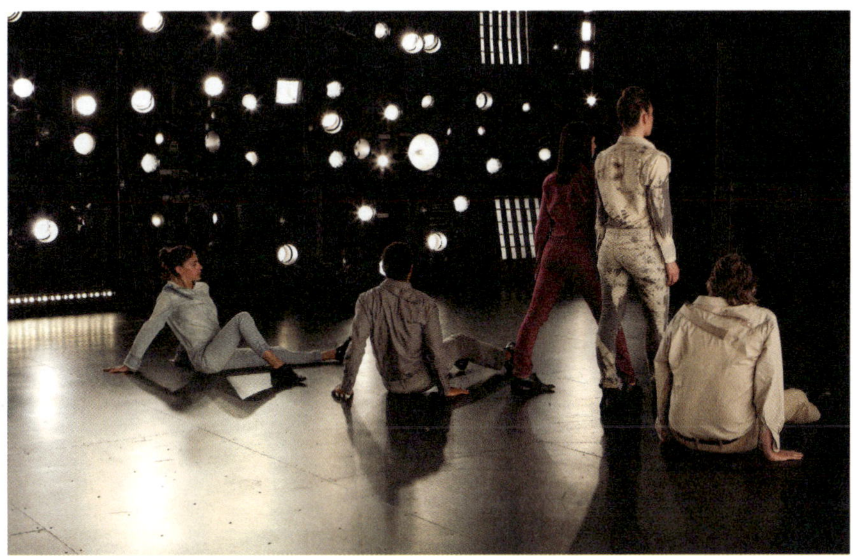

Maria Hassabi, *Premiere* (2013), performance view.

Although Hassabi had previously reimagined pieces for presentation outside the performance space—both in museums and out of doors—*Intermission* was her first work designed for gallery viewing: performed on a loop for the entirety of exhibition hours, neither timed nor ticketed. Its title makes clear, however, that the theater was never far from her mind. And, indeed, after this "break," the choreographer returned to her chosen forum with *Premiere*.

At a moment when the visual arts and performance are struggling to incorporate the latest digital technologies and make allowances for viewers' increasingly dispersed attention, *Premiere* strips everything away and asks audiences to sit and focus—a concentrated stillness that parallels that of the performers. While this can be a challenge, it is also a luxury: a pause, when we have time to observe and absorb every movement.

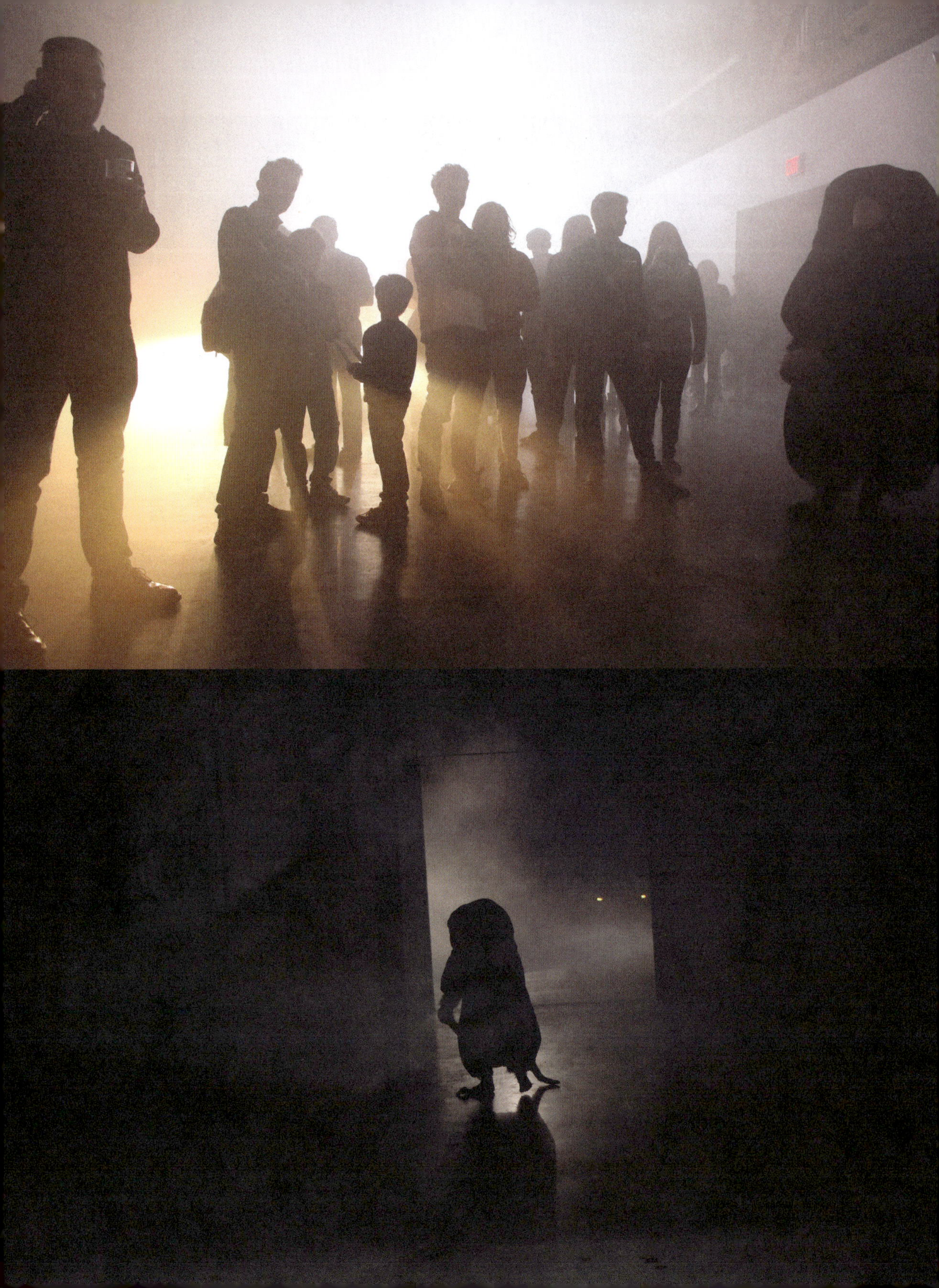

PHILIPPE QUESNE

BIVOUAC

On a chilly weekend afternoon, in a remote location in Brooklyn, a group of intrepid spectators waited for a bus to take them on a journey to an unknown destination. On board, French stage director and visual artist Philippe Quesne welcomed the audience and informed them that they would be part of an experiment called *Bivouac*, named for a camping term describing a temporary encampment for mountaineers or soldiers. The spectators also learned that the performance relied on their participation and that they would create group scenes for the camera, which would be disseminated via social media to generate rumors about the work. In other words, the afterlife of the performance was the reason for the event.

The group was taken on a bus ride through the streets of Red Hook at sunset. A curious movie of a human-sized mole on a construction site played on overhead monitors, accompanied by an eerie soundtrack on the sound system. Acting as tour guide, Quesne directed the group's attention to the sights: the harbor, the panoramic views of the shimmering Manhattan skyline, and the Statue of Liberty. Deeply influenced by Samuel Beckett and his perplexing *Waiting for Godot* (1953), Quesne's slow ride was an extension of his earlier absurd and disconcerting works in which performers look for something that is never entirely revealed. For *Bivouac*, the spectators-turned-performers also found themselves looking for something that might or might not reveal itself.

Thirty minutes into the ride, the human-sized mole from the movie suddenly appeared on a street corner and guided the driver to the doors of a darkened warehouse, which opened to allow the bus to enter. Inside, a pristine, white cube gallery was filled with thick smoke, and a theremin-player (Dorit Chrysler) performed as passengers dismounted. There, Quesne orchestrated a series of tableaux vivants, emphasizing the "role" of the audience in coming together as performers in this piece, thus inverting traditional expectations of audience and performer. As he does in so many of his works, Bivouac bounced back and forth between make-believe and seeing-is-believing, exposing the mechanics of illusion.

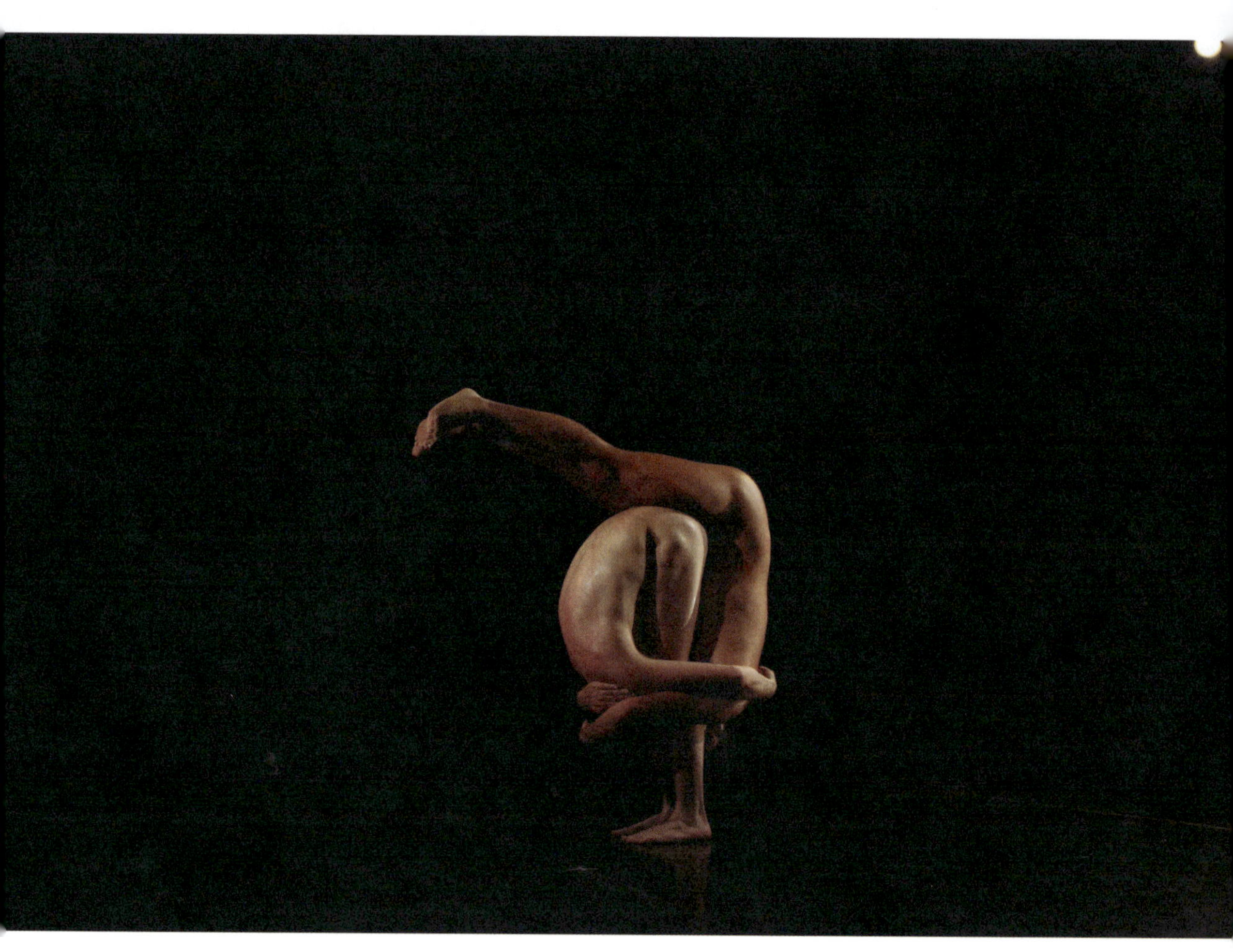

PIETER AMPE AND GUI GARRIDO/CAMPO

STILL STANDING YOU

They say it's a man's world, but that doesn't mean men have it easy. Friendship, for example, between two men is always a complicated affair: be close but not too close; touch but not too much; be understanding but never emotional. Above all, stay on top. How this translates into dance is the stuff of Belgian artist Pieter Ampe and Portuguese artist Gui Garrido's hilarious and provocative choreography jointly known as CAMPO.

In *Still Standing You*, the two performers use their own relationship as the point of departure for a duet that elicited laughter, gasps, and unreserved cringing from audiences in the studio space of the Martha Graham Dance Company (formerly the space of Merce Cunningham Company), converted to a black-box theater for the performance.

Wearing street clothes, the performance began with Ampe lying supine on the floor with his legs extended into the air, supporting Garrido, perched on top of them as though casually sitting on a stool. Garrido warmed up the audience with jokes about their trip to the U.S. and the gala opening of the biennial, while Ampe's legs began to shake from the physical strain of holding him up. "This is Pieter," said Garrido from above, as though introducing a favorite pet, just before attempting to stand straight up on top of Ampe's skyward-stretching arms and then taking a hard spill onto the floor.

Seizing Ampe's legs and dragging him roughly, Garrido soon helped catapult Ampe into a position clutching Garrido's back with his legs wrapped around his waist, carrying both sexual and childish connotations. Ampe soon transformed from victim to aggressor, hissing and clawing in the direction of the audience like a bearded Tyrannosaurus rex. Later, with Garrido splayed on the floor, Ampe jumped up and down on top of him, literally testing how much physical pain his partner could stand. Who held the power in this relationship shifted constantly, often in surprising ways—when Ampe pulled a limp Garrido offstage by the arm and leg, like an animal who had captured his prey, they circled back onstage again in the same way, but this time with Garrido raising an arm and leg into the air

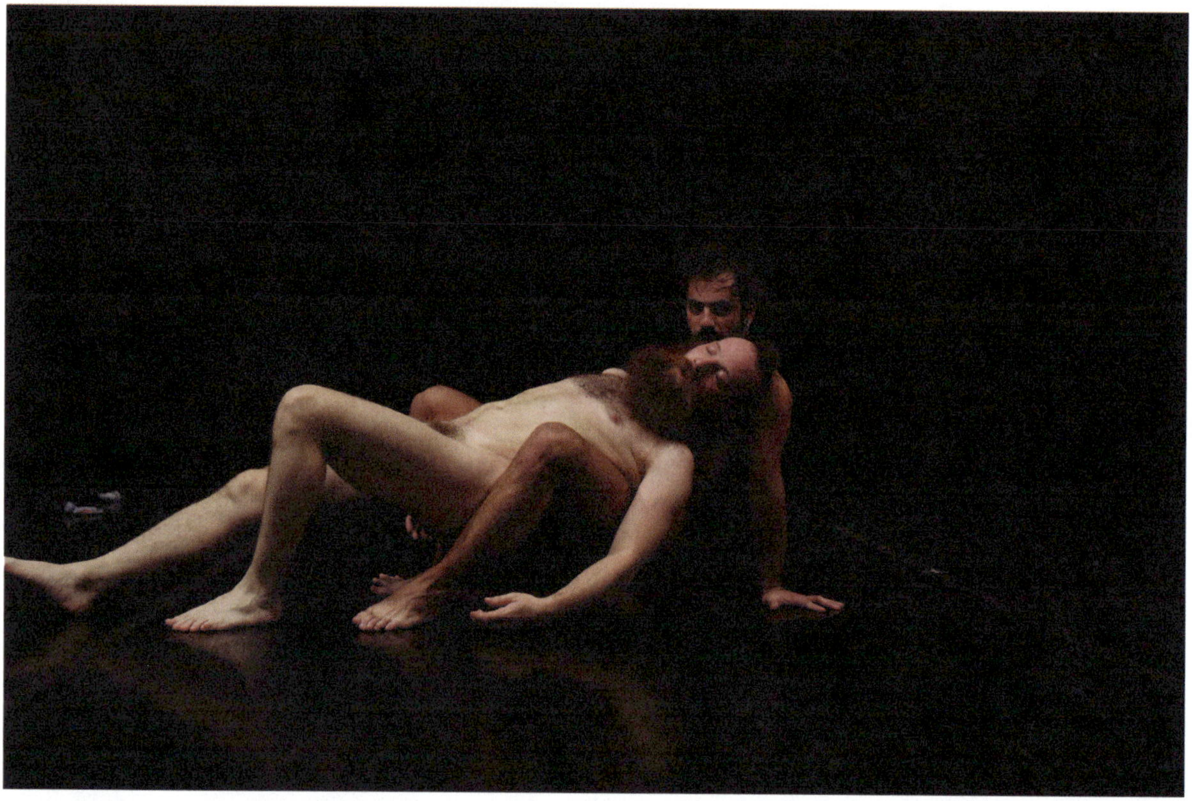

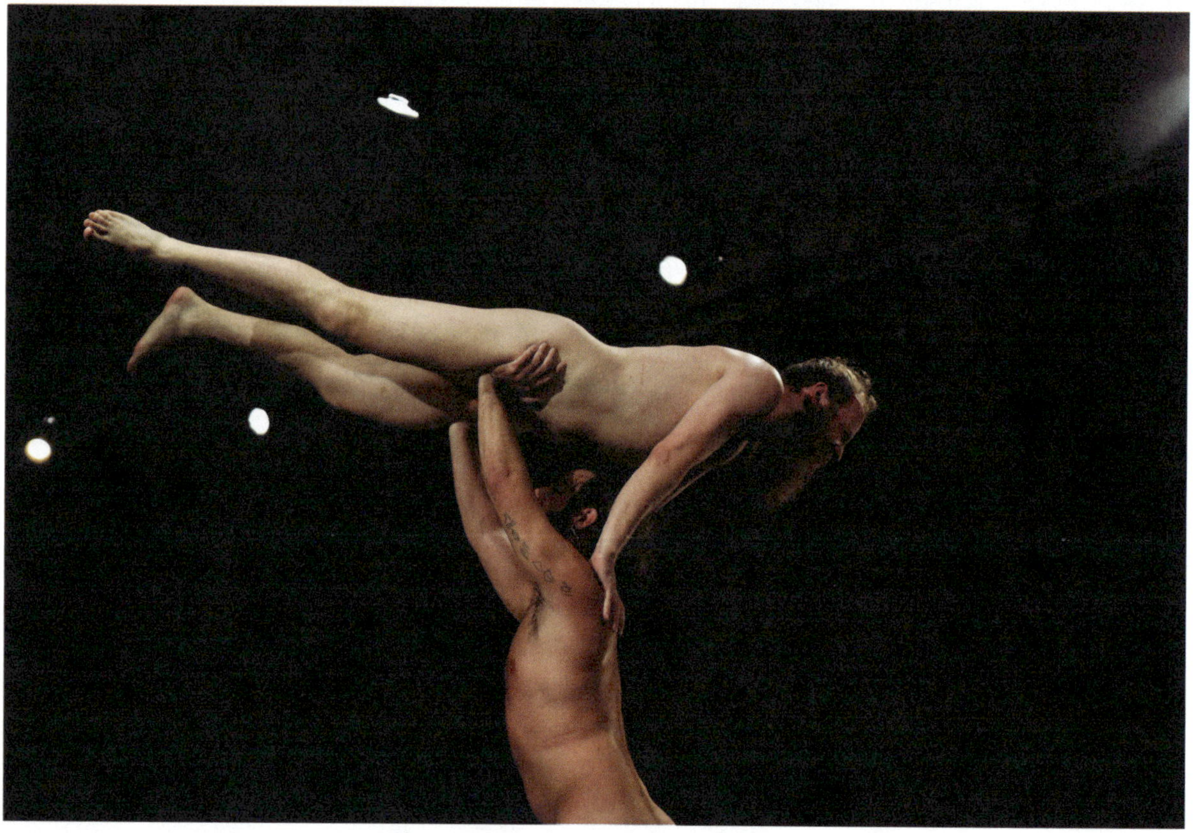

as Ampe spun him around, becoming an Olympic ice dancer in his climactic turn. It might have seemed like a contest in which strength decided all—until a clever maneuver by one man reframed the entire dynamic. New Rule: if you can't win the game, change the rules.

The high point of all this roughhousing was when the two stripped each other of their clothing, howling and wailing like ninjas throughout, finally showing their naked and vulnerable masculinity. They then launched into attacking each other's penises, enacting the worst fear of every man, including those in the audience. Initially playful, shaking each others' penises like businessmen shaking hands, the pair started slow-motion twisting and somersaulting, never relinquishing their grips on each other's members, as though playing a high-stakes game of Twister. The audience writhed and shrieked in empathy. In one unforgettable moment, Ampe pulled Garrido's foreskin out like the head of a microphone and screamed into it.

After the rowdiness of the first half-hour, these two naked, male figures gradually slowed, and their relationship began evoking various poses from art history. Ampe lounged between Garrido's legs on the floor in a shape resembling Manet's *Olympia* (1863). Garrido took Ampe in his arms, and the pair transformed into Michelangelo's *Pietà* (1498-99). Later, they made their own bodies more abstract, facing nintey degrees away from the audience to create linear shapes (inverted triangles, tightly stacked Ls) that read as purely graphic rather than representational. Quiet moments of extraordinary tenderness and intimacy—of the kind that could only be held between two real-life friends and rivals—gradually emerged.

Still Standing You unraveled ways in which masculinity itself is a performance. In the duet, CAMPO showed how every intimate relationship contains a kaleidoscope of contradictory feelings and ideas, as well as physical actions used to express them. Sometimes the difference between a hug and a choke is only a matter of degree.

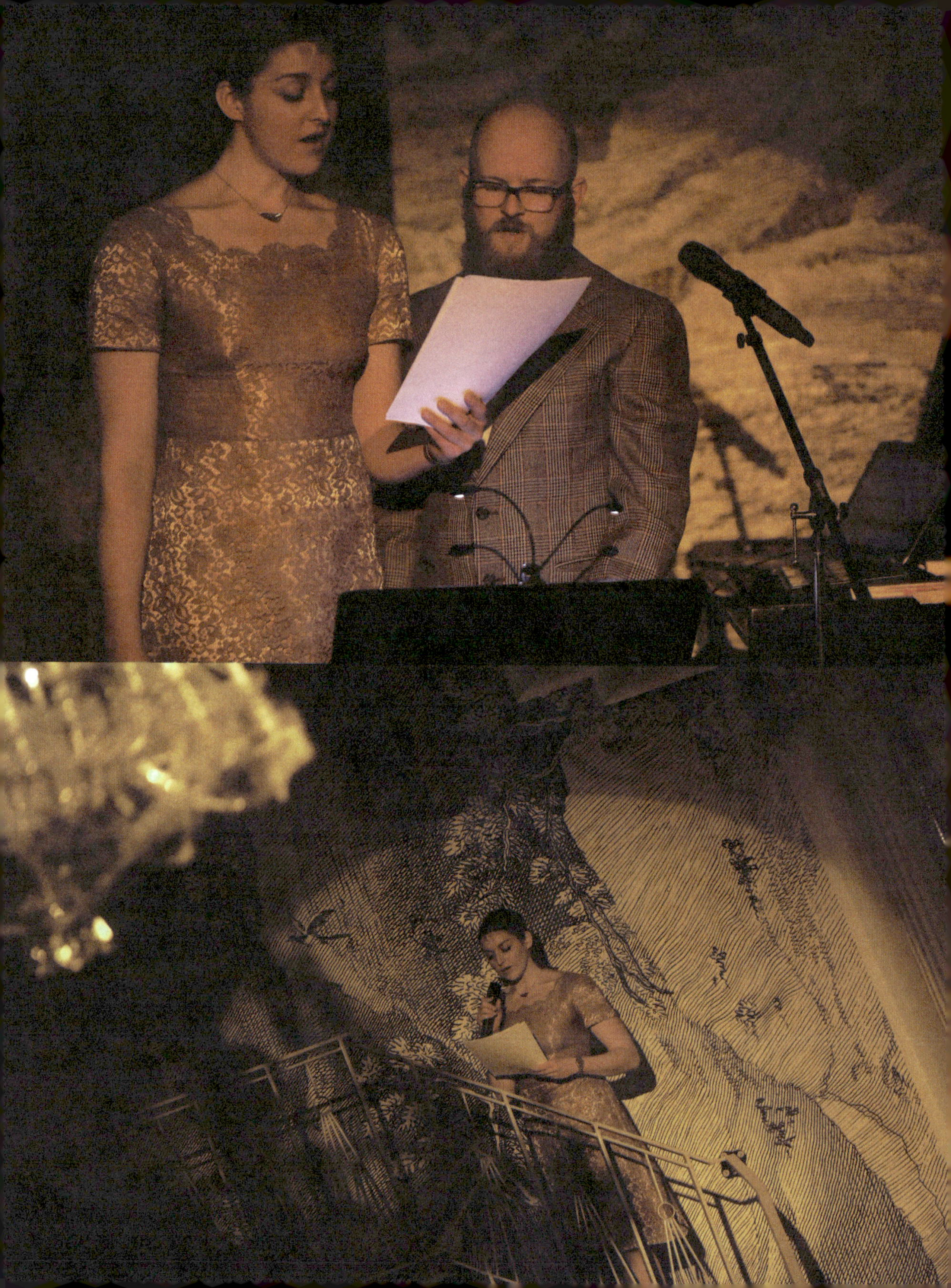

ELEANOR BAUER

BAUER HOUR

Primarily known as a choreographer and a dancer for austere avant garde artists like Anna Teresa De Keersmaeker, Trisha Brown, Xavier Le Roy, and Boris Charmatz, American-born, Brussels-based performer Eleanor Bauer has recently been experimenting with forays into more "entertainment"-based projects like *The Heather Lang Show By Eleanor Bauer and Vice Versus* (2009–2013), an outrageous talk show incorporating songs, fortune-telling, television commercials, and audience call-ins; and BAUER HOUR (2013–present), a peripatetic late-night variety show featuring interviews, scores, and set pieces with other artists, both of which have been presented at theaters, galleries, and performance spaces across America and Europe.

For Performa 13, Bauer presented a version of *BAUER HOUR* in which the setting and aesthetics of an old-timey variety show collided head-on with a seemingly unrelated text drawn from Bauer's year-long writing practice for her ensemble dance performance *Midday & Eternity (the time piece)* (2013). In this writing practice, Bauer and her dancers tried to capture the flow of their thoughts in rehearsal by writing in a "stream of consciousness" style, as an audio track of prerecorded spoken words related to time or physical movement practices played in the background. For Performa 13, some of the material that resulted was compiled into a long poem that Bauer read on stage.

Wearing a vintage bronze dress, Bauer stood under a spotlight in the faux *fin-de-siècle* grandeur of the newly renovated Bowery Poetry Club and recited this poem, which contained a mixture of speculative musing about the nature of time ("The organ stretches onward—it's the longest note ever played in the history of music—in the history of man—it's a song for the dinosaurs") and startling imagery that juxtaposed concrete memories with the more abstract language of time ("My mother had a premonition while her sister was pregnant that her sister was drowning at the bottom of a pool—My mother was able to save my aunt but unable to save the present tense").
Her vocal performance frequently began as one character and gradually transformed into that of another—the escalating rant of an

CURATED AND TEXT BY LANA WILSON △ BOWERY POETRY CLUB

auctioneer shifted into the rousing cries of an evangelist preacher or the tough New York cadences of a Rat Pack member moved into the gentle unmodulated babbling of a hyper-relaxed Californian. It was as though a wide cast of characters was taking turns reading a single continuous text. Throughout Bauer's verbalizations, composer Chris Peck was her musical sidekick, accompanying her on keyboard, singing songs with lyrics about movement and time, leading a brief trick-question trivia contest, and at one point joining Bauer on stage to dance in tandem, performing slow Bauhaus-style gestures in which the two mirrored each other's angular, mechanical-looking arm movements.

For Bauer, this performance of *BAUER HOUR* crystallized a moment in her career when she could address what she describes as a kind of "schizophrenia"—as an artist who has years of extensive training as a dancer, and a reputation as a performer in the avant garde dance world, how can she go beyond that world to follow other interests, particularly high-concept comedy? *BAUER HOUR* is part of her ongoing quest to understand the relationship between entertainment, with its expectations to instantly communicate with an audience, and conceptual art practices, whether in dance or visual arts, with their more opaque references and constructs, which are more likely to be incommunicable and intentionally so. Bauer's literal and symbolic search for a "voice" shows her to be an artist who is inspired by many different voices. They may share some connection, some large overriding themes—of the masochism of performing, or how an artist finds self-worth—or perhaps, as Bauer later said, "the only way to make sense of them is to keep moving through them all." Like a snapshot of a moment in time in one artist's lifelong search, this version of *BAUER HOUR* captured Bauer in pursuit of an idea, in a way that was both unexpected and bold.

(Above) Eleanor Bauer, *BAUER HOUR* (2013), performance view. (Below) Bauer's notes from talk at Performa Institute.   Photos by Paula Court

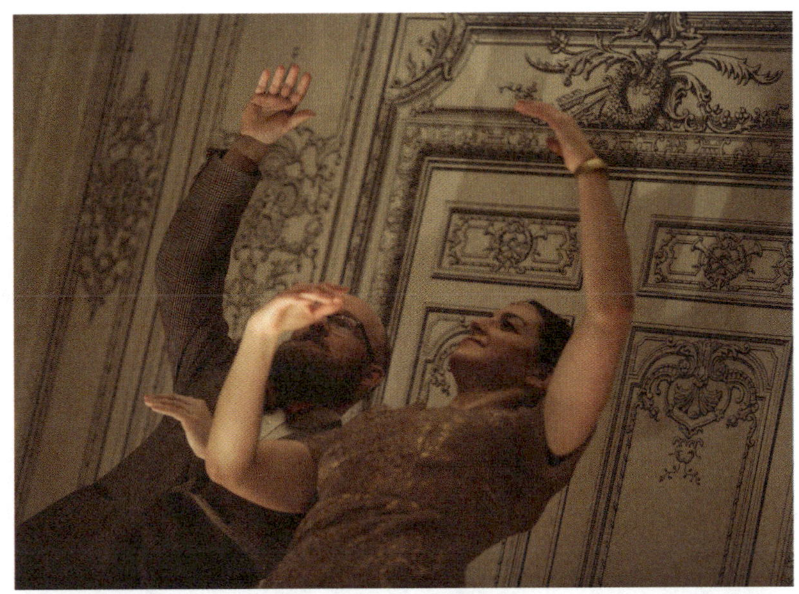

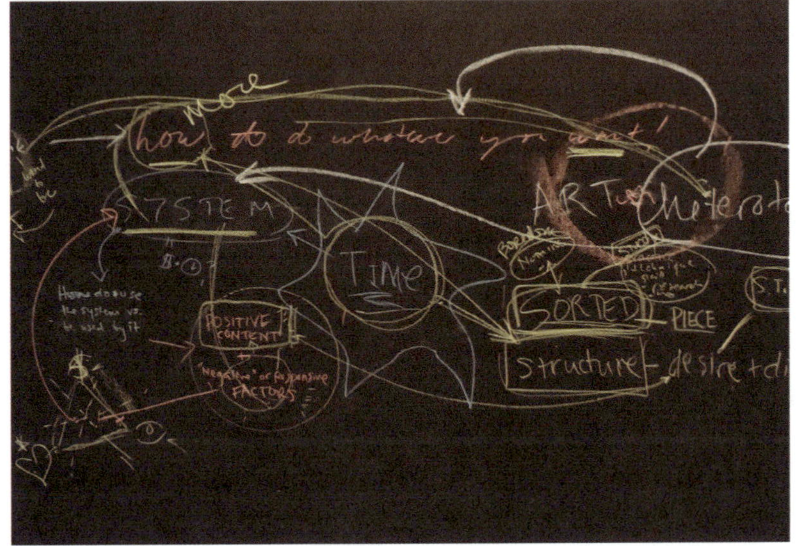
more
how to do whatever you want!
SYSTEM
ART
TIME
POSITIVE CONTENT
SORTED
PIECE
structure
desire
FACTORS

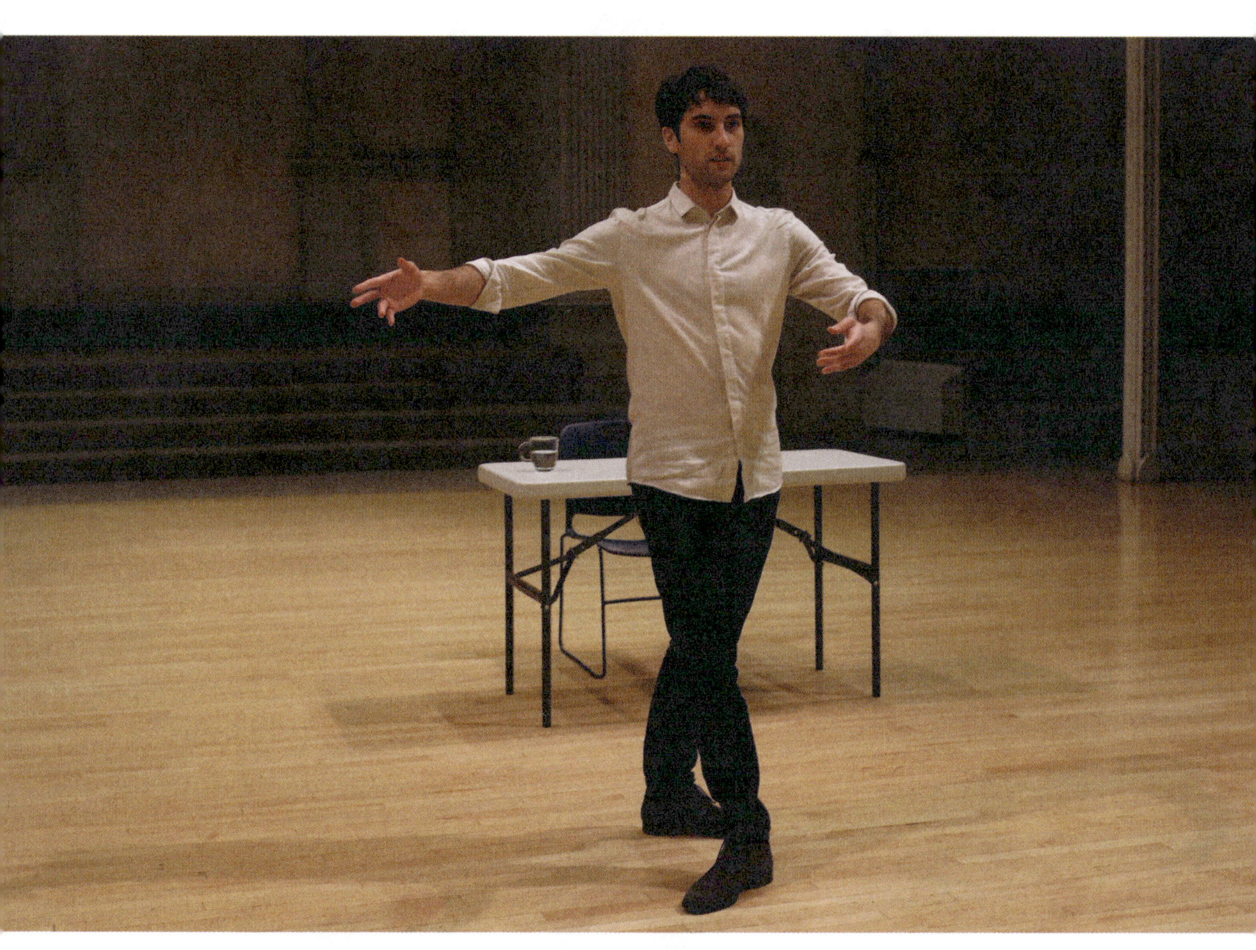

IDÉOGRAPHIE

Nurtured by the figures of "post-structuralism"—Gilles Deleuze, Jacques Derrida, Michel Foucault, and Julia Kristeva—French contemporary dance over the past two decades, spearheaded by Jérôme Bel, Boris Charmatz, Emmanuelle Huynh, and Xavier Le Roy, has offered challenging ways to reconsider the dancer's body and movements, as well as the politics of his/her presence on stage in a theater. Representing a younger generation, Noé Soulier extends this conceptual tradition, but shifts the subject matter to the logic systems of philosophers of language such as Ludwig Wittgenstein or J.L. Austin, and to inquiries in phenomenology (Edmund Husserl and Maurice Merleau-Ponty) as the starting points of his choreography.

Clad in tee-shirt and jeans, Soulier entered the brightly lit hall of St. Mark's Church, with its blond-wood dance floor and white-trellised balcony. He sat at a table, with a glass of water at hand, and began an hour-long performance, explaining to his audience that the content of the performance they were about to see was based on a collage of ten different texts ranging from the difficulties of "seeing and being" in one's body in Merleau-Ponty's *Phenomenology of Perception* (1945) to the life and times of a small female tick searching for blood in German biologist Jakob von Uexküll's texts.

As the performance progressed, *Idéographie* moved beyond the lecture format—designed to convey meaning—to an exploration of the melody of words and texts. Pacing the stage from table to chair and from chair to the front row of the audience, sentences were repeated, as if choruses of a song, cut and reassembled, blurring the original meanings into abstract phrases. In the final section, two solos emerged: one about Soulier's memories of learning how to perform a pirouette, which he demonstrated, the other examining the chain of muscles implicated in the action of grabbing, holding, and drinking a glass of water. With *Idéographie*, which etymologically means "a writing of ideas," Soulier played with the mechanics of movement and the thoughts that produce them, while creating a mental dance that pushed the boundaries of what choreography can be.

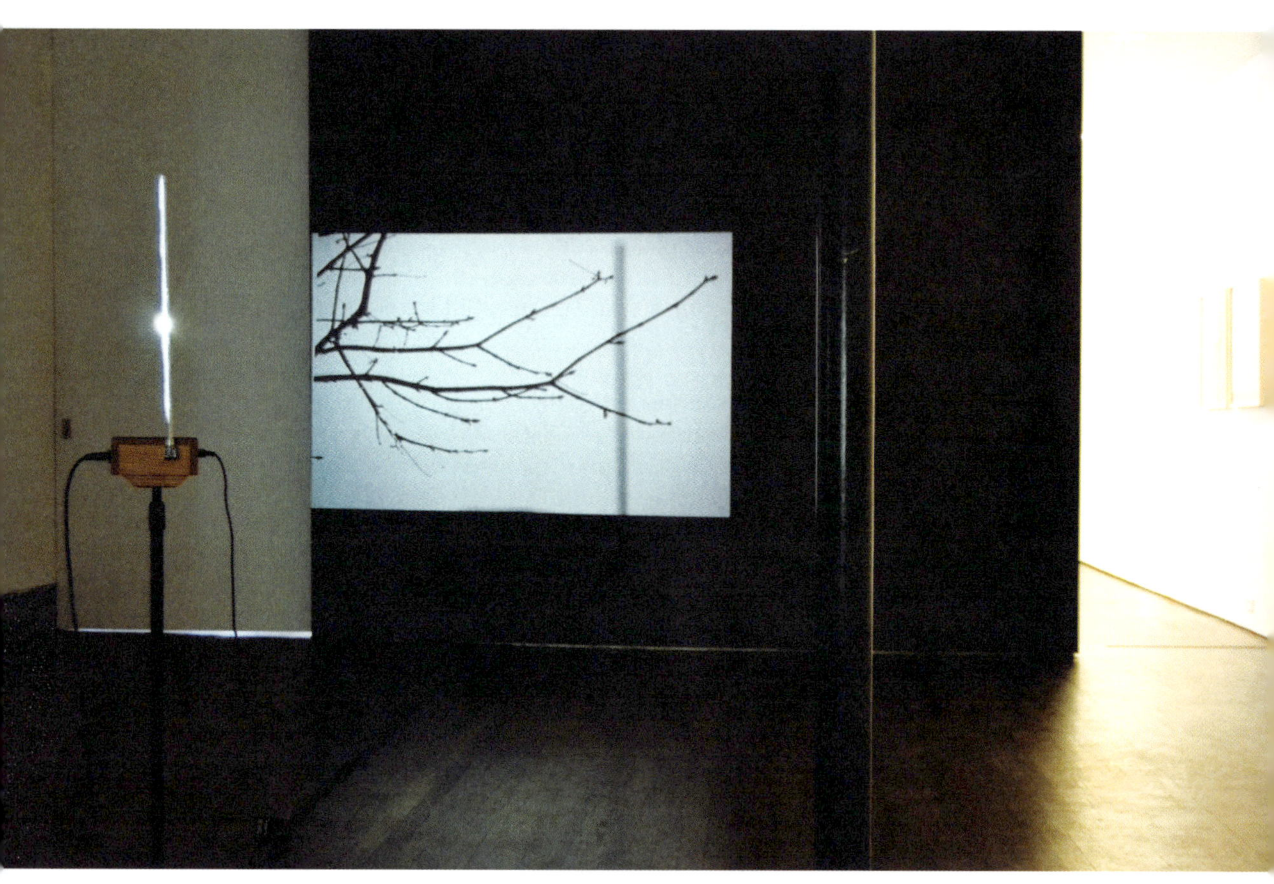

ATHANASIOS ARGIANAS

BRANCHING MUSIC
(UNDER THE TREES, ABOVE YOU)

Athens-born artist and composer Athanasios Argianas's work explores the ways in which we process and record natural, scientific, or social information, and the possibilities of transferring the notational structures of languages between acoustic and physical media. In *Branching Music (Under the Trees, Above You)*, Argianas transcribed the natural forms of a tree branch, projected on a wall of On Stellar Rays gallery, into a "score" performed nearby by theremin player Dalit Warshaw, who ran her hand over the branch images, literally "performing the image," while simultaneously generating sound.

Argianas determined parameters for movement: the length of each branch is a syllable; Warshaw's hands may pause at nodes or intersections. The natural ratios of tree branch lengths and angles created an index for the performer that, when combined with Argianas's compositional parameters, produced open-ended, improvisational compositions, at moments articulating clear tonality, and sometimes collapsing into noise. In his work, Argianas has made reference to early twentieth-century electronic instruments—such as the theremin and the ondes Martenot—experimental music and compositional methods from the 1960s, concrete poetry, the Constructivism of Naum Gabo, and Duchamp's *Machine Optique* (1920) and its circular deployment of language.

Against the wall, the performer's hands cast a visible shadow in contrast to the branches, creating choreography that joined natural form and mechanical technology. The ethereal sound of the theremin within the darkened gallery created a heightened perception of visual, acoustic, and social experiences, ranging from spirited and playful to hauntingly beautiful in its capacity to bridge the structures of musical and visual composition.

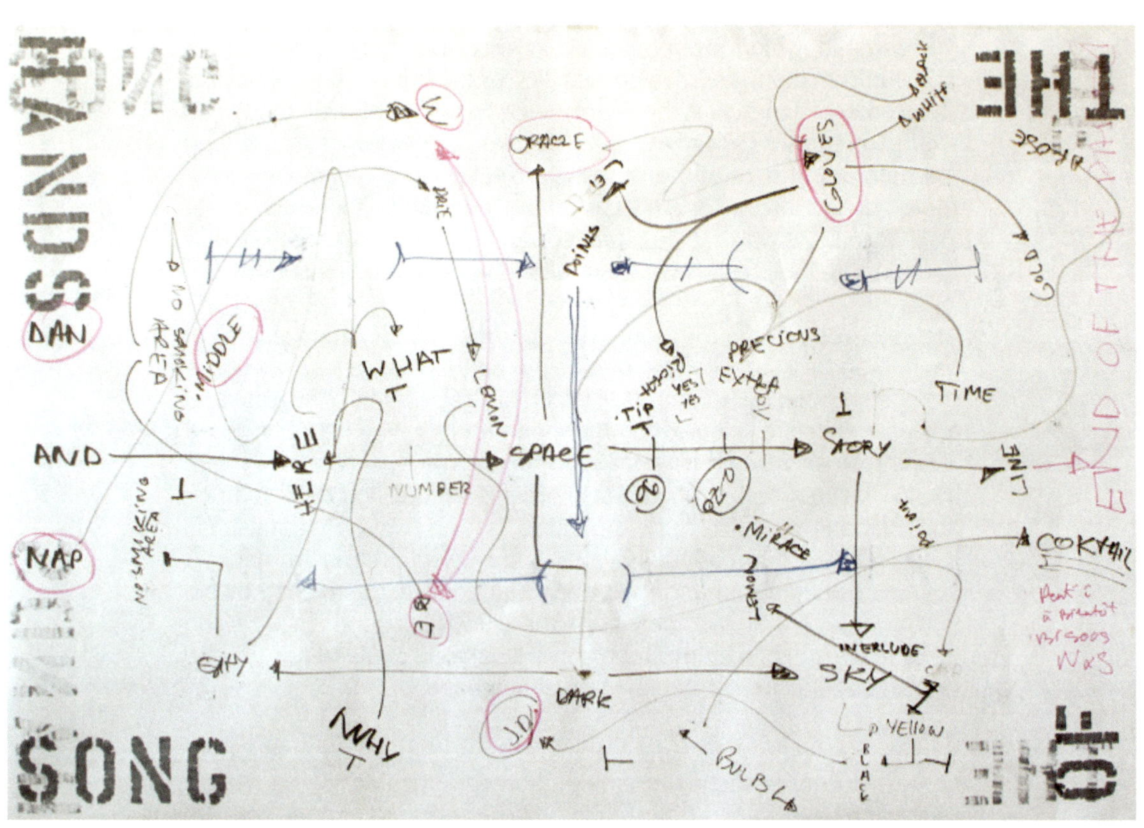
HANDS
DANCING
SONG
DAN
NAP
AND
THE
WHAT
HERE
MIDDLE
NO SMOKING AREA
NO SMOKING AREA
ORACLE
SPACE
NUMBER
LEMON
POINTS
LEFT
GLOVES
BLACK
WHITE
GOLD
PRECIOUS
EXTRA
YES
TIP
TIME
STORY
LINE
COCKTAIL
MIRAGE
INTERLUDE
SKY
DARK
WHY
BULB
YELLOW
END OF THE

JULIE BÉNA WITH ADRIEN VESCOVI

THE SONG OF THE HANDS

Paris-based artist Julie Béna's approach to performance—its execution and relationship to the audience—was developed early on under the many "big tops" of her childhood where she spent hours on the road with her mother, who worked in a traveling theatrical troupe. Béna's work, which includes impeccably crafted small sculptures as well as videos and photographs, uses the exhibition space, as she describes it, as her playground: each becomes a set for a sparse but elegantly lit installation and tableaux vivant that sometimes includes singers and actors. *The Song of the Hands* took place in a Brooklyn storefront that was set up to create the atmosphere of a speakeasy. Audience members were summoned from the dimmed and decorated waiting room to a curtained-off space. There they gathered intimately around the two performers: Béna, who narrated the tale of Dan and Nad, two characters lost on "eternal round-trips" in search of a place called Elsewhere, and artist Adrien Vescovi, who drew his interpretation of the pair's trajectory on a large tabletop pad. About the tension between external display and interior worlds, with one artist drawing and the other talking, the performance deals with translation from the verbal to the graphic. The poetic use of language in *The Song of the Hands* invoked the absurdities of orienting oneself, whether personally or geographically.

100% TRANSPARENT ● CURATED BY LINDA MAI GREEN

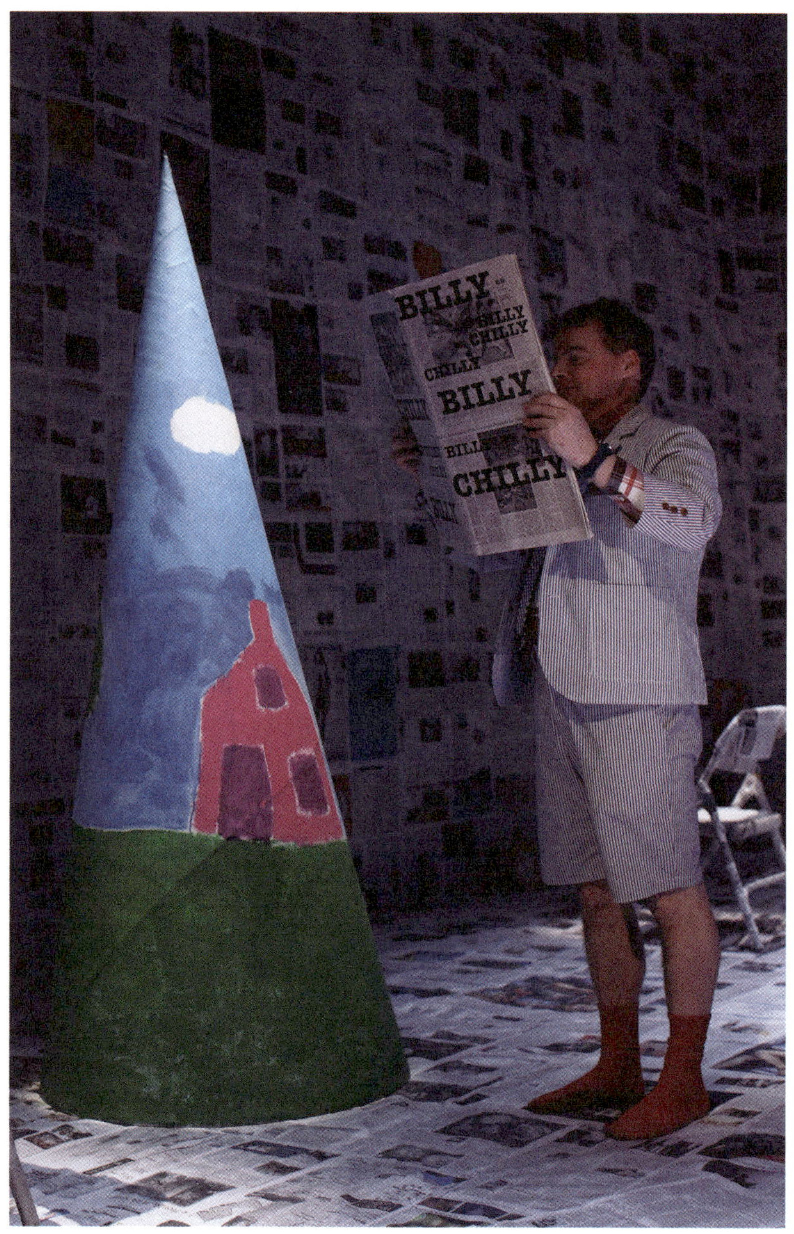
BILLY
CHILLY
CHILLY
BILLY
BILLY
CHILLY

CHRISTOPHER KNOWLES

THE SUNDANCE KID IS BEAUTIFUL

Christopher Knowles's 1973 poem *"Emily Likes the TV,"* written when he was thirteen years old, was the touchstone for Knowles' immersive exhibition-installation-live performance at WhiteBox. Moving through a colorfully decorated gallery space, tiled with newspapers from floor to ceiling, dotted with folding chairs, and punctuated with several of Knowles's signature painted objects—oversized cones and balls—and himself costumed to merge with his picture-book set, the wordsmith-collagist-performer stopped at different points in the room to theatrically recite selections from twelve separate texts.

Knowles's obsession with the sound of words, their visual appearance, and the ways in which their repetition could be made into pictures has become his signature ever since visionary performance and opera director Robert Wilson took him under his wing as a young boy. Incorporating Knowles' language puzzles into his seminal avant garde theater productions, including *A Letter for Queen Victoria* (1974), *the $ Value of Man* (1975), and his and Philip Glass's legendary opera *Einstein on the Beach* (1976), Wilson set the stage for the young Knowles' future experiments. These threads continue in his current work, *The Sundance Kid is Beautiful*, a line from *"Emily Likes the TV,"* which returns here as a central theme in Knowles' highly developed world of words.

Photo by Paula Court

Christopher Knowles, *The Sundance Kid is Beautiful* (2013), performance view.

CURATED BY BYRD HOFFMAN WATER MILL FOUNDATION ● WHITEBOX ART CENTER

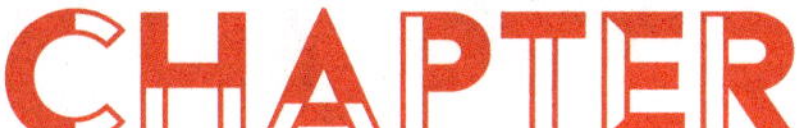

CHAPTER

6

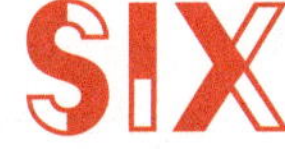

SIX

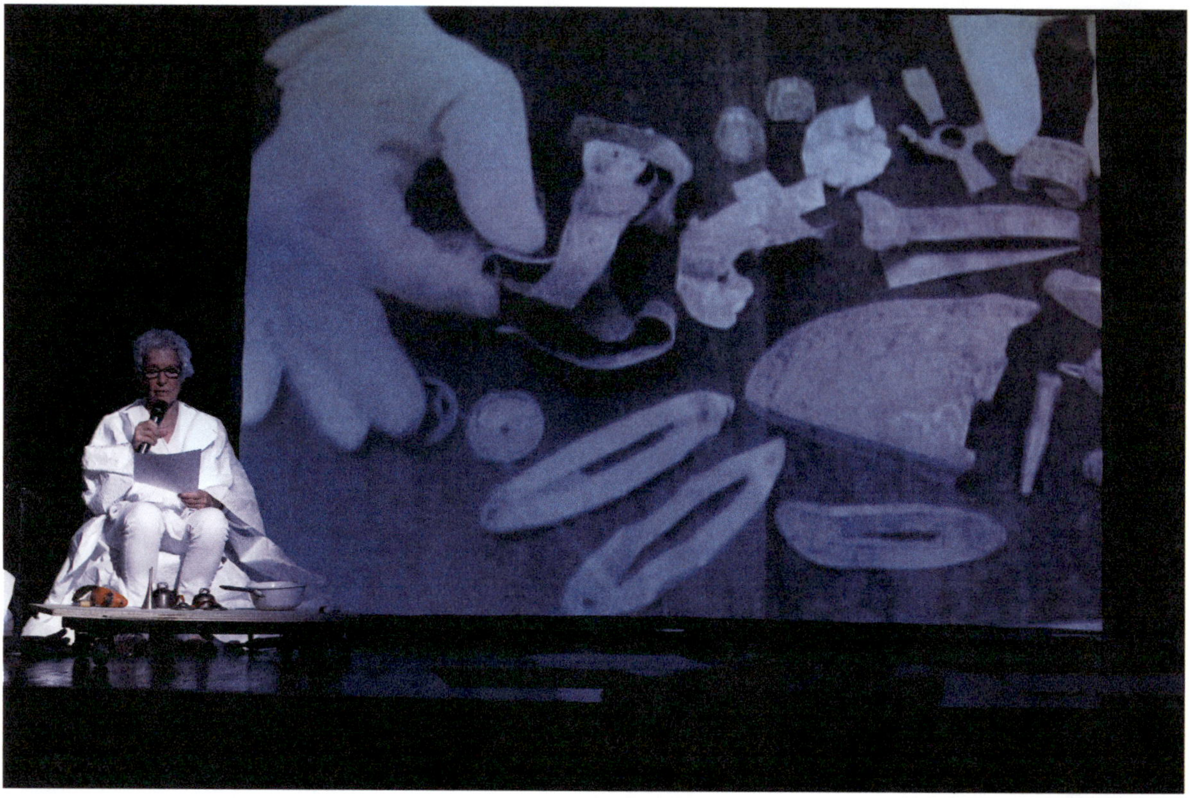

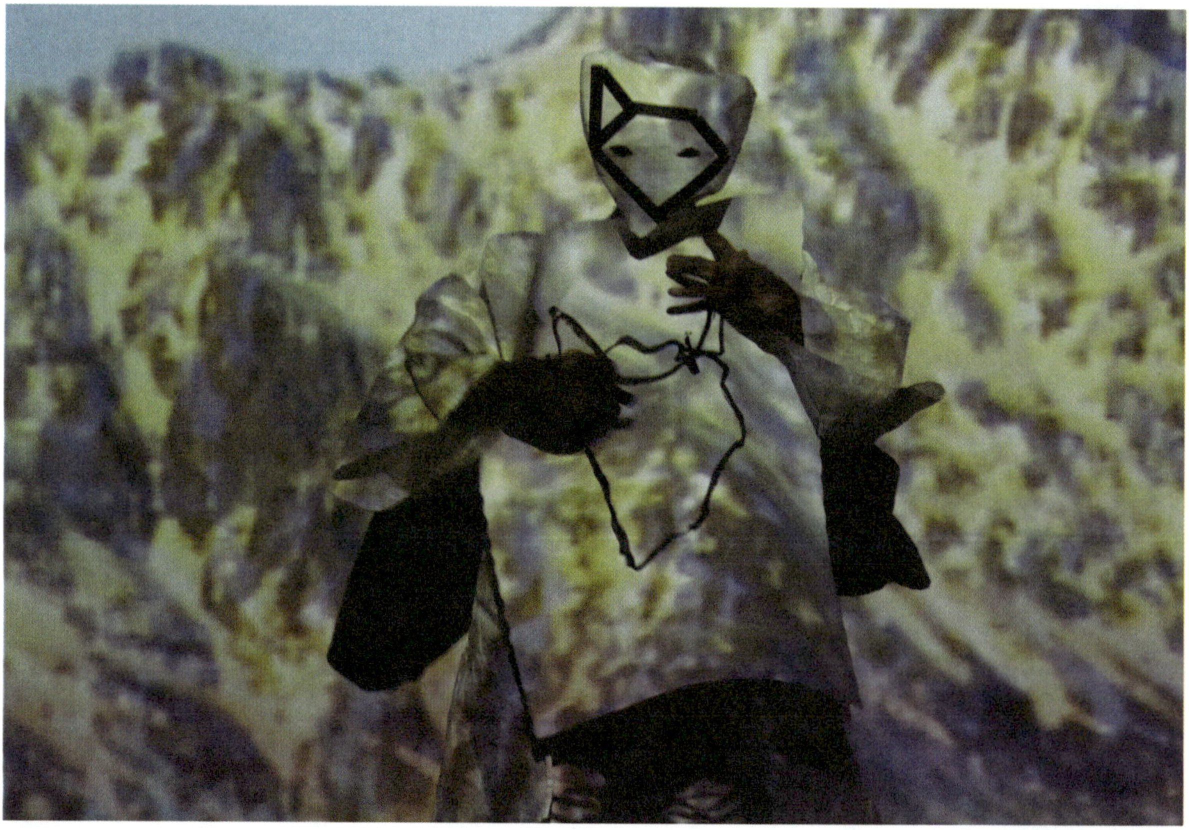

JOAN JONAS WITH JASON MORAN

REANIMATION

Joan Jonas has long taken inspiration from the Icelandic landscape and the great tradition of Icelandic storytelling—for instance, in her video and installation *Volcano Saga* (1989), about a woman whose dreams foretell her own future marriages (at least according to the dreams' interpreter). *Reanimation* is loosely based on *Under the Glacier*, a 1968 novel by Iceland's Nobel Prize-winning author Halldór Laxness, whose tale of a small Icelandic village where the renegade priest gives up burying the dead and leads his congregation in a return to paganism fed Jonas's own witty and poetic approach to what she calls the "miracle of nature." "Because glaciers are melting," Jonas remarked, she chose to incorporate aspects of this beautiful tale into *Reanimation*.

But while Laxness's words—such as his description of the interdependence of the dandelion and the honeybee, or of time as being "the one thing we can all agree to call supernatural"—are used in *Reanimation*, there is no novelistic narrative thread through the performance. Instead, the structure of the work seems essentially musical—appropriately enough, since it is a duet between Jonas and the pianist and composer Jason Moran, who appeared on stage with her throughout. This being their second collaboration—Moran also composed the music for *The Shape, The Scent, The Feel of Things* (2006)—they structured the sounds and images in tandem. "My work always divides into sections," comments Jonas, "and Jason has a different motif for each section." He plays a melody, she shows him images, "and we go back and forth," she says of their integrated way of developing individual ideas. As with many musical works, *Reanimation*'s great theme is essentially time—in this case, the contrast between the deep, slow time of a glacier and the urgent, subjective time of human need and desire.

Reanimation was not only a musical structure; space was just as important as time. But in the one as in the other, what emerged was a sense of contrast between the grand scale of landscape and the finitude of the individual. This sense emerged immediately, as Jonas appeared dwarfed by the apron stage on which she appeared.

A large screen behind her often displayed images of Iceland's wild terrain; standing at a drawing board with a camera trained on it, Jonas regularly attempted to trace the outlines of the landscape's features, to be superimposed on the photographic imagery simultaneously projected on the large screen and on her drawing board. But one image would switch to the next before she could finish adumbrating its contours. Suddenly, she would have to switch course in order to keep up with the change, and the resulting drawing would correspond to no one photographic source—thus the craggy side of a mountain might metamorphose into a horse. Perception inundates us with a flux of images we can only struggle to keep up with.

In another segment, Jonas, masked with an image of a white oversized fox, held up large sheets of paper in front of her body while frantically drawing outlines of a female figure on each before tossing it aside. The images that elude our grasp include our self-images. While the fox mask seemed to confer a sort of mythic eternity on the person of the performer, the frantic, seemingly frustrated gestures of her rough drawing communicated instead the sense of a mind and a hand racing ahead of themselves, unable to conjure the image conceived. This time, instead of a race between the human hand and an objective external image, it seemed to be a race between the hand and an inner desire.

A multilayered, approximately sixty-minute concert of words, movements, objects, images—both hand-drawn and technically mediated—and sounds both musical and otherwise, *Reanimation* succeeded in channeling Laxness's disquieting mixture of otherworldliness and irony. At times, Jonas seemed transfigured by a sort of shamanic intensity while at others, we saw her as a small, fragile, vulnerable human beset by the enormity of the world she is intent on perceiving and representing. Perhaps the ultimate realization is that one is no less magical than the other.

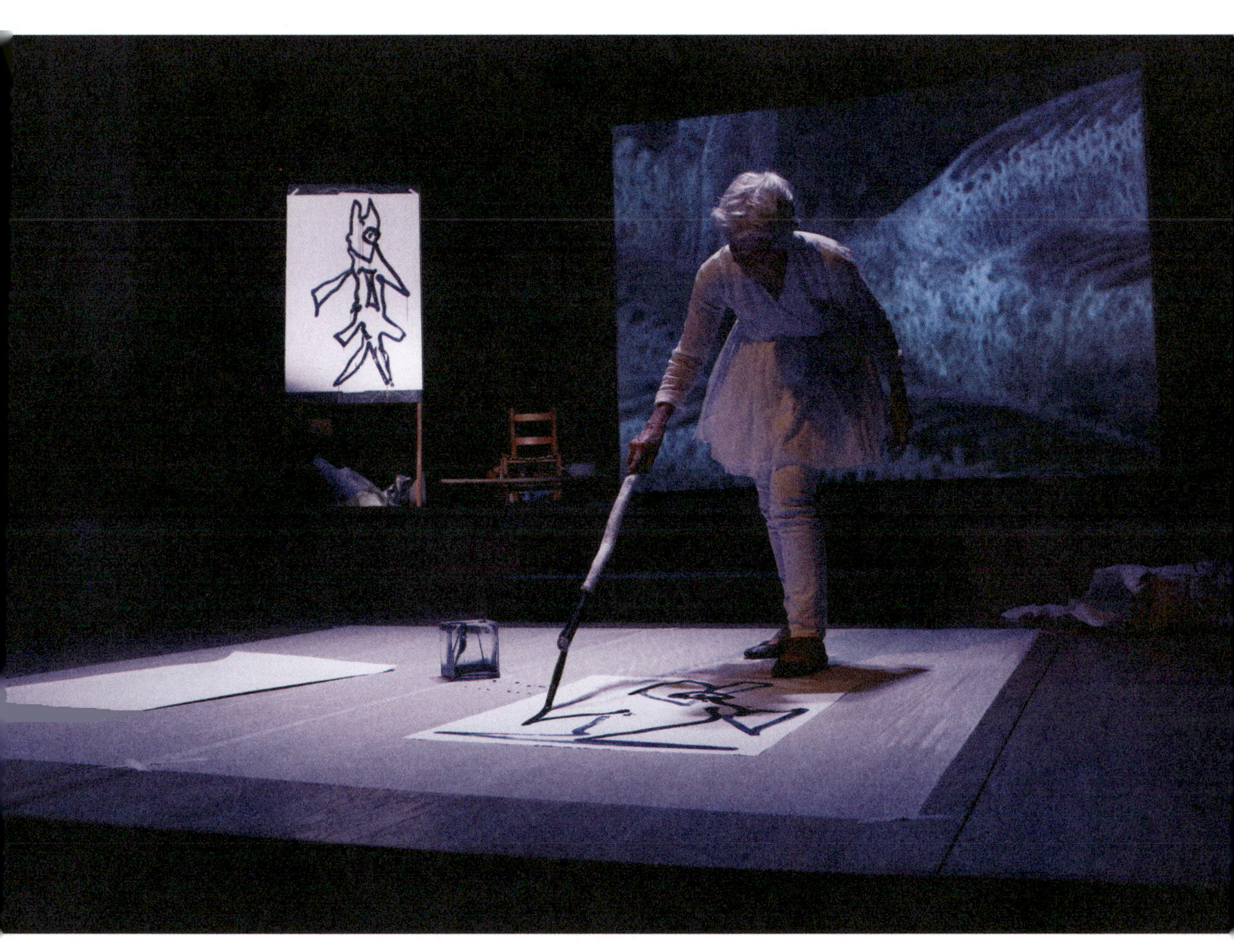

<h1 style="text-align:center">JOAN JONAS AND ROSA BARBA</h1>

<h2 style="text-align:center">IN CONVERSATION</h2>

Rosa Barba: Because I had never done a performance before, I was very sensitive to the audience—they were for me like actors too. For the first two nights, I was curious and the audience made me more present. How important is the audience to you?

Joan Jonas: Audiences are great if there is a correspondence—an energy. It's like teaching, you have to take control. If you depend on the energy of the audience, and sometimes that can happen, you can sink in too. There is a big difference with a Saturday night audience. The audience can be a difficult relationship. I can also be affected by something else and one performance can be better than another. You have to put your energy into the performance itself, not into what you think the audience is.

RB: But you are not on stage, which is a difference.

JJ: Right, you are not on stage, but directing the performance and looking at the audience … that's more difficult. You know, I don't wear my glasses when I am performing. I don't want to see faces.

I have only seen one of your pieces before, *The Empirical Effect* (2009), set in a volcanic landscape; this had a strong impression on me because it was an interesting subject, and there is something about the way you make your work—engaging groups of people—that is very different. Where was that shot?

RB: That was in Vesuvio in Naples, where I worked with people who had survived the last volcanic explosion. Making a film is a different approach than a performance, because although my films happen with people who are not actors, our works, they are documents that emerge.

JJ: I made a video called *Volcano Saga* (1989) in Iceland, based on an Icelandic saga called the *Laxdeala Saga,* but they are very different. *Volcano Saga* was a narrative, so while there may be commonalities between us, the structures are different—because I work with narratives, except in my installations. Although that's another kind of narrative, more similar to the way you constructed your piece at Anthology Film Archives—where people enter a space and they're surrounded by the piece, parts of the piece.

Landscape has always been a part of my work because it's a part of the space around us. So space is one of the main concerns in the work in relation to framing it and recording it as well as the space/place where it's presented or performed. I see the landscape as kind of a character, and it plays a very strong role.

RB: You also seem to be interested in wasteland or very spatial landscape. When you draw, you are also attentive to inscriptions of the landscape. I try to use my camera as a drawing instrument and I look for these inscriptions in the landscape. In *Reanimation*, you used your camera as a witness to the inscriptions you do in the performance.

JJ: Sometimes I draw for a video. For *Lines In The Sand* (2002-05), I drew in the sand and filmed it as I was drawing. And then sometimes the drawing is superimposed. Drawing is one of the main elements of my work, and I try and find different works of drawing in relation to the medium, the image, the situation, and the narrative, so drawing functions differently in each piece. The gesture of the drawing becomes part of that—the language. What I liked about your work is that you chose unusual locations, like the one on Second Avenue. The buildings were compelling where you chose to situate your action.

RB: I am always interested in buildings that have changed—when they don't have a specific function anymore, but lots of traces of what they may have been before remain. It's uncertain, a kind of suspended moment. In a way, you were drawing with the sound as well; it felt calming.

JJ: Yes, the sound is related to my body in the same way as the drawing. My whole body is involved with the gesture of the drawing, and the music has become the same, with Jason Moran's improvisation. I have to use my whole body to get the rhythm of that interaction. Jason says I am a percussionist: drummers use their whole body. I would have studied drumming if I knew that before. Jason improvises following consistent themes. We set the themes, timing, transitions, and signals. It is not music that is written down. The word improvisation is an interesting word; it means different things for different people.

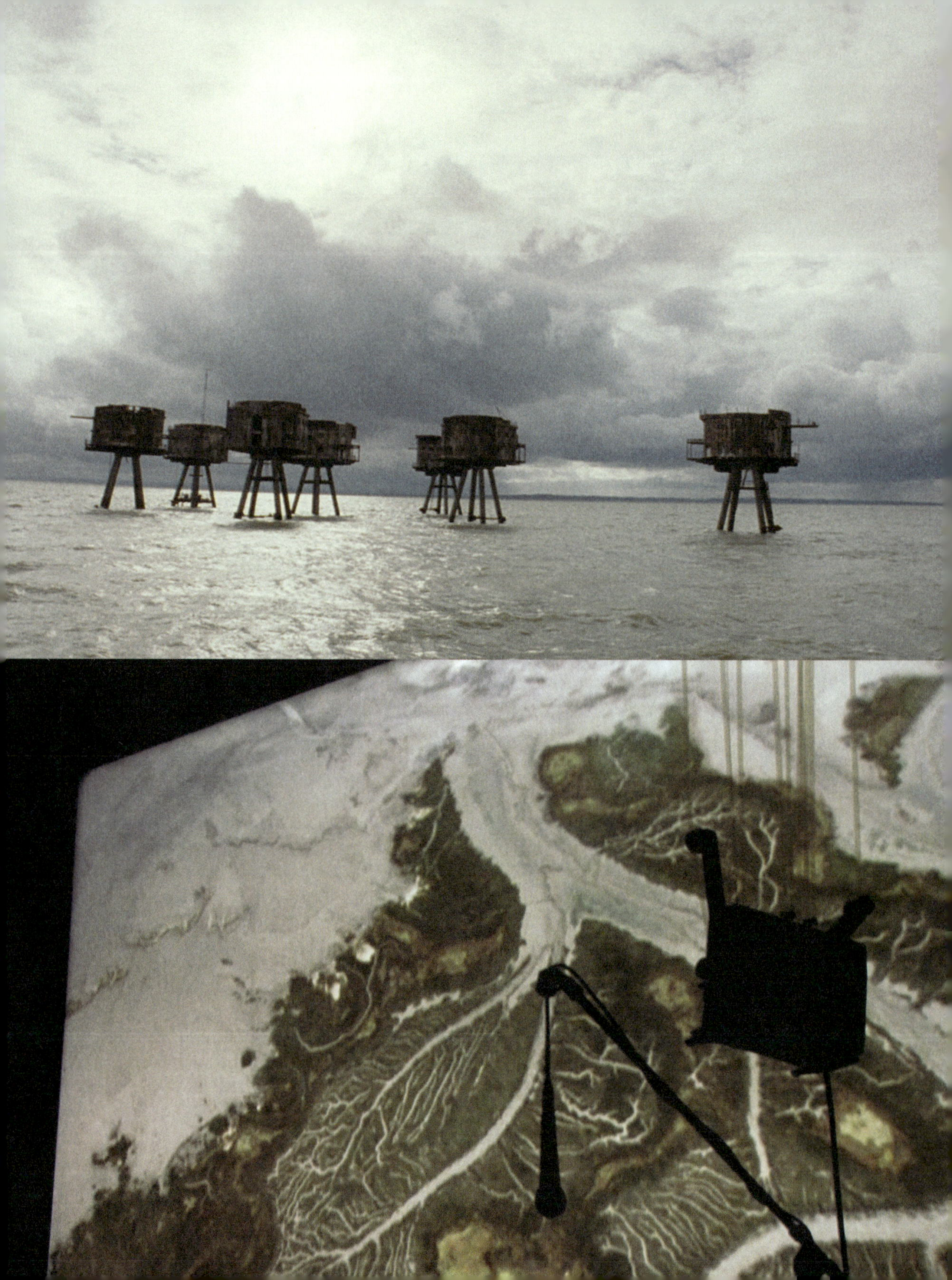

SUBCONSCIOUS SOCIETY—LIVE

In my work, I don't observe reality … I don't pose critical questions; I am trying to invent a utopia by showing political and social mechanisms set against technical mechanisms, which are themselves fragile.

—Rosa Barba

What I would like to do is build a cinema in a cave or an abandoned mine and film the process of its construction.

—Robert Smithson

Rosa Barba's work is odd, inventive, and philosophically rigorous in its examination of the technologies and effects of industrialization—especially analogue cinema. Born in 1972 in Agrigento, Italy (Barba lives in Berlin), her formal sensibility and interest in the material apparatus of celluloid film were shaped by the context of structuralist cinema from the era she was born into—for instance, the work of Michael Snow, Hollis Frampton, and Robert Smithson. Barba engages with the materiality of cinema as a sculptor who examines the effects of time and human intervention on the ravaged, lonely landscapes of industrial society, such as that found on the Kent coast in England.

Along with her ability to use the language and technology of analogue cinema within the conventions of sculpture and installation, Barba has a unique narrative imagination whose intent is not to mourn or even critique, but to create utopias and uncanny situations. *Subconscious Society—Live* was performed at Anthology Film Archives as a live event, an installation of objects, and a screening of a 35mm film called *Subconscious Society* (2013).

Before and after the film screening, the audience was encouraged to mingle among a range of meta-cinematic sculptures—conceptual contraptions which framed the fixed cinema seats. Among these sculptural elements was *Boundaries of Consumption* (2012), consisting of a 16mm projector laced with a filmstrip, a pulley, film cans, and metal globes with marbles. In the front of the room

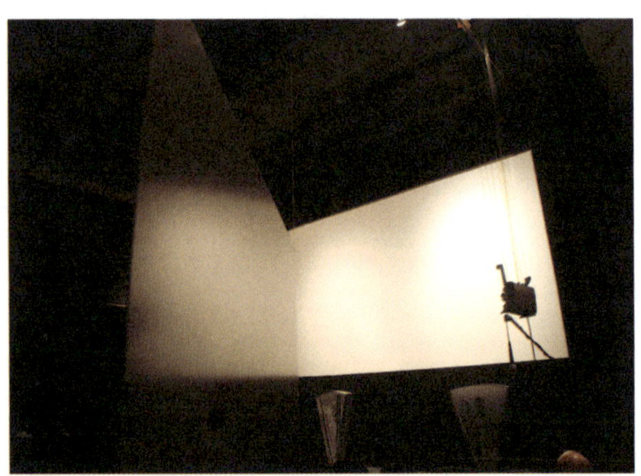
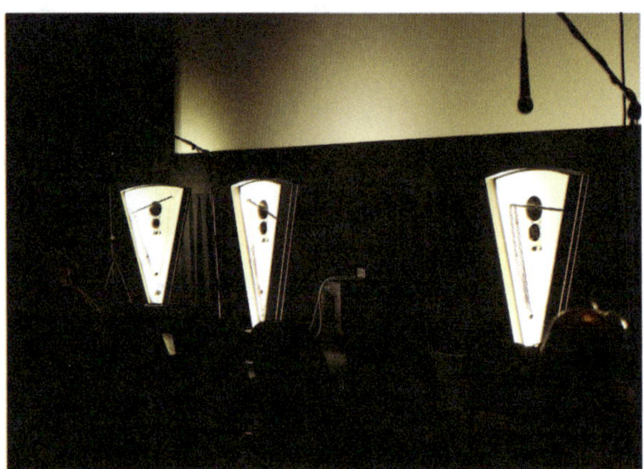
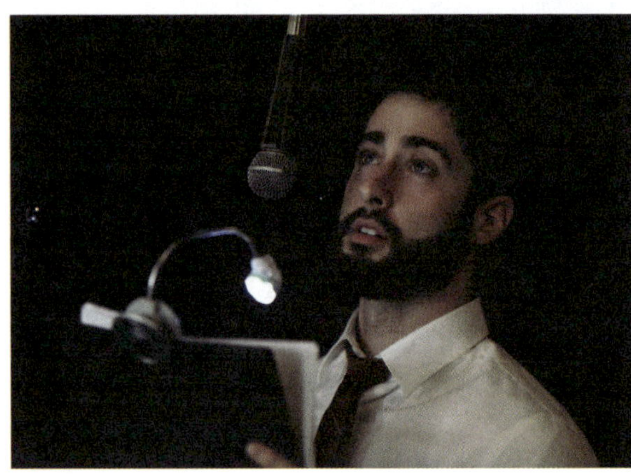
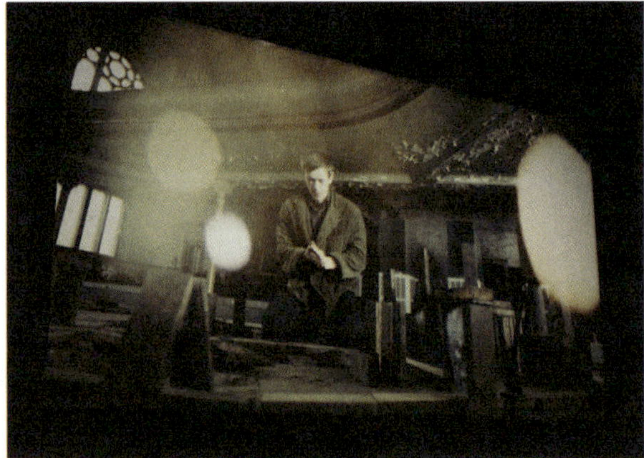

stood three upside-down triangular vitrines from Barba's 2013 solo exhibition *Subject to Constant Change* at Cornerhouse in Manchester and the Turner Contemporary in Margate, U.K. Each vitrine contained a backlit apparatus that had celluloid film leader threaded and running through a projector spool. The clear leader was marked with the word "red" (in red), "yellow" (in yellow) or "blue" (in blue), specific to each vitrine. Positioned to the right of the audience, midway into the seating and intervening into the orderly rows, was a screen on a tripod, on which text by Barba and quotes by Walter Benjamin flashed in black and white type. A lone 16mm projector attached to the ceiling by a loop of 16mm celluloid film dangled facing the audience to the right and diagonally aimed at the rear of the cinema. At moments ,while the audience watched the film in the dark theater, the projector would turn on, sending a pointed ray of light over the heads of the spectators, landing on the back wall in the shape of a rectangle of pure light onto the projectionist's booth. The effect of this light beam opened the scope of the room, expanding the space from the two-dimensional focus on the flat screen to the three-dimensionality of the physical space.

The actual 35mm film *Subconscious Society* was inspired by histories of industrialization in Manchester and the Kent coast. It is at once site-specific and unworldly—part science fiction (in feel), part absurdist play. The film "depicts a 'society' trapped inside a deteriorating interior where the characters explore what happens when objects lose their functions and meanings, while being hidden from the crumbling, abandoned world outside: rusting boats, collapsing piers and rollercoasters, and deserted buildings rising from the sea." The total effect of the projected 35mm film, with its odd, ungainly scenes of "the society" engaged in an absurdist auction of relics from the age of television, as well as crowded over a table in a planning session, or merely as still bodies standing rigid within the deteriorated church, did indeed evoke a subconscious society of profound complexity.

Subconscious Society was at once a multisensorial epic fusion of the live, the archived, and the staged; a repurposed industrial experience; and a philosophical meditation on the materiality of analogue cinema— built around a mythopoetic society of people and obsolescent technologies enclosed within the rusty architectures of monumental industrial decay.

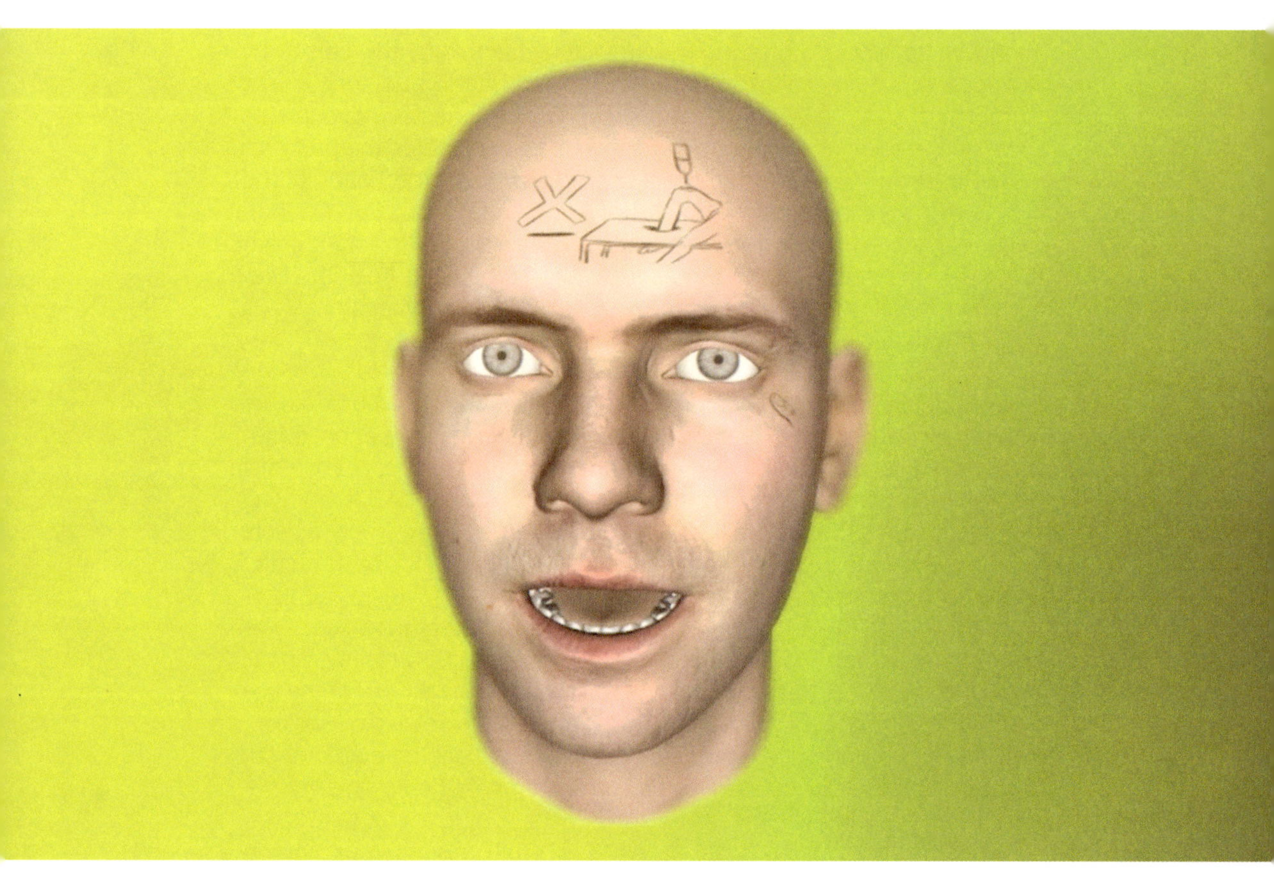

Taken from the Sanskrit word for "incarnation," and referring to an earthly manifestation of a deity, the word "avatar" has come to mean a digital alter ego, a computer-generated persona that inhabits a virtual world. Ed Atkins is known for the poetic ruminations of his own avatars who lament the isolation and longing produced by technological forms of communication. *Man of Steel* was a program of ten moving-image works, through which Atkins explored the deep disembodiment of contemporary avatars, presented in the isolating darkness of the cinema. The selection surveyed various uses of surrogates, characters, and doubles in relation to the affective dynamics of media technologies. Whether computer-generated, morphed, masked, or hand-drawn, the avatars in *Man of Steel* were cast as misanthropic figures, produced in and by the isolation of modern technological existence. Superman, that fundamentally duplicitous hero and alter ego of Clark Kent, served as a dubious archetype for *Man of Steel*, which captured how an avatar's displacement of agency can be equal parts disturbing and liberating.

The evening opened with two recent videos by young female artists— *Which Bitch is a Witch* (2001) by Tolia Astakhishvili and *Deportment* (2011) by Rachel Reupke. Where Astakhishvili exploits the amateur aesthetic of YouTube as she costumes herself in cheap wigs and make-up and adopts different accents, each asking the question of her title in a different way, Reupke uses digital manipulations to reverse figure/ground relationships in a romantic scene of a woman and a man at a candlelit table. After a brief musical interlude, an excerpt from Vito Acconci's *Theme Song* (1973) offered a crucial historic precedent for technological solipsism. Playing a creepy Lothario, Acconci attempts to seduce an imagined lover, for whom the camera is a surrogate. The artist performs the repetitive loneliness of desire accompanied by a romantic soundtrack. Amplifying Acconci's dissociated poetics, Atkins' recent works *Even Pricks* (2013) and *Warm, Warm, Warm Spring Mouths* (2013) amplify the tension between a seamless digital rendering of a body and the fragile emotions that emerge from its mouth. Atkins revels in the split between a fully digital subject and the dark intimacy of a self disconnected from whatever remains of the social world. Similarly, Peter Wächtler's digital animation *Untitled (Heat up the Nickel)* (2013) renders a world of despair in the drab colors and exaggerated figuration of German Expressionism, accompanied by the artist's voice chanting a fugue-like poem about drunken mishaps.

Where these artists seemed to disappear fully into their mediums, their bodies replaced by cameras and computers, others created new personas through physical transformations. In *Stomach Song* (1970), William Wegman frames his naked torso such that a "face" appears on screen. With nipples as eyes and navel as mouth, this "face" fills with expression produced by the physical exertions of Wegman's breath and vocalization. His stomach "sings" and his body becomes the ground on which another figure materializes. *Mrs. Peanut Visits New York* (1992-99), Charles Atlas's six-minute video of the legendary performance artist Leigh Bowery, captures the estranged glamour of Bowery walking around the rough post-industrial landscape of downtown Manhattan. Atkins found an unexpected precursor to Bowery's embrace of his own bodily imperfections in a classic Betty Boop cartoon of *Snow White* (1933), which in this context became a complex meditation on the pliable form of animation and the narrative power unleashed by the constantly shifting reflections of the Wicked Queen's magic mirror.

In the early twentieth century, Surrealists like Hans Bellmer and Max Ernst explored forms of doubling to conjure the odd sensations that Freud called "uncanny," or "the most remarkable coincidences of desire and fulfillment," as he defined it. One hundred years later, the ever-evolving digital universe suggests an increasing confusion between fantasy and reality. So, while Atkins' program notes related these melancholic, embattled figures to "the anonymous, grotesque trolls of online commentary," something heroic appeared here as well.

Mark Beasley: In response to your recent films *Us Dead Talk Love* (2012) and *Warm, Warm, Warm Spring Mouths* (2013), Performa invited you to curate an evening of film and video works at Anthology Film Archives that relate to one of the key aspects of your own work—that of "the avatar." What is it about the avatar that so appeals?

Ed Atkins: I suppose it's simply a conspicuously contemporary iteration of a character and its costume: the effect of donning something like a mask or a suit that changes a performance—most saliently something that really affords the performance of a role that might appear to be a fantasy of the actor. The idea of "the avatar" now feels solely attached to computer-generated movies and video games—but that's really just a historic slip. The *Man of Steel* program maintained the technological association, but also looked back through artists' moving imagery to understand a kind of performative cybernetics, where the camera becomes a mask. There's also the idea of the mirror—several of the works are to-camera performances, something that now feels superseded as a formal framework, subsumed by YouTube conventions. Understanding performance today is a different thing: in my works, at least, "the performance" could include that of the computer processor, in some direct synonym with the effort of performing within society, the effort it takes to maintain some sort of public mask. Avatars are simply a more literal form of the kind of fantastical "topiarizing" of self that happens—though not exclusively—within social media. That it can be seen to accelerate with technologies of representation and dispersion is no surprise.

MB: Can you unpack some of your thinking in relation to the title of the evening, *Man of Steel*?

EA: Well, *Man of Steel* is the name of the most recent Superman reboot, in nostalgic reference to a Kirby descriptor in the vein of "faster than a speeding bullet," etc. Superman seems like a more or less interesting fantasy, depending on the historical moment. For me, it was both an introduction to a fantasy of power, agency, etc. and something more ironic. Many of the performances in the program are

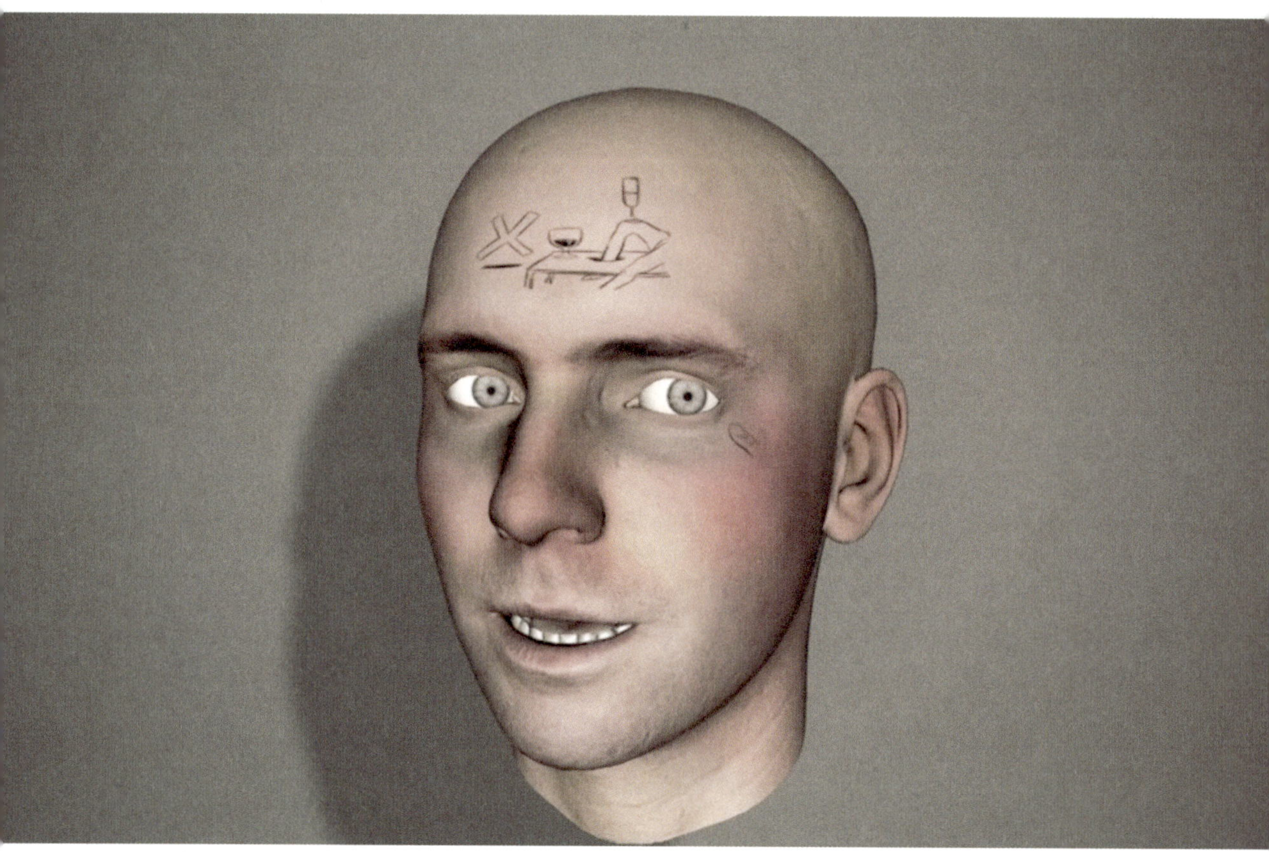

pretty grotesque—or, if not grotesque, perverse in relation to idealized forms of bodies, relations, performances. *Man of Steel* is a bit sneery, but for me did a pretty good job of underscoring, albeit opaquely, what was the impossible immortality erroneously offered by technology, representation, fantasy, ignorance, and desire.

MB: Your program incorporated a number of takes on the avatar, from the first historical instances of rotoscoped animation cells, where tracings mark the film allowing digital avatars to be included in scripted performances. This embrace of the essential aspects of an avatar was enlightening. Can you touch upon some of the works and why you selected them, specifically the rotoscoped works?

EA: That piece—*Snow White*—is a Betty Boop vehicle from the Fleischer Brothers; its stories are various and complex. Needless to say, it's not Disney's *Snow White*. My interest is specifically in the Cab Calloway performance in the middle of the cartoon, where he sings and dances in his inimitable way, as an infinitely plastic, boozy ghost. It's the most staggering sequence I know—its effect, the uncanniness, the imagination, the deeply moving relation between the ghost, Cab, the Fleischers, the original performance that was rotoscoped in order to maintain its particulars with such vivid accuracy. It's an exemplary bit of avatar performance. It describes what is possible and why one might want to have some sort of plastic, fantastical surrogate: someone, or something, that can bend and twist and completely contort himself to better manifest the feel of the performance, to sustain the assault of representation. It's something tonally and materially inspirational for my CGI videos. The piece by Rachel Reupke, *Deportment* (2011), is also a particular favorite. Silent, almost entirely still—perhaps more still than still—it's waylaid with the sadness of performance, a kind of socially determined masochism which, over a brief number of scenes, becomes increasingly uncomfortable, even impossible—as the female protagonist is being progressively augmented in increasingly brutal ways. The final inter-title—"My father says I have the perfect walk"— perfectly describes the devastation wrought by fantasy—in this case that of a father and a prospective male lover.

MB: I was particularly taken by the work of Peter Wächtler, as it offered a very bleak and pessimistic narrative, very un-Disney. His *Untitled (Heat up the Nickel)* (2013) didn't offer redemption or cathartic reflection. Was that something you were drawn to? How does it relate to your work?

EA: That film is more concerned with deliberate perversion of idealized aesthetics and technology. Avatars are fantasy-based mainstream moving-image forms, but Wächtler produces a consuming, interiorized monologue of self-loathing. Its abjection springs from the break between his incessant narrative and the form it takes as a cartoon. That and the interminable "It work…," repeated throughout. I attempt something related, pitting the aesthetic against itself, to reveal some impossible idealization offered as succor by that aesthetic. That sounds paradoxical—and maybe it is; it's that sort of paradox that breaks sufficiently and offers some sort of abjection. I've always found that stuff at least more accurate and certainly deeply moving. To see that kind of technique—cartoon, CGI—fail or dawdle or perform a wayward kind of uncertainty about itself, seems to open the possibility of thinking about how these kinds of images function otherwise.

MB: Interspersed between other works, you placed karaoke heads, friends of yours who sang along with avatars, from digital avatar to flesh. Were they asked to sing specific types of songs?

EA: They were all me—I didn't manage to get much out of friends! The songs I sang through the CGI heads were pretty much wallowing, male eulogies. In connection with the title, *Man of Steel*, I figured that these men singing—my singing—would be the point when predominant fantasies, desires, and myths were unraveled. They were funny to me, though I'm not entirely sure they had that effect on the audience. Again, undermining dominant aesthetics welded to certain social, industrial, and economic structures (and the cultures that proliferate them) felt like the most interesting thing to do. That the voice is *a cappella*, mine, untrained, and, insofar as this is possible, unaffected, it felt like I could collapse the veneer, my own emotional manipulations —I love those songs, even understanding their connivances—and find something more structural and also more affecting.

MB: The key moment for me was when the "life" onscreen became the "life" in the theater, when you stood up and sang along, unamplified, with one of your digital avatars—*Big Louise* by the singer and composer Scott Walker. We'd discussed a live aspect to the presentation, and considering all the live encounters I experienced in the biennial, it felt like one of the most alive; it had a strong impact. How was it for you?

EA: It felt important. To have that drop and shift of register. To undermine something of the cinematic clinch and return to something physical, an embodied thing; something I would have to do too— something that might reiterate a complicity. I suppose it's a familiar kind of drop, like that curtain pulled back to reveal the real Wizard of Oz—but a drop that works the other way too: that I would be as much subsumed into the image of the avatar as it, he, would be into me. The scale, too, felt important: that I would just be there in the cinema and, at the right point, stand up and sing the overdub of the mouthing head on the screen. Its aliveness would be understood in

Courtesy of Ed Atkins

Ed Atkins, Man of Steel (2013), video stills.

relation to everything that went before, which of course is less than dead. Then I sat down and the Fleischers' *Snow White* returned to recover the myth, only with the aftertaste of that live, embodied, and messy intervention.

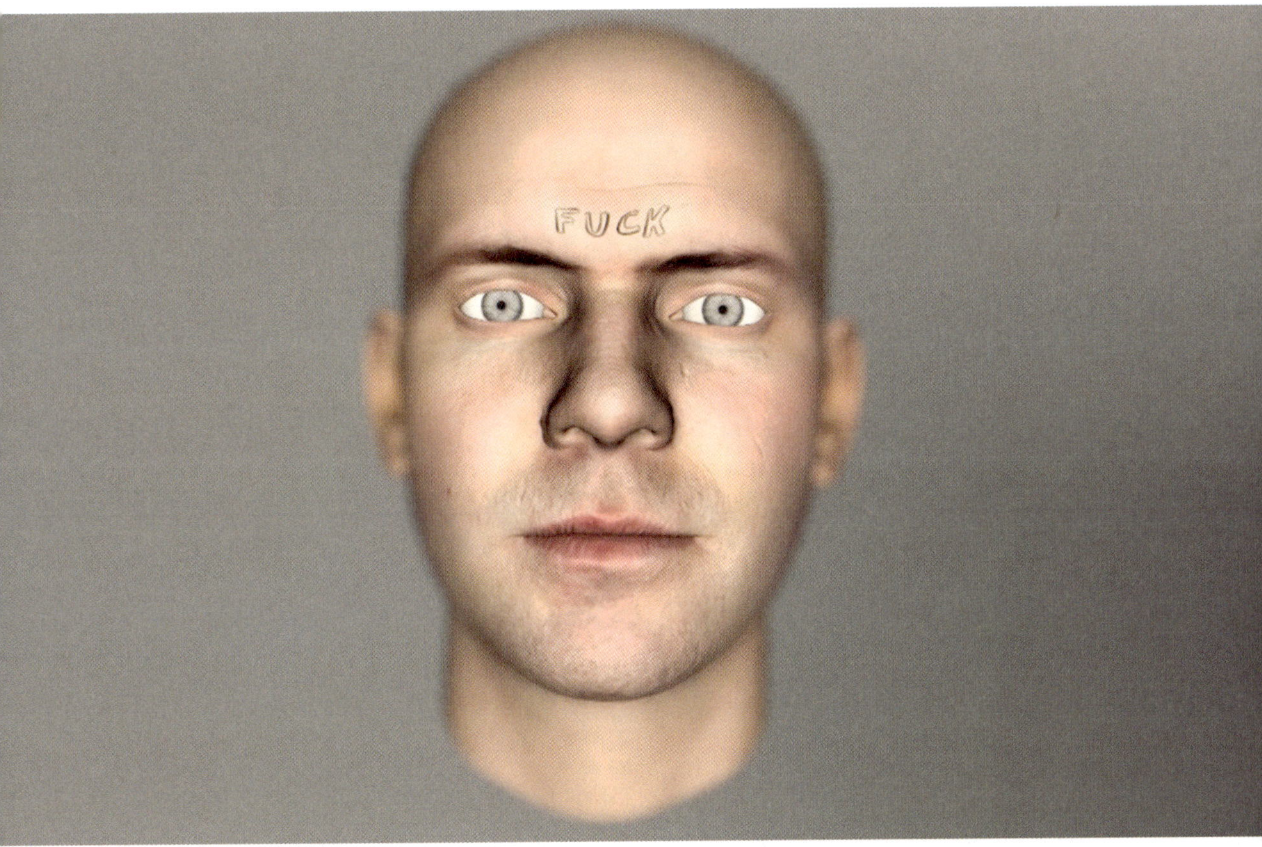

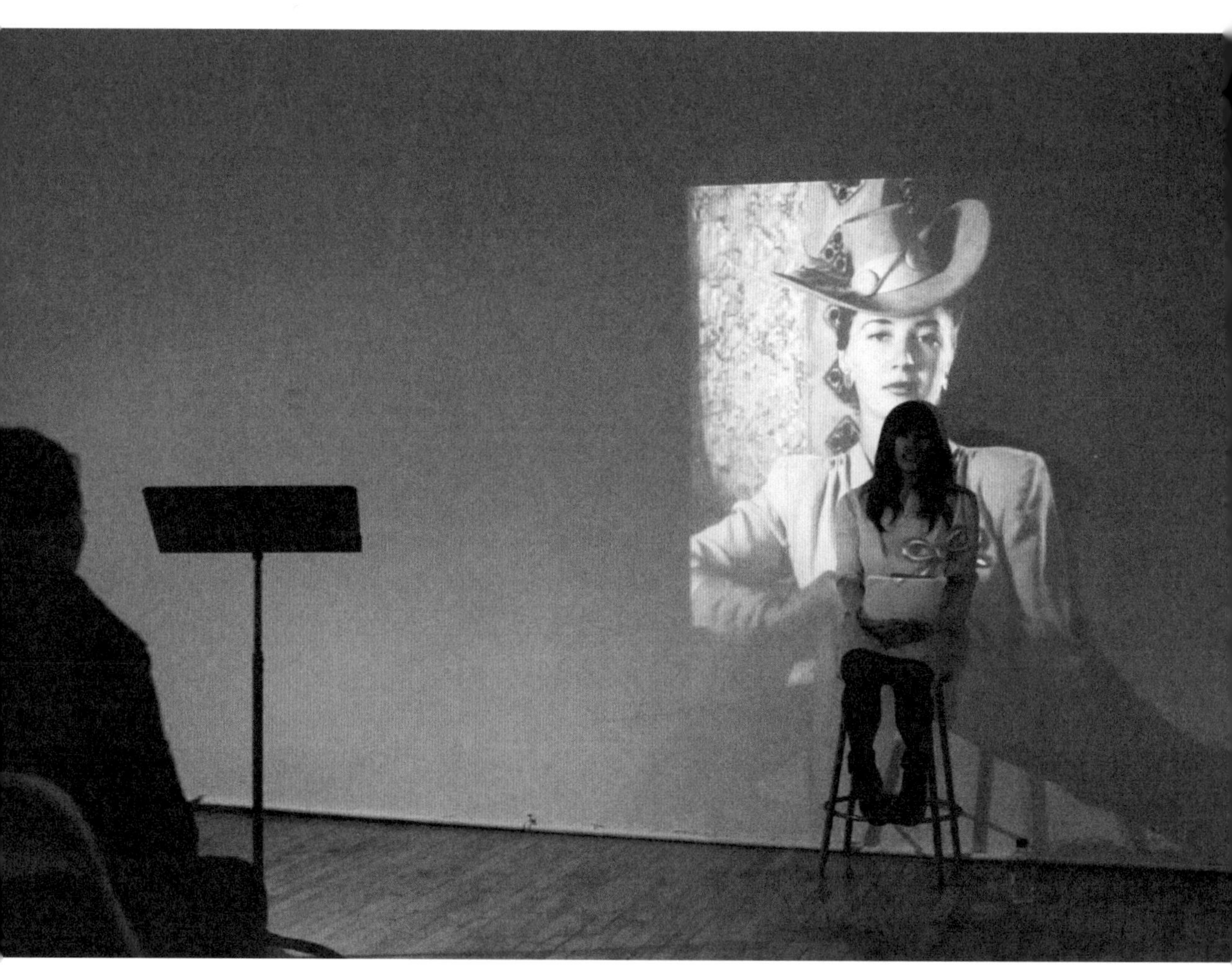

WOMAN IN SOMBRERO, WOMAN IN SOMBRERO

Photo by Steven Probert

Jill Magid, Woman in Sombrero, Woman in Sombrero (2013), performance view.

Luis Barragán (1902-88), a towering figure of Mexican Modernism and a triumphal twentieth-century architect who won the Pritzker Prize in 1980, left behind a complex and contested legacy. Besides the physical record of his work, the extant buildings that dot the environs of Mexico City and Guadalajara (where he was born), there lies a curious fact: Barragán's personal archive of papers and the copyright for the reproduction of many of his designs and images are owned and controlled by Frederica Zanco, the wife of Rolf Fehlbaum, chairman and founder of Vitra, the furniture manufacturer with a design museum based in Weil am Rhein, Germany. How this happened is a strange confluence of private opportunity and public neglect—one that makes us question copyright and corporate power relating to intellectual property, individual creative vision, and how history is made.

Jill Magid is an artist who engages with formal structures and systems of control to explore boundaries and limitations, probing them for meaning and social significance. Magid has investigated the limits of the law to confront the global inconsistencies of various systems, especially with regard to intellectual property and anomalies relating to access to an artist's work for the purposes of display and distribution. Magid initially knew little about Barragán, but she is represented in Mexico City by a gallery located on the same block as the sumptuous architectural gem Casa Luis Barragán, formerly the architect's private residence and now frequented by admirers. In her work, Magid explores the emotional, philosophical, and legal tensions between the individual and the "protective" authorities and institutions by highlighting systemic loopholes that allow her to continue to work where legal obstructions might impede her vision.

For *Woman in Sombrero, Woman in Sombrero*, Magid read from letters between herself and Zanco, surrounded by photographs, drawings, and other notations directly related to her research on Barragán and constituting a concurrent exhibition of the same name. In response to the possessive custodial claims of Zanco, Magid constructed

ART IN GENERAL

CURATED BY ANNE BARLOW / TEXT BY STEVE PULIMOOD

a semi-fictional narrative in which she, the artist, imagines herself as Barragán's lover, engaged in a ménage à trois with the copyright holder in Germany. Sitting in front of the audience, with a slideshow of the architect's photographs—including many of the thoroughbred racehorses which Barragán shot based on his interest in the animals—projected directly onto Magid's body, she performed a one-woman act, an epistolary monologue read aloud. Playing upon the implied impropriety of someone who "owns" someone else, her tone was seductive and throughout she was masked by the projected imagery of what had caught the architect's eye.

An act of investigation, intended to explore the restrictions on Barragán's legacy and his place in history, *Woman in Sombrero, Woman in Sombrero* prompted Magid to frame images of the architect's works, literally book pages from publications where the images are already copyright-cleared, taking the Barragán materials owned and held in Switzerland and using them in her work. Withholding permission to reproduce Barragán's imagery has, many claim, impeded the legacy of the architect by threat of legal action. Magid recognized the limits of control in the protocol and, as *The New York Times* noted, she has produced "a series of provocative artworks about Barragán that drift surreally somewhere between fact and fiction, the past and the present, and Mexico and Switzerland." She has done so by incorporating models of his furniture into her work, sometimes wrapped like a Christo, using ready-made books of his work previously given copyright permission, clearing images, which Magid has reframed, highlighting what she is not permitted to shoot herself, thereby, accessing Barragán's work and using it in her work despite the limitations imposed by the copyright holder. Magid's exploration of Barragán constitutes a confident critique of what happens when culture is compromised and when a creative legacy becomes private property restricted in the public domain.

Photo by Steven Probert

Jill Magid, *Woman in Sombrero, Woman in Sombrero* (2013), installation view.

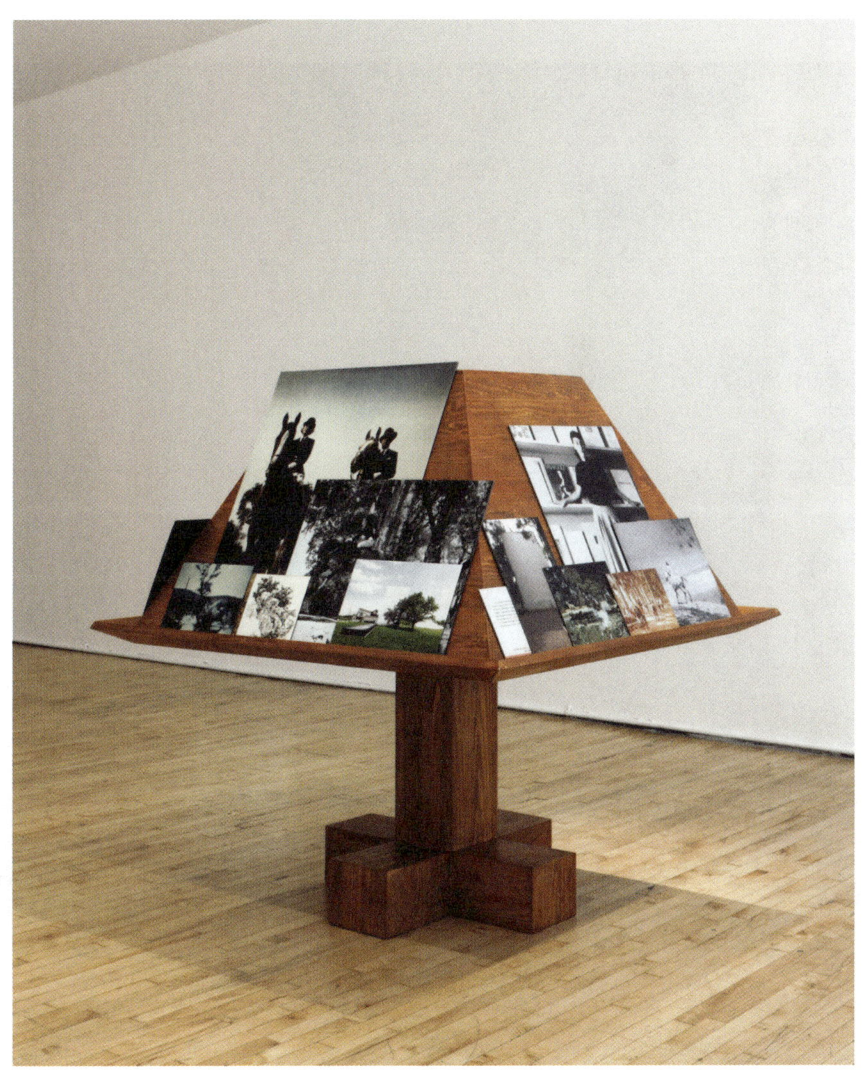

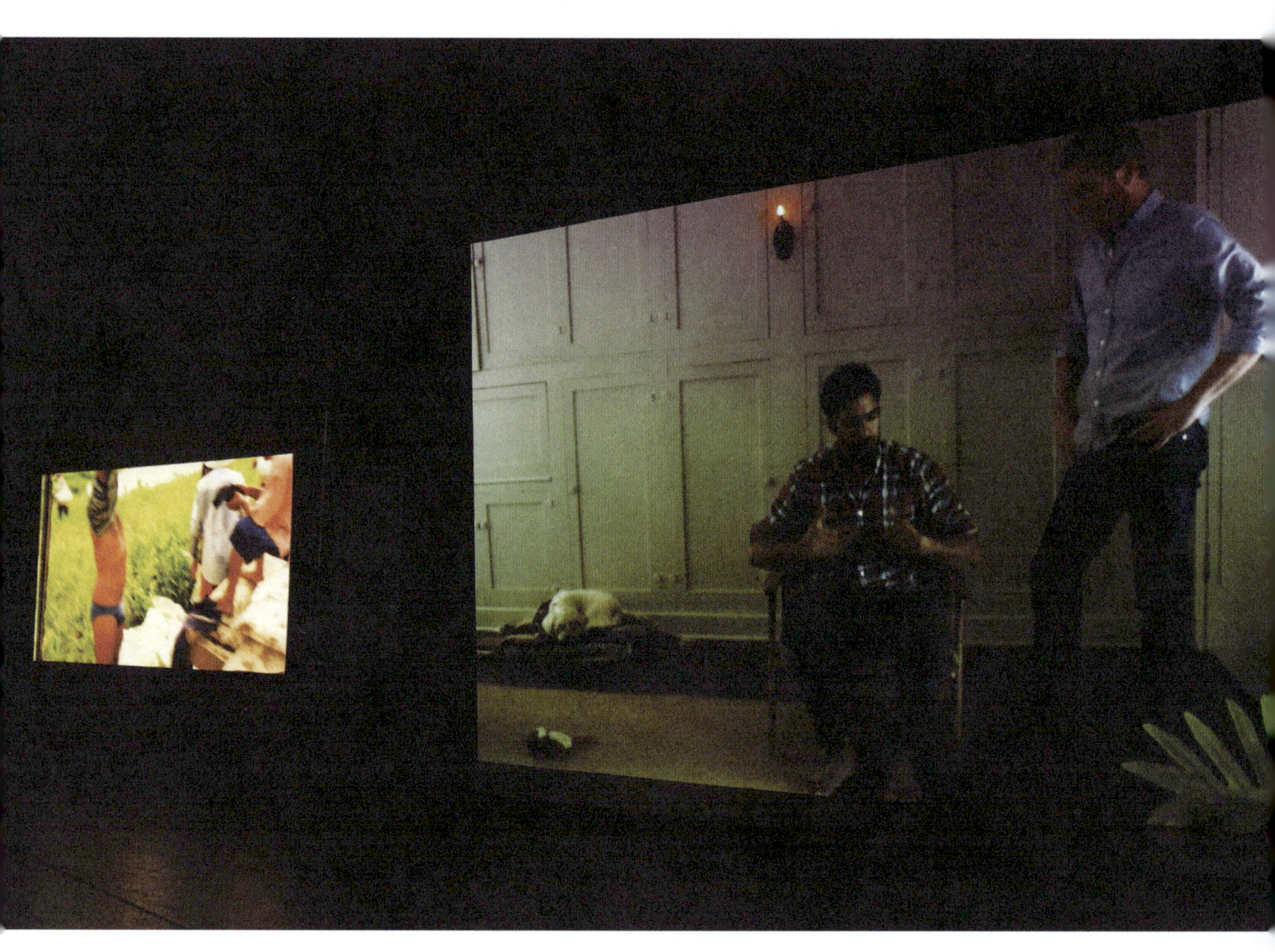

A SHAKY PICTURE HAS NO WEIGHT

Vishal Jugdeo's *A Shaky Picture Has No Weight* wove together live performance, prerecorded video, and mechanical props to form an abstract narrative that followed Jugdeo and his partner in their desire to know each other better and strengthen their relationship.

The performance began with the audience sitting in darkness on the stage of Abrons Art Center. Jugdeo's voice described a surreal dream that suddenly appeared vividly on the screen. The footage was from the artist's travels earlier in the year to British Guyana, the birthplace of his parents and a country he was visiting for the first time. The next thirty minutes intertwined video of the Caribbean landscape and village scenes with vignettes of the couple in their Los Angeles apartment playfully then tensely arguing. The pair was present, standing on stage but hidden by the projection screen, seen only as reflections in angled mirrors on either side.

Their dialogue on screen and on stage was circular, casual, and unscripted and then turned melodramatic. Probing questions about how to relate were answered by video clips from Guyanian bars and stories from villagers. A mechanical lamp stand balancing a globe wobbled across the stage, perfectly mirroring the moon on the screen above for a few luxurious moments, and other objects dropped from the ceiling unexpectedly to punctuate the scene. This constant channel-switching from live to scripted, domestic to exotic, was juxtaposed with props that grounded the audience in the moment while also articulating the surreal tension between the couple. The crux of *A Shaky Picture Has No Weight* was how the ebb and flow— moments of stillness and synchronicity followed by self-reflexive chaos—stood in for the uncertainty and emotional complexity of two people getting to know one another.

CURATED BY SUMMER GUTHERY △ ABRONS ARTS CENTER

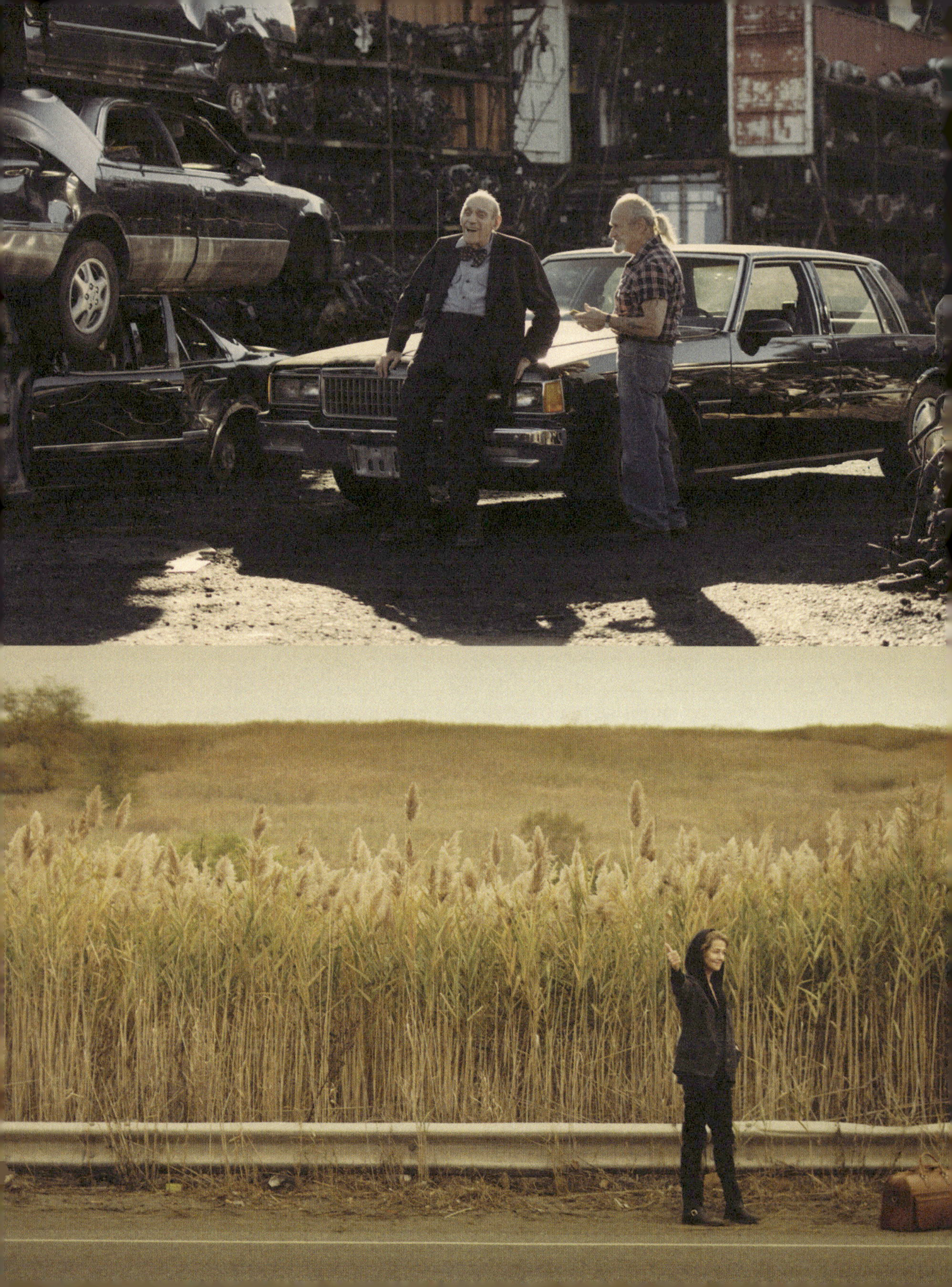

Three characters populate Agnieszka Kurant's ten-minute film *Cutaways* (2013). Played by Dick Miller, Charlotte Rampling, and Abe Vigoda, these characters were reclaimed from the notorious cutting room floor, having been edited out of the final cuts of the feature films for which they were originally created: *Pulp Fiction* (1994), *The Conversation* (1974), and *Vanishing Point* (1971). Working in collaboration with the famed film editor Walter Murch (who edited *The Godfather* (1972) and *Apocalypse Now* (1979)), Kurant revived these figures, twenty, forty, and forty-two years later, respectively. Kurant wrote a new script for them to interact with each other and cast the original actors to perform their roles again, picking up on the scene from which they had been cut out.

Kurant's use of the same actors shifted the focus from the original narratives to the process by which those narratives, and the films that resulted, were shaped—namely through editing. By cutting, pasting, deleting, and reorganizing raw film material, the role of an editor is to constantly move between presence and absence, making decisions about what to keep and what to omit.

For Kurant, editing is a sculptural process. Kurant first explored the artistic and political implications of editing in 2011 in her piece *103.1,* exhibited as part of her 2013 SculptureCenter exhibition, *exformation.* (The work was originally titled *88.7*—the title changes according to the frequency on which the work's radio content is broadcast). The silences that comprised the audio component of *103.1,* taken from recorded political speeches, do not represent the absence of noise, but rather convey "room tone"—the recorded sound whose characteristics derive from the location of the microphone within a space. Another term for room tone is "presence." We hear presence when speech or music is absent. Presence is given specific form by the shape, proportion, and material of the room in which the recording is made. Absence becomes presence.

This paradox is metaphorically fertile for Kurant, who has been working with what she has termed "phantom capital" for some time. In projects such as *Phantom Library*, begun in 2011, and her maps of phantom islands, the artist has explored the ways fictions, hypotheses, rumors, and memes gain currency in the real world. For example, *Political Map of Phantom Islands* (2011) shows nonexistent islands that appeared on geographic, political, and economic maps beginning in the fifteenth century, with some appearing as recently as the 1940s. These phantom islands may be the products of navigational errors, optical illusions, or willful fabrications to justify expeditions. With mythical histories, sovereign claims, and pure fictions, these phantom islands, by the mere assertion of their existence, accrue value that has an impact in the social, economic, and political arena.

Cutaways is a logical extension of these "Phantom" works and of *103.1*, in which nonentities are realized as art. The absence made present in these works may be considered "exformation," a term coined by the Danish science writer Tor Nørretranders to describe explicitly discarded information, or the shared context that makes information intelligible. Nørretranders argues that thought is actually the process of deleting extraneous data that we undertake in order to comprehend the world and communicate with one another. Our subjectivity is formed by exformation and the information we divest ourselves of influences our behavior in significant ways.

The final scene of *Cutaways* takes place in a junkyard, which is a resonant setting for this film about discarded footage. Not only does the film rescue these roles from "the dustbin of history," but the junk dealer recognizes the potential in scrap to still be transformed into capital. By reclaiming remainders of film history, Kurant makes the ironic comment that late capitalism—in its ability to commodify information and even "exformation"—has achieved the ultimate dematerialization of the art object.

Agnieszka Kurant, *Cutaways* (2013), video stills.

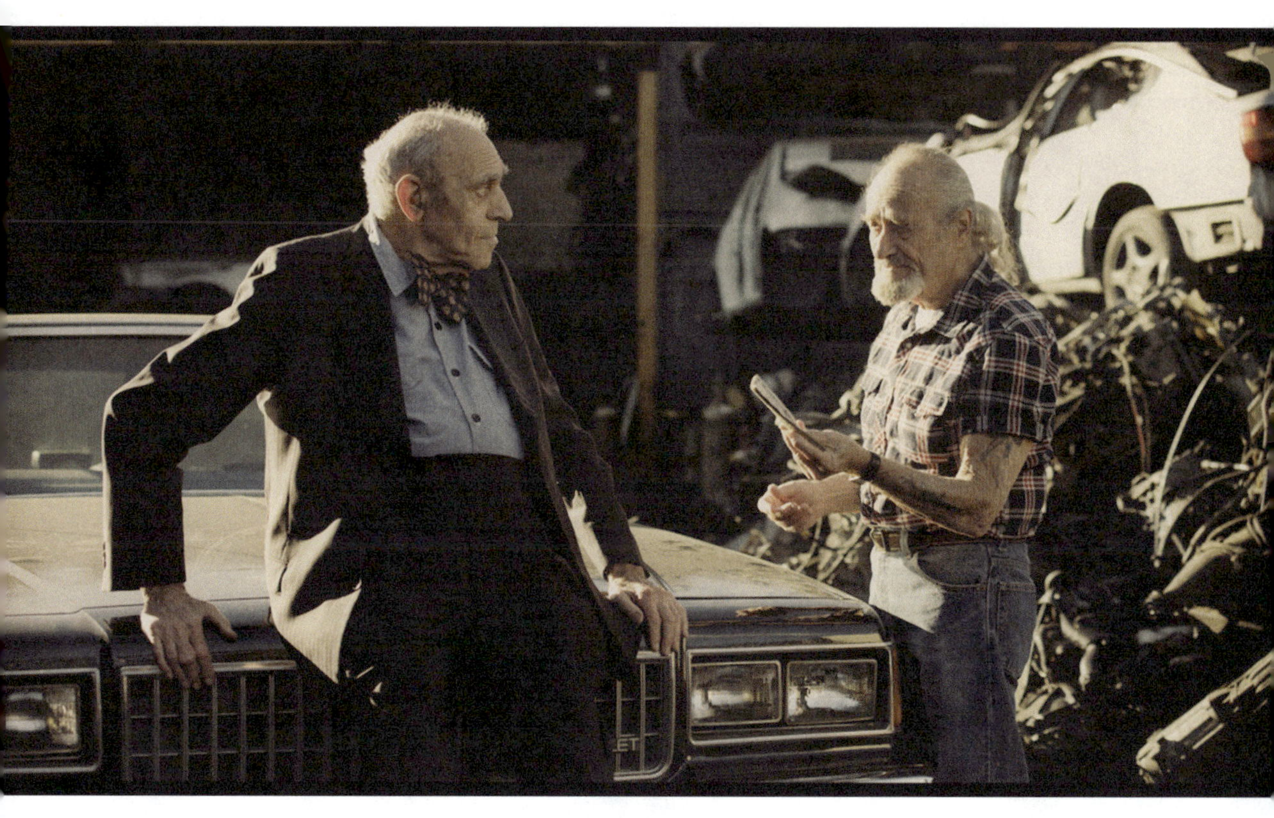

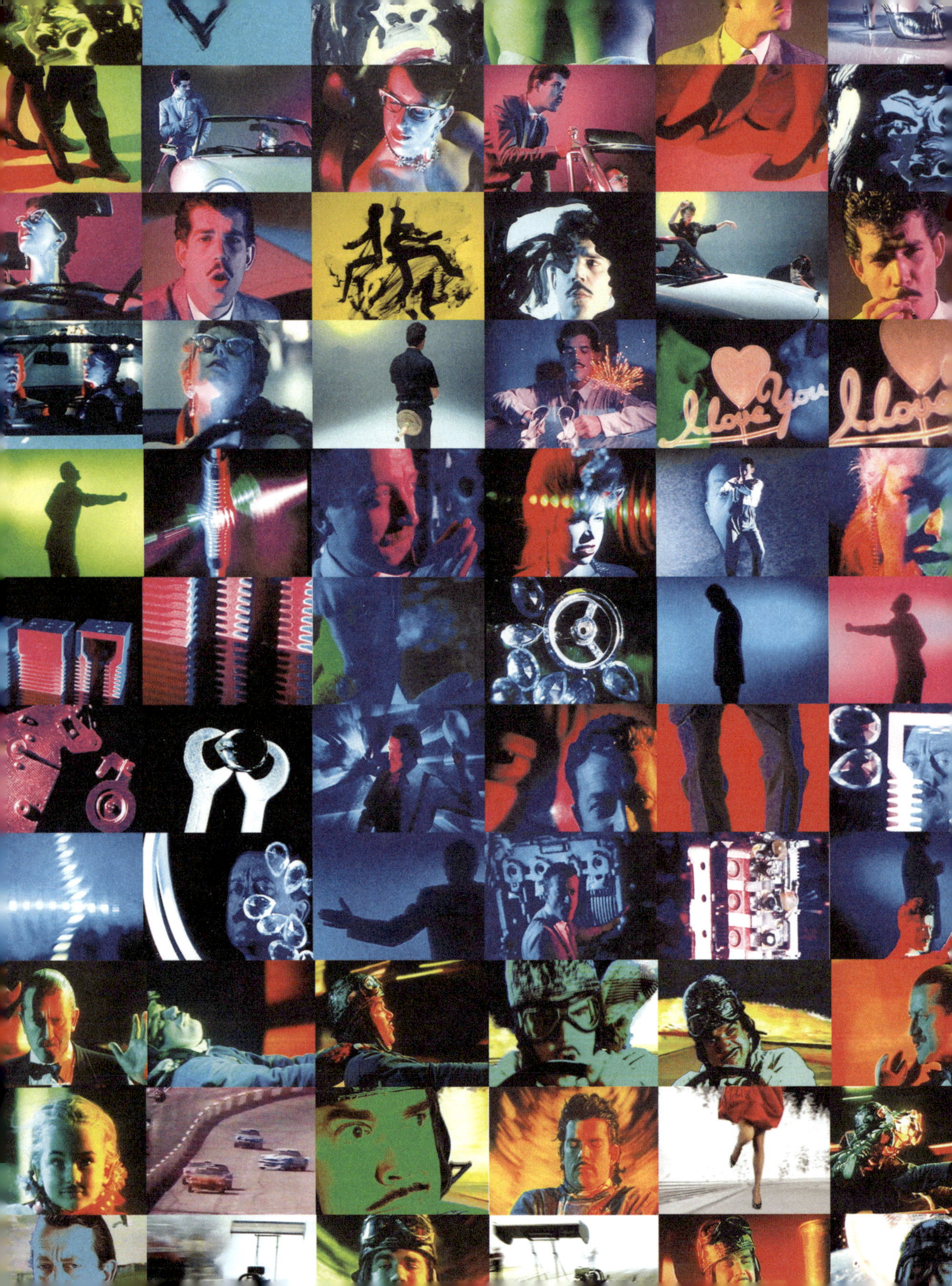

DIETER MEIER

YELLO VIDEO PERFORMANCES

There's plenty of evidence of what can occur when musicians try to make visual art—with rare exceptions is this enticing; one exception being Captain Beefheart aka Don Van Vliet. And when visual artists make music? The cupboard is equally bare. But say "Hello!" to Dieter Meier, who presented the evolution of his *Yello Video Performances* at WhiteBox Art Center over a period of nineteen days and participated in a Q&A about what Meier described as his "wholly accidental career."

Meier's father, a Zurich millionaire, let his son do as he pleased. So he made avant-garde movies in the late-1960s and '70s and segued into performance art when he attended a reception at the New York Cultural Center in early 1971, holding a handgun. A sign nearby read THIS MAN WILL NOT SHOOT, but his expression was such that the placard seemed unconvincing. He appeared at dOCUMENTA (5) the following year, but abruptly quit what he calls the "art race" not long after. As Meier explained, his inheritance was a factor, "If you know that you can survive without doing anything, then in your mind it has to be something very, very special. And this can kill you, because nothing is good enough."

So … what next? Movie projects were still a go. Sometimes Meier would perform in front of the screen. "I would play a guitar with one string, I would use my voice," he says. "I would use noise." A producer put him together with a punk band. Then he did gigs with several bands in '77 and '78, recording his first single, "Cry For Fame." That was how he met Boris Blank, a fanatic for playing with sounds. Yello was born.

Yello—a squished "yelled hello," a Meier joke—appeared in New York at the Roxy on the same bill as Afrika Bambaataa. There was wild applause when Diane Brill announced their presence to the crowd of a thousand, but silence greeted them as they arrived on stage. "They knew the song," Meier says. "And there were two Swiss faces." It had been assumed Yello were black rappers from the West Coast. Ironically, now Roxy houses a location of the international blue chip gallery, Hauser & Wirth, as the art world that Meier left is devouring everything in its path.

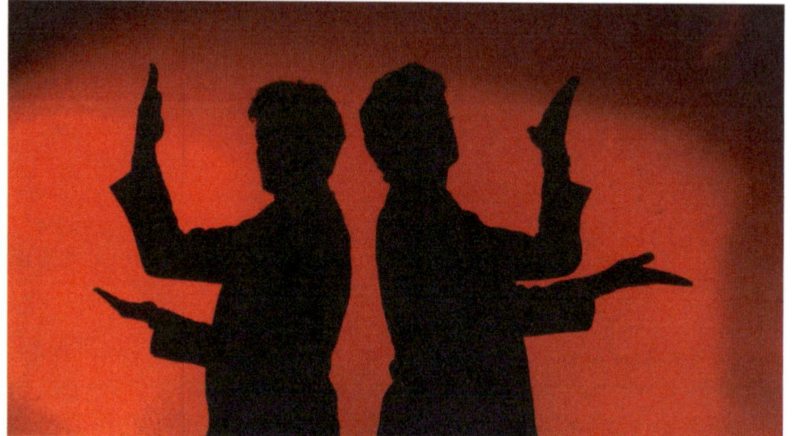

In a time when rockers everywhere were aping the Americans and Brits, Yello was a progenitor of electro and a distinctively Euro band. "And there we were, selling millions of records," said Meier—enough records to make his inherited wealth irrelevant. He channeled his Dadaist sensibility—he *is* Swiss—into a gush of videos that became staples of early MTV. If you missed *Yello Video Performances,* there's sufficient evidence to be discovered online.

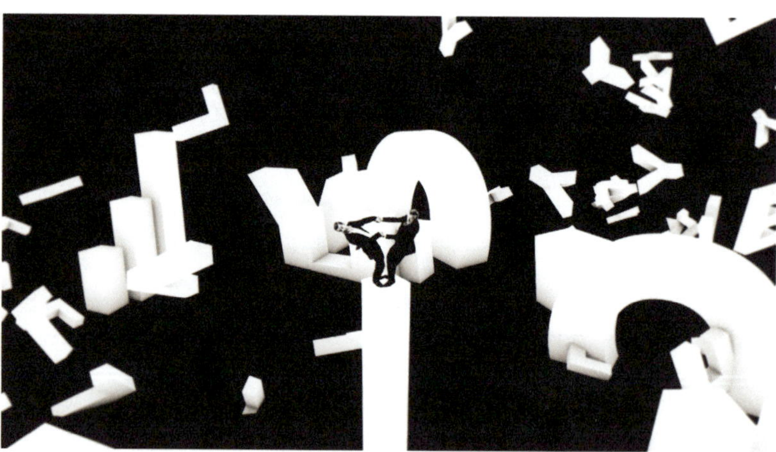

Courtesy of Yello

(Left, above) *Yello The Evening's Young* (1981) (Left, below) *Yello Tiger Dust* (2009), video stills. (Right, above and below) *Yello Tied Up* (1988), video stills.

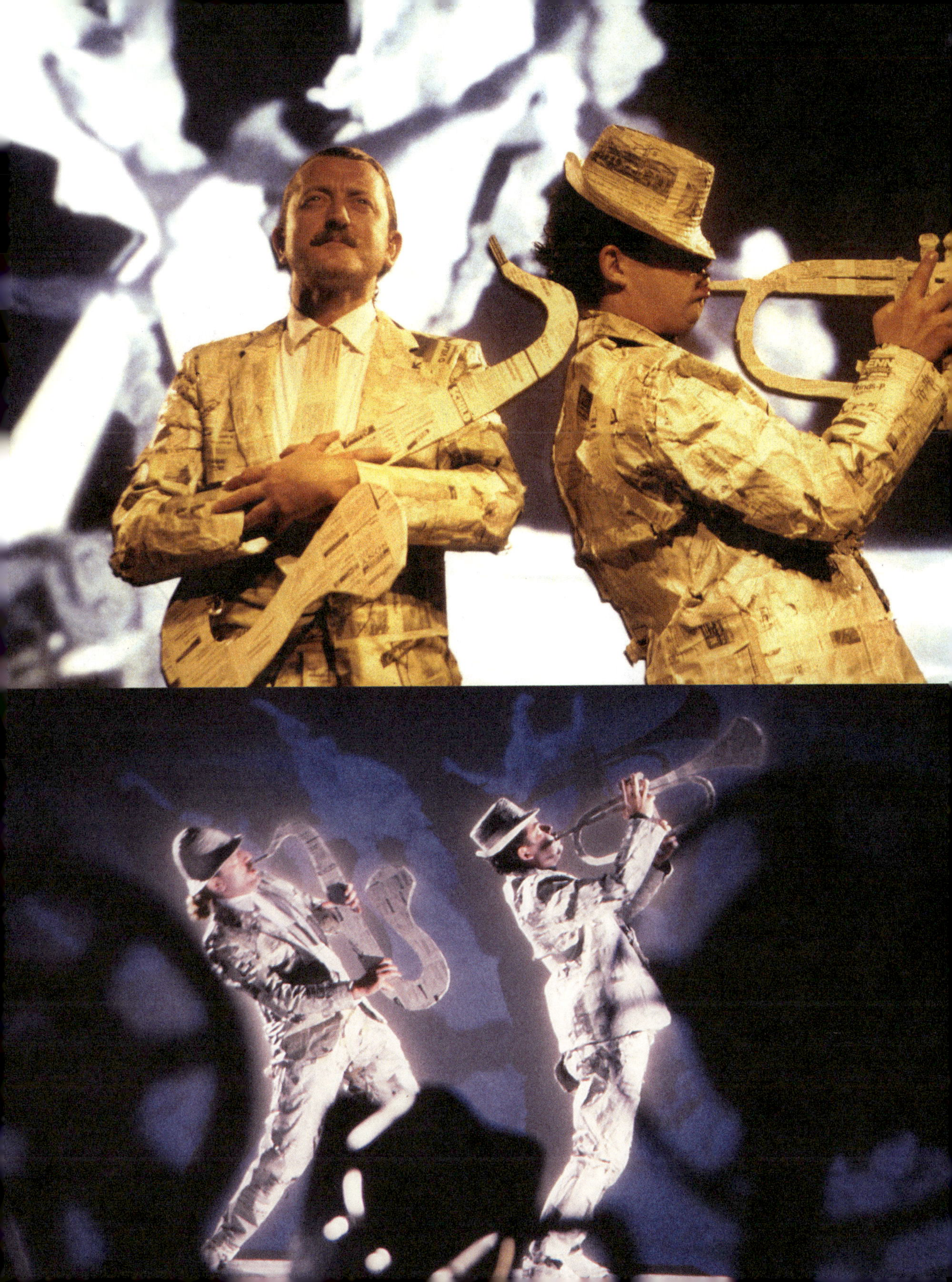

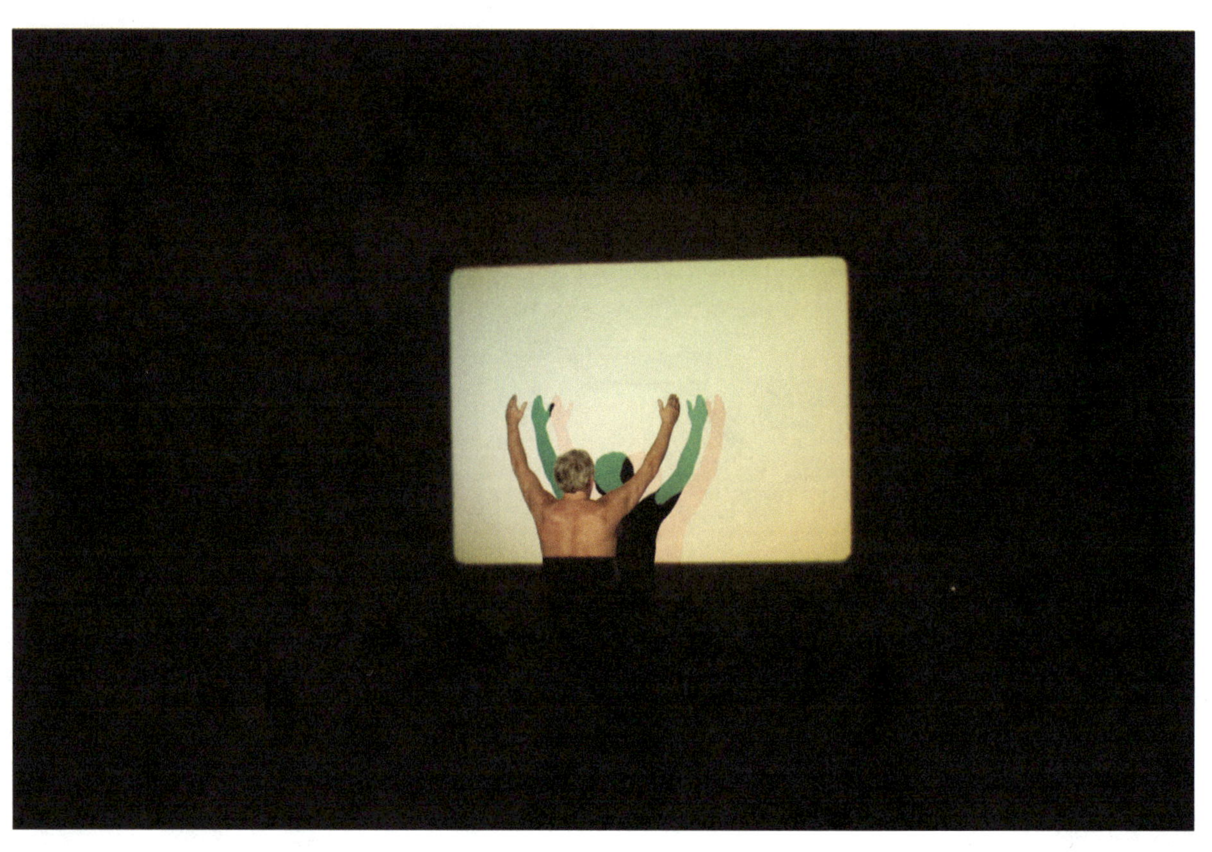

**MALCOM LE GRICE, GUY SHERWIN,
LYNN LOO, AND KEITH ROWE**

MAN WITH A PROJECTOR

The British scene of post-war experimental film anchored in the London Film Makers' Co-op (founded in 1966) radically transformed the dialogue around the cinematic experience, epitomized by the work of artists Malcolm Le Grice and Guy Sherwin. Both trained as painters, and their transition to film showed a sensitivity to materials—of color, projected light, and the medium of celluloid itself—and both pushed the parameters of live projections and film performances.

Man With a Projector, an evening of key works from their repertoires, took its title from Sherwin's 1976 performance *Man with Mirror*, itself a sly reference to Dziga Vertov's seminal film *Man with a Movie Camera* (1929). Sherwin opened the program with *Man with Mirror*, a work in which he stood in front of a Super 8 projector holding a two-sided panel, white on one side and mirrored on the other. Projected onto him was his image from forty years ago that, as he slowly rotated the panel, he caught on the white screen or reflected in the mirror. Then, London-based filmmaker Lynn Loo joined Sherwin to recreate two of their recent performances, *Vowels* and *Consonants* (2005), which involved an impressive installation. With its six 16mm projectors—made up of six films, each inscribed on a celluloid strip with typewritten letters that appeared on-screen in chance combinations of embryonic words. With *Mobius Loop* (2007), Sherman and Loo placed colored gels in the projector's light path, producing color-field-like blocks that coalesced in contrasting colors.

Malcolm Le Grice's *Horror Film 1* (1971) featured the artist bare-chested, interacting with his shadow on a screen. As his torso disrupted three beams of different-colored light from three film projectors, Le Grice adjusted the size of his shadow, resulting in a dance between the figure of a man and the interplay of geometric shapes. *After Leonardo* (1973-2013), another seminal Le Grice work, involved the participation of British musician Keith Rowe. Rowe's live improvisation, with a guitar laid flat on a table, included other sound devices. A worn-out close-up of the Mona Lisa, a reproduction itself, was pinned to the wall and became the focus of a *mise-en-abyme* that played with the idea of infinite live and recorded reproductions of that enigmatic smile.

CHAPTER

7

SEVEN

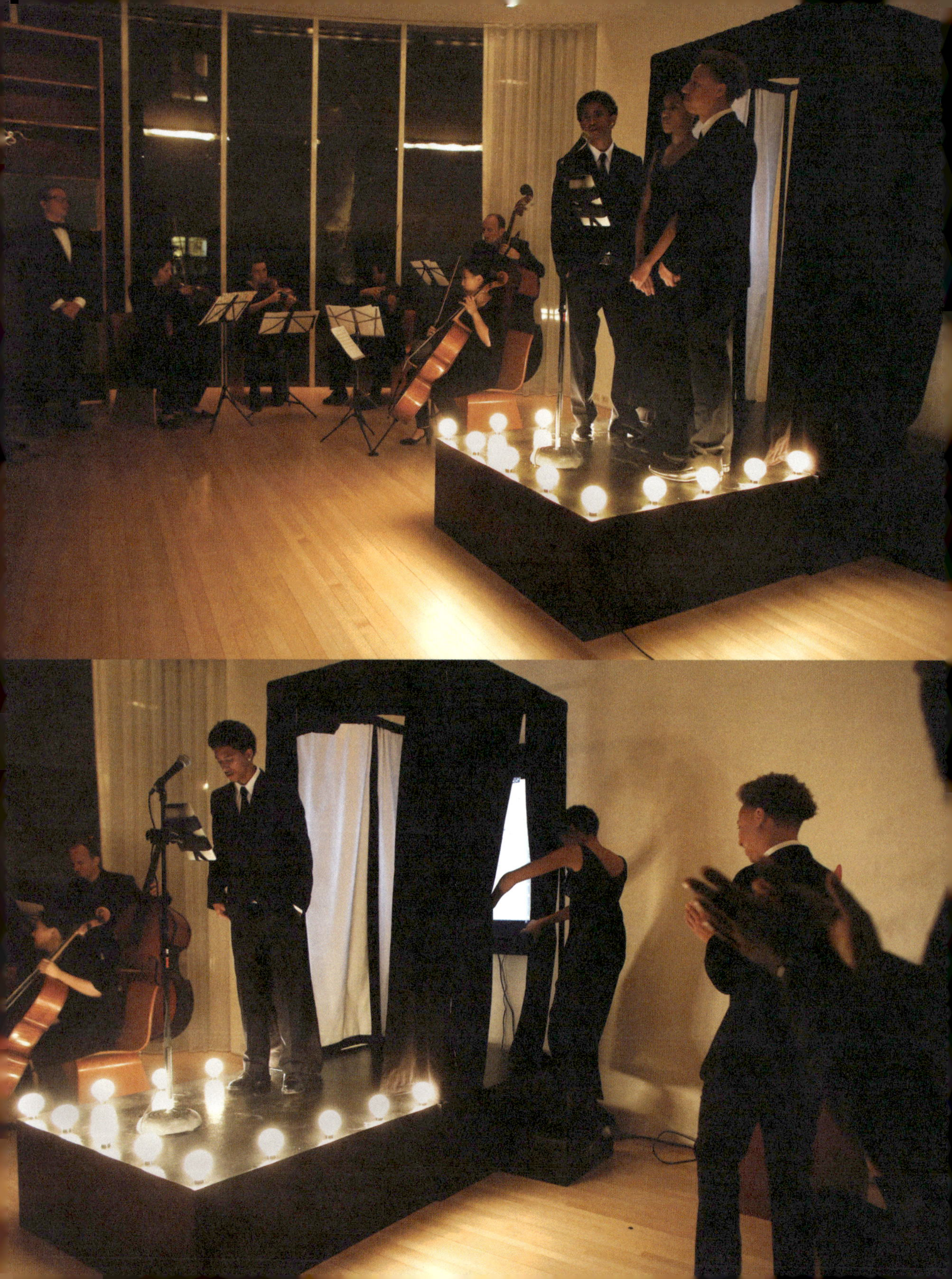

DERRICK ADAMS

ONCE UPON A TIME ...

Throughout his career, Derrick Adams has worked with micro/macro systems of representation, observing how practices in different ideological spheres overlap, while applying such intersections to form critiques of dominant ideologies. For *Once upon a time …,* Adams drew inspiration from the Calder Foundation's archives to explore the question of how we engage with and reinterpret overlooked histories.

In this performance, Adams simulated an African American practice of children reciting culturally significant historical texts on stage at community-sponsored talent shows that often supplement public education curriculums. Typically, the mastery of knowledge is displayed to an audience composed of community members, so the performance is less voyeuristic than most, representing a shared connection between the performer and the audience. For *Once upon a time …,* Adams employed teenagers to study and enact four poems by poets who were precursors to, or figures of, the Harlem Renaissance: Gwendolyn Bennett, Paul Laurence Dunbar, Langston Hughes, and Claude McKay. Facing the audience from a miniature, black-curtained stage, the young adults dramatized the poets' powerful internalizations while accompanied by a string quintet, evoking the theatrical endeavor. The original musical score was conceived in collaboration with composer Philippe Treuille and reinterpreted as a dialogue about sound between Calder and his friend, the composer Edgar Varèse, with related archival images of drawings by Calder projected behind the performers on stage. Overlapping aesthetic genres of presentation, from the cinematic and literary to the performative and auditory, Adams juxtaposed audience experiences related to simulation and authenticity, simultaneously questioning prevalent structures of public education and aesthetic production.

TEXT BY KATHERINE COHN ● CALDER FOUNDATION AT SALON 94

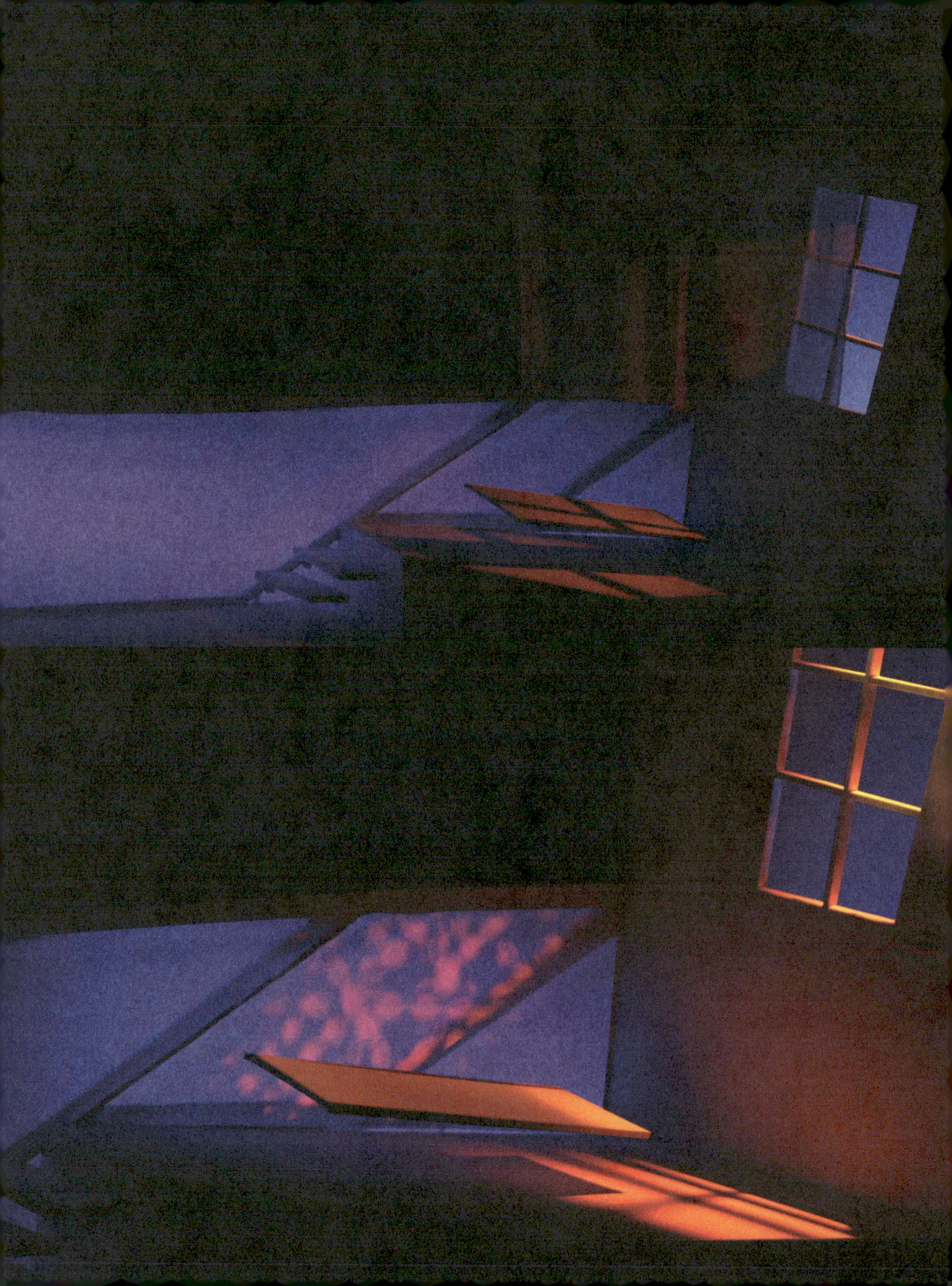

GABRIEL LESTER

SUPER-SARGASSO SEA (PHANTOM PLAY #1)

A popular form of live entertainment in the eighteenth and nineteenth centuries, "phantasmagoria" used proto-projectors to cast shadows that formed images such as skeletons and ghosts onto walls, smoke, or screens in ways which anticipated twentieth-century film and entertainment culture. Phantasmagoria explored what would become conventional in early film production—camera movements such as "transformations," "disappearances," and "superimpositions"—terms that described early techniques in film. These were frequently used in "trick" films developed by Georges Méliès at the turn of the last century. The "Super-Sargasso" is another such term, thought of as the spontaneous, anomalous teleportation of an object into another dimension. Charles Hoyt Fort, the American writer and researcher of anomalous phenomena, introduced the term Super-Sargasso to describe a "place" where things disappear to, or come from when they reappear. The Super-Sargasso Sea from which the term derives its name is situated in the Atlantic near the Bermuda Triangle. Dutch-based artist Gabriel Lester borrowed this term to describe his play in which no actors were featured, but the sounds of actions, lighting, and shadow play provided clues for the audience to imagine the narrative.

Super-Sargasso Sea (phantom play #1) is a "script for the subconscious," as Lester describes it, and was created by sampling, sequencing, and editing sound and computer-programmed colored stage lights of varying luminosities to intrigue audiences. Lester calls it a "film-in-mime," because it reminds him of a mime-play with no actors—a play to be experienced and imagined purely and solely within the audience's imagination.

As Adam Kleinman insightfully wrote, "Thinking is hard. The brain links inputs to ideas, but needs to do so quickly. If not, you'll overload. Snap judgments follow preconceived notions so as to limit processing power to get you through the day." The playbill (its very existence emphasized the theatrical nature of this play) listed the small cast: a scientist, his fiancée, their baby, a dog, and a cat. While following many of the conventions of a traditional play, this work also resonated as a playful evocation of the senses, with, for example, the sound of doors opening and closing, and the echos of footsteps climbing in and out of the apartment followed by the sounds of two car accidents (sirens and heart monitors at a hospital). In this story, the projected couple dies in two fatal and separate accidents, leaving their firstborn (named "Creature") an orphan. Lester admits to being inspired by *Frankenstein* (1818) and its theme of creation. All took place on an angular set that seemed like a giant sculpture, with a suspended bed and a living room, a front door, window blinds, and a clock—indeed all the trappings of a domestic life, which gave expectant viewers from an attention-deficit age the task of imagining how these physical elements projected meaning into the play.

Recalling early film history with its interest in magic, mime, illusion, and spatial dynamics, Lester's deceptively simple phantom play not only provided clues to his interest in old film genres, but also showed his mastery of cinema's codes, tools, and conventions, including optical trickery and other sophisticated variations of tension, suspense, and drama.

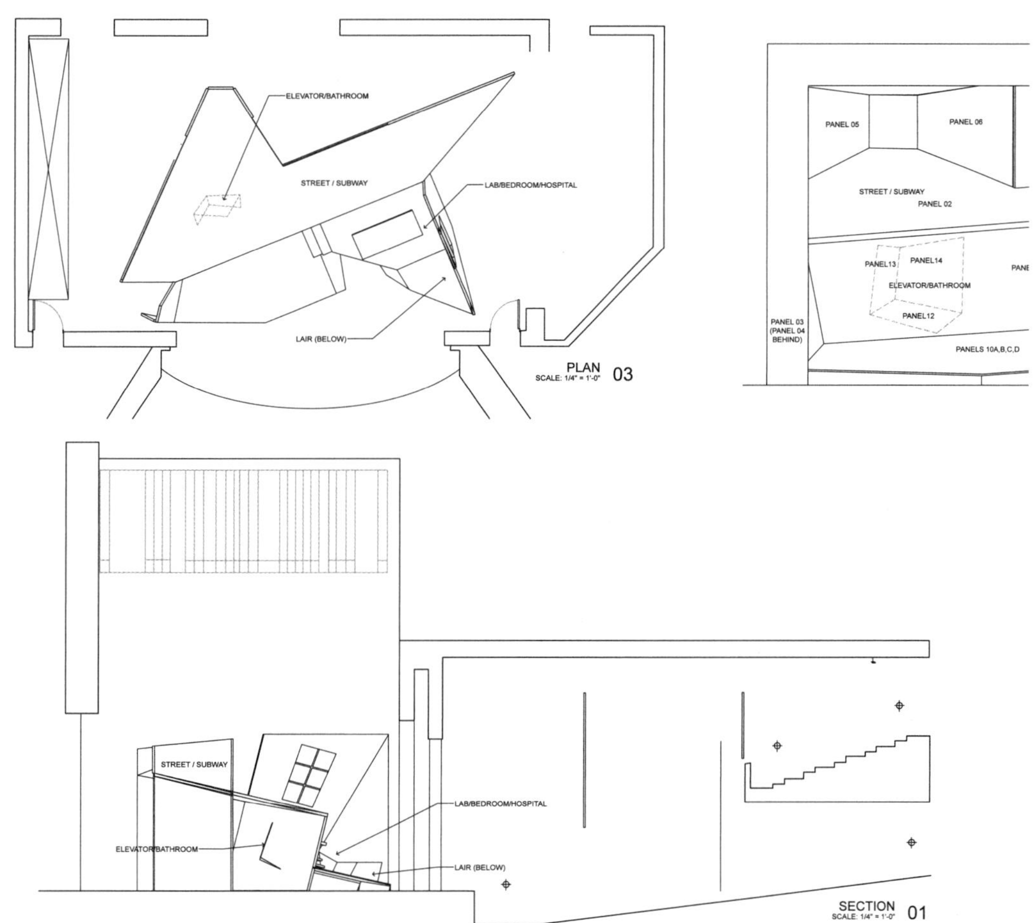
ELEVATOR/BATHROOM
STREET / SUBWAY
LAB/BEDROOM/HOSPITAL
LAIR (BELOW)
PLAN
SCALE: 1/4" = 1'-0"
03
PANEL 05
PANEL 06
STREET / SUBWAY
PANEL 02
PANEL13
PANEL14
ELEVATOR/BATHROOM
PANEL12
PANE
PANEL 03
(PANEL 04
BEHIND)
PANELS 10A,B,C,D
STREET / SUBWAY
ELEVATOR/BATHROOM
LAB/BEDROOM/HOSPITAL
LAIR (BELOW)
SECTION
SCALE: 1/4" = 1'-0"
01

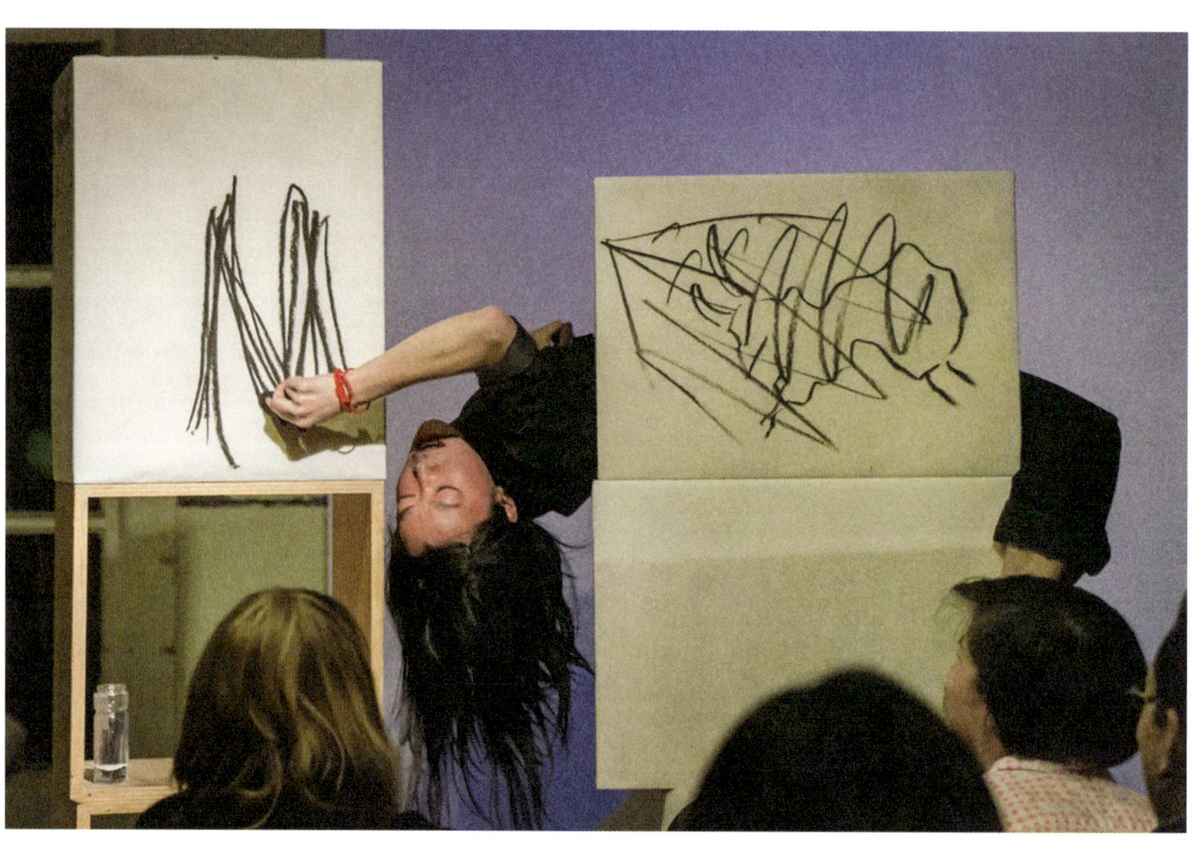

WE LIVE WITH ANIMALS

We Live with Animals was an installation and a night of storytelling and performance in that installation as well as a series of tours throughout New York City co-curated by Denise Hoffman and Catherine Seavitt Nordenson that commemorated human-animal experiences in the city and explored multifaceted aspects of "animal" as experienced in evolving everyday practices of living with and imagining the urban animal kingdom.

On the walls of Van Alen's backroom gallery, twelve commemorative bronze plaques, designed like those commonly seen affixed to historic buildings, were hung under spotlights. Each plaque highlighted a human-animal encounter in one of the five New York City boroughs. On display alongside the plaques was a large map identifying the exact location of the encounters, from Sludgie, a minke whale who was trapped in the Gowanus Canal, to Ming, a Bengal tiger discovered by the NYPD in a public housing building on 141st Street.

Set within the installation, visitors gathered on pillows for an evening of literal and fantastical storytelling by artist Aki Sasamoto, storyteller Adam Wade, multimedia artist Tamar Ettun, veteran news photographer John Roca, visual and performing artist Pat Oleszko, and Animal Care & Control of NYC Executive Director Risa Weinstock. Each story explored the relationship between animals and humans in the urban realm—exotic and domestic, hidden and in plain sight. Each transformed our understanding of nature, provoked new relationships with the animal kingdom, and offered access to under-explored worlds in the built environment of the metropolis.

Aki Sasamoto announced that she hated animals and elaborated on her least favorite type, the human mosquito. Adam Wade reflected on how his first great New York romance ended because of five cats and a poorly placed litter box. Tamar Ettun recounted the story of her relationship with an opossum as she projected a video shot from the perspective of roadkill. Pat Oleszko, wearing a turkey hat, talked about the city's changing neighborhoods and dressing up as a turkey with the hope of sneaking into the Macy's Thanksgiving Day parade. Risa Weinstock presented a range of animal stories, from escapees of slaughterhouses to pets expelled from domestic homes each year. John Roca described watching the NYPD scale a building to tranquilize a tiger held captive in an apartment in a dense public housing block.

That weekend, through a series of tours led by Brandt and Nordenson, commemorative plaques were installed in the five boroughs. Sites included three in Queens: homing pigeons in Ozone Park, a runaway peacock in Flushing, and an alligator discovered under a parked Datsun in Astoria. Three sites were in Lower Manhattan and Brooklyn: a bee swarm at South Street Seaport, a minke whale in the Gowanus Canal, and a "bat condo" in Carroll Gardens. And four sites were in Upper Manhattan and the Bronx, where plaques were installed for a coyote pack on Broadway, a tiger in Harlem, feral roosters in the Bronx, and a beaver at the New York Botanical Garden.

We Live with Animals was part of *Elsewhere: Escape and the Urban Landscape*, a multiyear initiative of Van Alen Institute exploring escape in the urban environment. *Elsewhere* is comprised of competitions, public programs, and research that investigate key questions of the contemporary urban experience. How and why do we escape from urban life? What prompts us to escape *to* the city? What forms of escape can we find within the urban environment? And how might the experience of going "elsewhere" contribute to our well-being?

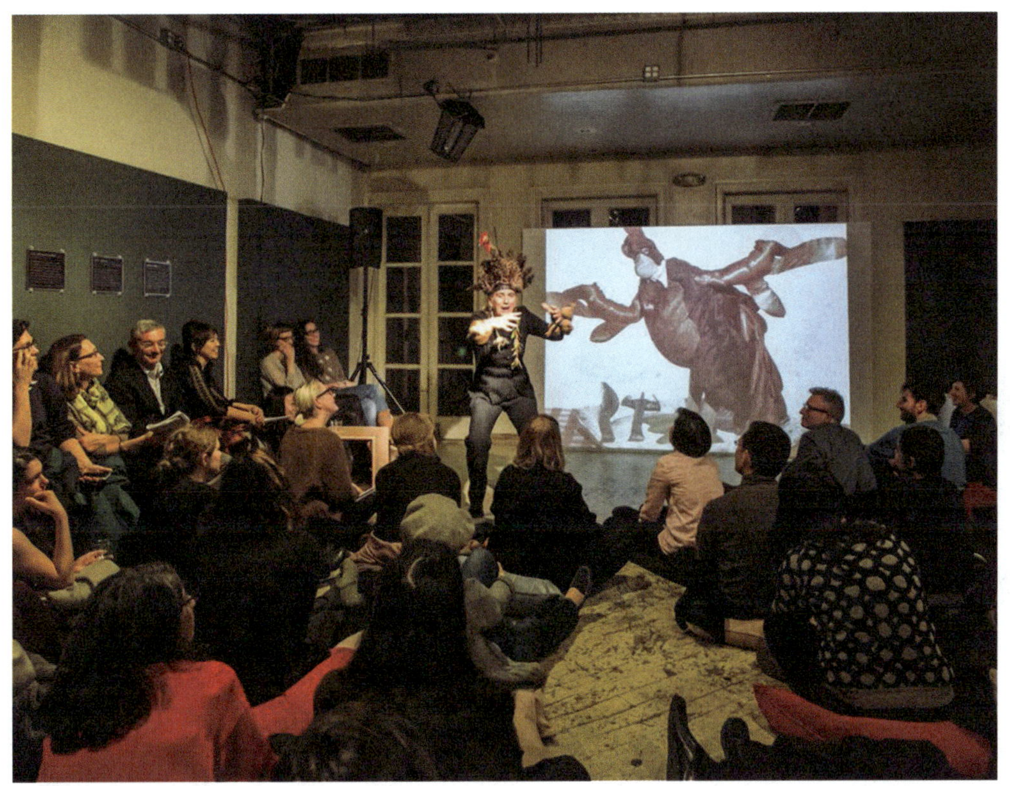

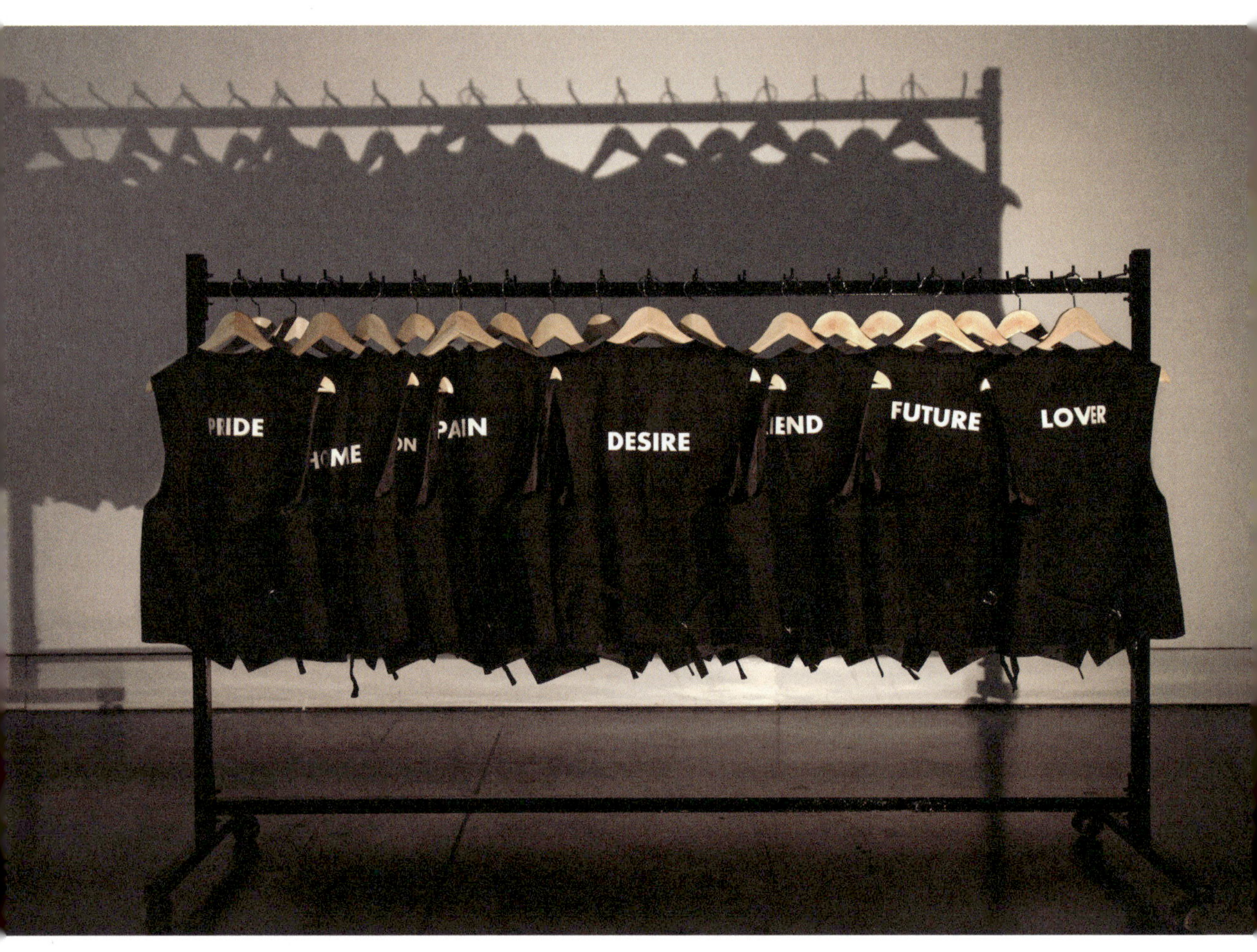
PRIDE
HOME
ON
PAIN
DESIRE
IEND
FUTURE
LOVER

A crossover between psychodrama therapy, theater, and authentic participation, Einat Amir's *Our Best Intentions* was at once a participatory performance and a video installation—a cinematic version of the work. After signing a waiver, donning black vests with words like "mother," "desire," "awkwardness," and "pain" written on the back, and entering a setting reminiscent of a reality TV show or sitcom, one suspected the performance was being filmed.

Our Best Intentions established a situation where the difference between performance and authenticity was effectively foreclosed, as participants were simultaneously the "content" and "viewers." There was no audience beyond the twenty participants. "Interpreters," who had been exposed to Amir's process during earlier performances, became professional facilitators, leading participants through different activities and scenarios and organizing groups into four staged areas that were recognizable as a dining room, bedroom, living room, and study.

First, the dining room interpreter asked her group to introduce themselves, and after a few quick warm-up activities, they enacted a scenario in which one of them entered into dialogue with his dead sister, who was played by another member of that group. Next, in the bedroom, practice exercises took place for the duration of the allotted time, seemingly without purpose. The interpreter, a drama coach, led the group through a mishmash of wordplay, free-association games, improvisation, and physical movement. It wasn't until the third group in the living room was activated that the words written on the vests came into play and gained meaning during another psychodrama role-play scenario. When the facilitator asked the group to strike a pose resembling or embodying the word they each wore, the "Father" sat on top of the armchair, while the "Mother" kneeled by the coffee table in a subservient manner, offering a glimpse at Amir's working premise that there may not be any contradiction between performance and authenticity. Finally, in the study, the interpreter whispered instructions to her group, their actions looking like a contemporary dance performance to the other participants, who were left unaware of what exactly was taking place.

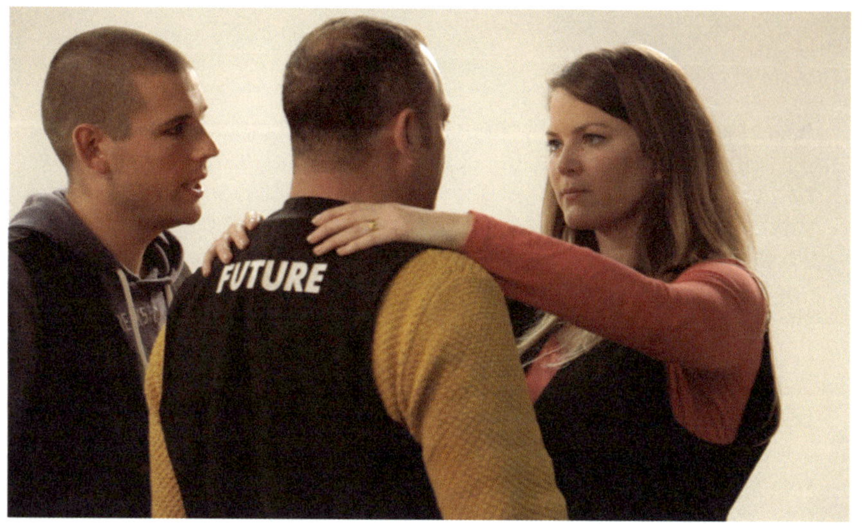

Our Best Intentions built on theater and psychology's historical relationship to achieve a contemporary art experience aimed at audience participation, leading to a meaningful and transformative performance. Amir's efforts succeeded in the creation of an intimate, familiar setting, where a group of strangers shared personal stories, emotionally connected, physically interacted, played, and ultimately performed the "self." The stage and direction Amir provided extended contemporary cultural conditions in which we ostentatiously present and share our personal selves and actively "like" and interact with others, while also frantically protecting our privacy.

Einat Amir, *Our Best Intentions* (2013), performance and video installation.

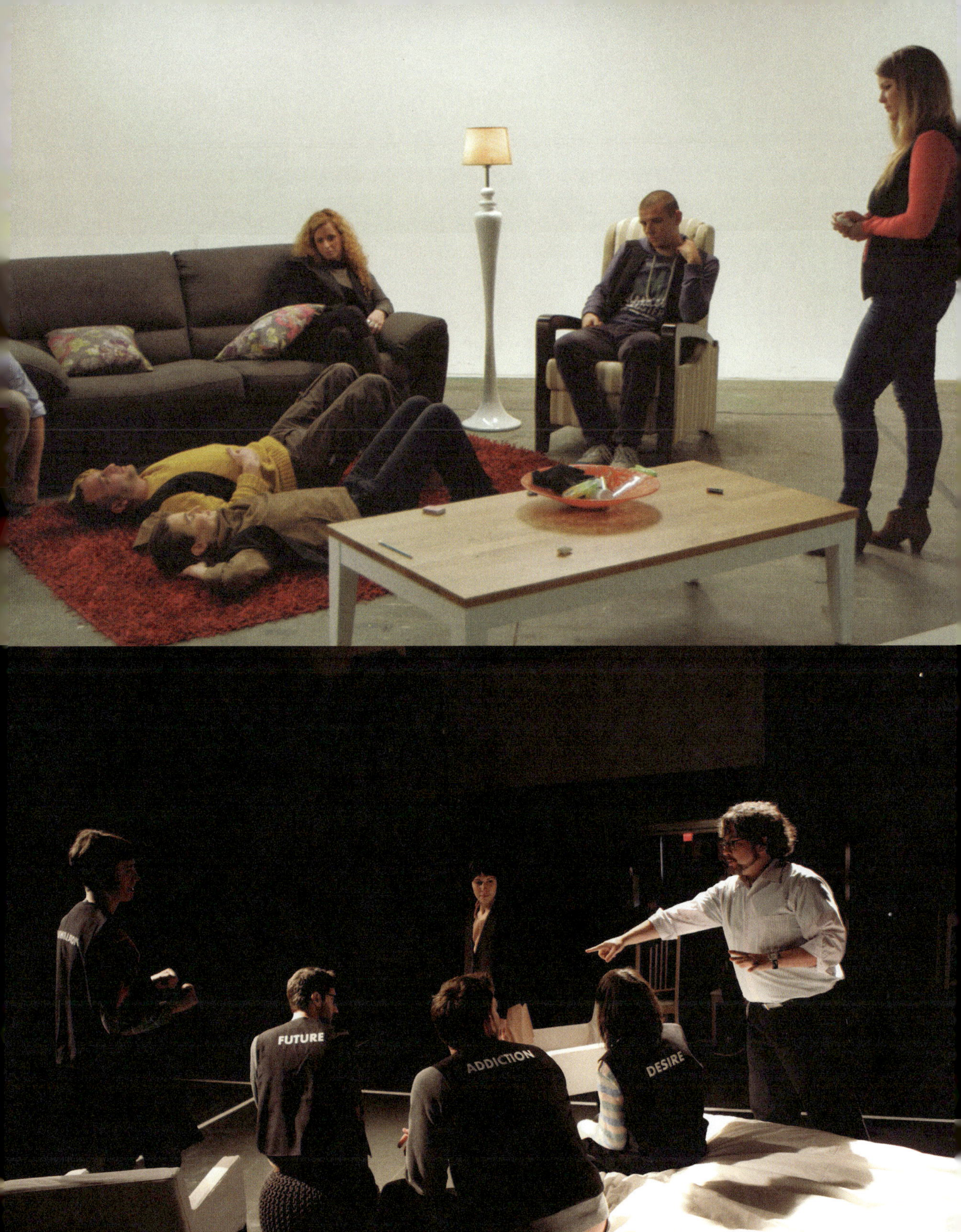
FUTURE
ADDICTION
DESIRE

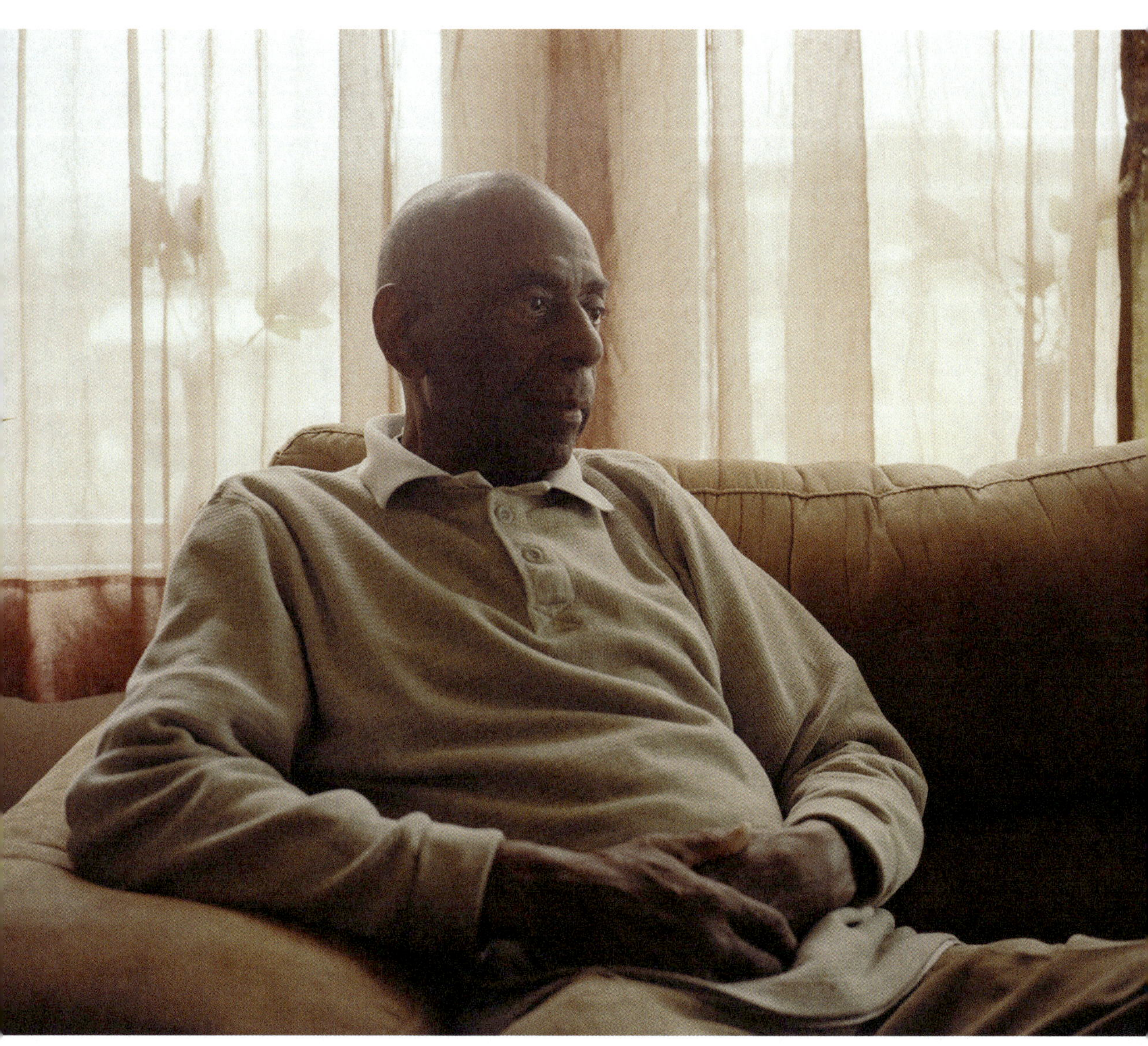

    Clifford Owens

FIVE DAYS' WORTH

Photo by and courtesy of Clifford Owens

Clifford Owens, *Five Days' Worth (Dad)* (2013), archival pigment print (detail).

Clifford Owens' *Five Days' Worth* was a site-specific project realized over five consecutive evenings in response to the intimate industrial loft space at 10 Greene Street in SoHo occupied by Third Streaming. While conceived as one artwork, the newly commissioned piece was structured in five distinct parts—a single performance per day, each of which pivoted on a distinguishing factor from Owens's previous performances. This was the most personal work Owens had conceived to date, meditating on self-reflexive themes of emotional, inspirational, and artistically influential importance to him.

Five Days' Worth was reminiscent of *Anthology* (2011-2012), Owens's compelling, paradigmatic, and infamous artist residency and suite of performances with a culminating exhibition at MoMA PS1 curated by Christopher Lew. *Anthology* used scores Owens secured from a range of black artists in an effort to build, imagine, and consolidate work about black creative production in performance art. It also carried the artistic trace of his *Photographs with an Audience*, an ongoing series of instigations begun in 2008, which Owens choreographs with spectators by asking questions, provoking responses, and staging postures in front of his camera, capturing the actions as intimate portraits.

Five Days' Worth was a point of departure for the artist, as it was realized outside of the white cube space of a gallery or museum, which is typically the context for Owens' performances. Throughout the series, Owens activated objects and staged conflicts and resolutions. He used the occasion and context of the project as the basis to create new photographs, videos, and sound works.

In the Dark was the opening night performance, during which the gallery was converted into a pitch-perfect black space—with absolutely no light or sound entering or leaving it. From 8pm to 10pm, participants (taken from a line that wrapped around the block and up the creaky stairs of the building) entered individually, each staying alone in the black room with Owens for varying amounts of time. Their interactions were recorded by multiple microphones: one placed on Owens and the others located throughout the space. The performance culminated with a congregation of those remaining in line being asked

CURATED BY ADRIENNE EDWARDS ● THIRD STREAMING

to form a circle, respond to Owens's verbal provocations, and perform a series of gestures until the lights came on.

The second event was private, entitled *Waiting for David (Hammons)*. In a sense, it was the final act of a durational performance with a Leica point-and-shoot camera loaded with a roll of color 35mm film and four cans of Café Bustelo, some filled with coffee, others filled with black beans, with one can containing a spliff placed in a prescription pill bottle. These were delivered in a black reusable bag—a knock-off Louis Vuitton purse from around the corner on Canal Street—that was filled with bike locks and heavy bike chains and a "Ghana Must Go" bag filled with over twenty new and used beanies, skull caps, and men's knitted hats, which were sent to Hammons over the course of several days via an amenable proxy collector, A.C. Hudgins. From midnight to 2 am, a group including me, Owens, Yona Backer (founder of Third Streaming), Natasha Bunten (the series producer), and Owens's supporter Matthew McNulty, among a few others, waited for David, who, of course, and as far as we know, never came. We did receive a nice bag of treats, along with the gifts, which were returned through Hudgins on the day of the performance, except for the cans of Café Bustelo.

Owens requested performance scores—prompts or texts from women with whom he had been romantically involved—for *Letters from My Lovers*, performed on the third day. Presented in vignettes, the artist auditioned and selected four women performance artists to enact the scores as he imagined them, each wearing differently colored lingerie. In response to the score "Lifted, Hanged, Your Pendent Self, Suspended at the Edge of the Cliff," a woman dressed in black lingerie beat a four-foot-tall piñata, custom-made in Owens's image, until it burst. Following Mathew McNulty's instructions, another woman alternated taking a spoonful of honey and a sip of brandy while playing a recording of Yugoslavian singer Silvana Armenulic's "Sta ce mi zivot." In the next act, a woman either masturbated in total darkness or was engaging in sex acts with Owens or faking sounds of a sexual encounter. In the last, an actress along with Owens reversed roles as they fed one another, as well as audience members, a mix of Korean, Czech, Middle Eastern, and Mexican food, a selection reflecting the ethnic backgrounds of the four former lovers who wrote the scores.

Dad, the fourth performance in the weeklong program, was a poignant tribute to the artist's father and, though less obvious, also a self-reflexive meditation on his own role as a parent to his two sons. Visually, the piece referenced Owens's father's involvement with the Nation of Islam: the gallery floor was covered in brightly jewel-toned Islamic prayer rugs sourced from an Islamic supply store in Flushing, Queens, and ultimately donated to a mosque and community center in Brooklyn. Facing East toward Mecca and featured on one of the gallery's white walls was a triptych of photographs with Owens on the right side of a couch facing his dad, an *in situ* photograph of a painting of a seminal leader of the Nation of Islam, Elijah Muhammad, in the center, and the artist's father seated on the left of a couch turned toward Owens. An audio recording was heard of Muhammad's last speech for Saviours' Day from 1974, which I sourced from my local Nation of Islam store on Nostrand Avenue in the Bedford-Stuyvesant neighborhood of Brooklyn. Owens emerged after about twenty minutes dressed in white and asked the more than eighty people gathered there if they had any questions about his father. While he responded, he photographed the audience, meandering among them, selecting subjects as he went along. Artist Terry Adkins played saxophone in the background.

Come to Me, the culminating performance, involved a series of participatory actions with the audience, who were required to bring an object, a text with instructions or actions, or anything else they wished to have Owens perform or engage with. In his typical fashion—both in terms of his performance aesthetics and his classic all-black attire— the artist laughed, cajoled, and instructed the crowd of more than 100 people, collecting items such as a church fan; a can of Spam; sheet music; letters; a feather; a bottle of glue; a miniature American flag in the red, black, and green color scheme of Pan-Africanism; condoms; a pink razor and shaving cream; and an electric cord. Owens played and made assemblages with these objects on a wooden table, while outright refusing others. All the while, Owens was amicable and warm, smoking a cigarette and placing drink orders from the bar, as his assistant snapped images and he exercised total control of the room.

Five Day's Worth was presented as related programming for the exhibition *Radical Presence: Black Performance in Contemporary Art New York City* presentation at the Studio Museum in Harlem and New York University's Grey Art Gallery, following its debut at the Contemporary Arts Museum Houston.

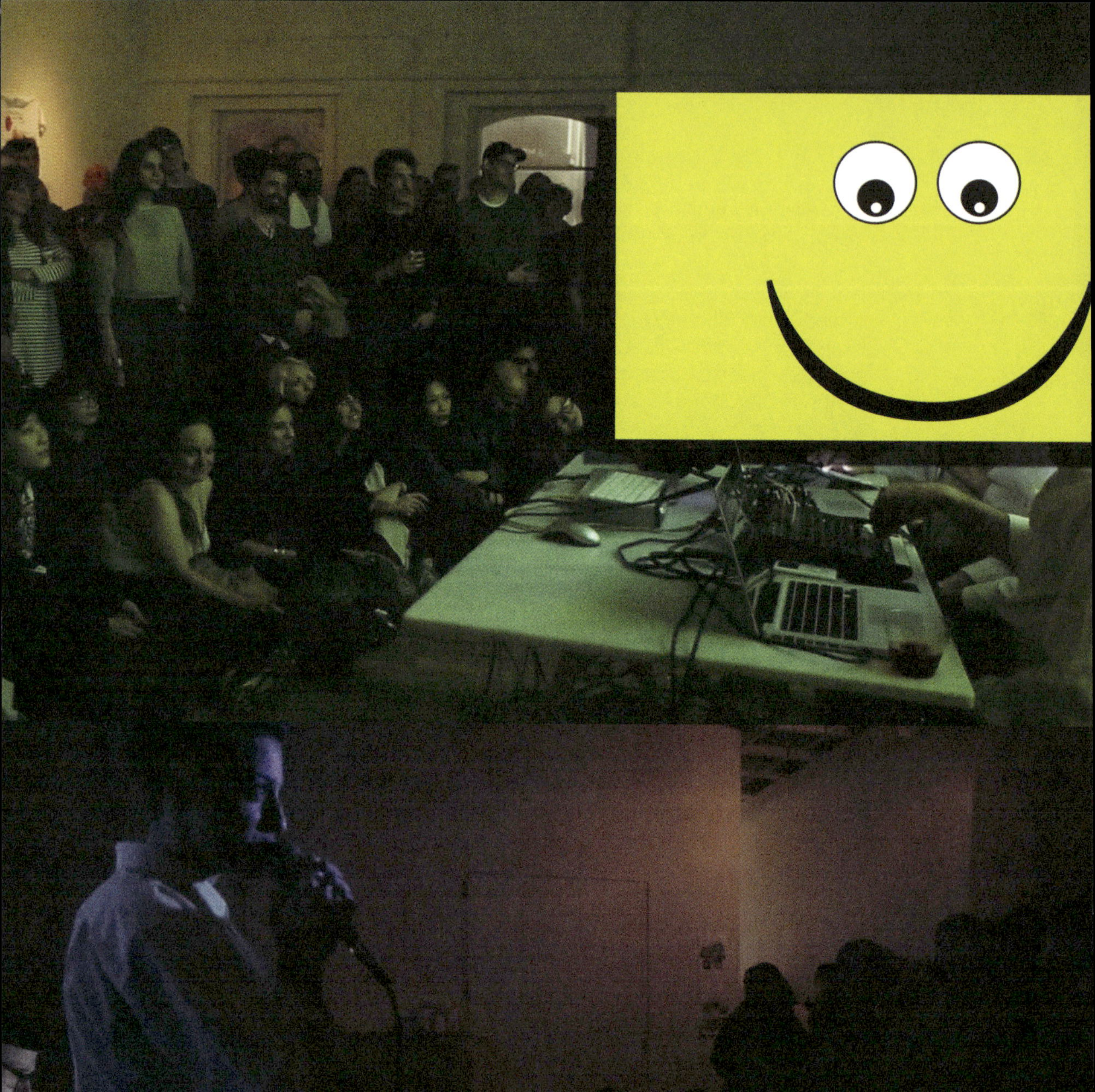

MICHAEL BELL-SMITH, SARA MAGENHEIMER, AND BEN VIDA

BLOOPERS #0

Sarah Magenheimer, Michael Bell-Smith, and Ben Vida, are a performance collective that operates as a band under the name Bloopers #0, sat in front of a large screen with laptops and microphones, all formally dressed in white button-down shirts and black pants. "Why do we hate some objects and love others?" Magenheimer intoned, swaying in front of projected footage of young men with baseball bats smashing mailboxes, which sprayed animated fireworks and dollar bills into the air whenever they were hit.

A crowd of 100 or so pressed into the main room of Four81 Broadway. For the artists, who site as influences Nam June Paik's 1973 Neo-Dada video collage Global Groove, Robert Ashley's 1984 television opera *Perfect Lives*, and the stand-up comedy of Andy Kaufman, they strive to "use contemporary pop music and its social spaces"—house parties, clubs, and the Internet—"as a framework for an expanded performance event." The hour-long performance oscillated between original dance music, slideshows of Internet ephemera, and spoken word, quoting from TK, creating a "multilayered dance party with distractions."

TEXT BY LIZZIE FEIDELSON / CURATED BY TRIPLE CANOPY ● FOUR81

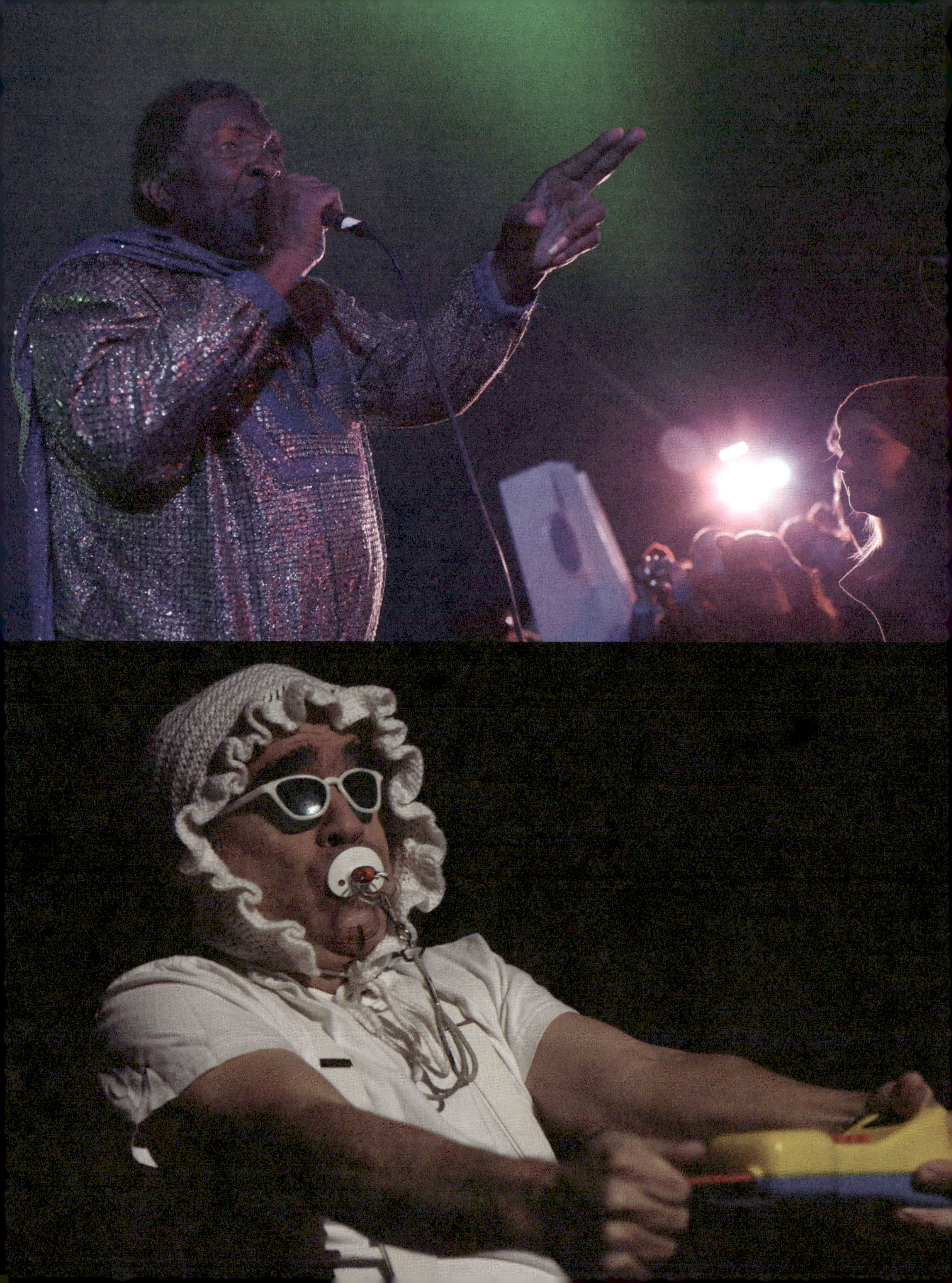

BLOWFLY AND MICHAEL SMITH

AN AFTERNOON OF HUMOR

Artist Michael Smith and the famed American rapper/artist Blowfly's performances were presented as part of the Mike Kelley retrospective at MoMA PS1, the largest exhibition of Kelley's work to date. Regarded as one of the most influential artists of our time, Kelley (1954–2012) produced a body of deeply innovative work that mined American popular culture and experimental music.

As Kelley's friend and sometime collaborator, Smith presented "Mike" and his diapered counterpart, "Baby Ikki," who appeared in Kelley and Smith's 2009 project *A Voyage of Growth and Discovery*. "Mike" sings a series of dirty limericks—an Eighteenth century form of lyric poetry often lewd and with humorous intent, favored by the English working class—a form of poetry that Kelley's used to great effect in his seminal video and performance work *Day is Done* (2005–2012). Blowfly, the "Original Rapper," was also a favorite musical act of Kelley's, who enjoyed the obscene and bawdy humor in the rapper's sexually explicit parodies of popular songs, such as his take on Brook Brenton's classic 1962 R&B track, "A Spermy Night In Georgia."
After the performance, Michael Smith and Jayson Musson, the creator of Hennessy Youngman and his "Art Thoughtz" series, discussed the use of humor in Mike Kelley's work.

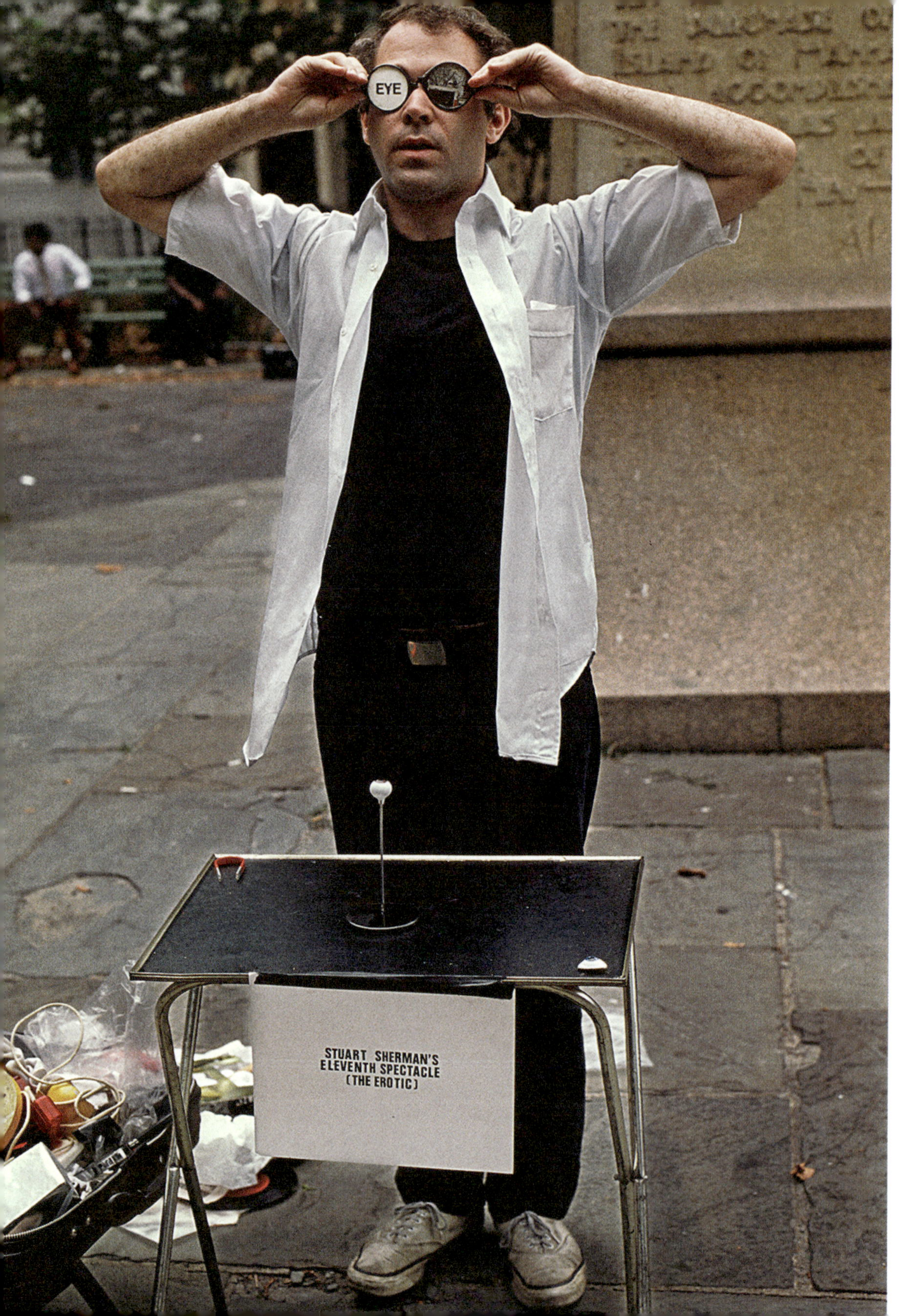

EYE
STUART SHERMAN'S
ELEVENTH SPECTACLE
(THE EROTIC)

SPECTACLE: A PORTRAIT OF STUART SHERMAN

British artist and filmmaker Robin Deacon was profoundly inspired in the mid-'90s by a two-week residency led by artist Stuart Sherman (1945–2001) in the Time-Based Art Department at the University of Wales. Deacon subsequently spent years studying and emulating Sherman's performance practice, and from 2006 to 2012 delved deeply into Sherman's work, creating a film, publishing papers and viscerally experiencing the work through re-enacted performances. Deacon began to recognize patterns. Through such mimetic action of doing and translating he gained an understanding of Sherman's work. Deacon's feature-length documentary, *Spectacle: A Portrait of Stuart Sherman* (2013), reflects this deep and internalized relationship to Sherman, exploring the unique nuances within the complex layers of meaning and humor in his work, and revealing biographical details through Sherman's many friends and collaborators.

Sherman began performing on the streets of New York City in the mid-'70s and became known for his one-man performances using a suitcase full of props and a small folding table. In *Spectacle* he is described as a "briefcase artist." Sherman manipulated a cast of small objects (eye glasses, playing cards, wind-up toys, telephones, and tape recorders, among other things) as moving parts of a greater whole, released from conventional functions and put into play in a fast-forming construction of visual meaning. His artistic pursuit centered on giving a physical shape to thoughts. In this way, Sherman created a language through his objects and actions, illustrating his view of the world in these "Spectacles." Sherman described this as "I'm doing what I'm doing and they are, in a sense, eavesdropping."

"I have succeeded when my own consciousness has been contradicted."
—Stuart Sherman

"A man on a mission but it was a quiet mission."
—Ken Ross, Collective for the Living

*Quotes above from *Spectacle: A Portrait of Stuart Sherman*.

Photo by John Matturri

Stuart Sherman, *Eleventh Spectacle (The Erotic)* (1979).

CURATED BY JAY SANDERS / TEXT BY GRETA HARTENSTEIN ● ABRONS ARTS CENTER

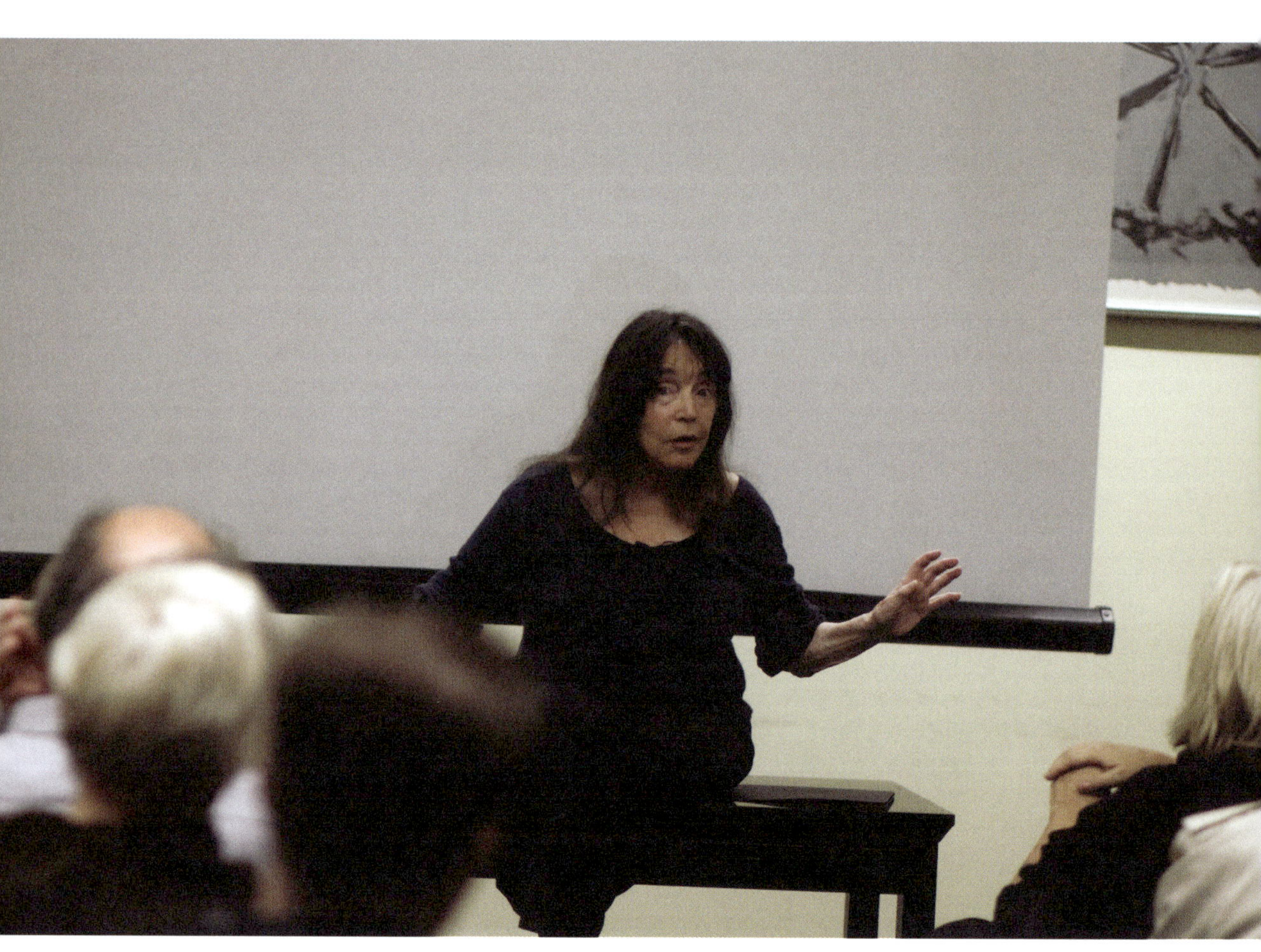

AN AFTERNOON WITH ELEANORA ANTINOVA/ 24 HOUR BALLAD

Coinciding with Performa 13, the exhibition I curated, *Multiple Occupancy: Eleanor Antin's "Selves,"* was on view at Columbia University's Wallach Art Gallery, displaying how conceptual artist Eleanor Antin animated personae of different genders, races, professions, and historical eras in her work from 1972 to 1991. Antin's early integrations of visual art, performance, and theater reverberate today, particularly in the work of the performance collective "My Barbarian," whose members, Malik Gaines, Jade Gordon, and Alexandro Segade, have worked with Antin on several projects. This connection moved Columbia and Performa 13 to present a pair of events: a multimedia presentation through which Antin revisited her persona Eleanora Antinova, the fictional ill-fated African-American ballerina of Diaghilev's Ballets Russes, and a public conversation among Antin, Gaines, and Segade. The latter two also produced *24 Hour Ballad* for Performa 13, independently from Antin, and as Courtesy the Artists. For this work, a rotating group of invited artists and musicians explored a narrative folk ballad, "Black is the Color (Of My True Love's Hair)," through a series of continuous performances over a calendar day. This was part of Courtesy the Artists' larger consideration of the ways that notions of folk, predicated on an authorless mode of affective political engagement, might serve a contemporary model of art production within the community.

In 1999 Gaines and Segade first encountered Antin's work during her retrospective at the Los Angeles County Museum of Art and found the work "revelatory" for its successful integration of Conceptual Art, performance, and theater. In 2012, the three artists collaborated when Gaines and Segade produced a new version of Antin's 1979 performance-play hybrid *Before the Revolution* for the Getty's *Pacific Standard Time* Performance and Public Art Festival. Shortly thereafter, Antin played a central character in My Barbarian's video *Universal Declaration of Infantile Anxiety Situations Reflected in the Creative Impulse* (2013). Across generations, Antin and My Barbarian have developed corresponding models of performance that rely on theatrical techniques such as character, costume, and voice to make visible the act of inhabiting different subject positions, distinguishing between, as Gaines has put it, "identification as a process" and "identity as a fixed state."

Originally staged in 1979 at The Kitchen, *Before the Revolution* centers on the conflict between Antinova's longing to play the part of Marie Antoinette and Diaghilev's contention that because she is black she can play only exotic types such as Cleopatra and Pocahontas. In the work's early productions, Antin played Antinova, applying makeup to her white skin to assume the part of the black ballet dancer and performing alongside a cast of five nearly life-sized Masonite puppets. By embodying the subject position of a black woman, from which she enacted the desire to occupy that of a white woman, Antin proposed that identity and performativity are mutually reinforcing. For the 2012 production of *Before the Revolution*, it was decided that Antinova should be played by an African-American actress (Danielle Watts) in recognition of the shifting significations of cross-race performance over the last thirty-plus years.

The reciprocal relationship of identity and performativity central to *Before the Revolution* frames My Barbarian's *Universal Declaration*. The video endows the labor of performance with a matrilineal heritage. Its thirty minutes are composed of five episodes in which the members of My Barbarian enact imagined historical vignettes with their maternal art historical forbears: Antin plays Eleanor Roosevelt and Mary Kelly is Mary Cassatt. Additionally, My Barbarian performs scenes with their biological mothers that explore fraught maternal experiences. The video ends in a black-box theater where a choreography of role-playing unfolds as Gaines, Gordon, and Segade take turns assuming the physical positions of mother and son in Michelangelo's *Pièta*. In *Universal Declaration*, it is precisely by destabilizing the mother figure and presenting motherhood as a subjective site open to multiple identifications that My Barbarian extends its maternal artistic lineage into the present moment, newly formulating the questions that Antin and Kelly's work explores.

Toward the end of *Before the Revolution*, Antin interrupts the work's narrative flow, addressing the audience as Eleanor Antin (not Eleanora Antinova) to recount an incident when she was unable to cash a check because a bank manager could not read her signature. The stakes of legible identity are poignantly conjured through what Antin designates as "the space between me and my name." If that space is by nature unstable, it has been consistent in remaining one of the most fertile environments for performance, as the work of My Barbarian—and Courtesy the Artists—makes vividly clear.

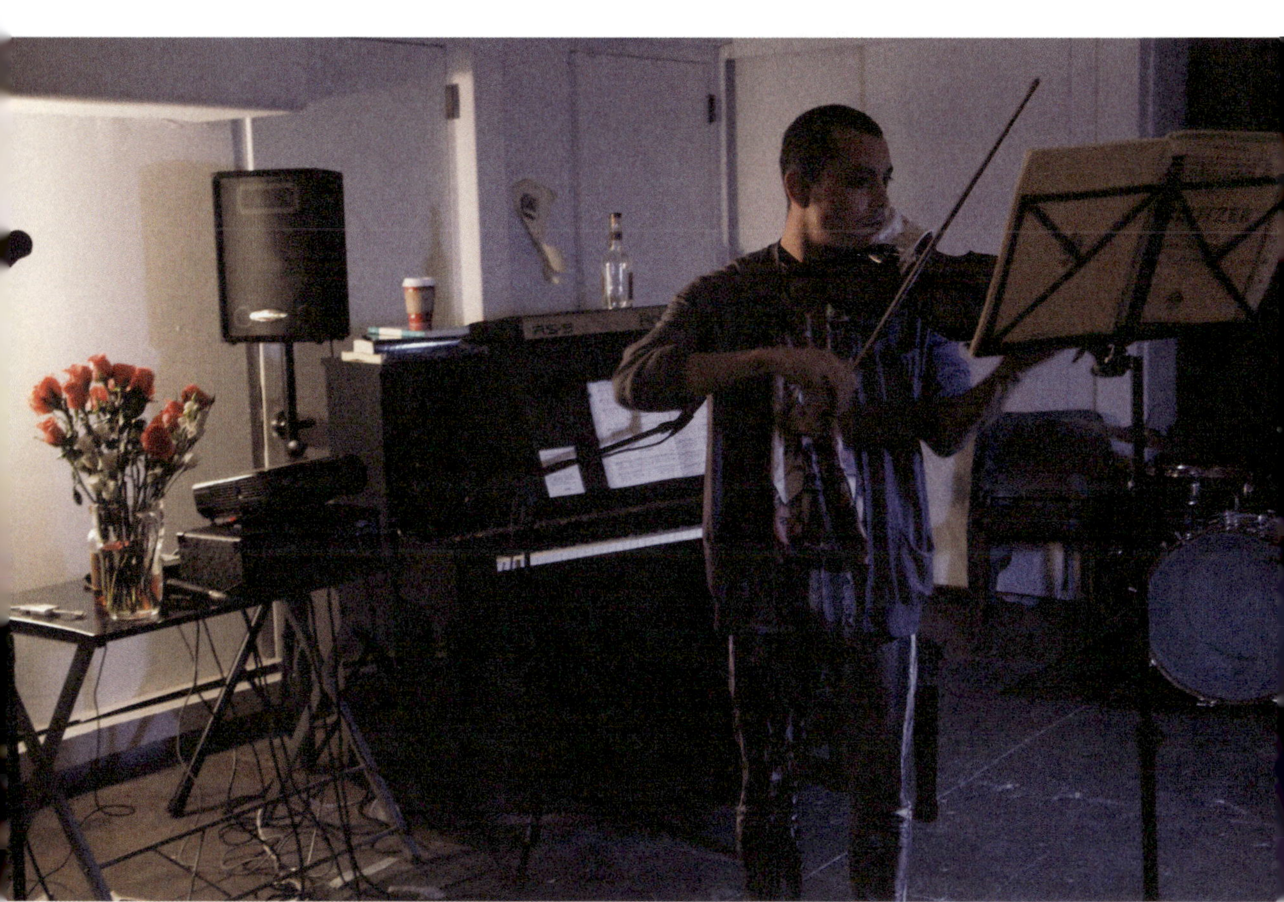

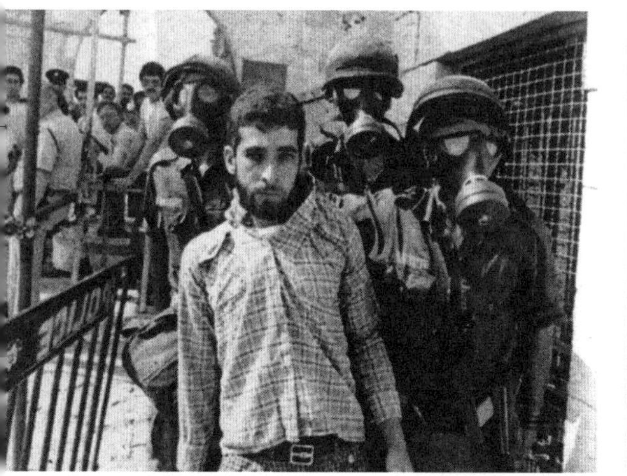

Here is what we have to offer you in its most
elaborate form- confusion by clear sense of purpose.

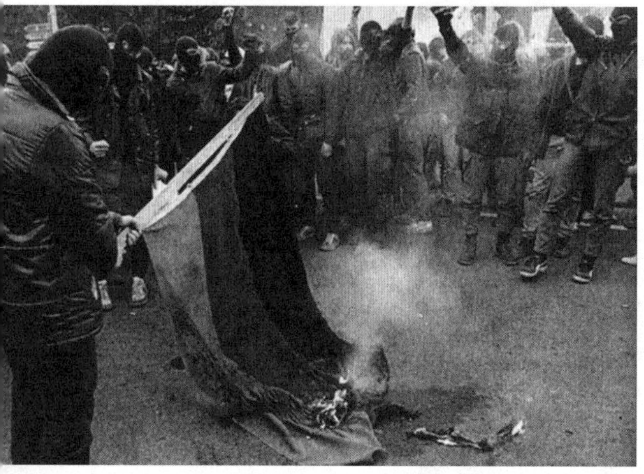

I try to turn something meaningless
into a meaningful thing.

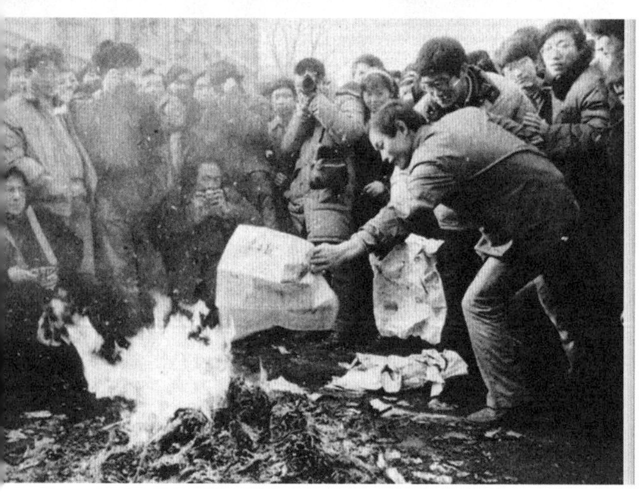

"Rejecting" something is a way of coming into relati
with it, getting involvedwith it, keeping it in play
somehow, at least I think that's what it is for me.

FAILED TO BIND

The melodic clicking of three 35mm projectors formed the baseline soundtrack to Dani Gal's performance-lecture *Failed to Bind* that was presented at the Goethe-Institut. Images of political conflicts from the past and present flashed across the wall, projected in sporadic yet carefully composed sequences. Culled by Gal from German newspapers and the Internet, slides of weaponry and military clashes were interspersed with close-ups of faces expressing anguish and compassion. A female narrator read Gal's script, essentially an assemblage of quotes Gal collected from artist interviews and writings—merging the narrator's voice with the steady rhythm of the projectors.

Failed to Bind illustrates Gal's continued interest in mining history to explore the human condition in times of conflict. His ongoing project *The Historical Records Archive* (2005) is an audio collection of major political speeches and important moments of the twentieth century. Gal's lauded film *Night and Fog* (2011) reconstructs the covert disposal of Adolf Eichmann's ashes off the coast of Israel through the eyes of a policeman, a Holocaust survivor. He often intertwines sounds—monologues, orchestral scores, and even silence—with provocative and poetic imagery to create multifaceted and unexpected narratives. Archival materials, such as letters and interviews, have provided inspiration, sometimes literally word for word, for the dialogue in Gal's films and installations. In *Failed to Bind*, Gal explores how art discourse can confront and connect with real events. By juxtaposing words with imagery, Gal aims to quiet the authoritative voice of history so new meaning can emerge from both the writings and photographs. The quotes, collected from artists working around the globe from the 1960s to today, cover a range of critical topics related to art production and processes, from reflections on creativity and image making to philosophical musings on self-awareness, anonymity, and technology. Although the statements and images represent a fifty-year span of history, in tandem they create a timeless, universal account of struggle and empathy.

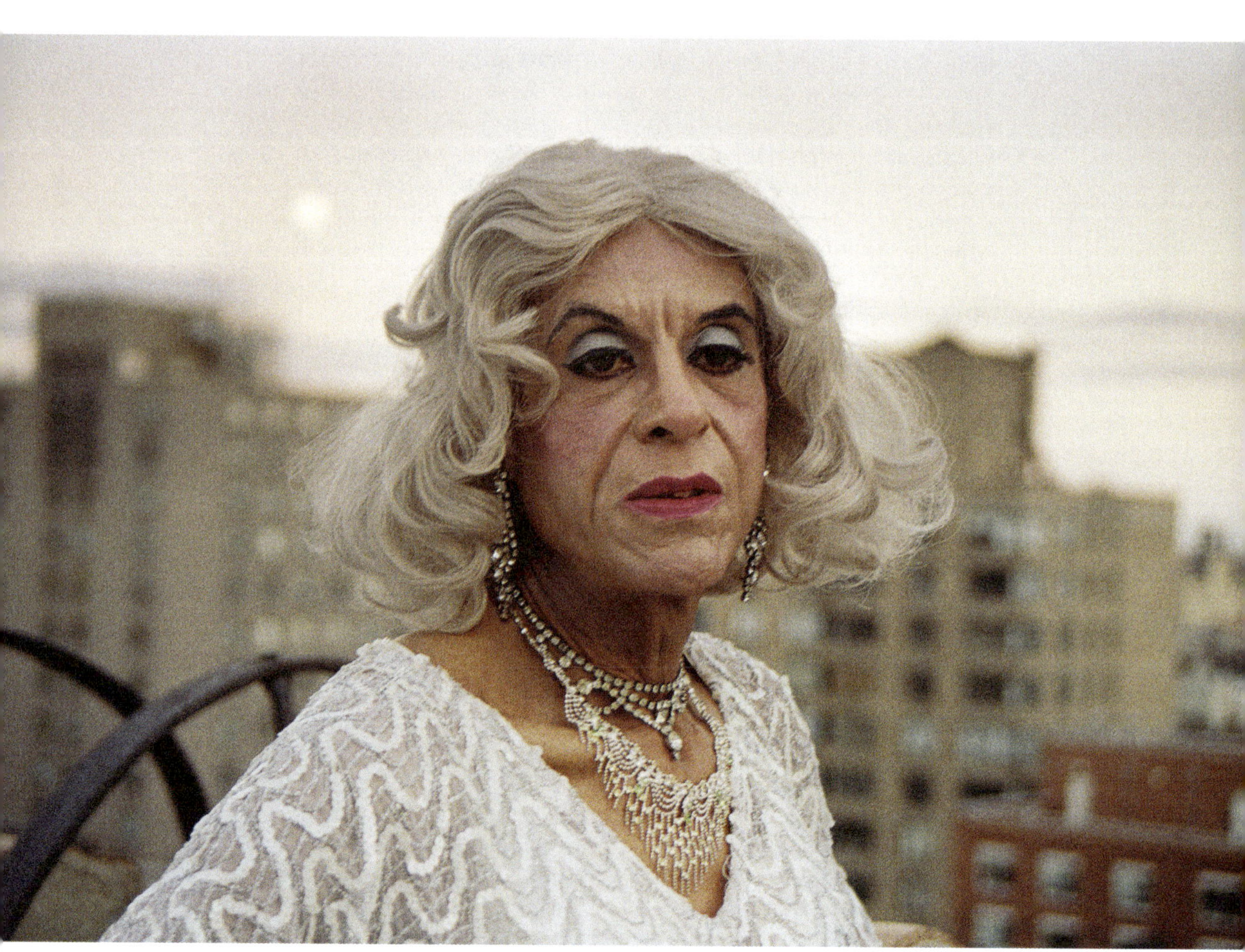

Legendary underground performer René Rivera (professionally known as Mario Montez) was an original "Superstar," which, according to Andy Warhol, in a June 1977 interview with Glenn O'Brien in *High Times*, was a term coined by Jack Smith. After meeting in 1960 through Reese Haire, a mutual friend and a photographic subject of Smith's, Rivera became Smith's muse and lover, posing in photographs as one of Smith's "Superstars of Cinemaroc" subsequently published by Piero Heliczer in *The Beautiful Book* (1962) and Ira Cohen's *Gnaoua* (1964). He also appeared in Smith's 16mm feature *Flaming Creatures* (1963) as Dolores Flores. Smith urged Rivera to rename himself Mario Montez, venerating Maria Montez, the '40s Hollywood B-movie actress. Montez subsequently appeared in Smith's *Normal Love* (1963) and *No President* (1967), as well as numerous shorts. He became a flamboyant presence, prominent on the experimental and underground scene in New York throughout the 1960s and early '70s. Appearing in drag for photo sessions, on stage and screen, Montez simply called it "getting into costume"—eschewing the word drag.

As Edward Leffingwell writes in *Jack Smith: His Amazing Life and Times*, published on the occasion of the show *Flaming Creatures: The Art and Times of Jack Smith*, organized by MoMA PS1 in 1997: "By the mid-1960s, many of Smith's models, whom he labeled as a group, the 'Superstars of Cinemaroc'… went on to become the superstars of Andy Warhol's Factory. Even Smith himself fell into Warhol's orbit, acting in an unreleased early film, *Batman/Dracula*. The term 'superstar' as well as the very idea of Warhol's Factory— an avant garde, Bohemian simulacrum of the traditional Hollywood studio, consisting of an ensemble of essentially replaceable stars and starlets presided over by a charismatic auteur—were appropriated by Warhol from Smith's Cinemaroc."

Indeed, the stars Smith brought to *Batman/Dracula* (1964) all appeared in subsequent Warhol films including Montez, Tally Brown, Beverly Grant, and Naomi Levine. Smith, offended that Warhol chose not to edit or release *Batman/Dracula*, appeared only twice more for

Warhol, in *Camp* (1965) and *Hedy* (1966), both alongside Montez. Though weary of the schism between Smith and Warhol, Montez went on to act in further Warhol films, including *More Milk, Yvette* (1965) and *Chelsea Girls* (1966), for a career total of fourteen moving image works.

Throughout this creative period in the '60s and early '70s, Montez always had a day job, mostly clerical. Filming, whether with Warhol, Jose Rodriguez-Soltero, Avery Willard, Takahiko Iimura, Ron Rice, Bill Vehr, or Hélio Oiticica, would sometimes require late nights, but Montez would be ready for work in the morning. This life/art/work balance gave Montez the clarity he needed to work with a range of very different filmmakers. Montez appeared for Warhol in roles such as the shoplifting, face-lifted Hollywood starlet Hedy Lamarr in *Hedy*; as a hungry Lana Turner in *More Milk, Yvette*; and as banana-peeling bombshell Jean Harlow in *Harlot* (1964). For Smith, Montez danced in head-to-toe black in *Flaming Creatures,* and starred as the mermaid in *Normal Love* (1963). He also appeared in Ron Rice's *Chumlum* (1964) and as Marilyn Monroe singing in the unfinished and lost *MM* (1967) by Bill Vehr. Montez was Lupe Vélez in Soltero's dime-store Baroque classic *Life, Death and Assumption of Lupe Vélez* (1966). He also played craps in front of the Flatiron for Oiticica in the unfinished *Agripina é Roma-Manhattan* (1972).

Montez was a founding member of Charles Ludlam's avant garde Off-Off Broadway Ridiculous Theatrical Company founded in 1967 with defectors from John Vaccaro's Play-House of the Ridiculous. The term for the genre "Theatre of the Ridiculous" was credited to playwright Ronald Tavel, whose early productions were directed by Vaccaro, starred Montez, and included the campy *Life of Lady Godiva* (1966), *Screen Test* (1967), and Indira Gandhi's *Daring Device* (1967). Tavel marketed these plays with the catchphrase, "We have passed beyond the absurd: our position is absolutely preposterous."

In Ridiculous Theatrical Company productions, written mostly by Ludlam, Montez appeared as Delilah No. 1 in *Whores of Babylon* (1967); Lupe Vélez in *Big Hotel* (1967); Alice and Magnavox in *When Queens Collide* (1967); Carla in *Turds in Hell* (1969); High Priestess in *The Grand Tarot* (1969); and Lamia the Leopard Woman in *Bluebeard* (1970). Montez also appeared in *Vain Victory* (1971) alongside Jackie Curtis and in Harvey Fierstein's *In Search of the*

Cobra Jewels (1972) and *Euripides: The Trojan Women* (1972). In 1977, when he grew tired of the bankrupted, freezing city that New York had become, Montez simply disappeared.

Unseen for thirty years, new footage of Montez appeared briefly, fantastically, in Mary Jordan's *Dead Jack Theatre* for Performa 05 and in the documentary *Jack Smith and the Destruction of Atlantis* (2006). Conrad Ventur, a Brooklyn-based artist, subsequently met Montez following his appearance at the Columbia University conference *Mario Montez: Superstar*, which Ventur attended. Their introduction was orchestrated through the combined efforts of Marc Siegel, Callie Angell, Douglas Crimp, and Agosto Machado. The encounter was fortuitous, occurring at a moment in Ventur's artistic life when he was restaging Warhol's "Screen Tests" with Factory members. Their collaboration began soon thereafter, starting with Montez performing in a new screen test by Ventur.

Between 2010–13, Ventur traveled to Florida (and once to Berlin) to work with Montez, filming and photographing situations in which Montez danced in a backyard setting in Orlando dressed as Dolores

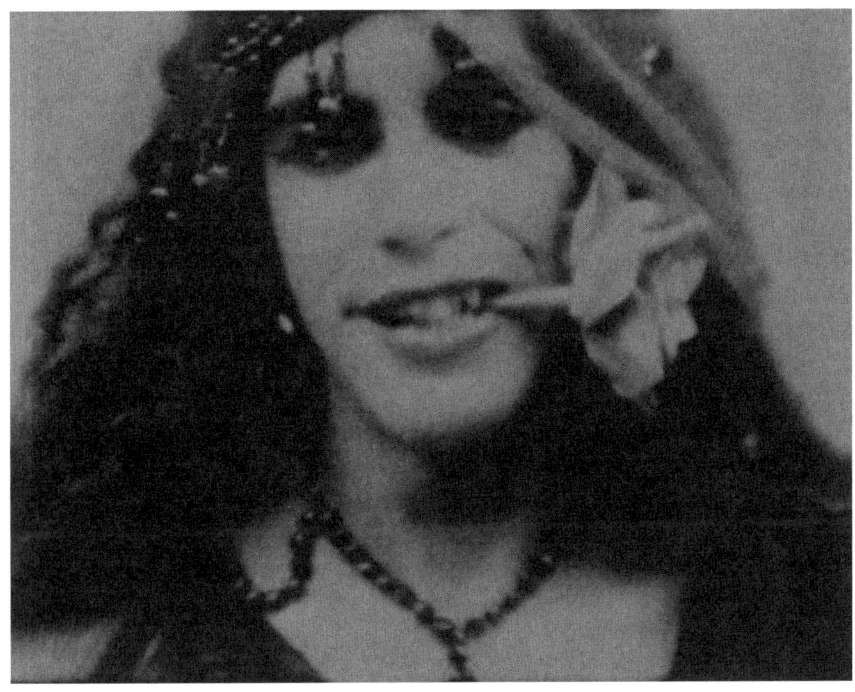

Flores from Smith's *Flaming Creatures*; looked longingly out of a window in Berlin wearing an elegant blue dress; sang "Besame Mucho" out of costume in a Berlin living room; drank ginger ale on a beach called Boca Chica in Key West; and listened to the radio while lounging poolside in Florida, among many other situations. These were effectively tests to get Montez ready for his return to stage and screen, as Ventur was planning a six-week multimedia performance environment at PARTICIPANT INC for Performa 13. With Montez as the star, the exhibition-as-performance site would have reunited actors from the original Ridiculous Theatrical Company and the renowned downtown theater La MaMa, alongside subsequent generations of performers, including Agosto Machado, Everett Quinton, Lola Pashalinski, Marti Domination, Paul Twinkle, and Brandon Olson, with musical interludes by a dozen others.

As preparations for his return to New York were underway, Montez died on September 26, 2013, having had a stroke several days before. The night before his stroke, Ventur talked with Montez on Skype about the set design and props that would be built in the gallery, including a fake palm tree, a Carmen Miranda-inspired oversized banana (Montez didn't like that idea, but Ventur loved it), and a giant volcano; and the scenes from their *Sunset Boulevard* (1950) and *Cobra Woman* (1944) remakes that would star Quinton. That night, Ventur began a preliminary design of the poster for *Mario Montez Returns*.

After the tragic and sudden departure of Mario Montez, we struggled with what we were capable of organizing without him. Ventur had come to love Montez as a friend, muse, grandfather, and drag mother collectively. Friends, cast, and crew all needed time to recalibrate and reflect. Three memorial screenings occurred on November 10, 17, and 24 as part of Performa 13.

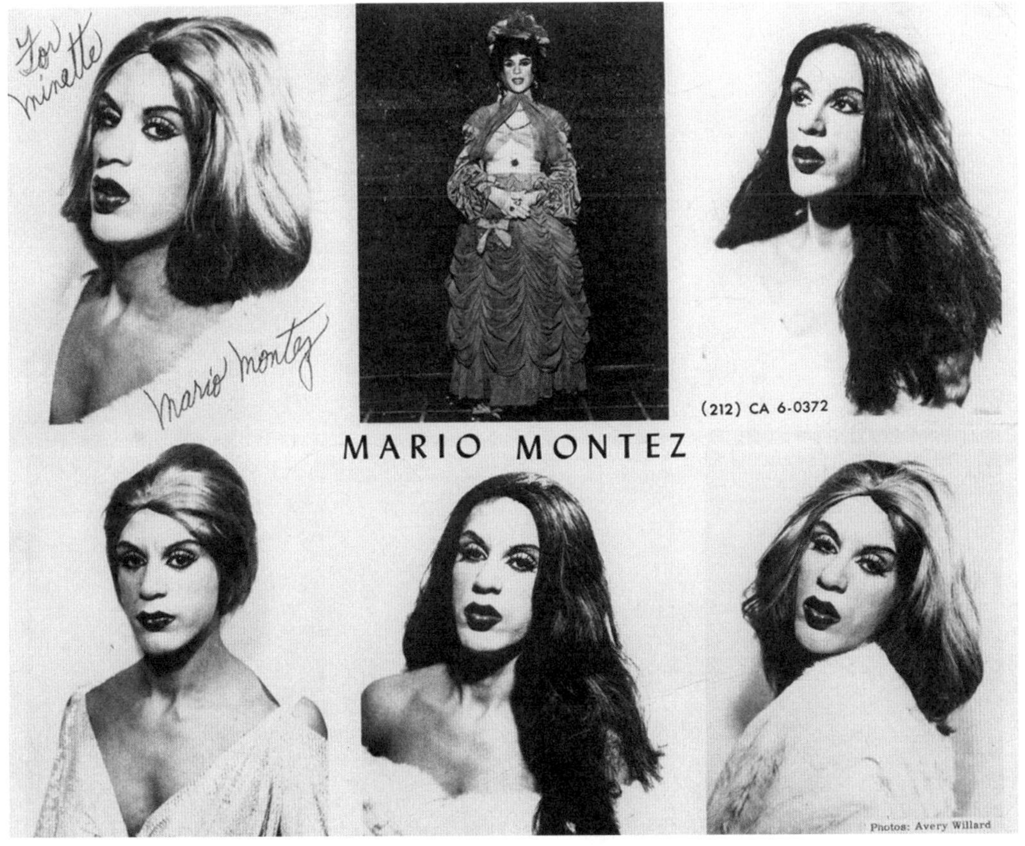

For
Minette
Mario Montez
MARIO MONTEZ
(212) CA 6-0372
Photos: Avery Willard

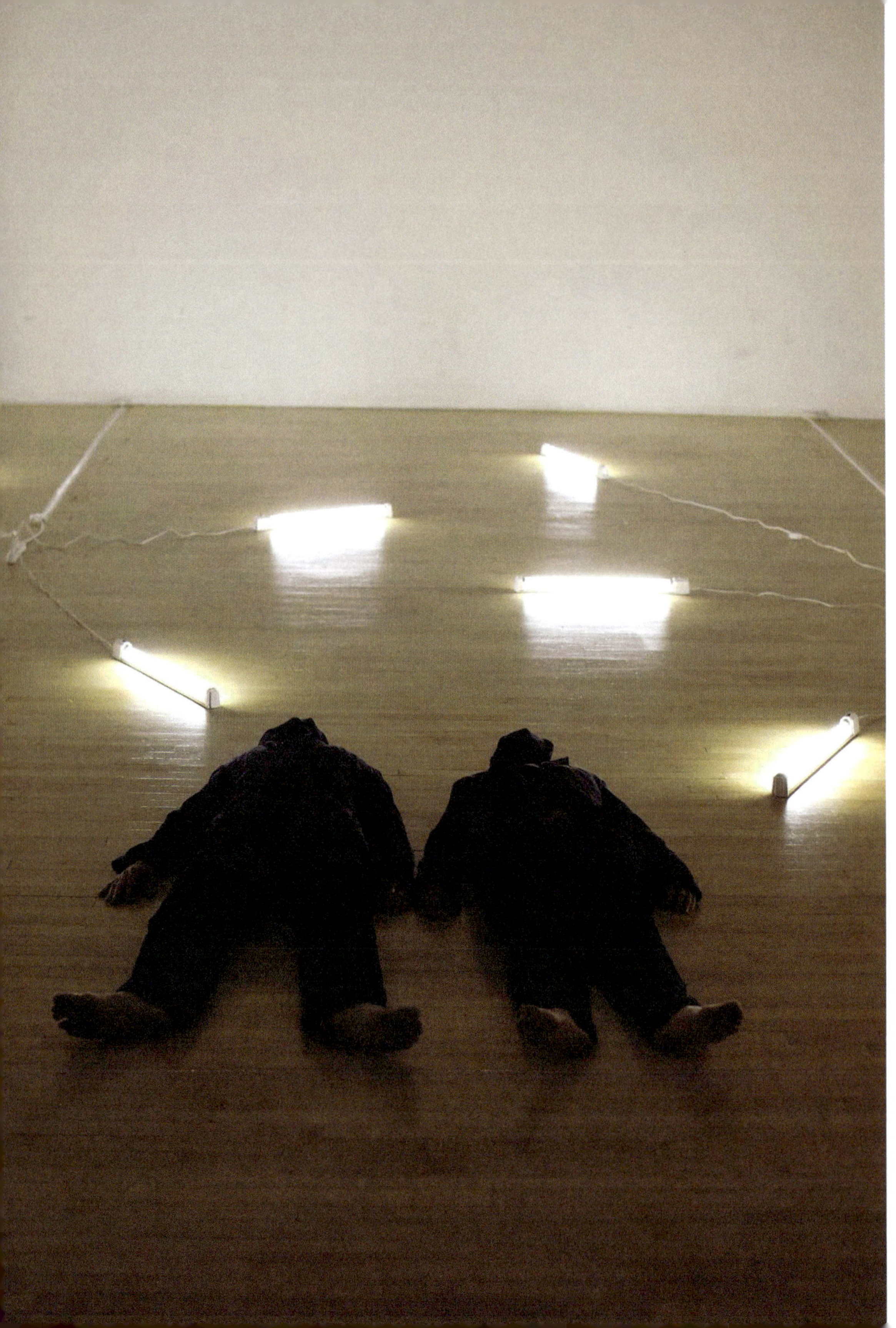

JULIE TOLENTINO

THE SKY REMAINS THE SAME

A Los Angeles-based artist with a history of engagement in contemporary dance, queer activism and extreme body art, Julie Tolentino has, since 2008, pursued an ambitious archiving project, which radically redefines the terms and conventions of archiving live art. Drawing directly from her relationships with past collaborators including Ron Athey, Franko B, David Rousseve and Stanley Love, among others, The Sky Remains the Same is an ever-evolving repository of performances contained and expressed through Tolentino's body. Anchored by individual contracts between Tolentino and these artists, each iteration of The Sky… is another negotiation around how one person's artwork enters into and lives within the body of another. The goal of the work is not to reproduce or "re-perform" a given performance, but to ask how traces of live events can carry on, beyond the bodies that first carried or received them. Working beyond conventional notions of archiving performance through material artifacts, video, photos, and other ephemera, Tolentino has conceived of an affective, unwieldy, yet deeply committed, mode of archiving, one that allows the past to literally live on.

On November 23, 2013, Tolentino presented the archiving of Lovett/Codagnone's *WEIGHTED*, one of three works chosen by the artist duo to be considered through the unique methodologies of The Sky… This archiving session was part of a residency organized in conjunction with the exhibition Performance Archiving Performance, a show that considered different artists' approaches to archiving as medium. Originally presented at Dixon Place in 2010, *WEIGHTED* was originally created as a duet for two masked performers—John Lovett and Alessandro Codagnone—utilizing minimal, repetitive movements and accompanied by a soundtrack that includes excerpts from The End of Imagination (1998) by Arundhati Roy. In this somber meditation that questions the concept of death as the ultimate failure of life, the artists take turns dragging one another's inert bodies through a series of positions. Performed in a room lit only by fluorescent lights arranged across the floor, the masked figure tasked with dragging his counterpart switches a light off between each turn until the room is completely dark.

For the New Museum iteration of Tolentino's *The Sky ...*, the artists chose to expand the notion of the body of the artist as an archive through dispersing their work across multiple bodies (all friends and colleagues). Constructed as a short duet with original music and sound design by CANDIDATE, the archiving of *WEIGHTED* was presented here as a durational repetition of the original score, performed in sequential pairings by John Lovett, Alessandro Codagnone, Julie Tolentino, Stosh Fila and Walter Dundervill. Fractured across multiple bodies, the work was then also multiplied.

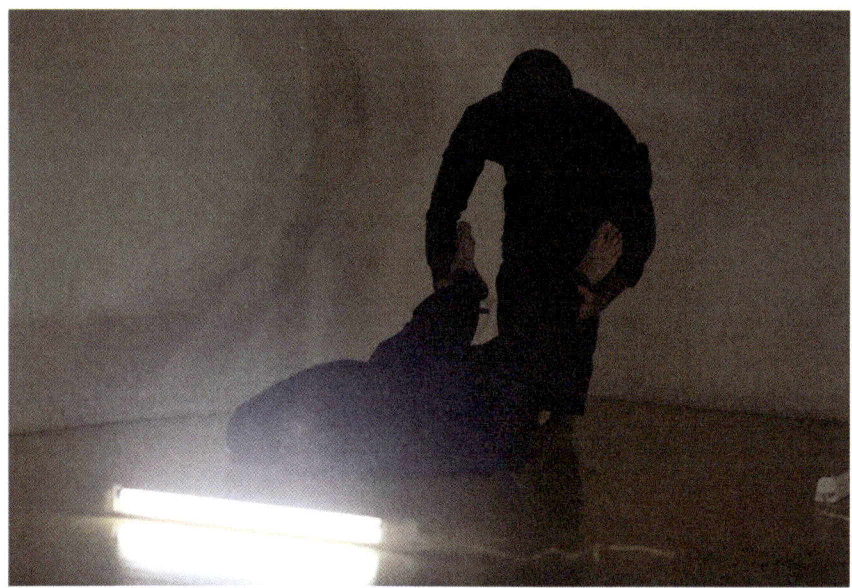

(Left) Julie Tolentino, *The Sky Remains the Same* (2013), performance view.
(Right) Lovett/Codagnone. notes for performance at the *New Museum*, 2013.

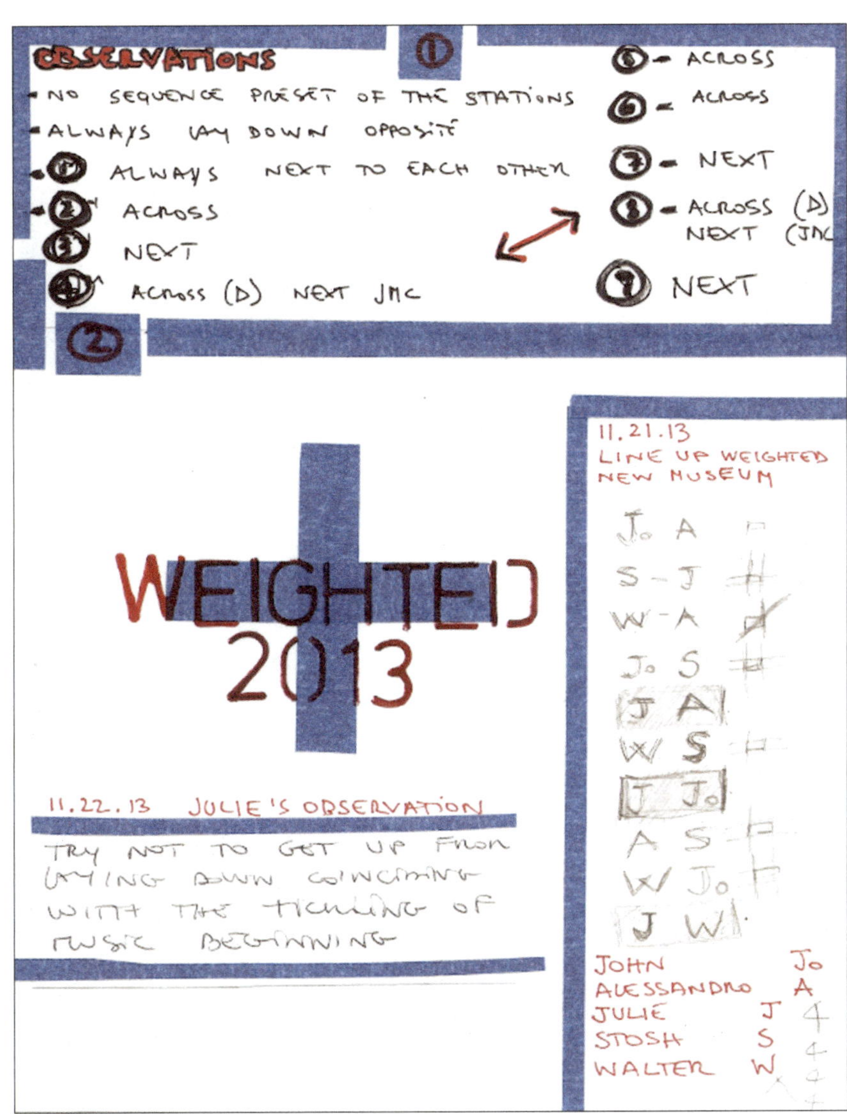

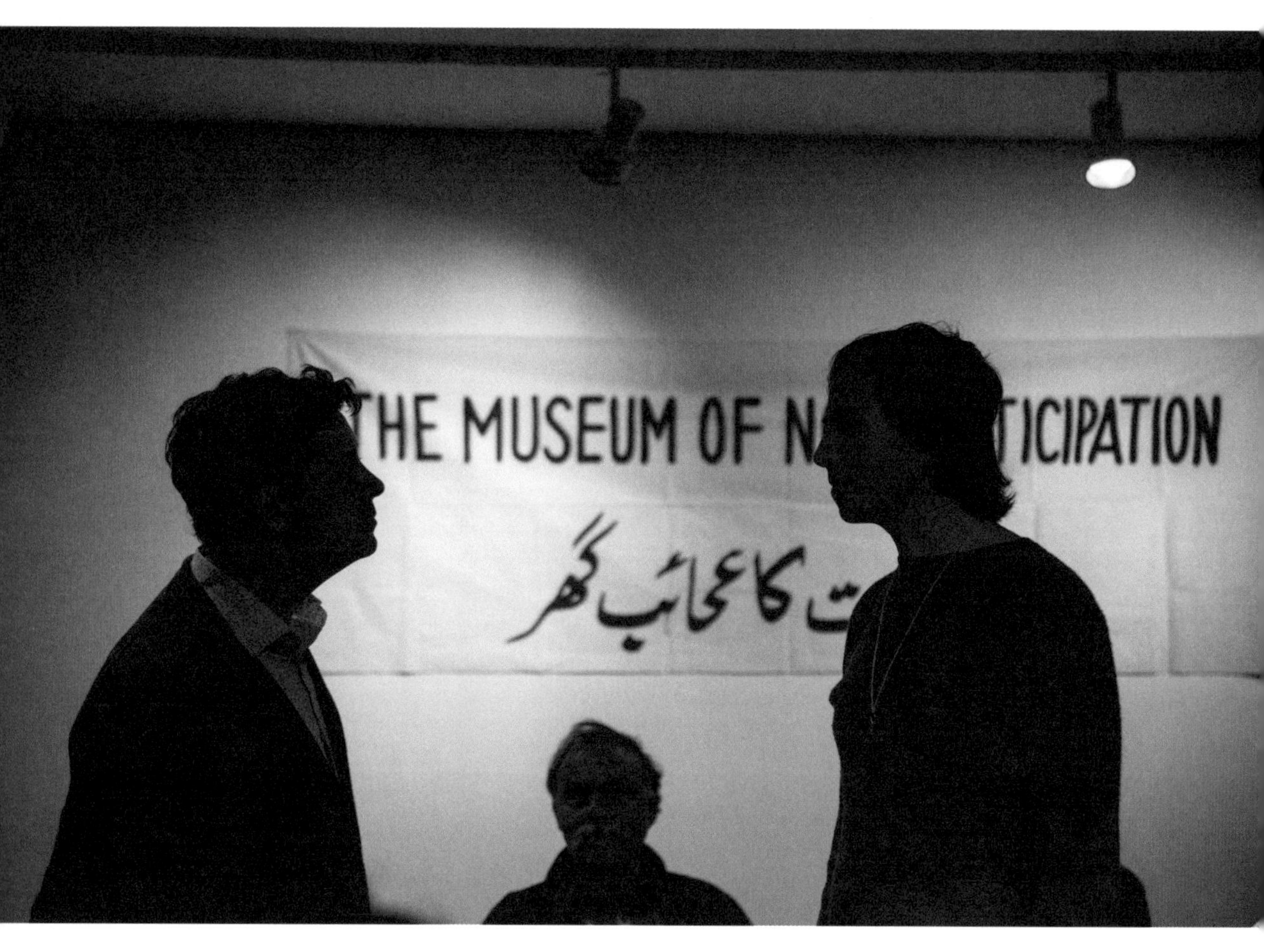

THE MUSEUM OF N   TICIPATION
ت کاعجائب گھر

KAREN MIRZA AND BRAD BUTLER

THE MUSEUM OF NON-PARTICIPATION: THE GUEST OF CITATION

The Museum of Non-Participation is a fictional museum initiated by London-based visual artists Karen Mirza and Brad Butler. Established in 2009 as a peripatetic space, the Museum of Non-Participation has manifested as a newspaper, site-specific interventions, a neon sign, exhibitions, and performances—always focused on the politics of participation at its hosting sites. Through assigned activities it serves to reveal, viscerally and directly, to audience and performers the underlying structures that guide social relations between people, cultures, and nations.

For Performa 13, Mirza and Butler invited New York City residents to work within *The Museum of Non-Participation* to create *The Guest of Citation,* an intervention into Bertolt Brecht's short play *The Exception and the Rule* (1929-30) using techniques developed by Brazilian theater director Augusto Boal whose "Theatre of the Oppressed" (1973) insisted on theater as a radical form of education through participation. The paradoxical dialogue between these two pedagogical theatrical forms were used by Mirza and Butler to create a tension, a condition of unmaking, through the praxis of Augusto Boal and the narrative of Brecht's *Lehrstücke* "learning play". This tension is also contained in the title of Brecht's work, where the "rule" referred to implies legal language or a directive, while the "exception" suggests being ungovernable. Taken together, Brecht suggests that the rule cannot exist without the exception, while Boal asks what qualifies as a state of exception, both politically and on stage.

Collaborating with ten players—a museum curator, docents, and interns as well as artists and performers who responded to an open call for actors and non-actors—Mirza and Butler led a four-day workshop of which the outcome on the fifth day was a collaborative public performance. The workshops sought to establish a space where institutional roles of curator/artist/producer/participant collapsed, and all would participate equally in the activities to come. Participants shared the roles in Brecht's text as well as those each play in daily life: labor lawyer, father, educator, student, playwright, and activist. Simultaneously, the players utilized movement and voice to question their own mutable political, social, and moral positions in the world. This process layered the contemporary complexity of the players' own experiences into Brecht's story of a merchant and his servant, drawing out the play's themes of capitalism and economics, labor and hierarchy, legislation and state ideology. The outcome was a group-authored structure of theatrical activities that merged the pre-existing script with improvisation in order to dissolve the boundaries dividing the audience and players.

The culmination of this activity was a two-hour public performance in the event space at the Museum of Arts and Design. Within this stark white room, usually used for income-generating rentals and board meetings, the players presented the final work in the round. Throughout the course of the performance, players cycled out as readers and performers. By repeatedly swapping out their roles, multiple players voiced single characters, while others spontaneously generated tableaux using only their bodies. The combination of theater forms and improvisation complicated the character roles of oppressors and oppressed within the text. As this lively interactive work unfolded, the workshopped structures became increasingly evident. Encouraging the audience to participate alongside the players, the work transformed the stage into a public forum to discuss our daily lives and the powers that shape them.

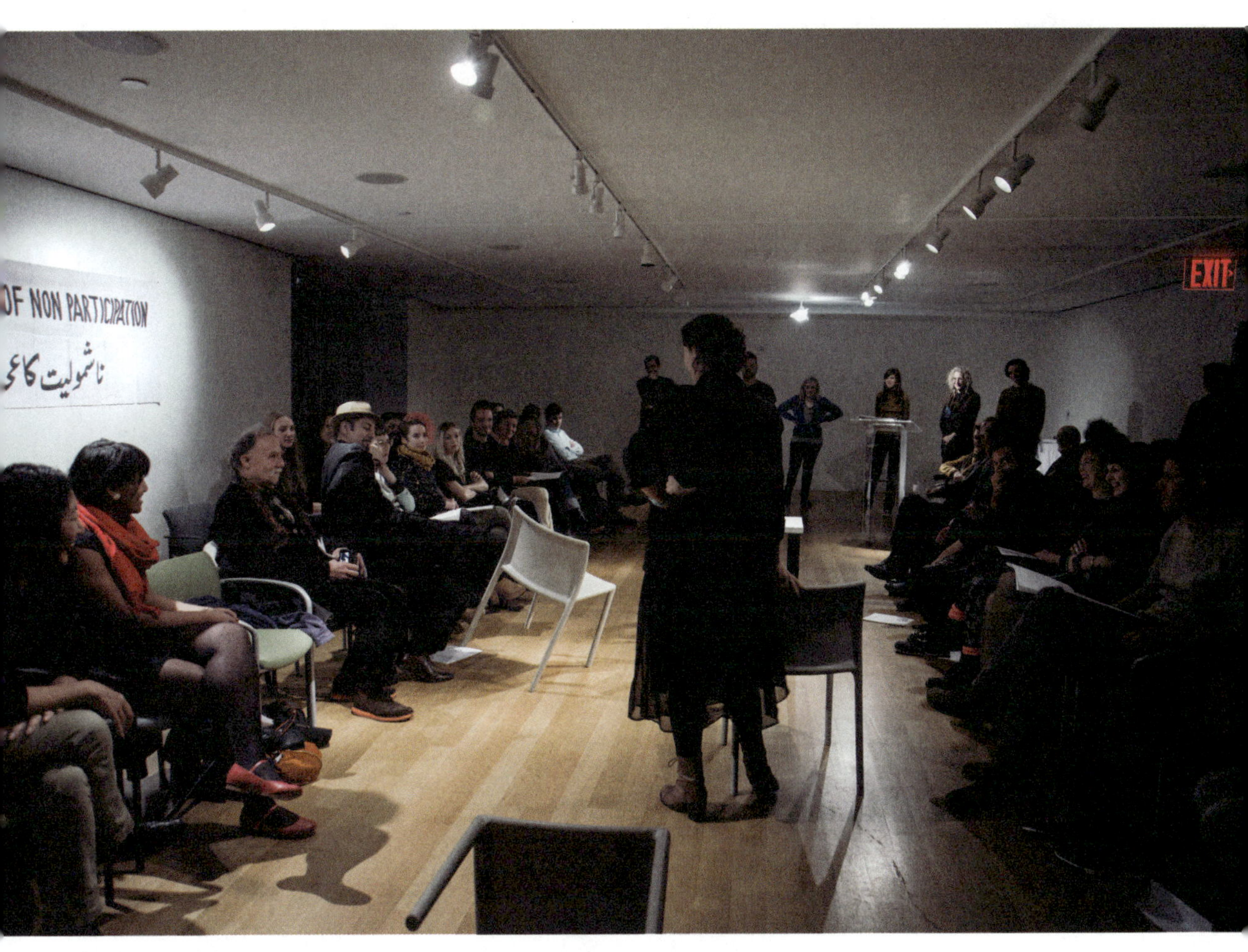

 The Museum of Non-Participation

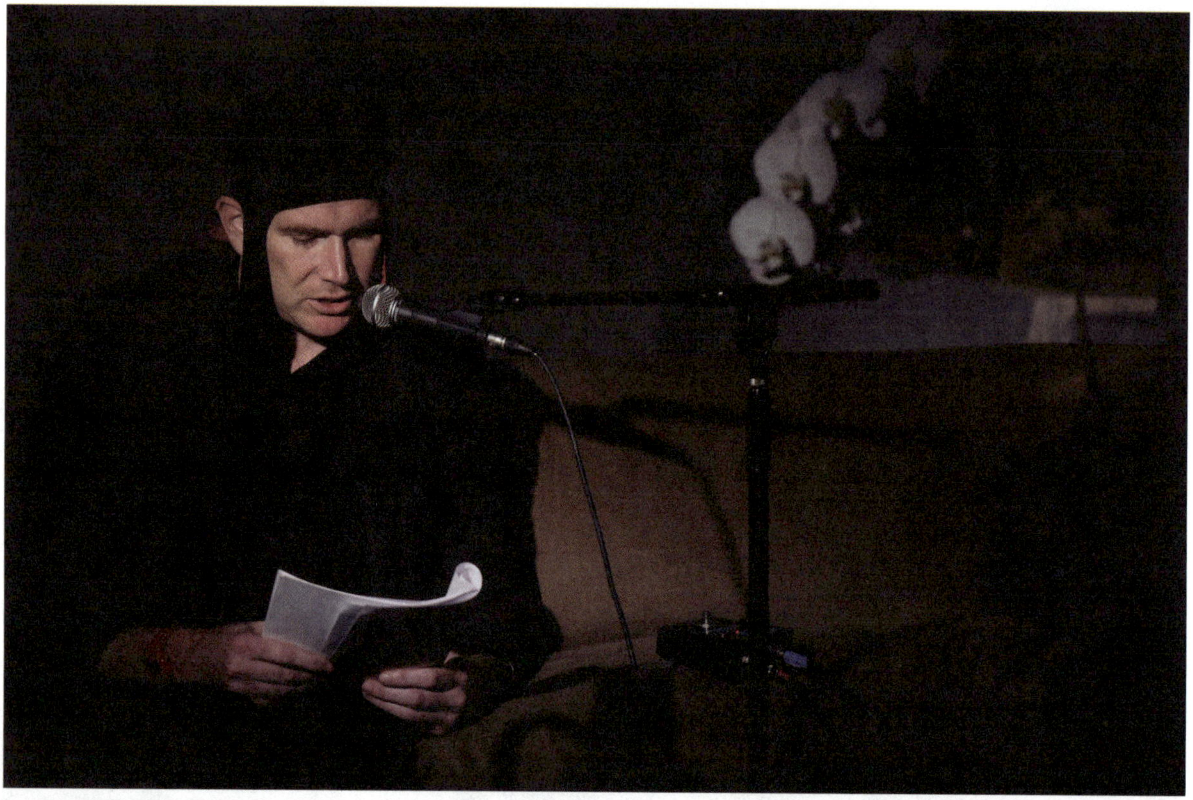

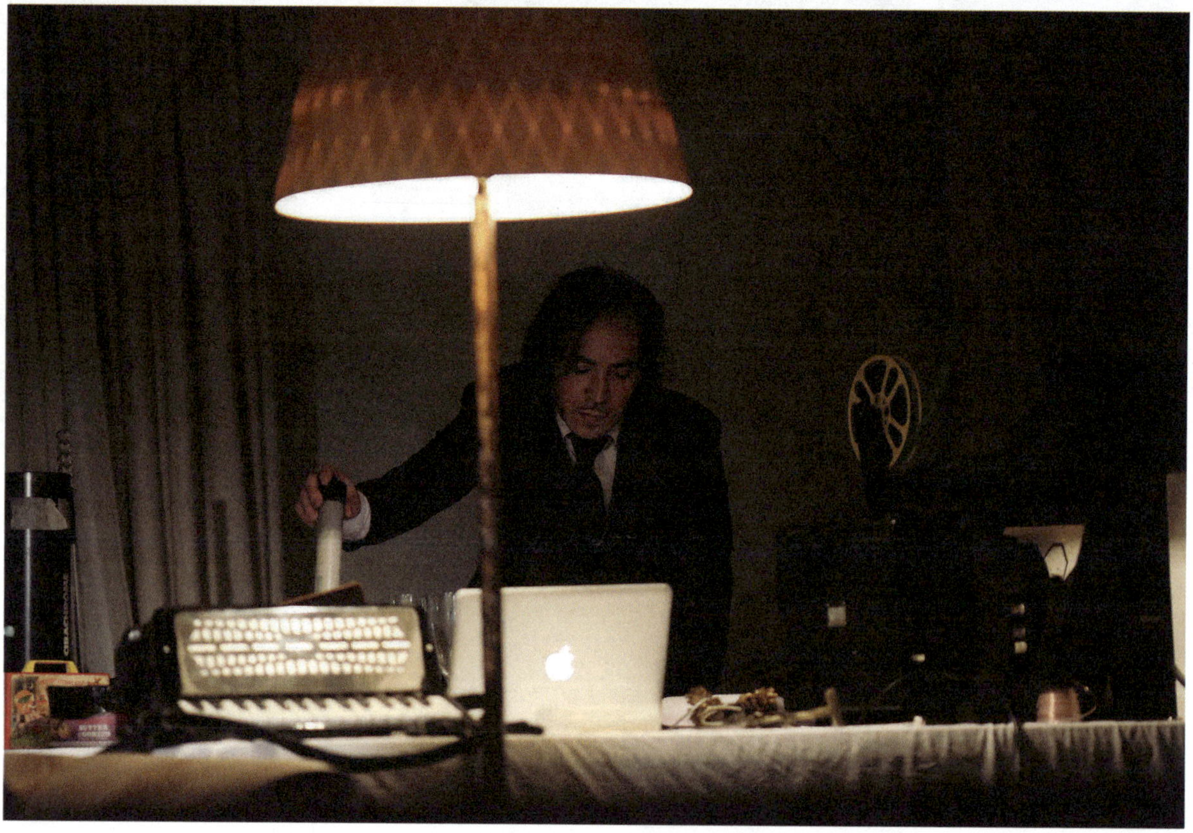

BEDWYR WILLIAMS

A BREAK IN

Soon after sunset on a still-bustling weeknight, Welsh artist Bedwyr Williams quietly "broke-into" a private home, slipping into a warmly lit, floor-through loft of a pre-war cast-iron building in SoHo, an impressive home belonging to two highly regarded contemporary art advisors and collectors. The "heist" was anything but spontaneous, Williams explained, and included him seducing the housekeeper to whom he eventually got close enough to copy her keys. The crime was not the bold pursuit of the priceless art adorning the white walls, nor of the elegant objects dotting the polished surfaces of the sweeping loft, but rather an ironic take on art's ineffable desirability.

Dressed in an expensive variant of the burglar's uniform—a black silk shirt, suit, and velvet cap—Williams settled on a taupe-colored sofa lit by a theatrical spotlight, an upright microphone at his side, and fifty plus people sitting in neat rows of designer chairs. Peering between columns, they leaned in when Williams began to read from his text; as in a surreal lounge act, with Foley sound effects made by musician Ian M. Colletti behind him, he reminisced about a glamorous party he had attended contrasting it with a coffee shop visit the day before.

Delivered by a seasoned performer fluent in absurd theater, *A Break In* was a deliciously self-deprecating forty-five minute monologue that was neither pure stand-up nor sermon, but an amalgam of the two. A site-specific radio play, it culminated in a melancholic reflection on the dollar value of artwork, implicating artist and audience in their participation in its material trappings.

CHAPTER

8

EIGHT

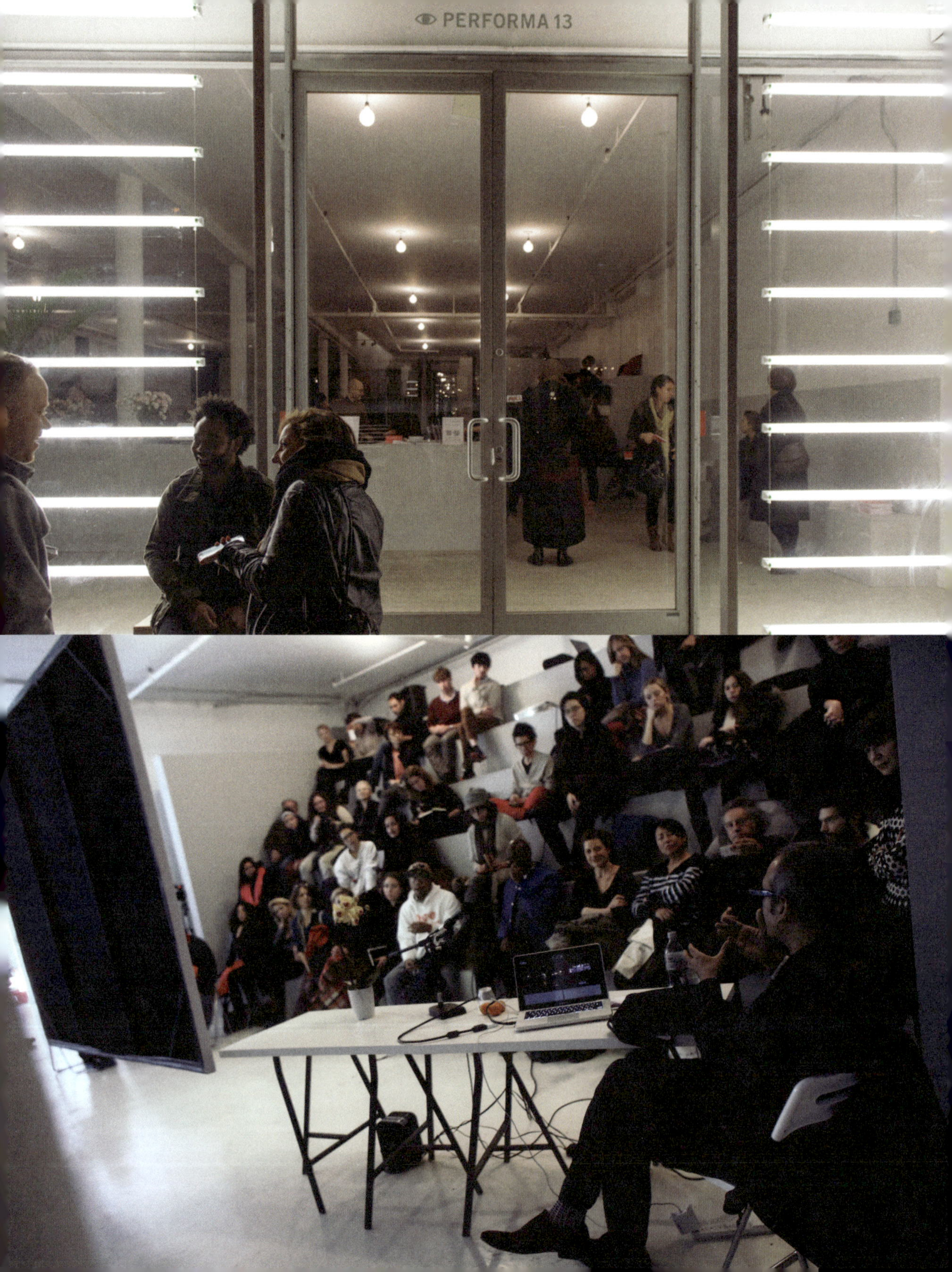
PERFORMA 13

PERFORMA INSTITUTE

PERFORMA HUB

Few people realize that a year and a half before the first Performa biennial in 2005, the profound, risky ideas that would come to inform and lead to the biennial's creation were nurtured through a series of innovative public talks and discussions, collectively called *Not for Sale*, held at New York University's Steinhardt School of Culture, Education and Human Development. These programs were at the vanguard, illuminating the most prescient issues concerning the role of performance in art history and contemporary art through field-changing discussions. This was evident from the start, having presented the first panel in April 2004 entitled *Curating, Conserving and Collecting Ephemeral Art*, a subject that many visual art organizations and museums are just grappling with after being exposed for the past ten years to Performa.

Our desire to give equal weight to our year-round program offerings and the biennial, as well as to provide the public with direct access to the intellectual, historical, and scholarly material that gives shape to the biennial led us initially, during Performa 11, to establish the Performa Institute. Since then, the Institute has continued its innovative educational initiatives, comprising year-round public programs, publications, a repository of digital and print archives, and fellowships, while also broadening its parameters to serve both as an incubator of radical ideas about art as well as an experimental laboratory for artists.

Located in the Performa Hub, the Institute built upon the dynamic programs of the previous biennial. Particularly through hosting a compelling array of seventeen master classes and talks led by biennial artists, including Rosa Barba, Jérôme Bel, Pedro Gómez-Egaña, Marthe Ramm Fortun, Subodh Gupta, Andy Holden and Peter Holden, Anna Lundh, Shana Lutker, Ryan McNamara, Benjamin Patterson, Eddie Peake, Alexandre Singh, and Tori Wrånes. They were invited to teach in the most creative and engaging fashion on any subject relevant to their artwork in general or to share their process for developing their Performa 13 projects. For instance, choreographer Eleanor Bauer, wielding nothing more than colorful chalk, launched the Institute with a dynamic group conversation on desire, dreams, and the discipline required to become an artist in *How to Do Whatever You Want*.

Biennial attendees also intimately engaged with the most prescient ideas concerning contemporary art and performance through thematic talks, lectures, panel discussions, and happenings. Explorations of new ways and means to manifest Twenty-first century life particularly resonated in programs on the Performa 13 theme of Citizenship. Driven by an interest in civic gatherings all over the world, historical and ongoing conversations that question the nature and effects of capitalism and the imperative to engage in utopian ideas, Raqs Media Collective's artist class, led by Shuddhabrata Sengupta, shared the triumvirate's process of research, speculation, and discovery that informed their rich, hybrid multi media Performa 13 Commission *The Last International*. While Cally Spooner explored the convergence of "liveness," authenticity, and speech acts in post-Fordist managerial and experience economies to consider the ways a performance artist emerges as an "immaterial laborer" extraordinaire.

Citizenship naturally suited the scope of Institute programming relating to the Polish Pavilion Without Walls. Art historian and curator Joanna Warsza's lecture, *Public Art in Poland After the Fall of the Wall*, traversed the landscape of public art in post-Communist Poland, revealing the social, cultural, and political idiosyncrasies of its post-socialist, turbo-capitalist, and westernized society. Warsza's talk was followed by Akademia Ruchu's artist class, uniquely situating and providing important context for avant garde art in Poland before and after 1989 through an evocative visual retrospective of the collective's work since 1974.

The importance of visionary imagination for curators today who are tasked with supporting and presenting art of many genres was part of the discussion between Norwegian curators, directors, and art historians Johanne Nordby Wernø and Solveig Øvstebø, who, as an element of the Norwegian Pavilion Without Walls, provided a tantalizing glimpse into the contemporary art scene in Norway and the vitality gained through international collaborations. Important questions such as: "What does it mean to stage an exhibition?" and "Can curating be defined as a performance?" permeated the panel discussion *Staging the Show: The Theater of Exhibition-Making* in which Jewish Museum deputy director and curator Jens Hoffmann alongside his collaborators Triple Candie elaborated on their dynamically theatrical approach, whether restaging an artist's work such as that of James Lee Byars or the development of the spatial design of their exhibitions.

Expanding the purview of the Institute from its pedagogical initiatives to become a locus where ideas about art making were not only discussed and debated but also took 3-D form, was an exciting new priority. This took the form of dynamic process-driven artist residencies and artist experiments loosely structured around Performa 13 biennial themes of the Voice and Citizenship, as well as Surrealism, the historical anchor.

The latest evolutionary step in the Institute's ongoing development featured its first-ever artist residency in which a work was created when Jennifer Wen Ma developed over eight days *Paradise*

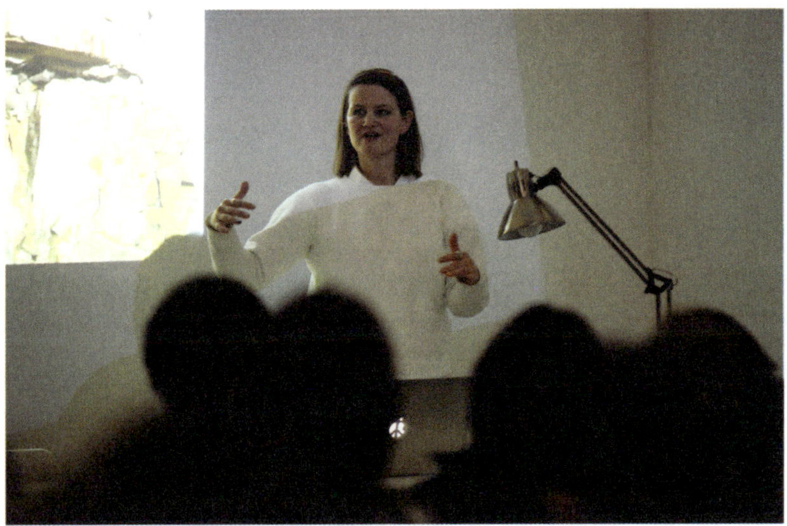

Interrupted, a contemporary Kunqu opera that remains a work-in-process. Wen Ma created a stunning large-scale black paper garden stage set with art students and the general public over the course of four days. She conducted a public two-day workshop and hosted a culminating evening event, featuring a preview performance by opera singer Qian Yi and a panel discussion with the core creative team. The panel's stimulating exchange addressed a range of topics such as the voice in Chinese and Western performance and the ways the female protagonist signifies the emotional and spiritual quests in the opera.

Derrick Adams presented *The Institution of Me*, a lively series of

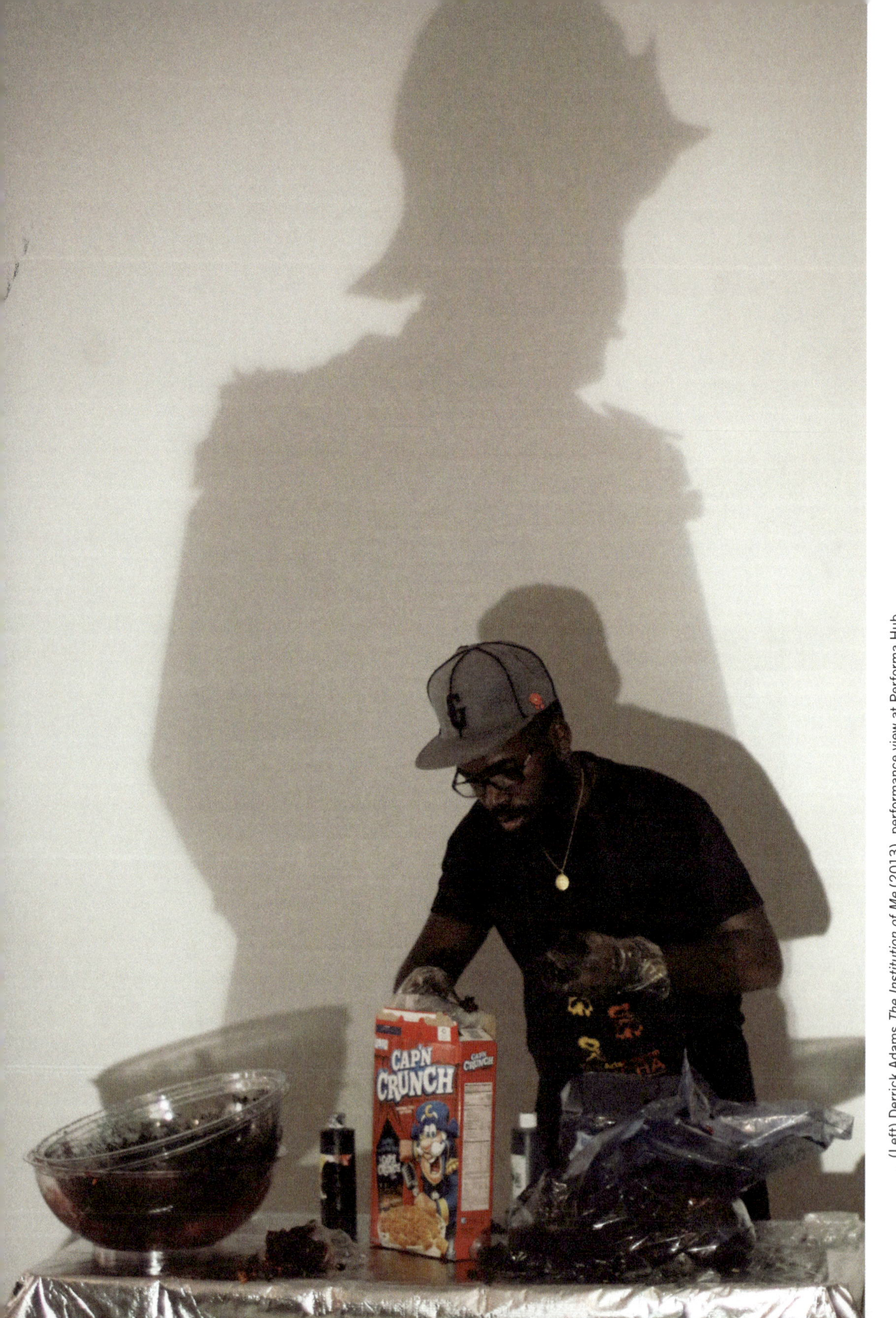

(Left) Derrick Adams *The Institution of Me* (2013), performance view at Performa Hub.
(Right) Siri Rishi Kaur, *Artist's Experiment: An Overnight Gong Symphony with the Free Seeker's Collective* (2013)

Photos by Paula Court

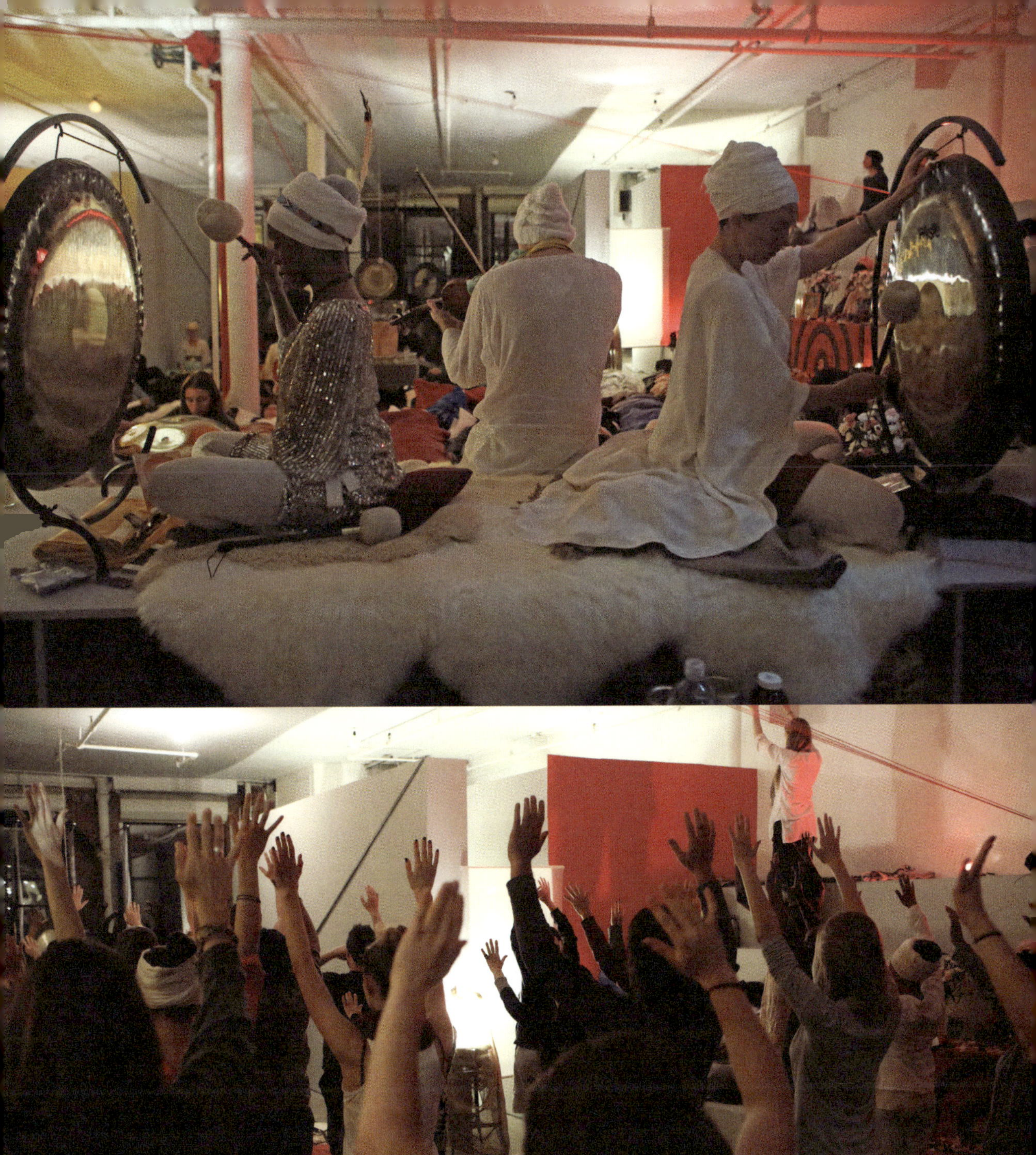

happenings-cum-art installations evolving from enlarged, projected silhouettes and using themes that emerged in *Get Ready for the Marvelous*, a February 2013 conference that explored the historical anchor of Surrealism in the African diaspora and its relevance to contemporary artists. Over the course of three evenings, Adams presented witty thirty-minute vignettes, each inspired by a different intriguing historical figure, including Pan-Africanist leader Marcus Garvey, Martinican Afro-futurist Robert Saint Rose, and Nigerian political activist and Afro-beat musician Fela Kuti.

Mothership of the Galactic Odyssey, an overnight immersion in the supernatural, the surprising, the sublime, and the wondrous, was inspired by a dream-space symphony of gongs, a flat circular metal disc that is a musical percussion instrument played with a mallet. Led by the Free Seeker's Collective, including yogis Siri Rishi, Dharam Singh, and Paramatma Siri Sadhana, participants settled in for an eight-hour sonic ritual, with their sleeping bags, yoga mats, and sheepskin rugs covering every inch of floor and seating space of the totally transformed Performa Hub.

Ahmet Öğüt debuted *The Silent University* in the United States, which has previously been established at the Tate Modern in London, Tensta Konsthall in Stockholm, and Stadtkuratorin Hamburg. *The Silent University* interactive half-day workshop, during which participants were educated on the challenges refugees face in transferring their education and skills upon relocating to the West. *Silent University Student ID Cards* were created, which provided for the loan and rebate of their time and skills at some point in the future by actively participating in this unique knowledge-exchange platform.

Institute programming also featured an inaugural collaboration with New York University's Fales Library & Special Collections. Organized in close partnership with Brent Phillips, audiovisual archivist at Fales, *Archive Fever* was a two-part series in documents from its archival collections in response to, and in expansion of, the biennial's themes in unusual and unexpected ways. The first program, *Documenting Free Speech,* presented video footage of Judson Dance Theater's 1970 performance of Yvonne Rainer's *Trio A* (1966), when five members performed nude with the American flag tied around their necks like a bib as a critical reflection on issues of censorship, patriotism, and obscenity during the Vietnam War. The documentary footage was shown alongside material from Judson Dance Theater's archives, including letters, photographs, and other documentation. The program also featured videos of the AIDS crisis from the Gay Cable Network Archive, including ACT UP shutting down Grand Central Terminal. Working against interpretation, *Queering the Archive* presented an excerpt of David Wojnarowicz's *Fire in My Belly* (1987) and Robert Blanchon's *let's just kiss + say goodbye* (1995) to explore questions of the legitimacy and authenticity of the queer artist's voice after death. The program focused on the presence of fragments in the archive to consider the ways in which incomplete projects are presented as fully realized works of art. In addition to screening Wojnarowicz's film and Blanchon's video, the scripts and written shot list were shared to illuminate interpretations that have adhered to the works.

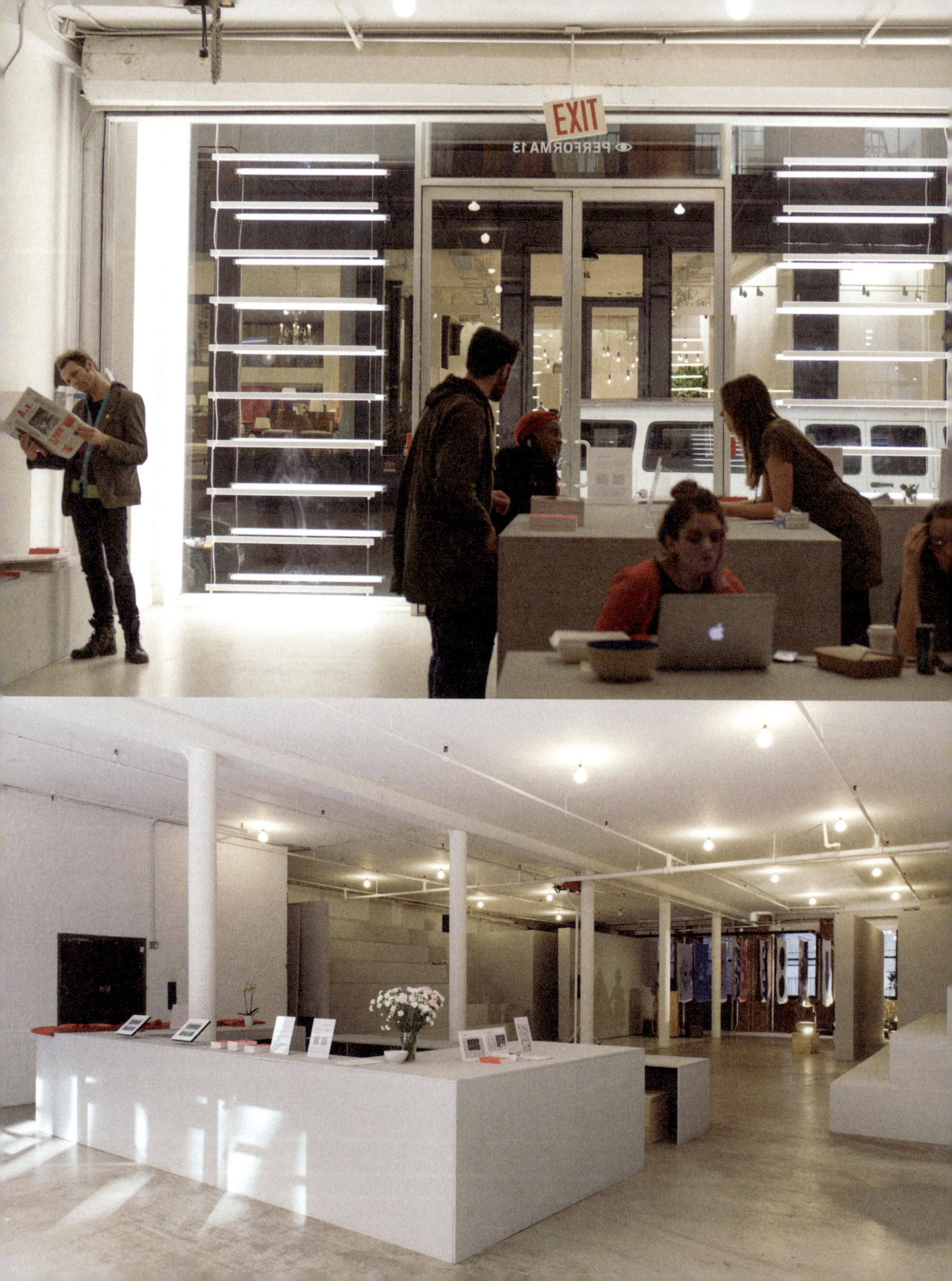
EXIT
PERFORMA 13

Photo by Chani Bockwinkel and Paula Court

Performa Hub interior views (2013).

PERFORMA HUB

DESIGN BY STUDIO MIESSEN

The Performa Hub 2013 was designed as a three-dimensional realization of the conceptual underpinnings of the organization that functions as Performa's headquarters during the biennial. Studio Miessen's Performa Hub was conceived as a linear space that attempted to condense all programmatic elements in a single discursive arena. It functioned as a truly live space capable of responding to the constantly shifting functional demands of the biennial. As Performa's central meeting place for discussion, information, and ticketing, the Hub consisted of a library and bookshop, a large-scale public coworking table, a performance and screening area, an exhibition space, and a classroom. It further allowed for press conferences, solo concerts, and public conversations, and was home to the classes, experiments, and residencies that made up the Performa Institute. The Performa team, artists, and volunteers were on hand to answer questions, provide recommendations, and offer insights into Performa 13.

STUDIO MIESSEN ◉ 13 CROSBY STREET

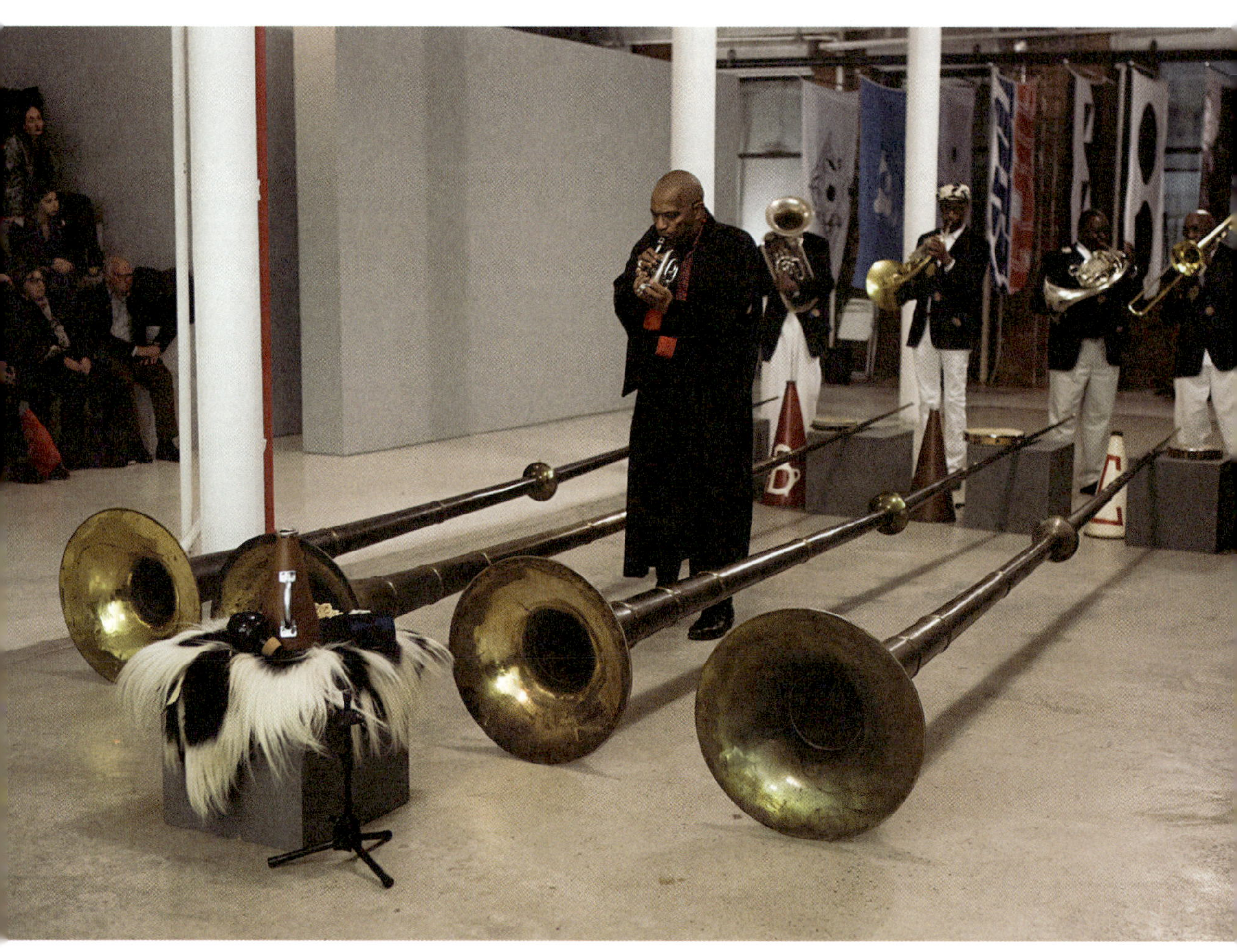

Terry Adkins's exploration of ideas, people, objects, places, archives, repertoires, and limits came full circle in his performance *Sacred Order of Twilight Brothers*, a recital of powerful voice and spectacular brass instruments, presented on the evening of November 18, 2013, to a packed house. Adkins energetically transformed the Performa Hub into a sensual installation. Attired in a black robe draped with a patterned red and black scarf, Adkins exuded shamanistic qualities. By his side was an altar, covered in black and white fur, on which a megaphone, an assemblage of miniature instruments, and other objects rested.

Adkins and the Lone Wolf Recital Corps members Vincent Chancey, Marshall Sealy, Dick Griffin, and Kiane Zawadi seduced the crowd by delivering a resonant and at times tense performance, which featured colossal eighteen-foot-long horns Adkins invented and called Arkaphones. The Corps was sharply dressed in white slacks with shirts and dark-colored blazers with slung sashes dotted with insignias, reminiscent of the garb worn by brass bands. Next to the performers were a tamborine and a megaphone, each varying in color and size, which Adkins had selected that morning, after considering several options.

This singular performance seemed to achieve the aims of Adkins's artwork, as he remarked, "My quest has been to find a way to make music as physical as sculpture might be, and sculpture as ethereal as music is. It's kind of challenging to make both of those pursuits do what they are normally not able to do." All except Zawadi had played the instrumental sculptures during their premiere in 1996 at the Whitney Museum of American Art's Philip Morris branch. The 1996 recital was dedicated to Adkins's father, Robert Hamilton Adkins, who had passed away shortly before that performance. The 2013 rendition was the first time these enchanting instruments were seen again in New York City since 1996. Adkins said of the Arkaphones, "I made them on the scale at which I thought angels would play them. … And so the Arkaphones actually represented the horns of the first four angels of the Last Judgment."

Terry Adkins, *Sacred Order of Twilight Brothers* (2013), performance view.

Photo by Chanti Brockwell

PERFORMA HUB

ORGANIZED BY ADRIENNE EDWARDS

Adkins passed away on February 8, 2014, making the Performa 13 event the last time he and the Corps would together play his treasured Arkaphones. Born in 1953, Adkins was deeply invested in visual art, music, and language. He emerged in the early-1980s in his native Washington, D.C., where he began making installations and reconstructing instruments to accompany his simultaneous practice as a musician. An immensely talented musician, Adkins played woodwinds, contrabass, pocket trumpet, and electronics. He was a charter member of Harmolodica with Yahya Abdul-Majid and collaborated with Sherman Fleming (aka Rod Force) in his AFRO (Anti Formalist Reclamation Organization). Upon moving to New York City in 1982, Adkins performed with Butch Morris, Jemeel Moondoc, Jamaaladeen Tacuma, Julius Hemphill, and Don Byron, among others. During a yearlong residency in Zurich in 1986, Adkins and his associate Blanche Bruce founded the multimedia performance collaborative the Lone Wolf Recital Corps, which staged emblematic concert performances, including the one which riveted the Performa 13 audience. Activating his sculptures with sound, Adkins engaged and reenacted the revised stories he traced and reimagined through, and as, history. His recital *Nenuphar* was concurrently on view at Salon 94 Bowery and Salon 94 Freemans during his Performa debut.

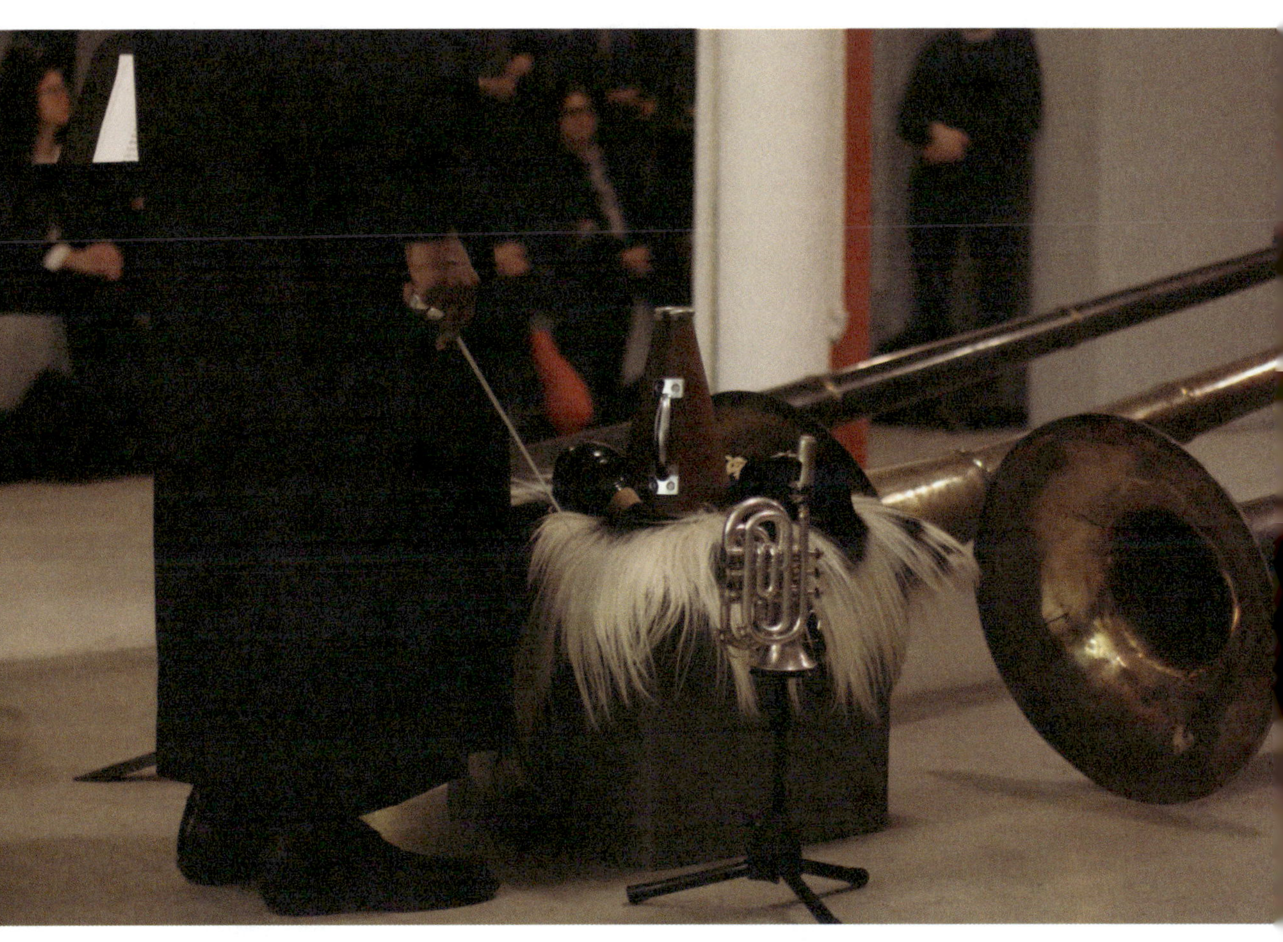

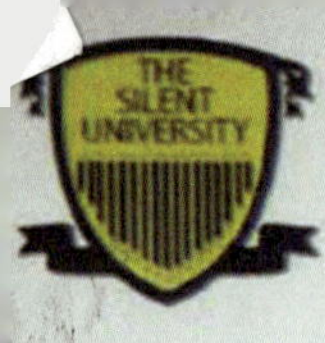
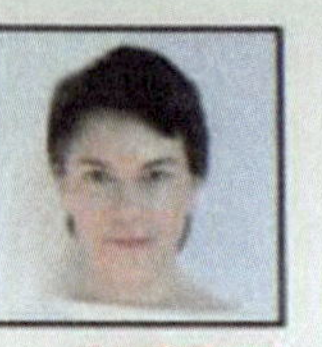
151120130044

NAME ANNA SERENKO
STATUS STUDENT
EXPIRY DATE 31-12-2019

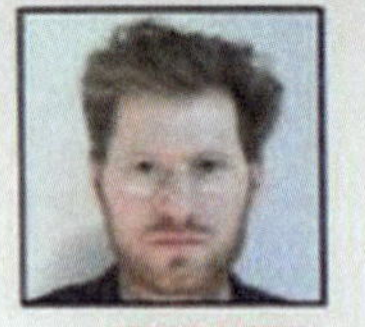
151120130081

NAME MICHAEL MANDIBERG
STATUS RESEARCHER
EXPIRY DATE 31-12-2019

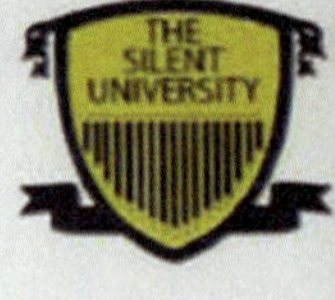
NAME PANH
STATUS STUD
EXPIRY DATE 31-

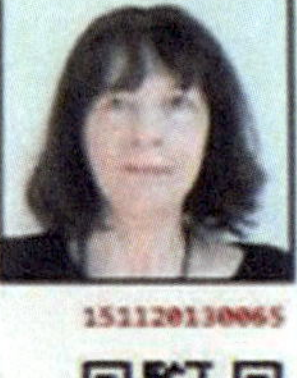
151120130065

NAME ANETA RADZIEJOWSKA
STATUS STUDENT
EXPIRY DATE 31-12-2019

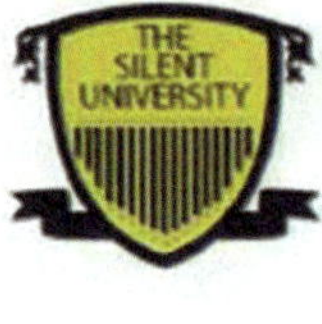
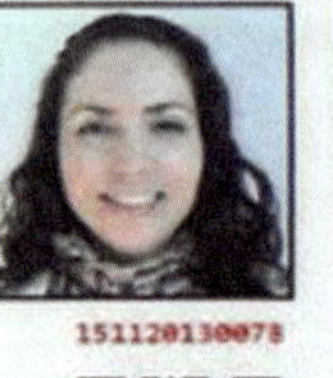
151120130078

NAME JUANA LOPEZ
STATUS STUDENT
EXPIRY DATE 31-12-2019

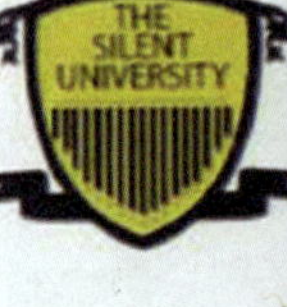
NAME JOSH
STATUS RESE
EXPIRY DATE 31-

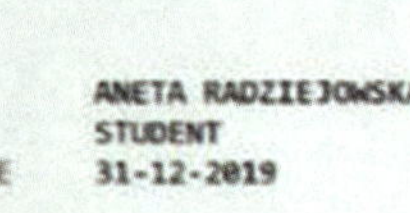

151120130084

NAME SUMMER GUTHERY
STATUS PRESS
EXPIRY DATE 31-12-2019

22FW03

This card is personal and non-transferable. Its use is subject to the Cardholder's knowledge and acceptance of the General Conditions of use.

This ID is your official Silent University ID Card and is issued for official purposes only.

NAME SON
STATUS PRES
EXPIRY DATE 31-

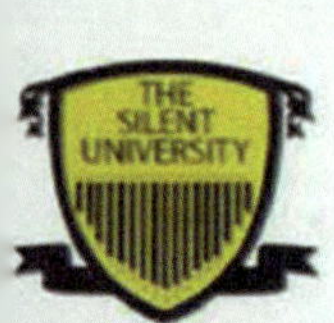
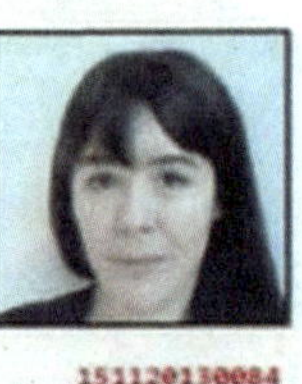
151120130042

NAME CLAIRE MIROCHA
STATUS CONTRIBUTOR
EXPIRY DATE 31-12-2019

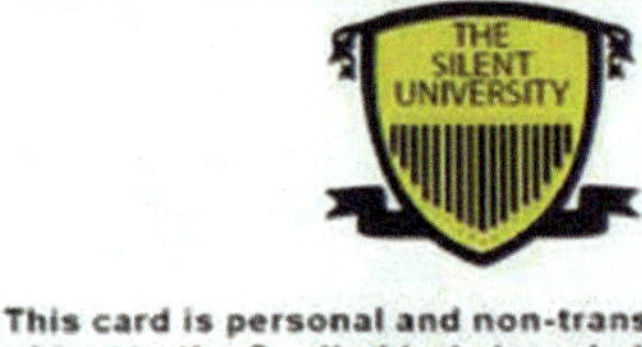
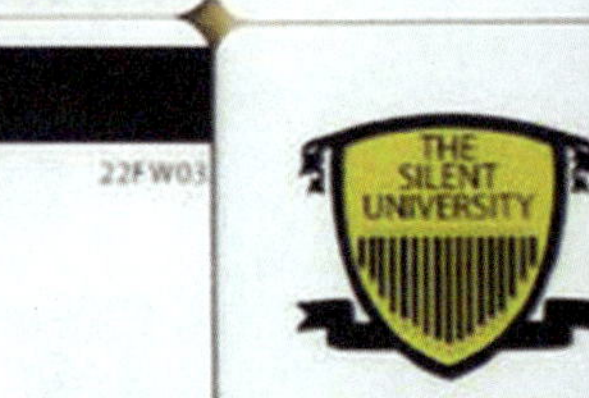
151120130085

NAME TALI WERTHEMIER
STATUS PRESS
EXPIRY DATE 31-12-2019

NAME CLA
STATUS RES
EXPIRY DATE 31-

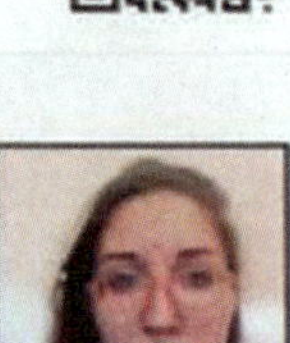
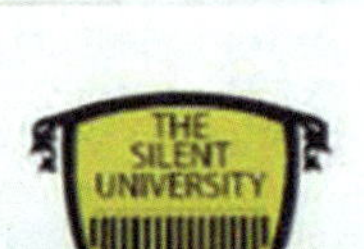
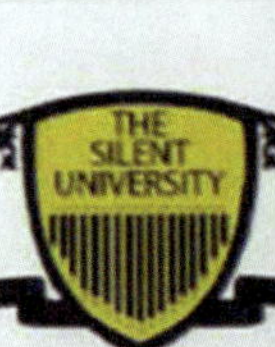

151120130036

NAME SIEBE TETTERO
STATUS PRESS
EXPIRY DATE 31-12-2019

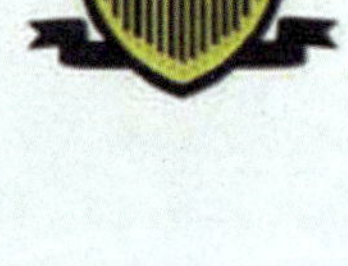
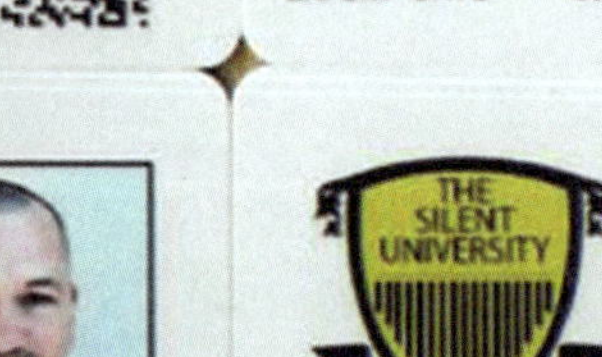
151120130064

NAME ALICE MCDERMID
STATUS STUDENT
EXPIRY DATE 31-12-2019

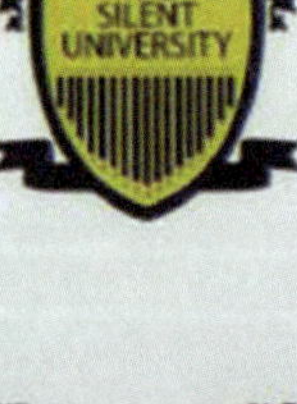
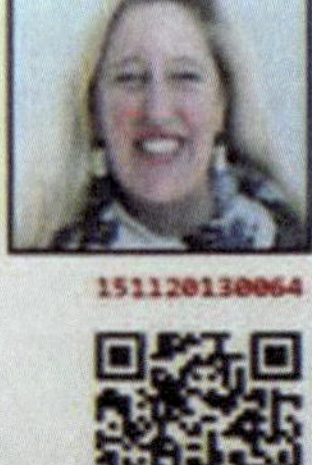
NAME JAC
STATUS STU
EXPIRY DATE 31-

ORGANIZED BY ADRIENNE EDWARDS / TEXT BY MARI SPIRITO

AHMET ÖĞÜT

DEFINE AND USE:
SILENT UNIVERSITY STUDENT ID CARD

Öğüt's one-day workshop for Performa 13 put significant focus on the purpose and intention of an ID card. *The Silent University Student ID Card* is distributed to anyone who registers as a user of *The Silent University*, who will loan time and skills to be exchanged at some unspecified future point. Around forty people, including students, academics, curators, writers, researchers, and artists, took part in the *Define and Use: Silent University Student ID Card* workshop, which involved and engaged the participants in the decision-making process of how to design, format, and use the *Silent University Student ID Card*. Set up in classroom style, open discussion provided insights into how different institutions organize their students and attempt to restrict or eliminate those who do not belong.

Silent University is a long-term education platform initiated by Kurdish artist and political activist Ahmet Öğüt for and by refugees, asylum seekers, and immigrants, currently operating in London, Stockholm, and Hamburg. These individuals have academic qualifications, knowledge, and skills from their homelands, but for many reasons are not permitted to work in their fields in the countries in which they now reside. *The Silent University* recognizes them as academics to share their knowledge, in their first language, and in this way to end the oppression that has been imposed on them.

Silent University Student ID Cards focus attention on permissions and the difficulties of being in or out of a given system with its nationalistic and bureaucratic barriers. These tools are employed by governing bodies, often regardless of individual consent or consideration. In the case of Öğüt's *Silent University Student ID Card*, this little plastic card becomes the reverse; it becomes a call for immediate acknowledgment of knowledge beyond its current oppressive structures of higher education and government protocols.

Ahmet Öğüt, *Define and Use: Silent University Student ID Card* workshop (2013).

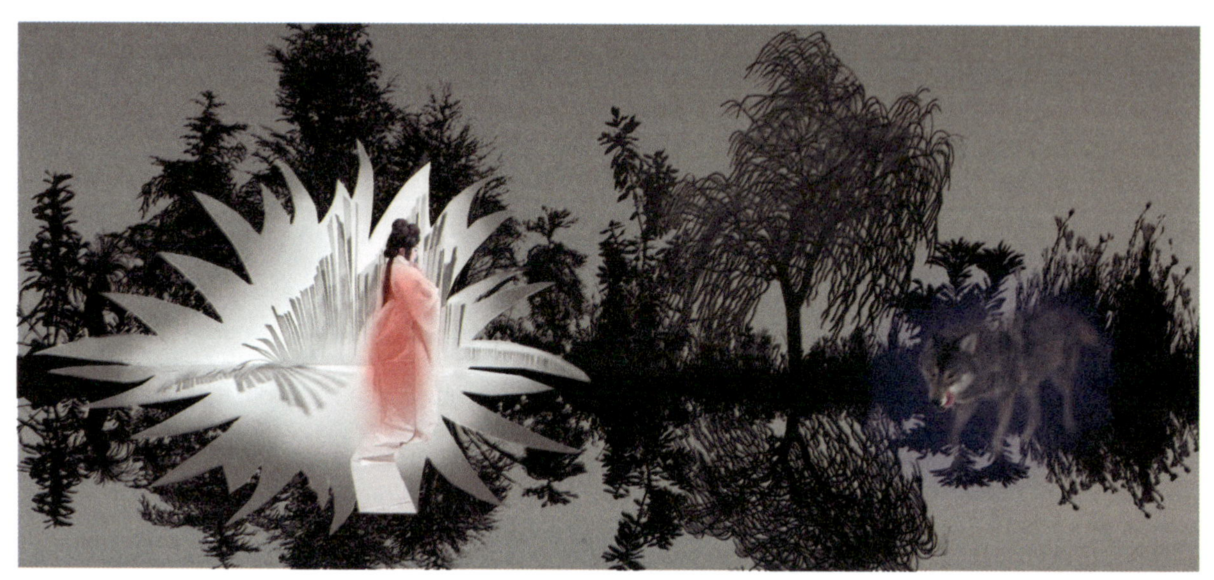

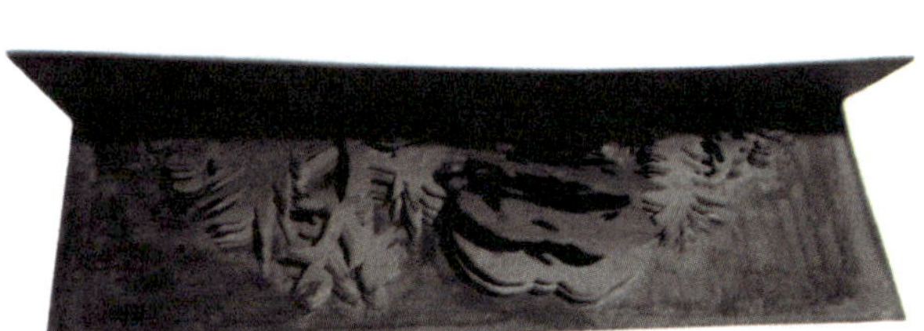

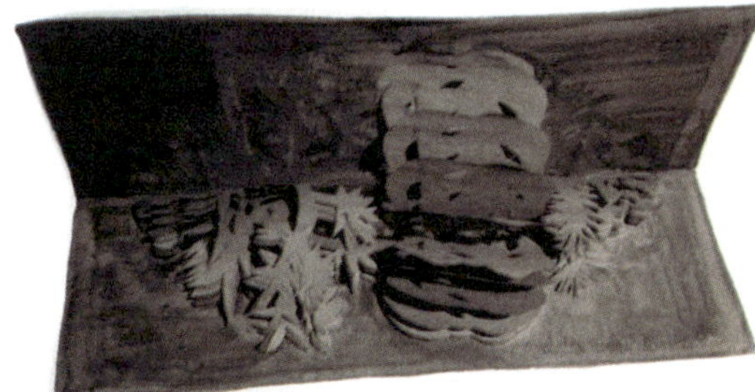

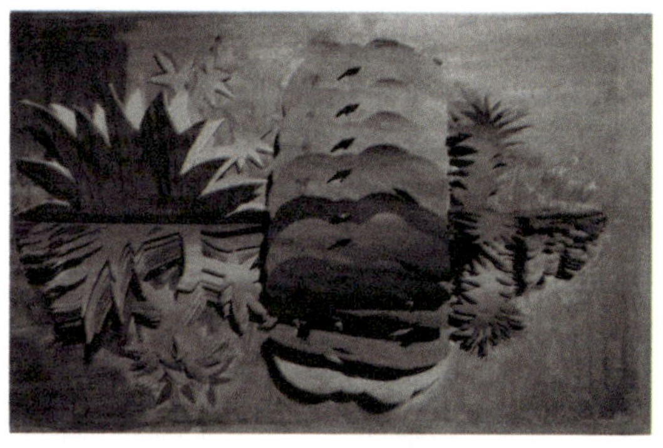

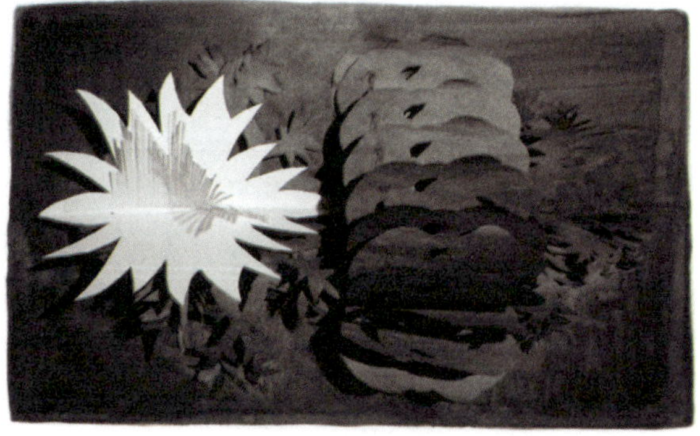

CURATED AND TEXT BY DEFNE AYAS ● PERFORMA HUB / PERFORMA INSTITUTE

JENNIFER WEN MA

PARADISE INTERRUPTED

How does a metaphor for an unattainable utopian ideal impact the individual psyche? How could one trace the original location of the Garden of Eden via vibrational qualities of voice? Can cross-cultural references to lost utopias such as Milton's *Paradise Lost* (1667), Hieronymus Bosch's *Garden of Earthly Delights* (1505), and Tang Xianzu's *Peony Pavilion* (1598) collide in an attempt to reconcile a 600-year-old Chinese opera tradition with that of the West?

Paradise Interrupted, a contemporary Kunqu opera by Chinese artist Jennifer Wen Ma, was presented as a three-part artist residency, over eight days at the Performa Institute. During the first four days, Ma created a large-scale three-dimensional paper garden stage set inspired by her research on the Garden of Eden, made from many layers of cut paper that opened like a honeycombed fan, but could also fold back into a flat, neat stack of papers. This kinetic sculpture was made by hand-cutting individual sheets of paper, and then gluing one sheet on top of another in a particular pattern to form the inner structure that allowed the paper to stand upright. The individual cuts produced the undulating forms of a garden, enabling Ma to create a landscape seemingly out of nothing, that could be lengthened or shortened depending on how far the form was pulled apart. Utilizing the Hub's architectural design, especially the cascading stairs, the garden was mounted vertically on the rise of the stairs and spilled onto the floor to extend toward the seated audience. This form was inspired by the tradition of Chinese landscape scroll painting: when a scroll is closed, it is an easily transportable cylindrical roll; once opened, it reveals a rich and varied world to the viewer—one that might extend to reveal a whole mountain range, even showing different seasons. Reference to Ma's own landscape ink paintings, frequently applied directly to plants and trees, in museums and outdoors, was further extended through the predominant use of black in the *Paradise Interrupted* garden, thus referencing another traditional Chinese art practice. With this performance, Ma not only turned a two-dimensional landscape painting into three dimensions, but also, with live performance, added a fourth.

Ma's *Paradise Interrupted* collaborators included renowned composer Huang Ruo and performer Qian Yi, lauded by *The New York Times* as "China's reigning opera princess," along with interactive multimedia artist Guillermo Acevedo and lighting designer Lihe Xiao. The role of the female protagonist as a symbol of emotional and spiritual quests was also considered in *Paradise Interrupted*, with all the visual elements in the opera responding to the woman's voice, whether a tree that sprouted from the ground in front of her, a garden that grew around her, or light that danced about her to form a vine, an animal, or a man. The highly abstracted and symbolic stage design, with minimal physical presence to restrict the drama, allowed the imagination of the audience to activate the stage as triggered by the music, lyrics, and codified choreography of the performers and the design of the accordion paper garden sculpture, all of which reflected on the artist's ability to fill a space but return to the void at will. Suggestion and stagecraft conjured *Paradise Interrupted:* Was the woman dreaming, remembering, or hallucinating, or did she have an actual encounter?

Ma's residency concluded with a public two-day workshop of rehearsals, leading to a brief fifteen-minute performance by Qian Yi set within the "walled garden" at the Performa Hub. The performance was followed by a panel discussion, which explored "the voice" in Chinese and Western operatic tradition (the former is delivered from the throat, while the latter technique uses the chest cavity to project the voice and is closer to the natural speaking voice of the performer).

Jennifer Wen Ma, *Paradise Interrupted* (2013), installation and performance views.

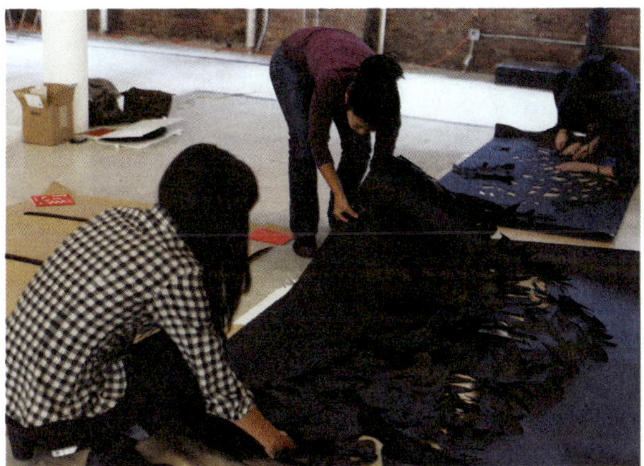
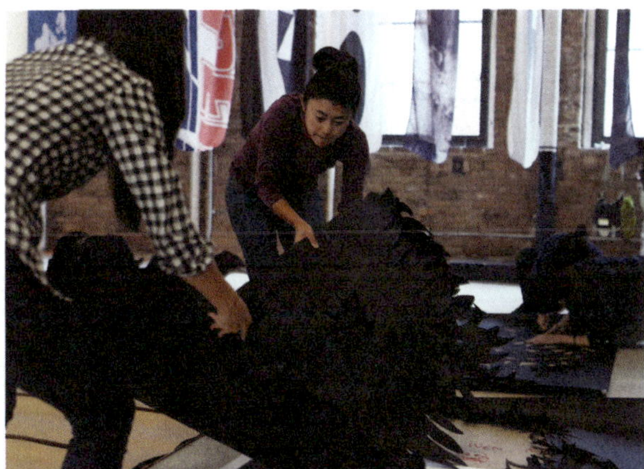
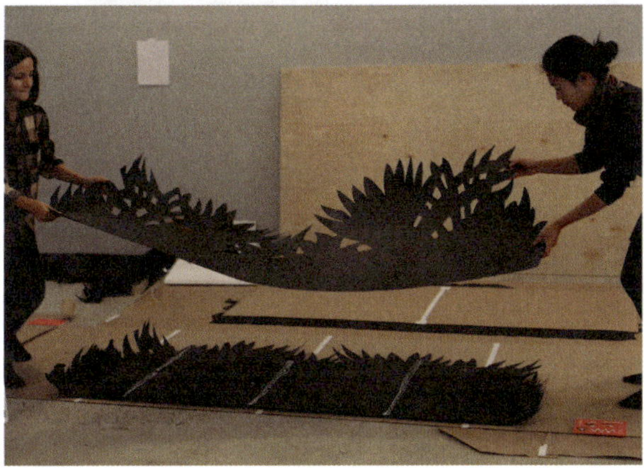
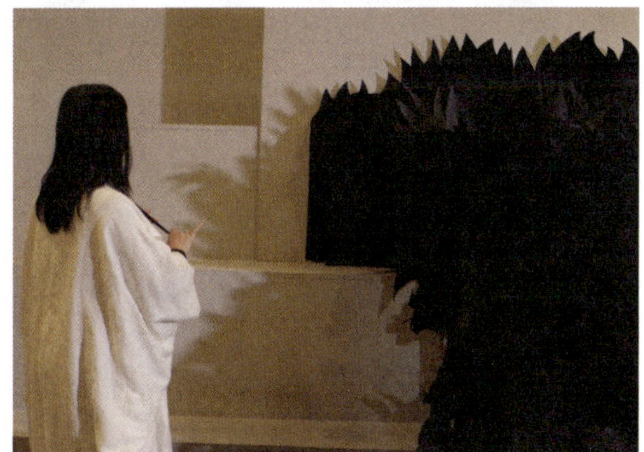

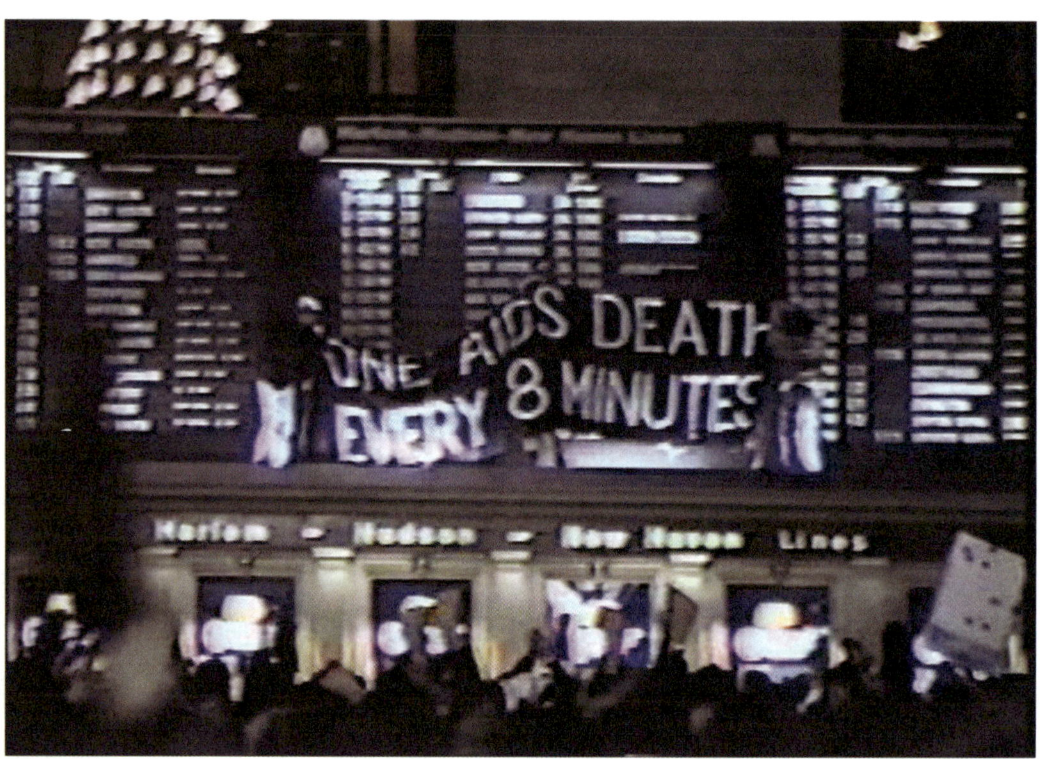

ONE AIDS DEATH EVERY 8 MINUTES
Harlem — Hudson — New Haven Lines

QUEERING THE ARCHIVE:
DAVID WOJNAROWICZ AND
ROBERT BLANCHON

Working against interpretation, *Queering the Archive*, an afternoon of short films and conversation, presented an excerpt from David Wojnarowicz's Super 8 "work-in-progress" *A Fire in My Belly* (1986–87) as well as Robert Blanchon's video work *let's just kiss + say goodbye* (1995) and the opportunity to consider the legacy of both artists, who died from complications related to AIDS (Wojnarowicz at age 38 in 1992 and Blanchon at age 33 in 1999). Labels such as "queer artist" or "AIDS artist" were discussed as potentially limiting to an artist's body of work, but also as an effective means to identify a particular community, and as such to consider a range of artwork, both conceptually and aesthetically, that conveyed the urgency of the times and the horrors of a health crisis that had both political and social ramifications.

Furthermore, the discussion focused on unfinished moving image works in the Wojnarowicz archive, such as the aforementioned *A Fire in My Belly*, raising the question as to whether it is appropriate to show Wojnarowicz's incomplete projects as fully realized works, as has occurred in several posthumous exhibitions. Wojnarowicz's original "shooting script" for *A Fire in My Belly*, which enumerates all the proposed themes the completed film planned to cover, was used to discuss this conundrum. Some contemporary critics now view the film as having to do with the AIDS pandemic, while in fact there is scant evidence of this.

Similarly, there is the problem of over-interpreting Blanchon's *let's just kiss*, a nine-minute video that focuses on the cutting and splicing of unintentionally amusing dialogue sequences from an array of gay pornography films. Blanchon isolated micro-narratives that are precursors to sex scenes and edited them into a fractured story of hypermasculine intimacy. Incorporated into the sound track is The Manhattans' soulful 1970s hit song of the same title, which imbues these brief meetings with a feeling of despair and melancholy. Is this work entirely—or actually—about AIDS? Or does such an interpretation minimize its central themes of sexual diversity, race, sex, love, objectification, and gender roles, as well as camp sensibilities?

One AIDS Death Every 8 Minutes, ACTUP, Day of Desperation at Grand Central Station (January 23, 1991). Courtesy of the Gay Cable Network Archive, Fales Library/New York University

ORGANIZED BY ADRIENNE EDWARDS / TEXT BY BRENT PHILLIPS ● PERFORMA HUB

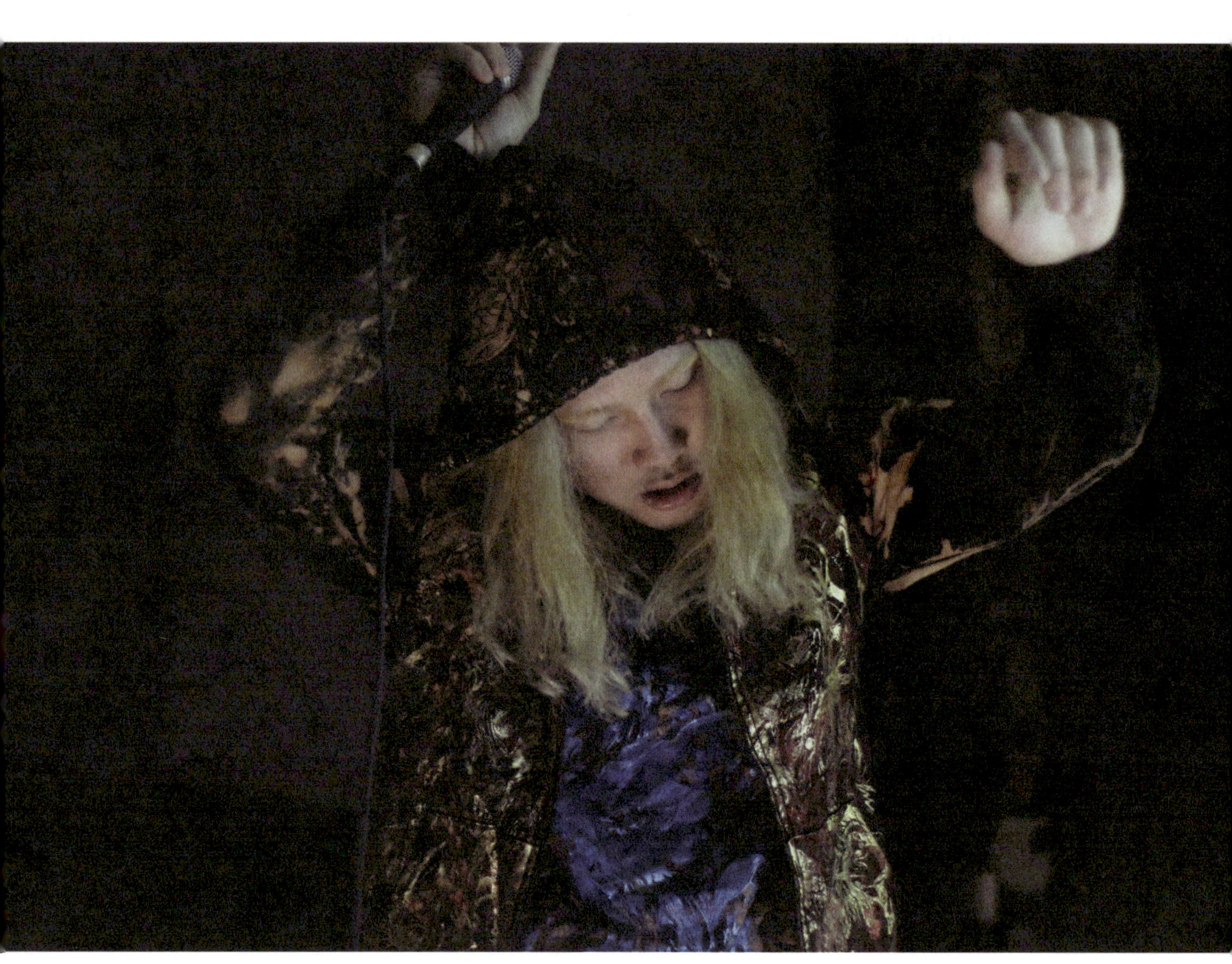

PERFORMA

AFTER HOURS

Evolving from the rich history of salon culture in 1930s Paris during the Surrealist era as well as New York's own infamous late-night scene of the 1970s and '80s, *Performa After Hours* was a post-show gathering each Saturday and Sunday night, for seven evenings. Audiences joined artists, curators, and organizers of Performa 13 for drinks, conversation, performance, and dancing at downtown bar and gallery Fig. 19. From lounge acts to music performances and an abstract drag show, *Performa After Hours* featured exciting emerging artists, including Korakrit Arunanondchai, Autre Ne Veut (billed as Ultra New View), Jesus Benavente, Guy Benfield, Helen Carmel Benigson, members of Chez Deep Colin Self and Alexis Penney, HARIBO, Ann Hirsch, Denise Musilova, RAF (Raphael Amadeus Frankenstein), Jimmy Raskin, and SADAF/Jealous Orgasm.

After Hours opened with a bang—performer SADAF's intoxicating dancing to intense, explosive percussion by Jealous Orgasm. Performance "supergroup" HARIBO with Raul De Nieves, Jessie Stead, and Nathan Whipple's blend of punk theatrics and pop operettas followed. It closed with a tongue-in-cheek sorrowful night of Ann Hirsch's take on foley sound, post-production sound effects, for soft-core porn and Guy Benfield's crooning goodbye.

Along the way, up-and-coming musician Autre Ne Veut performed a secret show just for the *Performa After Hours* audience with Butoh-inspired dance by Denise Musilova. Jimmy Raskin lectured on the eternal half-subject and the demise of poetry to a packed house. Korakrit Arunanondchai and Jesus Benavente dueled with cultural stereotypes of performance, culminating in a surprise appearance of a mariachi band. British performer Helen Carmel Benigson sang slick pop songs while getting a spray tan, with female weightlifters as her backup dancers. All the while, stylish lounge composer and self-proclaimed lifestyle professional, RAF (Raphael Amadeus Frankenstein) schmoozed the shoulder-to-shoulder crowd of revelers until the early morning hours.

ORGANIZED BY SUMMER GUTHREY △ VARIOUS LOCATIONS

ARTISTS BIOGRAPHIES

Derrick Adams (b 1970, Baltimore, Maryland) makes multidisciplinary work rooted in Deconstructivist philosophies and the perception of ideals attached to objects, colors, textures, symbols, and ideologies, and how these are formed.

AKADEMIA RUCHU (Academy of Movement) is a collective founded in 1973 by Wojciech Krukowski in Warsaw, Poland. For the past forty years, the collective has produced more than 600 happenings, theater performances, political actions, and anonymous interactions.

Paweł Althamer (b 1967, Warsaw, Poland) focuses on the communicative and community-forming power of art. Based on a participative approach, his work is realized through live sculptural and performative traditions.

Einat Amir (b 1979, Jerusalem, Israel) reflects on contemporary social and political issues, including power relations, sexuality, representation, and communication through video installations and live performances.

Pieter Ampe (b 1982, Burundi, Africa) is a dancer, choreographer, and performer focusing on the relationship between dance, masculinity, and collaboration. His past duet and group performances include partnerships with Guilherme Garrido, Alain Platel, and his brother Jakob Ampe.

Eleanor Antin (b 1935, New York) has worked in film, video, photography, installation, writing, and performance to reflect on history as a way to explore the present using the guise of famous theatrical personas.

Athanasios Argianas (b 1976, Athens, Greece) is a London-based musician, sculptor, and painter who explores the interchangeable relationship between sound and form.

Ed Atkins (b 1982, Oxford, UK) explores how digital forms of representation can create new versions of reality, through incorporating computer-generated characters in a combination of installations of video, photography, drawing, poetry, and collage.

Rosa Barba (b 1972, Sicily, Italy) is a Berlin-based filmmaker, fascinated by the materiality of cinema, who is recognized for her filmic installations and involved, fictitious narratives.

Eleanor Bauer (b 1983, Santa Fe, New Mexico) is a Brussels-based performer and performance-maker who works in the intersections of choreography, dance, writing, music, comedy, and performance art.

Jérôme Bel (b 1964, Montpellier, France) is a choreographer who produces conceptual works that explore the essence of dance and the mechanics of theater, skirting the line between the banal and the theatrical, and using humor to connect with his audience.

Michael Bell-Smith (b 1978, East Corinth, Maine) utilizes digital forms and imagery from video games, advertising, and corporate design to explore popular technologies in contemporary visual culture.

Julie Béna (b 1982, France) transforms the mundane into the dramatic by borrowing language from theater, games, and popular culture. In her performances, she often treats the exhibition space as a playground.

Blowfly (b 1939, Cochran, Georgia), AKA Clarence Henry Reid, is an American musician and songwriter often cited as the first rapper. His stage persona takes on theatricality through costuming, where he assumes alter egos, such as supervillains.

Paulo Bruscky (b 1949, Recife, Brazil) is a pioneer of art produced using electronic recording techniques; slide projection, fax, super 8 film, video, xerox, and offset printing.

Boris Charmatz (b 1973, Chambéry, France) seeks to integrate fine art and philosophy through choreography and is considered a leader of the French new wave and the movement of non-dance.

Elaine Chew (b Buffalo, New York) is a pianist and operations researcher who has built a career in mathematical and computational modeling of music and its performance.

Peter Child (b 1953, Great Yarmouth, UK) is a professor of music at MIT, Boston, who works with orchestra, chorus, solo voice, computer synthesis, and various chamber groups.

Courtesy the Artists is a collaboration between Malik Gaines and Alexandro Segade that invites artists and other cultural producers to interpret, react to, argue with, and take pleasure in historical works and texts that form dynamic foundations for present creative conditions.

Cricoteka (Centre for Documentation of the Art of Kantor) is a Polish-based cultural institution founded in 1981 by Tadeusz Kantor that focuses on the dissemination of the artist's works, both in the fields of theater and visual arts.

David Antonio Cruz (b 1974, Philadelphia, Pennsylvania) uses video, costume construction, performance, and painting to explore and redefine queerness, diaspora, and psychologically charged spaces.

Attila Csihar (b 1971, Budapest, Hungary) is a Hungarian black metal vocalist, best known for his vocal work on Mayhem's De Mysteriis Dom Sathanas album.

Jamal Cyrus (b 1973, Houston, TX) produces experimental performances that conflate cultural signifiers while embodying the musical and culinary contributions black people made to American culture.

Robin Deacon (b 1973, Eastbourne, UK) is an artist, writer, and filmmaker. His work encompasses live performance with a series of lectures, which explore journalistic and documentary approaches to arts practice.

Pete Drungle (b 1972, Chicago, Illinois) is a composer and pianist who has made music with Ornette Coleman, The Kronos Quartet, Yoko Ono, the Decoding Society, and others.

Zachary Fabri (b 1977, Miami, Florida) often addresses the relationship between the role of the individual and the integrity of community through performative work made specifically for video.

Ed Fornieles (b 1983, Petersfield, UK) addresses the ways people portray themselves in the real world and online, along with all the decoys, masquerades, and play-acting that constitute their public (and seemingly private) identities.

Marthe Ramm Fortun (b 1978, Oslo, Norway) brings canonized text and art historical references to a space of plurality through site-specific performances that explore how people engage with space in their everyday lives.

Dani Gal (b 1977, Jerusalem, Israel) is a Berlin-based artist who employs audio and video equipment to reinvestigate the past, creating a contrast with the history not yet written in our present.

Rainer Ganahl (b 1961, Bludenz, Austria) works in photography, video, and performance, dealing with the forms and content of education and politics at the intersection of linguistic and class issues.

Gui Garrido (b 1983, Portugal) is a Portuguese-born artist, dancer, and musician whose work in video and performance joins live music with visual experiences that draw on popular culture.

Pedro Gómez-Egaña (b 1976, Columbia) works in sculpture, video and phonography, and creates site-specific works with a focus on motion and temporality, while being motivated by the importance of time in cultural definitions of disaster, anxiety, and catastrophe.

Lina Viste Grønli (b 1976, Bergen, Norway) combines semiotic sculpture and collage techniques as narrative forms that deconstruct language and radically explore the arbitrary nature of meaning.

Subodh Gupta (b 1964, Bihar, India) is known for works that incorporate everyday objects, such as oxidized utensils, ubiquitous throughout India, to reflect on the economic transformation of his homeland.

Maria Hassabi (b 1973, Nicosia, Cyprus) is a director, choreographer, and artist who has developed a practice relating body and image, defined by sculptural physicality and extended duration.

Florian Hecker (b 1975, Augsburg, Germany) works with performance, installation, and digital music to make the physical presence of sound palpable, combining it with images subjected to the same digital processes used to create electronic music.

Andy Holden (b 1982, Bedfordshire, UK) is an artist, musician, and band manager whose work is characterized by internal references that have huge resonance in the world.

Will Holder (b 1969, Hertfordshire, UK) is a typographer and writer interested in conversation as a model for improvised publishing conditions—where the roles of author, subject, editor, and designer are improvised and shared.

Karl Holmqvist (b 1964, Västerâs, Sweden) blends poetry and pop music through remixed mash-ups based on the similar compositional structuring of both expressive forms, playing with designations of "high" and "low" cultural products.

Jenny Hval (b 1980, Oslo, Norway) is a transgressive artist who works in musical, literary, visual, and performative modes of expression, best known for her albums released under the moniker Rockettothesky.

Rashid Johnson (b 1977, Chicago, Illinois) is a sculptor and photographer who works in a wide range of everyday materials and is often identified with the post-black art movement.

Joan Jonas (b 1936, New York) is a pioneer of performance and video art, working in video, installation, sculpture, and drawing, often collaborating with musicians and dancers to realize improvisational works that disrupt the conventions of theatrical storytelling.

Vishal Jugdeo (b 1979, Regina, Saskatchewan, Canada) is an LA-based artist interested in productive miscommunication, slips in language, and how these can act as structural devices within narrative.

Angie Keefer (b 1977, Huntsville, Alabama) is a New York-based artist, writer, and editor whose speculative non-fiction traces themes and questions surrounding highly specialized information, navigating unfamiliar fields with the authority of an expert.

Jon Kessler (b 1957, Yonkers, New York) is known for his kinetic sculptures, which often combine centuries-old analog mechanisms with digital technology to explore the runoff of consumerist "post-utopian" societies.

Christopher Knowles (b 1959, New York) is a writer, painter, sculptor and performance artist, exploring the aural and visual elements of language through synesthetic works that conflate colors, words, and sounds.

Katarzyna Krakowiak (b 1980, Poland) explores sculpture and architecture through the use of various media, notably sound, to construct immaterial installations using radio waves and Internet links.

Agnieszka Kurant (b 1978, Lodz, Poland) is a Warsaw-based artist who often collaborates with scientists to investigate phenomena that exceed the logic of time, space, language, and knowledge.

Joan La Barbara (b 1947, Philadelphia, Pennsylvania) is a composer, performer, and sound artist who explores the human voice as a multifaceted instrument expanding traditional boundaries.

Malcolm Le Grice (b 1940, Plymouth, UK) is the influential modernist filmmaker whose work has explored the complex relationships between filmmaking in relationship to projecting and viewing processes as they constitute the medium of cinema.

Gabriel Lester (b 1972, Amsterdam, Netherlands) works across various disciplines, including cinema, music, performance, installation, sculpture, and architecture, to transform space and time through meticulously altering media and forms.

Molly Lowe (b 1983) works in costume, installation, sculpture, and video to create absurd and otherworldly performances focused on ensembles of nuanced and whimsical characters.

Shana Lutker (b 1978, Northport, NY) is an LA-based artist working in a range of media and inspired by historical documents, psychoanalysis, and the study of dreams.

Sara Magenheimer (b 1981, Philadelphia, Pennsylvania) is a Brooklyn-based artist. Her films attend to visual signs addressing materiality of manifestation with an interest in visual language rooted in the tradition of semiotics.

Jill Magid (b 1973, Bridgeport, Connecticut) explores the emotional, philosophical, and legal tensions between the individual and "protective" institutions, such as intelligence agencies or the police.

Jumana Manna (b 1981, New Jersey) explores the construction of human identity in relation to historical narratives and subcultural communities through multidisciplinary work that draws on sculpture and video.

Dave McKenzie (b 1977, Kingston, Jamaica) is a conceptual artist working in performance, photography, and video, who investigates complex representations of the self through abstract works.

Ryan McNamara (b 1979, Phoenix, Arizona) is known for blending different practices of dance, theater, and history in his situation-specific and collaborative works, creating social discourses surrounding participation within artistic production.

Dieter Meier (b 1945, Zurich, Switzerland) is a musician, a conceptual artist, and experimental filmmaker best known as one of the founding members of the pioneering Swiss electro-pop group Yello.

Jason Moran (b 1975, Houston, Texas) is a pianist, composer, and bandleader who mines a variety of musical styles to create adventurous and genre-crossing jazz performances.

Tameka Norris (b 1979, Agana, Guam) critiques the invisibility of blackness in popular cultural forms, using her work in performance, video, photography, and installation to look at social and political commentaries surrounding race.

Ahmet Öğüt (b 1981, Diyarbakir, Turkey) is internationally acclaimed for subtle references to complex topics, including religion, social/rural customs, and the specter of war, often with an edge of humor.

Clifford Owens (b 1971, Baltimore, Maryland) is a photographer, performance artist, and activist who advocates for the visibility and recognition of black performance artists in formal institutional settings.

Benjamin Patterson (b 1934, Pittsburgh, Pennsylvania) combines music, visual arts, and performance to create hybrid works that draw on the legacy of Fluxus to challenge traditional modes of art-making.

William Pope.L (b 1955, Newark, NJ) is known for provocative and often arduous performances steeped in dark humor that serve as commentaries surrounding labor, poverty, and race in America.

Philippe Quesne (b 1970, Les Lilas, France) designs opera, concerts, theatrical performances, and contemporary art exhibitions, and in 2003 founded the theater company Vivarium Studio.

Karol Radziszewski (b 1980, Bialystok, Poland) works with film, photography and installations and creates interdisciplinary projects. His practice extends to magazines, artist books and fashion as well as curatorial concept projects.

Maja Ratkje (b 1973, Trondheim, Norway) is a composer and performer whose music has served as the soundtrack for films, installations, dance, and other theatrical performances. She is a member of the Norwegian improv trio SPUNK.

Pedro Reyes (b 1972, Mexico) uses sculpture, video, and performance to explore the boundaries between the individual and the group, ordinary experiences, and extraordinary moments of interaction.

Aki Sasamoto (b 1980, Kanagawa, Japan) is a NY-based artist, who works in performance, sculpture, and dance that revolve around everyday gestures about nothing and everything.

Zeena Schreck (b 1963, San Francisco, California) is a Berlin-based artist, musician, and author, who serves as the spiritual leader of the Sethian Liberation Movement (SLM).

Guy Sherwin (b 1948) is a London-based artist whose works often use serial forms and live elements to engage with light, time, and sound as fundamental to cinema.

Alexandre Singh (b 1980, Bordeaux, France) is a NY-based visual artist and writer whose works draw on literature, performance, photo-conceptualism, and installation art, creating pieces which are characterized by obsessive detail and the interconnections between media.

Michael Smith (b 1951, Chicago, Illinois) has collaborated with a wide range of artists in many media as his performance persona Baby Ikki, whose bizarre and precipitous infancy is marked by conspicuous facial hair and oversized diapers.

Konrad Smoleński (b 1977) makes photography, video art, installation, performance, and happenings, while often using spectacular pyrotechnic effects, in contrast with a deficit punk aesthetic.

Noé Soulier (b 1987, Paris, France) questions how we perceive and interpret the gestures across multiple devices: choreography, installation, testing, and academic performance.

Cally Spooner (b 1983, Ascot, UK) works through film, broadcasting, novella-writing, and live events to explore political agency and activism in relation to movement and speech.

Sille Storihle's (b 1985, Tromsø, Norway) research-based practice takes form primarily as films concerned with history, gender politics, and the disputed position of knowledge production within the arts.

Squat Theatre (est 1970) is a theater company and collective formed in Budapest, Hungary, during the Cold War, whose core members included Stephan Balint, Peter Berg, Eva Buchmuller, Peter Halasz, and Anna Koos.

Radek Szlaga (b 1979, Gliwice, Poland) is a painter, illustrator, and author of sculptures, objects, and art books who exploits pop-cultural demons through the coupling of historical and religious symbols with images of contemporary compositions.

Theater HORA (est 1993, Zürich, Switzerland) was established by theater-pedagogue Michael Elber with the objective of promoting the artistic development of people with learning difficulties, providing opportunities to exhibit their extraordinary abilities to a wide audience.

threeASFOUR (est 2005, NY) is a fashion collection run by artistic trio Gabriel Asfour, Angela Donhauser, and Adi Gli, who collaborate on experimental and innovative designs that double as art works.

Julie Tolentino (b San Francisco, California) is a NY-based dancer and performance artist engaged with queer sexual subcultures, Eastern healing arts practices, AIDS, and queer cultural activism.

Guido van der Werve (b 1977, Papendrecht, Netherlands) works in a variety of mediums, including film, video, and artist's books, and is known for producing works that physically test his endurance.

Conrad Ventur (b Seattle, Washington) creates kaleidoscopic environments within the realm of expanded cinema that raise existential questions regarding sincerity, time and space, and the self.

Joanna Warsza (b 1976, Warsaw, Poland) curates performance and visual works that examine social and political agendas as a founder of the independent platform, the Laura Palmer Foundation.

Jennifer Wen Ma (b 1973, Beijing, China) fuses the mediums of installation, video, drawing, fashion design, performance, and public art, bringing together unlikely elements and creating sensitive and poetic works.

Bedwyr Williams (b 1974, St Asaph, UK) draws from the quirky banalities of his life to produce relational, comedic, and poetic installations and performances that deal with Welshness, otherness, and difference.

Tori Wrånes (b 1987, Kristiansand, Norway) works primarily with voice and sculptural installation, combining the two in dynamic live performances that stage character-driven and dreamlike fantasies.

C Spencer Yeh (b 1975, Taipei, Taiwan) is recognized for his experimental music projects, video, visual arts, and collaborations with other artists, that explore instances of sonic and visual intersections in typical and unexpected ways.

CURATORS & CONTRIBUTORS BIOGRAPHIES

Marc Arthur is Head of Research and Archives at Performa as well as an artist, scholar, and writer focused on theater, painting, sculpture, and dance. He is a PhD Candidate in Performance Studies at New York University.

Charles Aubin is Associate Curator at Performa. He is currently enrolled as a PhD student at the Royal College of Art, London, where his research explores the conceptual strategies of French choreographer Jérôme Bel.

Defne Ayas is Director and Curator of Witte de With, Center for Contemporary Art, Rotterdam, as well as the Performa Curator at Large. She has been a curator at Performa since 2005.

Kathy Battista is Director of Contemporary Art at Sotheby's Institute of Art, NY and Senior Research Fellow of the Centre for Global Futures in Art, Design and Media at the Winchester School of Art, University of Southampton.

Mark Beasley is a Curator at Performa as well as a writer and artist. He was awarded a Fine Art practice-based PhD from Reading University, and his first LP with the group Big Legs was released on Junior Aspirin Records in 2015.

Randi Grov Berger was the Performa 13 Coordinator for the Norwegian Pavilion and a Curatorial Fellow. She is Curator and Founding Director of Entrée, a non-profit exhibition space in Bergen, Norway.

Antonio Sergio Bessa is Director of Curatorial and Education Programs at The Bronx Museum of the Arts and teaches museum education at Columbia University's Teachers College.

Johanna Burton is the Keith Haring Director and Curator of Education and Public Engagement at the New Museum. She regularly contributes to Artforum, October, and Texte Zur Kunst.

Mary Ann Caws is a Distinguished Professor of Comparative Literature, English, and French at the Graduate School at CUNY. She is an expert on Surrealism and works on the interrelations of visual art and literary texts.

Travis Chamberlain is Associate Curator of Performance and Manager of Public Programs at the New Museum, where he oversees the Performance-in-Residence program.

Mary Ceruti is Executive Director and Chief Curator at the SculptureCenter and oversees all aspects of programming, planning, and organizational development.

Katherine Cohn is an MA candidate at Columbia University's Modern Critical and Curatorial Studies program and Cofounder of AD Projects, a curatorial collaborative dedicated to emerging American artists and experimental genres.

David Colman is a critic for *The New York Times* who covers a range of topics from art, music, and popular culture to selfies, fashion, and architecture.

Nikki Columbus is a writer who regularly contributes to *Artforum* and *Parkett* and covers exhibitions, openings, and events centered on performance and performative art, installation, film, and video.

Michael Connor is Editor and Curator at *Rhizome*. His work focuses on artists' responses to cinema and new technologies. He previously worked as Head of Exhibitions at BFI Southbank, London.

Adrienne Edwards is Curator at Performa. She is a PhD candidate in Performance Studies and a Corrigan Doctoral Fellow at New York University whose work focuses on artists of the African Diaspora and the Global South.

Sarah Farwell, Van Alen Institute is Program Manager and an urban planner, designer, and advocate for just cities. David van der Leer is Executive Director and a specialist in the contemporary urban condition.

Lia Gangitano is Founder and Director of PARTICIPANT INC, an education corporation and non-profit art space supporting emerging artists, curators, and writers in realizing ambitious and experimental projects.

Annie Godfrey Larmon is Assistant Editor at *Artforum*. She received an MA in Curatorial Practice from The Center for Curatorial Studies at Bard College. She is a regular contributor to *BOMB* Magazine.

RoseLee Goldberg is an art historian, author, critic, curator, and the Founder and Director of Performa. She is the author of *Performance Art: From Futurism to the Present* (Thames & Hudson, 2011), a key text for teaching performance in universities.

Thyrza Goodeve is a writer, artist, and interviewer who regularly contributes to *Parkett*, *Artforum*, and *Art in America* as well as various museum catalogues and book anthologies.

Summer Guthery was Assistant Curator for Performa 13 and is an independent curator and cofounder of JOAN, a non-profit art space in LA dedicated to promoting the work of emerging artists.

Anthony Haden-Guest is a writer, reporter, cartoonist, art critic, and poet who writes a weekly column on art-collecting for the *Financial Times* and regularly contributes to *Vanity Fair*, *The New Yorker*, *Esquire*, and *GQ*, among others.

Frank Haines merges a dizzying array of references, from history, mysticism, religion, pop culture, and the occult, into environments and performances uniquely his own invention.

Larissa Harris is Curator at the Queens Museum, where she has assisted in organizing a studio and artist services program as well as an artist residency in Corona, Queens.

Greta Hartenstein is Curatorial Assistant for Performance at the Whitney Museum of American Art who contributed to the 2013 exhibition *Rituals of Rented Island* on performance between 1970 and 1980.

Frank Hentschker currently serves as Executive Director and Director of Programs at the Martin E. Segal Theatre Center, an institute for theatre based at the CUNY Graduate Center.

Megan Heuer is a researcher on the topics of the intersections of film and the visual arts, the history and aesthetics of technology and museums, and the history of display.

Matthew Higgs is the Director and Chief Curator of White Columns, New York City's oldest alternative non-profit art space. He was previously curator at the Wattis Institute for Contemporary Arts.

Jens Hoffmann is Deputy Director, Exhibitions and Programs at the Jewish Museum, NY and Senior Curator-at-Large at the Museum of Contemporary Art Detroit.

Ana Janevski is Associate Curator in the Department of Media and Performance Art at MoMA. Previously she was Curator at the Museum of Modern Art in Warsaw, Poland.

Siri Rishi Kaur is a KRI-certified Kundalini Yoga teacher at Golden Bridge Yoga in NY. Her classes have a deep emphasis on allowing the flow of creativity and expansion through the heart.

Thomas J. Lax is Associate Curator in the Department of Media and Performance Art at MoMA. Previously he was Assistant Curator at the Studio Museum in Harlem, where he organized Radical Presence: Black Performance in Contemporary Art.

Emily Liebert is a Curatorial Assistant at MoMA in the Department of Painting and Sculpture. She recently completed a PhD at Columbia University in the Department of Art History and Archaeology.

Matthew Lyons is Curator at The Kitchen, one of the oldest non-profit art spaces in New York City. He has previously curated exhibitions at Paula Cooper Gallery, Eleven Rivington, and Apexart.

The M6: Meredith Monk Music Third Generation is a vocal ensemble dedicated to continuing the legacy of legendary composer/singer/director Meredith Monk. In 2007, The M6 formed to benefit from direct coaching from Monk.

Lasse Marhaug is a Norwegian composer and performer. Since the early 1990s, he has been a pioneer in the Norwegian noise and experimental music scene, contributing to over 300 releases.

Candice Madey is Founder and Director of On Stellar Rays gallery. She has previously worked at Christie's, The Wexner Center for the Arts, and Akron Art Museum.

Laura McLean-Ferris was a Performa 13 Curatorial Fellow and is an independent writer and curator who regularly contributes to *Art Review*, *Art Monthly*, *Frieze*, *Mousse* and the Tate Collections. She is the U.S. Editor for *Flash Art*.

Carlos Mínguez-Carrasco is Associate Curator at Storefront for Art and Architecture. He has been appointed Chief Curator of the 2016 Oslo Architecture Triennial with the After Belonging Agency.

Karen Mirza and Brad Butler's multi layered practice consists of filmmaking, drawing, installation, performance, and curating. Their work challenges participation, collaboration, and the traditional roles of the artist as producer and the audience as recipient.

Joanna Montoya is a Curatorial Assistant at The Jewish Museum, NY, where she manages the artist submission program. She received her MA in Curatorial Studies from the Center for Curatorial Studies at Bard College.

Hanne Mugaas is Director and Curator at the Kuntshall Stavanger in Norway, an art space dedicated to work which promotes audience engagement through public art initiatives.

Esa Nickle is Producing Director at Performa, where she is responsible for the production of all Performa programs. She has overseen five biennials and over 300 commissions, premieres, projects, international pavilions, tours, special projects, and events.

Johanne Nordby Wernø is Director and Curator of UKS, Unge Kunstneres Samfund, in Oslo as well as a regular contributor to *Morgenbladet*, *Billedkunst* and *Artforum*.

Jerzy Onuch is a performance artist and curator. He was Director of the Polish Cultural Institute in New York and between 2005 and 2010 was the Director of the Polish Institute in Kyiv, Ukraine.

Brent Phillips is the Media Specialist and Processing Archivist at Fales Library and Special Collections at the Elmer Bobst Library at New York University.

Eriola Pira is a NY-based curator and writer and is the Program Director of the Young Visual Artists Awards, a network of artist awards in Central and Eastern Europe with a residency program in New York.

Steve Pulimood is Owner and Director of gallery ROOM EAST. He is an art historian, writer, and critic who has written for *T Magazine* and *Art in America*.

The Raqs Media Collective was founded in 1992 and enjoys playing a plurality of roles, often appearing as artists, occasionally as curators, and sometimes as philosophical agent provocateurs.

Paramatma Siri Sadhana is a certified KRI Kundalini Yoga teacher at Golden Bridge Yoga in NY, who has taught and studied in India, Europe, and the Americas.

Jay Sanders is Curator and Curator of Performance at the Whitney Museum of American Art. He co-organized the 2012 Whitney Biennial, including a wide array of live performances.

Barry Schwabsky is Art Critic for *The Nation* and Co-editor of international reviews for *Artforum*, as well as an art historian and poet who has taught at New York University, Pratt Institute, and Yale University.

Rebecca Shaykin is the Leon Levy Assistant Curator at The Jewish Museum, who oversees the ongoing rotating exhibition *Sights and Sounds: Global Film and Video* of media art from around the world.

Mari Spirito is Founding Director of Protocinema, a transnational experiment making nomadic exhibitions in NY and Istanbul—a non-profit with a hands-on Education Program.

Hrag Vartanian is Cofounder and Editor-in-Chief of *Hyperallergic*. He has been a guest commentator on WNYC and KCRW, as well as other national and international media outlets.

Ben Vida produces electronic compositions that utilize analog and digital synthesizing technologies, with a focus on aural phenomena and sound localization.

Adam Wade is a fixture in the NYC storytelling and comedy scenes, having won twenty SLAMS at The Moth. He performs a monthly solo show titled *The Adam Wade from NH Show* at the Theater Under St. Marks.

Allison Weisberg is Founder and Executive Director of Recess Activities, Inc, a non-profit artists' workspace open to the public that promotes the work and practice of emerging artists.

Lana Wilson is an award-winning filmmaker known for her 2013 documentary on abortion providers titled *After Tiller*. She also served as the Film and Dance Curator at Performa.

Catherine Wood is Curator of Contemporary Art and Performance at Tate Modern, London, where she founded the live program. She regularly contributes to *Afterall, Frieze, Art Monthly, Kaleidoscope, Untitled,* and numerous exhibition catalogues.

Jake Yuzna founded the first cinema program at the Museum of Art and Design, where he continues to head the institution's experimental cultural production initiatives.

Joanna Zielinska is an art historian, writer, and Chief Curator at the Centre for the Documentation of the Art of Tadeusz Kantor-Cricoteka in Krakow, Poland.

PERFORMA 13 CONSORTIUM
100% Transparent
Abrons Arts Center
Angel Orensanz Foundation
Anthology Film Archives
Art in General
Affirmation Arts
Bowery Poetry Club
Brooklyn Academy of Music
Clemente Soto Vélez Cultural
& Educational Center
Columbia University
Community Church of New York
Connelly Theater
Danspace Project
El Museo del Barrio
Electronic Arts Intermix
Eyebeam Arts + Technology Center
Fridman Gallery
Goethe-Institut New York
Grey Art Gallery
Guggenheim Museum
The High Line
Hunter College
Institute of Fine Art
The Jewish Museum
Luhring Augustine Gallery
Martha Graham Dance Studios
Martin E. Segal Theatre Center
Miriam and Ira D. Wallach Art Gallery
Museum of Modern Art
MoMA PS1
National Academy Museum
NeueHouse
New Museum
New York Live Arts
New York Ethical Culture Society
On Stellar Rays
PARTICIPANT INC
Pioneer Works
Queens Museum of Art

Recess
Roulette
Salon 94
Studio Museum in Harlem
Swiss Institute
TEMP Art Space
The Kitchen
Third Streaming
Times Square Alliance
Van Alen Institute
Whitebox Art Center
White Columns

CURATORS
Chief Curator
RoseLee Goldberg
Performa Curators
Defne Ayas
Mark Beasley
Adrienne Edwards
Charles Aubin
Lana Wilson
Summer Guthery
Laura McLean-Ferris

PAVILIONS WITHOUT WALLS
Curators For Norway
Randi Grov Berger
Will Bradley
Hanne Mugaas
Anna Szefer Karlsen
Lasse Marhaug
Aaron Schuster
Johanne Nordby Wernø

Curators For Poland
Paulina Babecka
Fabio Cavallucci
Joanna Kiliszek
Jerzy Onuch
Joanna Warza
Joanna Zielinska

Consortium Curators
Sergio Bessa
Johanna Burton
Mary Ceruti
Travis Chamberlain
Michael Connor
Deb Cullen
Sherry Dobbin
Sara Farwell
Lia Gangitano
Linda Green
Larissa Harris
Frank Hentschker
Matthew Higgs
Judy Hussey-Taylor
Ana Janevski
Thomas J. Lax
Matthew Lyons
Carla Peterson
Juan Puntes
Jed Rapfogel
Eliza Ryan
Jay Sanders
Agueda Sanfiz
Jenny Schlenska
David van der Leer
Allison Weisberg
Jake Yunza

ABOUT PERFORMA

Performa is a multidisciplinary non-profit arts organization dedicated to exploring the critical role of live performance in the history of twentieth-century art and to encouraging new directions in performance for the twenty-first century. Part of Performa's mission is to present a biennial of visual art performance in New York City that illuminates the critical role of performance in the history of art as well as its enormous significance in the international world of contemporary art.

Performa is the brainchild of art historian and curator RoseLee Goldberg, whose definitive book, *Performance Art: From Futurism to the Present* (1979 & 2000), pioneered the study of performance art and has been translated into eleven languages. Ms. Goldberg's writing, as well as her activities as curator at The Kitchen in the late 1970s, has shaped the public's view of live performance as a visual art form for almost thirty years. In 2001, Ms. Goldberg originated and produced visual artist Shirin Neshat's first live performance, *Logic of the Birds*, with critical and popular success in both New York and London. The idea to create the Performa biennial, with specially commissioned new performances at its core, evolved from this highly successful production. Ms. Goldberg is Founding Director and Curator of Performa, which was founded in 2004.

Board of Directors

Noam Andrews
Laurie Beckelman
Irving Benson
Todd Bishop
Amy Cappellazzo
Toby Devan Lewis (Honorary Chair)
Wendy Fisher
Stephanie French
Emily Glasser
RoseLee Goldberg
Jeanne Greenberg Rohatyn (Chair)
Ronald Guttman
Barbara Hoffman
Rashid Johnson
Aditya Julka
Michael Kantrow
Edward Tyler Nahem

Founding Director's Circle

Toby Devan Lewis
Wendy Fisher
Jeanne Greenberg Rohatyn &
Nicolas Rohatyn
Ronald & Amy Guttman
Hauser & Wirth
Rashid Johnson
Nancy & Fred Poses
Valmorbida & Co.
White Cube

Producers Circle

Shelley Fox Aarons & Philip Aarons
Mimi Brown & Alp Ercil
Melva Bucksbaum & Raymond Learsy
Olivia Douglas
Gilbert Mackay Foundation

Executive Staff
RoseLee Goldberg, Founding Director and Curator
Esa Nickle, Producing Director and International Affairs

Curatorial Staff
Defne Ayas, Curator at Large
Mark Beasley, Curator
Adrienne Edwards, Curator
Charles Aubin, Associate Curator
Lana Wilson, Film and Dance Curator

Administrative Staff
Marc Arthur, Research and Archives
Franck Bordese, Director of Finance and Operations
Luisa Gui, Development & Special Events
Job Piston, Communications Associate and Special Projects
Jennifer Piejko, Editor, Performa Magazine

The Performa 13 Team
Jessica Massart, Communications Manager
Summer Guthery, Assistant Curator
Laura McLean-Ferris, Curatorial Fellow
Mike Skinner, Technical Director
Randi Grov Berger, Curatorial Fellow and Coordinator for the Norwegian Pavilion
Monika Rendzner, Production Fellow and Coordinator for the Polish Pavilion
Robert Wuss, Lighting Designer
Bret Tonelli, Production Assistant
Tali Wertheimer, Membership and Special Events
Anna Cline, Development Assistant
Julia Simpson, Production Manager
Elizabeth Feidelson, Production Manager
Cian McConn, Production Manager

Cara Stewart, Curatorial Assistant and Artists Liaison
Kristina Valberg, Hub Coordinator
Todd Feinstein, Box Office Manager
Hayley Samvee, Box Office
Debbie Huang, Production Assistant and Website Coordinator
Melissa Negro, Website Coordinator
Cora Walters, Communications Intern
Amanda Ryan, Curatorial Assistant
Paula Court, Archival Photographer
Chani Bockwinkel, Assistant Photographer
Pierce Jackson, Performa TV
A Practice for Everyday Life, Design
Fitz & Co. Public Relations
Perry Garvin Studio, Website Design
Yeju Choi, Designer in Residence
Darling Green, Logistics and Construction
Polemic Media, Video Documentation
Charles Dennis, Video Documentation
Kathryn Bown & Olivia Paige Ross, Interns

Performa Commssions + Projects were generously supported by the Andy Warhol Foundation for the Visual Arts, Toby Devan Lewis and The National Endowment for the Arts, Art Works.

COMMISSIONS
Paweł Althamer's Biba Performa, a Performa Commission, was supported by The Trust for Mutual Understanding, Foksal Gallery Foundation (Warsaw), neugerriemschneider (Berlin), Fundacja Sztuka i Współczesnosc, CCA Ujazdowski Castle, Polish Ministry of Cultural and National Heritage, and Tilton Gallery. In collaboration with Noah Fischer, Roman Stanczak, Rafal Zwirek, the Aaron Burr Society, and Szymon Althamer and Bruno Althamer. Production: Esa Nickle and Monika Rendzner. Additional thanks to Materials for the Arts and Socrates Sculpture Park.

Rashid Johnson's *Dutchman*, a Performa Commission. Director: Rashid Johnson. Assistant Director: Alex Ernst. Lula: Tori Ernst. Clay: Kevyn States. Curator: Adrienne Edwards. Additional thanks to Sheree Hovsepian and Julius Johnson for the support.

Ryan McNamara, ME M: *A Story Ballet About The Internet*, a Performa Commission, was supported by Performa Producers Circle members Philip and Shelley Fox Aarons, and Performa Patrons Ellen Sue Cantrowitz, Raphael Castoriano, Glori Cohen, Corina Larkin and Nigel Dawn, Susan Seelig and Laura Skoler. Choreography: Ryan McNamara in collaboration with the performers. Project Manager: Sam Roeck. Lighting Design and Technical Director: Robert Wuss. Construction: Nathaniel De Large and David Kirshoff. Musical Arrangement: Ryan McNamara. Performers: Reid Bartelme, Kim Brandt, Jimmy Burgio, Andrew Champlin, Jason Collins, Carrie Ellmore-Tallitsch, Fana Frasier, Frank Lombardi, Mickey Mahar, Waldean Nelson, Miki Orihara, Sabine Rogers, Jen Rosenblit, Natasha Stagg, Sonia Stagg, Brandon Washington, Joshua Weidenmiller, Emily Wexler, and Nikki Zialcita. People Movers: Ben Rosenberg, Emily Smith, Heather Donahue, Honey McMoney, Patrick Gallagher, Shane Rutkowski, Esther

Clowney, Damani Pompey, Edward Shenk, Allison Brainard, Sigrid Lauren, Alberto Hamonet, Jamie Simone, Thurmon Green, Nathanial De Large Music: John Carpenter, Janet Jackson, Stevie Nicks, The Field, Ciara, Dave Brubeck, Cory Daye, The Breeders, Dolly Parton, Miley Cyrus, Zok Zok, David Bowie, Malcolm McLaren, Liz Phair, Diana Ross and The Supremes, Tangerine Dream, The Turtles, Steely Dan, Frankie Goes To Hollywood, Yes, Drake, Rex the Dog, Shakatak, Still Going, Dennis Parker, John Barry, Michael Nyman, Kelis, TLC, The Carpenters, Whitney Houston, Samara Davis, Katy Perry, Aaliyah, Madonna, The Zombies, Deee-Lite, Duran Duran, Lady Gaga, Blondie, Boston, Fleetwood Mac, Beyonce, and Freddie Mercury. Additional thanks to the entire Performa staff, especially RoseLee Goldberg, Esa Nickle, Bret Tonelli (design of people movers), Lizzie Feidelson (production), and Bob Wuss (technical production) and his team. He would also like to thank Janet Eilber, Scout McNamara, Tuck Stephenson, Sam Roeck, David Velasco, Isabel Venero, Anna Sperber, moshiner7, Stefan Gunn, Intrack Tires, Myles Ashby, Christopher Schulz, Bradley Teal Ellis, and Pierce Jackson.

Subodh Gupta's *Celebration,* a Performa Commission, was supported by Hauser & Wirth, The Asian Cultural Council, and Nature Morte. Thank you to Tracy Candido (Production Manager) and Tom Barr (Front of House) and the entire kitchen crew. Produced by Esa Nickle with Bret Tonelli. Additional thanks to James Lavender, Julia Lenz, and David Shull.

Florian Hecker's *CD – A Script for Synthesis,* a Performa Commission, was co-presented by the Solomon R. Guggenheim Museum, New York. Curated by Mark Beasley. Supported by Sadie Coles HQ, London; Editions de Parfums Frédéric Malle; Galerie Neu, Berlin; Institut für Auslandsbeziehungen; IFF; Kvadrat and Meyer Sound. Synthetic paper booklet designed by NORM, Zurich. Libretto by Joan La Barbara. Performers: Biraj Barkakaty, Amy Carrigan, Valerie Kuehne, Brian McCorkle, Brian Rady, Jean Carla Rodea, Jean Carla Rodea, Kamala Sankaram, and Tatyana Tenenbaum Produced by Esa Nickle with Julia Simpson Technical Direction by Mike Skinner. Thank you to Reza Negarestani, Charlotte Rampling, Carlos Benaïm, Joan La Barbara, Pauline Daly, Alexander Schröder, Thilo Wermke, Miguel Abreu, Shelley Fox Aarons, RoseLee Goldberg, Robin McKay, Olivier Pasquet, Paul Pinto, and Nat Trotman. Additional thanks to PRG.

Alexandre Singh's *The Humans,* a Performa Commission, was supported by Performa Producers Circle members, Metro Pictures, Sprueth Magers, Mimi Brown, and Alp Ercil. The Humans is co-commissioned by Performa and Witte de With (Rotterdam), and co-presented in New York with Brooklyn Academy of Music. Curated by Defne Ayas. Written and directed by: Alexandre Singh. Costume Design: Holly Waddington. Light Design: Guus van Geffen. Music: Gerry Arling, Touki Delphine (Rik Elstgeest and Bo Koek) in collaboration with Annelinde Bruijs, Robbert Klein, Amir Vahidi. Mask design: Alexandre Singh. Set design: Alexandre Singh, Jessica Tankard. DRAMATIS PERSONAE: Ms.Chief: Simona Bitmaté. Harry Foulbreech: Jesse Briton. Pantalingua: Elizabeth Cadwallader. Tophole: Sam Crane. Charles Ray: Phillip Edgerley. Vernon/31: Ryan Kiggell N: Flora Sans. CHORUS: Sanne den Besten, Annelinde Bruijs, Folkert van Diggelen, Dook van Dijck, Sanna Elon Vrij, Loulou Hameleers, Lucia Kiel, Suzanne Kipping, Robbert Klein, Gerty Van de Perre, Lucas Schilperoort, Amir Vahidi. HUMANS: Duchess: Annelinde Bruijs. Crone: Sanne den Besten. Splingebottom: Jesse Briton. Bullen: Dook van Dijck. Vermillion: Phillip Edgerley. Strumpet: Loulou Hameleers. Frau: Lucia Kiel. Fingerer: Ryan Kiggell. Hag: Suzanne Kipping. Bertrand: Robbert Klein. Dandy: Lucas Schilperoort. Wife: Gerty Van de Perre. Husband: Folkert van Diggelen. Macaire: Amir Vahidi. Bray: Sanna Elon Vrij. Produced by Maaike Govwenburg Alexandre Singh was invited by Witte de With Center for Contemporary Art, to develop The Humans at Witte de With from April 2012 to January 2013, after which he continued to work on the play in Rotterdam. Special thanks to Joe Mellilo, Alice Bernstein, Amy Cassello and the team at BAM Fisher.

Rosa Barba's *Subconscious Society— Live,* a Performa Commission, was co-presented by Anthology Film Archives. Supported by Institut fur Auslandsbeziehungen, The Dena Foundation for Contemporary Art, Galleria Gió Marconi, and Vistamare. Composition Sound: Jan St. Werner. Field Recordings: Matt Wand. Foley: Ian M. Coletti. Sculptures, written, and directed by: Rosa Barba. Choir: Rosanne Rubino, Frank Lyon, Hallie Cooper-Novack, Lori Felipe-Barkin, Elann Danziger, King David, Matt Ziegel, and David Michael Di Gregorio. Projectionists: Sarah Halpern, Merten Houfek, Tim White, and Genevieve Havemeyer-King. Production: Mike Skinner, Jeremy Johnston, Bret Tonelli, Julia Simpson, Brian Wenner, Cara Stewart, Jared Haberer, and Neil Brown. Curatorial: Laura Mclean-Ferris and Henriette Huldisch. Special thanks to: RoseLee Goldberg, Esa Nickle, Giuliana Settari, Jed Rapfogel, Tim Keane, Anthology Film Archives, Franck Bordese, John Mhiripiri, Sung Hwan Kim, Uma Sofia, Lauren Wright, and Sarah Perk.

Eddie Peake's *Endymion,* a Performa Commission, was co-presented with Swiss Institute, New York. Supported by White Cube Gallery, Galleria Lorcan O'Neill, Valmorbida & Co., Abdullah AlTurki, AliaAl-Senussi, and Indoo Sella di Monteluce. Devised and directed by Eddie Peake. Musicians: Tim Goalen, Gwilym Gold, and Alexis Nuñez. Dancers: Eric Berey, Ann Chiaverini, Mary-Elizabeth Fenn, Djassi Johnson, Alex Romania, Tara Sheena, and Melissa Ullom. Make-up: Adam de Cruz. Production: Susanna Greeves, Esa Nickle, Mike Skinner and Lizzie Feidelson. Additional thanks to: Susanna Greeves, Celia Hempton, Prem Sahib, everyone at Performa, the Swiss Institute, Galleria LORCAN O'NEILL, and White Cube.

Shana Lutker's *The Nose, The Cane, The Broken Left Arm,* a Performa Commission, was supported by Susanne Vielmetter Los Angeles Projects and Andrea Krantz and Harvey Sawikin. Curated by Summer Guthery. Residency support provided by Pioneer Works, Center for Art and Innovation. Written and directed by: Shana Lutker. Narrator: Joey Frank. Actor 1: Adrian Jevicki. Actor 2: Jennifer Kraus. Actor 3: Maarouf Naboulsi. Piano: Denise Fillion, Julia Den-Boer. Lighting Design: Chris Kuhl. Projectionist: Tim White. Prop Master: Emily Kohl-Mattingley. Stage Manager: Lillie DeArmon. Lighting Assistant: Rachel Fraley. Interns: Molly Belsky and Cullen Welch. Thank you to RoseLee Goldberg, Summer Guthery, Esa Nickle, Bret Tonelli, and everyone at Performa; Dustin Yellin, Gabe Florenz, Ella Marder, Joey Frank, Tom Beale, Hannah Garner, and everyone at Pioneer Works; Susanne Vielmetter and everyone at Susanne Vielmetter Los Angeles Projects; Michael Liu and Theatre 80; Adrian Jevicki, Emily Spivack, Vishal Jugdeo, Virginia Poundstone, Lauri Firstenberg, Mika Yoshitake, Lizz Wasserman, Isaac Resnikoff, Kris Paulsen, Ry Wharton, Barbara Seiler, Reto Thuring, Christopher Kreiling, Eric Schmalenberger, David Matorin, Vernon Downey Jr., Emily Kohl-Mattingley, La Mama, Molly Belsky, and Cullen Welch.

Marianne Vitale's *The Missing Book of Spurs,* a Performa Commission, was presented by MV Studio. A work by Marianne Vitale with an original score by Mike Stroud of Ratatat. Starring: Todd Colby, India Menuez, Walter Cambin, Cole Mohr, Caleb Addison, Billy Cancel, Janelle Miau, William Burgess, Jingles Boiler, Olimpia Dior, Bennett Williams, with Michael Gerner, Bogdan Teslas Kwiatkowski, Susannah Liguori, Amanda Topaz, Anat F., Chicton Atkinson, Janet Castel, Barbora Venckunaite, Chloe Rossetti, Victoria Crowbar, Simone, Stephen Franco, Cole Blumstein and Adrian Caridi. Costumes: Diva Pittala and Francois Hugon. Make-Up and Hair: Andrea Helgadottir. Lighting: Kiki Lindskog, Matthew Reily, and Ross Epps. Sound and Light Coordination: Rosey Selig-Addiss. Sound Tech: Tommy Malekoff. Thanks to the Performa team. Special thanks to: RS Studio, Fairsbie Tabs Inc, Knoblodge Productions, and Manducatis Rustica.

Raqs Media Collective's *The Last International,* a Performa Commission, was supported by Frith Street Gallery, +91 FOUNDATION, and The Asian Cultural Council. Image & sound: Umang Bhattacharyya. Writer: Himali Installation & moving images: Singh Soin. Theatre Director: Zuleikha Chaudhari. Sound Design: Ish Sherawat. Video Editing: Rajan Kumar Singh. Animators: Manas (Pencil Tribe), Satya, Viveka Chauhan, Mayur, Vivek and Rahul. Colorist: Pradeep Gosain. Drummer: Ravi Makhija. Produced by Esa Nickle with Bret Tonelli, Lizzie

Feidler, and Robert Wuss. With help from Zach Rockhill and Joe Diamond. Chorus: Samuel Alper, Heloisa Chagas, Lucia Cousins, Matthew Holbert, Susan O'Doherty, Stacey Osei-Kuffour, Jeremy Rafal, and Zachary Segel.

Tori Wrånes' *Yes Nix,* a Performa Commission, was supported by the Norwegian Consulate General in New York, The Office for Contemporary Art Norway (OCA), and Performing Arts Hub Norway. Curated by: Mark Beasley Directed by: Tori Wrånes. Assisted by: Gustav Gunvaldsen. Lighting Design: Kyrre Heldal Karlsen. Electronics: Hanne Holstø. Saw: Jan Erik Mikalsen. Saw: Natalia "Saw Lady" Paruz. Performers: Biraj Barkakaty, Meaghan Burke, Bob Carlsen, Amy Carrigan, Isabel Castellvi, Natalie Galpern, Amanda Gregory, Mini Gu, Kendrew A. Heriveaux, Brian Maurice Kinnard, Kjersti Kveli, Mariana Luna, Brian McCorkle, Masami Morimoto, Morgan O'Hara, Émilie Pictet, Paul Pinto, Brian Rady, Jean Carla Rodea, Reya Sehgal, Aliza Simons, Angeli Sion, Sarah Small, Gisburg Smialek, Tatyana Tenenbaum, William McCauley, Barbara Etra, Geraldine Visco, Bernie Brendell, Bob Johnston, Alex Fox, Eileen Aubi, Joe Harkins, Katinka Mann, Joe Mann, Anne Bassen, Donna Swensen, Lucy Fielding, Pat Lewis, Roger Greenawalt, Jan Erik Mikalsen, Hanne Kolstø. Producer: Esa Nickle with Cian McConn. Technical Director: Mike Skinner. Sound Design: Daniel Smith. Assisting Sound Design: Thorolf Thuestad. Assisting Lighting Design: Sarah Gosses. 2nd Assistant to Artist:

Pål Halvorsen. Stylist: Sara Dunn. Tailoring for Tori's upside-down costume: Lars Nord Studio. Headpieces: Ashley Ruprecht for Faeth Millinery. Rigging: Joe Diamond, Anton Lundkvist, and Brian Owens. Additional thanks to: SIR Stage37 Staff, Jelena Milanovic, Thomas Glans, Ann Cathrin, November Høibo, and Ann Karen Hytten.

The Performa 13 Hub at 13 Crosby Street, A Performa Commission. Designed by Studio Miessen: Markus Miessen and Diego Passarinho. Construction: Darling Green. Hub Coordinator: Kristina Valberg. Special thanks to Noam Andrews and Lisamarie Dixon.

PREMIERES
Cally Spooner's *And You Were Wonderful, On Stage,* a Performa Premiere, was co-presented by National Academy Museum and in collaboration with Stedelijk Museum, Amsterdam. Curated by Charles Aubin and Laura McLean-Ferris. Supported by MOT International. With thanks to Annie Godfrey Larmon, Wysing Art Centre, and KW Institute Berlin. The project's preliminary structure was commissioned by the Stedelijk Museum, Amsterdam, co-curated by Annie Godfrey Larmon and Hendrik Folkerts. Performed by: Kendra Jo Brook, Yael Dray-Barel, Rhiannon Drake, Natalie Galpern, Natalia Miranda-Guzmán, Helen Hart, Adriana Jones, Jane Jourdan, Kjersti Kveli, Piya Malik, Jenny Minton, Maria Pietranera, Megan Schubert, Ilaria

Tarozzi, Rebecca Thorn, Chloé Turpin, and Reya Sehgal. Arranged by: Peter Joslyn. Devised and arranged with: Rhiannon Drake, Helen Hart, Jenny Minton. Piya Malik, Rebecca Thorn and Chloé Turpin. Choreography by: Adam Weinert. Costumes designed and made by: Malene List Thomsen. Produced by: Edd Hobbs and Cian McConn. Special thanks to Marshall Price.

Einat Amir's *Our Best Intentions,* a Performa Premiere, was presented by Artis with support from Affirmation Arts, the Ostrovsky Family Fund, Outset Contemporary Art Fund, Franklin Furnace Fund supported by the Lambent Foundation and NYC Department of Cultural Affairs, Artport, the Petach Tikva Museum of Art, and the Consulate General of Israel in New York.

Joan Jonas's *Reanimation,* a Performa Premiere, was co-presented with Roulette. Featuring Jason Moran. Supported by United States Artists' Friends Fellowship; the Council for the Arts, Massachusetts Institute of Technology; the Galeria Raffaella Cortese, Milan; the Galleria Alessandra Bonomo, Rome; the Wilkinson Gallery, London; and Galerie Yvon Lambert, Paris. Special thanks to Anne Katrine Dolven. Conceived and directed by: Joan Jonas. Text: Halldór Laxness. Performer: Joan Jonas. Singer: Ande Somby. Video Technician: David Dempewolf. Camera: Joan Jonas. Video Editors: Joan Jonas and David Dempewolf. Assistant to Joan Jonas and Stage Manager:

Coral Turner. Thanks to Jim Stanley, Loren Mullins, and Sarah Scandiffio. *Reanimation (In a Meadow)* was originally created for Documenta 13 in 2012 and presented as an installation in a custom-built cabin in the Karlsaue Park in Kassel, Germany. Its New York premiere at Performa 13 was reconfigured as a live performance for the stage.

Jérôme Bel and Theater HORA's *Disabled Theatre,* a Performa Premiere, was co-presented with New York Live Arts. Supported by FACE (French American Fund for Contemporary Theater), Pro Helvetia, Stadt Zürich Kultur, Kanton Zürich Fachstelle Kultur, Stiftung Denk an Mich, Ernst Göhner Stiftung. Concept: Jérôme Bel, Remo Beuggert, Gianni Blumer, Damian Bright, Matthias Brücker, Matthias Grandjean, Julia Häusermann, Sara Hess, Miranda Hossle, Lorraine Meier, and Tiziana Pagliaro. Dramaturgy: Marcel Bugiel. Assistant to Jérôme Bel: Maxime Kurvers. Production Management: Ketty Ghnassia. Artistic Director Theater HORA: Michael Elber. Actors Training Theater HORA: Urs Beeler. General Manager Theater HORA: Giancarlo Marinucci. Assistance and Translation: Simone Truong or Chris Weinheimer. Produced: Theater HORA – Stiftung Züriwerk(Zurich). Coproduction: Theater HORA, R.B. Jérôme Bel, Festival AUAWIRLEBEN (Berne/ Bern), Kunstenfestivaldesarts (Bruxelles/ Brussels/ Brüssel), Documenta 13, Festival d'Avignon, Ruhrtriennale, Festival d'Automne à Paris, Les Spectacles vivants – Centre Pompidou (Paris), La Bâtie – Festival de Genève, Hebbel am Ufer (Berlin). Thanks to Carla Peterson and the NYLA Team.

Maria Hassabi's *Premiere,* a Performa Premiere, was co-presented with The Kitchen. It was also a co-production of Kunstenfestivaldesarts (Brussels, Belgium), Kaaitheater (Brussels, Belgium), Steirischer Herbst (Graz, Austria), and Dance4 (Nottingham, UK). Supported by the Lower Manhattan Cultural Council's Extended Life Program. Additional funding by the MAP Fund, the Jerome Foundation, LMCC Manhattan Community Arts Fund, and Mertz Gilmore Foundation's Late-Stage Production Stipends. PREMIERE was developed through residencies at Kaaitheater (Brussels, Belgium), Pa-f (St Erme, France), and Mount Tremper Arts (New York). Directed by: Maria Hassabi. Performers: Biba Bell, Hristoula Harakas, Robert Steijn, Andros Zins-Browne, and Maria Hassabi. Sound Design: Alex Waterman. Lighting Design: Zack Tinkelman and Maria Hassabi. Styling: threeASFOUR. Dramaturgy: Scott Lyall. Production Assistants: Meghan Finn and Kate Ryan.

Molly Lowe's *Hands Off,* a Performa Premiere, was co-presented with Recess at Temp Art Space. Co-curated by Charles Aubin and Allison Weisberg. Supported by Ronald & Amy Guttman. Vocals: Brian Belott and Gelsey Bell. Actors: Emily Vetsch, Caterina Nonis, Dean Linnard, and Britt Moseley. Production help: Zeven Rodriguez, Britt Moseley, Claire Beaumont, and Melissa Beck. Special thanks to: Recess Art, Temp Space, Performa, Pioneer Works, Nancy Hechinger, Peter Lowe, Jason Flietz, Jon Kessler, Liz Magic Laser, and Ryan Sullivan.

Philippe Quesne's *Bivouac,* a Performa Premiere, was co-presented with Pioneer Works, Center For Art And Innovation. Curated by Charles Aubin. Supported by the French-American Fund for Contemporary Theater, a program of FACE. Conception: Philippe Quesne, in collaboration with César Vayssié (videography), Martin Agryroglo Callias Bey (photography), Marc Chevillon (technical direction), and Corinne Petitpierre (costume design). Special guest: Dorit Chrysler. Additional thanks to: Aymar Crosnier, Vivarium Studio's Board Chairman, and the team at Pioneer Works, Center for Art and Innovation.

Pieter Ampe and Guilherme Garrido's *Still Standing You,* a Performa Premiere. Curated by Lana Wilson. A CAMPO production supported by Flanders House. Thank you to Martha Graham Studio. Production assist from Lizzie Feidler.

Relâche, La Boum, Featuring *Re: Re: Re: Relâche* by Ryan McNamara with Andrew Champlin, V'erdre Green, Jordan Isadore, Burr Johnson, Frank Lombardi, Samuel Roeck, Adam Weinert, and Enrico Wey. Special appearance by Laura Skolar. The Furniture Orchestra: Luciano Chessa,

Conductor; Alex Waterman, Orchestral Bureaucracy. Baton; Piano; Quijada: Luciano Chessa, Flute: Jessica Schmitz, Oboe: Rachel Seiden; Bassoon: Sara Schoenbeck, Clarinet: Vasko Dukovski, Trumpet: Peter Evans, Trombone: Max Seigel, Horn: Kate Sheeran, Violin: Pauline Kim Harris, Violin: Rachel Golub, Viola: Dana Lyn, Cello: Alex Waterman, Bass: Bob Hart, Harp: Shelley Burgon, Piano: Marc Peloquin, Percussion: David Shively, Bass: Christ van Voorst van Beest. Additional performances by SIA, and aerialists Francis Stallings and Juanita Cardenas. Photo Booth with Jonathan Hokklo. Producer: Esa Nickle. Technical Director: Mike Skinner. Production Architect: Francesca Fornasari. Production Assistant: Bret Tonelli. Set fabrication: The Lighting Syndicate. Food: Bite. Event Planning: MF Productions. Special thanks to: FITZ & Co. for providing public relations services, SIR for their generosity, and Pace Gallery and Stacy Wakefield for designing the program.

PERFORMA 13 Opening Night
Performances by Gelsey Bell, Stine Motland, Brian Belott and the Wordless Chorus, Paulo Henri Paguntalan, NaTasha Williams, Paolo Henri, and Ashland Mines (DJ TOTAL FREEDOM). Curated by Mark Beasley and Esa Nickle. Technical Director: Mike Skinner. Lighting Designer: Robert Wuss. Production: Julia Simpson. Food Design: BITE. AV Tech: Viper. Support: MF Productions. Program Design: Yeju Choi. Additional thanks to Artists: Iona Rozeal Brown, Ragnar

Kjartansson, Shirin Neshat, and Elizabeth Peyton. Sponsorship: AOL Inc., Paddle8, Martini, and Absolut.

PERFORMA 13 Grand Finale - Presentation of the Malcolm McLaren Award.
Grand Finale took place at Performa Hub on November 24, 2013. Hosted by Glenn O'Brien and Young Kim. Performances by Gay Dog (Mykki) Blanco, No Bra (Susan Oberbrecke), and DJ Justin Strauss. Curated by Mark Beasley. Thanks to: Glenn O'Brien, Young Kim, Christian Marclay, Linda Yablonsky, Adam Pendleton, and Lawrence Kumpf. Techical direction by Mike Skinner and Bob Wuss. Production by Julia Simpson. Sponsored by Absolut and Vinyl Factory.

PROJECTS
Flag New York City, a Performa Project, was co-presented by Entreé as part of the Norwegian Pavilion Without Walls. Curated and produced by Randi Grov Berger. Supported by The Office for Contemporary Art Norway (OCA), Norwegian Consulate General in New York, and Arts Council Norway. Artists involved are: Jørund Aase Falkenberg, Azar Alsharif, Rosa Barba, Javier Barrios, Are Blytt, Marco Bruzzone, Danilo Correale, Espen Dietrichson, Leander Djønne and Lars Korff Lofthus, Ida Ekblad, Sammy Engramer, Serina Erfjord, Juan Pedro Fabra Guemberena, Kjersti Foyn, Ulrika Gomm, Steinar Haga Kristensen, Jeannine Han and Dan Riley, Tamara Henderson, Lisa

Him-Jensen, David Horvitz, Marianne Hurum, Toril Johannessen, Annette Kierulf and Caroline Kierulf, Ingeborg Kvame, Erik Larsson, Else Leirvik, Malin Lennström-Örtwall, Gabriel Lester, Lewis and Taggart, Klara Sofie Ludvigsen, Anna Lundh, Cato Løland, Cameron MacLeod, Sanya Kantarovsky and Liz Magic Laser, Jumana Manna, Dillan Marsh, Kyle Morland, Santiago Mostyn, Randi Nygård, Raqs Media Collective, Borghild Rudjord Unneland, Athi-Patra Ruga, Arne Rygg, Andrea Spreafico, André Tehrani, Sandra Vaka Olsen, Mathijs van Geest, Kjersti Vetterstad, Lina Viste Grønli, Christian von Borries, Bedwyr Williams, Magnhild Øen Nordahl, and Stian Ådlandsvik.

Konrad Smolenski and Radek Szlaga's *TRIBUTE TO ERRORS AND LEFTOVERS,* a Performa Project, was co-presented by The Adam Mickiewicz Institute and Fridman Gallery as part of the Polish Pavilion Without Walls. Curated by Charles Aubin. Featuring Dean Spunt. Technical production by Mike Skinner and Daniel Smith. Produced by Monika Rendzner. Thank you to Iliya Fridman.

Jumana Manna & Sille Storihle's *The Goodness Regime,* a Performa Project, was co-presented with Kunsthall Oslo as part of the Norwegian Pavilion Without Walls. Curated by Will Bradley. Supported by Norwegian Consulate General in New York and The Office for Contemporary Art Norway (OCA). Produced by Esa Nickle and Randi Grov Berger.

Voice is the Original Instrument,
a Performa Project, featuring
performances by: Maja Ratkje, Joan la
Barbara, and The M6: Meredith Monk
Music Third Generation, Supported
by Norwegian Consulate General in
New York and Music Norway. Curated
by: Mark Beasley. Producer: Julia
Simpson. Technical Director: Mike
Skinner. Sound Engineer: Justin Frye.
Additional thanks to: Peter Sciscioli;
Meredith Monk/The House Foundation.

In Tones from Light to Dark: A Concert,
a Performa Project, was co-presented
by Henie Onstad Center. Supported by
Norwegian Consulate General in New
York and Music Norway. Credits: Jenny
Hval, Stine Motland and C. Spencer
Yeh, and Void Ov Voices (Attila Csihar).
Jenny Hval's band: Håvard Volden
and Kyrre Laastad. Organized and
curated by: Mark Beasley and Lasse
Marhaug. Producer: Julia Simpson.
Technical Director: Mike Skinner.
Sound Engineer: Justin Frye. Additional
thanks to: Ingrid Moe, Anne Hilde
Neset; O.C.A.; Milena Høgsberg; James
Hoff; Chuck Moses (Viper Sound).

Eleanor Bauer's *The Poetry Episode-
Bauer Hour,* a Performa Project.
Conceived and performed by:
Eleanor Bauer and Chris Peck.
Poetry: Eleanor Bauer. Music: Chris
Peck. Curated by Lana Wilson.
Akademia Ruchu's *Chinese Lesson/
Chinska Lekcja,* a Performa Project,
was co-presented by the Polish
Cultural Institute New York and The
Martin E. Segal Theatre Center at

The Graduate Center, CUNY. Part
of the Polish Pavilion Without Walls,
was supported by the Polish Cultural
Institute New York, Fundacja Sztuka i
Współczesnosc, CCA Ujazdowski Castle,
and the Polish Ministry of Cultural
and National Heritage. Performers:
Janusz Baldyga, Jolanta Krukowska,
Wojchiech Krukowski, Cezary Marczak,
Zbigniew Olkiewicz, Jan Pieniazek,
Jaroslaw Zwirblis, and Krzysztof
Zwirblis. Thanks to Frank Hentschker.

Pete Drungle's *Dream Sequences For
Solo Piano,* a Performa Project, was co-
presented with Roulette. Video Editing by
Toby Rymkus. Curated by Lana Wilson.

Noé Soulier's *Idéographie,* a Performa
Project, was co-presented with Danspace
Project. Supported by FUSED. Curated
by Charles Aubin and produced by
Danspace. Thanks to Judy Hussie-Taylor.

Karol Radziszewski's *Kisieland,* a
Performa Project, was co-presented
with the CCA Ujazdowski Castle.
Coordinated by Marc Arthur.

Akademia Ruchu's *The Market of Toys,*
a Performa Project, was co-presented
by Times Square Alliance. Supported by
the Polish Cultural Institute New York,
Fundacja Sztuka i Współczesnosc, CCA
Ujazdowski Castle, the Polish Ministry
of Cultural and National Heritage,
Times Square Arts, Artplace and NEA
Artworks. Produced by Esa Nickle with
Paulina Bebecka and Monika Rendzner.
Performers: Janusz Baldyga, Jolanta
Krukowska, Wojchiech Krukowski,

Cezary Marczak, Zbigniew Olkiewicz,
Jan Pieniazek, Jaroslaw Zwirblis,
and Krzysztof Zwirblis. With
Agata Bebecka, Paulina
Bebecka, Emma Faith Hill, Adela
Janickova, Ida Krajewska,
Briana Leatherbury, Ricardo
Seiça Salgado, Martyna Sara
Sowa, and Alexa West.

Katarzyna Krakowiak's *The Great and
Secret Show / The Look Out Gallery,* a
Performa Project, was part of the Polish
Pavilion Without Walls. Co-presented
with Moynihan Station, Storefront for
Art and Architecture, and the Adam
Mickiewicz Institute. Special thanks
to Ralf Meinz, sound designer, and
Andrzej K. Klosak, PhD, MSc, Ing, Arch
(archAKUSTIK). Technical Director:
Mike Skinner, Production by: Monika
Rendzner and Joe Diamond with
additional assistance from Martin Layh.
Supported by the Moynihan Station
Development Corporation. Special
thanks to Michael Evans and Fred
Bartoli and Carlos Minguez Carrasco.

Marthe Ramm Fortun's *Inverted Sky,*
a Performa Project, was co-presented
with MTA Arts for Transit & Urban
Design and Unge Kunstneres Samfund
(UKS) as part of the Norwegian Pavilion
Without Walls. Curated by Johanne
Norby Wernø. Supported by Norwegian
Consulate General in New York, The
Office for Contemporary Art Norway
(OCA). Produced by Randi Grov Berger.

Jennifer Wen Ma's *Paradise Interrupted,*
was co-presented with Witte de With at

Performa Institute. Curated by Defne Ayas, Director of Witte de With Center for Contemporary Art. The final full production of *Paradise Interrupted* is co-commissioned and co-produced by Spoleto Festival USA, Lincoln Center Festival, and National Kaohsiung Center for the Arts.

Frank Haines & Zeena Schreck's *Live From the Eye of the Storm,* a Performa Project. Curated by Mark Beasley. First percussion: Hisham Bharoocha. Second percussion: Anders Hermund. Stage set design: Frank Haines. Zeena's wardrobe: Ohne Titel. Production: Mike Skinner, Guy Weltcheck and Bret Tonelli.

Man with a Projector: Featuring Malcolm Le Grice, Guy Sherwin, Lynn Loo, and Keith Rowe, a Performa Project, was co-presented with Eyebeam Art + Technology Center. Curated by Charles Aubin. Thanks to: AL Rees, LUX and Gil Leung, Roddy Schrock, the Eyebeam Team, and Sabel Gavaldon. Technical Production: Mike Skinner, Sarah Halpern, Daniel Neumman, and Tim White.

Lina Viste Gronli, Peter Child, and Elaine Chew's *Practicing Haydn,* a Performa Project, was supported by Norwegian Consulate General in New York, The Office for Contemporary Art Norway (OCA). Co-presented with Kunsthall Stavanger as part of the Norwegian Pavilion Without Walls on the occasion of the relaunch of the Kunstall Stavanger. Curated by Hanne Mugaas. Produced by Esa Nickle and Randi Grov Berger.

Bedwyr Williams's *A Break In,* a Performa Project, was supported by Thea Westreich. Foley effects by Ian M. Coletti. Curated and produced by Mark Beasley. Special thanks to the Westreich Team.

Vishal Jugdeo's *A Shaky Picture Has No Weight,* a Performa Project, was supported by Champions of Culture—Justin Gilyani and Heather Harmon—and Thomas Solomon Gallery. Curated by Summer Guthery. Produced by Abrons Arts Center.

To Breathe is Not Enough, a Performa Project. Curated by Mark Beasley. A concert featuring Karl Holmqvist, Will Holder, and Angie Keefer. Curated and by produced by Julia Simpson.

Cricoteka's *Can Objects Perform?,* a Performa Project. Curated by Maaike Gouwenberg and Joanna Zielinska. Co-produced by Cricoteka Centre for the Documentation of the Art of Tadeusz Kantor in Krakow. Featured the work of Marvin Gaye, Chetwynd, Dominika Laster, Nathaniel Mellors, Agnieszka Polska, Salon de Fleurus, and Catherine Sullivan, with a live performance by Shana Moulton.

Gabriel Lester's *Super-Sargasso Sea (phantom play #1) – 2013,* a Performa Project, was supported by the Mondriaan Fund and Kingdom of the Netherlands. Curated by Defne Ayas. Produced by: Esa Nickle and Bret Tonelli. Architecture: Peter Zuspan/ Bureau V. Light Design: Gertjan Houben. Music: Job Chajes. Phanthom: Jonas Lund. Special thanks to Marco

Giacomelli, Larissa Harris, Uri Rapaport, Mickey Smit, and Abrons Arts Center.

Ed Atkins's *Man Of Steel,* a Performa Project, was co-presented with Anthology Film Archives. Curated by Mark Beasley. Producer: Julia Simpson. Anthology Archives: Jed Rapfogel. Film Programmer Program: *Which bitch is a witch?* – Tolia Astakhishvili, 2000, 3'07. *Deportment* – Rachel Reupke, 2011, 3'32. *Theme Song* – Vito Acconci, 1973, 33'15 (excerpt). *Warm, Warm, Warm Spring Mouths* – Ed Atkins, 2013, 12'50. *J.P.* – Steve Reinke, 2002, 6'53. *Stomach Song* – William Wegman, 1970, 01'21. *Untitled (Heat up the Nickel)* – Peter Wächtler, 2013,   11'26. *Mrs. Peanut visits New York* – Charles Atlas, 1999, 6'05. *Even Pricks* – Ed Atkins, 2013, 7'32. *Snow White* – Dave Fleischer/Roland Crandall, 1933, 7'. Additional thanks to: RoseLee Goldberg. Esa Nickle, James Richards, Tim Keane, EAI, LUX, Criterion Pictures, UCLA Film and Television Archive.

Pedro Gómez-Egaña's *Object to Be Destroyed,* a Performa Project, was supported by Bergen Kommune, Norwegian Consulate General in New York, and The Office for Contemporary Art Norway (OCA). Curated and produced by Randi Grov Berger with Bret Tonelli. Co-presented as part of the Norwegian Pavilion Without Walls. Concept and direction: Pedro Gómez-Egaña. Performers: Mina Nishimura, Ximena Garnica, Matthew Davis, Carlos Maria Romero, Elaine Kwon. Dramaturgical Advisor: Bojana Bauer. Off-Site Technical Assistance: Stefan Törner. Co-produced with Entrée.

Two Arrabalesques's *A Surrealist Café,* Generously supported by Spain Culture New York-Consulate General of Spain: member of the network Spain Arts & Culture, Martin E. Segal Theatre Center at The Graduate Center, CUNY, and Ronald & Amy Guttman. Curated by Charles Aubin and Marc Arthur. Special thanks to Mel Gordon for envisioning the evening, Frank Hentschker, Martin E. Segal Center, CUNY, Águeda Sanfiz of the Spain Culture New York-Consulate General of Spain, Íñigo Ramírez de Haro, Consul for Cultural Affairs at Consulate General of Spain in New York, and to Amanda Ryan, Performa 13 curatorial Intern.

Three Duets, Seven Variations, a special series for the Performa 13 biennial, pairing six intergenerational artists for seven programs, was presented as part of *Radical Presence: Black Performance in Contemporary Art.* This program was organized by Adrienne Edwards, Performa, and Thomas J. Lax, The Studio Museum in Harlem. *Radical Presence* was curated by Valerie Cassel Oliver, Senior Curator, Contemporary Arts Museum Houston, and presented in New York in two parts: Part I at New York University's Grey Art Gallery (September 10–December 7, 2013) and Part II at The Studio Museum in Harlem (November 14, 2013–March 9, 2014). Co-organized by the Grey Art Gallery, NYU; The Studio Museum in Harlem; and Performa. The program included: Tameka Norris's *Untitled,* 2012, was presented at The Studio Museum in Harlem. Senga Nengudi's RSVP, 1976 and 1976-77, a Performa

Project, was presented at The Studio Museum in Harlem.

Pope.L's *Cage Unrequited* was presented at Clemente Soto Vélez Cultural and Educational Center, Production: Lydia Grey. Production assistant: Lizzie Feidelson.

Jamal Cyrus's *Texas Fried Tenor,* 2012, was presented on the High Line in partnership with High Line Art. Technical production: Mike Skinner and Chuck Moses (Viper). Special thanks Cecilia Alemani.

Benjamin Patterson's *A Penny for Your Thoughts* was presented on the High Line in partnership with High Line Art. Special thanks Cecilia Alemani.

Benjamin Patterson's *Pond* was presented at the Grey Art Gallery, NYU. Zachary Fabri's Shiny Shoes, a Performa Project, was presented at The Studio Museum in Harlem.

Terry Adkins's *Sacred Order of Twilight Brothers* was presented at the Performa Hub. Pocket Trumpet, Voice, and Percussion: Terry Adkins. Arkaphone, French Horn, Voice, and Percussion: Vincent Chancey. Arkaphone, French Horn, Voice, and Percussion: Marshall Sealy. Arkaphone, Trombone, Voice, and Percussion: Dick Griffin. Arkaphone, Euphonium, Voice, and Percussion: Kiane Zawadi. Voice, and Percussion: Blanche Bruce. Curated by Adrienne Edwards.

CONSORTIUM
Boris Charmatz's *Flip Book Part of*

Musée de la Danse: three collective gestures. The conversation at The Donald B. and Catherine C. Marron Atrium, MoMA's Atrium, was led by Ana Janevski, Associate Curator, Department of Media and Performance Art. Organized by Ana Janevski (Associate Curator), Jill Samuels (Performance Producer), Martin Hartung, and Leora Morinis (Curatorial Assistants, Department of Media and Performance Art, Museum of Modern Art) in collaboration with Boris Charmatz (Director), Sandra Neuveut (Deputy Director) and Martina Hochmuth (Production Director, Musée de la Danse/Centre Chorégraphique National de Rennes et de Bretagne).

Unconscious Media (Experiments In Intermedial Activism). Produced by WhiteBox Art Center, Live Web Conference/Performance, featuring artists Raul Marroquin, Ellen K. Levy, and Hans Breder. Additional contributors: Herman Rapaport and Igor Molochevski. Special performances include Caridad Botella, Yolanda Duarte, and Carlos Cuellar Brown.

Paulo Bruscky's *Game-Performance* was presented by the Bronx Museum at Macombs Dam Park. Curated by Sergio Bessa.

Dieter Meier's *Yello* was presented at Whitebox Art Center. Curated by Juan Puntes.

Rainer Ganahl's *COMME Des MARXISTES,* A Fashion Project By Rainer Ganahl was presented by White Columns. Curated by Matthew Higgs.

Dave Mckenzie's *All The King's Horses None Of His Men* was presented by Third Streaming. Curated by Adrienne Edwards. Thanks to Yona Backer and Natasha Bunten.

Squat Theatre, featuring Eva Buchmuller, Anna Koos, and Jay Sanders, was presented in collaboration with the Whitney Museum of American Art, where an installation by Squat Theatre was included in the exhibition *Rituals of Rented Island: Object Theater, Loft Performance, and the New Psychodrama—Manhattan, 1970–1980,* organized by Jay Sanders, Whitney Museum of American Art Curator of Performance.

Jill Magid's *Woman In Sombrero, Women In Sombrero* was presented by Art in General. Exhibition curated by Anne Barlow.

Ed Fornieles' *New York New York Happy Happy* was commissioned by Rhizome, the leading organization supporting contemporary art engaged with technology.

Eleanor Antin's *An Afternoon With Eleanora Antinova (A.K.A. Eleanor Antin)* was presented by The Miriam and Ira D. Wallach Art Gallery at Columbia University.

Derrick Adams's *Once upon a time…* was commissioned by the Calder Foundation and hosted by Salon 94. It was accompanied by an original musical score conceived in collaboration with composer Philippe Treuille that reinterprets a dialogue on sound between Calder and composer Edgard Varèse.

threeASFOUR's *Fest* was designed in collaboration with Breads Bakery, Naama Shefi, Studio Christian Wassmann, Bradley Rothenberg, and Oliver Halsman Rosenberg and conceived in relation to threeASFOUR: MER KA BA. It was presented by the Jewish Museum and Art Production Fund.

Conrad Ventur's *Tribute To Mario Montez,* curated by Lia Gangitano, was supported by the Franklin Furnace Fund supported by Jerome Foundation, the Lambent Foundation, The SHS Foundation, and by public funds from the New York City Department of Cultural Affairs in partnership with the City Council. The Tribute featured films that were among Montez's favorites of the myriad in which he starred, by Jose Rodriguez-Soltero, Jack Smith, Andy Warhol, Ron Rice, Avery Willard, and Takahiko Iimura.

Fernando Arrabal's *Fernando Arrabal: About Alfred Jarry And 'Pataphysique* was presented in collaboration with Spain Culture New York-Consulate General of Spain and Martin E. Segal Theatre Center.

Eleanor Antin's *Eleanor Antin In Conversation With Malik Gaines And Alexandro Segade* was presented by Columbia University.

Dani Gal's *Failed To Bind* was presented by the Goethe-Institut New York.

Courtesy The Artists (Malik Gaines and Alexandro Segade)'s *24 Hour Ballad* was presented at Recess. Curated by Allison Weisberg.

Aki Sasamoto, Adam Wade, and Tamar Ettun's *We Live With Animals* was supported by NYSCA. Presented by Van Alen Institute and co-curated by Denise Hoffman Brandt and Catherine Seavitt Nordenson.

Robin Deacon's *Spectacle: A Portrait Of Stuart Sherman* was presented at Abrons Arts Center by the Whitney Museum of American Art. Curated by Jay Sanders.

Athanasios Argianas's *Branching Music (Under The Trees, Above You)* was presented by On Stellar Rays. Theremin: Dalit Warshaw.

Joan Jonas: *Reanimation,* a film directed by Rima Yamazaki, was presented by Anthology Film Archives.

Eric Duncan's *Sunday Night Fever.* DJs: Eric Duncan (Dr. Dunks/Rub N Tug), Spencer Sweeney (Santos/Gbe), Matthew Higgs (White Columns), Nick Relph (Gbe).

Clifford Owens's *Five Day's Worth,* was presented by Third Streaming. Curated by Adrienne Edwards. Thanks to Yona Backer and Natasha Bunten.

Martha Graham Dance Company's *Surreal Graham: Herodiade and Spectre-1914.* Artistic Director: Virginie Mecene. RITUAL TO THE SUN: Music: Carl Nielsen. Costumes: Halston and Martha Graham. Original Lighting:

Beverly Emmons. Premiere: February 26, 1981, John F. Kennedy Center for the Performing Arts, Washington, DC. "Thank you for all the Acts of Light which beautified a summer now past to its reward." – Emily Dickinson III. Chief Celebrants: Vera Paganin, and Gildas Lemonnier. Alexandre Balmain, Adam Dickerson, Constance Dolph, Stephanie Fuentes, Timothy Kochka, Brice Payet, Jaclyn Rea, and Anja Zwetti. I. Pan and Syrinx, Op.49; II. Andante lamentoso (At the Bier of a Young Artist); III. Helios Overture, Op.17. Recorded by the Danish Radio Symphony Orchestra conducted by Herbert Blomstedt, courtesy of EMI Classics. I and II used by arrangement with G. Schirmer, Inc., agents in the United States for Edition Wilhelm Hansen A/S-Denmark, publisher and copyright owner.

Karen Mirza And Brad Butler's *The Museum Of Non Participation: The Guest Of Citation* was commissioned by Risk & Reward 2013, the Museum of Art and Design. Curated by Jake Yuza.

David Antonio Cruz's *Takeabite: The Opera* was commissioned by El Museo del Barrio with additional funds courtesy of Franklin Furnace.

Dieter Meier In Conversation With Anthony Haden-Guest was presented by Whitebox Art Center.

Michael Bell-Smith, Sara Magenheimer, and Ben Vida's *Bloopers #0* was commissioned and presented by Triple Canopy, and was hosted at Four81 Broadway by Jack Chiles and Mila Giesler. Julie Béna (In Collaboration With

Adrien Vescovi) *The Song of the Hands* was presented by 100% Transparent at 38 Marcy Avenue, Brooklyn. Curated by Linda Green.

Pedro Reyes's *The People's United Nations (pUN)* was supported by Mexico's National Council for Culture Arts (CONACULTA), Jacques, Natasha Gelman Trust, BBVA Bancomer, and The Mexican Cultural Institute of New York. Special thanks to Lisson Gallery; Galeria Luisa Strina, Sao Paulo; LABOR Gallery, Mexico City; SOMA Summer, Mexico City; and Casa Vecina, Mexico City.

Julie Tolentino's *The Sky Remains The Same: How Do You Map The Sky?* was presented by the New Museum. Artist archived three works selected for her by the artists Lovett/Codagnone, presented as part of a residency for *The Sky Remains the Same,* November 11–24, 2013, at the New Museum. The archiving process for this particular group of works is constituted by a series of open studios, panels, and public performances.

Agnieszka Kurant's *Cutaways,* a screening and conversation between Agnieszka Kurant and Manuel Cirauqui moderated by Mary Ceruti. Presented at Neuhouse by SculptureCenter.

Christopher Knowles's *The Sundance Kid is Beautiful* was made possible in part from a generous grant from WorldStage, with further support from the American Friends of the Louvre and Gavin Brown's Enterprise, New York. Staged: Noah Khoshbin. Produced: Andrew Gilchrist. Dramaturgy: Lauren

DiGiulio. Design: Eugene Tsai. Lighting Design: John Torres. Sound Design: Bryce Kretschmann. Costume Design: Kevin Santos. Set Construction: Stephen Crawford. Developed at The Watermill Center and Commissioned by the Byrd Hoffman Water Mill Foundation, Gavin Brown's Enterprise, New York, in association with The Martin E. Segal Theatre Center at The Graduate Center, CUNY, Change Performing Arts, and Dissident Industries.

Guido Van Der Werve's *Fourth Annual Running To Rachmaninoff Run.* The run began at Luhring Augustine, 531 West 24th Street and ended at Kensico Cemetery, Valhalla, NY

Blowfly And Michael Smith's *An Afternoon On Humor* were co-presented with MoMA/PS1 and revisited the two-day experimental music festival co-curated by Mike Kelley and Mark Beasley for Performa 09.

PERFORMA 13 SUPPORT
Lead support has been provided by
Toby Devan Lewis
Lambent Foundation
Fund of Tides Foundation
The Royal Norwegian Consulate
General in New York
AOL
The David and Elaine Potter Foundation
The Andy Warhol Foundation
for the Visual Arts

Major support (below $40k)
has been provided by
The National Endowment for the Arts
French American Cultural Exchange
The Office for Contemporary Art Norway
Paddle8
Prohelvetia

Additional support (below $20k)
has been provided by
Absolut
The Vinyl Factory
Christie's
The Mondriaan Fund
The Asian Arts Council
the Adam Mickiewicz Institute
The Trust for Mutual Understanding;
FUSED: French U.S. Exchange in Dance
a program of the National Dance Project/
New England Foundation for the Arts
and the Cultural Services of the French
Embassy in New York
The Dutch Consulate in New York
The Consulate General of Israel in
New York
CCA Ujazdowski Castle
ifa (Institut für Auslandsbeziehungen)
New York State Council on the Arts
New York City Department of Cultural
Affairs

Supreme
Music Norway
The Dena Foundation for
Contemporary Art
Abdullah AlTurki
Alia Al-Senussi
Susan D. Bowey
Ellen Sue Cantrowitz
Glori Cohen
Elizabeth Dee
Michele Oka Doner and Frederick Doner
Galleria GiO Marconi
Julia Fowler
Champions of Culture Justin Gilyani &
Heather Harmon
Frances Kazan
Young Kim
Corina Larkin & Nigel Dawn
MOT International
Tracey & Phillip Riese
Carol Rollo
Alexander S.C. Rower
Arlene J. Shechet & Mark Epstein
Indoo Sella di Monteluce
Sue Stoffel
Thomas Solomon Gallery
Tauck Family Foundation
Bill Todd, Vistamare
Helen Warwick
Thea Westreich
Performa Board of Directors
Performa Founding Director's Circle
Performa Producers Circle
Performa Curators Circle and
Performa Visionaries

Mike Skinner, of the beatific smile, generous goodwill, and enveloping warmth, was our producing partner for every Performa biennial since the very first, Performa 05, in November 2005. Working most closely with Esa Nickle, Mike provided us with a confidence and a sense of the infallible, knowing that every Performa Commission, event, conference, lecture, or concert would be delivered seamlessly, on time and without a hitch—sometimes three or four times a night throughout three weeks of the Performa biennial, no matter the demands of each artist in realizing their complex and complicated dreams. Mike's intuitive understanding of tech riders and sound equipment, and his ability to translate artists' ideas into fully fledged productions, has been essential to Performa's commissioning program and is forever woven into our history. He will be missed with every Performa biennial and every Performa event going forward.

ACKNOWLEDGMENTS

Writing the Performa book after the biennial is a necessity because none of the material in these pages existed before the biennial itself. All the work that we present is live, so creating a finished catalogue before the biennial would be like providing a roadmap but leaving out entirely the exciting tales of the roads taken. It takes time to sift through thousands of photographs, hundreds of hours of videos, multiple reviews, interviews, texts, drawings, and tangential histories relevant to each event before the material can begin to settle into the shape of a book.

This process is an unending conversation with artists, curators, writers, and audience members. We thank each and every one of them for taking the conversation back to 2013, but also for bringing it forward into the present, rethinking earlier ideas and finding new ways of relating to them now. The entire team who works on this book gets caught up in the "then and now" pendulum, and each of us comes to understand that this constant shift is in fact how history is written.

My thanks are too many and too profound to suffice, but, in no order, please know how much I value each and every one of you and your capacity to interpret and report on cultural history as it is in the process of being made. Performa curators Adrienne Edwards, Mark Beasley, Defne Ayas, Charles Aubin, Lana Wilson, and producer and sometimes curator Esa Nickle; contributors including Jens Hoffmann, Jennifer Piejko, Hrag Vartanian, Catherine Wood, and Nikki Columbus; editor Kathleen Madden; designer Robin Cameron; photographer Paula Court; Performa archivist Marc Arthur; Performa TV director Pierce Jackson; and communications associate and my right hand, Job Piston. This book is a composite of ideas, of different viewpoints, and specializations in many media, based on the work of remarkable artists, just like Performa itself.

Performa and this book could not be produced without Performa's extraordinarily generous Board of Directors, headed by Jeanne Greenberg Rohatyn (Chair) and Toby Devan Lewis (Honorary Chair). My family, in every way, provides the essential landscape of possibilities for me to act; my heartfelt thanks to Dakota, Zoe, and Pierce Jackson.

Performa also remembers Peter B. Lewis, whose encouragement of Performa from the start helped make the difference between idea and reality, and David Tieger, similarly a steadfast champion of our mission; Terry Adkins, who gave his last beautiful recital at the Performa Institute in November 2013; and Wojciech Krukowski, who described his first visit to New York for Performa as a dream come true. We miss these wonderful individuals who mean so much to us all.

Finally, this book is released with a very special thank you to our co-publisher, Gregory R. Miller & Co. Our collaboration is a meeting of minds and imagination. It is an immense pleasure to work with Greg and his team.

RoseLee Goldberg, Founding Director and Curator, Performa

INDEX